GEORGE B. McCLELLAN

THE YOUNG NAPOLEON

GEORGE B. MCCLELLAN
THE YOUNG NAPOLEON

STEPHEN W. SEARS

TICKNOR & FIELDS
NEW YORK
1988

———————

LIBRARY OF CONGRESS CATALOGING-IN-PUBLICATION DATA

Sears, Stephen W.
George B. McClellan: the young Napoleon.

Bibliography: p.
Includes index.
1. McClellan, George Brinton, 1826–1885.
2. Generals — United States — Biography.   3. United
States. Army — Biography.   4. United States — History —
Civil War, 1861–1865 — Campaigns.   I. Title.
E467.1.M2S43   1988   973.7′3′0924   88-2138
ISBN 0-89919-264-5

Printed in the United States of America

Q 10 9 8 7 6 5 4 3 2 1

Maps by Marsh Communications

In memory of Robert S. Fletcher

CONTENTS

MAPS

INTRODUCTION

WHEN MAKING WAR, General George Brinton McClellan was a man possessed by demons and delusions. He believed beyond any doubt that his Confederate enemies faced him with forces substantially greater than his own. He believed with equal conviction that enemies at the head of his own government conspired to see him and his army defeated so as to carry out their traitorous purposes. He believed himself to be God's chosen instrument for saving the Union. When he lost the courage to fight, as he did in every battle, he believed he was preserving his army to fight the next time on another and better day. Throughout the Civil War he labored under a burden of controversy as heavy as Pilgrim's bundle. While he basked in the appellation given him by his admirers — the Young Napoleon — he was called by a legion of derisive opponents Young McNapoleon.

General McClellan was seldom out of the public eye during the war years. At the age of thirty-four he was named commander of the North's largest army, and then commander of all the Northern armies. At thirty-five he fought the longest and largest campaign of the time, and then the bloodiest single day of battle in the nation's history. At thirty-seven he ran for the presidency against Abraham Lincoln, and it required an act of political suicide by his party to ensure that he would not win. However all these actions may be judged for good or ill, George McClellan's importance in shaping the course of the Union during the Civil War was matched only by that of President Lincoln and Generals Grant and Sherman.

Few of those who commented on General McClellan, in his day and afterward, have been neutral toward him, and as a conse-

quence their interpretations of his actions, even their recital of
the facts of his life, have varied widely. As is true of any life so
filled with contradiction and controversy, an understanding of
the man is best found in original, primary sources, and this biography is drawn entirely from such sources.

They are a remarkably rich and varied lot — in many instances
previously untapped — and they cast new light on old contentions. McClellan was said, for example, despite all his faults to
have been the best commander the Army of the Potomac ever
had, yet on the evidence he was inarguably the worst. The record
is equally clear that it was his own decisions, rather than those
of the government, that doomed his grand campaign to end the
war. Contemporaries charged him with being secretly in sympathy with the secessionists, but in truth there was no one who
was more loyal and patriotic. He has been portrayed as a political
innocent caught up in the schemes of party, when in fact he was
a partisan Democrat in knowing and deliberate opposition to the
Republican administration that employed him.

The historian James Ford Rhodes once wrote that "no man
can go unscathed if his acts are interpreted by his innermost
thoughts." However true that may be, history can be grateful
that in George McClellan's case it is these innermost thoughts,
so well expressed in the full record of his letters and other writings, that finally reveal the measure of the man. If that measure
is not how he himself believed history would judge him, it is
representative of yet one more of his delusions.

ONE

THE MAKING OF A SOLDIER

CONDITIONAL CADET McClellan was disheartened by everything about his first two weeks at West Point except the spectacular setting. He was desperately homesick and his feet hurt from drilling in shoes that were too tight, and he was nearly ready to pack up and return to Philadelphia. "I am as much alone as if in a boat in the middle of the Atlantic, not a soul here cares for, or thinks of me — not one here would lift a finger to help me," he wrote his sister Frederica. "I am entirely dependent on myself . . . & take the blame of all my mistakes. . . ." He had to put his letter aside to answer the drill call, but when he returned he was rejuvenated; with new shoes his awkwardness disappeared and he outdid everyone. "You can't imagine how much more inspirited I feel since I have acquitted myself handsomely at this mornings drill," he told Frederica. He was sure now that he could do his duty "as well as anyone who ever did go through here." George Brinton McClellan would rarely lack confidence in his soldierly abilities, and this first experience of doubt was typically brief.

His homesickness may be accounted for by his age. At just over fifteen and a half, he was the youngest of those who arrived at West Point in June 1842 to seek places as fourth classmen in the Military Academy. His confidence grew when he passed the physical examination — thirty of his potential classmates failed, he noted — and then the entrance examination. One hurdle remained, but his promise was such that in his case the authorities waived the minimum entry age of sixteen. On July 1 he was admitted to the class of 1846.[1]

In a brief sketch of his boyhood, written late in life, George

McClellan traced his interest in West Point back to the age of ten, when a fellow student at a private school in Philadelphia, Alfred Sully, son of the prominent painter Thomas Sully, had received an Academy appointment. There was an ancestral military background of sorts — the Mclellans of Scotland fought in support of the Stuart kings — but the only American McClellan of direct ancestry to take up arms before young George was his great-grandfather, Samuel McClellan, of Woodstock, Connecticut. Samuel served in the militia in the French and Indian War, and shortly before the Revolution raised a troop of horse at Woodstock. A family tradition of dubious authority placed him in the Battle of Bunker Hill. At any event, he served in the local militia for the remainder of the Revolution. Although not called to action during any of the British raids on Connecticut, he was a capable enough administrator to rise in rank to brigadier general of militia by 1779. He was married to a descendant of Governor William Bradford of Plymouth Colony, lived out his life much honored and respected, and was known to his posterity, including his great-grandson, as General Sam.

The succeeding generation remained in Woodstock, where General Sam's sons James and John founded the Woodstock Academy. The sons of James McClellan, George and Samuel, made their careers in medicine and sought a wider world. George, the father of Cadet McClellan, graduated from Yale College in 1816 and earned his medical degree from the University of Pennsylvania three years later. He set up a surgical practice in Philadelphia, specializing in ophthalmology. A man of great energy, he founded the Jefferson Medical College and headed its faculty, maintained a substantial practice, edited a medical journal, wrote on the principles and practice of surgery, and kept a stable of fast trotters.

Dr. McClellan moved in the upper rank of Philadelphia society and numbered among his acquaintances such notables as Daniel Webster. Regarded as charming and courtly of manner, he was also stubbornly opinionated and not amenable to compromise, traits that in 1838 led to his departure from the medical school he had founded. In that day the rewards of medicine were not great, even for someone of Dr. McClellan's stature. His assumption of his father's considerable debts and the cost of a medical education for his eldest son, John Hill Brinton McClellan, created financial pressures, and no doubt the prospect of a free education helped steer his second son and namesake toward West Point.[2]

In 1820 Dr. McClellan had married Elizabeth Steinmetz Brinton, of a leading Philadelphia family, and the couple produced five children: a daughter, Frederica; then three sons, John, George, and Arthur; and finally another daughter, Mary. From the evidence of her letters, Elizabeth McClellan was a woman of culture and refinement, and she saw to it that her children had the best education Philadelphia could offer. In a draft of his memoirs, General McClellan remarked that "before I went to West Point I had received an excellent classical education, was well read in History for a boy, and was a good French scholar."

George Brinton McClellan was born on December 3, 1826, and at the age of five attended what was called an infant school. This was followed by four years in the private school of Sears Cook Walker. Walker was a Harvard graduate and a man of considerable scientific attainment — "far above the grade of an ordinary scholastic," in McClellan's words — who would go on to important work with the United States Naval Observatory and the Coast Survey. Leaving Walker's school at age ten, young George next took instruction from a private tutor whom he described as "a one eyed German Jew by the name of Schiffer . . . , a magnificent classical scholar & an excellent teacher. We were obliged to converse in Latin & French, and at an early age I became a good scholar in the classics. . . ." In 1838 he enrolled at a preparatory academy of the University of Pennsylvania directed by the Reverend Samuel W. Crawford. Two years later, at the age of thirteen, he entered the university.

He resigned himself without enthusiasm to a career in the law, but after two years there he changed his goal to the military. "The youth has nearly completed his classical education at the University," his father wrote the secretary of war in the spring of 1842, "and desires to go through the West Point school for the serious purpose of devoting his life to the service of the Army of the U. States." There was some delay in his acceptance by the Academy, Dr. McClellan told the secretary, and he had requested President John Tyler's "kind consideration of my son's application. . . ." Whether Tyler actually endorsed young McClellan is not known, but thereafter his nomination and acceptance proceeded without a hitch.[3]

Little is recorded of George McClellan's youth beyond his schooling. His sister Frederica remembered him fondly if uncritically as "the brightest, merriest, most unselfish of boys ..., fond of books & study — & also of fun & frolic, & always the 'soul of honor.' " He would recall childhood visits to his grandparents' home in Woodstock, but for the most part the McClellans' New England heritage became submerged in the Southern-oriented society of antebellum Philadelphia. (Some two decades later, General McClellan revealed how far he had departed from his family roots when he wrote disgustedly of "pestiferous wooden nutmeg, psalm singing yankees. ...") An incident suggestive of his forming character is one he himself related years later. At the Reverend Crawford's academy, when he was twelve or thirteen, he was accused of an offense he had not committed and made subject to punishment. "My father had told me not to permit myself to be whipped," he wrote, so when Dr. Crawford approached him with his rattan switch, "I met him with a kick & went out of the school." After a few days the dispute was mediated — there is the implication that his father intervened in his behalf — and he was readmitted at Dr. Crawford's "request." McClellan concluded his recollection of the episode with the remark that he "never had any more trouble with the rattan."[4]

During his first two months at West Point, in the summer encampment of 1842, Cadet McClellan learned the fundamentals of soldiering in the regimen known as the School of the Soldier: the proper uniform, the use of musket and bayonet, the basic marching drills. The entire Corps of Cadets lived in tents in imitation of campaign conditions, with the plebes subjected to the harassing orders of smugly superior upper classmen. They were assigned to companies by height; McClellan, one of the smallest plebes as well as the youngest, found himself near the foot of the class, in stature, in C Company.

He had few complaints about the routine, he wrote home, except for the food, which was a universal complaint. He customarily skipped the Sunday dinner of pickled beef and potatoes, and observed that no bread ever reached the mess tables "younger" than a day old. Encampment life was not all drill and rigor. Superintendent Richard Delafield may have been "very economical with us" in regard to food, McClellan wrote, but he was indulgent in other matters. There was seldom any problem with obtaining permission for visits by relatives and friends, or in off-duty hours to go boating on the Hudson or to see the local sights. By the end of the summer he felt at home at the Academy. He carried his musket and wore his uniform with pride, he wrote his mother, and boasted that he was becoming as tough as a pine log.[5]

The academic year began in September, and the cadets moved indoors to Spartan, drafty rooms in the stone barracks. Their twelve-hour days continued, but now it was two or three hours of drill and nine or ten of study and classroom recitation. The first year's curriculum was limited to two subjects — mathematics (algebra, geometry, and trigonometry) and French — but for many of the plebes it was a year of agony.

West Point was in theory an egalitarian institution, having at any one time a cadet from each congressional district plus a limited number of at-large appointees, and the comparatively easy entrance examination affirmed the principle. Classroom work, however, soon revealed the great disparity in educational opportunities across the country in the 1840s. For a George McClellan, educated at the best schools in Philadelphia, privately tutored and with two years of college, the classroom held no fears. For a Thomas J. Jackson, his classmate from rural Virginia for whom any mathematics beyond simple arithmetic and any language beyond English were utter mysteries, it was a struggle for survival. The physical and academic examinations proved too much for more than a third of the appointees of 1842, including one of McClellan's roommates. Just 83 of the 134 June arrivals survived the first year. McClellan would rank third in class "order of general merit"; Jackson fought his way to fifty-first place.

Cadet McClellan sometimes worked only as hard as was necessary to get by. At the examinations in January 1843 he stood first in mathematics but eighth in French, a subject in which he came to the Academy exceedingly well prepared. "I never studied at all at home," he admitted in a letter to his brother John; "now I do study a little (not much I must confess)," although he added that he was taking more pains with his work than formerly. Many years later, Charles S. Stewart, recalling their academic rivalry in the class of 1846, would say of McClellan, in praise that was somewhat faint, "He was well educated, and, when he chose to be, brilliant."[6]

George McClellan entered West Point a gentleman as well as

a scholar, and his friendships reflected that fact. Thomas Neill, also the son of a Philadelphia doctor and a year behind McClellan at the Academy, described the caste system that prevailed. "The distinction here is very marked indeed," he wrote in an 1843 letter. "In almost every class those who are gentlemen associate together, and have nothing whatever to do with those forward, impudent fellows who never can be gentlemen." Social status was only a part of the distinction. As McClellan explained to his brother, commonly held beliefs, attitudes, and politics cemented the associations. "Some how or other I take to the Southerners," he wrote; "almost all my associates — indeed all of them — are Southerners; I am sorry to say that the manners, feelings, & opinions of the Southerners are far, far preferable to those of the majority of the Northerners at this place." Among his new friends were the Virginians Dabney Maury and his roommate Ambrose Powell Hill (but not that other Virginian, roughhewn Tom Jackson), Cadmus Wilcox of North Carolina, and James Stuart of South Carolina, with whom he roomed for much of his time at West Point and who became the closest friend of his early life. Like most of George McClellan's views, which, once fixed in his mind, rarely changed, his sympathy with Southern attitudes would remain constant — with the singular exception of the matter of secession.[7]

In their second year cadets completed work in mathematics (more geometry, then calculus and surveying) in preparation for the scientific and engineering courses of their final two years. They also finished their study of French, the goal of which was to make them, if not fluent, at least conversant with French military and engineering treatises. There was instruction in English composition and grammar, and the first of two years of drawing, a preparation for later work in military and civil engineering. Robert Weir, a talented artist in his own right, headed the Department of Drawing. Sympathetic to the fact that artistic ability was not something learned, like French grammar, by "boning," Weir generally passed any cadet who tried his best, whether the results were recognizable or not. Drawing was the only course in his Academy years that McClellan failed to master. As a third classman he ranked eighteenth in the subject, although he was third in overall class standing. The next year's curriculum stressed science: chemistry and what was called natural and experimental philosophy, a catchall term embracing mechanics, acoustics, optics, and astronomy. McClellan's rank in drawing that year slipped to twenty-third, and his overall class position fell one place, to fourth. He described drawing — figure, topographic, and landscape sketching — as "hard work" and was glad to have it behind him. That year he was appointed cadet sergeant in C Company.

The summer encampments progressed from the infantry's School of the Soldier in the first year through the increasingly complex field maneuvers of the School of the Company, the School of the Battalion, and the "evolution of the line" in the second and fourth years. (In the third summer there was a two-month furlough, one of the most eagerly awaited events of a cadet's West Point experience.) Artillery instruction followed a similar pattern, advancing from the duties of the gunner through those of the gun crew and finally the battery. There was work as well in entrenching, pontoon bridging, and fortification. Second classmen were taught riding, but there was no instruction in cavalry tactics.

Life at all times was governed by rote and discipline. Reveille was at five in the morning in summer and at six in winter. The drum signaled every activity through the day. Even the call for church, where attendance was required, was by drum; the cadets fell in and were marched into the chapel, where they sat in assigned places to hear strict High Church Episcopal sermons. Demerits were factored into the formula for class standing, and were handed out for sloppiness of dress, badly cared-for equipment, tardiness, and similar violations. The most serious offenses, such as drunkenness, could lead to court-martial and possible dismissal. Discipline was so constant that on the few occasions when it was relaxed the men sometimes "kicked up an awful row," as Cadet Thomas Neill described it. He calculated that during one Christmas and New Year's period fully half the cadets were drunk at one time or another, and were saved from punishment only by friends covering up for them.[8]

The youthful-looking McClellan, short and compact of build, with gray eyes and dark hair, attracted much favorable notice at West Point. Erasmus Keyes, his artillery instructor, wrote that "a pleasanter pupil was never called to the blackboard." Dabney Maury, his friend from Virginia, thought he bore "every evidence of gentle nature and high culture, and his countenance was as charming as his demeanor was modest and winning.'' His academic rival, Charles Stewart, remembered him as generous and honorable, with not ''a mean thought in him.'' Yet he was far from stuffy. He himself reported that on New Year's Eve in his plebe year he and half a dozen friends risked demerits to enjoy an after-hours supper of oyster pies, most likely procured from the famous off-limits tavern in nearby Highland Falls run by Benny Havens.[9]

His private face was not always so cheerful as his public one. In 1845, when he was a second classman, McClellan believed himself the victim of the faculty's injustice. He wrote his mother that in the recent January examinations he had finished second in both chemistry and natural philosophy. But with second came second-class treatment. Even when he had a better recitation than the man ahead of him, he did not receive as good a mark ''& have to get a much better mark to rise him; if I were already above him, I could distance him, I think.'' He decided that ''toiling up hill is not what it is cracked up to be!''

This was part of a forming and almost morose view of the unfairness of life, an attitude expressed in a letter dating from the time of his complaint of academic injustice. Early in 1845 he learned of the death of his three-year-old niece, Lizzie English, and he composed a letter of condolence to Frederica that was darkly fatalistic in outlook. ''A long struggle in this world is all that life consists of,'' he wrote, and he speculated that if happiness existed at all, it was merely ''a forgetfullness of trouble & absence of misery.'' In her brief life Lizzie had experienced the only pure happiness, that of innocence; perhaps death was best for her, sparing her the burden of cares and disappointments that was her inevitable lot. He had seen much of men in his few years, he told Frederica, ''& from the low opinion I have formed of them'' he rated Lizzie's chances for a happy life, had she been spared to marry, as a thousand to one. To be sure, his tone was in part simply an eighteen-year-old's awkward groping for some way to give comfort in the face of death. But it was as well a forecast of mature attitudes. ''I know not what fate has in store for me, . . .'' he wrote in his earliest example of self-fulfilling prophecy; ''I only know that I must expect the hardest trials a proud spirit can bear before I can effect anything.''[10]

Nearly all cadets who commented on the subject regarded their final year, as first classmen, as by far the most stimulating of their four years at West Point. There was classroom work in infantry and artillery tactics; mineralogy and geology; ethics, a heading that covered the study of constitutional and international law, logic, and moral philosophy; and the course that by the mid-1840s was an institution at the Academy, Dennis Hart Mahan's Military and Civil Engineering and the Science of War. Cadet McClellan declared himself "passionately fond of Military Engineering, & Military Tactics."[11]

It was primarily under Mahan that West Point's dual themes of engineering and military command came together. Graduating first in the Academy class of 1824, Mahan had spent four years of study in France, considered at the time the fountainhead of the military art, and in 1832 he was appointed professor of Military and Civil Engineering. He held the post for thirty-nine years, and it was he who added "and the Science of War" to the course title. In his war lectures he took the main elements of European military thought, primarily French, and distilled them for an American context. His teaching notes became two long-lived textbooks, *A Complete Treatise on Field Fortification* (1836) and *An Elementary Treatise on Advanced-Guard, Out-Post, and Detachment Service of Troops* (1847), an oddly titled volume that was in fact his formulation of strategy and tactics. While *Out-Post*, as the cadets called it, was not published until a year after McClellan graduated, he and his classmates used a lithographed version in substantially the same form.

Mahan's influence on his students would later receive considerable attention in debates on whether this or that Civil War general utilized one or another classic — or antiquated — strategy in his campaigns. However, Mahan's teaching was very much attuned to West Point's primary rationale in the period: to produce engineers capable of military command, rather than officers with engineering skills. In his year-long course, students met daily for an hour and a half (three hours for sessions devoted to engineering drawing) and were instructed in civil engineering, architecture, stonecutting, machinery, and permanent and field fortifications. There was but a single week devoted to the science and art of war — six hour-and-a-half meetings. Nine hours was hardly enough time to indoctrinate students with any particular theory of war. Mahan could do little more than introduce the subject.

On the other hand, to the best of his students Dennis Hart Mahan was an inspiring teacher (among the so-called Immortals at the foot of the class he induced terror), and after graduation many picked up where he had left off and pursued the study of military history and grand strategy on their own. In George McClellan Mahan saw that he had an exceptional student, one who would in fact lead the class in his department. Fifteen years later, when McClellan became a general, Mahan wrote him that of the small group he had marked out for high command "the luck has been singular that I find some of you turn up as I hoped for."[12]

By the spring of his final year it was obvious that McClellan would finish very near the top of his class. He had hopes for first place and the first choice of branches: engineers, topographical engineers, ordnance, or a line assignment in the artillery, infantry, or dragoons. The Corps of Engineers was almost invariably the election of any cadet who had the choice. "We were taught with every breath we drew at West Point ... that the engineers were a species of gods ... ," wrote John Tidball of the class of 1848. Encouraging McClellan to select the engineers was Lieutenant Gustavus W. Smith of the engineering faculty. McClellan related that Smith had taken a personal interest in him earlier in the year, invited him to his home, "& since then has been the kindest friend I have had on the Point." Another direction was suggested by his old private school teacher, Sears Cook Walker, who urged McClellan to seek assignment to him at the Naval Observatory. He declined; he was certain that the engineers promised the best avenue to the further study of his passion, military science. It was the elite corps, he told his mother, and "everything is expected of them in time of trouble."[13]

A time of trouble was very much on his mind in that spring of 1846, as rumors swept through West Point of an impending clash with Mexico over the disputed Texas boundary. Many of the cadets and faculty had friends among the officers in General Zachary Taylor's force of regulars on the scene, McClellan wrote, and there was much concern. At the same time, he and his classmates were excited by the prospect of war. There was the promise of action, of putting their training to use. There was also the promise of advancement. The army was notorious for its glacial pace of promotion in peacetime. With no compulsory retirement, officers could stay on in service to die with their boots on while those below them were stranded in grade until a vacancy opened. As a result, many West Pointers did their required four years' service after graduation and then resigned to put their excellent engineering training to use in civilian life. McClellan had expected to follow the same path, although in the direction of the law; "it is quite probable that I shall have a shingle up when 25 or 26," he wrote in March 1846. But a war could change everything, bringing with it an expansion of forces and the probability of rapid advancement.

When the news came of clashes on the Rio Grande and of President James Polk's war message, McClellan burst out in youthful enthusiasm to Frederica, "Hip! Hip! Hurrah! War at last sure enough! Aint it glorious!... Well, it appears that our wishes have at last been gratified & we shall soon have the intense satisfaction of fighting the crowd — musquitoes & Mexicans &c.... You have no idea in what a state of excitement we have been here." No one knew whether the whole class would be ordered to Texas, or whether they would remain at home to drill the 50,000 volunteers the president had called for. Although not yet a regular, McClellan had a regular's contempt for "fancy volunteers," as he termed them. If there was any hard fighting to be done, he predicted, it was the regulars who would do it.[14]

In June 1846, on the eve of graduation, McClellan delivered his valedictory address as president of the Dialectic Society. The Dialectic represented the intellectual cream of West Point's upper classmen, with membership by invitation. The group met every Saturday evening to hear and discuss papers by its members and to debate issues of the day. In his address McClellan described the Dialectic's literary pursuits as "essential to the man who would bear the character of an accomplished & polished gentleman...." He spoke of the place of the military in society and of his view of the essentials of command. "War is the greatest game at which man plays, & officers sustain the most important parts in it," he said, and as future officers his listeners must mitigate the "miseries of the contest" whenever possible. They must control and motivate their men, and he reminded them of Napoleon's "thrilling proclamations which imposed new ardor into the worn out frames of his troops. . . ." In closing, he turned to a matter he regarded with grave concern — the growth of divisive sectionalism across the country.

By most testimony, sectionalism had not yet struck deep roots at West Point. McClellan's classmate Truman Seymour of Vermont recalled that such questions were rarely discussed in his time at the Academy. Another contemporary, John Tidball of Ohio, thought what regional differences there were involved merely distinctive speech and diet and the Southerners' fascination with politics. Yet in 1843 the superintendent had found it necessary to refuse the Dialectic Society permission to debate the constitutionality of nullification, and certainly George McClellan thought the sectional issue potentially dangerous enough to devote the peroration of his address to it. If it ever happened, he said, "that party or sectional spirit should rise so high as to bring upon us the horrors of a civil war, . . . let the army, united as one man, throw its weight into the scale, & the result cannot be doubtful. . . . Let us hope that the army will ever incline to the conservative party, to that one whose motto shall be 'The Union, one & indivisible.' " In conclusion, he borrowed from the Gospel of St. Mark, as would Abraham Lincoln a dozen years later: "Remember the proverb — 'A house divided within itself, must surely fall.' "[15]

McClellan felt that his overall accomplishments entitled him to first place in the class of 1846, but he had to settle for second, behind Charles S. Stewart. He did not accept the verdict gracefully. "I must confess that I have malice enough to want to show them that if I did not graduate head of my class, I can nevertheless do something," he wrote his family. In later years he could look back on that pledge with satisfaction. Forty-four of his fifty-eight classmates would fight in the Civil War, and of those, six served under him as generals in the Army of the Potomac: Jesse Reno, Darius Couch, Truman Seymour, Samuel Sturgis, George Stoneman, and George H. Gordon. Four others fought against him as generals in the Army of Northern Virginia: David R. Jones, Cadmus Wilcox, George Pickett (the class Immortal, dead last), and Tom Jackson, seventeenth in class rank and destined for military fame as Stonewall. Of the future Union generals in other classes at West Point during McClellan's four years there, he would command nineteen of them in the Potomac army, including William Franklin, Ambrose Burnside, Fitz John Porter, Winfield S. Hancock, William F. Smith, Charles P. Stone, John Gibbon, and Alfred Pleasonton. Others he would face in Confederate gray during the war were G. W. Smith of the faculty, Simon Bolivar Buckner of the class of 1844, and A. P. Hill, who had fallen back to the class of 1847 because of illness. Charles Stewart would serve under him as well, as a captain of engineers.[16]

On July 1, 1846, the new graduate was commissioned a brevet second lieutenant in the Corps of Engineers, and a few days later, on leave in Philadelphia, he received orders to report back to West Point for duty with the newly formed Company of Engineer Soldiers. This was to be the elite company in the elite corps of the army, he told Frederica, "all that I could hope, ask, or expect; it is exactly what I desired."

The engineer soldiers were intended to be jacks of all trades, able to construct military roads, bridge rivers, erect fortifications and batteries, and lay out siege lines. Recruits had to be American-born, single, active and able-bodied, educated at a minimum in reading and writing, and to have a "mechanical trade." While they were not required to resemble the Apollo Belvedere, Mc-Clellan wrote, they did have to be several cuts above the usual enlistees and were expected to earn their extra pay. Captain Alexander J. Swift, a West Point instructor in engineering, headed the new company. McClellan's friend G. W. Smith was second in command, and he was the third-ranking commissioned officer. Some two months were allotted for organizing, equipping, and drilling the company before it embarked for "the seat of war" in Mexico.[17]

The young second lieutenant plunged enthusiastically into his new duties as organizer and drillmaster. He had the recruits on the field by eight in the morning and continued with them until the supper hour, giving instruction in both the infantry drills of the School of the Soldier and the specific skills of field engineering. After supper, McClellan wrote, "we go to Capt Swift's & read 'sapping & mining,' until tattoo, I then go down to tattoo, roll call, & my day's work is over." He was pleased with the company's progress — it could soon assemble a pontoon bridge as fast as the famous French corps of pontooners, he boasted — and by September he pronounced his men ready and eager for a fight. If the war did not end before they reached it, he wrote, "I'll be most confoundedly mistaken if we dont thrash them 'some.'"

Even in these busy weeks McClellan did not forget that his commission was that of a gentleman as well as an officer. He assured his mother that he had upheld the proper tone of Philadelphia society when it was momentarily brought "below par" by an acquaintance of his father's he encountered at the hotel on the Academy grounds. The man had clapped him on the shoulder and called him George and otherwise acted "entirely too familiar & impertinent to suit my taste," he related. "I looked at him, & spoke to him in a way to astonish him a little ... and I have been 'Mr. McClellan' ever since." Had the man acted at all decently, he would have humored him for his father's sake, he explained, but he believed in propriety "& intend to follow it out always." Nor did a gentleman go to war without proper personal service. He and G. W. Smith arranged with McClellan's brother-in-law in Alabama to borrow his black servant Songo to handle their horses and organize their mess when they reached the war zone.[18]

The engineer company with its three officers and seventy-one rank and file sailed from New York on September 26, 1846, and reached Brazos Santiago, near the mouth of the Rio Grande, two weeks later. McClellan landed well prepared for action, with a double-barreled shotgun, two pistols, a saber, a dress sword, and a bowie knife. The water at their camp was bad, strong winds blew sand into everything, and, in a journal he began keeping, he condemned Brazos Santiago as the worst port on the Texas coast. He also complained that they had arrived too late to take any part in the recent American victory at Monterrey. An armistice was now in force, creating uncertainty about the company's future role.

The Mexicans' surrender at Monterrey on September 24, combined with their defeats at Palo Alto and Resaca de la Palma the previous May, appeared to secure General Taylor's hold on the disputed triangle of Texas land between the Rio Grande and the Nueces that had triggered the war in the first place. There was still the Mexican presence in California and the vast territory west of Santa Fe, but various land and naval expeditions were preparing to deal with that. The navy also had the Mexican ports of Tampico and Vera Cruz under blockade. Zachary Taylor, with his victories and his catchy nickname, Old Rough and Ready, was already being talked of as the Whigs' best candidate to unseat the Democrats in 1848.

While Taylor marked time awaiting Washington's reaction to the armistice, McClellan was stricken with dysentery and malaria, which kept him in hospital quarters for nearly a month. He was nursed through the worst of it by his classmate Jimmy Stuart, newly arrived with his regiment of Mounted Rifles. The malaria would recur in later years—he called it his "Mexican disease"—often at critical times in his military fortunes. His recovery in mid-November coincided with a major shift in war plans. Taylor's armistice was disapproved, he came under a cloud for granting it, and a new campaign took shape under the personal direction of the army's general-in-chief, Winfield Scott.[19]

At six feet five inches and 250 pounds, Scott towered over the military establishment of his day in fact as well as in intellect. He had gained a reputation for his victories at Chippewa and Lundy's Lane during the War of 1812, and added to it by promoting a new sense of professionalism throughout the regular army in the years between that war and the conflict with Mexico. He was named head of the army in 1841. Everything about Scott was outsized, including his vanity and his political ambition— like Taylor, he was a Whig—but in matters of strategy he was eminently clear-headed. Rather than continue the peripheral campaigning in Mexico's northern provinces, he gathered forces for a thrust inland from Vera Cruz directly on Mexico City, reasoning that the enemy would mass all his forces to defend his capital and thus lay himself open to total defeat. With Vera Cruz known to be heavily defended, the port of Tampico, midway down the coast from the Rio Grande, was made the staging area for the expedition. The division of volunteers under General Robert Patterson was ordered to Tampico by road, its way prepared by the Company of Engineer Soldiers.

The 400-mile advance to Tampico was generally without event, and McClellan had opportunity to observe the volunteers and their civilian-soldier officers, or mustangs, as the regulars called them, after the unkempt and intractable Texas mustangs many of them rode. Mustang ineptitude was an article of faith among West Pointers. They noted with amusement that fortifications erected by troops under Gideon Pillow, President Polk's one-time law partner, were ditched on the inside rather than the outside, and were totally inadequate in any case. A story made the rounds that Jimmy Stuart had mounted a stunted Texas mustang and jumped Pillow's lines in one easy bound. The volunteers, known as Mohawks for their wild-Indian ways, had already compiled an ugly reputation in their camps on the Rio Grande. "They think nothing of robbing & killing the Mexicans," McClellan wrote a month after his arrival.

On the march this "Continental Army," as he sarcastically termed it, was in his eyes an appalling sight. He recorded in his journal finding himself one day in the middle of one of its columns, "and the Lord deliver me from ever getting into such a scrape again. Falstaff's company were regulars in comparison with these fellows — most of them without coats; some would have looked much better without *any pants,* than with the parts of pants they wore; all had torn & dirty shirts — uncombed hair — unwashed faces — they were dirt & filth from top to toe." If they were attacked, their defeat would be certain. Military appearance was always a matter of great importance to George McClellan, and he never lost the conviction that before a man could begin to fight like a soldier he must look and be equipped like one.[20]

The company reached Tampico on January 24, 1847, and remained there for a month while men, equipment, and transportation were assembled for the Vera Cruz expedition. McClellan was back with the regulars now, including a number of his West Point classmates, and he decided that for a subaltern of twenty this was soldiering at its best. His servant, Songo, proved to be an expert scrounger, considerably easing the burdens of life in the field. He wrote his mother that, in spite of the volunteers, he had enjoyed the "charm & excitement" of the march. "I could live such a life for years & years without becoming tired of it. . . . You never saw such a merry set as we are — no care, no trouble — we criticize the Generals — laugh & swear at the mustangs & volunteers, smoke our cigars & drink our brandy, when we have any. . . . We are living on the fat of the land — game, oysters, vegetables of all kinds, champagne &c &c, warm baths when we want them. . . ."

Lieutenant McClellan's plaints about political generals were not so offhand as his letter suggests. He had earlier asked his father to pull all the strings possible to get him a captaincy in one of the ten new regiments of regulars that Congress had authorized. When he found he was too late, he fired off a letter bitterly critical of the administration. He could not imagine a "weaker head" for the government than President Polk, he wrote; even a petty Italian city-state would display more energy in prosecuting the war. Worst of all were the commanders of the new regiments, "deficients of the Mil. Academy, friends of politicians, & bar room blaguards. . . ." He could not understand how anyone believed that putting a uniform on a civilian made him an officer. "The climate of Spitzbergen and Arabia are not more different than the characteristics of a Civil & a Military man," he wrote, "& as well might we expect those climates to change in an hour, as to see a citizen become a good officer without years of training." He had yet to see war, but he was convinced that it was a matter for professionals; civilians could not understand it, or be permitted to direct it.[21]

Although still short of supplies and equipment, Scott elected to mount his attack before the approaching yellow fever season imperiled the whole offensive. By early March the warships and transports carrying the 13,000-man expeditionary force were assembled off Vera Cruz. A landing site was chosen in a small roadstead three miles south of the city, and on the morning of March 9 the first wave of regulars, including McClellan and his engineer company, boarded surfboats for the run into the beach.

"At last all was ready," he wrote in his journal, "but just before the order was given to cast off a shot whistled over our heads. 'Here it comes' thought everybody 'now we will catch it.' " To their astonishment, it was the only shot fired at them. They scrambled ashore unopposed and secured the beachhead. "Our company & 3rd Artillery ascended the sand hills & saw — *nothing*," he wrote. The Mexicans' failure to challenge the landing was fatal to their defense of Vera Cruz. Within four days the Americans had drawn their lines around the fortified city. Scott rejected a frontal assault in favor of a formal siege.

The Vera Cruz siege was an acid test for the new army professionalism advocated by the general-in-chief. The chief engineer himself, Colonel Joseph G. Totten, headed the contingent from the Corps of Engineers, which included Captain Robert E. Lee; both were members of what Scott called his "little cabinet" of advisers. Other engineers whose paths would cross McClellan's in the future were First Lieutenants P. G. T. Beauregard and Isaac I. Stevens. McClellan and his classmate John G. Foster were the most junior of the ten engineers active in the siege. The topographical engineers at hand included Captain Joseph E. Johnston and Second Lieutenant George G. Meade. Shortly after the landing, Captain Swift of the engineer company fell ill — he would die in New Orleans several weeks later — and G. W. Smith took over the company, with McClellan as second-in-command. They would have much to do, for Scott intended his engineers not only to lay out siege lines and construct batteries but to act as his eyes as well.

The engineer soldiers' first task was to rough out access roads to the infantry and battery positions, and McClellan and Smith took the occasion to reconnoiter well in advance of their lines. They were spotted, and McClellan remarked of his first time under fire that bullets came "whistling like hail" around his head. During one of these expeditions he located the city's main aqueduct, and soon Vera Cruz's principal water supply was cut off. "It was upon reporting to Col. Totten on this night (12th) that he said that I (& G.W.) were the only officers who had as yet given him any information of value — that we had done more than all the rest &c &c," he wrote proudly.

For the remainder of the siege he erected mortar batteries under Captain Lee's direction. The working parties were mostly volunteers, and much of the labor was done under cover of darkness. Some daylight work was necessary, however, and one of Scott's staff recorded in his diary the arrival of Lieutenant McClellan at headquarters one evening: "His clothes were very much torn, and he said laughing that the Mexicans had been firing at his party nearly all day without hitting a man." Sleep, already at a premium during the siege, was made more difficult by the innumerable sand fleas that plagued the besiegers. McClellan and Smith came up with the idea of greasing their faces with salt-pork fat and crawling into large canvas bags, which they tied snugly around their necks. This kept the fleas at bay while they slept, causing the insects (so Dabney Maury claimed) to redouble their efforts "on us of the line who had no canvas bags."

The siege train proved inadequate, and Scott arranged to borrow heavier ordnance from the navy. While these guns were being brought ashore, those already in battery were ordered to open fire on the afternoon of March 22. "The command 'Fire!' had scarcely been given," McClellan wrote, "when a perfect storm of iron burst upon us — every gun & mortar in Vera Cruz & San Juan, that could be brought to bear, hurled its contents around us — the air swarmed with them.... The recruits looked rather blue in the gills when the splinters of shells fell around them, but the veterans cracked their jokes & talked about Palo Alto & Monterey." He went forward to observe the fall of their shot and pronounced the effect "superb." As the bombardment continued around the clock, he came under fire repeatedly while strengthening the battery positions and repairing damage caused by enemy fire. The naval battery, when it opened on March 24, was decisive. "The superiority of our fire was now very apparent," he noted. A truce was granted the Mexican garrison on March 26, and the next day it surrendered.[22]

Once Vera Cruz was secured and the batteries dismantled, Scott lost little time moving his army inland to higher and more healthful ground to avoid the yellow fever scourge. His line of advance was along the National Highway toward Mexico City, 250 miles distant. But in mid-April 1847 he came up against an extremely strong Mexican position at the village of Cerro Gordo, 50 miles from Vera Cruz, where the highway climbed through a narrow defile descriptively named the Devil's Jaws. General Antonio Lopez de Santa Anna massed 12,000 men and abundant artillery at the defile and promised to destroy the barbarian invaders from the north.

Cerro Gordo was a battle that George McClellan would long admire as a tactical masterstroke. Fourteen years later he would speak of pulling off "a Cerro Gordo" of his own during his first Civil War campaign. Ironically, his role in the actual battle was far from any scene of glory. To his utter disgust, he found himself with the least competent of the mustang generals, who was assigned the least promising phase of Scott's battle plan.

The plan evolved largely from bold reconnaissances made by Beauregard and Lee of the engineers. Lee succinctly summed up the problem they faced: "The right of the Mexican line rested on the river at a perpendicular rock, unscalable by man or beast, and their left on impassable ravines...." However, they discovered a tortuous route that promised to turn Santa Anna's left flank, and a substantial force led by regulars was assembled for the movement. To distract the Mexicans, four regiments of Pennsylvania and Tennessee volunteers under Gideon Pillow were to make a demonstration against the opposite flank. Lieutenant McClellan and ten of his engineer troops were ordered (as he described it) "to go with Gid Pillow & the Mohawks.... The idea of being killed by or among a parcel of volunteers was anything but pleasant." He took it as an ill omen when in a preliminary skirmish a Mexican round shot "came about as near my head as would be regarded agreeable in civil life...."

The diversionary movement on April 18 immediately went awry when Pillow ignored the route laid out for him, missed the enemy flank entirely, and instead ran up against strongly posted batteries at the center of the Mexican line. Coordination among the four regiments evaporated. One attacked unsupported and was driven back, and another dutifully endured an artillery barrage while waiting in vain for the order to return fire. McClellan did what he could to sort out the tangle, the natural result, he wrote angrily, of Pillow's "folly, his worse than puerile imbecility...." Pillow sent him to General Scott to plead for a reinforcement of regulars. Scott refused, and McClellan noted in his journal that the commanding general did not seem surprised at his report of the defeat. As it happened, Pillow's check had no effect on the battle, for the main flanking attack was spectacularly successful and Santa Anna's army fled Cerro Gordo in rout. Soon white flags were flying from the works. McClellan had to explain to one of the puzzled volunteer officers that they signified surrender.[23]

Scott's campaign came to an involuntary halt after Cerro Gordo while he struggled with manpower problems. The enlistments of most of his volunteer units had expired, and in spite of his entreaties they refused to see the campaign through. McClellan would face a similar frustration with three-month volunteers in 1861 and be reminded of the intractability of Mohawks. Soon a third of the army was on its way home. At Puebla, ninety miles from Mexico City, Scott impatiently marked time for nearly three months while waiting for replacements.

McClellan left no contemporary account of his part in the remainder of the Mexico City campaign. He stopped making entries in his journal, and none of his letters for the period has survived. However, he did recall for a biographer years later one incident in which he took obvious pride. He was with the lead division approaching Puebla when warning came of an imminent Mexican attack. He rode forward to reconnoiter, but discovered no enemy except a Mexican cavalry captain on a similar mission. The captain wheeled his horse about and raced away. McClellan gave pursuit, mounted on a fast mare he had obtained from his brother-in-law to use ''in *action* & on extraordinary occasions.'' He rode the Mexican down and forced his surrender, then nearly lost him as he bolted off in another attempt to escape. Once again McClellan's horse proved the faster, and he retrieved his prisoner and brought him triumphantly back to the column.[24]

He occupied his off-duty hours at Puebla by reviewing the sixteenth-century conquest of Mexico by Cortés, whose invasion route the Americans were following. At a local seminary he purchased a first edition of Bernal Díaz's classic account of the conquest, which he discovered while searching ''for something readable among their shelves of bad theology.'' Yet he would not remember the months at Puebla with any pleasure, for it was there that a letter reached him from Philadelphia announcing the death of his father. Dr. George McClellan had died without warning on May 9, 1847, at the age of fifty, leaving his wife with two minor children, ages seven and five, and assets — his trotting horses and a manuscript on surgical practices — considerably short of meeting the debts he had accumulated. McClellan was stunned by the news. G. W. Smith recalled that ''for several days he would see no one & was inconsolable.'' Even five months later, in a letter to his brother John, he could hardly bring himself to write of their father, whom he called ''as noble a being as ever graced the earth.'' He would take joint responsibility for the debts, he told John, ''whether it will be a work of five or of twenty years for me to pay off my share....''[25]

On August 6 the brigade of future president Franklin Pierce reached Puebla, raising Scott's strength to some 10,700. Santa Anna was known to have at least twice that number. Expecting no further reinforcements — convinced, in fact, that for political reasons the Democratic administration, chary of his success, was withholding support — Scott put his army on the march for Mexico City the next day. To make full use of all available manpower, he called in his garrisons and cut his communications with Vera

Cruz, determining to live off the countryside. If not as dramatic a gesture as Cortés's burning his ships to demonstrate to his men that there would be no turning back, it was an exceptionally bold move for a general of that day. When told of the decision, the Duke of Wellington is supposed to have exclaimed "Scott is lost!"

McClellan was probably employed to some extent in reconnoitering the approaches to Mexico City, but the primary scouting was done by Lee and Beauregard. Selecting the southern approach, Scott encountered the first serious opposition near the village of Contreras. Again McClellan found himself under the orders of Gideon Pillow, and it very nearly cost him his life. What he would remember about the first day of the Battle of Contreras, August 19, was his narrow escapes.

Sent forward on a reconnaissance to develop the Mexican position, he ran into skirmishers and had his horse shot out from under him. Pillow ordered the battery of Captain John Bankhead Magruder to keep the Mexican defenders occupied while infantry circled around to take their position in flank and rear. Magruder's four 12-pounders were supported by a battery of light mountain howitzers under Lieutenant Franklin Callender. In posting the section of Magruder's guns commanded by his classmate Tom Jackson, McClellan had a second horse killed under him, this time by a round shot. Badly outnumbered and outgunned, the American batteries were pounded mercilessly. An eyewitness, Daniel Harvey Hill of the 4th Artillery, wrote, with the bluntness of a regular, "Certainly of all the absurd things that the ass Pillow has ever done this was the most silly. Human stupidity can go no farther than this. . . ." The commander of Magruder's other section was mortally wounded, and McClellan took over for him. Then Callender of the howitzer battery went down, and he assumed that command. At some point during the bloody afternoon he was knocked down by a grapeshot, but the force of the blow was taken by the hilt of his sword and he escaped with a bruise. At nightfall the batteries were finally withdrawn, "in somewhat crippled state," as Magruder phrased it. For his efforts McClellan earned a mention in dispatches.

Like Cerro Gordo, the mismanaged holding operation against the Mexican center at Contreras had its rewards. Early on August 20, in just seventeen minutes, the position was stormed from the rear and Santa Anna's troops routed. Scott was relentless in pursuit. That afternoon he hurled every available man against the next blocking position, at Churubusco. "A tremendous fight came off," Colonel Ethan Allen Hitchcock of Scott's staff wrote in his diary. It is not known what role McClellan played in this headlong assault, but he was certainly under fire, and would earn a brevet promotion to first lieutenant "for gallant and meritorious conduct" in the battles of Contreras and Churubusco. In his official report, Brigadier Persifor F. Smith wrote of G. W. Smith and McClellan, "Nothing seemed to them too bold to be undertaken or too difficult to be executed...."[26]

Scott granted the Mexicans an armistice following Churubusco in expectation of a peace agreement, but it was soon apparent that Santa Anna was using the time only to strengthen the defenses of his capital. Fighting resumed in September, and Scott pressed ahead with plans to seize the formidable bastion of Chapultepec, commanding the final approach to the city's gates. "If we carry Chapultepec, *well;* if we fail or suffer great loss, there is no telling the consequences," Colonel Hitchcock noted in his diary when the decision was made.

During the night of September 11, McClellan and the engineer soldiers went to work laying out four batteries of siege guns intended to reduce the bastion's fortifications. Two of the batteries were finished rapidly and opened the next morning. The other two, in more difficult sites, had to be completed in daylight under enemy fire. Lee directed the work, with McClellan as his assistant, and by dawn on September 13, the day selected for the assault, they had all their guns in action. At 8:00 A.M. the gunners ceased their fire and the infantry was ordered forward. By 9:30 two divisions of volunteers, spearheaded by regulars using scaling ladders, had broken through the defenses and planted their flags atop the heights of Chapultepec. As Santa Anna's men fled toward the city, McClellan joined William Worth's division of regulars in pursuit.

Worth's objective was the San Cosme city gate, which could be approached only over a narrow causeway through swampy marshlands. The Mexicans' artillery commanded the causeway, and their infantry had the cover of houses lining it on both sides for nearly a mile. McClellan and the engineer troops took the lead in the house-to-house fighting, breaking through the common walls with pickaxes. Light howitzers, one directed from a church

belfry by a 4th Infantry quartermaster, Ulysses S. Grant, cleared
the rooftops. Successively outflanked by these tactics, the enemy
was forced back until by nightfall the San Cosme gate was in
Worth's hands. At the same time, a division of volunteers under
John A. Quitman seized the Belem gate. In the early morning
hours of September 14 word came that Santa Anna had evacuated
the city with what was left of his army. Shortly after daylight
the American flag was raised over Mexico City's central plaza.
The peace process would now begin in earnest.[27]

"I feel so glad and proud that I have got safely through the
battles in this war, that it will take a heavy, heavy shock to make
me despond," McClellan wrote John from Mexico City a few
weeks later, and he added, "Thank God! our name has not suffered, so far, at my hands." He had reason for pride. His personal
courage had been amply demonstrated. In the Vera Cruz siege
and at Cerro Gordo and the battles for Mexico City he had done
his duty and more, often under severe enemy fire; Chapultepec,
in fact, would earn him a second brevet promotion, to captain.
Yet his accomplishments were those of a very junior officer, far
removed from any real command or planning responsibility. General Scott's cabinet of advisers did not include twenty-year-old
lieutenants hardly a year out of West Point. McClellan had no
illusions about his record. On his return from Mexico, when the
leading citizens of Philadelphia honored him with a presentation
sword, he found the ceremony something of an embarrassment.
"They will humbug me into the belief that I am somebody," he
told his mother; ". . . it actually causes a kind of feeling of shame
to rise in me this being rewarded for doing a subaltern's duty in
such a small business. . . ."[28]

For much the same reason, it is hard to imagine that Mc-
Clellan's future opponents, such as Beauregard or Joe Johnston
or Robert E. Lee, discovered the inner secrets of his military
character during the campaign. They may have noted his bravery,
to be sure, but everyone was brave; 452 brevets for gallantry
were distributed among the 523 West Point graduates who served
in Mexico. McClellan also made the most of his opportunities, but
that was to be expected of a West Pointer. On his record he could
best be described as "promising." Nor did the youthful lieutenant learn anything very revealing about these more senior officers. Like everyone else, he admired Lee's daring reconnaissance

efforts throughout the campaign, but that he deduced nothing in particular from this demonstration of personal bravery is evident in his analysis of Lee, a year into the Civil War, as "*too cautious & weak*" when faced with responsibility.

Still, McClellan drew certain lessons from the Mexican War that became embedded in his military thinking. One was a thorough contempt for the civilian management of the conflict. This was a view hardly unique among the regulars, but he did not confine his opinions to campfire conversations or private letters. Exercising the certitude of youth, he put them on paper for the benefit of a United States senator.

The immediate reason for his letter, he wrote on October 31, 1847, was to protest the awarding of an undeserved commission in the Mounted Rifles — his friend Jimmy Stuart's unit — to the mountain man and scout Kit Carson. He then lunged into a ringing condemnation of civilian officers of every stripe: "In the name of God, Sir, does the History of the world present such another instance as that of our govt., which having at its disposal men trained to be soldiers from their boyhood who were educated expressly for the army, in probably the best Military Academy in the world, passes over these men ... & goes behind the curtain, into county courthouses, & low village bar rooms to select her generals, her colonels & all the officers of her new regiments?" He concluded with harsh indictments of the two political generals, Patterson and Pillow, under whom he had served. No doubt he took comfort when three months later the Senate disapproved Carson's commission.

If his view of mustang generals was not at all tempered by events since the march to Tampico, he apparently resigned himself to the necessity of volunteers in the ranks in a war emergency. As he had witnessed, the hard fighting they displayed in the closing battles for Mexico City demonstrated that they could gain a battlefield education. In a memorandum on the lessons of the Mexican War he composed early in 1848, he insisted that in the best of all worlds "it is barely possible to make a decent soldier even of Infantry in 5 years, much less of Engineers, Artillery and Dragoons. ..." What he urged — and would continue to urge in the years ahead — was a peacetime army with half-size companies but numerous enough in regular officers to be doubled in an emergency through rank-and-file volunteering while utilizing its cadre of trained officers to turn the new levies into soldiers. "Last not least," he wrote, "if citizens must be appointed they should in every case go in below those already in service — that is to say as 2nd Lts, not as generals." However professionally ideal this last notion may have been, it exhibited an artless view of the political realities of building a wartime army.[29]

He also learned much from Winfield Scott. Scott's rejection of costly head-on assaults in favor of siege tactics, as at Vera Cruz, and of turning movements, as at Cerro Gordo, seemed to him worthy of emulation. So was the careful preparation before taking the offensive, as at Puebla. In February 1848, after Scott was relieved by President Polk — another example of political chicanery, McClellan thought — there was a final review in his honor in Mexico City. He took the salutes of his troops from a balcony, McClellan wrote, and "the noble old fellow must have felt that even if the administration has relieved him from commanding they could not weaken the hold he has upon the respect & affection of every man in the army." That relationship between general and private was another lesson carefully noted.

Other elements of Scott's generalship, however — his boldness in breaking with conventional military wisdom, his relentless pressure applied to a wavering foe — apparently made less impact on his young subordinate. McClellan later praised Scott as "the General under whom I first learned the art of war," but he would be selective in applying that art. The best explanation for this selectivity may be his agreement with his friend Joe Johnston, who wrote him in 1856, "I hope it may never be my lot to fight troops much better than el señor Mexicans — there is no comfort like that of going into battle with the certainty of winning."[30]

The eight months McClellan spent in Mexico City while peace was made fully compensated him for any campaign hardships. He and G. W. Smith and the engineer company were quartered in the palatial home of the former Mexican chief of staff, and he had just enough to do — he was acting quartermaster for the company — to remind him that he was still a soldier. He went sightseeing in and around the capital, attended the opera regularly, and visited the Aztec Club, a convivial gathering place for officers, where, he wrote home, "we will meet none but gentlemen." He went on to detail his daily life on occupation duty:

"G.W. and myself have fine tablecloths, china plates, cups &c (gilt at that), excellent knives & *silver* forks. We have omelette every morning for breakfast, soup, ducks, snipe &c &c for dinner.... *Aint* I glad I'm alive. I tell you that one cant tell what fine fun it is to live until he has been through about 6 battles!" A romance with a señorita named Nachita rounded out this soldier's dream. "Not many so good & pretty as Nachita in this world of ours," he would recall. After he left Mexico City, Jimmy Stuart assured him that his farewell note "was delivered to N——a, who as report stated, cried uninterruptedly for the space of a week ... but as she has done the same thing several times before for others, don't cut your throat...."

At last the peace treaty was signed and the occupation ended. As sorry as he was to leave Mexico City, McClellan wrote, he was sorrier at the ending of a unique comradeship: "The attachments formed in a campaign with men by whose side you have fought, ... with whom you have exulted in the moment of victory & whom you have met day after day — such attachments cannot be severed without a pang." In June 1848 his orders came to report with the Company of Engineer Soldiers to West Point. The great adventure was over, he told his mother: "I suppose I must make up my mind to pass the rest of my life in a very tame & humdrum manner."[31]

TWO

ON PEACETIME SERVICE

LIFE in the peacetime army was a tremendous letdown for an ambitious twenty-one-year-old subaltern fresh from the triumphs of a foreign war. McClellan was too bored even to keep up a journal. In a rare entry, written in September 1849, he summed up the lessons of fifteen months of garrison duty at West Point: "Mc thinks that he's booked for an infernally monotonous life for the remainder of his natural existence...."

He did his best to win a change of scene. In appealing to the chief engineer, Brigadier Joseph G. Totten, for an assignment on the Pacific Coast, he claimed it was for the good of the service; the army gained nothing by posting him with the engineer company, "a mere matter of dull routine & duty...." Totten was unmoved. He pointed out that the new company commander, Captain George W. Cullum, was occupied with his duties on the West Point faculty, and with G. W. Smith on extended leave, McClellan was the company's only experienced full-time officer. McClellan read between these lines that dull routine was likely to be his lot for some time to come.[1]

Although the army's official register listed him as a member of the Military Academy's engineering faculty, McClellan did not in fact instruct cadets during his West Point assignment. They may have observed him directing practice field operations — pontoon bridging, for example — but his only classroom work was with the Company of Engineer Soldiers, to whom he taught mathematics and practical engineering. He was highly sensitive to the distinction, which led to acrimonious debate with both the Academy administration and the Engineer Department in Washington. The argument began with his arrival from Mexico in June 1848 and was still an issue three years later, when he moved on to his next post.[2]

The Academy superintendent, Captain Henry Brewerton, was something of a martinet, and McClellan bristled when he was ordered about like a junior member of the faculty. He maintained that as an officer of the engineer company he was subject only to General Totten's orders; where the company was stationed had no bearing on the matter. Totten negotiated a truce between the two that lasted more than a year, but war broke out anew in November 1849, when McClellan was called on to explain his absence at compulsory chapel. He dissented at length and took the case to Totten, who diplomatically replied that, although he was technically in the right, he should voluntarily abide by Academy rules. He would be only too happy to do so now that the principle was settled, McClellan wrote. He had raised the objection only to protest ''an order entirely repugnant to my feelings & conscience.''

Captain Cullum fell ill, and on June 18, 1850, McClellan became acting commander of the Company of Engineer Soldiers. From that post he continued his skirmishing with Brewerton. They debated the location of a storage shed for the company's equipment, with McClellan taking his case to Totten in seven pages of exhaustive argument. Nothing less than his reputation was at stake, he insisted. This badly placed shed would catch everyone's eye, ''& I will be accused of ignorance, apathy or neglect....'' He lost that case, but fared better when he took issue with the right of the Academy to apply rules for cadets to the men of the engineer company. Like his father, he had no taste for compromise, and carried all disputes to the limits of appeal. ''I don't think that I am of a quarrelsome disposition,'' he remarked to his sister-in-law, Maria, '' — but I do have the luck of getting into more trouble than any dozen other officers....''[3]

He also continued to seek a new assignment. His proposal for a manual of siege engineering had him studying abroad at the best French military schools. He was turned down, but he won a favorable response from Winfield Scott to his plan for translating a leading French manual on bayonet tactics. When it was reported in 1851 that Congress might authorize a new regiment of dragoons, he applied for a captaincy. The legislature failed to act. Meanwhile he campaigned to raise the Company of Engineer

Soldiers to parity with the other service branches. He called for an Engineer School of Practice, operating (and commanded) independently at its own station. "The proper time for instruction in pract. eng. would be after Cadets have graduated in the course of eng., & at a post affording proper facilities to Officers, Cadets & Soldiers," he explained. "Nothing whatever of the slightest importance, in this branch, can ever be done at this post."

McClellan pressed his case in a tone so demanding that the long-suffering Totten lost patience and forwarded his proposal to Secretary of War Charles M. Conrad with the comment that it was unmilitary and improper. In his endorsement Conrad agreed: "Its tone is very objectionable. The writer assumes to speak on the important subject it refers to more authoritatively than his rank & experience entitle him to. . . ." The young second lieutenant (his brevet captain's rank was honorary only) showed no tolerance for criticism. In a letter to a friend he dismissed Totten and Conrad as old women, and to his brother John he summed up his view of such matters: "I don't care much for anybody's opinion, as long as I am in the right." Implicit in the remark was his confident judgment of what was right.[4]

However much he chafed at the "indifference, stolidity & fogiesm" of the peacetime army, McClellan fully enjoyed the convivial society at West Point. After growling at his lot, he wrote his sister-in-law, "what pleasure it is to get with some comrade of the war & talk ('gas' as we say) over old times." He later numbered two of the faculty instructors, William Franklin and Fitz John Porter, among his closest friends. He also saw much of Dabney Maury, who brought his hunting dogs with him from Virginia and added a touch of sporting flavor to the scene. They hunted and fished and rode all across the scenic Hudson highlands. The slightest excuse was enough to begin popping corks, Maury recalled. In a letter written a few years later he shared a reminiscence of these times with McClellan: "How you and I went to church tight on Xmas eve . . . & how we then went to my room 'to take a quiet glass of punch' together and how we sat the punch in a tumbler on the coal fire to heat it and how it blazed up and astonished us and the dogs who were dozing on the hearth. . . ."[5]

McClellan had as well the pleasure of an unofficial postgrad-

uate course in the art of war conducted by Dennis Hart Mahan.
Mahan's Napoleon Club, open to the faculty and other officers
stationed at West Point, met regularly to hear and discuss papers
on Bonaparte's campaigns. McClellan prepared two such papers,
on the Battle of Wagram and on the Russian campaign of 1812.
He considered them major efforts. In the spring of 1851 he told
Maria that he had just presented a 111-page paper — probably
the one on the Russian campaign — to the Napoleon Club. ''I
have been working hard at it . . . & the ink was hardly dry on the
last part when it was read,'' he wrote. ''. . . I've been so intently
occupied with the one subject, that I have thought of but little
else.'' He added that the club members ''compliment me by saying that it gave a clear explanation of the campaign — so I am
contented.''

He continued to study military history on his own. Dabney
Maury wrote of him that he had ''the happiest faculty of ac-
quiring knowledge I have ever known. . . . He would often sit late
with a jovial party, and then go to study while we went to bed,
and be up in the morning, bright as the brightest.'' In a notebook
he jotted down observations on generalship from Marshal Saxe's
eighteenth-century classic on the art of war, *Mes Rêveries*.
McClellan made note of the French marshal's admonitions that
a general must take care of his men, always maneuver so as to
retain the option of accepting battle, observe the enemy's behavior with care, strike at the proper place at the right time, and
''know how to profit by the favorable moment, which decides the
success of a battle.'' His notes concluded with a quotation from
Saxe on the fruits of victory: ''If you gain a victory, profit by
it. I do not conform to the praiseworthy custom of contenting
yourself with the possession of the field of battle.'' McClellan's
later detractors would have been surprised to learn that he was
aware of this particular principle of warfare.[6]

To keep up with affairs in the world beyond West Point he
subscribed to the British magazine *Blackwood's* and followed
domestic matters in the pages of several newspapers and maga-
zines. His viewpoint was unwaveringly conservative and nation-
alistic. During the debates that produced the Compromise of 1850
he wrote his mother, ''The Union is not dissolved yet — I suspect
that there are too many sensible people in this large country to
consent to any such madness as that,'' and he applauded a speech

that "gave it to the South with about as much vim as they deserved."

Abolitionists were anathema to him, however. He had no patience with Northern defiance of the Fugitive Slave Act, noting with approval the capture and return of the escaped slave Thomas Sims in Boston in April 1851. "The abolitionists are making a great fuss," he wrote of the case. "Is it not shameful that such speeches should be tolerated? It is rank & open treason — neither more nor less." He hoped that "really intelligent" Bostonians would disavow such radical agitation. Although he tended to follow in the footsteps of his father, a staunch Whig partisan, his principles dictated his politics. He had favored the Whig Zachary Taylor for president in 1848, but in a local election a few years later he supported the Democratic backer of the Compromise over a Whig who was a professed abolitionist.[7]

In June 1851 McClellan was relieved from duty at West Point and ordered to Fort Delaware, a masonry work under construction on an island in the Delaware River, forty miles downstream from Philadelphia. It was a typical Corps of Engineers assignment for a junior officer and a far remove from the postings he had sought, yet to his surprise he liked it, at least at first. The pace was not overly demanding — Fort Delaware had been under construction since the late 1830s — and he had time to study and read and to learn German. The island, which went by the homely name of the Pea Patch, was a sportsman's paradise. "I have gone on the principle of making myself perfectly acquainted with my duties before I go to amusing myself," he wrote home. "I shall soon be able to work it so as to fish & shoot without interfering with my work." His one sadness in this otherwise pleasant summer was the news of a clash in the Oregon country between the Mounted Rifles and hostile Indians. "On the 18th of June 1851 at 5 in the afternoon died Jimmy Stuart, my best & oldest friend," he recorded in his journal.[8]

McClellan celebrated his twenty-fifth birthday on December 3, 1851, and reviewed his prospects. During the winter, assigned to duty in Washington to prepare his bayonet manual for publication, he appealed directly to General Totten for a more challenging appointment. He wrote John of his ambition: "There is much to be done & reputation to be gained. Am I not right, as long as I am a soldier by profession, to sacrifice personal comfort to the prospect of active service & gaining a reputation?" Good fortune came to him almost immediately. On March 5, 1852, he was ordered to report to Captain Randolph B. Marcy at Fort Smith, Arkansas, to serve as engineer, commissary, quartermaster, and second-in-command on an expedition to discover the sources of the Red River.[9]

Marcy, who turned forty as the expedition was being assembled, was a West Pointer and veteran of long and varied frontier service with the 5th Infantry. He was best known for having reconnoitered immigrant routes from Fort Smith to Santa Fe and El Paso three years earlier. This added much to the knowledge of the Texas border country, leaving the upper Red River area as the largest blank on the maps of the region. His task was to fill in this blank and describe the country and its resources for future travelers and settlers. McClellan reported for duty at Fort Smith on April 1. The party — four officers, 5th Infantry rank and file, and hunters and Indian guides — totaled seventy-five. They took with them a light 6-pounder fieldpiece to keep hostile tribes at bay.[10]

At Fort Washita, 150 miles southwest of Fort Smith and the jumping-off place for the expedition, McClellan met Mrs. Marcy and her younger daughter, Fanny. They were due to leave for the East, and he found Mary Marcy "a most pleasant & kind lady." The Marcys' other daughter, sixteen-year-old Mary Ellen, was at school at the Hartford Female Seminary in Connecticut. He was shown a daguerreotype of Ellen, as she was called, or sometimes Nelly, and thought her quite pretty. He was in fact impressed with all the Marcys. After the party was on the trail a week, he wrote his mother that Randolph Marcy "is one of the finest men I ever met with, & never saw one better fitted to conduct such an expedition."[11]

McClellan was equally pleased with his assignment, writing John that he would not have missed the opportunity for anything in the world. On May 7, camped "this side of nowhere," they were nearing what he described as the "Ultima Thule of the whites — all beyond is new, & unexplored. . . ." A month later, in the Texas Panhandle, they encountered the tracks of a large Indian war party. This inspired "a general cleaning of rifles & pistols," he noted in his journal, but they continued on their way without event. Among his duties was keeping a detailed daily meteorological record and helping to collect mineral samples.

On June 16 the party reached the source of the north fork of the Red River, and in honor of his second-in-command Captain Marcy named a pretty little tributary McClellan's Creek. Turning southward, they traced the main branch of the Red to its source. ''The scenery equals in beauty & wildness any that I ever beheld,'' McClellan wrote of Palo Duro Canyon in the Panhandle. The sight moved him to an imaginative eloquence: ''The immense bluffs tower above us on every side, & assume every shape that fancy may suggest — here you see a huge castle with a magnificent gothic entrance — there is an immense fortress, to which Cologne or Schweidnitz is but a plaything — on this side a beautiful East Indian temple. . . .''

Reaching civilization again on July 28, they were startled to be greeted as returned from the dead. Some days before, a report reached one of the frontier outposts that the expedition had been ambushed by 2,000 Comanches and massacred to the last man. The story had been a week-long sensation across the nation. McClellan blamed the hoax on ''a set of scoundrels, who seek to keep up agitation on the frontier in order to get employment from the Govt. in one way or other.'' He remarked sardonically that the hoaxer must have decided that ''we could not use the 6 pdr on account of the ground being too unobstructed, & not being able to see the Indians, for the reason that the sun was under a cloud. . . .''

Randolph Marcy proved to be one of the few superiors McClellan ever served under without friction. But even Marcy was briefly the object of his wrath. When McClellan was told (falsely, as it turned out) that his role in the expedition would be slighted in Marcy's Red River report, he snapped that he would never fall so low ''as to need the praises of any Captain of Infantry to help me along in the world — one of these days I may have the gentleman serving under me.'' He was glad to know, when the facts of the case were clear, that his trust in Marcy as ''an honorable gentleman'' was not misplaced.[12]

Parting from the captain in Arkansas, McClellan set off for the Gulf Coast with orders to report to General Persiphor F. Smith, commanding the military department of Texas. Through the fall of 1852 he acted as Smith's aide on a lengthy inspection tour of frontier posts. He liked the roughhewn western life. ''I can't stand inactivity," he wrote his mother from San Antonio, "& the very short rest of one week I've had here only makes me long for the march again." He sent his sister-in-law a wry account of a night in the raw settlement of Lamar, where he and the general shared quarters with an array of Texas fauna. First came a pair of deer "accustomed to sleep in my bed," he wrote, then "a force of 5 pigs, presently came in a pair of calves, then a dog moved in to drive them out — so the night passed,... how glad we were when daylight came & we bade adieu to Lamar!" That fall he received a copy of *Bayonet Exercise,* his first published work. He also arranged to pay off the last of his share of his father's debts by the sale of the 160 acres of bounty land awarded to Mexican War veterans.[13]

In October 1852, month-old orders from Washington caught up with McClellan, directing him to make a survey of rivers and harbors on the Texas coast. Totten explained that Congress had called for "such information by actual examinations and surveys as will permit projects of improvement to be made...." McClellan's first reaction was negative — he described the project to John as "this confounded river & harbor business" — but on reflection he saw a silver lining. For the first time in his army career he would be in charge rather than acting as an assistant.

He quickly mobilized resources for the new project. He requested the Coast Survey to send him whatever charts it had on Texas, purchased a small schooner, hired an assistant and six men, and set up his survey headquarters at Corpus Christi. These efforts took him to New Orleans, where he looked up his fellow engineer from the Mexican War, P. G. T. Beauregard. It was a new experience for him, he wrote his mother: "Stayed with Maj. Beauregard at his rooms, & took our meals at a French Restaurant — found it the most pleasant possible way of living for a Bachelor." During his survey work he also became acquainted with another Mexican War veteran, Captain Don Carlos Buell, whom he described as "one of the best men in the army."[14]

After a personal inspection and interviews with ship's pilots and others involved in the coastal trade, McClellan concluded that improving navigation on Texas's rivers and harbors was a matter of considerable complexity. The numerous sandbars were powerfully acted upon by tides and currents and winds, he wrote Totten. "These changes are constantly occurring, & these sudden variations have taken place as far back as the recollection of the Pilots &c extend.'' Displaying a solid grasp of engineering analysis, he explained that dredging alone would not solve the problems and that more complicated techniques were needed.

By March of 1853 he was completing the survey field work and preparing to write his report. He would be happy to be done with the project, he told Maria: ''Altho' I am glad to have had it, for the sake of learning something new, yet I must confess that I prefer prairies & pack mules, to the briny & a sail boat.'' He grew a mustache and in his spare hours continued his study of the art of war. He focused on the works of Antoine Henri Jomini, the Swiss military analyst whose studies of Napoleon and his campaigns were regarded as authoritative. ''The Jomini I have wanted badly,'' he wrote in acknowledging the arrival of one such volume from home.[15]

On April 7 McClellan arrived at Indianola, Texas, and found a telegram forwarded to him by Beauregard in New Orleans. It was from Isaac Stevens, one of the engineers he had served with in the Mexico City campaign, offering him a place in the most ambitious exploration yet undertaken by the army. Stevens explained that he had resigned his commission to become governor of Washington Territory, and was in charge of surveying a route for a transcontinental railroad from St. Paul, Minnesota, to Puget Sound. McClellan would command the far western half of the survey, exploring inland from the coast through the uncharted Cascade Range. ''The exploration arduous & will bring reputation,'' Stevens assured him. In his covering letter Beauregard termed it an excellent opportunity: ''I was on the point of answering *yes* for you.... I will take the liberty to advise you to accept his offer....'' McClellan promptly accepted, and in any case he soon received a telegram from General Totten ordering him to the duty. The order was issued before his letter of acceptance could have reached Washington, he told his younger brother, Arthur, and that suited him fine: ''If the duty should not be a pleasant one I cannot blame myself....'' This was written with tongue in cheek; later he would contrive to take the question seriously.[16]

The Stevens expedition was one of four such reconnaissances ordered by Jefferson Davis, secretary of war in the new administration of Franklin Pierce. The transcontinental railroad had become one of the most hotly debated topics in Congress. The one thing the legislators agreed upon was the need for a rail line to the Pacific. There was nothing like a consensus on the route it should follow, however. The possible expansion of slavery along a southern route was one of the argued questions, but not the only one. Every city and town on the fringes of settlement from New Orleans to St. Paul lobbied to be the eastern terminus of the trans-Mississippi line. The issue was at once sectional, political, and economic, and the result was a hopeless deadlock.

The Pacific Railroad Survey Act of March 1853 was designed to take the matter out of the halls of Congress and place it in the hands of the army. It was hoped that the western landscape itself would resolve the deadlock; the army expeditions, operating with scientific detachment, would by a process of elimination decide the best route in terms of practicality and cost. Setting out from St. Paul, Stevens was to survey the most northerly of the potential routes, between the 47th and 49th parallels, rendezvousing with McClellan east of the Cascades. A second expedition would follow a central path, and two others would trace more southerly routes. McClellan was ordered to report to Stevens in Washington and be prepared to sail soon afterward for the mouth of the Columbia via Panama. He completed his rivers and harbors report and on April 25 took leave of Texas. "EN ROUTE FOR OREGON!" he wrote in bold letters in his journal that day.[17]

In Washington McClellan conferred with Stevens and received his instructions, which granted him considerable leeway in carrying out his primary mission to "thoroughly explore" the Cascades from the Columbia River northward to the 49th parallel, "making detailed examination of the passes & obtaining full information in relation to the range in general." He sailed from New York on May 20, 1853, on the steamer *Illinois* for the Isthmus. On Panama's Pacific coast he took passage for San Francisco and from there for the army's Fort Vancouver on the Columbia. The voyage took almost six weeks, and he no doubt passed part of the time reading two books he had acquired, Lewis and Clark's history of their expedition, and Washington Irving's *Astoria,* an account of John Jacob Astor's fur-trading venture on the Columbia.[18]

He took three more weeks to assemble and equip his party at Fort Vancouver. Among those he called on for help were two more officers whose paths he would later cross, Charles P. Stone, the post's ordnance officer, and Ulysses S. Grant, the quartermaster. (As a member of the expedition recalled it, Grant went on a drinking spree, which the greatly annoyed McClellan neither forgave nor forgot.) To his mother he described the pleasure he expected in being the first to explore much of the Cascades: "No one but the Indians knows anything about the country between Mt. Rainier & the boundary. I shall be pleased as a child with a new toy when I get started...." It was the independence of command that he welcomed the most. "I've a good saddle — a fine command — a new country — hard work & plenty of responsibility on my shoulders — what more could one ask?"

When he set off for the Cascades on July 18, 1853, his party totaled sixty-one, with 160 horses and pack mules and three months' rations. George Gibbs, a scientist of reputation in the Northwest, served as geologist and ethnologist, and the party's doctor doubled as naturalist. The expedition, nearly as large as Captain Marcy's Red River exploration and modeled on it, included twenty-nine soldiers from the 4th Infantry at Fort Vancouver as escort. A party of such size had been no handicap on the Red River, but traversing mountain country proved to be another matter.[19]

After tracing the course of the Lewis River across the Cascades, the expedition turned northward and made its slow way along the eastern face of the range. For the first month it averaged only five miles a day. Finally McClellan realized he had overprepared, and reduced the number of animals by half and sent the infantry escort back to Fort Vancouver. "I've just returned from the mountains & a glorious old range it is — to look at; but awful to travel in," he wrote John on September 18. "... Now, with my reduced party, I shall have little else than pack mules & can travel much more rapidly." He took particular pride in naming one of the most impressive peaks he sighted Mount Stuart, after his dead friend Jimmy Stuart.

He found only two passes he considered even remotely feasible for a railroad — at the headwaters of the Naches and Yakima rivers — but both presented problems. The more difficult of the two, the Naches Pass route, would require at least five tunnels and many cuts through solid rock, he noted in his journal; he doubted he would "ever ride down the valley of the Nachess in a Railroad car." He was even more concerned by what the Indians had told him and by what he took to be snow marks on the trees. This indicated a winter snow depth in the Cascade passes of at least twenty feet, he concluded. He followed neither pass much beyond the summit of the range, and at Yakima Pass he was content to observe the surrounding area rather than explore it.

Discovering no other passes as he continued his northward course, McClellan met Governor Stevens and his party from St. Paul on October 18 at Fort Colville, near the Canadian border. At first their relationship was cordial enough, but when Mc-Clellan learned that Stevens expected him to test the passes he had found by a winter crossing and march to Puget Sound, he decided the governor was playing to his constituents in a dramatic but unnecessary gesture. ''Political barbecue & the devil played generally tonight,'' he wrote in his journal on October 28; '' — all well enough in its way, but don't like the way at all. Politics & surveys don't agree well together.'' Arguing that his animals were in no condition to risk the deep snow he expected to encounter, and that in any case his report should be accepted as fully meeting the needs of the survey, he got the order rescinded. The combined parties set out on the long way around the Cascades, via the Columbia.

Stevens was not prepared to give up his scheme, however, and at Fort Walla Walla he announced that one of his own men, Frederick W. Lander, would go through Naches Pass. McClellan was coldly furious at what he took to be an insult to his credibility and refused Lander any assistance, ''since the order has been given in direct opposition to my own judgment. . . .'' On November 9 he recorded in his journal, ''I have done my last service under civilians & politicians. . . . I will not consent to serve any longer under Gov. S. unless he promises in no way to interfere — merely to give the general orders & never to say one word as to the means or time of executing them.'' In assuring himself that he was blameless, he revealed another fixed characteristic — a bent for self-deception: ''The great consolation is that I was detailed in this service without either my knowledge or consent. . . .''[20]

In January 1854 he and a small party set out from Puget Sound on orders from Stevens to investigate the western approach to Yakima Pass. In his state of mind, he was not inclined to be bold. Well short of the pass snow was encountered to the depth of a foot and increasing. This confirmed to his satisfaction that the snow at the summit must be twenty to twenty-five feet deep, he reported to Stevens. ''I reluctantly determined to return — being forced to the conclusion that if the attempt to reach the pass was not really impracticable, it was at least inexpedient. . . .'' Dissatisfied with this effort, Stevens sent his own men through the pass, where they found an accumulation of six or seven feet of light snow and concluded it would not unduly hamper a rail crossing.

In his official report, McClellan declared it ''very evident'' that in the Cascades between the Columbia River and the Canadian border only Yakima Pass was ''at all practicable for a Railway.'' A crossing there would be expensive in money, time, and labor, however. He recommended instead a route that followed the Columbia — considerably longer, to be sure, but more economical to construct and with fewer wintertime problems. He defended his cursory explorations as justified by the extent of unknown territory he had to cover. The finding of Stevens's men he dismissed as a fluke, for he understood the season was unusually dry; with more data, he was sure, ''the statement of the Indians will be found to be quite near the truth.''

Although he stated these conclusions with his usual confidence, McClellan had in fact made reconnaissances empty of any real accomplishment. As Stevens's men demonstrated, he failed to document accurately the explorations he did make. Furthermore, he failed to discover three passes much superior to the Yakima route. Stampede Pass, just five miles to the south, would one day carry the Northern Pacific across the range. The main highway in the area would run through Snoqualmie Pass, five miles to the north. Thirty miles to the north, the Great Northern would cross the Cascades at Stevens Pass.[21]

This poor showing was due primarily to a prevalent, stubborn caution. His delay in reducing the party to manageable size sharply limited the time available for exploration. His willingness to accept the fanciful tales of his Indian informants in advance of — and instead of — actual investigation led him to discount evidence to the contrary. (This was not a result of inexperience; during the Red River expedition predictions made by Indians proved just as exaggerated.) His dispute with Stevens furnished him with one more excuse to close ranks against any opinion other than his own.

As it happened, McClellan would escape the Pacific railroad survey with nothing more damaging to his professional reputation than Isaac Stevens's displeasure. His dismal record as an explorer was not recognized at the time, and in any case it was obscured by the overall failure of the army surveys to advance the cause of a transcontinental line. Enough was found in favor of each of the four routes that no clear-cut choice emerged. Jefferson Davis's obvious bias toward the southernmost route contributed nothing to a spirit of compromise, and the congressional deadlock persisted. It would not be broken until 1862, after the Southern states had left the Union — and the Congress.

McClellan's relations with Governor Stevens, meanwhile, went from bad to worse. To document his final report, Stevens asked his subordinates for their expedition journals. McClellan not only refused to part with his journal — not a surprising position, considering the acerbic comments about the governor it contained — but in addition asked that his name appear "as seldom as possible" in the final report. Stevens assured him he would receive fair credit for his achievements, and called again for the journal; he would settle for a copy, with personal matter deleted. Terming this "the Gov's declaration of war," McClellan replied in a letter rude to the point of arrogance. What he dreaded, he wrote, was more of the "indiscriminate & unlimited praise" notable in the governor's preliminary report; "this redundant & resonant commendation bestowed upon those engaged in a very ordinary duty necessarily brings ridicule upon all concerned." To anything further, "I can pay no attention. As for my own journal, you cannot have it."[22]

Among the letters waiting for him when he returned to New York in April 1854 was one from his mother, who said she had recently seen a good deal of the Marcy family. "As to Miss Nelly, she is beautiful," she wrote; the young lady had heard so much about him from Captain Marcy that she declared "she was just ready to fall in love with you." The twenty-seven-year-old first lieutenant — notice of his promotion reached him during the Pacific railroad survey — hastened to make the acquaintance of eighteen-year-old Ellen Marcy.

They met in Washington, probably in the last week of April, and for George McClellan it was quite simply love at first sight. On May 14 he wrote Mrs. Marcy, ''You may think me to be very disinterested in desiring to see much of you & Miss Nelly ... now let me place myself in the confessional & say that I am selfish in the whole matter. The honest truth being that altho' I have not *seen* a very great deal of the little lady mentioned above, still that little has been sufficient to make me determined to win her if I can.'' Since Captain Marcy was stationed in Texas and he wanted to ''avoid sailing under false colors,'' he was requesting permission to court her daughter.

Mrs. Marcy did nothing to discourage the suit, and her husband was nothing less than delighted with it. Ellen Marcy was an attractive, vivacious young woman who was the apple of her father's eye and the subject of his anxious matchmaking. On June 18 he wrote his wife that he had just had a letter from Lieutenant McClellan ''and I am glad to learn that he was pleased with my dear Nelly.... I hope she will like him for he is talented, good looking, agreeable and in every respect preferable to another officer that I know of, and I cannot conceive how she can think otherwise.'' He pointed out that the lieutenant was ''one of the most brilliant men of his rank'' in the service, came from a good family, and was a staff officer and thus able to provide a wife with a good home; altogether, he concluded, McClellan was a catch ''that any young lady might justly be proud of.''

The young lady, however, had a different view of the matter. On a morning in June, in Washington, McClellan confessed his love for her and proposed marriage. To his dismay, she rejected him. Years later he could reminisce with equanimity about ''that awful morning when I had the confidential interview with you, when you did *not* love me, by a great deal.'' At the time he was furious with himself, he told Mrs. Marcy, for ''making a very great blunder & doing a very foolish thing in the way of pushing too far & too quickly....'' He would bide his time and pray for a change of heart. Meanwhile, it was with some relief that he received orders from Secretary of War Jefferson Davis sending him far from the scene of his failure.[23]

On June 28, 1854, McClellan set sail from Norfolk, Virginia, in the frigate *Columbia,* ''destination mysterious & unknown — to outsiders,'' as he phrased it. His secret assignment was to select and survey an anchorage and coaling station suitable for the navy's use in the Dominican Republic. Since 1849, when the California gold rush focused attention on crossings of the Isthmus, including the possibility of an interocean canal, Great Britain and the United States had been sparring for position in the area. The Clayton-Bulwer Treaty of 1850, renouncing domination of Central America by either nation, did not satisfy Secretary Davis. He wanted to put the American fleet on an equal footing with the Royal Navy in the Caribbean by establishing an island base to match British-controlled Jamaica. McClellan was to lay the groundwork for negotiations with the Dominican government.

The *Columbia* paid a courtesy call at Santo Domingo, and McClellan went ashore in civilian clothes, avoiding the authorities so as not to call attention to himself. The amount of space in his journal devoted to the city's defenses suggests unofficial instructions from Davis, who was apparently considering possible alternatives should negotiations fail. The *Columbia* then called at the Bay of Samaná, on the northern coast of the island, which McClellan pronounced the best location for a naval base. Here again he noted the local defenses, remarking that he had no trouble circumventing the guards "& did all I wished." He reported that all the fortifications he saw were "entirely out of repair & present no obstacle of consequence to an enterprising force." In mid-August the *Columbia* sailed for home, and by early September he was back in Washington. Nothing came of the project, and his report would not surface publicly until 1870, when President Grant unsuccessfully attempted to annex the Dominican Republic.[24]

By now Jefferson Davis was treating McClellan as a protégé. "The Secy expressed himself as being very much pleased with the result of my summer's work, & the manner in which it had been conducted," he wrote Mrs. Marcy. A month after his return from the Caribbean, Davis put him to investigating the nation's established railroads, collecting data on construction methods and costs so that (as McClellan described it) "the Secretary may come to some definite conclusion about the different Pacific routes. . . ." This assignment proved to be of considerably more value to him than to the secretary. Whereas the transcontinental railroad question remained in abeyance, the study added a good deal to McClellan's knowledge of railroad engineering — "a new pursuit to me," he wrote, "should I ever desire to leave the army."

That thought was increasingly on his mind. He considered several positions in civilian life, and in the case of one of them — a railroad job — was on the point of resigning his commission, but it fell through at the last moment. The failure of his suit for Ellen's hand disturbed him greatly; he was unused to failure. He could not get the "little Presbyterian," as he called her, out of his thoughts. Life was unjust, and he told Mrs. Marcy that his sole consolation in the affair was "in giving my vanity so good a lesson that it is not probable that I shall soon forget it." All in all, he admitted, the past year was not one he looked back on with satisfaction. What finally kept him in the service and renewed his taste for new experiences was a promotion and Jefferson Davis's interest in his career.

McClellan had been seeking rank in a new regiment since the Mexican War, and in 1855 he succeeded at last. Congress was persuaded that a larger army was necessary to oversee the great territorial gains of the Mexican peace settlement, and it authorized two new infantry and two new cavalry regiments. Early in the year McClellan saw his brother John off to Washington to pull strings "with some of his political friends" for one of the available commissions. While this may have helped, Davis's support was crucial, and on March 3, 1855, George McClellan was appointed captain in the new 1st Cavalry. It had taken him more than six years to climb in regular army rank from second to first lieutenant; he made the jump to captain in less than two. His next assignment was added proof that his military star was on the rise.[25]

Davis was an activist war secretary, much concerned with keeping the army up to date in tactics and weaponry and logistics, and in March 1855 he won President Pierce's approval to send a military commission to study the latest developments in Europe. It was also to observe at first hand the war then being fought in the Crimea. The senior members of the commission were two veteran officers who had been first in class at the Military Academy, Majors Richard Delafield (class of 1818) and Alfred Mordecai (class of 1823). McClellan was selected as the third member, and for a newly minted captain not yet thirty it was opportunity come knocking. "Of course I feel much flattered by the choice," he wrote. Their sailing date was set for April 11. It was his ninth assignment in the less than seven years since his return from Mexico, and the one that, more than any other, firmly fixed his reputation as an expert on the art of war when in 1861 war came to America.

In a daguerreotype taken two months later in Warsaw, Captain McClellan stands in full dress uniform beside Mordecai and Delafield, looking intently into the camera. The mustache he grew in Texas is complemented by a small beard in the imperial style popularized by the Emperor Napoleon III. He is five feet, eight inches tall, according to his passport, and his slim youthfulness and full, dark hair point up the generation's difference between him and his dignified, white-haired colleagues. He took the contrast seriously, writing John not long afterward of his impatience with "these d —— d old fogies!! I hope that I may never be tied to two corpses again — it is a hell upon earth. . . ."[26]

His impatience was not entirely personal. The trip had begun well enough when London promised the commissioners full cooperation in any inspection of the British forces besieging Sevastopol, in the Crimea, but when they sought the same courtesy in Paris, they ran into a snag. There followed three weeks "filled with vexatious delay & annoyance" (in McClellan's phrase) while the matter was debated. He passed his time taking in the sights. He was presented to the royal family at the Tuileries, and described Louis Napoleon for his mother as a "stolid stupid looking man not showing the remotest sign in his face of the ability he undoubtedly possesses — nothing of the royal in his bearing." To Mrs. Marcy he sent a careful description of the Empress Eugénie and her gown, which he invited her to share with Ellen. The authorities finally set their terms: any visit to the French lines in the Crimea was conditional on their pledge not to visit the Russian positions subsequently; unlike their British allies, the French apparently believed the Americans would reveal military secrets to the enemy. Unwilling to accept this arrangement, McClellan, Mordecai, and Delafield set off to petition the Russians.

Reaching St. Petersburg in mid-June via Berlin and Warsaw, they encountered a bureaucracy to rival the French. They were granted an audience by Alexander II readily enough, but their application to visit Sevastopol disappeared into the Russian labyrinth. In the meantime, they zigzagged across northern Europe from Moscow to Danzig to Stettin to Berlin, collecting material on Russian and Prussian military installations for their report. "Waiting for something to turn up," McClellan wrote in exasperation from Berlin in late August. Finally the response came from St. Petersburg: like the French, the Russian generals refused to let the Americans view their lines if they intended going on to the other side. When the news came that the Russians had given up Sevastopol on September 11, 1855, and fallen back, the commissioners decided to accept the French conditions and limit their visit to the Allied camps. They hoped an inspection of the abandoned Russian works would be adequate for their report.[27]

On October 8 the party landed at Balaclava, scene of the famous charge of the Light Brigade a year earlier, and made their camp with the British. It was McClellan's intention to write a critique of the Sevastopol siege for his report, and he toured the lines from one end to the other, making notes, sketching features of the works in his journal, and talking to Allied officers. There was still some firing from the new Russian positions. "Some few shells burst near enough to remind me a little of Vera Cruz," he wrote John. "Thank heaven I shall not return without having been under fire, even if it were a trifling matter indeed." Sevastopol itself had been battered to pieces by the year-long siege and reminded him of descriptions he had read of Pompeii. He watched with particular interest the technique of a French general reviewing the Imperial Guard: "... galloped to the right of the line & passed slowly along & then by the rear — each battalion presenting arms & the field music playing as he passed...." He took particular care to examine the logistics of the siege, from horse-transport ships to hospitals. When they left after twenty-five days, he felt confident that he had absorbed the lessons of the long and bloody contest; in 1862, drawing his own siege lines at Yorktown on the Virginia peninsula, he was satisfied that he was avoiding the mistakes of Sevastopol.

During the six months that followed, the investigators continued their travels, inspecting the fortifications and facilities of the Austrian, Prussian, French, and British armies. Having finally viewed the scene of the Crimean fighting, McClellan began to feel more generous toward his colleagues. "We have been getting on much more pleasantly of late," he wrote home from

Vienna in December 1855. He composed long, chatty letters to
Mrs. Marcy from the capitals of Europe, describing all he saw
and experienced. He supposed that Ellen still regarded him with
"the most perfect indifference," he wrote, but he hoped they
could at least remain friends. The only possible way to her heart,
he had concluded, was through her mother.

He made it a point to visit Waterloo and other famous battlefields. "Oh what zest it will give to my reading hereafter...,"
he told John. "Having seen so many of the places ... connected
with the great events of the wars of the Revolution & Empire, I
can now almost imagine that I was a spectator of the great drama."
By the time they sailed for home on April 19, 1856, McClellan
had experienced a year-long Grand Tour of England and the
Continent.[28]

Jefferson Davis was agreeable to McClellan's request that he
be posted in Philadelphia to prepare his report, and in the spring
of 1856, quartered in his mother's house, he began work. His
colleagues were to focus on their specialties — Mordecai on ordnance, Delafield on fortifications — while he dealt more generally
with the organization of Europe's principal armies, paying particular attention to engineer troops and cavalry. He had brought
back with him from Europe nearly a hundred books and manuals
on topics ranging from field rations to veterinary medicine. With
his facility for languages, those in French and German posed no
problems; for those in Russian he simply set out to teach himself
the language. He remarked somewhat coyly to Mrs. Marcy that
on a brief trip to Washington he had encountered numerous
eligible young women, but "I hurried back here & am devoting
myself to the Russian language — not ladies." Less than three
months after embarking on his study, he had translated one 300-
page Russian volume and was starting on a second. As a result,
his description of the Russian army was the most comprehensive
available to American readers.

McClellan's report, published as a congressional document in
1857, opened with a critical analysis of the siege of Sevastopol,
followed by a detailed account of the organization of the armies
of Europe's major powers. It concluded with his proposed manual
for American cavalry serving in the field, which he had adapted
from the Russian cavalry regulations. The army would adopt his
manual, and also the famous McClellan saddle, which remained

standard issue for as long as there was horse cavalry. Delafield described McClellan's saddle for Jefferson Davis as a derivation from "the Hungarian plan as adapted in the Prussian Service with such modifications as his observations in other armies of Europe suggest as valuable. . . ." It is something of a curiosity that the American cavalry arm utilized a tactical manual and a saddle developed by an officer who had never served — and would never serve — a day with the cavalry.[29]

In technical and administrative matters, George McClellan's military education was greatly advanced by his European experience. At installations all across Britain and the Continent he had witnessed how professional armies were trained and administered. The transport and supply of the Allied forces in the Crimea by sea offered him lessons to ponder when planning the Peninsula campaign of 1862. Although the Sevastopol siege was over by the time he reached the scene, the logistical framework that had supported it was still in place, as were the officers who had operated it. He also observed at first hand that field fortifications, if manned by good troops, were of more value than previously supposed. Of the Russian works he wrote, "They were attacked as field works never were before, and were defended as field works never had been defended." When viewed as training for the role of military executive, his experience on the commission put him in a class by himself in comparison with other future Civil War generals. As a reviewer wrote in 1861 of a reissue of McClellan's commission report, "A prime interest attaches to this work, because, unconsciously, the author has given us, in advance, his repertory of instruments and principles. From the written word we may anticipate the brilliant achievement. . . ."

Two important areas, however, had not attracted McClellan's attention. For all the detail he amassed on the administration and equipment of foreign armies, he gave hardly a mention to the subject of high command. The ranks and numbers of officers on general staffs were listed, but not how this important innovation operated in the directing and moving of armies. On achieving high command himself, McClellan would lament nothing so much as the lack of an operations staff and the instructed officers to man it.

Furthermore, in his critique of the Crimean War he made no mention of the most forceful lesson it had to offer. It was the first war in which the rifled musket was used to any extent. The combination of a rifled barrel and Captain Claude Minié's bullet that on firing expanded into the rifling grooves produced a weapon with far more velocity and accuracy than the old smoothbore. The effective range of the infantryman's basic arm was now between two and three times greater than before. In the Crimea the impact of the new weapon, even in limited numbers, was most noticeable in the several battles that preceded the siege of Sevastopol. Because McClellan arrived too late to witness either battles or siege, the potential effect of the rifled musket on future tactics escaped him. Although he wrote of Russian attacks resulting in "terrible losses," he attributed their failure to maneuvers made "in too heavy and unwieldy masses." During his later inspection of installations in France he noted in his journal, "Experiments are being made with a view to adopt rifled weapons for all arms of service," but he was silent on the implications of this armaments revolution. As a consequence, neither he nor those who read his report were stimulated to rethink tactical doctrine as a result of the Crimean War. Whatever advantage he would have as a military administrator in 1861, he possessed no more tactical insights into the war to come than did any of his fellow (or opposing) generals. [30]

McClellan's military commission report was the capstone of his peacetime army career. On November 26, 1856, he wrote the adjutant general in Washington of his intention to resign his commission, effective January 15, 1857. At the age of thirty he embarked on a new career in civilian life. "I fancy you were rather surprised at my sudden departure from my old paths," he wrote Randolph Marcy; " — I was rather so myself — it was a sudden thing, done almost upon the spur of the moment, & under the influence of a combination of circumstances ... which I regarded as making it obligatory upon me to take the course I have done."[31]

THREE

LIFE IN A CIVILIAN WORLD

McCLELLAN'S DECISION to leave the service surprised his army friends. J. K. Duncan, his second in command on the Pacific railroad survey, wrote him from New Orleans, "We all wondered here what induced you to take off the harness; — a young captain — chock full of big war science — the Secty. for a patron...." McClellan never recorded his specific reasons for resigning, but a major factor was certainly the limited future the army seemed to offer after his return from Europe. His regiment, the 1st Cavalry, had the thankless task of trying to keep peace in "Bleeding Kansas" between free-soil and proslavery parties. "Soldiers were never on more disgusting service," Joe Johnston wrote from Kansas, and warned him about the 1st Cavalry's colonel, Edwin V. Sumner. Any officer serving under Sumner, who had joined the army in 1819, had to learn to cultivate the pose "that he is utterly ignorant, professionally — & that his colonel is not," Johnston explained, and added " — the last most difficult." Such a pose was unimaginable for anyone of George McClellan's sensibilities.[1]

During the summer and fall of 1856, while writing his military commission report, McClellan had canvassed acquaintances for likely jobs. He considered engineering work on a mint in Philadelphia and on an addition to the Treasury building in Washington. His Mexican War comrade G. W. Smith, now a civil engineer, introduced him to the noted ironmaster and business leader Abram S. Hewitt, and the position he finally took — chief engineer for the Illinois Central Railroad — he owed primarily to strong recommendations by Hewitt and by another New Yorker, Samuel L. M. Barlow.

Samuel Latham Mitchell Barlow, who like McClellan was thirty, was a rising young corporation lawyer in Wall Street. Active in Democratic politics as well as in business circles, he specialized in railroad affairs. He was a cultivated bon vivant, with a taste for fine paintings and first editions, and he and McClellan became lifelong friends. They had first met two years earlier, when McClellan was investigating railroad construction methods for Jefferson Davis. Barlow's motives in this case were not entirely altruistic, for through McClellan he hoped to forge a link between the Illinois Central and the Ohio and Mississippi, a road in which he held a substantial interest.[2]

The main line of the 704-mile-long Illinois Central ran the length of Illinois north to south, connecting Chicago with Cairo, where the Ohio River enters the Mississippi. It was the first of the great land-grant railroads, originally endowed with 2,595,000 acres of government land, and when McClellan took up his duties in Chicago in January 1857 its affairs were prospering. Traffic revenues and land sales were on the upsurge, its bonds were selling at par, and its common stock had reached 120. "The work will be rather harder than commanding a company of cavalry — but it affords brighter prospects in the future," he told Randolph Marcy. He welcomed the authority, the luxury of making decisions without having first to refer everything to the adjutant general or the secretary of war: "I feel already as if a heavy load was removed from my shoulders." His salary was $3,000 a year, more than twice his army pay, and there was the promise of an advancement to vice president at $5,000 if he proved himself. Marcy was quick to pass these particulars on to Ellen.

McClellan proved to be an active and able executive, and within a year he was named vice president of the road. He made regular tours of inspection in his private car to oversee operations and maintenance, reviewing all the details personally. He found the people in the interior of the state "rather primitive in their appearance & habits," he wrote Ellen, but they were beginning to recognize him as one of the "powers that be," and at the village hotels a prairie chicken or a quail would be set aside for his supper. A cook and a housekeeper made his life in Chicago more civilized, yet something was missing. Adopting a platonic tone, he asked Ellen, "Can't you find among your acquaintances some quiet young woman of a moral turn of mind, who can sew on buttons, look happy when I come home, drive off my neuralgia, & make herself generally useful (including going to market) who will come out on speculation. . . .''[3]

After he had spent six months on the job, however, signs of boredom began to appear in his letters. He wrote Fitz John Porter that he feared his heart was not as much in his work as it should be, and he wondered whether he had made a mistake by leaving the army. What he missed most was the comradeship. He began to consider a return to military service, but in an army of a different sort and in a different arena — a filibustering expedition into Spanish America.

Whether McClellan would have actually joined one or another of these private armies as a soldier of fortune bent on overthrowing governments, had circumstances taken a different turn, must remain an open question. Certainly he was interested enough to maintain a correspondence with leaders and potential leaders of the movement, including the future Confederate generals J. K. Duncan, Mansfield Lovell, G. W. Smith, P. G. T. Beauregard, and Joseph E. Johnston, and to suggest more than once that he was on the verge of accepting a position of high command.

Most of those who became filibusters acted out of a thirst for power or adventure or profit or to open new regions for slavery. McClellan's motives, as far as he stated them, seem to have been of a higher order. In speaking of intervening in strife-torn Mexico, for example, he told Mansfield Lovell, ''Now is the time to pitch in and help the liberals. . . .'' The evidence suggests that he aligned himself with those in the 1850s who believed it was America's manifest destiny to extend its influence and power southward. As Duncan phrased it in a letter to him, it was a matter of conquest and regeneration : ''Spanish America from Mexico to the extreme southern point of South America, must sooner or later be overrun and receive the impress of a higher race than its present mongrel occupants. . . .''

Through the summer and fall of 1857 Duncan kept McClellan informed of the fortunes of William Walker, the most celebrated of the filibusters, who had recently been expelled from Nicaragua after seizing control of that country with his private army during a local civil war. Walker and his chief lieutenant, Charles Henningsen, were back in the United States, seeking men and money and arms for an attempt to retake Nicaragua, and in New Orleans

Duncan was recruiting for the expedition from among the "old crowd" who had fought in the Mexican War and on the frontier.

"You, Lovell, G.W. and myself are anything but satisfied with our present occupations," he wrote McClellan on July 23; here was "a chance to try what that European experience of yours amounts to. The fact is Mac, if we dont embrace some chance like this, our day and generation will pass amidst the quiets of peace, . . . our lives will be devoted to the accumulation of dollars and cents." Nicaragua was only the beginning. "There is a vast empire — a new world in fact before you, if you have only the heart to dare and the head to execute."

On August 19 he wrote again to say that he had signed up 500 men and was encouraged by McClellan's response: "Our opinions are common in regard to the objects and merits of the expedition. . . . We are both willing to go with a suitable force, properly officered, organized and equipped. . . . We only differ in our views of the leader." McClellan had likened Walker after his expulsion to a dead fighting cock in the pit. Duncan proposed that they treat him simply as a figurehead, to be replaced should he blunder. If all continued to go well, he wrote, "you can decide whether you are *in* or *out*. If in, say the word and you shall be *No. 1* above Henningsen & myself." A few days later he elaborated on these plans in a meeting in New York with McClellan and Beauregard.

In the event, McClellan did not have to make any decision. "Hang up your sword old fellow . . . the thing will 'bust,' has bust or ought to do so," Duncan advised him on November 9. He explained that Walker's financial support had abruptly disappeared in the financial crisis — the Panic of 1857 — that struck the nation in late August. Further, President James Buchanan let it be known that the government opposed more filibustering in Nicaragua. In the face of these setbacks, Duncan withdrew from the project, promising vaguely "a new, different and better programme," and McClellan soon enough lost interest. Joe Johnston thought him wise to stay clear of Walker, whom he termed "a mere robber, with robbers for his associates," and in fact Walker's dream of a Central American empire came finally to nothing. He died under the guns of a Honduran firing squad in 1860.[4]

Any boredom McClellan felt toward his job evaporated under the impact of the Panic of 1857. The Illinois Central was badly positioned to ride out the financial storm. Most of its debt was in bonds and short-term notes, and after widespread runs on banks and other sources of credit by panicked depositors, it suddenly found itself with far more obligations than cash to meet them. Nor could it collect on many of its own accounts. On August 28 McClellan described the situation succinctly for one of his subordinates: "The pressure is so very great in the money market that it is almost impossible to raise money on any terms to meet payments." The railroad's directors and its president, William H. Osborn, bombarded him with demands to ship every dollar he could scrape up to the New York office.

He responded by reducing purchases, halting construction, and putting off all maintenance not related to safety. However, when New York's demands for cash continued, accompanied by proposals to cut service and wages drastically, he dug in his heels. Characteristically, he began to view the arguments of others as challenges to his personal integrity. He told Osborn that "no one in N.Y. can judge of what reductions ought to be made so well as I can here"; surely he was to act as he thought best rather than "cut down everything, root & branch...." To one of the directors he explained, "If I fail to comply with any suggestions or orders it will be because I see such good reason for my course that I am willing to risk my reputation & position on the issue."[5]

These efforts fell short, and on October 10, 1857, the Illinois Central resorted to the device of assignment to prevent collapse. This was not a declaration of bankruptcy — the railroad's assets far outweighed its liabilities — but rather the legal assignment of the company to a committee of officers and directors so as to gain a respite from its creditors. McClellan was named chairman of the committee. In Chicago, far from the scene of the panic, he reported that the employees and the public were "incredulous even yet" at the news. The railroad's bonds and stock fell to half their early 1857 prices.

Called to New York for emergency action on the crisis, he continued to oppose demands to curtail service and slash wages further. In his view, eliminating scheduled trains was "equivalent to surrendering our position as a first class road...." Already the company's laborers were working for only a dollar a day, he said, hardly enough to live on. To give force to his arguments and to take "an independent position that I might freely express whatever opinions mature reflection might dictate,'' he announced that he would accept no salary for the duration of the crisis. Fortunately, the financial panic subsided within a matter of weeks. The strenuous efforts of Osborn restored the railroad's credit, and by the end of 1858 the assignment was lifted and the line restored to normal operations. A few months later dividends were being paid again.[6]

William Osborn was strong-willed and aggressive, the sort almost sure to clash sooner or later with anyone who valued his own views as highly as did McClellan, and during the Illinois Central's ordeal the two began to strike sparks. With this conflict added to his general restlessness, McClellan decided to seek a change. He wrote a friend in the Corps of Engineers, who a year earlier had offered him work on the Treasury addition, to ask if there were still any openings. There was nothing ''worthy of your acceptance,'' he was told. In the meantime, he resolved to try to return to the army, just then undergoing an ordeal of its own — a potential shooting war with the Mormon settlers of Utah Territory. If the situation in Utah worsened, he told Mrs. Marcy, ''I have determined to give up my present position with all its advantages of high pay &c., & reenter the service at least until the trouble is over. I cannot bear the idea of my old friends being on campaign without me.'' To Ellen he wrote plaintively that he had no ties to bind him, no desire for wealth without a wife to share it: ''I would rather be in Utah now than anywhere else.''

Conflict between the Mormon leader Brigham Young and the federal government — it ultimately came down to who would govern Utah Territory — had sharpened in 1857 to the point where President Buchanan sent out a new territorial governor escorted by three regiments of regulars under Colonel Albert Sidney Johnston. In October the expedition's supply trains were captured and burned by Mormon irregulars, and Johnston had to go into winter quarters at Fort Bridger, a hundred or so miles short of Salt Lake City. (Randolph Marcy would make a dramatic march through winter snows to open a new supply line, winning most of what little acclaim the expedition achieved.)

When Congress convened in December, the Mormon War — as yet a bloodless war — was a main topic of concern, and Buchanan sought authorization for ten new regiments. McClellan hurried to Washington to try for a colonelcy and the command of one of them. Early in 1858 he told Samuel Barlow that he had marshaled the support of such prominent senators as Jefferson Davis, Stephen A. Douglas, and John J. Crittenden, and of Vice President John C. Breckinridge; he also expected congressional support from his home state of Pennsylvania.

While still in the army he had once compared Congress in session to the animal performances in a bear garden, but he had since become adept at political lobbying and thought his chances for a commission were good. "Railroading is all very well," he wrote Barlow, " ... but I like the old business better — & if you can get me back into the service, I trust I do not flatter myself, when I say that you will make a pretty good soldier out of a d —— d bad railroad man. . . . Life is too short to waste in bickering about cross ties & contracts — I cannot learn to love it. In God's name give me all the help you can — I should die out here in another year."

G. W. Smith, now an Illinois Central director, told McClellan that President Osborn and the board were decidedly unhappy with the prospect of his resigning. Public confidence in the railroad's recovery effort was sure to be shaken if the head of the new management committee left, and Smith warned him that the directors would refuse to accept his resignation. He also reminded him of the understanding reached when he was hired that he would remain with the line for at least three years. McClellan was undeterred. "The attractions of the drum & fife have not at all lessened since I wrote you," he told Barlow on February 12. Finally it was Congress that decided the matter. It rejected Buchanan's ten-regiment proposal and authorized only two new regiments of volunteers, if and when the Mormon situation grew critical. Even those proved unnecessary, for the Mormon War was soon ended by negotiation and without bloodshed.[7]

Frustrated in his effort to return to the regular army, McClellan looked once more to filibustering as an escape from the toils of a business life. He corresponded with Mansfield Lovell, who described a plan to raise an army of 4,000 Americans to enter the civil war then convulsing Mexico on the side of Benito Juárez and his reforming liberal party. "If we could raise money I would send you a call in less than 3 months," Lovell promised. "Depend upon it, my dear Mac, that if there is a remote possibility of effecting the purpose, it will be done; and you will be one of the leaders.'' A few days later, on February 28, McClellan wrote Ellen, "The prospect for new regts is gloomy, but I think I see a faint glimmering hope of seeing service again — on fields where I have fought before — in a righteous cause & with fair prospect of distinction. The old brain will not rot — the old ambition, the old first love will return — & you need not be surprised to hear one of these days that I am again in harness.''

Mexico, however, like Nicaragua and Utah, provided no relief for his discontent. Joe Johnston wrote him from Vera Cruz that there was no chance for their schemes. Neither side in the Mexican conflict wanted filibusters in their ranks, he explained; they would rather risk defeat by their Mexican enemies than be supplanted in control by Americans. "Our castles in the air, my dear Mc, are blown away. You'll have to consent to becoming a rich civilian instead of a member of a small but select party of maintainers of human liberty.'' Except for a militia commission in the Chicago Light Guard, McClellan had to content himself with the role of armchair general.[8]

His avocation continued to be the study of war, as it had been since his days at West Point, and he read widely on the subject in a growing personal library that already numbered several hundred volumes. He owned copies of all the important studies of the campaigns and generalship of the Napoleonic Wars. Other masters of war, such as Caesar, Marlborough, and Frederick the Great, were represented on his shelves, as were the leading military theorists. His tastes ran also to the major historians — among them Herodotus, Xenophon, Tacitus, Gibbon, and Macaulay — and to a wide assortment of works of literature, philosophy, religion, and science, but always he returned to the military arts. When reading of Marlborough's campaigns, he wrote Ellen on one occasion, he found that "the old profession stirs my blood & delights me more than any other pursuit. Yet I cant come down to taking any interest in pipe clay & garrison duty — it is war on a large scale that interests me. . . .''[9]

However much he may have disliked the businessman's role, McClellan made his mark as a railroad executive in this period. In January 1858 he virtually doubled the reach of the Illinois Central by contracting with a group of steamboat owners to carry freight and mail and passengers on a regular schedule between the railroad's southern terminus, at Cairo, and Memphis, Vicks-

burg, and New Orleans. He was so confident of his judgment that
he signed the contracts without consulting the board of directors.
This occasioned sharp exchanges with several directors, but
McClellan's plan, if not his methods, gained the board's approval.
Building on this New Orleans connection, he envisioned new trade
for the railroad with the Texas coast, Cuba, Mexico, and Central
America. A few months later he went to New Orleans to investigate a rail connection between that city and Cairo. He reported
that the route would be "a perfectly safe investment." Although
the link-up would not be completed before the Civil War, in the
postwar years the process McClellan initiated carried the Illinois
Central's tracks to New Orleans.[10]

His position with the railroad brought him together with several men, in addition to Barlow, who would have a part in shaping
his role in the Civil War. In Chicago he gained enough regard
for the work of Allan Pinkerton, the private detective under
contract with the Illinois Central and other railroads to protect
their property, to entrust him with his intelligence gathering in
1861. In these years he also formed a close friendship with the
future Army of the Potomac general Ambrose Burnside, who
wrote him in May 1858 seeking a job. Burnside had graduated
from West Point a year after McClellan and left the army in
1853 to produce a breech-loading carbine of his own design, but
the Panic of 1857 threw him into bankruptcy. McClellan not only
found him a place as cashier in the railroad's land department
but invited the Burnsides to share the large house he had taken
on Chicago's lakefront. "Mac" and "Burn" were soon as close
as McClellan and Jimmy Stuart had been. He confided to Ellen
that of all the men he knew, he valued Burnside's friendship and
respect the most. "Why, that honest, true, brave old Burnside is
worth a legion of those paltry butterflies that flutter around ball
rooms," he wrote. "... If ever a man went to heaven he will
surely go there...."[11]

He was less impressed with Abraham Lincoln, who represented
the Illinois Central in a number of legal cases during McClellan's
tenure with the railroad. This was hardly surprising, for politically the two had nothing in common. McClellan was by now
settled firmly into the camp of the conservative Democrats, and
he actively supported Stephen A. Douglas in his 1858 Illinois

senatorial contest against challenger Lincoln. During the campaign he made his private car available to Douglas, and on at least one occasion traveled with him to the scene of one of the famous Lincoln-Douglas debates.

In drafting his memoirs, he recalled that Douglas was up most of the previous night drinking and talking politics, and was "somewhat affected by the large amount of whisky he had taken, & looking unkempt and sleepy. He, however, retired to my private cabin, and soon emerged perfectly fresh and ready for the work before him. . . ." In the debate, McClellan wrote, "Douglas' speech was compact, logical & powerful — Mr. Lincoln's disjointed, & rather a mass of anecdotes than of arguments. I did not think that there was any approach to equality in the oratorical powers of the two men. . . ."

His vote for Douglas in this contest was the only one he would cast in a major election until after the Civil War. In addition, he told his daughter with great satisfaction some years later, he frustrated an attempted Republican voting fraud and saved a county for Douglas. Tipped off that an Illinois Central special train had been chartered to carry supporters of the Lincoln ticket into a neighboring county to vote illegally, he told the road's superintendent, "I don't care how you accomplish it but that train must *not* reach its destination." On Election Day, halfway into the journey the special's locomotive "broke down" and the would-be voters were stranded miles from anywhere until the polls closed.[12]

During and after the war, in private notes and correspondence, McClellan made no secret of his contempt for Lincoln as his social and intellectual inferior. In notes for his memoirs, for example, he remarked that Lincoln the president "was not a man of very strong character, & as he was destitute of refinement — certainly in no sense a gentleman — he was easily wrought upon by the coarse associates whose style of conversation agreed so well with his own." This was the impression he formed on first meeting Lincoln, and, typically, his mind was not changed by closer acquaintance. A clue to his view of Lincoln in these years is in a letter he received in 1861, on the eve of the war, from his friend John M. Douglas, an Illinois Central director. The president-elect, Douglas wrote, "is not a bold man. Has not nerve to differ with his party and its leaders. . . . O Mc you and I both know L and we do know that he can not face the opposition which would rise if he were to take the right stand. . . .''[13]

"I am leading a very different life from the old one — work, work, work!" McClellan wrote Ellen in February 1858. "Care & anxiety enough to make good old Job fretful. . . .'' Even though he had managed finally to establish a two-way correspondence with Ellen — a letter from her, he wrote, was like "the balm of Gilead'' — she gave no outward sign of a change of heart. His efforts to enlist sympathy for his bachelor's existence grew increasingly transparent. He described lonely games of chess played against himself and thanked her for an introduction to a young woman of her acquaintance, but observed that the less he saw of "articles of that nature, the less likely will my vanity be to receive decidedly unpleasant shocks.'' He dreaded to think of the future: "It seems so blank — no goal to reach, no object to strive for!" Her replies to such plaintive calls are not preserved, but apparently his tactics had some effect, for she did not stop writing.

Perhaps one reason Ellen Marcy continued to keep the love-struck McClellan at arm's length was the sheer number of suitors paying her court. Before she was twenty-five she had received (including McClellan's) at least nine proposals of marriage. The Marcy family knew almost everyone in the tightly knit world of the pre–Civil War army, and any officer stationed in Washington or passing through made it a point to call on Mrs. Marcy and her pretty elder daughter. Ellen was also a very visible figure on the capital's social scene. Her later photographs, showing her with severely coiffed hair and without a hint of animation, do her injustice. Her swains spoke of her charm and lively conversation; one wrote longingly of her "soft, sweet, gentle smiles.''

Her suitors came in all ages and circumstances. One, signing himself simply "Charlie,'' wrote at great length to convince her that his childhood infatuation had matured into true love. W. J. A. Fuller, perhaps inspired by Longfellow's recently published "The Courtship of Miles Standish,'' concocted an elaborate proposal on behalf of a "rich client'' before confessing that it was in fact he who sought her hand. Two young lieutenants of the 5th Infantry, her father's regiment, hoped that the connection would cause her to look favorably on their proposals. Captains Marcus Simpson and Gordon Granger, McClellan's contempor-

aries at West Point, sent her love letters and romantic poetry
from their distant postings in the West. One of her most tenacious
suitors was Captain John G. Barnard, who was old enough to be
her father (he had graduated from West Point a year after Randolph Marcy) and showed a persistence similar to McClellan's
after he was rejected. Barnard would become McClellan's chief
engineer in the Army of the Potomac and eventually one of his
sharpest critics. Whether Ellen ever harbored reciprocal feelings
for any of these suitors is not known. It was a different case with
Ambrose Powell Hill, whom she fell in love with and agreed to
marry.[14]

A. P. Hill, described by McClellan at the time as "one of my
oldest & best friends," began courting Ellen when he was posted
to Washington in 1855. In the spring of 1856 he proposed, she
accepted, and he wrote to Captain Marcy to ask for her hand. In
striking contrast to their reaction to McClellan's suit two years
earlier, Marcy and his wife threw up adamant opposition. All
the captain's protective instincts were aroused: Lieutenant Hill
was a line officer with no particular prospects, and to marry him,
he warned Ellen, was to resign herself to "a life of exile, dep-
rivation and poverty." He wanted better for her, he said, and
sternly forbade her to see Hill again.

Mrs. Marcy was even more vehement in her view of the match.
Her objection, as Hill later described it, was that, because of a
certain youthful indiscretion, "my health and consitution had
become so impaired, so weakened, that no mother could yield her
daughter to me, unless to certain unhappiness." This Victorian
circumlocution referred to venereal disease, which Hill had contracted while he was on leave from West Point and about which
Mrs. Marcy had somehow learned. In the face of this united
parental opposition, Ellen ended the engagement, although with
great reluctance. One of those she wrote to for counsel was
McClellan. He blandly advised her "to govern yourself by the
dictates of your good sense & true woman's feeling." Her mother
chastised her for her choice of suitors. She had just seen Captain
McClellan after his return from Europe, Mrs. Marcy wrote Ellen
in the fall of 1856: "How very kind he is; oh, Nell such a treasure
as you have lost forever — you can't realize now — but the time
is coming sooner or later just as sure as you live when you will
regret if ever a woman did — mark my words."[15]

Ellen's suitors might come and go, but McClellan was always there, biding his time. He continued his courtship by mail, and at last, more than five years after his dogged pursuit began, he was rewarded. In the fall of 1859 Randolph Marcy was ordered to a new posting at St. Paul, Minnesota, and he took his family with him. McClellan invited them to stay at his house when they reached Chicago. In expectation of seeing Ellen again, he wrote to assure her that he was still a bachelor ("I don't know where Mrs McC is — do you?") and that he had given up all thought of returning to the army. He dropped a broad hint about his idea for improving his lot: "I can certainly imagine a state of affairs that would make civil life more pleasant than the Army in Peace — perhaps you will not sympathize with any such notion as that. However, we will talk over these and many other things when we meet. . . ."

They met in Chicago on October 20, and when the Marcys boarded their train for St. Paul four days later, McClellan went with them. A good deal of talking was evidently done, for on the second day of the journey he proposed marriage once again, and this time Ellen accepted. Her parents approved without hesitation. "How dear to me is the recollection of that trip in the cars . . . ," he wrote her a month after their engagement. "If we have fifty years the remembrance of that trip will ever be among our most pleasant thoughts. . . ."

George and Ellen McClellan would have twenty-five years together rather than fifty, but by all accounts they always treasured that remembrance. They were utterly devoted to each other. "My whole existence is wrapped up in you," he told her; he hoped he might "yet play my part on the stage of the worlds affairs & leave a name in history, but Nelly whatever the future may have in store for me *you* will be the chief actor in that play. . . ." For the first time in his life, he confessed, he wanted to open himself completely to someone else: "In talking or writing to you it is exactly as if I were communing with myself — you *are* my *alter ego,* darling. . . ." Returning to Chicago, he began his lifelong habit of writing at least once every day during their separations, and insisted she do the same. Then and later, he faithfully recorded all that he saw and felt and believed, and his letters are mirrors of self-revelation. He kept nothing from Ellen that he did not keep from himself.

During the seven months of their engagement, McClellan underwent an evangelical religious regeneration that fundamentally affected his outlook on life. In contemplating marriage to his ''little Presbyterian,'' he wrote, ''the mere thought of uniting your pure religious soul to an unrefined irreligious immoral or tainted man is to me sacrilege itself.'' He gratefully adopted the rigid Calvinism of her faith as his own. However unjust and unfair life on earth might be, he could now look beyond it. ''I believe that we are to be united *forever*,'' he explained, ''& that our union *on this earth is only a state of preparation for our union through eternity in a higher & better state.*'' This had come about not by chance but by predestination, an example of God's will acting on those He elected. That election was irresistible and unquestioned: ''My instinct, my intellect both tell me that . . . the hand of fate seems to have concerned itself & preserved us for each other.'' When, eighteen months later, he was in fact called to the world's stage, he accepted that, too, as God's will.[16]

They were married on May 22, 1860, at Calvary Church in New York. The groom was thirty-three, the bride just turned twenty-five. Among the groomsmen were G. W. Smith, McClellan's West Point friends Cadmus Wilcox and Henry Clitz, and Seth Williams, his future adjutant. General-in-Chief Winfield Scott headed the guest list, which included Confederate generals-to-be Joe Johnston and D. H. Hill, Richard Delafield from the European military commission, classmate Alfred Gibbs, and Gordon Granger, one of Ellen's failed suitors. After a reception at the Fifth Avenue Hotel, the couple boarded the evening train for Chicago. In his diary McClellan called it the day of his life: '' !!May 22!! Le jour de ma vie.'' Two weeks later he wrote his mother, ''You can scarcely imagine how changed everything seems to me now. . . . I believe I am the happiest man that ever lived & am sure that I have the dearest wife in all the world.''[17]

A month after the wedding, McClellan had a letter from Samuel Barlow relating a plan to restore the Ohio and Mississippi Railroad to solvency. A victim of the Panic of 1857, the line was in receivership under the care of William H. Aspinwall, a New York businessman and financier. A superintendent was wanted to operate the line, which ran 340 miles between Cincinnati and St. Louis, and Barlow assured him, ''There is no one here talked of but yourself.'' McClellan promptly expressed his interest. What he called his "naturally defiant disposition" had brought him into growing conflict with William Osborn of the Illinois Central, and he was ready for a change.

The arrangements were soon completed. McClellan took the post of superintendent at $10,000, double his Illinois Central salary and one of the highest of any railroad executive in the country, on the understanding that he would shortly be advanced to the presidency of the road's eastern division in tandem with Barlow, head of the western division. "I feel rejoiced to see this long looked for event accomplished — the road in the hands of a master," Aspinwall told Barlow. McClellan's satisfaction may be imagined from a letter he received from his brother John: "I was not surprised to hear of your leaving the Illinois Central after the little you told me in N York as I then foresaw you could not get along with such a man, as I suppose Osborn to be.... This time you will be head of the *concern* and will have no one to interfere with you in any shape or manner." In August 1860 McClellan left Chicago and the Illinois Central and moved to Cincinnati to take up his new duties.[18]

Personally, at least, the Cincinnati period was one of the happiest times of McClellan's life. He rented a comfortable house and cultivated a circle of business acquaintances, and he and Ellen maintained a busy social calendar. He could afford and he enjoyed the pleasures of table and wine cellar and fine cigars. In these civilian years the slim figure of his army days broadened and thickened, and this full-fleshed stockiness made him seem shorter than he actually was. Although he welcomed playing host to old army friends passing through Cincinnati, he did not take up a role with the local militia as he had in Chicago. Offered the command of the company of Guthrie Grays, he begged off because of business pressures.

Indeed, his business affairs produced no satisfactions comparable with those of his personal life. The Ohio and Mississippi had a debt of almost $10 million, and its president, Joseph W. Alsop, urged on him "a rigid economy ... until we can free ourselves from pressing and immediate claims." It was the Illinois Central situation all over again. Advanced to the head of the eastern division, he once more became entangled in a personality clash. In this instance he got on well enough with the top management of Alsop, Barlow, and Aspinwall; his dispute was with an operations superintendent. After Fort Sumter he would draft a letter of resignation, giving as his reason that his orders were being ignored, "a course which must inevitably destroy the interests of all concerned...." (Barlow persuaded him not to act so hastily, and he did not resign until early 1862.) As Aspinwall later told him, the Ohio and Mississippi "first & last has caused both you & all connected with it, no little trouble."[19]

The sectional conflict that was becoming acute after Lincoln's election captured more and more of McClellan's attention. He wrote Barlow from Cincinnati in the last days of 1860, after South Carolina had seceded, that he was following events closely. "The feeling of *all* people here is that the North West will do justice to the South if they will give us time," he explained. Midwestern Republicans he talked to joined him in supporting the constitutional amendments recently proposed by Senator John J. Crittenden of Kentucky as a basis for compromise, including extending the line of the Missouri Compromise to the Pacific, forbidding slavery north of the line but permitting it to the south, as well as an adjustment of fugitive slave laws to the South's advantage. But if Southerners "go off half cocked & listen to nothing but the Republican politicians at Washington...we will meet the consequences unitedly, let it be war or peace — but the general opinion is that it will be *war*."

He wrote to his brother-in-law in Alabama that he still hoped for a compromise that would isolate the fanatic "ultras" of both sides. If the border states could be satisfied, "I think the further steps of satisfying all the other slave states save South Carolina will not be difficult." Yet he sensed how powerful were the tides of sectionalism, and when he took his house in Cincinnati, he recalled, he insisted upon a clause in the lease "releasing me from the obligation in the event of war."[20]

McClellan would never waver in his conviction that mutual fanaticism had brought the nation to this pass. Two years later, in command of the Army of the Potomac, he told Navy Secretary Gideon Welles that above all things he hoped to capture Charleston, South Carolina, so that he could demolish it. "He detested, he said, both South Carolina and Massachusetts, and should rejoice to see both States extinguished," Welles wrote in his diary. "Both were and always had been ultra and mischievous, and he could not tell which he hated most." In drafting his memoirs,

McClellan described these extremists as "overzealous & excitable, some of them narrow minded fanatics, some mere 'busy bodies,' others designing & troublesome knaves. . . ."

But if in his mind Northern abolitionists and Southern fire-eaters bore equally the moral guilt for the coming of the war, he was in no doubt where his own duty lay. He was unalterably opposed to secession. "Southerners were the aggressors in withdrawing from the Union," he wrote. After Fort Sumter was fired on he told his old friend Fitz John Porter, "I throw to one side now all questions as to the past — political parties etc — the Govt is in danger, our flag insulted & we must stand by it." Thus he was infuriated by the later accusation that in 1861 he had entertained an offer to fight for the Confederacy. He labeled it a deliberate and politically motivated slander by the New York abolitionist press he despised.

To be sure, several future Confederate generals did seek his advice — and his support — on the eve of the war. Cadmus Wilcox wanted his views on whether force would be used on the seceding states. He urged Wilcox to "stick to the Union to the last for it is both right & politic." He sympathized with A. P. Hill's decision to go with his home state of Virginia, but said that by the same token his own belief in states' rights obliged him to remain loyal to the North. On the day after Fort Sumter surrendered, Mansfield Lovell wrote that he and G. W. Smith had sworn they would never submit to "throat-cutting" abolitionists who sought to give blacks "political & civil equality with the white man," a doctrine they insisted the South would resist to the death. "I trust that mature reflection and close investigation of the whole subject will result in your siding with us," Lovell concluded. This invitation was both vague and entirely unofficial — Lovell and Smith did not themselves join the Confederacy until the war was five months old — and it was as close as McClellan came to being offered a high place in the Southern army.[21]

That he would be offered a high place in the Federal army no one in the service doubted. The variety of his assignments, particularly his year of observation of Europe's armies, had ranked him as one of the military intellectuals of the prewar army. He was widely considered to be, as J. K. Duncan had phrased it, "chock full of big war science." In addition, his four years as a railroad executive promised competence in the vital area of military logistics.

It was therefore no surprise that with the firing on Fort Sumter George McClellan quickly became the most sought-after former officer in the North. By the time the war was a month old he was, at the age of thirty-four, a major general both of regulars and of volunteers and was outranked in the United States service only by the general-in-chief himself, Winfield Scott.[22]

FOUR

THE CALL TO WAR

ON APRIL 15, 1861, the same day that Mansfield Lovell wrote McClellan in the hope of enlisting his sympathy for the Southern cause, Major Fitz John Porter urged him to take his stand for the Union. The president had called for troops to suppress the insurrection, and Porter told McClellan he must help "counterbalance" the impact of three other prominent former army officers — Jefferson Davis, Braxton Bragg, and P. G. T. Beauregard — casting their lot with the Confederacy. "We now need the sterling men of our country to act at once," Porter wrote, and pressed him to take a high command in the volunteer forces to be raised in his home state of Pennsylvania or in Ohio. William F. (Baldy) Smith, another friend from West Point days, had the same advice. Smith had it on good authority that President Lincoln was considering naming McClellan a brigadier general in the regular army, and suggested he seek rank at least that high in the volunteers as a bargaining point.[1]

As it happened, the three Northern states with the largest military contingents all sought McClellan's services. Ohio's bid was the most determined. Governor William Dennison enlisted his advice on defending Cincinnati, thought to be a tempting target for any Confederate offensive west of the Alleghenies. McClellan suggested planning an extensive system of fieldworks: "There is only one safe rule in war — i.e. to decide what is the very worst thing that can happen to you, & prepare to meet it," he told the governor. Cincinnati's leading citizens petitioned Governor Dennison, President Lincoln, and General-in-Chief Scott to name him commander of Ohio's troops.

Pennsylvania, meanwhile, did not stand idle. Robert Patterson, general of militia, offered him the post of chief engineer in the state forces, but McClellan (as he later wrote) "did not exactly fancy the connection." His opinion of Patterson, the Mexican War mustang general, had not softened with time. He looked with more favor on an "intimation" that he was being considered for higher command as head of the Pennsylvania Reserves. On April 18 he wrote Fitz John Porter in Washington that he would take the post if asked. Let General Scott say a word in his behalf to Andrew G. Curtin, Pennsylvania's governor, and "I think the matter could be easily arranged. ... I much prefer the Penna service...." He was proud of his home state, he told his wife, "& would like to make it proud of me."

Hearing nothing from Curtin after almost a week, McClellan determined to go to Harrisburg to discuss the matter in person. On April 23, at Governor Dennison's request, he broke his journey at Columbus to report on the state of affairs in the Ohio Valley. The governor displayed a considerable talent for persuasion. He offered McClellan the command of Ohio's forces, and the bargain was quickly struck. In a matter of hours Dennison pushed a special bill to that effect through the legislature, and that evening the former captain of regulars became a major general of volunteers.

An odd twist of fortune had intervened in the case. Governor Curtin had acted promptly enough in deciding on McClellan for the Pennsylvania command, but by some slip-up his telegraphed offer was addressed to Chicago instead of Cincinnati. It caught up with McClellan only on April 24, the day after he had accepted the Ohio post. That day, too, he was notified that Governor Edwin Morgan of New York wanted him for the command of that state's troops. So it happened that George McClellan began his Civil War career in the western theater of operations rather than the eastern, a circumstance that would radically accelerate his climb to high command.[2]

McClellan did not waste a moment taking up his duties. On the night of his appointment he wrote a lengthy situation report to Winfield Scott. He called for arms and equipment of every kind for the Ohio men flocking to the colors in numbers far exceeding Lincoln's call. He understood that 10,000 muskets had been promised; twice that number was needed simply as a beginning, as well as five million cartridges. "I have never seen so fine a body of men collected together — the material is superb, but has no organization or discipline," he wrote. He would establish a camp of instruction, and requested that experienced officers be assigned to him, among them Fitz John Porter and Randolph Marcy. He told General Scott he took it as his duty to defend Cincinnati and the line of the Ohio River.

Jacob D. Cox, an Ohio legislator newly minted as a brigadier in the state militia, was with him frequently in these first weeks of the war, and he was impressed by what he saw. He described McClellan as "rather under the medium height, but muscularly formed, with broad shoulders and a well-poised head, active and graceful in motion." From the first, Cox recalled, he made a strong impact on those around him: "Personally he was a very charming man, and his manner of doing business impressed every one with the belief that he knew what he was about." This look of competence would remain one of McClellan's most noticed characteristics. "There is not a weak line in his face," wrote the future Civil War historian John C. Ropes on meeting him in 1863. "All is strength and self-possession, and I think rectitude of purpose is clearly shown...."

On McClellan's first day on the job, he and Cox investigated the stock of arms at the state arsenal. They found nothing more than a few boxes of rusty smoothbore muskets, several badly corroded 6-pounders used for decades to fire salutes during militia musters, and a heap of mildewed and useless harness. After the abbreviated inspection, McClellan glanced around the nearly empty, echoing arsenal and remarked dryly, "A fine stock of munitions on which to begin a great war!"[3]

Just then and for a week to come, McClellan was out of direct communication with Washington. The capital's rail and telegraphic links with the North had been cut by Maryland secessionists, and until they were restored he and Governor Dennison acted on their own initiative. It was clear enough that their first priority was to get the enlistees into camp for training. The president had called up 75,000 militia for three months' service, and Ohio's share was thirteen regiments — some 10,000 men in all. When thousands more volunteered, Dennison accepted them all. "The lion in us is thoroughly roused," he told Secretary of War Simon Cameron. By the time the telegraph and the mails to Washington were operating again, the state had twenty-two regiments in training, and the legislature had appropriated $3 million to support them. In McClellan's mind this was only a start. He based his plans on having 30,000 men under his command from Ohio alone.[4]

He established his main camp of instruction near Cincinnati, naming it Camp Dennison. On April 30 Cox led the first trainload of men from Columbus to the site. McClellan had his engineering officer, William S. Rosecrans, waiting for them with a trainload of lumber. By nightfall the men had laid out their camps and erected huts, and the next day they began drilling. Each train brought more recruits. McClellan faced a complicated administrative task. There were state militia units, militia mustered into federal service for three months under Lincoln's first call, and (after May 3, when the president recast the North's manpower needs) volunteer regiments enlisted in federal service for three years. He had already shifted his headquarters from Columbus to Cincinnati and was generating a growing flow of orders, reports, requisitions, and strategic plans.[5]

He demonstrated a prodigious capacity for work, going frequently to Camp Dennison to judge for himself the progress of troop training and living conditions and morale. Schools of instruction were begun for the volunteer officers, most of whom knew no more of drill than did their recruits. He made it a point to be seen often by the men, and on horseback he was an impressive martial figure. Joseph Alsop and other Cincinnati "railroad friends" had presented him with a big dark bay named Dan Webster, which became his favorite mount. He sat tall in the saddle, a journalist decided, because "he was commenced for a tall man and built for one, as far down as his hips. . . ." As soon as the recruits were capable of the simplest marching evolutions, he began the practice of holding reviews, as much for the purpose of being known by those in the ranks as to evaluate their progress. He was conducting such a review when a *New York Tribune* correspondent introduced him to eastern readers. The *Tribune* reporter observed that General McClellan "is personally extremely popular, army officers and men and everybody seem to have entire faith in him."[6]

When McClellan came to write his memoirs, an exercise he began immediately after the war in a mood of bitterness, he painted a vivid picture of the constant struggle he waged against blundering and incompetence during his first two months of command. That picture remained essentially intact in *McClellan's Own Story* when it was finally published in 1887, after his death. In it he recorded "the apathy and contracted views" of those in authority in Washington, and their unwillingness to furnish him the staff officers and matériel needed to train and equip his troops. Repeatedly — four times within the space of six pages — he wrote of having to act entirely on his own for the good of the country, without orders or guidance from General Scott. His opening campaign, he insisted, was, "from the first to last, undertaken upon my own authority and of my own volition, and without any advice, orders, or instructions from Washington. . . ."[7]

This picture seriously distorts the facts of the matter, but it does accurately reflect the origins of McClellan's conflict with Winfield Scott. At first he was flattered by evidence of the general-in-chief's confidence in him. "I believe your appointment as commander in chief of the forces in the West secure," his detective friend Allan Pinkerton wrote him from Washington after seeing Lincoln. "I learned that Genl Scott had told the President that he considered you an abler officer than Beauregard &c &c." Pinkerton's information was correct. On May 3 McClellan was put in command of the Department of the Ohio, consisting of the states of Ohio, Indiana, and Illinois; later the department would be expanded to include portions of western Pennsylvania and western Virginia and, later still, the state of Missouri.

McClellan wrote Scott to assure him of his "implicit confidence in the General under whom I first learned the art of war. . . ." On May 14 he received the ultimate soldier's honor — appointment as major general in the regular army, then the service's highest official rank. Only Scott, a major general since 1841 and a lieutenant general by brevet, outranked him. He owed his new position and promotion in no small measure to Treasury Secretary Salmon P. Chase, a former governor and senator from Ohio, who had made him his protégé.[8]

In keeping with what was by now a virtually predictable character trait, McClellan's "implicit confidence" in his superior did not last very long. The first rift came over staffing. During the time he was cut off from Washington, he had snared several unassigned officers passing through Cincinnati and put them to work. He was angered when Washington did not initially approve this improvisation, although in the end he did not have to give them up. He failed to get two of the officers he specifically requested for his staff — Fitz John Porter and West Point classmate Jesse Reno — but he was given Randolph Marcy and the others he sought, and instead of Porter obtained his second choice, Seth Williams. (In the case of his father-in-law, Marcy, he went out of channels with a personal appeal to President Lincoln "that he may be assigned to my command as the Chief of my staff.") The large number of officers resigning to join the Confederacy, Scott's adjutant wrote him, "sufficiently explains the necessity for asking you to do as well as you can with the talent and zeal you can find in your command." Assuming priority for himself, McClellan had little sympathy for the personnel problems of the high command.[9]

One officer he did not seek for his staff was Ulysses S. Grant, former captain in the 4th Infantry. Casting about for a role in the war, Grant called at McClellan's Cincinnati headquarters to offer his services but was told that the general had just gone out. He waited two hours, asked that McClellan be informed that he had called, and returned the next day, with the same lack of result: the general again had gone out. "McClellan never acknowledged my call, and, of course, after he knew I had been at his headquarters I was bound to await his acknowledgment," Grant recalled. McClellan remembered the incident differently in his memoirs, claiming that he was away from Cincinnati at the time, but in any case he did not follow up on the matter. Grant was known in the old army as a drinker and McClellan would not have forgotten his spree at Fort Vancouver during the Pacific railroad survey in 1853, and he no doubt considered this reason enough to avoid an interview. Grant began his Civil War career with a field command as colonel of an Illinois regiment.[10]

A second point of contention was Scott's timetable for filling McClellan's requests for arms and equipment, ranging from heavy artillery to armored gunboats. Even though army headquarters had to grapple with the threat of imminent secession by Maryland and Missouri and a hostile force twenty-five miles from the capital, it managed within a month to supply more than 25,000 muskets to Ohio's troops and, a week or so later, to mount the first heavy guns on the Ohio River frontier. McClellan was intolerant

of any delay, however. ''The apathy in Washington is very singular & very discouraging,'' he confided to Governor Dennison
on May 13. ''. . . I can get no answers except now & then a decided
refusal of some request or other — perhaps that is a little exaggerated, but the upshot of it is that they are entirely too slow for
such an emergency, & I almost regret having entered upon my
present duty.''[11]

This sense of emergency went to the heart of his dispute with
General Scott, then and later. While he was in charge of the
Department of the Ohio, the Ohio Valley was the scene of a crisis
of the highest priority. When he was named to command the
Army of the Potomac, the center of crisis moved with him to
Washington. Scott shared neither of these views, and in any case
he believed McClellan had ample authority to act and sufficient
forces to meet whatever enemy he might encounter. On May 20
McClellan complained that he had ''as yet received neither instructions nor authority'' to deal with the imminent threat to his
department. ''My hands are tied until I have one or the other.
Every day of importance.'' Scott replied that he was surprised
by such a complaint. Citing chapter and verse of his orders, he
wrote, ''It is not conceived what other instructions could have
been needed by you.''

For the moment McClellan avoided an open break with the
general-in-chief. On May 24 he attended a meeting in Indianapolis with the governors of the states in his department — Dennison of Ohio, Oliver P. Morton of Indiana, and Richard Yates
of Illinois — and they composed a ''memorial'' that Yates was
to deliver personally to Scott in Washington. In it they urged a
plan of campaign for the western theater and a substantial increase in McClellan's forces. The next day McClellan telegraphed
his confidant Dennison, ''Genl. Scott is as you are aware eminently sensitive, and does not at all times take suggestions kindly
from military subordinates especially when they conflict with his
own preconceived notions.'' Because of the need for Scott's ''hearty
cooperation'' in future military operations in the West, he went
on, Governor Yates should be cautioned that in Washington he
was ''not to use my name in such a way as to disturb the sensitive
complexion of the General's mind.''[12]

Even as he set up a program for troop training, McClellan was
giving thought to a strategy ''intended to relieve the pressure

upon Washington, & tending to bring the war to a speedy close."
On April 27, just four days after taking command, he sent his
proposal to Scott. As a first step, he wrote, key points along the
Ohio River frontier must be garrisoned, most notably Cairo, at
the junction of the Ohio and the Mississippi, and Cincinnati, near
the eastern end of the defensive line. Troops would be stationed
at key railroad junctions between these two points, ready to move
rapidly to any threatened area. In addition to these garrisons,
he called for an 80,000-man "active army of operations" to take
the offensive under (he presumed) his command. He anticipated
ending the rebellion by either of two strategic movements.

If cooperation with the eastern army at Washington was wanted,
McClellan would "with the utmost promptness" cross his army
into western Virginia and follow the valley of the Great Kanawha
River through the Alleghenies for a thrust on Richmond. "I know
that there could be difficulties in crossing the mountains," he
admitted, "but would go prepared to meet them." His alternative
proposal was designed for war on a larger canvas: an advance
from Ohio southward through Kentucky on Nashville, Tennessee.
"Were a battle gained before reaching Nashville," he wrote, he
would then move against Montgomery, Alabama, at that time the
capital of the Confederacy. After a simultaneous offensive by
the eastern army into South Carolina and Georgia, the combined
armies would go on to seize the South's Gulf ports — Pensacola,
Mobile, New Orleans. "The 2nd line of operations could be the
most decisive," he concluded.

McClellan's plan is noteworthy for being the first recorded
attempt at an overall strategy for prosecuting the war. In light
of his reputation in the old army as a first-rate military intellect,
however, it was surprisingly impractical on the face of it, as
General Scott was quick to point out. George McClellan was known
to be a quick study, but this was an instance of too much haste,
of too much extemporizing in plotting grand movements.

His proposed advance through the valley of the Great Kanawha, for example, called for a longer march than Scott's army
had made to Mexico City in 1847, facing far more inhospitable
conditions, with six or seven times as many men to feed and
supply. It was an area without railroads, and except for the first
seventy miles, where the Great Kanawha was navigable, everything would have to be carried by wagon. Annotating the plan

for the president, Scott pointed to its dependence on "long, te-dious, & *break down* (of men, horses & wagons) marches."
McClellan intended the movement on Nashville to be supported
by rail, but here too supply was the central problem, and Scott's
most telling criticism was the failure to use any of the rivers in
the western theater either as highways of invasion or as efficient
supply routes. Even allowing for the imperfect knowledge of
war's realities that prevailed in 1861, McClellan's grand strategy
presented an obvious logistics nightmare.

Scott responded with a campaign plan of his own, designed in
his words "to envelop the insurgent States and bring them to
terms with less bloodshed than by any other plan." It had two
main elements: a blockade of the South's Atlantic and Gulf ports,
and an expedition down the Mississippi to New Orleans, using
the 80,000 men McClellan proposed but supporting them by water
with a fleet of gunboats and supply vessels. Enemy positions
would be turned, and a "cordon of posts at proper points" would
keep the river open and the Confederacy permanently split. Months
would be required to drill the troops and assemble the shipping
for the movement; he set a target date of November 10. McClellan
was surely pleased to read Scott's assurance "that you are likely
to bear an important if not the principal part in this great ex-pedition," and that the general-in-chief's "great confidence in
your intelligence, zeal, science, and energy" was undiminished.

Scott's scheme for crushing the rebellion in the coils of eco-nomic strangulation rather than by pitched battle was leaked to
the press, where it was derisively labeled the "Anaconda Plan."
He had predicted that his greatest obstacle would be "the im-patience of our patriotic and loyal Union friends. They will
urge instant and vigorous action, regardless, I fear, of conse-quences...." The rising clamor in the North for one decisive
battle in Virginia to end the war bore out his prediction. Replying
to Scott's letter, McClellan acknowledged "the wisdom of your
intentions & recognize the propriety of all your military dispo-sitions...." He added, prophetically, that reconciling the public
to "necessary delay" would be no easy task.[13]

The administration's most immediate concern was keeping the
border state of Kentucky in the Union. "I think to lose Kentucky
is nearly the same as to lose the whole game," Lincoln wrote. The
divisions running so deep within the state were symbolized by its

political leadership. Governor Beriah Magoffin called for a special convention to consider an ordinance of secession, only to be blocked by moderates in the legislature. One of Kentucky's senators, John J. Crittenden, was celebrated for his strenuous efforts to find a compromise that would have headed off the war; the other senator, John C. Breckinridge, would become a major general and secretary of war in the Confederacy. The state's home guard under McClellan's old army friend Simon Buckner was suspected by Unionists of being readied to join the Confederate service, and they formed their own body of pro-Union militia as a counterweight.

On May 20 Governor Magoffin proclaimed Kentucky officially neutral, but few expected that fragile compromise to last long. Gideon Pillow, the mustang general so much scorned by McClellan during the Mexican War, positioned his Tennessee troops along the southern border. McClellan did the same with his forces along the Ohio River line. "From reliable information I am sure that the Governor of Kentucky is a traitor," he informed Washington. "Buckner is under his influence, so it is necessary to watch them." While he considered his troops still too raw to take the offensive, he hoped their mere presence just across the river would reassure Kentucky's Unionists and bluff its secessionists.[14]

For the moment he confined his efforts in Kentucky to gathering intelligence, putting Allan Pinkerton in charge of what he described as his secret service. In addition to sending out agents, Pinkerton made an undercover journey of his own through Kentucky, Tennessee, and Mississippi, and at Memphis penetrated the Confederate high command (by his own account) to the extent of taking a brandy and water with General Pillow. Of more real value were the dozens of reports of Confederate movements and secessionist political activities that McClellan received from a network of loyalist correspondents. He sent two members of his staff, Orlando Poe, of the topographical engineers, and Thomas M. Key, a former Cincinnati judge and legislator, into Kentucky (in Poe's case, into western Virginia as well) to evaluate Unionist sentiment. Key's findings were regarded as important enough that he was sent to Washington to report directly to the president.[15]

The Northern response to Governor Magoffin's neutrality proclamation began to take on an aggressive edge. A shipment of

5,000 muskets arriving in Cincinnati was earmarked for distribution to the home guard of loyalist Kentuckians. McClellan pressed ahead with making an armed camp of Cairo, the western gateway for any advance into Kentucky, and initiated the arming of river steamers to strengthen its defenses. He notified Washington that the Union men of Kentucky were determined to fight it out, and that he had promised them that if the Confederates violated the state's neutrality, "I would cross the Ohio with 20,000 men, if that were not enough with 30,000, & if necessary with 40,000, but that I would not stand by & see the loyal Union men of Kentucky crushed. . . . I hope yet to pay a visit to the Hon Jefferson Davis at Montgomery."[16]

In western Virginia the question was not whether there would be hostilities, but how soon. Geographically and culturally the region was more a part of the Ohio Valley than of the Old Dominion, and there was strong opposition to the ordinance of secession passed in Richmond on April 17. The fact that the Baltimore and Ohio, the main rail artery between the eastern theater and the Ohio Valley, crossed this corner of the state was reason enough that the North could not permit it to fall under Confederate control. During the first month of McClellan's command he had the benefit of an undeclared truce until Virginians voted on the secession ordinance in a referendum scheduled for May 23. He was careful to take no overt action before the election but did what he could to be ready if Southern forces broke the truce.

His memoirs to the contrary, he was fully empowered by Scott to counteract any such move. The general-in-chief confirmed in a telegram to Governor Dennison (who passed it on to McClellan) that a Union countermove in western Virginia was "within the competency of Gen McClellan to whom please refer." In the referendum, as expected, a large majority of Virginia's voters ratified secession except in the far western counties, where Unionist sentiment predominated. The next day Scott telegraphed McClellan that the Confederates were putting troops into the area at Grafton, on the Baltimore and Ohio, and asked, "Can you counteract the influence of that detachment?"[17]

The dispatch reached McClellan in Indiana, where he was conferring with the state governors in his department. After assuring Scott "Will do what you want," he hurried back to Cincinnati. He was at home on Sunday afternoon, May 26, when he learned from his intelligence sources that the Confererates were burning bridges on the Baltimore and Ohio. He quickly put into motion plans already made. Grafton was a key junction point on the railroad, where a branch ran westward to Parkersburg on the Ohio and the main line ran northwestward to Wheeling. He ordered the 1st Virginia at Wheeling — something of a shell regiment, containing far more Ohioans and Pennsylvanians than Unionist Virginians — to entrain for Grafton, backed up by the 16th Ohio from across the river. Two other Ohio regiments were sent toward Grafton on the Parkersburg branch. Reinforcements were put on alert in Indianapolis. When his telegraphic orders were on the way, he recalled, he sat down at the dining room table, "with the ladies of my family chatting around me," and composed proclamations to be issued to his army and to the inhabitants of Virginia.

The troops were cautioned to safeguard the persons and property of all civilians they encountered, whom they were rescuing "from the grasp of armed traitors." In his proclamation to the people of western Virginia he expanded on this theme. He noted their strong Unionist stand in the secession referendum, and said that his troops were entering the region to lift from their shoulders "the yoke of the traitorous conspiracy dignified by the name of the Southern Confederacy." He then took it upon himself to clarify the North's war aims. All rights and all private property would be religiously respected: "Notwithstanding all that has been said by the traitors to induce you to believe that our advent among you will be signalized by interference with your slaves, understand one thing clearly — not only will we abstain from all such interference but we will on the contrary with an iron hand, crush any attempt at insurrection on their part."

In a letter to Lincoln a few days later, he explained that there had been no time to clear his proclamation with the president in advance: "I prepared it in great haste & on such a basis as my knowledge of your Excellency's previous course & opinions assured me would express your views...." If he had misjudged the case, "a terrible mistake has been made, for the proclamation is regarded as expressing the views of the Presdt, & I have not intimated that it was prepared without authority."

With the exception of the gratuitous pledge to put down slave insurrections with an iron hand, the proclamation was not out of line with Lincoln's policy of keeping slavery from becoming a primary issue in these early months of war. Its real significance was that George McClellan, a general in the field, publicly committed himself to protecting Southern slavery by means of the Union army. If a majority of Northerners took no particular offense at this at the time, a powerful and very vocal antislavery minority would forget neither the proclamation nor its author. William Howard Russell, the noted correspondent sent by the *Times* of London to cover the American war, thought that to go on record proclaiming slaves to be private property was an "atrocious" act on a Northern general's part. However that may be, the proclamation served notice that here was a general who saw in army command something more than simply obeying orders and dealing in purely military matters.[18]

Grafton was occupied without a shot fired as the few Confederates there retreated eighteen miles southward to the village of Philippi. The burned Baltimore and Ohio bridges were rebuilt, and McClellan sent in reinforcements and a West Pointer, Thomas A. Morris, to take command of the expedition. At dawn on June 3, after marching all night in a drenching rainstorm, two of Morris's columns converged on the unsuspecting Southerners encamped at Philippi and routed them. After a round or two from his gun, an Ohio artillerist wrote, "Out they swarmed, like bees from a molested hive. This way and that the chivalry flew, and yet scarcely knew which way to run." Six Rebels were killed and a substantial stock of supplies lost, against the Federals' loss of one man wounded. "Your dispatch about the Phillippi affair last evening created a lively sensation of pleasure here," William Rosecrans wrote McClellan from Washington. It was a sensation across the rest of the North as well, with the newspapers christening it the "Philippi Races" and playing up this first victory over the secessionists as a major event. On June 11 delegates from Virginia's western counties met in convention in Wheeling, set up their own provisional state government, and named Francis H. Peirpoint governor. For McClellan it was an entirely satisfying way to begin a campaign.[19]

While he pushed troops and supplies into western Virginia to protect the Baltimore and Ohio and prepare for a renewed offensive there, McClellan gave thought to the complexities of Kentucky's situation. On June 20 Kentuckians would go to the polls to pick members of Congress, and on August 4 to choose a new state legislature, and he was well aware of the delicate diplomacy required of him until these elections clarified the question of union or disunion. He wrote the president that his proclamation to Virginians on noninterference with slavery "has produced the happiest effect" in slave state Kentucky. In the meantime, should his old commander of Mexican War notoriety breach that state's neutrality, he would "endeavor to find means to cause Genl Pillow to repeat his Cerro Gordo movement. . . ."

He advised Washington to move slowly. The people of Kentucky, he told General Scott, "desire to remain in the Union *without a revolution, under all the forms of law & by their own action"* — that is to say, without threat to the institution of slavery — and they should be treated with the "utmost delicacy" until the elections were over. If the state's neutrality was broken, let it be broken by the South. "I trust, General, that my action in the Grafton matter will show you that I am not given to procrastination but I feel so keenly the vital importance of keeping Kentucky in the Union that I must urge delay until we know exactly what we are doing."[20]

The matter took a new turn on June 7, when McClellan met with Simon Buckner, commander of Kentucky's home guard. The two had known each other since West Point, and they talked at McClellan's house in Cincinnati through the night and until five the next morning. McClellan later told General Scott that Buckner initiated the meeting, and he agreed to it primarily in the hope of "reclaiming" his old friend for the Union cause. He did not mention that he had received advance notice of Buckner's views from his aide Thomas M. Key, who met at length with the Kentuckian the night before in Louisville. Key hurried off a report to McClellan that spelled out Buckner's plan for maintaining Kentucky's neutrality. "The main result of my conference with Genl Buckner," he wrote, "is that if Kentucky is let alone by the U.S.," the state government would continue to submit to federal laws, make no attempt to initiate secession, and abide by the will of the people as expressed in the forthcoming elections. If the Confederacy sent in troops, "Kentucky would at once take arms against them."

In his brief account of the meeting for Scott, McClellan reported little more than Buckner's promise that his state forces would oppose any invasion from Tennessee, and, if necessary, would call on the Federals to help drive out the invaders. Certainly he and Buckner came to a broader understanding than that. The one witness present, a mutual West Point friend named Samuel Gill, gave it as his understanding that, while McClellan was not "stipulating for the Government," he would for the present "act in accordance with the general views expressed by Simon." For his part, Buckner saw their meeting as affirming the points he had already discussed with Thomas Key. In his report to Governor Magoffin, however, Buckner termed their understandings stipulations, as if they had made a treaty to ensure Kentucky's neutrality. Magoffin released the letter to the newspapers, and McClellan found a storm whirling about his head.

The Buckner letter, a Kentucky Unionist warned him, "is doing you the gravest injury possible. The indignation is as great in Ky as north of the Ohio. The Cabinet disavows your stipulations." Newspapers editorialized that by seeming to recognize Kentucky's neutrality officially, General McClellan was playing into the hands of the disunionists; the North, they argued, could no more recognize neutrality than it could recognize secession. McClellan denied the implication, insisting that his meeting with Buckner was informal and entirely unofficial, nothing more than an exchange of views between friends. Buckner's letter, he telegraphed General Scott, "fills me with astonishment. I can scarcely believe what he wrote. It is an entire misconception & is incorrect throughout."

If he was not quite the innocent victim of circumstance he professed to be, McClellan actually agreed to nothing that contradicted administration policy toward Kentucky. "It seems to me," he wrote, "that there must finally be a collision between the two parties, in Ky, & that we must throw our weight into the scale." The Buckner affair obscured the fact that when that day came, the Federals would be ready to act, thanks in good measure to McClellan's preparations. Yet once again, he as a field general had thrust himself into the middle of a political issue. There were those in the Republican party with strong views on making hard war who would find in the Buckner meeting evidence that McClellan was willing to compromise with enemies of the Union. Allan Pinkerton cautioned him that the affair had created great excitement and ''evil disposed persons are using this to your injury at Washington.''[21]

Another correspondent advised him that nothing would remove any tarnish from his reputation more quickly than winning a battle, and he was preparing to attempt exactly that. On June 20 he set out to take personal command of the campaign in western Virginia. His departure for the front was announced, and at every stop his train made between Cincinnati and Marietta he was welcomed as a conquering hero. The journey was a ''continuous ovation,'' he told Ellen. ''Gray-headed old men & women; mothers holding up their children to take my hand, girls, boys, all sorts, cheering and crying, God bless you! I never went thro' such a scene in my life & never expect to go thro' such another one.'' He hoped he could live up to their expectations.

In a letter to her mother-in-law written a few days later, Ellen described the general as ''very well & in excellent spirits and is I suppose very anxious for a fight.'' She prayed for a short campaign and his early return. Since her father was serving on McClellan's staff, her mother and her sister, Fanny, had come to stay with her in Cincinnati. She described herself as ''heartily tired'' of her husband's absence, ''in wretched spirits most of the time, and generally disquieted.'' She did not enjoy robust health, and in addition, she was in the sixth month of pregnancy with her first child, and in these hot summer months she was often at the soothing mineral baths of nearby Yellow Springs. McClellan wrote to her at every opportunity, at least once a day, and when the telegraph crews kept pace with the army he wired her daily to assure her of his health and safety.[22]

General Robert E. Lee, in command of Virginia's forces, responded to the Philippi defeat by sending in reinforcements under new commanders to try to retrieve the Confederacy's fortunes in western Virginia. In addition to the Baltimore and Ohio route, there were two other practical passages through the mountains of the region: the valley of the Great Kanawha, which McClellan had proposed for his advance on Richmond, and a turnpike connecting Parkersburg on the Ohio with Staunton in the Shenandoah Valley. Former Virginia governor Henry A. Wise, with the Wise Legion he had raised, would operate in the Great Kanawha Valley. Lee sent his adjutant, Robert S. Garnett, to hold the

Parkersburg-Staunton turnpike. Garnett established blocking positions at key passes in Rich Mountain and Laurel Hill, near the
town of Beverly. McClellan, with the bulk of the available forces,
took personal charge of the campaign against Garnett. The Kanawha assignment went to Jacob Cox, with troops to about the
strength of a brigade.

Reaching Grafton on June 23, McClellan spent the next two
weeks bringing up supplies and putting his forces into proper
order for the offensive. He was convinced that very little was
done or done right unless he personally supervised it. He wrote
Ellen that volunteers in this war posed the same problems as
volunteers in the Mexican War: ''Everything here needs the hand
of the master . . . so difficult is it to get these Mohawks in working
trim.'' Nevertheless, he remained as impressed with the potential
of the recruits as when he first took command. In a report to
Treasury Secretary Chase, his patron in the Cabinet, he wrote,
''We have the most magnificent material for an army that was
ever brought together — give me three months in a camp of instruction after this little campaign is over & I would not hesitate
to put these men at the best of European troops.'' He expressed
no concern about either the strength or the capability of the
enemy, and scoffed at the Confederate boast that one Rebel soldier was the equal of three Yankees. In describing for Chase his
plan for snaring Garnett's army, he commented, ''I hardly hope
that they will be foolish enough to fall into the trap — whether
they do so or not I shall then advance . . . & drive them into &
across the mountains.''

The first year of the Civil War saw a flood of proclamations
and addresses issued by generals on both sides, more than a few
of them laced with bombast, and McClellan's were about average
on that score. The address he issued to his troops at Grafton on
June 25, for example, expanded on the soldierly qualities he
expected of those under his command, and concluded with a gran-
diloquent declaration of purpose: ''Soldiers! I have heard that
there was danger here. I have come to place myself at your head
and to share it with you. I fear now but one thing — that you
will not find foemen worthy of your steel. I know that I can rely
upon you.''

This was deliberately Napoleonic in intent and, as Jacob Cox
remarked, composed for stage effect, yet it was perfectly attuned

to the hour and to the mood of the North. George McClellan knew
how to make new soldiers believe in themselves. Even the better
civilian intellects were not immune. "How like the sound of the
silver trumpets of Judah . . . ," wrote Sophia Hawthorne, wife of
New England's celebrated man of letters, of one of McClellan's
addresses. "I conceive an adoring army following the lead of
such a ringing of true steel.'"23

In a proclamation to Virginia's civilians, McClellan repeated
his pledge to protect private rights and property. "The beneficial
effect of this course has been everywhere apparent," he assured
Governor Dennison. Implicit in such proclamations was his belief
that secession was an aberration: once the federal government
demonstrated that it was capable of stamping out armed rebellion,
he was certain that secession's supporters would realize their
delusion and gladly return to the Union. Until that day, they
should be made welcome under a policy of reconciliation and not
be persecuted because of their beliefs. "All private property
whether of secessionists or others must be strictly respected, and
no one is to be molested merely because of political opinions,"
he wrote a local official. Depredations committed by his troops,
he warned, would not be tolerated. He court-martialed a company
of the 19th Ohio — three-months' men from Cleveland, where
antislavery sentiment was strong — for robbing the home of a
Virginia secessionist. "I have been obliged to inflict some severe
punishments & I presume the Abolition papers of the Western
Reserve will be hard down on me for disgracing some of their
friends guilty of the small crime of burglary," he told his wife.
"I believe the Army is beginning to comprehend that they have
a master over them who is stern in punishing & means what he
says.'"24

In outlining his plan of operations for Scott's adjutant, McClellan
made it clear that he was taking as his model the general-in-
chief's Mexican War campaign. "Say to the General . . . ," he
wrote, "that I am trying to follow a lesson long ago learned from
him — i.e. — not to move until I know that everything is ready,
& then to move with the utmost rapidity & energy." Not even a
chance for a brilliant stroke would induce him "to depart from
my intention of gaining success by manoeuvring rather than by
fighting; I will not throw these men of mine into the teeth of
artillery & intrenchments, if it is possible to avoid it." He found

Garnett's dispositions to be similar to those of Santa Anna in 1847, and "if possible I will repeat the manoeuvre of Cerro Gordo."

To defend what he termed the "gates to the northwestern country," General Garnett had positioned most of his troops at Laurel Hill, on the road leading southward from Philippi to Beverly, over which he expected the Yankees to come. He had also to consider the possibility that McClellan might approach Beverly from the west, on the main Parkersburg-Staunton turnpike, and posted a detachment under Colonel John Pegram where the pike crossed Rich Mountain.

It was not unlike a problem posed in Professor Mahan's Science of War course at West Point, and McClellan responded with a classic textbook solution. Thomas Morris with a single brigade was to advance from Philippi on Laurel Hill and, without attacking, attract Garnett's attention; in the military parlance of the day, he was to "amuse" the Confederate general. Meanwhile, with three brigades, McClellan would advance along the turnpike toward Rich Mountain and attempt to turn Pegram's position, getting into his rear at Beverly and cutting the communications and escape routes of both enemy forces.[25]

His confidence in his soldiers was offset by a considerable lack of confidence in his officers. Of the four brigadiers under his immediate command — Morris, Rosecrans, Newton Schleich, and Robert L. McCook — he had nothing good to say about three of them by the time he had been in the field ten days. On July 3 he wrote Ellen, "I have not a Brig Genl worth his salt — Morris is a timid old woman — Rosecranz a silly fussy goose — Schleich knows nothing. . . ." He did not confine his displeasure to private remarks to his wife. One evening during the advance on Rich Mountain, some of Rosecrans's men camped beyond the stopping point specified for them. Pointing out that this might tip off his intentions to the enemy, McClellan issued his subordinate a rebuke so sharp that Rosecrans appealed to him to delete it from the record; he did so, but was satisfied that he had made his point. Rosecrans, he told Ellen, was "very meek now after a very severe rapping I gave him a few days since."

Thomas Morris, who had managed the Philippi surprise attack skillfully, came in for a rapping even more severe, and one that remained on the record. Morris discovered that the Confederates were at Laurel Hill in more force than expected, that indeed

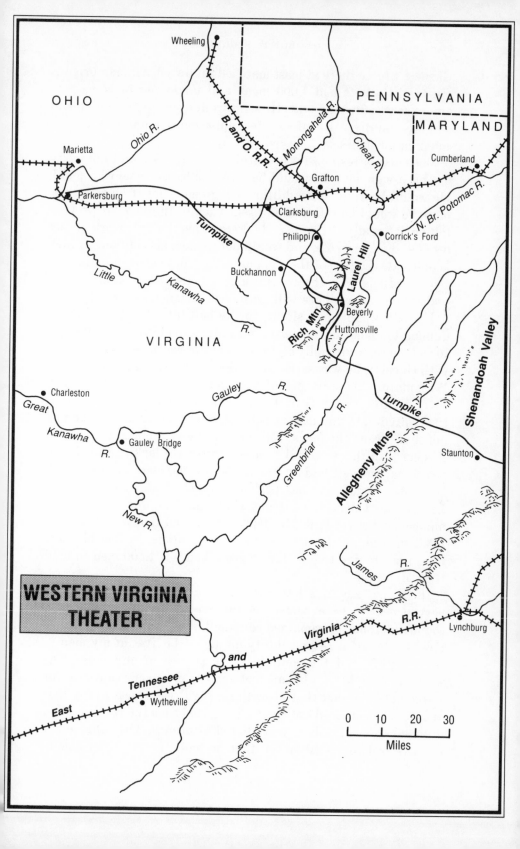

OHIO

Wheeling

PENNSYLVANIA

MARYLAND

Marietta

Ohio R.

B. and O. R.R.

Monongahela R.

Cheat R.

Cumberland

Parkersburg

N. Br. Potomac R.

Grafton

Turnpike

Clarksburg

Corrick's Ford

Philippi

Little

Kanawha

Buckhannon

Laurel Hill

R.

VIRGINIA

Rich Mtn.

Beverly

Huttonsville

Charleston

Gauley

R.

Shenandoah Valley

Great

Kanawha

Gauley Bridge

Greenbriar

R.

Turnpike

Allegheny Mtns.

R.

Staunton

New R.

James

R.

WESTERN VIRGINIA
THEATER

Virginia

and

R.R.

Lynchburg

Tennessee

East

Wytheville

0   10   20   30
Miles

Garnett's force there at least matched his own 3,500-man brigade (in fact, Garnett had 4,000 men) and might not be so easy to amuse as was first thought. He sent his findings to McClellan and observed mildly, "I confess I feel apprehensive unless our force could equal theirs. . . ."

McClellan's response was scathing. If Morris could not carry out his assignment, he would be replaced by someone who could. He would be given one additional regiment, but if he asked for more he would be relieved and sent back to Indiana. "I propose taking the really difficult & dangerous part of this work on my own hands," he wrote, and would not weaken his column, "which is to decide the fate of the campaign. . . . I have spoken plainly — I speak officially — the crisis is a grave one, & I must have Generals under me who are willing to risk as much as I am. . . ."[26]

His risk was in fact slight, for he had intended from the beginning to undertake no movement until he had sufficient strength to make success virtually certain. As he approached the showdown with Garnett, he was satisfied on that score. In addition, he told Washington, his opponent had committed the cardinal military sin of dividing his army in the face of a superior foe. He estimated the Confederate numbers at between 6,000 and 7,000, and he was not that far off the mark. Neither army was adept at paperwork this early in the war, and precise figures are lacking, but it appears that Garnett had a total of about 5,300 men, against which McClellan could marshal perhaps 11,000 of all arms. Leaving 4,000 under Morris to confront what was thought to be an equal number at Laurel Hill, McClellan calculated that his remaining 7,000 gave him at least a two-to-one advantage. In fact his edge was closer to five to one, for Pegram had but 1,300 men to hold Rich Mountain.[27]

In the privacy of a letter to his wife McClellan revealed the nervousness to be expected on the eve of his first battle as a commander, but he remained confident of the outcome. "I realize now the dreadful responsibility on me — the lives of my men — the reputation of the country & the success of our cause," he wrote on July 5. ". . . I shall feel my way & be very cautious, for I recognize the fact that everything requires success in my first operations. You need not be at all alarmed as to the result — God is on our side." Publicly he radiated assurance. Although he put it on record for Washington that he had "great difficulties to meet,'' he announced that his men were eager for the fight. Arriving before Rich Mountain, he telegraphed: ''I think I can turn his position — feel sure of success in any event.'' He was already planning the next phase of his campaign — an advance either into the Shenandoah Valley or into eastern Tennessee, as the general-in-chief should prefer.[28]

Once committed to the offensive, McClellan moved swiftly. He arrived in front of Rich Mountain on July 9, established by a reconnaissance the next day that Pegram was in a well-fortified position at the foot of the mountain, and by the evening of July 10 had worked out a plan of attack. Rosecrans learned that a young Union man named David Hart, who lived on a farm at the crest of the mountain, had offered his services as a guide. He called him in and found he knew of an obscure pathway that turned the enemy's left flank and came out at the Hart farm on the mountaintop. He took the youth to McClellan, who questioned him closely and then approved the plan. Rosecrans assembled just under 1,850 infantrymen from his brigade and at first light on July 11 set off up the mountainside. McClellan ordered him to report progress hourly, and it was agreed between them that when the sound of Rosecrans's guns announced his attack on the rear of Pegram's entrenchments, he would attack from the front with the other two brigades.[29]

Rosecrans predicted that he might open his attack by ten in the morning, but the hour came and went in silence and McClellan waited impatiently with the troops he had readied for his assault. It was raining heavily. At last, about 1:00 P.M., a message arrived from Rosecrans. Written at eleven o'clock, it announced that the flanking party was just then within sight of the mountain crest. The climb had been longer and rougher than anticipated and sending back progress reports was difficult, and Rosecrans said he would send another courier when he had something to report. At 2:30 the boom of artillery and the rattle of musketry from Rich Mountain was clearly heard in McClellan's camp. Rosecrans was obviously engaged with the enemy; the question was where. The only certainty was that he was not attacking the rear of Pegram's entrenchments as expected.

John Beatty, an officer in the 3rd Ohio, recalled that when the sound of battle was first heard, McClellan and his staff came galloping up to his forward position. The men tensed for action,

Beatty wrote, but McClellan ''sat there with indecision stamped on every line of his countenance.'' Although written well after the fact, Beatty's recollection was probably accurate enough; certainly McClellan at that moment was perplexed. The battle was not going according to plan. To attack now would be to throw his men against an entrenched enemy in an uncertain situation, at the risk of perhaps heavy casualties. On the other hand, Rosecrans might be in serious trouble and in danger of being cut to pieces behind enemy lines unless the main column came to his aid.

He elected to make no attack, but instead to wait for word from Rosecrans. The flanking party would have to fend for itself. It was late in the day before the firing died out. In the meantime, McClellan's topographical officer, Orlando Poe, found a position for artillery to take Pegram's line under an enfilading fire. If the flanking movement had indeed failed, McClellan would pursue the battle the next day by shelling the enemy out of his works.

A burst of cheers from Pegram's lines late in the afternoon suggested to McClellan a Confederate success in the battle on the mountain. This was as much bluff as anything else, for the Rebels had nothing to cheer about. Early that morning Pegram had gotten wind of the Federal flanking movement from a captured courier and sent a party under Captain Julius de Lagnel back up the mountain to the Hart farm to guard his rear. De Lagnel threw up a rough breastwork of logs and with 350 men and one gun engaged Rosecrans in a fierce firefight. The outcome was never in doubt, but by the time Rosecrans organized his assault, overran the position, and pulled his victorious troops together for further action, the afternoon was nearly gone. There was no sign of any attack by McClellan, and he decided he had done all he could for one day.

With a plan gone awry recriminations were sure to follow. In his account of the battle written three days later, McClellan glossed over the matter, but in his report on his wartime service, published in 1864, he acknowledged hearing Rosecrans's engagement, the sound of which was ''distant and stationary,'' and added that Rosecrans failed to communicate and ''failed to carry out his orders to move on the rear of Pegram's works.'' (In a draft of his memoirs these failures were termed ''extremely censurable.'') For his part, Rosecrans testified before a congressional committee that it was McClellan who deserved censure. The moment he heard the sound of battle, he "was bound, as a military man, to have made the attack in his front, for the purpose of preventing the enemy from falling on me with too heavy a force. . . ."

Behind the recriminations was the fact that in this first test as a battlefield commander McClellan took resort in caution when his plan miscarried, leaving a portion of his army in possible peril. He had conceived his campaign on a skillful reading of the position and resources of the enemy, demonstrated equal skill in administering his own army, outmaneuvered his opponent, and then brought him to battle under circumstances in which (in his own words) "I had provided against & foreseen every contingency. . . ." Yet when the enemy confronted him with the unexpected, he halted and waited to see what the next day would bring.[30]

To be sure, as events unfolded McClellan's decision became nothing more than a footnote to the history of the campaign, of interest only as a possible precedent for the future. The Confederate defense of the Parkersburg-Staunton turnpike collapsed like a house of cards following Rosecrans's victory. Most of Pegram's surviving troops were able to evacuate Rich Mountain that night, but after they wandered aimlessly without rations or hope, Pegram sent word to McClellan that he was ready to surrender. On July 13 he and almost 600 officers and men laid down their arms. It is unlikely that more than a third of Pegram's original force of 1,300 finally escaped. Realizing that his own communications were now threatened, Garnett evacuated Laurel Hill. Morris pursued closely, and near Corrick's Ford on July 13 Garnett was mortally wounded while directing a rear-guard action. "Our success is complete & secession is killed in this country," McClellan telegraphed Washington. It was a measure of his achievement in making this a campaign of maneuver rather than of fighting that the single, decisive battle involved hardly 2,200 men.

He hoped to make his victory complete by cutting off Garnett's column as it made a long detour trying to reach the safety of the Shenandoah Valley. He ordered the various Union garrisons guarding the Baltimore and Ohio to use the railroad's rolling stock to mass on the enemy's escape route. Nothing went quite right, however. The scheme was complicated, everyone involved was inexperienced, and in the end the Confederates evaded the trap.

McClellan found much to criticize in this episode, and when he decided that General Cox was also acting too slowly in the Great Kanawha Valley, he exploded. "In heaven's name give me some General Officers who understand their profession," he telegraphed Washington. "I give orders & find some who cannot execute them unless I stand by them. Unless I command every picket & lead every column I cannot be sure of success." This was an ungenerous judgment. His harsh reprimands of Cox in official dispatches, for example, were based on an unsubstantiated report that he had "suffered a detachment of his command to be badly routed and whipped. . . ." In fact Cox outmaneuvered his opponent — turning the enemy's flank as ably as Rosecrans did at Rich Mountain — and gained all the objectives McClellan had assigned him.

From these supposed shortcomings of his subordinates came perhaps the major lesson McClellan drew from his western Virginia campaign — the conviction that he must supervise personally every aspect of a military operation. "More than that," he told Ellen on July 21, "I don't feel sure that the men will fight very well under anyone but myself. They have the utmost confidence in me & will do anything I put them at." There was a certain hypothetical quality to this statement, for he had neither witnessed nor directed any fighting.[31]

The campaign also revealed in McClellan a penchant for aggrandizement. "I am more than satisfied with you," he announced to his troops in an address issued on July 16. "You have annihilated two armies, commanded by educated and experienced soldiers, and entrenched in mountain fastnesses fortified at their leisure." He continued in this vein until every soldier in his command was surely filled with pride in himself and in the general commanding: "Soldiers! I have confidence in you, and I trust you have learned to confide in me." (One purpose of this flattery may have been to persuade the three-months' men to stay on until the campaign was done, but in this he would be disappointed. "I have as yet found but few whose patriotism is sufficient to induce them to remain beyond their time," he wrote Ellen in disgust.) In addition to multiplying his accomplishment into the annihilation of armies, he gave Washington a new count of the enemy he had faced. He told army headquarters that "captured official papers show Garnetts force to have been 10,000 men." He arrived at this inflated figure by including four regiments of Confederate reinforcements, none of which had reached Garnett.[32]

Just then no one cared about such conceits, for overnight he had become the North's first battlefield hero. Detaching strategically vital western Virginia from the Confederacy was recognized as a major achievement. The telegrapher handling his communications reported that "the success of Gen. McClellan's movements is eliciting great enthusiasm through the country." General Scott wired him that he, the president, and the Cabinet "are charmed with your activity, valor, and consequent successes. . . ." As for finishing up the campaign, Scott added, "we do not mean to precipitate you, as you are fast enough." Congress adopted a joint resolution of thanks for his achievements. Future archenemies were full of praise in his hour of victory : "McLellan is doing a good work in Western Virginia," wrote the radical Republican senator from Michigan, Zachariah Chandler, and Horace Greeley's *New York Tribune* editorialized, "We like the works and ways of Gen. McClellan. . . . May his shadow never be less!" The *Louisville Journal* termed his campaign "a piece of finished military workmanship by a master hand." The *New York Times* announced, "We feel very proud of our wise and brave young Major-General. There is a future before him. . . ." The *New York Herald* headed a column of fulsome praise "Gen. McClellan, the Napoleon of the Present War."[33]

In the bright afterglow of victory McClellan put his displeasure with Winfield Scott behind him. "I value that old man's praise very highly," he wrote Ellen. He thanked the general-in-chief for his commendation : "All that I know of war I have learned from you, & in all that I have done I have endeavored to conform to your manner of conducting a campaign. . . . It is my ambition to merit your praise & never to deserve your censure." He sent Randolph Marcy to Washington with the report of his operations and several Confederate flags captured on the battlefield. President Lincoln was reported "much pleased" with the trophies. McClellan instructed Marcy to tell General Scott "that I think a movement through Kentucky, Western Tennessee and Northern Alabama would be decisive of the war."

His old friends P. G. T. Beauregard and Joe Johnston soon enough ended talk of decisive campaigns. Scott had discussed with McClellan a plan to bring his army eastward to act in concert with Robert Patterson "to bag Johnston" (as Scott phrased it) in the Shenandoah Valley. Irvin McDowell's army at Washington was to dispose of Beauregard at Manassas Junction, twenty-five miles west of the capital. Johnston, however, demonstrated that like McClellan he knew how to amuse an opponent. He slipped away from the befuddled Patterson and joined Beauregard at Manassas. On July 21 McDowell attacked the combined Confederate forces along Bull Run, and by day's end the Federals were beaten and in flight back to Washington.

The news of Bull Run ran across the North like a shock wave, shattering confidence in a quick and comparatively bloodless end to the rebellion. Secretary of War Cameron concluded that McDowell, tarred with defeat, must be replaced and a new start made. On July 22 a telegram from Washington was handed to McClellan at Beverly: "Circumstances make your presence here necessary. Charge Rosecrans or some other general with your present department and come hither without delay."[34]

FIVE

BUILDING AN ARMY

For the second time George McClellan made his way to a new military command to the accompaniment of what he himself called "one continuous ovation." He traveled by special train on the main Pennsylvania line from Wheeling through Pittsburgh, Philadelphia, and Baltimore and on to Washington, and at every stop crowds alerted by telegraph nearly overwhelmed him with their enthusiasm. He arrived late on the afternoon of July 26, 1861, and was welcomed as the conquering hero of western Virginia.

The next morning he called on President Lincoln, who received him cordially and described his new command: head of the Division of the Potomac, comprising McDowell's army and the defenses of Washington. The rest of the day was a continuous round of conferences and inspections, and that night he sat down to record it all for Ellen. "I find myself in a new & strange position here — Presdt, Cabinet, Genl Scott & all deferring to me — by some strange operation of magic I seem to have become *the* power of the land," he wrote in pleased amazement. "I almost think that were I to win some small success now I could become Dictator or anything else that might please me — but nothing of that kind would please me — *therefore* I *won't* be Dictator. Admirable self denial!" He was confident that he had already discovered the causes of the Bull Run defeat, and that he could turn this army around and lead it to victory.

McClellan, a student of Roman history, referred to dictatorship not in its modern totalitarian sense but in its original meaning of a temporary expedient in time of crisis. Many in Washington did indeed see him as the savior of the Republic. When he visited the Senate to urge passage of a bill he had drafted for enlarging his staff, the legislators crowded around to remark that he looked too young to be an old soldier, and to declare him responsible for the fate of the nation. "I began to feel how great the task committed to me . . . ," he told Ellen. "Who would have thought when we were married, that I should so soon be called upon to save my country?"

A few days later he attended a state dinner at the White House in honor of Prince Napoleon, cousin of France's Emperor Napoleon III, and was again a center of attention. He found it strange to enter the room "with the old General leaning on me — the old veteran (Scott) & his young successor; I could see that many marked the contrast." At dinner he was seated next to the prince's aide, Colonel Camille Ferri Pisani, with whom he spoke at length in his fluent French. The British ambassador, Lord Lyons, who had been observing the adulation lavished on McClellan for the past week, assured the colonel that he was conversing with the next president of the United States. McClellan responded, Ferri Pisani wrote, "with a fine, modest, and silent smile."[1]

General Scott seems to have felt as a matter of principle that at thirty-four McClellan was too young to deserve command of an army, but in the event he raised no actual objection. Nor were there real grounds for objection: once the decision was taken to replace McDowell, McClellan was the logical and all but inevitable choice to succeed him. His record and reputation in the old army were already recognized by appointment to a rank second only to Scott's. As head of the Department of the Ohio he had demonstrated real ability as a military executive. In western Virginia, if he did not actually direct any battles, he planned and executed — and won — the campaign with incisive skill. That by itself uniquely qualified him for the post. At the time and place, considered on his merits, he was the best man for the job.

It became part of the McClellan dogma that when he took command at Washington (saving the capital for the first time) he found a helpless city, defended by a mere collection of regiments "cowering on the banks of the Potomac," easy prey for even a single regiment of Rebel cavalry. That was hardly the case. He knew very well that old acquaintances such as William T. Sherman and William B. Franklin and Ambrose Burnside, or tough regulars of the stripe of Andrew Porter and George Sykes and Henry J. Hunt, would never allow troops to remain cowering on the riverbank half a dozen days after the battle. Positions were manned and there were eighty-eight pieces of artillery in the forts on the Virginia side of the river, no call had gone out for Patterson's force in the Shenandoah Valley to act as emergency reinforcement, and General Scott gave his assurance that the city was in no immediate danger.[2]

If the crisis was something less than he would have history believe, McClellan still found too few hours in the day to accomplish all that he judged needed to be done. One of his first tasks was restoring a sense of order in Washington itself. The city was overrun with soldiers: three-months' men, their terms up, setting out for home; new regiments flooding in from the North; and a backwash of the stragglers and dispirited from the battlefield, a distressing number of them officers, wandering about the streets and public places. McClellan made Andrew Porter provost marshal and gave him a squadron of regular cavalry, and in short order the hardbitten troopers emptied the barrooms and hotel lobbies and sorted out the lost and strayed and sent them off to the outlying camps. No soldier was allowed in the city without a pass. Just three days after Porter's appointment, McClellan could boast that Washington was "perfectly quiet." It was hard to tell, he wrote his wife, that a regiment was stationed there, much less an army. On August 1 the *New York Tribune* titled an editorial from the capital "Confidence Renewed" and lauded the young general and "the admirable system of discipline he has put in force."

He was meanwhile inspecting the camps and the fortifications, seeing and in turn being seen, just as he had done at Camp Dennison in Ohio. On one of these tours he was in the saddle twelve hours, leaving his staff trailing far behind by the pace he set. The men took to calling him "Little Mac" and raising a cheer when they saw him, and his acknowledgment soon became his trademark: snatching off his cap, he would raise it high above his head and give it a jaunty twirl. Often he stopped to chat casually with a squad or a company. He might ask the men if they were "ready for a brush" with the Rebels, and when they shouted that they were, he promised to risk it with them. To another company he pledged no more Bull Run retreats: "Boys, every foot of ground taken by us hereafter will be held." Watching one of these encounters, a sergeant in the 2nd Michigan decided that it must be the general's intention to inspect personally every regiment in the army. Before he made his presence felt, the sergeant noted in his diary, that army was "a great, green, overgrown, loose concern. . . . There is a great improvement since he took command. The men begin to feel more confidence." On August 5 an editor at the *New York World* wrote Cabinet member Montgomery Blair, "It is evident that Genl McClellan has done more in ten days towards organizing the advance than Scott did in ten weeks."[3]

These deliberate efforts to restore morale were matched by a demonstration of his stand on discipline. Two regiments, the 2nd Maine and the 79th New York Highlanders, resorted to mutiny to bring attention to their various grievances; heading the list was their term of enlistment, which they said was three months and the army said was three years. McClellan's response was prompt and blunt. Sixty-three of the Maine soldiers were sentenced to grim imprisonment in the Dry Tortugas, off the Florida Keys. The New Yorkers were confronted by a detachment of regulars and the announcement that they would be fired on if they did not obey orders instantly. "The gentlemen at once laid down their arms," McClellan wrote. The ringleaders were imprisoned, and he took away the Highlanders' colors until they proved by good behavior that they deserved them back. It was a sobering lesson in implacable military justice. He blamed the episode on the "utter worthlessness of the officers of these rgts — we have good material, but no officers."[4]

Lincoln had asked him for his thoughts on a strategy for suppressing the rebellion, and on August 2 he obliged the president with what he described for Ellen as "a carefully considered plan for conducting the war on a large scale . . . ." He was invited to read it to the Cabinet the next day.

McClellan rejected General Scott's thesis of applying concentric pressure on the Confederacy in favor of a single massive army — his army — operating as a juggernaut to "crush the rebels in one campaign. . . ." This army was to have 273,000 men and 600 guns. A large naval force would provide waterborne communications and mount diversionary attacks on the Southern coastline. Other logistical needs would be met by railroads. He made Richmond his primary target, to be followed by an advance on Charleston and Savannah and then a march across the Deep South to seize Montgomery, Pensacola, Mobile, and New Orleans. Operations in the western theater — the centerpiece of Scott's Anaconda Plan — would be secondary or diversionary. Counting the necessary garrison troops and a "strong reserve," he would be personally commanding perhaps three quarters of the 500,000 troops Congress had authorized. He furnished no timetable, but it must have gone without saying that training and equipping this grand army could hardly be accomplished before the spring of 1862. In such a conception time counted for less than execution.

The immense massing of fighting power, the focus on the Confederacy's vital points, the large-scale maneuvering to render the outcome all but inevitable, owed much to his study of Baron Jomini, the Swiss military theorist and interpreter of Napoleon. The memorandum also revealed important and fundamental principles of George McClellan's own military thought, principles that outlasted the hard reality of his situation as he would presently perceive it.

Central to his strategic concepts was that all operations elsewhere be secondary and in support of his own; and that to persuade the rebellious states "of the utter impossibility of resistance," they must be subjected to overwhelming defeat at a time and on a battlefield of his choosing. One Napoleonic grand army, perfectly prepared, and one grand campaign, perfectly executed and with nothing left to chance, and the secession impulse would be crushed. If at the same time Southern civilians and their property (including their slaves) were rigidly protected — a civil war, he wrote, was after all a contest for the minds of a whole people — the Union might be restored with harmony and without social upheaval.

This was and would remain a crucial element of McClellan's military strategy. Revolutionary political objectives such as the abolition of slavery must not be allowed to embitter the contest and leave the South no choice but to fight to the death for independence. In such an event, he believed, the North might not have the resources to prevail; only in a strictly limited war was victory certain. As it was, he admitted that the force he recommended was large and the expense great, but he posed the alternative: "Shall we crush the rebellion at one blow, terminate the war in one campaign, or shall we leave it as a legacy for our descendants?''[5]

Rather than living in the field with his army, McClellan made his headquarters in the capital, in the spacious house owned by the navy's Captain Charles Wilkes, on Pennsylvania Avenue at 19th Street on Jackson Square, two blocks from the War Department. He took rooms on the second floor for his personal quarters. The first floor was taken up by staff offices and the telegraph room. General and staff took their meals at a restaurant around the corner on I Street operated by the free mulatto Wormley, one of Washington's best-known caterers, or had them sent in when military business was pressing.

It became McClellan's daily routine to hold a staff conference after breakfast, then to see visitors and conduct business, and in the afternoon to ride out for inspection tours or reviews at the camps north of the city or across the Potomac in Virginia. ''I *must* ride much every day for my army covers much space,'' he told Ellen, ''& unfortunately I have no one on my staff to whom I can entrust the safety of affairs — it is necessary for me to see as much as I can every day. . . .'' The general and his aides, usually rushing along at a gallop, were soon a familiar sight on Washington's avenues. On at least two occasions he made aerial observations from Professor Thaddeus Lowe's hydrogen balloon. He seldom returned from his tours before nine or ten at night. Following another staff conference, he customarily worked until the small hours of the morning. He delegated little authority and set a pace as if driven, and by the end of August he was in a state of exhaustion so severe that he fell ill for the better part of a week, probably with the recurrent malarial fever he called his Mexican disease.[6]

The public was eager for impressions of the new commander of its principal army. (On August 20 that army officially took the name he had chosen for it: the Army of the Potomac.) Soon after arriving in the capital he invited war correspondents to his headquarters to discuss the need for self-censorship in reporting military news, and when he came into the room sweat-stained and dusty from an inspection tour, wearing no mark of rank, a journalist wrote that he could have passed for a private soldier. He exhibited no more pretense of speech than of dress, and made a good impression because of it. He even essayed a little humor.

In answer to a question about whether drawings of the Washington fortifications in the illustrated weeklies were revealing military secrets, he replied that he had no objection to them at all: in their improbability they were more likely to confuse the enemy than to enlighten him.

To meet the demand for his likeness he was persuaded to visit Mathew Brady's photographic studio, and his carte de visite portraits were soon offered for sale across the North. Like many another general, Union and Confederate, he struck some poses for the camera with his right hand thrust into the front of his uniform coat in imitation of Napoleon. William Howard Russell of the *Times* of London thought in fact that McClellan had a Napoleonic look about him "in actual weight and breadth," with the same tendency toward embonpoint. Following the lead of the *New York Herald,* newspapers began praising him as the "Napoleon of America" or the "Young Napoleon" and comparing his rapid climb to high command with Bonaparte's. Russell described him as " 'the little corporal' of unfought fields," and predicted that shaping the Army of the Potomac into a fighting force would require herculean labors. He detected an anxious look about the general's eyes.[7]

The anxiety was real, for within ten days of his arrival in Washington McClellan became convinced that he was about to be attacked. The Confederate army at Manassas Junction and Centreville grew in his mind's eye more menacing each day. On August 4 he put his forces on a forty-eight-hour alert. On August 6 he extended the alert. On August 8 he announced to General Scott a state of emergency. His intelligence sources confirmed that an attack was imminent: "I am induced to believe that the enemy has at least 100,000 men in our front. Were I in Beauregard's place, with that force at my disposal, I would attack the positions on the other side of the Potomac and at the same time cross the river above the city in force." His army, outnumbered two to one, could not withstand such an offensive. Every available reinforcement must be rushed to the capital without an hour's delay, and all nearby military commands placed under his control. That night he wrote his wife, "I have hardly slept one moment for the last three nights, knowing well that the enemy intend some movement & fully recognizing our own weakness."

Of all the appraisals of the enemy that he would make during his months of high command, this first one was pivotal. It fixed the pattern for those that followed : he was heavily outnumbered; he must be immediately reinforced at whatever cost to other operations; he was solely responsible for the fate of the nation; he must have full and unfettered control to meet the crisis. A man of George McClellan's inflexible certitude could not tolerate dissent from these conclusions. A captive of his pride, he could never admit error by retreating from them. From that day forward, the Confederate army he faced would never number (by his count) fewer than 100,000 men, and frequently it would number a great many more.

The reality of these figures was never as he stated and the unfavorable odds he cited were typically the reverse, and blame for this continuing intelligence fiasco most often falls on Allan Pinkerton, whom he put in charge of his military intelligence gathering. Yet there is nothing to show that Pinkerton had any part in this crucial August 8 estimate. The detective had only just arrived in Washington, and he made no report on the situation in Virginia until the end of August. Crediting Beauregard with 100,000 men poised for attack was McClellan's own analysis.

The Confederates did indeed hope to take the offensive, but even so modest a goal as raising their forces to 60,000 before winter proved to be beyond their resources. McClellan's view of their numbers may be glimpsed in the account of one Edward B. McMurdy, a deserter from Beauregard's army at Manassas. McClellan interviewed McMurdy early in August as to "the strength, plans &c of the Rebels" and then took him to General Scott, where they were joined by President Lincoln and Secretary of State William H. Seward. "They thought my views of the resources of the Rebels to be extravagant," McMurdy recalled, but McClellan did not : "Gen McClellan told me that I had saved Washington City and in all probability the very existence of the Government...."[8]

McMurdy's description of divided counsels within the Federal high command was true enough. General Scott was incensed at the charge that Washington stood in imminent peril. He would have welcomed a discussion of the matter with his subordinate, he told Secretary of War Cameron, but instead McClellan had issued what amounted to an indictment of him and in the bargain made sure that the president received a copy of it. "I am confident in the opposite opinion," Scott wrote. "... I have not the slightest apprehension for the safety of the government here." In view of his age and ailments and the disrespect of his junior, he asked to be put on the retired list.

For his part, McClellan concluded that once again he had a superior who stood in his way. Reporting to Ellen a discussion of the problem with Secretary Seward, he wrote, "How does he think that I can save this country when stopped by Genl Scott — I do not know whether he is a *dotard* or a *traitor!* ... I am leaving nothing undone to increase our force — but that confounded old Genl always comes in the way — he is a perfect imbecile. He understands nothing, appreciates nothing & is ever in my way."

In fact, although he was seventy-five years old and physically infirm and irascible, Winfield Scott understood the situation very clearly. Before Bull Run, Federal intelligence had estimated the Confederates under Beauregard and Johnston at about 35,000, and nothing that happened during the battle or afterward persuaded Scott that this figure was very far wrong. Now came McClellan to insist that in just eighteen days after accepting battle with that number the enemy was able to triple his forces, and the old general simply refused to credit such miraculous arithmetic. (As late as October, the Rebel army confronting McClellan totaled fewer than 45,000 men.) The president tried to mediate between his warring commanders, but Scott was adamant. It was obvious that in his failing health he could not remain at his post, but he was determined to stay on long enough for General Henry W. Halleck, a writer of military texts and a favorite of his, to arrive from California to take his place as general-in-chief.[9]

There is no evidence that McClellan deliberately fabricated the figures he cited or the dangers he thought they posed. On the contrary, it is clear enough from his letters to Ellen — "*you,* who share all my thoughts," he told her — that his self-deception was total. "I am here in a terrible place — the enemy have from 3 to 4 times my force — the Presdt is an idiot, the old General in his dotage — they cannot or will not see the true state of affairs ...," he wrote her on August 16. On August 19 he credited the Confederates with 150,000 men against his 55,000, and the next day he wrote, "If Beauregard does not attack this week he is foolish...." Only when the week passed uneventfully did he begin to feel somewhat easier. On August 25 he announced, "I can surely beat M de Beauregard should he arrive to pay his respects.... Last week he certainly had double our force."

Such letters, often written after midnight at the end of a grueling day, suggest a mental exhaustion edged with hysteria. He did not confine this near panic to private correspondence, however. Two weeks later he once more raised the alarm, this time directly to the secretary of war. He warned Cameron that the enemy had now readied 130,000 men for an offensive, including a column of 100,000 to strike at Baltimore and cut off Washington. It was said that their invasion would be signaled by the secret passage of a secession ordinance by the Maryland legislature, and he organized the arrest of disloyalists among the legislators. On September 13 he told Cameron that reinforcements were pouring into Virginia from all across the Confederacy, and "it is evident that the decisive battle of the War is soon to be fought in this vicinity...." He counted his own field army "for active movements" at some 81,000 men (or only 60,000, depending on the attack route the Rebels chose) and added, "The enemy probably have 170,000!"[10]

In calculating these desperate straits, McClellan adhered to his "one safe rule of war" — be prepared for the worst. What was a normal precaution, however, now became for him an obsession, a self-fulfilling prophecy; in preparing for the possibility of the worst, he came to anticipate and then to expect the worst. By his reckoning, his adversary would gamble everything in one desperate bid for victory, abandoning all his vital interests and throwing every soldier he had against the Army of the Potomac. He counted the forces he could marshal against this onslaught more conservatively. His army, even on defense, numbered only what remained after deducting the sizable garrisons protecting Washington, Baltimore, and every other area deemed vital. In his system of military arithmetic, the other man took all the risks.

George McClellan was by no means the only Civil War general to believe he was outnumbered when he was not, but he was the only one to believe it so obstinately and for so long. Virtually all of his strategic and tactical decisions as commander of the Army of the Potomac were those of a general confronting an enemy substantially superior in numbers, and when viewed from that perspective his decisions are for the most part essentially sound.

He maintained that no other general facing what he believed he faced could have done better. Referring to these early months of command, he would write that during the Revolution General Washington was also "constantly hounded & abused . . . for slowness & inaction. All now see that he was right, & I trust that the time will come when it will be equally evident to all that I was right in doing as I did."

In a virtual act of metamorphosis he had assumed an altered military character in moving from the Department of the Ohio to the Division of the Potomac. In western Virginia, operating with a known superiority of forces against opponents of only modest ability, he commanded with confidence; his only question about the outcome was how complete his victory would be. In Washington that confidence rapidly vanished.

This was certainly owing in part to his judgment of the generals he now faced. Beauregard and Joe Johnston — later joined by G. W. Smith — had been as respected as any officers in the old army, an opinion he shared ("I know full well the capacity of the Generals opposed to me," he told Samuel Barlow, "for by a singular chance they were once my most intimate friends"), and he had little hope that against them he could pull off another Cerro Gordo maneuver so easily. He believed their immense army to be highly trained, the product of a militant South that had begun preparing to fight well before Fort Sumter. Confederate morale, too, was superior, raised to a peak by Bull Run. He was certain his one-time patron Jefferson Davis was perceptive enough (like McClellan himself) to see eastern Virginia as the primary theater of war and to mass his best generals and his best soldiers for the contest there. McClellan's sense of responsibility for the fate of the nation — he could conceive of no one else meeting such a challenge — bred an anxiety so suffocating that at times it unbalanced his rational thought.

Once he fixed this picture of the enemy in his mind he never altered it. From the first days of his command to the last he was incapable of imagining that the problems in his own army that drove him to bitter complaint — poor and unenterprising officers, ill-trained and undisciplined soldiers, bad staff work, inadequate supplies — might confront his opponent as well. Indeed, the Confederates as he saw them sometimes assumed superhuman qualities: if McClellan imagined it to be even theoretically possible for them to transfer an army from one theater of war to another, to move a column with instant decision at lightning speed, to feed and forage and arm forces vastly superior to his own, he supposed it was actually so. One of his legacies to the Army of the Potomac would be an inbred sense of inferiority.

A more subtle and more deeply ingrained strain helped warp his reason. Whenever George McClellan found events turning against him — as they had during the Pacific railroad survey in 1853, for example — he fell back on the rationalization that he had not sought his role but was ordered to it, and not being responsible, he was not to blame. In the crisis he invented for Washington in 1861, he employed the same rationalization but raised it (as it were) to a higher power. He came to believe it was predestined that he should command, just as it was predestined that he be united with Ellen in this world and the next; he had been elected by God to save the Union.

"I feel that God has placed a great work in my hands — I have not sought it — I know how weak I am — but I know that I mean to do right & I believe that God will help me & give me the wisdom I do not possess," he wrote Ellen soon after raising the alarm with General Scott. At the height of his rage with Scott and administration leaders for their failure to recognize the crisis, he wrote, "I have one great comfort in all this — that is that I did not seek this position, as you well know, & I still trust that God will support me & bear me out — he could not have placed me here for nothing." He saw divine reasoning at work: "My previous life seems to have been unwittingly directed to this great end, & I know that God can accomplish the greatest results with the weakest instruments — therein lies my hope."

Taking the role of God's chosen instrument might be dismissed as nothing more than a harmless conceit but for the effects it produced on his generalship. It was at once the prop for his insecurity and the shield for his convictions. With Calvinistic fatalism he believed his path to be the chosen path; anyone who raised criticisms or objections — whether president or Cabinet officer or legislator or editor or fellow general — was at best ignorant and misguided and at worst a traitor. It was inevitable that he soon detected as many enemies at his back as he found in front of him.

Equally damaging, this messianic complex influenced his view of the foe. Once persuaded that Providence had called him to save the nation, McClellan could scarcely acknowledge that it was he who commanded the larger battalions; the Lord might move in mysterious ways, but that it was necessary for Him to act through McClellan to preserve the Union from an outnumbered enemy was surely not one of them. Mr. Lincoln perceived this trait very clearly, if not the cause of it, when he later remarked ruefully that should he accede to General McClellan's newest call for 100,000 fresh troops, the general would come back the next day with the news that the enemy now numbered 400,000 and he could not advance without reinforcements. Hardly a week after his proposal for one massive army that would sweep everything from its path as it marched across the South, McClellan became certain that it was his fate to be outnumbered.[11]

Whatever reinforcement might be needed for this delusive state of mind was furnished by Allan Pinkerton. Pinkerton concealed his secret service headquarters within the provost marshal's office, concealed himself behind the cover name E. J. Allen, and went to work with an energy that rivaled McClellan's. He drew his information from two sources: interrogation of those who came from behind enemy lines — prisoners, deserters, refugees, fugitive slaves — and from spies who slipped into and out of Confederate territory under various guises. His findings were not limited to enemy units and numbers and armaments, but included such things as the quality of rations, military and civilian morale, arms manufacture, supplies of salt and lead, uniforms, Richmond food prices, and the like. His reports ran to thirty and forty pages or more of the most specific detail and the closest calculation. Great effort and considerable risk were involved in gathering this intelligence, and it had every appearance of authority. Some of it was indeed correct and even perceptive, especially those parts dealing with civilian matters. Most of what related to Confederate armed forces was woefully wrong.

Each step in Pinkerton's collection of this military intelligence was marked by error, adding up finally to colossal error. The problem began with Pinkerton himself. He had an affinity for cloak and dagger and was adept enough at counterespionage work, an activity not unlike the uncovering of burglary rings that had been a specialty of his detective agency before the war. In dealing with military intelligence, however, he displayed a singular inability to separate probable fact from improbable rumor. He and his interrogators wielded the power of judge and jury over those brought to them for questioning: on their recommendation a Rebel deserter might be paroled or sent to a prisoner-of-war camp; a civilian refugee might go free or face espionage charges. As a consequence, self-interest inspired eager-to-please refugees to multiply regiments into brigades, and high privates to elevate rumor, the common coin in every army, into sworn fact. "The deserters and negroes generally told us much more than they knew in order to secure a welcome," an astute observer remarked, but Pinkerton and his questioners were not so discerning.

The failings of Pinkerton's spies were of a different sort. They operated mostly in Richmond, and on those rare occasions when they found a safe excuse to visit Confederate units in the field, they seldom had the opportunity to see beyond those individual units. Their results did not match their enterprise. One agent used his wife as his courier and made reports in tiny handwriting on scraps of paper "that she might so secrete them about her clothing as absolutely to defy detection." He claimed to have seen a "calculation" by a regimental adjutant that put the total of Confederate troops in Virginia in late August at 160,000, certainly one source for McClellan's alarming warnings to Secretary Cameron. Apparently no one questioned how such a low-level officer could have access to the highest-level headquarters information.

A Pinkerton spy of more ambition was Frank M. Ellis, who posed as a supplier of special paper and ink for the printing of bank notes. By Pinkerton's account, Ellis dined in Richmond with President Jefferson Davis, Treasury Secretary Christopher G. Memminger, and Secretary of War Judah P. Benjamin. Whatever accuracy Ellis achieved in his accounting of conditions in the Southern capital was not matched by his estimates of military forces in the field, however. On October 28, for example, he reported the main army at Manassas Junction and Centreville to be 80,000 strong. Confederate returns for October 31 record the total of effectives in that force as 44,131. A month later Ellis put the figure at 77,000, which Pinkerton endorsed: "I respectfully submit that it is a very close comparison with the *real strength* of those forces." The actual figure on that date was less than 42,000.[12]

In a comparison of the Pinkerton reports with these returns, a pattern emerges of error compounded by error. A basic error was regularly overstating the number of Confederate regiments, a miscalculation made worse by his agreement with McClellan to add 5 percent automatically to the manpower totals to compensate for regiments missed in the counting. (As Pinkerton explained, it was a "certainty" that the enemy had additional forces, which must be included "for the sake of safety."). This inflated number of regiments was then multiplied by an estimate of regimental manpower that was itself persistently inflated. Even Pinkerton's arithmetic was faulty. In a major report on Confederate forces in Virginia in early October 1861, for example, he explained that he was reducing his totals by 15 percent to allow for the sick, so as to produce the actual number of troops McClellan might face in battle. In fact, he reduced his totals by one-fifteenth, a rather different matter. On this error alone, he increased his already inflated estimate of Southern fighting men by better than 8 percent.[13]

McClellan accepted these reports with no more critical analysis than went into their making. They were, after all, exactly what he expected: confirmation of his own conclusions. Pinkerton, faithfully following the rules and the precedents established by the general commanding, was happy enough to produce no surprises. When a conflict in figures did arise, McClellan prepared for the worst and accepted the higher figure. Prince Napoleon returned from a visit to Manassas and told *Harper's Weekly* that the Confederate troops there came to 60,000, most of them ragged and hungry. McClellan put the prestige of his position behind a warning to Cameron that he was facing battle outnumbered by a force almost three times that size.

On one occasion, when the Pinkerton spy Timothy Webster delivered a count of the total of Rebel forces in all of Virginia that was close to the mark — 123,000, only about 10,000 too high — it was passed over in favor of a far higher count. "I think they have from 180,000 to 200,000 men distributed north of Richmond towards Washington," General William Franklin told a congressional committee. "I get my information from officers connected with General McClellan's staff." Uncritical newspapermen spread the myth. The managing editor of the *New York Tribune* took Secretary Cameron to task for a slowdown in recruiting "when we are so constantly outnumbered by the rebels."[14]

The atmosphere of crisis he generated added a special urgency to McClellan's efforts to enlarge and perfect his command. When the pace of volunteering did not meet his expectations, he called on the president to institute a draft. "We must have men without delay," he insisted. The army's rate of growth soon picked up, although it was still exceeded in his imagination by that of the enemy. He inherited from McDowell some 51,000 men. In mid-September, when he expected daily to have to fight the decisive battle, there were 122,000 present for duty. A month later the total rose to more than 133,000, by the first of December to nearly 170,000, and by the end of the year to nearly 192,000. To be sure, not all of these troops were yet properly armed or drilled, probably one in ten had duties that would keep him off the firing line when there was fighting to be done, and McClellan customarily assigned between 50,000 and 60,000 to garrison duty. Each step in the process had become for him a uniquely personal achievement. "The Army of the Potomac is my army as much as any army ever belonged to the man that created it," he would say when looking back on his work.[15]

This personal identification was deliberate. He had not forgotten the lesson of General Scott's hold on his army in the Mexico City campaign. He believed morale was related directly to the confidence officers and men felt in the general commanding: if they believed in him they would believe in the tasks he set for them. He invariably got on better with subordinates than with superiors. When he was with his officers, one of them recalled, he seemed to have a "royal faculty" for remembering names. Among the men in the ranks he set out to be a figure as familiar as their company commanders. General John Gibbon would record an incident while on campaign when McClellan shook an enlisted man's hand and congratulated him on the fight his brigade had just made, and in no time at all the news of it had spread all through the brigade. That, Gibbon remarked, was how to win the confidence of soldiers.

"You have no idea how the men brighten up now, when I go among them — I can see every eye glisten," McClellan told Ellen on September 11 after a ceremonious review. "Yesterday they nearly pulled me to pieces in one regt. You never heard such yelling," and he added, "I did not think the Presdt liked it much." The cheering was not invariably spontaneous. "General Smith required his division to cheer McClellan," Brigadier George G. Meade wrote his wife after one of these reviews; "not being posted in the programme," his own troops remained silent. A veteran recalled that in the field it was customary for the general commanding to wait until the army was on the march and then ride forward to the head of the column, preceded by an officer shouting, "McClellan's coming, boys! McClellan's coming! three cheers for McClellan!" After a time, the man wrote, some came to regard this as "clap-trap and humbug," yet the cheering never stopped.

However grave McClellan's inner concerns, they did not betray his outward manner. Henry W. Bellows of the U.S. Sanitary Commission, a civilian group devoted to the welfare of the troops, met McClellan in mid-September and was struck by his presence. He radiated an air of self-possession, even self-complacency, Bellows thought: "There is an indefinable *air of success* about him and something of the 'man of destiny.' " The chaplain of the 1st Minnesota was convinced that the men had implicit confidence in their general, "& his presence is greeted with the enthusiasm that the soldiers of France always exhibited toward Napoleon." Looking back on these months, the 13th Pennsylvania's chaplain wrote, "The truth is, our magnificent army much needed a transcendent leader, and the crisis prompted us both to crave and expect one fit for the occasion — one whom we could afford to idolize." In such a setting the conviction grew in the Young Napoleon's mind that he was indispensable to this army and to its chances of victory.[16]

It was this deliberate effort to personify the army in the figure of its commander that would make George McClellan unique among Civil War generals. The personal stamp he put on the Army of the Potomac would be, for good or ill, a lasting one. In other respects, his administration of the Potomac army was entirely conventional, tending if anything toward the conservative.

The regular army of 1861 possessed the administrative machinery, once it was expanded, to feed, clothe, shelter, and arm the volunteer forces being mobilized. Operationally, however, it had no comparable machinery to plan campaigns or to move and direct troops in the field beyond the person of the general commanding and his aides. McClellan would later find much to criticize about operating an army by the book, but at the time his impulse toward reform was brief and largely meaningless.

He made a start at operational reform by centralizing intelligence gathering, then defeated his purpose by putting the undiscerning Allan Pinkerton in charge. Congress saw the logic of his proposal to enlarge army staffing and within a few days approved the necessary legislation, but McClellan simply increased the number of his aides without making them responsible for particular operational duties. His appointment of Randolph Marcy to the new post of chief of staff seemed a promise of genuine innovation, but he watered down the promise by delegating to Marcy little authority. Even the smallest details of military routine continued to require the attention of the general commanding. McClellan never lost the mistrust of subordinates' abilities that marked his western Virginia campaign, and at critical moments in the field he would often be found bogged down in administrative details.

He kept the key function of strategic planning entirely to himself. There is no evidence that he took even such confidants as Marcy, Fitz John Porter, and William Franklin entirely into his confidence. It would be only under extreme pressure from the president that he finally offered anything more detailed than vague promises of forthcoming advances during his first six months of high command.

As new regiments arrived in Washington from the Northern states, they were given a minimum of drill at a basic-training command headed by Silas Casey, a veteran officer well known in the old army as a disciplinarian and drillmaster. They were next assigned to brigades and then divisions for stepped-up training. As he had done at Camp Dennison, McClellan established instructional schools, directed by his brigadiers, for the volunteer regimental and company officers. Their schooling ranged from field drills to recitation in tactics and army regulations. For the time being, the division was to be the largest command unit. McClellan intended to postpone a corps organization until he could select corps commanders on the basis of battlefield experience. This decision, which he clung to stubbornly, reflected his confidence in controlling personally an army of at least ten divisions (the number it had reached by mid-October) in at least one major battle.[17]

In McClellan's mind, the need for what he called "instructed officers" was fully as great as the need for troops. West Pointers, in or out of service, were in demand, and state governors sought far and wide for anyone with any military experience at all to lead the volunteers. Numerous regiments were headed by the men who raised them, and often enough their patriotism far outweighed their soldierly abilities. An effort was made in Congress to disband the regular army entirely and distribute its commissioned and noncommissioned officers among the volunteer forces. The army establishment strongly opposed such an innovation. General Scott wanted each Union army to have at its core a trained nucleus of regulars who could be relied upon in any emergency. It was widely believed that only the steadfastness of the regulars at Bull Run had saved the capital from capture by the victorious Rebels.

McClellan favored this policy as well, and called for all available regular units to be assigned to his army. At the same time, he had long insisted in his proposals for army reform that command go only to instructed officers. Thus he supported a congressional authorization for transferring regular officers to the command of volunteers whenever feasible. He endorsed, for example, a plea by Governor John A. Andrew of Massachusetts to put a regular, then on recruiting duty, in charge of one of the state's new regiments. "I do not think it possible to employ our Army officers to more advantage than in comdg Divisions, Brigades & Regts of new troops," McClellan told Secretary Cameron. In fact, even had the old army been disbanded, there were far too few regular officers to meet the needs of the Army of the Potomac. Between the demands of frontier defense, the needs of other armies, and the large number of regulars captured by the seceding states, there were only thirty-six companies — just over three and a half regiments — of infantry regulars available in the East in the fall of 1861 when the Potomac army was being assembled. "We have almost *none* of the old troops at our disposal," McClellan reminded Cameron.[18]

He put regulars to the best use in the artillery. It was his goal to attach four batteries to each of his divisions, one of the four being a regular army battery to furnish a leavening of experience and training; its senior officer was to be the divisional artillery commander. McClellan lavished his highly developed sense of order on the artillery, laboring to standardize gun types, equipment, and training. By mid-October the nine poorly equipped batteries he inherited from McDowell had multiplied in number by three and in efficiency by considerably more. He saw artillery superiority offsetting the supposed disparity in infantry.

In sharp contrast was his handling of the cavalry. Federal cavalry labored under severe handicaps to begin with — among them a shortage of arms and equipment and the inability of most Yankee cavalry recruits to care for or even to ride their horses — made all the worse by the organizational scheme he imposed on it. McClellan's ideas for the use of cavalry were conservative in the extreme. In his prewar cavalry manual he had focused almost entirely on guard duty and posting to prevent surprise enemy attacks. The two pages he devoted to reconnaissance did not have the cavalry operating in any independent way. In instructions he wrote for his officers soon after taking command, the cavalry's primary duty was defined once again as guarding against surprise. While the Confederate army commander Joe Johnston was establishing an operationally independent cavalry brigade under J. E. B. Stuart, McClellan was scattering what cavalry he had broadcast throughout the army. His cavalry head, George Stoneman, was merely an administrator, and the one cavalry brigade formed was temporary and only for training purposes.

The consequence was that the Potomac army's cavalry became little more than an adjunct of infantry commanders. A trooper in the 1st Pennsylvania recalled that in his first year of service, "the cavalry were for the most part scattered about and used as escorts, strikers, dog-robbers and orderlies for all the generals and their numerous staff officers from the highest in rank down to the second lieutenants." There were many reasons for the superiority of the Southern mounted force (Jeb Stuart being one of them), but as important as anything else was McClellan's failure to give his cavalry any tactical independence. He later wrote sarcastically that on the Peninsula his cavalry arm was "so ridiculously insufficient" that it was fortunate Stuart rode around his army only once, but this disguised the fact that the Federals were hamstrung tactically in trying to confront Stuart on anything like equal terms.[19]

Although Congress would reject a proposal by McClellan for enlarging the Corps of Cadets at West Point and accelerating the program of study there to increase the supply of officer candidates, it did enact legislation that enabled him to weed out the worst of the volunteer officers flooding into his army. Commanding generals were authorized to establish military boards to examine officer qualifications, and on September 20 McClellan appointed two such boards for the Army of the Potomac. The effects were immediate and dramatic. Within a week, twenty-seven officers in a single division, including two regimental colonels, resigned rather than face the humiliation of a board review; in less than two months the total number of resignations in the Potomac army reached nearly 170. Since virtually none of these officers had yet been under fire, their failings were in the fundamental areas of discipline and taking care of their men.[20]

It had meanwhile occurred to Secretary of State Seward to resolve the command problem by recruiting officers from Europe's armies, and dozens of soldiers of fortune began arriving on American shores. It was soon apparent that most of them, as McClellan put it, "had left their own armies for the armies' good...." Under Seward's direction, an effort was even made to persuade the celebrated Garibaldi to take a Federal command. The scheme foundered when Garibaldi insisted on assuming Scott's post as general-in-chief, along with the power to abolish slavery by his own fiat. The hero of the Hungarian revolution, György Klapka, set equally high terms, including a $100,000 bonus, for ending the threat to the Union. "He failed to state what provision he would make for me," McClellan wrote; he presumed it would depend on how good an impression he made on the Hungarian.

His staff was not without an international flavor, however, thanks in good measure to its three princes of the House of Orléans. The Prince de Joinville and his two youthful nephews, the Duc de Chartres and the Comte de Paris, pretender to the French throne, arrived from their English exile soon after Bull Run to observe the American war. When they approached McClellan regarding positions on his staff, the Comte de Paris recorded in his diary, the general "seemed astonished and flattered" and promised to consult the president. To the delight of the young princes, the matter was arranged "with perfect tact," and they were named staff aides with the rank of captain. Joinville took no official position, but his military background as a vice admiral in the French navy made him, in McClellan's eyes, a valued private adviser. The young princes served in a variety of staff roles, including the summarizing of Pinkerton's intelligence reports, and were known to the troops, inevitably, as Captain Chatters and Captain Perry.[21]

It was an essential of McClellan's strategic plan that Washington be a fortified citadel, both to shelter his army against attack and later to leave him free to embark on a campaign of maneuver. The ring of fortifications grew apace with the army. General John G. Barnard, the one-time suitor for Ellen's hand, was put in charge of what he termed this "immense work." The task consumed a great deal of McClellan's time as well, for scarcely a shovelful of dirt was turned without his approval, and he laid out many of the works personally. Before the end of 1861 there were forty-eight forts and strongpoints encircling the city. Most of the intended 480 guns were in place, Barnard reported, requiring 7,200 artillerists to man them. Incorporated within these lines were Upton's and Munson's hills, outposts within sight of the Capitol that the Rebels finally abandoned late in September. "They can no longer say that they are flaunting their dirty little flag in my face," McClellan wrote to his wife.[22]

During this busy period when he was building his army and forming his picture of the enemy, McClellan took the equally momentous step of involving himself directly in the politics of the war. He recorded in his memoirs that shortly after reaching the capital he had "interviews" with several prominent abolitionists, Senator Charles Sumner of Massachusetts being the one he mentioned by name. Expanding on the views expressed in his western Virginia proclamations, he made certain these men understood, he wrote, "that I was fighting for my country & the Union, not for abolition and the Republican party."

George McClellan shared his opinions and epithets on race with most of his countrymen — "I confess to a prejudice in favor of my own race, & can't learn to like the odor of either Billy goats or niggers...," he wrote shortly after the war — but he nevertheless deplored the inhumanities of the slave system. He saw it as an institution recognized in the Constitution, however, and entitled to federal protection wherever it existed. That did not mean that in any peace settlement he might draw up the peculiar institution would be allowed to return to its old ways. "When the day of adjustment comes," he assured Ellen in mid-November

1861, "I will, if successful, throw my sword into the scale to force
an improvement in the condition of those poor blacks." Had it
been his fortune to lead the North to victory and arrange the
terms of peace, he later wrote, he would have insisted on gradual
emancipation, guarding the rights of both slaves and masters, as
part of any settlement.

In the event, he said, these radical Republicans rejected his
arguments and favored immediate abolition, without thought to
the convulsion it would cause in American society. As he later
put it, "The Radicals had only the negro in view, & not the
Union...," and in a passage deleted from *McClellan's Own Story*
by his editor he wrote, "They cared not for the results, knew
little or nothing of the subject to be dealt with, & merely wished
to accomplish a political move for party profit, or from senti-
mental motives." Under such terms, he vowed to Ellen, "I will
not fight for the abolitionists...." A staff officer recalled him
saying, at about the same time, that if his superiors "expected
him to fight with the South to *free the slaves,* they would be
mistaken, for he would not do it."

It is not certain whether McClellan initiated these conversations with Sumner and his colleagues — his is the only account
of them — but it is clear enough that he took the opportunity to
step well beyond the usual limits of military command to define
politically what he would and would not fight for. To be sure,
his views were well within the mainstream of conservative Northern opinion, yet to beard these radicals deliberately — especially
Charles Sumner, one of the more formidable figures in American
politics — was a tactic bordering on the foolhardy. In saying he
would not fight for the Republican party he was implying (as
his listeners easily grasped) that his commitment was to the Democrats and their policies. General McClellan made no secret of
the fact that he was (so to speak) marching off to war under the
banner of the opposition party.

"I & the country paid dearly for this first expression of my
views," he later wrote, and whatever the truth of that may be,
he was hardly the innocent victim of the transaction. William H.
Aspinwall, his mentor from the Ohio and Mississippi Railroad,
warned him, "Don't allow any one to mix you up with any side
issue... avoid all complications with any party," but McClellan
did not heed his advice. Of his involvement with politics it would

be said (he was one of those to say it) that his partisan Democratic friends were his own worst enemies. Yet they, like Pinkerton in his role in intelligence gathering, became scapegoats in a chain of events that McClellan himself initiated.

From the moment he reached Washington he saw it as part of his mission to lead the nation on fields political as well as military, yet he invariably reacted with hurt at what he considered politically motivated attacks on him. After conversing with him on the subject, Samuel Barlow assured an acquaintance that the general had no ambitions for the presidency, but wanted only to lead the army and pursue his own policy in prosecuting the war, regardless of the administration's wishes. Perhaps McClellan best stated how he viewed his role in the Civil War in another passage deleted from his memoirs before publication. Had he been recalled to army command in 1863 or 1864, he wrote, "I would have held myself bound as a soldier to carry out the orders of the Govt, while always doing my best to keep its policy in the right direction."[23]

On October 7, in an editorial titled "Generals and Critics," Horace Greeley's *New York Tribune* took to task those newspapers "which evince impatience at Gen. McClellan's inactivity...." The *Tribune* dismissed "the palpable inadequacy" of such criticism and counseled patience: the general commanding knew best when his army would be ready for battle. Beyond the irony that the *Tribune,* in time to become McClellan's most unrelenting critic, was one of his strongest early supporters, the editorial pointed up the pressures beginning to build for an advance by the Army of the Potomac. These pressures stemmed in part from heightened expectations. The grand reviews McClellan staged, each one larger than the last, were well attended and widely reported, and whatever the true condition of the army, to untutored eyes the troops looked ready for battle. To McClellan's eyes they were far from ready. When the army was finally organized and disciplined and armed to his satisfaction, he wrote Ellen on October 6, "I will advance & force the rebels to a battle on a field of my own selection. A long time must yet elapse before I can do this, & I expect all the newspapers to abuse me for delay — but I will not mind that."

The drilling continued as autumn advanced and the weather

remained favorable, and the complaints grew more strident. On October 12 Senator Zachariah Chandler, who three months earlier had expressed his pleasure with the western Virginia campaign, wrote of his change of heart: ''I am greatly dissatisfied with Genl McLelland. He seems to be devoting himself to parades & military shows instead of cleaning the country of rebels.'' His fellow radical from Ohio, Senator Benjamin Wade, was of like mind. Wade complained that the Army of the Potomac's only activity was issuing periodic bulletins that Washington was safe and all was quiet on the Potomac. It appeared to him, he wrote Chandler, that ''the General is determined his troops shall all be veterans before he permits them to come under fire, or into a skirmish seriously.''[24]

The navy would no doubt have seconded Wade's assessment. It had for some months wanted to recapture Norfolk and the nearby navy yard, which had fallen to the Confederates soon after Fort Sumter. Intelligence sources, including Pinkerton spies, reported that the Rebels had raised the scuttled steam frigate *Merrimack* and in Norfolk's dry dock were converting her into a powerful ironclad, and the navy was intent on destroying this threat to the blockade.

There was much to recommend a joint army-navy expedition against Norfolk. It could be launched and supported from the Federal bases at Fort Monroe and Newport News, close by on the tip of the Virginia peninsula, and the fleet controlled the local waters. If it did no more than destroy the *Merrimack* in a hit-and-run raid, the expedition could claim an important victory, boosting Northern morale and relieving the pressure on General McClellan to do something. The navy put forward plans for the operation and attracted the support of McClellan's chief engineer, John Barnard, but each time the scheme reached the general commanding, he put it aside. First he could spare no troops so long as the enemy host threatened Washington. Then he wanted to wait for the Union's own ironclad, the *Monitor*, to be completed so that she could lead the attack. Finally he thought by a flanking movement he could induce Norfolk to fall without a battle. He would have occasion to regret his shortsightedness.[25]

The navy was equally intent on breaking the Confederate blockade of the lower Potomac, for which it was taking increasingly sharp criticism in the press. Keeping open the water route to the capital was in fact as much the task of the army as of the navy; preventing batteries from being erected on the Virginia shore, or destroying them after they were built, required a joint effort. McClellan at last agreed to cooperate, and promised 4,000 troops for a landing on September 30 at Mathias Point, a particularly threatening battery site. The navy arrived with gunboats and landing barges, but the troops failed to appear. Lincoln and Gustavus Fox, the assistant navy secretary, went to McClellan's headquarters to seek an explanation. McClellan said his engineers did not see how all the troops could be landed. Fox assured him that the navy would take the responsibility, and McClellan rescheduled the operation for the next night. Once again no troops appeared. Fox was told the general had come to fear that a major engagement might result. The Rebels were thus allowed without hindrance to close the Potomac to all but warships. One of the Confederate artillerists wrote that the Yankees "seem signally wanting in enterprise," and so it seemed to many in the North as well. McClellan professed indifference. Once his grand campaign against Richmond began, in due course, the enemy gunners would have to give up the Potomac blockade or risk being cut off.

Thus two favorable chances were missed for what Cabinet member Edward Bates termed "some dashing expeditions — some victories, great or small, to stimulate the zeal of the Country, and ... to keep up the credit of the Government." McClellan undertook on his own initiative to create a third chance, and the result was a defeat almost as humiliating as Bull Run.[26]

During the first two months or so of his Potomac army command, McClellan devoted his energies to securing Washington and the army from expected attack. It was mid-October before he felt strong enough to venture small advances. When it was reported that the Confederates had pulled back somewhat and reduced the garrison at Leesburg, the anchor of their line on the upper Potomac, he grew more bold. He sought to maneuver them entirely out of the upper Potomac area by pushing a reconnaissance in force up the Virginia side of the river as far as Dranesville, a dozen miles from Leesburg. He accompanied George McCall's division in the advance, and on October 19 wrote Ellen,

"I hope to make them abandon Leesburg tomorrow." The next day he ordered Charles P. Stone, whose division guarded the Maryland side of the Potomac, to find out if the occupation of Dranesville "has the effect to drive them away. Perhaps a slight demonstration on your part would have the effect to move them."

Stone took this to mean that he was to send a reconnaissance of his own across the river toward Leesburg, backing it with the threat of a crossing in force. He also took it for granted that McCall would continue to threaten Leesburg. McClellan, however, left General Stone to his own devices, as General Rosecrans had been left on his own at Rich Mountain. Without waiting to learn what effect his maneuvers had on the enemy — and without notifying Stone — he ordered McCall back to the Washington lines. The Confederates were now free to concentrate on any force that might cross the river, an advantage that Stone never suspected.

One additional blunder was still needed to produce a military disaster, and it was furnished by the civilian-in-arms commanding one of Stone's brigades, Colonel Edward D. Baker, a United States senator of note and one of President Lincoln's closest friends. The impulsive Baker went beyond his orders in crossing the Potomac on October 21, and his men were soon pinned against the river at a place called Ball's Bluff, under fierce attack and with too few boats to make a rapid evacuation. Baker was killed and defeat became rout as desperate men by the hundreds tried to swim to safety. "The river now seemed covered with heads and was as white as a great hail-storm where the rebel bullets struck," a Massachusetts soldier wrote. The final casualty toll reached 921. A substantial number of the more than 700 listed as missing were drowned. Bodies washed ashore at Washington for some days.

McClellan called Ball's Bluff a butchery and sent a circular to his generals, assuring them that the fault lay with Baker, the amateur soldier. He told his wife that the operation "was entirely unauthorized by me & I am in no manner responsible for it." Baker's inexperience was beyond doubt the immediate cause of the defeat, yet neither McClellan's orders nor his actions absolved him of responsibility. He later insisted he never intended that Stone send troops across the river and so had no reason to keep McCall's division standing by, yet his vaguely worded orders failed to make that clear. Stone based his movements on the assumption that McCall was within easy supporting distance on the Virginia side of the river. The Ball's Bluff fiasco, wrote a Federal officer, was "plainly an unpremeditated and unprepared effort," a matter of considerable discouragement to Northerners, who noted that it took place three months to the day after the Bull Run fiasco.[27]

Meanwhile, the conflict between McClellan and Scott had worsened with each passing day. It was by now simply a struggle for power, and McClellan treated the old general with studied neglect and contempt, making little effort to keep his attitude secret. Their dispute had boiled over at a conference on September 27 attended by the president and several Cabinet members. Scott made bitter complaint that he was told nothing of the numbers and condition and position of the Army of the Potomac, although his subordinate was quick to report such information to civilians in the administration. At the conclusion of the stormy meeting, Scott confronted McClellan and told him that when he arrived in Washington "you had my friendship and confidence. You still have my confidence." "I kept cool, looked him square in the face, & *rather* I think got the advantage of him," McClellan boasted to Ellen. He accepted the encounter as the general-in-chief's declaration of war. Scott wrote Cameron a few days later that only his concern for Northern morale prevented him from courtmartialing his army commander for insubordination.

The battle lines were drawn for all to see. "The country is rife with reported misunderstandings between Gens Scott and McClellan," the astute political observer Thurlow Weed warned the administration. "This is damaging." The Comte de Paris recorded in his diary that within the army it was believed Scott was thwarting McClellan at every turn: "I heard generals say, 'If in 10 days McClellan is not Commander in Chief, the army shall have something to do with the matter,' leading one almost to glimpse the prospect of an 18 Brumaire." He also understood that McClellan forced the issue by threatening to go into winter quarters, or even to resign, unless he was upheld. However the pressure was applied, it was effective. At a Cabinet meeting on October 18 it was agreed to accept Scott's resignation. The news was leaked to McClellan, and the next day he wrote Ellen that the general would retire, but not in favor of Henry Halleck as

Scott had wanted. The victory was his, and he expected to be general-in-chief within a week.[28]

Ball's Bluff postponed the changeover and at the same time increased demands for it. Strange alliances resulted. On October 25 three Republican leaders of what presidential secretary John Hay called the Jacobin Club, the radical senators Wade of Ohio, Chandler of Michigan, and Lyman Trumbull of Illinois, descended on McClellan with a fierce determination to get the war moving. They railed at him until one in the morning. Wade insisted even a defeat was better than a stalemate, for it would stimulate enlistments. With Ball's Bluff fresh on his mind, the general replied that he preferred fewer recruits before a victory than many after a defeat. He deflected the impatient senators by explaining that General Scott was the great obstacle to the advance of the Army of the Potomac. They left promising to make common cause with him in a ''desperate effort'' to depose Scott.

McClellan had meanwhile allied himself with Edwin M. Stanton, a prominent lawyer, Democrat, and attorney general in Buchanan's Cabinet, whom he met through their mutual friend Samuel Barlow. Stanton assisted him in preparing what McClellan described as an important paper ''intended to place on record the fact that I have left nothing undone to make this army what it ought to be & that the necessity for delay has not been my fault.'' In the paper, addressed to Secretary Cameron, he declared that the Confederate army on the Potomac was at least 150,000 strong, ''well drilled & equipped, ably commanded & strongly intrenched.'' He rated his own field army at half that size. Reinforcements must be rushed to the Army of the Potomac from all other commands, which would go on the defensive. If all his stipulations were met, including ''unity of action & design'' directed by ''a single will,'' he promised an advance no later than November 25. At the same time he wrote privately to his wife, ''It now begins to look as if we are condemned to a winter of inactivity. If it is so the fault will not be mine. . . .''

On the evening of October 31, the day he submitted his paper to Cameron, he learned that Scott's retirement would take place the next day and that he was to be named general-in-chief. ''I feel a sense of relief at the prospect of having my own way untrammeled,'' he wrote Ellen when he heard the news, but he assured her that he felt no sense of gratified vanity or ambition.

The Comte de Paris thought the appointment potentially a major event in the nation's history, and in his diary assessed its implications: "Called at so youthful an age" — McClellan would not turn thirty-five for just over a month — "to his nation's highest military position by the will of public opinion, not by what he has done, but by what is expected of him, he is obliged to act."[29]

SIX

GENERAL
OF ALL THE ARMIES

ON THE MORNING of November 1, 1861, a White House messenger brought McClellan official notification of his new post. "I have designated you to command the whole Army," the president wrote. "You will, therefore, assume this enlarged duty at once, conferring with me so far as necessary." For the general order he issued on assuming the command, McClellan composed a fulsome panegyric to General Scott. It was overly rhetorical, he confessed to Ellen, "but I wrote it *at* him — for a particular market!" That evening Mr. Lincoln called at headquarters to assure him of his support. McClellan replied that the appointment greatly relieved him : "I feel as if several tons were taken from my shoulders today. I am now in contact with you, and the Secretary." The president expressed concern about the "vast labor" involved in the dual role of army commander and general-in-chief. As John Hay recorded it, the general responded quietly, "I can do it all."[1]

In predawn blackness the next morning, in a driving rainstorm, McClellan and his staff rode to the depot to see Winfield Scott off on the train to New York. In their black rubber havelocks and slickers, swords and spurs clattering as they strode along the platform, general and staff seemed to a newspaperman like the black knights of yore. The old warrior greeted the new with great politeness and wished him well. "Carry out your own ideas, and you will conquer," Scott told him in parting. "God bless you." Despite the contrived farewell address he had written, McClellan found himself genuinely moved. He told Ellen it was a lesson he would not forget. "I saw there the end of a long, active & ambitious life — the end of the career of the first soldier of his nation — & it was a feeble old man scarce able to walk. . . . Should I ever become vainglorious & ambitious remind me of that spectacle.''

A delegation from his home city of Philadelphia called at headquarters the following day to honor him with a presentation sword. ''The war cannot last long,'' he said in a brief acceptance speech. ''It may be desperate. I ask in the future, forbearance, patience, and confidence. With these we can accomplish all. . . .'' The remarks were widely quoted by a generally approving press. His words, Greeley's *New York Tribune* editorialized, ''are welcomed everywhere, and are indicative of vigorous and decisive work.'' The *New York Times* thought the public had ''all the confidence in General McClellan which it would be safe for any man in his position to enjoy.''[2]

The position of general-in-chief was ill-defined and largely what the man who occupied the post made of it, or was allowed to make of it by a particular president or secretary of war. Winfield Scott had run the peacetime army as if it were a fiefdom, and for much of the decade of the 1850s, in part because of a long-running feud with Secretary of War Jefferson Davis, he kept his distance from the War Department by maintaining army headquarters in New York. As it happened, managing an army of some 16,000 men scattered to the farthest frontiers and contending primarily with Indians was not such a taxing job that War Department and army headquarters needed to work together in perfect harmony. The coming of war changed all that.

Scott had long since moved his headquarters back to Washington, but had continued to maintain his administrative staff separate from that of the War Department. It was a system quickly overwhelmed by the demands of mobilization. ''I find the 'Army' just about as much disorganized as was the Army of the Potomac when I assumed command — everything at sixes & sevens — no system, no order — perfect chaos,'' McClellan exclaimed to his wife after laboring eighteen hours on his first day on the job. ''I *can* & *will* reduce it to order — I *will* soon have it working smoothly.''

His first step was to eliminate the separate staff and files of the commanding general and center all functions of the office at the War Department, on 17th Street near the White House. He conducted business there through the army's adjutant general

and spent the rest of his time at Potomac army headquarters, on
Jackson Square, or visiting the camps ringing the city. The firm
hold he took on his new duties suited the secretary of war well
enough. Simon Cameron was considerably more adept at managing Pennsylvania politics than at administering the War Department, and he was engulfed by the complexities of the huge
wartime expansion. He had little time and no inclination for
military planning. "Anxious to aid you with all the powers of
my Department," he had written McClellan. "I will be glad if
you will inform me how I can do so." This attitude made him,
in the general's eyes, the ideal superior. Thus encouraged, he
interpreted his role as being exclusively in charge of the military
management of the war. With Cameron supplying arms and men,
he would personally direct strategic planning and oversee the
operations of all the armies.[3]

He faced a particular challenge in his dealings with the army's
administrative bureaus, the semi-independent bodies that his old
West Point instructor Dennis Hart Mahan had warned him were
"miserable nests of petty intrigues." In the chain of command
the heads of these bureaus — ordnance, commissary, quartermaster, paymaster, chief engineer, surgeon general, and adjutant
general — reported to the secretary of war rather than to the
general-in-chief, but McClellan used his mastery of the ins and
outs of the military bureaucracy to handle them with considerable
success.

He worked personally with the pedantic adjutant general, Lorenzo Thomas, and was attentive to protocol and tact in corresponding with the ultraconservative ordnance head, James W.
Ripley, and venerable Joseph G. Totten of the Corps of Engineers.
He worked around the incompetent surgeon general, Clement A.
Finley, by appointing the reform-minded Charles S. Tripler medical director of the Army of the Potomac. It was his good fortune
that Montgomery C. Meigs, the army's best staff officer, was
quartermaster general. For all his bureaucratic skills, however,
the lack of an operational staff meant that effective coordination
with the bureaus was dependent on McClellan's personal efforts.

His immediate need was for information from the field, and
telegrams went out to every subordinate commander. "Please
report by telegram in cipher the numbers, position & condition
of your troops...," a typical dispatch read. "State your situa-

tion & intentions — the same with regard to the enemy. Report
at least once each day by telegram, & by letter.'' He reshaped
the western commands and put new men in charge — Henry W.
Halleck, General Scott's favorite, at the head of the Department
of Missouri to manage operations in that crucial border state and
in the Mississippi Valley ; and Don Carlos Buell, the acquaintance
from his Texas days in the old army, at the head of the Department of the Ohio to direct affairs in the equally crucial border
state of Kentucky.[4]

A week after his appointment as general-in-chief, McClellan
outlined for his friend Samuel Barlow his thoughts on conducting
the war. The next battle would be fought in Virginia and decide
the struggle, he explained. ''My intention is simply this — I will
pay no attention to popular clamor — quietly, & quickly as possible, make this Army strong enough & effective enough to give
me a reasonable certainty that, if I am able to handle the form,
I will win the first battle.'' Let there be no doubt, he wrote, that
when he was ready to strike a blow ''it will be heavy, rapid, &
decisive,'' whatever the season.

Until that day came, he wanted the support of Barlow and his
influential political friends to keep the conflict within proper
limits. ''Help me to dodge the nigger — we want nothing to do
with him. *I* am fighting to preserve the integrity of the Union &
the power of the Govt — on no other issue.'' Abolitionism must
not be allowed to embitter the conflict and interfere with his
scheme for peace and reunion ; the slavery issue must remain
''incidental and subsidiary.'' He believed that under his influence
Lincoln was of a like mind : ''The Presdt is perfectly honest &
is really sound on the nigger question — I will answer for it now
that things go right with him.''

Barlow replied that McClellan's letter had greatly encouraged
him. A single victory like the one he described, the Democratic
leader agreed, and the South would surely be willing to return
to the Union, provided of course that the North made certain
constitutional accommodations on the issues that divided the sections. Such accommodations might include (as he wrote another
friend) the requirement that future presidents be elected, and
future slavery legislation be passed, by majorities in both the
free and slave-holding sections. The letter was passed on to the

administration with the notation that it came from "the particular friend of Genl. McClellan...."[5]

At the same time, McClellan's strategy for prosecuting the war
underwent revision and refinement. In October he had promised
the impatient radical senators a prompt advance by the Army of
the Potomac in return for their help in removing Winfield Scott
from his path. On the eve of becoming general-in-chief he had
assured Secretary Cameron that if Union forces elsewhere went
on the defensive and sent him enough reinforcements to match
Joe Johnston's army at Manassas man for man, he would fight
the decisive battle near Washington before winter. Now he quietly
abandoned all such thoughts. He issued no orders to other commands to send forces sufficient for him to take an immediate
offensive. Instead they were to act in concert as part of a larger
plan drawn from the grand design he had composed for the president early in August.

In Missouri, Halleck was instructed to make it his first order
of business to untangle the rat's nest left by his predecessor, John
C. Frémont; he was then to organize his command for future
movements along the western rivers. In the Department of the
Ohio, Buell was given Knoxville, Tennessee, as his objective, a
choice dictated by military and political factors in equal measure.
East Tennessee was believed to be heavily Unionist in sentiment,
and Mr. Lincoln was anxious to "liberate" this portion of the
Confederacy at the earliest possible moment.

On this point McClellan and the president were in perfect
agreement. The seizure of Knoxville would cut the South's only
direct rail connection between Virginia and the western theater,
a matter of critical importance in his strategical design. When
in due course he made his own advance, he considered it essential
to prevent the enemy from calling in reinforcements from the
West to oppose him. He would further isolate the Confederates
in Virginia by striking at their railroad communications south
of Richmond with an amphibious force being readied by his old
friend Ambrose Burnside. He authorized planning for still another coastal expedition, this one aimed at New Orleans; once he
had matters in hand in Virginia, he intended to command it
personally. To forestall any threat to his grand design by intervening European powers, he pressed for stronger harbor defenses

in the North's seaboard cities. He privately set April 1862 as the target date for delivering the decisive blow in Virginia, which he predicted to a newspaper reporter would mark the Waterloo of the rebellion.[6]

With detective Pinkerton reporting that the fortifications of Centreville and Manassas Junction mounted some 200 guns and appeared more formidable each day, McClellan grew increasingly reluctant to make his campaign in that direction. No matter what approach he contemplated there, he envisioned being outflanked or attacked in detail by Johnston's host. Should he attempt to repeat his western Virginia success by "amusing" the Rebels with a part of his force while attacking their communications with the rest, he would be committing the error of dividing his army in the face of a superior foe. Even the lesser goal of destroying the Confederate batteries along the lower Potomac called forth from him an involved scheme employing no fewer than 118,000 men.

After waiting a month for a plan of action from his new general-in-chief, Lincoln sought to break the deadlock by suggesting a movement on the line of the Occoquan River against Johnston's supply line. In any such advance, McClellan replied on December 10, the Rebels "could meet us in front with equal forces *nearly.* . . ." But, he assured the president, "I have now my mind actively turned towards another plan of campaign that I do not think at all anticipated by the enemy. . . ."[7]

In his preoccupation with delivering the single war-ending blow, McClellan concluded that, as matters stood, Richmond was a far more likely place to gain the victory than Washington. The plan he hinted at to Lincoln was a strategic turning movement by way of lower Chesapeake Bay. The objective was to reach Richmond before Johnston could get there from Manassas to save his capital, thus forcing him into a battle on McClellan's terms. It was classic Jominian strategy.

As early as August, William Aspinwall had pointed out the Chesapeake to him as "a shorter & safer road" to Richmond than the overland route, and now, late in November, McClellan began giving it serious thought. He sought the views of his chief engineer, John Barnard, on shifting the theater of operations southward to the James, York, or Rappahannock rivers. Barnard was doubtful; transferring an army of 100,000 men to that line, he wrote, "I look upon as almost impracticable, if not otherwise imprudent." Undeterred, McClellan put Stewart Van Vliet, the Potomac army's quartermaster, to studying shipping needs, and explored naval cooperation with Flag Officer Louis M. Goldsborough of the Atlantic blockading squadron. He ordered his topographical engineers to assemble all the information they could find on the geography and topography and weather patterns of coastal Virginia as far inland as Richmond.

In a bid for support, he also confided his new scheme to his most vocal supporter in the Cabinet, Secretary of the Treasury Chase. He explained that he would land a powerful expeditionary force at Urbanna, near the mouth of the Rappahannock, and rapidly march the fifty miles to Richmond. Chase was gravely concerned about the strain the war effort was putting on the nation's financial structure; he said that after about mid-February of 1862 he did not see how he could raise any more money to pay for a conflict that seemed to have no end in sight. McClellan vowed he would be in Richmond before that date. On the strength of this pledge Chase assured the Northern masters of capital and credit that they could rely on the general's "activity, vigor and success." It was yet another promise that mortgaged McClellan's credibility.[8]

In his general-in-chief's role he was thrown into daily contact with what, in a fit of exasperation, he called the "wretched politicians" of the administration. The president might come by at any hour to consult him or to get the latest military news, and often called him to Cabinet meetings. The only Cabinet secretary he thought well of was Chase, his patron. He tolerated the compliant Simon Cameron (while referring privately to his rascality), and he credited Postmaster General Montgomery Blair with sense and courage, although disliking him personally. His view of other Cabinet members was decidedly uncharitable. He described Secretary of State Seward to Ellen as "a meddling, officious, incompetent little puppy," and termed Secretary of the Navy Gideon Welles an old woman and Attorney General Edward Bates an old fool. For all his professed reverence for constitutional principles, he had lost none of the contempt for civilian control of the military he had first displayed during the Mexican War.

It became his habit, when in company with politicians, to say as little as possible. Secretary Seward's eighteen-year-old daughter Fanny first met him when he called on her father on a military matter. "General McClellan spoke but little, in a low pleasant voice — what he said was very brief . . . ," she recorded in her diary. The historian George Bancroft was also introduced to McClellan that winter, on a visit to his headquarters in company with the president. Lincoln did most of the talking, Bancroft wrote his wife: "Of all silent, uncommunicative, reserved men, whom I ever met, the general stands among the first. He is one, who if he thinks deeply, keeps his thoughts to himself."[9]

McClellan found Lincoln the president no particular improvement on Lincoln the Illinois lawyer. When he came to write his memoirs (by which time his hatred of Edwin Stanton knew no bounds), he would profess shock at Stanton's abusive comments about the president during these fall months of 1861, especially his observation that the explorer Paul Du Chaillu had been foolish to search darkest Africa for the gorilla when he could have easily found that creature in Springfield, Illinois. In fact, McClellan had promptly adopted Stanton's characterization for his own, referring to Lincoln in his letters as the "original gorilla" and "nothing more than a well-meaning baboon."

What he particularly resented was the president's habit of visiting him unannounced. On one occasion he told Ellen that to get any work done he had concealed himself at Stanton's house "to dodge all enemies in shape of 'browsing' Presdt etc. . . ." A short time afterward, General Samuel P. Heintzelman recorded in his journal that he had encountered Lincoln at headquarters reviewing the military situation on a map of Virginia, "making remarks, not remarkably profound but McClellan listened as if much edified." After seeing Lincoln out, McClellan turned to Heintzelman and remarked, "Isn't he a rare bird?"

His famous snub of the president was a direct consequence of this attitude. On November 13 Lincoln, Seward, and John Hay paid an evening call on the general-in-chief and were told that he was attending an officer's wedding. They had been waiting in his parlor an hour when McClellan returned, passed by the parlor door, and went upstairs, ignoring his orderly's announcement that the president and secretary of state were waiting to see him. After half an hour the orderly was sent upstairs to remind the general of his visitors; he returned to say that McClellan had gone to bed. Hay termed it "unparalleled insolence" and "a portent of evil to come." (It was not an isolated incident. A month or so earlier, William Howard Russell of the *Times* of London noted in his diary a scene at headquarters when the president was sent away by the announcement that General McClellan had gone to bed and would see no one.) Lincoln took no apparent offense, and indeed he returned the next evening for a discussion of future operations, but the contempt inherent in the snub could hardly have escaped him.[10]

This arrogance, rarely displayed so publicly, marked the most unpleasant side of George McClellan's character. Yet the relationship between president and general was more ambiguous than such patronizing actions might suggest. Often enough the issue was nothing more weighty than some offense to McClellan's patrician outlook. "I never in my life met anyone so full of anecdote as our friend Abraham," he wrote his wife after one of Lincoln's visits, adding that the stories "were as usual very pertinent & some pretty good." When the storytelling was displayed on a public occasion, however, it violated McClellan's standards for presidential dignity. Describing a Sunday reception at Seward's, he wrote, "I found the 'Gorilla' again, & was of course much edified by his anecdotes — ever apropos, & ever unworthy of one holding his high position." At other times during this first winter of the war he was persuaded that the president was his "kind true friend" whose "confidence has upheld me," and that he exhibited perfectly sound views on certain matters — such as, just then, his attitude toward the slavery question. Looking back on their wartime relationship, he wrote, "I never had any trouble with Mr. Lincoln when I could meet him face to face; the difficulty always came behind my back. I believe he liked me personally, & he certainly was always much under my influence when in personal contact."

For his part, Lincoln spent far more time and effort in dealing with General McClellan than with any other of his generals throughout the four years of war. He patiently reasoned with him and flattered his ego and defended him against his critics. "Don't let them hurry me, is all I ask," McClellan pleaded at one point, and the president replied, "You shall have your own way in the matter, I assure you." Possibly this attitude of deference was a mistake, the result of one of Lincoln's rare misjudgments of the character of those with whom he dealt. Perhaps less familiarity might have bred less contempt on McClellan's part.

On the other hand, even in the best of times McClellan could never find it in himself to regard the president as his social or intellectual equal. In this instance, as in so many others, he displayed no flexibility of mind or judgment, no room for the change of an opinion once formed. In his final days of command of the Army of the Potomac he was echoing his first days when he wrote, "There never was a truer epithet applied to a certain individual than that of the 'Gorilla.' " Because of this conceit — and of considerably greater consequence to his military career — he never took the president fully into his confidence. "The General's single mistake, that was the source of all his misfortunes, was his distrust of Lincoln," the newspaper editor Alexander K. McClure wrote Ellen many years later. Had he reciprocated Lincoln's friendship, McClure thought, "he could have mastered all his combined enemies." [11]

The burdens of his new office did not prevent him from staging the grand reviews that were now a trademark of the Army of the Potomac. He was always the most dramatic figure at these events as he galloped across the reviewing grounds at the head of his escort. His mounts, Dan Webster and another big bay named Kentuck, the gift of Union men in Kentucky, were thought to be the finest horses in Washington. "As soon as he made his appearance, coming over the hill, the whole division took off their hats, and commenced whorahing," a Michigan sergeant wrote. "McClellan took his cap off and held it up the whole length of his arm, and rode rappidly along the line. . . . He has that peculiar look about him, which fascinates all beholders, and it seems as tho he were conscious of the fact."

The grandest of the grand reviews was held on November 20. Seven divisions, some 65,000 men, wheeled through their maneuvers in a scene that *Harper's Weekly* called "brilliant beyond description." It was the review of the French Imperial Guard McClellan had seen in the Crimea, multiplied many times over. Bands played and fifteen batteries of artillery crashed out salutes and massed cavalry thundered past. President Lincoln, Cabinet secretaries, and the diplomatic corps headed the dignitaries in attendance. Newsmen estimated the spectators at 30,000. Mc-

Clellan wrote Ellen that he had never seen so large a review in
Europe carried out with such precision : "I was completely satisfied & delighted beyond expression."[12]

His domestic life took a decided turn for the better when Ellen
was at last able to join him in Washington. Except for a brief
meeting at the time he was called to the capital from western
Virginia, they had been apart since late June. On October 12 she
gave birth to a daughter, christened Mary but always called May.
Ellen recovered her strength slowly, and it was almost two months
before she could make the journey from Cincinnati. In expectation of her arrival, McClellan rented what he described as "a
very good house" at the corner of H Street and 15th, acquired
a domestic staff, and early in November moved there from Army
of the Potomac headquarters on Jackson Square. Sharing the
house with him were his father-in-law, Randolph Marcy, and his
younger brother, twenty-two-year-old Arthur, who had been appointed to his staff with the rank of captain. On December 4
McClellan took a special train to Baltimore to pick up Ellen and
meet his daughter for the first time and bring them to Washington.

The McClellans were active in the capital's winter social season.
Ellen was charming as a hostess and sought after as a guest. "Her
manners are delightful; full of life and vivacity, great affability,
and very ready in conversation," General George Meade reported
to his wife after one of Ellen's receptions. Another hardbitten
regular, E. O. C. Ord, admitted to his wife that when Mrs. McClellan
brought in the baby for the company to admire, he melted at the
sight. He took little May in his arms, "and my heart was home
in a minute." McClellan wrote lightheartedly that Ellen's social
calendar was so crowded that her wardrobe was reduced to "the
condition of Miss Flora McFlimsey" and required renewal. Such
was his pride in her that he staged a review of Fitz John Porter's
division especially in her honor. "We had a great deal of fun ...,"
Ellen wrote in delight to her mother-in-law. "I had a Maj. Genl's
salute of seventeen guns given me as we drove in to the grounds
& altogether we had a very exciting & merry day."[13]

The session of Congress that opened on December 2 was soon
a forum for public debate on the war effort — and on General
McClellan as well. To Republican radicals the regular bulletin
"All quiet on the Potomac" was now a mockery. They made it

clear that the continued idleness of the Army of the Potomac had
ended whatever sense of common purpose they once shared with
the general. They could not see, they said, that the army had
done anything since General Scott's retirement but stage reviews.
Federal judge Joseph Casey appraised the mood in Washington
and on December 11 wrote a friend, ''It cannot be disguised that
there is springing up again both in Congress & the Country a
good deal of restlessness & impatience, at the apparent inactivity
of the immense army we have in the field.'' Horace Greeley's
once-patient *New York Tribune* now concluded that winter was
the best time to campaign in the South. "Let us end the war!"
it demanded.

McClellan's partisans rushed to his defense, adding to the political cast of the debate. The *Journal of Commerce* wanted it
known that there was a growing abolitionist plot against the
general stemming from the fact that ''he is known to be sternly
opposed to anti slavery schemes. . . .'' The *New York Herald* issued a pointed warning that unless congressional radicals ''speedily draw in their horns,'' they would find in George McClellan
as formidable an opponent as Parliament had found in Oliver
Cromwell. Samuel Barlow cast an eye on these exchanges and
told his friend Edwin Stanton that if the public perceived ''the
whole abolition pack'' snapping at the general's heels, it might
not be such a bad thing. Any discrediting of the radicals would
be the Democrats' gain.[14]

The congressional debate took more concrete form with the
appointment on December 10 of the Joint Committee on the Conduct of the War, headed by Republican radical Benjamin Wade
of Ohio. A few days before Christmas the committee organized
for business and invited McClellan to be its first witness. He
agreed to testify on December 23, but on the appointed day he
was too ill to appear. His illness grew worse, and doctors were
called in. Their diagnosis was typhoid fever.

For two weeks the high command functioned only on matters
of daily routine. Chief of Staff Marcy also fell ill with typhoid.
On December 27 President Lincoln told a visitor that the general-
in-chief ''is now quite sick.'' Newspapermen tried to confirm
persistent rumors that his condition was critical and that he was
not expected to live. Three homeopathic physicians from New
York hurried to the capital to care for him. (In common with

his religious regeneration, McClellan owed his conversion to homeopathy to his wife. All the Marcys were advocates, and one of the three physicians called in was General Marcy's brother. Homeopathic medicine was not universally admired, however, and General Meade remarked that among McClellan's friends belief in his "claimed extraordinary judgment" was shaken.) In fact McClellan was not near death at any time, and after a week or so he began to transact a limited amount of routine business. But it was not until January 6, by his own admission, that he ventured any serious work, and even then he apologized for lacking "strength enough to write a fuller and more intelligible letter...."[15]

The most serious consequence of his illness was the harm it brought to his military fortunes. It could not have come at a worse time. Had he appeared, as planned, as the first witness before the Committee on the Conduct of the War, he almost certainly could have defused or deflected some of its hostility. He might have explained the strategic situation and his reasons for delaying the advance of the Army of the Potomac, and given assurances of his plans to coordinate the movements of all the armies. To be sure, by his own statements and those of his supporters his stance on the politics of the war was now too well known for him to escape entirely the enmity of such committee members as Ben Wade and Zach Chandler, who were committed to believing the worst of him. At the very least, however, he could have provided an authoritative background against which the testimony of other witnesses had to be judged.

Instead, by the time he finally appeared before the committee, in mid-January, it had already heard testimony from a parade of his division and brigade commanders. Some were determinedly loyal to McClellan and others were critical, and a few said they knew he was maturing his plans but refused to say more without his permission. But one thread ran through all their testimony: whatever the plan of action for the Army of the Potomac might be, nothing much was being done to implement it, and General McClellan — who, rumor had it, was on his deathbed — had kept its most significant details entirely to himself.

The possibility that the sum total of war planning might go to the grave with the general greatly disturbed Senator Wade. The country was spending itself into bankruptcy on its army, he said, yet the capital was virtually under Confederate siege and "Europe is looking down upon us as almost a conquered people" and debating entry into the war on the side of the South. "How can this nation abide the secret counsels that one man carries in his head, when we have no evidence that he is the wisest man in the world?" Wade asked; were he a Napoleon or a Wellington he would feel easier, but thus far "we are not sure of that."[16]

Although the committee took testimony in closed session, it was quick to make its findings known to the president. At a meeting at the White House on the last day of the year Wade violently attacked McClellan for his apparent inactivity. Investigating matters for himself, Lincoln telegraphed Generals Halleck and Buell in the western theater to ask if they were prepared to act in concert during the general-in-chief's illness. Halleck replied that he knew nothing of Buell's plans and in any case was not yet ready to cooperate, and he warned against "too much haste." Buell understood that any instructions for concerted action would come from headquarters in Washington.

The committee resumed its attack a week later, at a meeting with the president and his Cabinet. Wade and Chandler demanded that Irvin McDowell replace McClellan as head of the Army of the Potomac. Secretary Chase defended McClellan as the best man for his place, but admitted that he "tasked himself too severely" by acting as both general-in-chief and commander of the Union's largest field army. Lincoln sent McClellan a note of warning that he had better go before the committee the moment his health permitted.[17]

From the first, McClellan had given the impression of being the very model of a strong, active general-in-chief. He reorganized the office to function efficiently, and established priorities for allocating arms and equipment. He called on his field commanders for a steady flow of information on which to base decisions, and closely followed the fortunes of each of them. Most important, he developed an overall strategic design for making war on the Confederacy from tidewater Virginia all the way to Indian Territory. If in this design all other commands were to act for the benefit of his Army of the Potomac, at least they would be applying pressure on the Rebels simultaneously at many points. This principle was just as the president himself had worked it out. The North must make its greater strength an "over-match" for the enemy, he wrote Buell and Halleck, and it seemed to him "this can only be done by menacing him with superior forces at *different* points, at the *same* time;... if he *weakens* one to *strengthen* the other, forbear to attack the strengthened one, but seize, and hold the weakened one...."

Yet as Lincoln discovered (along with Senator Wade and the committee), not only was very little being done to carry out this strategic plan, but there seemed to be no knowing when anything might be done. Secretary Chase may or may not have told him of McClellan's pledge to be in Richmond by mid-February, but in any case the president had seen a full month pass since the general mentioned to him a new plan of campaign for the Army of the Potomac, and nothing more had been said of that. It was all too evident that there was no sense of purpose or unity in the western theater. In exercising high command, General-in-Chief McClellan was less decisive than he seemed; he preferred expressing hopes and making suggestions to issuing orders and setting timetables.[18]

When Halleck and Buell made it clear they did not intend advancing any time soon — in fact, Buell confessed, he strongly opposed the move on East Tennessee that both Lincoln and McClellan set such store by — the president became greatly troubled. On January 10 he wrote on a letter from Halleck detailing all the problems he faced, "It is exceedingly discouraging. As everywhere else, nothing can be done." Afterward he went to the office of the army's quartermaster, Montgomery Meigs, and poured out his distress. "General, what shall I do?" he asked. "The people are impatient; Chase has no money and tells me he can raise no more; the General of the Army has typhoid fever. The bottom is out of the tub. What shall I do?"[19]

That evening, acting on Meigs's advice, the president called together an informal council of war at the White House. From the Potomac army he summoned Generals Irvin McDowell, its former commander, and William Franklin, known to be a confidant of McClellan's. Secretaries Chase and Seward and Assistant Secretary of War Thomas A. Scott represented the Cabinet. According to McDowell's notes, Lincoln opened the meeting by recounting the bad news flooding in from every quarter, and observed that as far as he could tell, the nation's war machine was stalled on dead center while the general-in-chief lay ill. He had called at McClellan's house, but "the general did not ask to see him," and he remarked that if McClellan was not going to use the army any time soon he wanted to borrow it, "provided he could see how it could be made to do something." If the command were theirs, he asked the two generals, what would they do with the Army of the Potomac?

McDowell replied that he would keep Washington as his base, force the Confederates at Manassas Junction and Centreville out of their fortifications by attacking their supply line, and give battle — which, had he known it, was exactly what the president had proposed to McClellan back in early December. Franklin, who knew from McClellan something of his Urbanna plan, recommended instead an advance on Richmond from the lower Chesapeake. Lincoln told them to study the matter more fully and report back the following day.

Before this second meeting Secretary Chase was visited by two men close to McClellan, Edwin Stanton and staff aide Thomas M. Key, and it is likely that he told one or both of them about the president's war council. In his memoirs McClellan credited Stanton with informing him of the "grand conclave" called without his knowledge. He also wrote that Stanton (who, unlike the president, apparently had no trouble gaining admittance to the general's bedside) warned him that his enemies were counting on his death and already dividing up his "military goods and chattels."

On Sunday morning, January 12, McClellan appeared unannounced at the White House. He wrote later that it was only with some effort that he "mustered strength enough" for the carriage ride, but he exaggerated the hardship. He had ventured out as early as January 7, and the day after seeing the president he would write Buell, "I am now quite well again, only somewhat weak." There is no doubt that for some days past he could have arranged to receive Lincoln and relieve his mind by explaining his plans. However that may be, on this Sunday morning he revealed to him for the first time the outlines of his Urbanna strategy.

The following afternoon an enlarged war council met for what proved to be the last time. It was divided equally between civilians and soldiers — Lincoln, Chase, Seward, and Montgomery Blair, the one West Pointer in the Cabinet; and Generals McDowell, Franklin, Meigs, and McClellan. McClellan soon made it clear that he viewed the proceedings with sullen resentment. For his benefit the president recited his reasons for assembling the council and then called on McDowell and Franklin to review the military options they had discussed. McClellan responded (in a tone McDowell described as cold and curt), "You are entitled to have any opinion you please!" and lapsed back into silence. He made no further comment as the discussion continued. Meigs pulled his chair up next to McClellan's and whispered that Lincoln expected something from him; by remaining mute he was being disrespectful to the commander-in-chief. Could he not consider a move against Manassas? McClellan replied that the latest reports put the enemy there at 175,000, too many to attack. In any case, if he revealed his plans now, they would be in the *New York Herald* the next day. The president could not keep military secrets; he even told them to Tad, his eight-year-old son.

Chase finally asked him directly where and when he intended to advance with the Army of the Potomac. After a long and uncomfortable pause, McClellan replied that it was necessary to act first in Kentucky, and he was pressing General Buell on that. As for his own plans, he was unwilling to reveal them unless ordered to do so by the president. "No General fit to command an army will ever submit his plans to the judgment of such an assembly," he said; ". . . there are many here entirely incompetent to pass judgment upon them; . . . no plan made known to so many persons can be kept secret an hour. . . ." Lincoln asked if he had at least fixed a particular time to open his campaign. He said he had. "Well," the president said, "on this assurance of the General that he will press the advance in Kentucky, I will be satisfied, and will adjourn the Council."[20]

McClellan's refusal to discuss even generally plans that were by then hardly a secret to anyone in his audience was an example of a willful stubbornness that was becoming increasingly noticeable. John Barnard labeled it childish obstinacy, and Jacob Cox called it obstinacy "of a feminine sort." Both men were unfriendly critics when they made these comments, but even as close a friend as Ambrose Burnside would record that he once had to stay up until three o'clock in the morning to argue McClellan out of some particularly self-destructive position. His conduct at the war council exasperated his ally Chase. "Well, if that is Mac's decision, he is a ruined man," he remarked. Chase overstated the case — the next day McClellan wrote a friendly note to Lincoln, saying that he was working hard to "carry out the promise I made to you yesterday" — but the war council nevertheless marked an important first step in his parting from the administration. He saw only conspiracy in the episode, with McDowell, the radicals' favorite, angling for command of the Army of the Potomac. He assigned that general to the ranks of his enemies, and was a long time forgiving his old friend Franklin. Recalling the incident seven months later, he wrote Ellen, "I do not at all doubt Franklin's loyalty now. . . . ''21

January 13 proved to be a day crowded with momentous events. That evening, as McClellan dressed for dinner, Colonel Key of his staff appeared at his house on H Street with the news that Simon Cameron had resigned and the president had named Edwin Stanton to be secretary of war. A few minutes later Stanton himself arrived. He said he would accept the position only if the general approved. As McClellan recalled the conversation, Stanton pledged "all his time, intellect, and energy to my assistance," and promised that together they would soon bring the rebellion to an end. McClellan urged him to accept. The next day the president called at H Street to explain that he had refrained from consulting him on the appointment so as to give the general's opponents no cause to say he had dictated the choice. In any event, he assumed there would be no objection to a close friend as head of the War Department. McClellan no doubt agreed, for he wrote Samuel Barlow soon afterward that Stanton's appointment "was a most unexpected piece of good fortune," and he hoped it would also have a good effect on the country.22

Stanton wasted no time in acting on his pledge of support. He was back at McClellan's the following evening to introduce Malcolm Ives, a correspondent for James Gordon Bennett's *New York Herald.* According to Ives, Stanton and McClellan said they so valued the continued backing of the nation's largest newspaper that they wanted it to have the inside track on all military news. After Stanton left, McClellan treated the reporter to a three-hour briefing. The day before, he had refused to discuss war plans with President Lincoln and his chief advisers on the ground that anything he said would end up in the next issue of the *Herald.* Now he presented that newspaper with what was certainly the largest official leak of military secrets in the entire course of the Civil

War. "What I declined communicating to them," he told Ives, "I am now going to convey through you to Mr Bennett... *all* the knowledge I possess myself, with no reserve...." He detailed the most current reports from Halleck and Buell in the western theater, from Burnside's expedition newly arrived on the North Carolina coast, and from other operations under way or planned in South Carolina, Florida, and against New Orleans. He explained how all this meshed with his own plans for a great offensive against Richmond. "They must be beaten and they *shall* be beaten in Virginia, and then I will knock them to pieces at New Orleans," he declared. He was confident that Mr. Bennett would use this information wisely and not reveal its source.

McClellan continued to brief Ives on a regular basis, furnishing him with copies of dispatches from the field and even proposing to plant stories in the *Herald* "to help me throw dust in the eyes of the enemy." He arranged to alert Bennett in a special telegraphic code the moment his offensive opened. When a hitch developed in getting all this inside information to the paper through Ives, he ordered Randolph Marcy, who was recuperating from his typhoid fever in New York, to see Bennett and assure him of his desire "to communicate fully & unreservedly ... — I am anxious to keep Mr B. well posted & wish to do it fully...."

Ives cautioned his editor that General McClellan was "as guileless and innocent as a child, and we must be careful not to injure him, even to promote Herald interests." It appears, however, that the innocent in the affair was reporter Ives. McClellan found James Gordon Bennett's abhorrence of abolitionism, stated frequently and pungently in his editorials, as welcome as the editor's praise for his generalship. Having already sought the aid of Barlow and his political allies to help him "dodge the nigger" and prevent slavery from becoming a major issue in the conflict, he was hardly so naïve as to cultivate one of the most powerful voices in the press for any lesser purpose.

That he was using Ives for his own designs is evident in the carefully fashioned account he gave the reporter of his January 15 testimony before the Joint Committee on the Conduct of the War. As he told it, the committee members received him "with the most marked courtesy," with Chairman Wade declaring their desire to sustain him in all matters relating to the war. Wade simply wanted him to be aware of the country's financial problems, of the fear of foreign intervention, and of the desire of the people for some sign of military progress. McClellan replied that he fully understood and sympathized with these "embarrassments," and assured the committee that action would be forthcoming soon. That had concluded the interview on a note "satisfactory to all parties," he told Ives. He gave the *Herald* permission to make any use it wanted of his account.

No transcript of McClellan's testimony is on record, but it was described very differently by Senator Chandler. By his account, when the general explained that he could not advance until his line of retreat was secure in case of a check on the battlefield, Chandler interrupted to say that what he really meant was that "before you strike at the rebels you want to be sure of plenty of room so that you can run in case they strike back!" Wade added, "Or in case you get scared." Comparing notes afterward, Chandler told Wade that the general's testimony struck him as "infernal, unmitigated cowardice." Whatever the actual tone of the session may have been, it was certainly not as harmonious as McClellan wanted the *Herald* to believe.[23]

In addition to investigating the Army of the Potomac, the congressional committee looked into the battle at Ball's Bluff the previous October that had taken the life of one of its own, Senator Edward Baker. Responsibility for the disaster, the committee soon concluded, fell on Colonel Baker's superior, Brigadier General Charles P. Stone. It was already well known that Stone returned fugitive slaves to their masters and had gotten into a hot fight it with no less than Senator Charles Sumner, and the committee found witnesses willing to question not only Stone's military competence but his loyalty as well. Tales were told — at second and third hand, to be sure — of mysterious meetings under flags of truce between Stone and Confederate officers from across the Potomac, of suspected secessionists who were issued passes, of sealed letters passed through the lines, and other such suspicious matters. When Stone himself testified, he was told nothing of the case being built against him. On January 27 the committee went to Secretary of War Stanton with the testimony branding General Stone a traitor. The next day Stanton sent a directive to McClellan that Stone be relieved of his command and placed in arrest.

McClellan ordered Stone to Washington but did not immediately arrest him. Instead he went personally to the committee's rooms in the basement of the Capitol and argued that Stone should be recalled and allowed to know the evidence against him so that he might respond to it directly. On January 31 Stone went before the committee a second time, but again no specifics were given him; if he learned the names of witnesses from his command, Chairman Wade said, he might take reprisals. Stone could do little but offer a general defense of his loyalty.

He was further hamstrung by orders from army headquarters. Earlier he had sought a court of inquiry after an attack on him by the noisy Republican representative from New York, Roscoe Conkling, but one of McClellan's staff warned him off. "Your military superiors are attacked," he was told, reason enough to keep silent. When he went before the committee he was under orders not to reveal military details of the Ball's Bluff affair. The general-in-chief might believe Stone innocent "of all improper motives" (as he later wrote him), but he had no intention of taking his place on the block. One of Stone's officers told Attorney General Bates of discussing the case with McClellan about this time. "They want a victim," McClellan remarked. "Yes," the officer replied, " — and when they have once tasted blood, got one victim, no one can tell who will be the next victim!" With that, Bates recorded in his diary, "the Genl. colored up, and the conversation ceased."[24]

By now McClellan realized that General Stone was nothing but a stalking horse in a larger game. Stone was (like McClellan himself) a conservative Democrat and less than enthusiastic about the antislavery movement, and by the committee's reckoning these factors by themselves made him suspect. The army's high command, in short, was to be tested by powerful voices in the Congress as much for political beliefs as for military skills. McClellan began to look for a way out of this entanglement, and he found it in a report from Allan Pinkerton.

On February 6 Pinkerton sent him the results of an interrogation of one Jacob Shorb (also known by several aliases), a refugee from Confederate-held Leesburg on the upper Potomac. Shorb recounted the same gossip and campfire rumors retailed earlier by the committee's witnesses. He said he had heard that Rebel officers described General Stone as *"a brave man and a gentleman,"* surely a proof of disloyalty. Even Pinkerton had doubts about Shorb — "his general appearance did not impress me very favorably," he noted — but McClellan talked to him and then passed on the interrogation report to Stanton. The secretary called for Stone's immediate arrest, and McClellan issued the necessary orders. Stone was locked away in Fort Lafayette in New York Harbor. The Pinkerton report that put him there went into the army files with the endorsement "Full account of Gen. Stone's treachery."

Charles Stone would spend 189 days in military prisons before he was finally released, in August 1862. No charges were ever filed against him, in clear violation of the Articles of War. McClellan wrote Stone after his release that on several occasions he had tried to get him his day in court, but without result. At the same time, he was careful to keep his distance from the case. No doubt he would have agreed with Attorney General Bates, who saw in Stone's imprisonment a grim shadow of "congressional interference with the command of the army" reminiscent of Revolutionary France.

It was as yet still a shadow. "It is all important that you should have the full confidence of the community in your plans," George Gibbs, an old friend from the Pacific railroad survey, wrote McClellan, "but it is very certain that that confidence is already weakened & that in Congress . . . you have strong & active enemies." It was not too late to counter this, Gibbs said. McClellan had always excelled in winning people's trust; now was the time to recognize "their right to be assured that you are entitled to their confidence. . . . Dont fail us now through any error."[25]

SEVEN

THE GRAND CAMPAIGN

THE ADULATION he experienced during his first weeks of command in Washington was sure to fade in time, but McClellan was not prepared for the criticism of the Potomac army's inactivity that began to build week by week in the new year. "You have no idea of the pressures brought to bear here upon the Government for a forward movement," he wrote General Buell on January 13, 1862. Secretary of War Stanton was outspoken on the subject. He moved into Cameron's office on January 20 in a whirlwind of activity. General McClellan's army, he told the *New York Tribune*'s Charles A. Dana a few days later, "has got to fight or run away; ... the champagne and oysters on the Potomac must be stopped." At first he was rather less peremptory in dealing with the general, however, and on January 29 McClellan could write Randolph Marcy, "I am getting on very well — Stanton's appointment has helped me infinitely so far, & will still more in the future." These were the last kind words he would ever have for Edwin M. Stanton.

Stanton's immediate goal was an agreement on a strategic design. At his urging, McClellan met with the president and argued the case for his Urbanna movement against Richmond. Lincoln continued to favor keeping the army between Washington and the enemy, and outflanking the Manassas-Centreville force along the Occoquan River line. McClellan resented having to debate the matter at all. The president, he later wrote, assumed the role of strategist "& talked about 'my' plan as if he really supposed himself capable of conducting great operations." He set to work drafting a long and closely reasoned paper in defense of his Urbanna plan.[1]

As winter rains turned Virginia's roads into quagmires, it became apparent that the army would not be moving any time soon. McClellan began to consider a radical change in carrying out his strategy — the transfer to Kentucky of a major part of the Army of the Potomac for an early offensive in the western theater. "My mind is more & more tending in that direction, tho' not fully committed to it," he wrote Stanton on January 26. He would want to move as many as 70,000 infantry and 250 guns by rail and steamboat, he said, and would assume the overall command there in person. Assistant Secretary of War Thomas A. Scott was sent west to work out the logistics of the move. "It is an immense undertaking," Scott reported, "*but can be done.*"

McClellan never elaborated on this remarkable scheme, but it can be assumed that he saw two major advantages to it. By taking command personally, he could finally press Buell and Halleck into acting in concert, and at the same time ensure that his cherished objective of cutting the Confederacy's main east-west rail artery was carried out in advance of his move on Richmond. Indeed, once Federal forces were astride that railroad from Knoxville to Memphis, he might even utilize the eastern end of the line to transfer troops from Buell's army into Virginia through Lynchburg to cut off the enemy's retreat from Richmond. It was a truly Napoleonic concept.

On February 6 Barlow wrote him that he had heard it was Stanton's opinion "that you should go to Ky. *if* there is to be action there & none for the present in Va." Barlow believed the secretary was acting from the best of motives and "is really desirous of your distinguishing yourself in the war...." It is probable, however, that even then McClellan was turning away from the notion. For one thing, events in the West had begun to move without him. For another, the president was once more applying pressure for an advance by the Army of the Potomac. On February 20 McClellan dismissed the last traces of the idea. "At present no troops will move from East," he telegraphed Thomas Scott. "Ample occupation for them here." He also rejected the thought of making a brief trip to Kentucky to confer with his generals. Secretary Stanton had embraced the western plan so wholeheartedly as to suggest he originated it, and he seems to have argued the case with some heat. "I have not been able to impress the importance of this movement on General Mc-

Clellan ... nor to induce him to give the orders ...,'' he complained to Scott; ''I hope very speedily that he will change his notions on this subject. ...'' In a conversation with General Heintzelman he expressed his general dissatisfaction with how the high command was being run.

It was hardly a month after his taking office, and already he and the general-in-chief were at odds. Whether it was this issue or some other, however, they would sooner or later have found something that divided them; two such dogmatic temperaments were bound to clash. With his ''impulsive and energetic'' singlemindedness (as Gideon Welles described it) and his determination to reassert the authority of the War Department, Edwin Stanton may well have reminded McClellan of the Illinois Central's William Osborn, and he drew the same conclusion: anyone who did not support him in every respect and without exception must be against him.[2]

In the continued absence of a specific strategic plan from McClellan, Lincoln again took the initiative. His war order of January 27 specified George Washington's birthday, February 22, as the starting date for a general advance by Federal land and naval forces. Four days later, a supplementary order assigned the Army of the Potomac to move against the communications of the Confederates at Manassas Junction and Centrevillethe Occuquan plan he had been pressing on McClellan since early December. As soon as he received the order, on the morning of January 31, McClellan hurried to the White House to protest. He asked if he might submit his objections in writing. The president agreed, no doubt in some anticipation of finally seeing, after three months, something concrete in the way of a war plan from his general-in-chief.

The twenty-two-page paper in McClellan's handwriting that was laid on Secretary Stanton's desk on February 3 was drawn from the defense of his Urbanna plan he had begun drafting some days earlier. It began with a review of the events of the past six months, and then analyzed in detail the failings of the president's Occoquan plan. Any advance from Washington, McClellan wrote, must involve an intricate and careful series of movements to prevent the ''masses of the enemy'' from falling on an unprotected flank or an unsupported column. ''It is by no means certain that we can beat them at Manassas,'' he warned, but even assuming a victory there, the results would be limited: possession of the battlefield, the securing of the Potomac line, the prestige of avenging Bull Run — "important results it is true, but not decisive of the war. . . ." Substantial Confederate forces would probably escape, leaving the Potomac army to make a slow and costly overland pursuit toward Richmond.

He painted the prospects for his Urbanna plan in brighter colors. An advance from the mouth of the Rappahannock "affords the shortest possible land routes to Richmond, & strikes directly at the heart of the enemy's power in the East." The roads in the region were sandy and well drained and passable in any season of the year. He promised to leave Washington fully garrisoned, but in any event the Rebels would have no choice but to rush to the defense of their capital, only to find the Army of the Potomac already there in "a position selected by ourselves. . . ." They would have to make a hopeless attack, disperse, or surrender. With the initiative firmly in his hands and his flanks and communications secure, he wrote, "I regard success as certain by all the chances of war."

He went on to sketch the subsequent and inevitable collapse of the Confederacy. With Richmond in hand, a great arc of Union power would stretch from Burnside on the North Carolina coast through the Army of the Potomac in Virginia to Buell in Tennessee and Halleck on the Mississippi. After Charleston and other Atlantic ports were secured, the final steps would be "to advance our centre into South Carolina & Georgia; to push Buell either towards Montgomery, or to unite with the main army in Georgia; to throw Halleck southward to meet the Naval Expedition at New Orleans." He would stake everything on this outcome.

Lincoln's war orders had not of course been made public, but insiders picked up hints of his actions and of the recent war council meetings, and Senator Lyman Trumbull, for one, saw all this as most promising. He told Illinois governor Richard Yates that the president "seems to be waking up to the fact . . . that the responsibility is upon *him*, & I think he has resolved hereafter not to content himself with throwing all army movements on the Generals commanding, on the ground that he is no military man." Whether the Union's soldiers and sailors actually all moved forward in unison on Washington's birthday was less important to Mr. Lincoln than the need to stir General McClellan to action, and in that he had succeeded. Here was finally a plan of action for the Army of the Potomac, and if it was not the plan he would have preferred, at least it could be discussed and decisions made. As for the operations in the western theater, McClellan wrote Halleck, "It is very desirable to move all along the line by the 22d February, if possible."

McClellan's February 3 strategy paper confronted the president with a clear choice: he could either defer to his general-in-chief's conviction that the road to victory must begin with an advance on Richmond by way of the lower Chesapeake ("I will stake upon it the success of our cause"), or he could replace him with another general willing to campaign against the enemy's army in the immediate vicinity of Washington. There is no evidence that Lincoln seriously considered removing McClellan over this issue. What he insisted on, however, was a guarantee that the capital not be left in danger when McClellan took the army down the Chesapeake.

The president had reason to be concerned, for in accepting McClellan's view of the strategic situation, he was also accepting his view of the enemy. If the Confederate army on the Potomac was indeed as large as McClellan reported, and well led and well drilled and well equipped, could it not seize Washington in what the military textbooks he had been studying called a coup de main? McClellan might be right that instead General Johnston would rush southward to save Richmond (he "*must* do this"), but was this an absolute certainty? Mr. Lincoln would keep a very careful eye on the dispositions for guarding the capital.

The first need for the proposed offensive was shipping, and Stanton put Assistant Secretary of War John Tucker in charge of collecting an immense fleet of steamships, sailing vessels, barges, and tugs. McClellan intended to embark the initial force for Urbanna from Annapolis, directly on Chesapeake Bay. Once outflanked by the Urbanna landing, the Confederates (so he reasoned) would have to abandon their batteries on the lower Potomac, and his forces could then use the more direct river route from the capital.[3]

Events in the West suddenly started moving with a rush. This came about not so much from anything McClellan (or the president) willed, but because a Confederate deserter from Manassas reported that General Beauregard was being sent to Kentucky

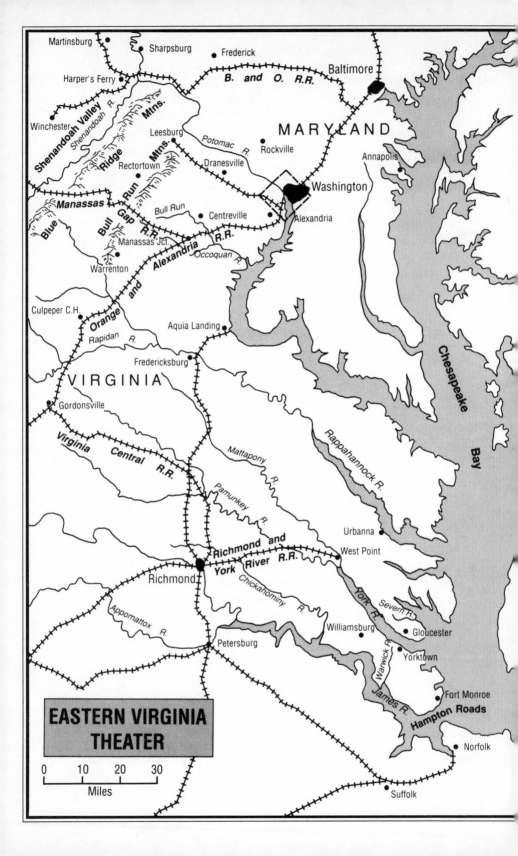

Martinsburg
Sharpsburg
Frederick
Baltimore
Harper's Ferry
B. and O. R.R.
MARYLAND
Winchester
Shenandoah Valley
Shenandoah R.
Mtns.
Leesburg
Potomac R.
Rockville
Annapolis
Ridge
Mtns.
Rectortown
Dranesville
Washington
Manassas
Bull Run
Centreville
Alexandria
Blue
Bull Run Gap R.R.
Manassas Jct.
Alexandria
Occoquan R.
R.R.
Warrenton
Orange and
Culpeper C.H.
Aquia Landing
Rapidan R.
Fredericksburg
VIRGINIA
Gordonsville
Virginia Central R.R.
Mattapony R.
Rappahannock R.
Pamunkey R.
Urbanna
Richmond and
West Point
York River R.R.
Richmond
Chickahominy R.
Appomattox R.
Williamsburg
Gloucester
York R.
Severn R.
Petersburg
Yorktown
Warwick R.
James R.
Fort Monroe
Hampton Roads
Norfolk
Chesapeake Bay

EASTERN VIRGINIA THEATER

0   10   20   30
Miles

Suffolk

and would take fifteen regiments with him. The story was half right, the fifteen regiments being simply a camp rumor, but the prospect of the famous Beauregard coming his way with a column of reinforcements was enough to persuade General Halleck to act before they arrived. He approved a plan that Brigadier Ulysses S. Grant and Flag Officer Andrew H. Foote had drawn up for a joint army-navy attack on Fort Henry, on the Tennessee River just below the Kentucky line. The fort surrendered on February 6, and ten days later nearby Fort Donelson, on the Cumberland, was also in Grant's hands, along with more than 12,000 of its defenders. With astonishing swiftness the center of the Confederates' line was pierced and the way to Tennessee thrown open.

McClellan could take no credit for initiating this offensive, but once it began he spent hours in the telegraph room pressuring his two generals, Halleck and Buell, to work in tandem. The advance up the rivers had pushed Buell reluctantly into an advance of his own, from central Kentucky toward Nashville, and he and Halleck did not see eye to eye on all matters. "There is evidently a little desire on the part of General H. to out general General B.," Thomas Scott warned Washington, and McClellan alternately calmed one and pushed the other. He displayed more confidence than Halleck in Grant's ultimate success in besieging Fort Donelson. "I have taken such steps as will make Grant safe & I think force the evacuation of Donelson or its surrender," he assured Stanton, and before the news of that surrender reached him he had cleared the telegraph wires for a three-way "conversation" with Halleck in St. Louis and Buell in Louisville on their next moves.

After Buell occupied Nashville on February 25, McClellan returned to the more leisurely policy of writing letters to his generals with ideas and suggestions for future movements. He thought Halleck might concentrate on taking Memphis and opening the Mississippi. It would be best if Buell moved on Chattanooga. He preferred discussing these matters to issuing directives. "Do write me fully your views as to future movements in the West," he urged Halleck. He deflected that general's effort to gain overall command of the western theater, intending to continue directing from Washington whatever joint action might be needed. That direction would have to wait, however, for at present he was fully occupied with the details of his own offensive.[4]

The rush of Union victories — in addition to Forts Henry and Donelson and Nashville, successful battles were fought at Mill Springs in eastern Kentucky and at Roanoke Island in North Carolina — brought a surge of optimism to the North. Under the heading "The End at Hand," a *New York Times* correspondent wrote, "The highest military authorities of our Government believe the Confederate rebellion to be hopelessly overthrown." The *Journal of Commerce* remarked on the efforts of the general-in-chief "and the debt of gratitude which the nation owes to him for all this success." The humorist Robert Henry Newell's commentator Orpheus C. Kerr assured his readers that General McClellan's genius "is equal to fifty yards of the Star Spangled Banner. His great Anaconda has gathered itself in a circle around the doomed rabbit of the rebellion, and if the rabbit swells he's a goner."

Among McClellan's detractors, however, these victories only made the continued idleness of the Army of the Potomac all the more noticeable. "We heard the echoes of victory from the West," Secretary Chase wrote, "but all was quiet on the Potomac." With McClellan's Urbanna scheme necessarily a secret, those wanting action, particularly newspaper editors, said it was time and past time for the Potomac army to take the field against an enemy within easy reach just twenty-five miles from the capital. To some, the failure to do so meant that General McClellan's heart was not in the war. Editor Richard Smith of the *Cincinnati Gazette* wrote a friend that before Fort Sumter McClellan was heard to say that the South was in the right and that the nation was best off when ruled by Southern Democrats. "Can the ethiopian change his skin or the leopard his spots?" Smith asked. Horace Greeley, completing his about-face, suspected the general of an even baser motive. The *Tribune* wondered if he was holding back from a concern "that he would be likely to kill several thousand good voters, whom he might need in 1864 when he runs for President as the candidate of the reunited and reinvigorated Sham Democracy."

In reply, the *Journal of Commerce* assured its readers that the general "has no selfish ends, . . . no political anticipations to gratify." Having months before declared his party allegiance in the house of his enemies, however, it was inevitable that McClellan would be judged by the company he kept. Samuel Barlow, a leader of the conservative Democratic faction in New York and a man hated by the radicals (so he told McClellan) in the same way the devil hated holy water, found it necessary to write the newspapers branding as "wicked" and "simply absurd" attempts to put his political sentiments into the general's mouth.

George Gibbs, his old friend from the Pacific railroad survey, hoped McClellan would reject all political partisanship in favor of political persuasion. Gibbs wrote him that Senator Solomon Foot, a moderate Republican from Vermont, told of being turned away from McClellan's headquarters because the general commanding was conferring with Samuel S. Cox and Clement L. Vallandigham, Democratic politicians regarded by Gibbs as so lukewarm toward the war that he characterized them as "dogs." He wanted McClellan to make it a point of meeting instead with Republican moderates like Foot: "Talk to them openly and candidly — tell them why you have not done this & why you have done that.... If you leave here with your rear undefended, your tenure of office is not worth a week's purchase." McClellan continued to cultivate support in the newspaper war, but if he made any effort to strike an alliance with congressional moderates it is not on the record.[5]

On February 19 Ben Wade and Andrew Johnson of the Joint Committee on the Conduct of the War called on Secretary Stanton to complain of the continuing Confederate grip on the Potomac above and below Washington. Stanton agreed that this partial blockade of the capital was irksome and humiliating. McClellan happened to be at the War Department just then, and Stanton called him in. McClellan explained that he was aware of these problems and was planning to act on them as soon as his preparations were complete. He said he could not order his men into hostile Virginia without the precaution of securing a line of retreat. This was just what he had told the committee more than a month earlier, and it infuriated Senator Wade. In what the committee's journal termed "pretty strong and emphatic language," he stormed at the general that he commanded 150,000 of the best troops in the world, who should be able to beat any force the enemy could bring against them, "and if any of them come back, let them come back in their coffins." McClellan said nothing. It did not escape his notice that Secretary Stanton made no effort to defend him. A few days later General Marsena Patrick recorded in his diary the talk around headquarters that Stanton was "running a jealous opposition to McClellan — sold out to the Tribune & thwarting McClellan in every possible way...." The general, it was said, was fully aware of the cabal plotting to remove him from command.

The unrelenting pressure to clear the upper and lower Potomac of Confederates — or simply the more general pressure to take action of any kind to demonstrate that the immense Army of the Potomac was good for something — put McClellan in a particular quandary. If his Urbanna strategy was to work, Joe Johnston must remain unsuspecting at Manassas and Centreville as long as possible. Even though the plan included a cavalry raid to destroy key railroad bridges north of Richmond, it was still an open question whether he could land and build up his forces by water faster than Johnston could withdraw to his capital by rail. Chief Engineer John Barnard warned him that this was the flaw in the plan. In any event, McClellan worried that any threat to either of Johnston's flanks might cause him to pull back and spoil everything, and he wrote later that in obeying the urgings of Lincoln and Stanton to act on the Potomac, he was going against his best judgment. At the time, however, he made no written protest that is on record. Indeed, in view of his determined pattern of reticence, it is not even certain that he discussed these concerns with them.[6]

The task on the upper Potomac was to reopen the Baltimore and Ohio's direct link to the Ohio Valley. Even as Senator Wade raged at him, the finishing touches were being put on a plan for rebuilding the railroad's demolished bridge at Harper's Ferry and protecting the line to the west, where Stonewall Jackson had been raiding it during the winter. On February 26, under McClellan's approving eye, Federal engineers threw a light pontoon bridge across the Potomac at Harper's Ferry, and elements of General Nathaniel Banks's division crossed into Virginia. "As they touched the sacred soil their enthusiasm knew no bounds, the bands played, and the air was filled with shouting," one of the engineers wrote in his diary. Telegraphing the news to Stanton, McClellan called for the engineers to be brevetted for the feat, and said the troops were "in the mood to fight anything."

The next day brought him a rude shock. To cross over the heavy reinforcements and supplies needed to take Winchester and hold the lower Shenandoah Valley against Jackson's incursions, a permanent bridge was to be constructed of timbers laid across canal boats anchored in the river. These craft had been floated to the site on the Chesapeake and Ohio Canal paralleling the Potomac and were to be passed through a lift lock into the river. Only when everything was ready for the bridge building was it discovered that the lock was six inches too narrow to admit the canal boats. After some hasty checking the red-faced engineers had to admit that the case was beyond saving. It seemed that this particular lock was designed to transfer the smaller craft that plied the nearby Shenandoah Canal. To the army engineers one canal boat looked much like another, and no one had thought to measure either boats or lock.

McClellan telegraphed Stanton that he was scaling down his plan: now he could maintain only enough troops on the Virginia shore to protect the railroad's construction crews while they rebuilt the Harper's Ferry bridge. Orders for the reinforcements were countermanded. Taking Winchester and sealing the Shenandoah Valley would have to wait.

In a fury, the secretary of war hurried to the White House with the dispatches. "It means that it is a damned fizzle," he said in reply to the president's question. "It means that he doesn't intend to do anything." Chief of Staff Marcy, who had remained behind to handle affairs at army headquarters, was called in for what presidential secretary John Nicolay termed "a long and sharp talk." The fact that Mr. Lincoln's temper was displayed so rarely was no comfort to poor Marcy. "Why in the Nation, General Marcy, couldn't the General have known whether a boat would go through that lock before spending a million dollars getting them there?" the president demanded. "I am no engineer, but it seems to me that if I wished to know whether a boat would go through a hole or a lock, common sense would teach me to go and measure it. I am almost despairing at these results. Everything seems to fail. The general impression is daily gaining ground that the General does not intend to do anything." Marcy started to say that he was sure General McClellan could explain everything, but Lincoln dismissed him brusquely.

The president had not entirely cooled off two days later when he described the affair for Senator Sumner. "He expressed himself angrily" and has made up his mind "to talk plainly" to the general, Sumner wrote. Horace White, a correspondent for the *Chicago Tribune*, wrote his editor that Lincoln "swore like a Philistine ... & there was wailing & gnashing of teeth among the imperial staff.... Inextinguishable laughter has been the result...." Before long it was all over Washington that the Harper's Ferry expedition had died of lockjaw.

As it happened, all the objectives of the expedition were in time carried out. The Harper's Ferry railroad bridge was reconstructed and the rest of the line put in order, and in due course General Banks occupied Winchester and the lower Shenandoah. Yet the impression lingered of ineffectual fumbling, of a grand scheme brought to ground ignominiously. "It was Ball's Bluff all over again, minus the slaughter," correspondent White remarked, and if that was an unjust appraisal, it was how a growing army of McClellan detractors viewed the matter.[7]

The day after he returned from Harper's Ferry, McClellan met with several of his officers to work out a plan to open the lower Potomac. Seizing the Rebel batteries there required (as he wrote General Halleck) "a movement of the whole Army in order to keep 'Manassas' off my back." He counted on the *Monitor*, the new Union ironclad of radical design then undergoing final trials at New York, to help reduce the batteries. If he could also keep the abolitionists off his back, he added, he would soon embark his army "for the region of sandy roads & short land transportation."

He went on to describe for Halleck his "undying hate" of the radicals who were doing their best to drive him from his command. George McClellan was not one to suffer criticism lightly, and in these difficult weeks he frequently grew angry and depressed. A few days later, attending the funeral of one of his officers, he confided to William Franklin that he almost wished it were he who was in the coffin. Ellen shared his sense of injustice at the attacks. She was greatly annoyed, she told her mother-in-law, "that any one should *dare* to breathe one word against a man who is so entirely pure & free from a selfish thought in this matter."[8]

McClellan called a meeting of his generals for the morning of March 8 to announce the Potomac operation. At an early hour that day, however, he was summoned to the White House for what he described in his memoirs as "a very peculiar" private interview. The president seems to have spoken plainly, as he had told Senator Sumner he intended to do. By McClellan's account, he expressed dissatisfaction with the outcome of the Harper's Ferry expedition, and then turned to what he termed "a very ugly matter." He had been told, he said, that the real motive behind McClellan's plan for taking the army down the Chesapeake was his "traitorous" intention to leave Washington open to capture by the enemy.

At this, McClellan wrote, he jumped to his feet and "in a manner perhaps not altogether decorous towards the chief magistrate" demanded a retraction of the charge. Lincoln explained that he was only repeating what others had said. "I warned him to be careful, & again told him that I would not permit him to cast the slightest doubt upon my intentions." He declared he would submit his Urbanna plan to a vote of his generals, who would be gathering shortly at headquarters, so that the president could decide for himself "whether I was a traitor or not."

An element of improbability marks McClellan's recollection of this interview. There is no evidence that either Lincoln or anyone else in the small circle who then knew of the Urbanna plan believed the general was a traitor, whatever else they may have thought of him. Perhaps the president tried to warn him — as he repeatedly warned him later — that in the highly charged political atmosphere of the time he could not protect him much longer unless he produced some prompt military success to silence the charges against his loyalty by radical critics. In any event, his effort at plain talk failed; all that McClellan took away from the encounter was the mention of disloyalty.

His twelve generals were surprised to find themselves constituting a council of war. McClellan outlined his scheme and then left them with two main questions to decide: whether the army should change its base of operations from Washington to the lower Chesapeake; and what was to be done about the Confederate batteries blockading the Potomac. The council favored the Urbanna movement by a vote of eight to four. Opposing it were Chief Engineer Barnard and the three senior generals, Edwin Sumner, Irvin McDowell, and Samuel Heintzelman; Erasmus Keyes, fourth in seniority, qualified his approval with the condition that the Potomac be opened first. Barnard, who considered the movement impractical, complained that the vote was taken with virtually no discussion; McDowell and Heintzelman saw it simply as a vote of confidence in the general commanding. That, Marcy had told Heintzelman and perhaps others, was the real issue before the council. A majority, by a vote of seven to five, also endorsed McClellan's view on the Potomac batteries, saying their destruction need not be the first step in the operation.

The generals were called to the White House to present their findings to the president and Secretary Stanton. Stanton questioned them sharply and at length to be sure they understood what they had voted for. Only McDowell and Sumner favored an immediate offensive to open the Potomac, which led Stanton to say to John Hay the next day "We saw ten Generals afraid to fight." Lincoln, on the other hand, was relieved that a decision was finally reached. "I don't care, gentlemen, what plan you have," McDowell quoted him as saying; "all I ask is for you to just pitch in!" McClellan's reaction is not on record, but he was surely pleased that he had been vindicated.[9]

Immediately following the meeting the president issued two additional war orders. The first organized the divisions of the Army of the Potomac scheduled to take the field into four corps, under Sumner, McDowell, Heintzelman, and Keyes. The forces on the upper Potomac would make up a fifth corps, under Nathaniel Banks, and the defenses of Washington were assigned to James S. Wadsworth. The second order directed that the capital be left "entirely secure" in the judgment of both McClellan and the corps commanders, and that the movement to the lower Chesapeake begin no later than March 18, ten days hence; no more than two corps were to embark, however, until the Potomac was opened to navigation.

Although McClellan predictably took offense at these presidential war orders, they were in fact simply restatements of his own views, or decisions made necessary by his obstinate refusal to act even when his best interests were at stake. The requirement that the capital be left secure did nothing more than affirm the pledge he had already made, and the order that the Potomac be opened was insurance in case his prediction that the Confederates would abandon their batteries proved wrong and the Federals had to return to the capital by the shortest route in an emergency. The March 18 deadline was based on the opinion of the generals at the war council and was within the timetable he had already privately established.

It was the order forming army corps without consulting him that particularly offended McClellan. Every military expert the president had consulted — including the members of the war council that day — recommended the appointment of corps commanders. McClellan had repeatedly promised to do so himself, yet kept putting it off until he had tested his generals in battle. But there had been no battles large or small, except Ball's Bluff, and carrying his promise to its logical conclusion (as Mr. Lincoln apparently did) meant that in the coming climactic fight for Richmond General McClellan would have to direct personally a dozen divisions, perhaps 130,000 men, on the field of battle. Even Napoleon had relied on his marshals, and the president thought it equal wisdom that the army's four senior generals serve the Young Napoleon as corps commanders. It is doubtful that McClellan could have ignored the army's reverence for seniority in making the appointments himself, but by acting earlier he might at least have won over these senior generals to his plans.

He was equally unhappy about the appointment of General Wadsworth, a wealthy New York landowner completely lacking in military training (and a professed abolitionist in the bargain). Yet this assignment, as bad as it surely was, need never have been made. Nearly two months earlier, on January 14, McClellan had written Major General John A. Dix, in command at Baltimore, to tell him that the "very delicate & responsible position" at Washington would be his when the army took the field. Dix, one of the administration's first military appointees, was energetic and capable and widely respected as an administrator. Nothing would have benefited George McClellan more in the crucial weeks to come than having his own man in charge of the capital's defenses; why he did not follow through on Dix's appointment when he still had the confidence of Lincoln and Stanton seems inexplicable.[10]

The answer may be (as Secretary Chase believed) that he was simply overtaxed. His records from this first winter of the war are filled with projects begun and not followed up, of promises made and not kept. Plans for seizing Norfolk, and with it the ironclad *Merrimack*, were often discussed, for example, but nothing ever quite came of them. "I will try to write more fully tonight," he assured Buell at one point; three weeks later when he fell ill the letter was still unwritten, and such delays were not uncommon in his dealings with subordinates. His reluctance to delegate authority meant that trivia in vast quantities crossed his desk every day. He immersed himself in the smallest administrative details, to the extent of arguing the cost of ordnance metal on behalf of a small Ohio foundry, or directing the president of the Baltimore and Ohio Railroad to a supplier of bridge-building equipment. He failed to follow up or develop a largely superficial report by the Corps of Topographical Engineers on the geography and topography of the Richmond area, so that one of his officers would subsequently label that theater of war *terra incognita*. No one was responsible for interpreting the mass of intelligence information, much of it contradictory, furnished by detective Pinkerton, unless it was the general himself, with the consequence that his view of Joe Johnston's army was as improbable in March 1862 as it had been in August 1861.[11]

Even as the war council was putting its stamp of approval on the Urbanna movement, the Confederates proceeded to upset all of McClellan's plans. The *Merrimack,* the constant subject of rumor and spies' reports over the past months, steamed out of Norfolk into Hampton Roads and destroyed two of the navy's big wooden frigates and drove a third aground. News of the disaster reached Washington the next morning, March 9. McClellan joined other officers and Cabinet secretaries at the White House that Sunday in an atmosphere of crisis. He telegraphed General Dix at Baltimore and other commanders in major seaboard cities to be on the alert should the *Merrimack* finish off the rest of the blockading fleet and go on a rampage up the coast. On Stanton's instructions he pressed arrangements to sink scows loaded with stone to block the Potomac if the Rebel ironclad tried to reach Washington. "I think we will find the danger less as we learn more . . . ," he told Stanton; "nevertheless we must take it for granted that the worst will happen." The one note of hope came late in the day with a report that the Union's ironclad *Monitor,* which had reached Hampton Roads the previous night, met the *Merrimack* when she reappeared and fought her to a draw.

Telegrams arrived from other quarters with equally startling news. General Banks reported the enemy abandoning his posts on the upper Potomac. From downriver came word that the Confederates had spiked their guns and demolished their battery positions along the lower Potomac. An outpost in Virginia reported the arrival of a contraband who said the Rebel army at Manassas Junction and Centreville was gone. McClellan hurried across the river to confirm the news for himself. "I am arranging to move forward to push the retreat of rebels as far as possible," he telegraphed the president and Secretary Stanton that evening.[12]

The next day the entire army at Washington, 112,000 strong, was in motion toward Manassas and Centreville. The lead divisions advanced in careful order, ready for battle. From the camps north of the capital long columns of marching men filled the city's avenues and crowded the bridges across the Potomac. In expectation of going to war, men made their wills and wrote their farewell letters. Sidewalks were thronged with scenes of tender leave taking. On H Street General McClellan made his parting from his wife, wrote a reporter, "according to the approved Hector and Andromache fashion." The Prince de Joinville encountered the general on one of the Potomac bridges in a jam of lumbering artillery batteries, "on horseback, with an anxious air, riding alone, without aids-de-camp, and escorted only by a few troopers."[13]

Like the Harper's Ferry expedition, however, the Manassas march soon concluded on a decided note of anticlimax. The Confederates had abandoned their fortifications without detection and with a twenty-four-hour lead slipped away southward to new positions behind the Rappahannock River. McClellan let them go unmolested. The latest intelligence estimates of the numbers Joe Johnston might bring against any pursuit ranged from 70,000 to 102,500; as a matter of course, he accepted the higher figure. (The actual count was less than 48,000.)

The scheme for a surprise landing on the Rappahannock at Urbanna was now gone beyond recovery. McClellan put the best possible face on his disappointment for his civilian and newspaper supporters. He explained to Barlow that his movements were responsible for driving the Confederates from their strongholds.

"History will, when I am in my grave, record it as the brightest passage of my life ..." he wrote; "all I ask of the papers is that they should defend me from the most malicious attacks...."

The malicious attacks were not long in coming. McClellan thoroughly inspected the enemy's works and pronounced them formidable. He could not mention what he had suspected for some weeks and what correspondents with the advance soon discovered — several dozen embrasures containing logs painted black, soon to be notorious as "Quaker guns." Militarily this wooden ordnance (as one paper called it) proved of no more consequence than the undersized lift lock at Harper's Ferry, but in the court of public opinion it counted as another considerable embarrassment. "We have been humbugged by the rebels," the New York diarist George Templeton Strong concluded, and it was a common enough opinion. A reporter for the *Tribune* was reminded of the Chinese trick of frightening enemies "by the sound of gongs and the wearing of devils' masks." McClellan wanted Secretary Stanton to understand that storming these works "would have been a desperate affair," which was no doubt true enough but overlooked the fact that the Occoquan flanking plan urged upon him for so long had nothing in it about assaulting fortifications head-on.

He quickly determined to proceed with a revised plan of campaign against Richmond, taking as his new base Union-held Fort Monroe, at the tip of the Virginia peninsula bounded by the James and York rivers. He had listed Fort Monroe as a "worst coming to the worst" alternative to Urbanna in his February 3 strategy paper, noting that it promised "complete security, altho' with less celerity & brilliancy of results...." Now it was his sole alternative to an overland march.[14]

He would undertake the campaign, however, solely in the role of army commander. On March 11, at a Cabinet meeting, the president announced his latest war order: "Major General McClellan having personally taken the field at the head of the Army of the Potomac, until otherwise ordered, he is relieved from the command of the other Military departments...." By the same order, General Halleck assumed overall command in the western theater. No new general-in-chief was named. Lincoln and Stanton would run the war themselves for the time being, and the phrase "until otherwise ordered" suggested that McClellan might well resume the post when his campaign was successfully completed. That, at any rate, was how he interpreted it. Former Ohio governor William Dennison was delegated to deliver the order personally to the general, and along with it the assurance that he retained the president's full confidence and would command the Potomac army wherever it might go.

When McClellan received a telegram from Chief of Staff Marcy summoning him to Washington to see Dennison on an urgent matter, he took it as the start of another move by those plotting his downfall. He was in a dispirited state of mind. He had endured having a mere civilian, albeit the commander-in-chief, challenge his best professional view of grand strategy, and after finally winning that battle had seen his hard-won plans upset by the enemy. His ego was bruised by Quaker guns and a too-small canal lock. He had had his army arbitrarily reorganized under generals for whom he had little use. Now, as he told a correspondent for the *New York World,* it seemed possible ''I should be denied the satisfaction of leading the Army of the Potomac to victory & of sharing the fruit of the work of many months.'' He replied to Marcy, ''I think the less I see of Washington the better,'' and remained in the field. That night he wrote Ellen, ''I regret that the rascals are after me again. . . . If I can get out of this scrape you will never catch me in the power of such a set again. . . .''

As a consequence, he first learned of his removal as general-in-chief from the next day's newspapers (a humiliation he later blamed on the administration). But when he finally met Dennison and learned the whole story he was reassured, and he wrote Lincoln to thank him ''most sincerely for the official confidence & kind personal feelings you entertain for me.'' He pledged that ''under present circumstances I shall work just as cheerfully as ever before. . . .''[15]

In time he would come to see this command change very differently, describing it as part of an intrigue ''to secure the failure of the approaching campaign.'' A better explanation is that the president believed it impossible for McClellan to fight his way to Richmond and at the same time successfully direct all the other Union armies. Another factor, according to a War Department official, was that pressure on the president and secretary of war had grown so unendurable that ''the only relief was by a change, which really does not injure McClellan. . . . If the movement is well managed . . . , he will no doubt regain his former standing & position.''

George McClellan's chief accomplishments during his four months as general-in-chief were the activist interpretation he gave to the position and the formulation of a grand strategy for prosecuting the war. For two years the Union cause would flounder until another general with the same vision, U. S. Grant, took over the post. Yet at the same time, McClellan's chief failing — his persistent unwillingness to make common cause with the civilians charged with managing the war — virtually nullified his accomplishments. By resolutely refusing to share with Lincoln either his knowledge or his confidence, by dismissing as mere clamor the concerns of public opinion and the political realities of the time, he squandered nearly all the trust and support that earlier had been his without question. When he wrote Barlow, on March 16, ''*The President is all right* — he is my strongest friend,'' he might have said more accurately that within the administration the commander-in-chief was now one of his very few friends.[16]

He called the corps commanders with him into council on March 13 and gained their unanimous vote in favor of the Fort Monroe plan. The president promptly endorsed the movement to the Peninsula, ''or anywhere between here and there,'' as long as the army set out at once and Washington and Manassas were left well garrisoned. The armada of vessels being collected at Annapolis was shifted to Alexandria, a few miles down the Potomac from the capital, and the army ordered there for embarkation.

The next day, in an address to his troops, McClellan announced that the moment for action had arrived at last. ''I will bring you now face to face with the rebels . . . ,'' he told them; ''ever bear in mind that my fate is linked with yours. . . . I am to watch over you as a parent over his children; and you know that your General loves you from the depths of his heart.'' In delivering the death blow to the rebellion he would demand of them ''great, heroic exertions, rapid and long marches, desperate combats, privations, perhaps.'' For his peroration he borrowed from Napoleon's address to his army after the Italian campaign: ''. . . . and when this sad war is over we will all return to our homes, and feel that we can ask no higher honor than the proud consciousness that we belonged to the ARMY OF THE POTOMAC.'' A man in an engineer regiment thought it right on the mark: "The document is quite Napoleonic in its style and sings finely."

On March 17, 1862, one day before the president's deadline, the first transports loaded with troops set sail from Alexandria for the Peninsula. "I shall soon leave here on the wing for Richmond — which you may be sure I will take," McClellan announced to Barlow. "The Army is in magnificent spirits, & I think are half glad that I now belong to them alone."[17]

EIGHT

ON THE PENINSULA

THE PASSAGE of the Army of the Potomac to the Peninsula was one of the spectacular sights of the Civil War. Day after day an enormous parade of ships shuttled back and forth on the Potomac and the Chesapeake — steamers of every description, sailing schooners, barges under tow — in all almost 400 vessels in an operation John Tucker of the War Department described as "without a parallel on record." In twenty days, Tucker reported, this armada transported 121,500 men, 44 artillery batteries, 1,150 wagons, nearly 15,600 horses and mules, and a mountain of equipment ranging from pontoon trains to telegraph wire. In the Hampton Roads anchorage the Prince de Joinville counted at any one time ships by the hundreds, with twenty or twenty-five big transports packed tight with troops waiting their turn to disembark. An English observer termed it "the stride of a giant."[1]

Yet behind the scenes these last weeks of March 1862 were a precarious time for George McClellan. Nathaniel Hawthorne, observing the scene in Washington, wrote home that "the outcry opened against General McClellan, since the enemy's retreat from Manassas, is really terrible, and almost universal...." Members of the Joint Committee on the Conduct of the War visited the abandoned Manassas fortifications, where they inspected the derisive wooden ordnance and were told that the enemy had been evacuating the position for three weeks before the general caught on to what was happening, and they returned in high dudgeon. On March 16 Samuel Ward, a lobbyist with good connections in the capital, told Samuel Barlow that McClellan was in disgrace with the president and especially with Secretary of War Stanton, who was heard to pronounce him "a dead failure." The next day

Republican radicals in the Senate were blocked only by parliamentary maneuvering from bringing to a floor vote a resolution calling for the general's dismissal.

To help him and the president manage the war, Secretary Stanton established the War Board, made up of heads of the army bureaus and General Ethan Allen Hitchcock, who had been General Scott's chief of staff in Mexico and who by reputation seemed to promise military advice of a high order. Hitchcock was sixty-three and in poor health, however, and the depth of his thinking would prove to be limited, perhaps not surprising in view of his profound interest in alchemy and the occult. Hitchcock was flabbergasted when, on March 15, without any preliminaries, Stanton offered him command of the Army of the Potomac. He hastily declined. "I am still uncomfortable," he wrote in his diary that night. "I am almost afraid that Secretary Stanton hardly knows what he wants, himself." As if to prove the point, not long afterward Stanton told Senator Orville Browning, an Illinois friend of the president's, that if he would propose to Lincoln that another old regular, Colonel Napoleon Bonaparte Buford, be made major general and head of the Potomac army, he would vigorously support the nomination.

It cannot be imagined that Lincoln knew of these offers beforehand, or that he would have given a thought to either one had he been told of them. Stanton's frantic, spur-of-the-moment actions were simply demonstrations of his complete loss of faith in General McClellan. The president continued to follow his own course in the matter. "He has declared so emphatically that he will not back down on Mac," Democratic senator Benjamin Stark wrote with satisfaction to Barlow, "that the hounds in and out of Congress have ceased their yelpings," although he feared "it is only for a time." In a conversation that Senator Browning recorded in his diary, the president explained that he had taken the measure of General McClellan as best he could and was satisfied that "he had the capacity to make arrangements properly for a great conflict...." As the moment for action approached, however, "he became nervous and oppressed with the responsibility and hesitated to meet the crisis," but he said McClellan now understood that he was expected to move, "and he must do it."[2]

In addition to arranging the transfer of the army to the Peninsula, McClellan had to give thought to Mr. Lincoln's injunction that no campaign was to begin "without leaving in, and about Washington" a sufficient force to ensure the capital's safety. This appeared to pose no problem. In voting their approval of the Peninsula plan, McClellan's corps commanders had specified that the Washington garrison be supported by an additional 25,000 men in "a covering force in front of the Virginia line." To meet this requirement McClellan assigned a brigade of General Banks's Fifth Corps to remain in the Shenandoah Valley to guard communications and ordered the rest of the corps to the area around Manassas Junction to serve as the capital's covering force.

After March 23, however, the problem suddenly became complicated. On that date, Stonewall Jackson attacked the Federals in the Shenandoah at Kernstown, near Winchester. As it happened, Jackson was sharply repulsed, but the incident was disquieting nonetheless. "His movement on Winchester was most mysterious to me," Chief of Staff Marcy observed, and so it seemed. McClellan directed that until Jackson was disposed of, Banks and most of his command would have to remain in the Shenandoah. That in turn upset his calculations for the Washington covering force, and to resolve the difficulty he resorted to juggling numbers, with grievous consequences to his credibility.[3]

Possibly he was impelled to this course by the president's announcement, on March 31, that he was detaching Louis Blenker's division from the Army of the Potomac to serve with John Charles Frémont, the radicals' threadbare hero, in a renewed advance on East Tennessee. Lincoln admitted that political pressure was behind the move, and although McClellan assured him that he would "cheerfully acquiesce in your decision without any mental reservation," he decided to cut a corner or two to prevent any further weakening of the Peninsula army.

In a report on April 1 to the War Department, he explained that he was leaving 18,000 men to garrison the Washington fortifications and some 55,500 more in a covering force, making a comforting total of 73,500. When Stanton and Lincoln looked more closely at these figures, however, they discovered the numbers did not mean exactly what General McClellan said they meant. Of that impressive covering force, for example, almost two-thirds was not "in, and about Washington" at all, but eighty miles away in the Shenandoah Valley. On further investigation, it became clear as well that the general had papered over a large enough number of cracks in his argument to make the whole report suspect. He had counted one of Banks's brigades twice. Four of General Wadsworth's Washington regiments were also listed in two places at the same time, and his garrison had 3,000 fewer men to begin with than McClellan gave it. A contingent of 3,500 men were recruits still in Pennsylvania, who might or might not appear as scheduled. Blenker's division was counted with Banks in the Valley (with Stanton's approval), but in due course it would have to join Frémont as ordered. When all this was sorted out, it was found that the general was actually leaving only 26,700 men at Washington and Manassas; of equal concern, most of the troops in the capital garrison were the rawest of recruits, mustered into service just a week or two earlier. "When the Presdt. became aware of this," Senator Sumner reported, "he was justly indignant."[4]

McClellan would argue that in fact the forces he left to defend Washington, and their placement, entirely met the case. For anyone to say otherwise, he wrote in his memoirs, "is an untruth which proves either complete ignorance or wilful malevolence." As he reckoned the situation, Johnston's army posed no further threat to Washington, for in withdrawing behind the Rappahannock it had destroyed the railroad bridge across the river. The Confederates would surely not campaign that way again without a railroad to support them. (General McClellan would never attempt such a thing, and he could not think so good a general as Joe Johnston would either.) "It seems clear that we have no reason to fear any return of the rebels in that quarter," he wrote Banks. If by some chance they did dare such a move, they would have to rebuild bridge and tracks as they came, giving Banks plenty of time to reach the scene from the Valley.

Having assured himself on that score, he made no effort to assure the president and the secretary of war, the two men who most needed to understand his reasoning, and as soon as he sent off his manpower report to the War Department he set sail in the steamer *Commodore* for Fort Monroe. By now his contempt for his civilian superiors outweighed even considerations of self-interest. "I feared that if I remained at Alexandria I would be annoyed very much & perhaps be sent for from Washn," he wrote

Ellen late that afternoon as the *Commodore* steamed down the Potomac. "Officially speaking, I feel very glad to get away from that sink of iniquity...."[5]

No doubt his confidence would have been greater had he successfully pursued the appointment of General Dix to the Washington command. As it was, Wadsworth and Hitchcock and the bureau generals of the War Board saw only that he had not obeyed the president's orders to the letter. What if the enemy was willing to give up Richmond and concentrate against Washington, Quartermaster General Meigs asked at one of the War Board meetings. "That would be an act of desperation," Hitchcock replied. "It is one which a great man would take," Meigs said.

The president, too, was gravely concerned that the Confederate army, which as far as anyone in the administration had been told still numbered up to 150,000 highly trained soldiers, might be sorely tempted to send a powerful force back from the Rappahannock to sack Washington. A sudden hit-and-run raid might not be militarily sound by McClellan's way of thinking, but it would have a disastrous political impact at home and especially abroad, where recognition of the Confederacy was under debate. It was a danger the administration could not ignore — indeed, in the next few weeks the Confederates would consider just such a move — and in that event General McClellan's dispositions would be sorely tested.[6]

McClellan reached Fort Monroe on the afternoon of April 2 and conferred into the early hours of the morning with his generals and Flag Officer Louis M. Goldsborough, commander of the blockading squadron at Hampton Roads. "The grass will not grow under my feet," he assured Ellen in his daily telegram, and he was as good as his word. He issued orders on April 3 for an advance to begin the following day against the Confederate stronghold at Yorktown. He would have 53,000 fighting men and a hundred guns for the work ahead. He was dismayed by notice from Washington that General John E. Wool would retain control of the Fort Monroe garrison, but Wool promised him full support. He told Ellen that he expected to have Yorktown in two days and then push on up the Peninsula. "The great battle will be (I think) near Richmond as I have always hoped & thought. I see my way very clearly...."[7]

His plan of operations had undergone certain revisions over

the past few weeks. One of the original attractions of the Peninsula route to Richmond was the promise that the navy's gunboats, in control of both the James and York rivers, would guarantee secure logistics almost to the gates of Richmond and at the same time guard the army's flanks as it advanced. The *Merrimack* changed that notion drastically by denying the James to the Union navy. McClellan suggested obstructing the Norfolk channel to bottle up the Rebel ironclad. The navy said it would be glad to cooperate in such a venture as soon as the army disposed of the batteries guarding the channel. The army replied it would attempt that if the *Monitor* would first reduce the batteries. The navy refused to risk any mishap to the *Monitor* as long as the *Merrimack* remained a threat. There the matter rested, and McClellan had to take the James River out of his calculations.

In outlining his plan to Secretary Stanton on March 19, he had named his immediate objective as West Point, where the Pamunkey and Mattapony rivers join to form the York. West Point was the terminus of the Richmond and York River Railroad, the means by which he planned to support his army in the final advance against the Confederate capital. The key to West Point, in turn, was the York. It was blocked near its mouth by batteries at Yorktown and Gloucester, between which the river narrowed to a channel only a thousand yards wide. Yorktown and Gloucester might be reduced by siege operations lasting several weeks, he said, or the blockade might be blown apart if the navy threw "its whole available force, its most powerful vessels, against Yorktown. There is the most important point — there the knot to be cut." Naval cooperation was an "absolute necessity" for prompt and decisive results.

It presently developed that once again the navy could not oblige General McClellan. Flag Officer Goldsborough was pledged to keep the *Merrimack* from cutting the army's supply line, and that required the full-time attention not only of the *Monitor* but of the largest of the navy's other warships as well. This left only the smaller wooden gunboats to cooperate with the army, and they were considered no match for well-sited shore batteries; in any case, their guns could not be elevated sufficiently to reach the batteries atop Yorktown's bluffs. Goldsborough promised full support for any landings the army might make to storm or turn these batteries, but a head-on attack by the gunboats was out of

the question. McClellan would later condemn Goldsborough as
"too timid," but at the time the flag officer's concern was understandable. The *Merrimack* was thought to be a genuinely fear-
some engine of war, and the pounding that Union gunboats had
taken in February at Fort Donelson — armored gunboats, it was
noted — could not be shrugged off. General McClellan had no
monopoly on overestimating Confederate prowess.

All this had been reported to him before he left Washington,
so he went fully prepared for siege operations. Orders had gone
out to assemble the heaviest ordnance available. On March 28 he
had written General Totten of the engineers that his campaign
would open with an advance on Yorktown and Gloucester, and
"this *may* involve a siege (at least I go prepared for one) in case
the Navy is not able to afford the means of destroying the rebel
batteries at these points." He would first attempt to seize Yorktown by maneuver, however. Expecting to find 15,000 Rebels
entrenched there, he planned to send a flanking column past the
citadel to cut it off from Richmond, "unless they abandon the
place on our approach."[8]

On the morning of April 5 his advance guard reported encoun-
tering a line of fortifications extending all the way across the
Peninsula, from Yorktown to the James. The Warwick River
flowed like a moat in front of these works, and much of the ground
was marshy and impassable. It was raining hard, and the roads
that were supposed to be firm and passable in all seasons were
already muddy bogs. Troops "were seen crowding the ram-
parts...," Fitz John Porter noted in his report of the day's
action. "Our fire was warmly returned...."

General McClellan professed surprise at these discoveries. He
claimed he had been misled into thinking he could outflank Yorktown, and it is true enough that his maps were inaccurate and
his topographic research faulty and Pinkerton's intelligence scanty
and three months out of date. Even so, that did not explain why
he had believed his old Mexican War comrade John Bankhead
Magruder, in command on the Peninsula, would be so incompetent a general as to leave Yorktown wide open to a turning movement. However that may be, he made no effort to test the actual
strength of Magruder's lines, and by midday orders had gone
back to Fort Monroe to bring up the siege train. "I cannot turn
Yorktown without a *battle,* in which I must use heavy artillery

& go through the preliminary operations of a siege,'' he explained to Flag Officer Goldsborough.[9]

Magruder had been known in the old army as Prince John for his theatrical flamboyance, and from the moment the first Yankee scouts appeared before his lines he exercised his special talents and stage-managed his 11,000 men into a force seemingly far more formidable. ''This morning we were called out by the 'Long Roll' and have been traveling most of the day, seeming with no other view than to show ourselves to the enemy at as many different points of the line as possible,'' an Alabama soldier wrote in his journal. ''I am pretty tired....'' That evening General Heintzelman observed in his journal, ''The enemy's force is much larger than we anticipated.''

The illusion Magruder created no doubt had its effect, but the strongest impact on McClellan's mind that day was made by his finding the enemy where he was not supposed to be. As he had demonstrated at Rich Mountain and would demonstrate again on other battlefields, he was invariably brought up short by the unexpected. Applying immediate and hard pressure to seek some weakness in these fortifications would cost lives, perhaps to no purpose. Besieging Yorktown was the safer and surer way; a siege was one kind of warfare George McClellan knew a great deal about and was certain he could win. With that, the English observer remarked, the stride of the giant became the step of a dwarf.[10]

A few hours after making his decision to put Yorktown under siege, McClellan received a dispatch from Washington announcing that McDowell's First Corps was being held back by the president, who (it was subsequently explained) regarded ''the force to be left in front of Washington insufficient to insure its safety....'' McClellan's reaction was disbelief and outrage. He pleaded with Lincoln to reconsider: if the order stood, ''in my deliberate judgment the success of our cause will be imperilled.... I am now of the opinion that I shall have to fight all of the available force of the Rebels not far from here. Do not force me to do so with diminished numbers.'' That night he wrote Ellen, ''It is the most infamous thing that history has recorded.... The idea of depriving a General of 35,000 troops when actually under fire!''[11]

The removal of McDowell's corps from his command became

the cornerstone of the case he built to convince history, the American electorate, and perhaps himself that a treasonous conspiracy was the cause of all his troubles on the Peninsula. In his report on his tenure as commander of the Army of the Potomac, published in 1864, he described how the loss of the First Corps frustrated his entire design for the campaign: "It compelled the adoption of another, a different and a less effective plan of campaign. It made rapid and brilliant operations impossible. It was a fatal error." To his political allies he cast it as part of the "abominable design" of the administration to ensure that he would not win the crowning victory at Richmond and reunite the Union on his own terms. His enemies in Washington, he assured Samuel Barlow in reviewing the campaign, "have done their best to sacrifice as noble an Army as ever marched to battle."

It was necessary for George McClellan to believe this premise if he was to continue to believe in himself, but the facts of the matter are considerably different. He was not forced to resort to a siege by the president's order, nor did it affect how the siege was conducted nor even how long it lasted. What made "rapid and brilliant operations impossible" was his own decision, already taken, to abandon any effort to turn Yorktown.

As he had scheduled it before leaving Washington, all of McDowell's troops would not be at hand for another ten days or two weeks; April 11 was the earliest the first contingent was slated to arrive. By then he supposed Yorktown would be bypassed, with any remaining defenders trapped there and certain of capture, leaving him free to use these three divisions to overrun Gloucester and in due course to advance up the north bank of the York to West Point and (as he told Stanton) "turn in that manner all the defences of the Peninsula." Now, brought up short before Yorktown, such a turning movement would only invite disaster. Even had McDowell's entire corps been his for the attempt, to land it on the other side of the York was to expose it to defeat in detail by the enemy host while the main body of the Army of the Potomac was immobilized in its Yorktown siege lines.

During the siege he repeatedly called on Washington to return to him all or part of the First Corps for a landing on the Severn River, behind Gloucester, but this had no more ambitious purpose than to assault Gloucester when he was finally ready to assault Yorktown. Release two or even one of McDowell's divisions to use against Gloucester, he asked Stanton on April 11, "& I will at once undertake it." He was more candid when he told his wife a week later, after Franklin's First Corps division was restored to him, "I will then invest Gloucester & attack it at the same time I do York." He thought for a time the new ironclad *Galena* might gain him control of the York and save something of his original plan, but she was delayed and nothing came of the idea. If it occurred to him to leave only a holding force in the trenches and throw the main weight of his army into the turning movement (a tactic that in due course General Lee would inflict on him), he left no record of it.[12]

His conspiracy theory was equally insubstantial. McClellan appears to have firmly and forever set his mind against "these traitors who are willing to sacrifice the country & its army for personal spite & personal aims" (as he described them for Ellen) when he learned from General Franklin the supposed inside story of the decision to withhold the First Corps. Franklin wrote him on April 7, "McDowell told me that it was intended as a blow to you. That Stanton had said that you intended to work by strategy, and not by fighting, that all of the opponents of the policy of the administration centered around you — in other words that you had political aspirations." It is possible that Stanton said something of the sort — it reflects what he had come to think of McClellan, and why he wanted to replace him — but it was hardly evidence that to achieve that goal he and President Lincoln were plotting the deliberate defeat of the Army of the Potomac before Richmond.

McClellan found support for his theory in tales of utter implausibility. He recorded a story told him years later, at third hand, that on the eve of the Peninsula campaign Stanton said to McDowell and Franklin (known to be a McClellan admirer) that his chief goal as secretary of war "was to ruin that 'damned McClellan' & prevent his success." In *McClellan's Own Story* he cited a former West Point professor as authority for Stanton's announcement to a group of the general's supporters about this time that the war must not end until the abolitionists achieved the upper hand, and consequently it was not administration policy "to strengthen Gen. McClellan so as to insure his success." Mr. Lincoln was at the meeting and "assented to this view of the case," McClellan wrote. (His editor deleted this reference to the president before publication.) In such accounts, Lincoln and Stanton were apparently willing to tell anyone and everyone of their treasonous plot directed at General McClellan and his army.[13]

Having elected siege warfare, McClellan soon displayed evidence to justify his decision. Prisoners taken in a skirmish on April 6 reinforced the illusion Magruder had created. One of them told a Pinkerton interrogator that Joe Johnston had already arrived with reinforcements, raising the number of Yorktown's defenders to 40,000, along with 500 guns; "in a few days" 100,000 Rebels would be manning the fortifications. On April 7 McClellan telegraphed Stanton, "It seems clear that I shall have the whole force of the enemy on my hands...," which he put at 100,000 "& possibly more." When all his own troops arrived, he would have only 85,000 men. Like his first report on the Confederate army, back in August 1861, this evaluation set the pattern for all that followed. When the Peninsula dispatches were made public in 1864, James Russell Lowell wrote that he had to go back to Cervantes's Don Quixote to find a self-deception comparable to General McClellan's.[14]

President Lincoln had meanwhile formed his own view of the situation, and he telegraphed McClellan that he had better break the enemy's lines at once. "They will probably use *time,* as advantageously as you can," he warned. Montgomery Blair, by now McClellan's only supporter in the Cabinet, offered him the same advice, and added, "I can see that the President thinks you are not sufficiently confident, & it disturbs him." In a letter written on April 9 Lincoln tried to reason with his general. Only the Confederates benefited by delay, he observed. "And, once more let me tell you, it is indispensable to *you* that you strike a blow. *I* am powerless to help this." He reminded McClellan that he had always insisted that carrying the campaign to the Peninsula was only shifting the difficulty, not surmounting it; he would find there the same army he had faced at Manassas, behind equally formidable works. "The country will not fail to note — is now noting — that the present hesitation to move upon an intrenched enemy, is but the story of Manassas repeated. I beg to assure you that I have never written you, or spoken to you, in greater kindness of feeling than now, nor with a fuller purpose to sustain you.... *But you must act.*" McClellan made no reply. He was committed to a siege, and if for no other reason his pride would not admit another course. He wrote Ellen he was tempted to tell the president that if he wanted the enemy's lines broken, "he had better come & do it himself."

In his letter Lincoln also raised the "curious mystery" of the number of troops in the Army of the Potomac. By the War Department's count, he wrote, 108,000 men had been sent or were en route to the Peninsula, yet General McClellan was reporting that when everyone arrived he would have only 85,000. Where were all these missing men? As it happened, they were not so much missing as invisible. The War Department was measuring McClellan's army by the aggregate number in it at a particular time — the officers and the fighting men, the noncombatants, those on special duty and on sick call and in the guardhouse — in short, everyone who had to be fed and equipped. Starting with the same returns, McClellan came up with a much lower total by counting only enlisted men actually present for duty. There was nothing really wrong with counting this way except, again, his obstinate refusal to explain what he was doing, and the result was to diminish his credibility even more.

Moreover, he was guilty of deliberate sleight-of-hand by not counting the enemy's army the same way he counted his own. On the Peninsula Allan Pinkerton provided him with estimates of aggregate strength (Pinkerton prided himself on ferreting out the supposed number of rations issued to Confederate troops), and consequently his totals, wildly overstated to begin with, were even more alarming when set against McClellan's way of counting the Army of the Potomac. It was one more of the misapprehensions and misunderstandings beginning to settle over the Peninsula campaign like a fogbank.[15]

By the time the president wrote his letter, the opportunity for quickly breaking through the Yorktown position was nearly gone. On April 11 Magruder reported having something over 31,000 men, and had substantially strengthened his lines. In any event, McClellan had decided from the first that he would make no assault until he had subjected the enemy works to a pulverizing bombardment by the biggest guns in the Federal arsenal, and that would take some time to arrange. All his energies were devoted to laying out battery positions and constructing earthworks and opening parallels. "McClellan is constantly at work...," one of Joe Hooker's soldiers wrote. "He looks much care worn and those who saw him at the commencement of the war say he looks five years older than he did at that time.'' He added that all the troops ''have every confidence in his ability.'' On April 19 McClellan wrote Ellen, ''I *do* believe that I am avoiding the faults of the Allies at Sebastopol & quietly preparing the way for a great success.''[16]

When Joe Johnston finally took command at Yorktown and inspected the lines and heard Magruder's account of the early days of the siege, he remarked ungenerously of his old friend, ''No one but McClellan could have hesitated to attack.'' For his part, McClellan was equally ungenerous in appraising another close acquaintance from the prewar army. He had learned, he wrote Lincoln on April 20, that Robert E. Lee was now in overall command on the Peninsula (actually Lee was Jefferson Davis's military adviser, in effect chief of staff of the Confederate army), and he believed this would benefit the North: ''I prefer Lee to Johnston — the former is *too* cautious & weak under grave responsibility — personally brave & energetic to a fault, he yet is wanting in moral firmness when pressed by heavy responsibility & is likely to be timid & irresolute in action.'' There is no knowing how McClellan arrived at this reading of General Lee's military character — it is all the more remarkable in light of his usual tendency to overestimate his opponents — but mercifully the president put the letter away among his papers and it went unremarked.[17]

As the immense labor of erecting the Yorktown siege batteries dragged on day by day through the month of April, Northern newspapers were once more filled with reports of Union victories on other fields. At Shiloh, on the Tennessee River, Grant repelled a powerful Confederate attack, although at fearful cost. Island Number 10, a stronghold in the Mississippi, fell to General John Pope. Fort Pulaski, guarding Savannah, and Fort Macon, on the North Carolina coast, were captured. On April 25 New Orleans surrendered to the naval squadron of Flag Officer David Farragut. Secretary Stanton was confident enough of final victory that he had closed enlistment offices throughout the North and sent back to the army the officers detailed to recruit replacements in their regiments. It was an imprudent and puzzling action; apparently he counted on McClellan's being replaced by another general who would successfully close out the war. ''Glorious news

come borne on every wind but the South Wind,'' John Hay wrote
John Nicolay; ''... the little Napoleon sits trembling before the
handful of men at Yorktown afraid either to fight or run. Stanton
feels devilish about it. He would like to remove him if he thought
it would do.''

The Young Napoleon did not lack for defenders, either in the
army or on the home front. The immensity of his task (as he
calculated it) went out in press dispatches for which Chief of
Staff Marcy was often both source and censor. The correspondent
of the New York Associated Press, for example, obviously had
an inside track when he announced that the Confederates had
100,000 men at Yorktown, ''the flower of their army,'' behind
entrenchments bristling with 500 guns. He was reminded of Sevastopol, ''which withstood a siege of months.'' Henry J. Raymond, the editor of the *New York Times,* inspected McClellan's
operations and, as Sam Ward reported to Barlow, ''returned
radiant nay positive of the success of your Achilles.'' Fitz John
Porter wanted Manton Marble, the editor of the *New York World,*
to be aware of the urgent need for ''a military man to direct
affairs at Washington.'' Stanton, he wrote, was an ass who would
ruin any cause, ''a politician who would sacrifice a million lives
for his own advancement. ...'' A sergeant in the 4th Michigan
expressed a common enough feeling in the army about the newspaper debate when he wrote home, ''Every word said against
McClellan by the *home guard* only strengthens the love, faith
and admiration of those under his command.''[18]

In the early hours of May 3, the twenty-ninth day of the siege,
McClellan wrote Ellen in a mood of depression: ''I feel that the
fate of a nation depends upon me, & I feel that I have not one
single friend at the seat of Govt — any day may bring an order
relieving me from command — if such a thing should be done
our cause is lost.'' In just two more days he would finally be
ready to open an immense bombardment from nearly a hundred
heavy siege guns and mortars. It was thought that Yorktown
could not hold out more than twelve hours under this fire. ''If
they will simply let me alone I feel sure of success ... ,'' he wrote.
The perfect quiet that prevailed made him suspect an enemy
sortie or even an evacuation: ''If either I hope it may be the
former. I do not want these rascals to get away from me without
a sound drubbing. ...''[19]

They could in fact get away from him any time they chose, for Yorktown was in effect under an open siege; General Johnston was not trapped there in the manner of General Cornwallis and his redcoats eighty-one years earlier. At first light on May 4 word came back to Federal headquarters that no sentries were visible in the enemy lines. The Comte de Paris awakened McClellan for his orders, but he was unimpressed by the reports and went back to sleep. "The American mind is slow to grasp an idea to which it is not accustomed beforehand," the young Frenchman remarked in his diary. Finally enough confirmation arrived to convince the last doubters that the Confederates were gone, but it was not until noon that a pursuit was organized. "I shall push the enemy to the wall," McClellan telegraphed Stanton.

After he had fully considered the events of the day, he assured Washington that Yorktown's defenses were "most formidable & I am now fully satisfied of the correctness of the course I have pursued. Our success is brilliant & ... its effects will be of the greatest importance." When Ellen offered but faint praise, he chided her for failing to appreciate "a great result gained by pure skill. ... I am content with what I have done, & history will give me credit for it." Reviewing the siege for Ambrose Burnside, he linked it with the Manassas evacuation as "my brightest chaplets in history. ..."

Yet he was disappointed, too. With Joe Johnston's entire army drawn up before him, 100,000 to 120,000 strong as he believed, he had grown confident that the decisive battle he hoped for would be fought on his own terms at Yorktown rather than at Richmond, and as a consequence he wÀs caught unprepared by the evacuation. There was no plan for an organized pursuit, no preparation for a flanking column to use the York to cut off the enemy. Franklin's division of reinforcements, kept aboard ship since its arrival, had disembarked two days before. He could only conclude, he told Ellen, that Johnston "must have been badly scared. ..."[20]

As Johnston's columns — some 56,000 men in all — withdrew up the Peninsula to Williamsburg and beyond, McClellan improvised a pursuit with his cavalry and five divisions of infantry. With them went no fewer than three corps commanders, headed by General Sumner. The general commanding remained behind at his headquarters to start a force up the York to West Point.

Almost nothing had been done to assemble transports or organize their loading for such a movement, and mistrusting his aides and his generals to carry out the task, McClellan immersed himself in staff work all that day and well into the next afternoon.

From early morning onward on May 5, while he pressed the embarkation of Franklin's division, the sound of battle was plainly heard from Williamsburg, a dozen miles to the north. "Enemy still at Williamsburg," he notified Washington at 9:00 A.M.; " — heavy firing now going on." He later made bitter complaint that had he only reached the scene of the fighting at noon rather than at 5:00 P.M., he might have gained a substantial victory; as it was, he said, no one informed him that he was urgently needed until it was almost too late.

The more fundamental question about his role that day was why he had waited to be summoned. Hearing the sound of battle continuously for seven or eight hours might have suggested to him something more than simply the rear-guard skirmishing he had expected, and it might have been a matter of some concern, since (as he informed Stanton that night) his army was "undoubtedly considerably inferior to that of the Rebels. . . ." He had no great confidence in Edwin Sumner's generalship to begin with; as he wrote Ellen the next day, Sumner "proved that he was even a greater fool than I had supposed. . . ." Yet once again he seemed incapable of reacting decisively when his enemy did something he had not anticipated — in this instance, turning back in force to administer a sharp check to Sumner.

When he finally arrived before Williamsburg late on that dark and rainy afternoon, he told Ellen, "I found everybody discouraged . . . no system, no cooperation, no orders given, roads blocked up etc. As soon as I came upon the field the men cheered like fiends & I saw at once that I could save the day." He sent in reinforcements and filled gaps in the lines as the fighting died out in the darkness, and during the night Johnston resumed his withdrawal. Although incensed at the "utter stupidity & worthlessness" of his corps commanders on the scene, he thought some good had come from the fight. "It is perhaps well as it is," he confided to Ellen, "for the officers & men feel that I saved the day. . . ."

He concluded that the condition of the roads made further close pursuit useless, and turned to his original plan of outflanking the enemy by way of the York River. Nothing came of the effort. When the cautious General Franklin landed his division near West Point on May 7 he encountered enemy fire and notified McClellan, "I congratulate myself that we have maintained our position." Soon Johnston's columns were out of danger, and he took up position behind the Chickahominy River, a winding stream that flowed north and then east of Richmond to the James and lay squarely across the Federals' line of advance.[21]

The occupation of West Point gave McClellan the terminus of the Richmond and York River Railroad, and on May 10 he set repair crews to work on the line and called for locomotives and rolling stock from Washington. His supply line would now run the length of the York and upstream on the Pamunkey to a new base at White House plantation, where the railroad left the riverbank and ran twenty-three miles westward to Richmond. At the same time, there was promise of still another route to the Confederate capital. Norfolk was evacuated on May 9, and two days later the *Merrimack*, which drew too much water to reach Richmond, was blown up by her crew. This gave him the option, McClellan explained to Stanton, "to change my line to the James River & dispense with the Railroad." It presently developed that the enemy would have something to say about that.

On May 15 a Union flotilla that included the ironclads *Monitor* and *Galena* steamed up the James with the intention of bombarding Richmond, only to be driven back eight miles short of its goal by Rebel batteries at a place called Drewry's Bluff. The navy concluded it could not take Drewry's Bluff by itself, and General McClellan said that just then he could not detach any troops to attack it from the land side. In any case, the Drewry's Bluff batteries were not the end of the problem. Flag Officer Goldsborough estimated that the channel was so effectively blocked that it would take "3 months of uninterrupted labor" to clear away the obstacles. This overstated the case, but even so the James River line to Richmond was not likely to be available to the Federals any time soon.[22]

For the three weeks following the battle at Williamsburg the campaign was all but static as McClellan edged his army up to the Chickahominy and began to secure crossings of that stream. Thousands of Yankee soldiers labored to establish supply depots and repair the railroad and to corduroy existing roads and cut new ones through the dense woodlands. In the endless mud and steady downpours of rain everything moved in slow motion. "Our progress has been slow," McClellan admitted to General Burnside on May 21, "but that is due to ignorance of the country ..., the narrowness, small number, and condition of the roads, which become impassable for trains after a day's rain, of which we have had a great deal." Secretary of the Treasury Chase, once the general's strongest advocate, complained the same day to Horace Greeley of the *Tribune*, "McClellan is a clear luxury — fifty days — fifty miles — fifty millions of dollars — easy arithmetic but not satisfactory. If one could have some faith in his competency in battle — should his army ever fight one — if not in his competency for movement, it would be a comfort."

Visitors arrived from Washington to view the campaign at first hand. The president and Secretaries Stanton and Chase spent several days at Fort Monroe and took part in the occupation of Norfolk, but General McClellan said his presence with the army was too important to confer with them. Lincoln remained through May 10, by which time McClellan had matters well in hand at the front, but still he made no effort to arrange a meeting and perhaps reach some understanding on the issues that divided them. Apparently he believed no understanding was possible. He was facing a desperate battle at Richmond against superior numbers, he told Burnside. "The Government have deliberately placed me in this position. If I win, the greater the glory. If I lose, they will be damned forever, both by God and men." Lincoln later told a newspaperman that he was dissatisfied enough with McClellan's lack of progress after Williamsburg that he considered replacing him.[23]

McClellan meanwhile was expressing optimism about the larger course of events. Barlow told him that Yorktown and Williamsburg had produced rejoicing among his supporters and despair among his detractors. "The most noisy abolitionists now fear to say anything openly & the politicians among them are trying to get on your side without delay," he observed. McClellan wrote Ellen, "I learn that the abolitionists begin to think that I am not such a wretch after all," and as evidence he pointed to a resolution, passed by the House of Representatives, commending him "for the display of those high military qualities which secure important results with but little sacrifice of human life." What

particularly pleased him about the resolution, he said, was its
sponsorship by Owen Lovejoy, a deep-dyed abolitionist representative from Illinois. He was pleased, too, when the president
repudiated a proclamation by General David Hunter that eman-
cipated the slaves in the area Hunter commanded. "I feared he
would not have the moral courage to do so," he told Ellen. Clearly,
any victory by General McClellan was coming to be seen as a
corresponding defeat for the abolitionists, and he was not at all
displeased by that development.

In point of fact, he was getting his way with the administration
more often than not. He removed one of his generals as unfit to
command, and made the dismissal stick despite the president's
concern about the reaction of the general's supporters in Congress. In the wake of the Williamsburg fight he complained bluntly
about the corps organization imposed on him and called for "full
& complete authority" to relieve incompetent senior commanders.
Lincoln acceded to this request as well, but coupled it with a word
of warning. He had heard, he said, that the general consulted
only with his favorites, Fitz John Porter and William Franklin,
rather than with his corps commanders, and he asked, "Are you
strong enough, even with my help — to set your foot upon the
necks of Sumner, Heintzelman, and Keyes all at once? This is a
practical and very serious question for you." McClellan pondered
the matter, and on May 18 ordered a general reorganization that
retained the three senior corps commanders but limited their
commands to two divisions each and established two new army
corps, under Porter and Franklin. This finally gave him, he later
wrote, two corps commanders he could trust.[24]

He was meanwhile sending one dispatch after another to Washington calling for reinforcements and predicting the most severe
consequences if they were not forthcoming. The battle for Richmond would be desperate beyond all reckoning, and every other
consideration must give way to this reality. The Confederacy was
calling in men from every quarter; Washington must do the same.
Detective Pinkerton soberly delivered estimates by local farmers
that Joe Johnston's army numbered 100,000 or 120,000 or 150,000
men, and McClellan soberly passed these findings on to the government. "If I am not reinforced," he warned Stanton on May
10, "it is probable that I will be obliged to fight nearly double
my numbers, stronger entrenched." He repeated this grim pre-

diction to the president four days later, and noted that he could bring only 80,000 men to the field of battle.

In these dispatches McClellan introduced a new wrinkle into the way he counted his strength. In reporting his field army for battle at 80,000, for example, he included as before only enlisted men and only those present that day for assignment, but he then reduced that number by one-sixth to allow for those whose duties did not actually put them on the firing line. This was yet another way of counting manpower, and it had its uses, but once again he did not explain his methods — and did not apply the same calculation to Johnston's army. His report could not have come as any comfort to those in Washington, where figures indicated that more than 128,000 Army of the Potomac soldiers were on the Peninsula, with 102,000 of them present and equipped for duty. Mr. Lincoln would be led to remark that when an army went into the field it dwindled like a shovelful of fleas pitched from one place to another.[25]

The management of military affairs by President Lincoln and Secretary Stanton in the coming weeks aroused great controversy (not the least of it initiated by General McClellan), but their major error of the campaign was committed right at the beginning and stemmed, ironically enough, from the best of intentions. In response to McClellan's calls for help, Washington sent word on May 18 that McDowell's First Corps would finally be sent as reinforcement. More than that, McDowell would be at the head of a virtual army, exceeding in numbers even what McClellan had asked for. It was a decision that profoundly affected events both on the Peninsula and in the Shenandoah Valley.

Following the dispatch of Franklin's division to the Peninsula in mid-April, McDowell's corps was brought back up to strength by assembling various units into a replacement division. Had these 30,000 men promptly marched southward from Fredericksburg (the president insisted McDowell go by land instead of water so as not to leave Washington uncovered), they would have reached McClellan no later than May 25. McDowell felt confident of carrying enough rations and forage for the three or four days needed to reach the York River supply line, and strong enough to handle the small Confederate force facing him south of Fredericksburg. In any case, as Lincoln observed, any enemy troops he met were that many fewer facing the army on the Chickahominy. His arrival would restore to McClellan the twelve divisions he had originally intended to move to the Peninsula, and perhaps then the campaign would proceed with at least some mutual trust restored between general and administration.

Instead, assured by Banks that Stonewall Jackson was no further threat in the Shenandoah, the president detached James Shields's division from Banks and assigned it to McDowell. A good deal of slippage occurred in the course of the transfer, however, and when the First Corps was directed to join the Army of the Potomac on the Peninsula, Shields was still two days' march away. One thing and another caused further delay, and in the end McDowell set May 26 as the earliest day he could finally start his enlarged corps, now 41,000 strong, on the roads to the Peninsula. In the meantime, General Banks was discovering that Jackson was someone to be reckoned with after all, and without Shields he had only a single division to meet him.[26]

McClellan reacted to the news of McDowell's orders with suspicion. He took it that McDowell, who he thought now more than ever was conniving to replace him as head of the Army of the Potomac, would have an independent command on the Peninsula, and he saw in this the hand of the Washington conspirators. "Stanton is without exception the vilest man I ever knew or heard of," he told Ellen when the secretary's dispatch reached him. Furthermore, he doubted that McDowell's troops could really march the fifty miles from one supply line to another in a matter of days, and he complained to Lincoln, "I fear there is little hope that he can join me overland in time for the coming battle." He was mollified when Lincoln assured him that McDowell would come under his orders upon arrival.

In his later accounts of the campaign McClellan ranked the order for McDowell to march overland to join him, instead of going by water, as yet another fatal blow. It forced him, he claimed, to remain on the Chickahominy, vulnerable to attack, rather than taking a new, safer base on the James. But at the time he gave no indication of wanting to shift his base from the York to the James. After the navy's fight at Drewry's Bluff demonstrated how much effort would be needed to open that route, he was satisfied with the line he had chosen. It offered a major and almost immediately usable advantage: a railroad to carry his heavy ordnance directly to the gates of Richmond should siege operations become necessary. That was a tactic that came naturally to his mind when confronting an enemy in far greater force than he possessed, and strongly entrenched as well. He was thinking of siege warfare when he wrote his wife on May 22 that the final battle would probably take place on the very outskirts of Richmond, "which must in that event suffer terribly, & perhaps be destroyed." He was not sure, he continued, "that I can control fully this army of volunteers if they enter the city on the heels of the enemy after an assault. I will do my best to prevent outrage & pillage, but there are bad men in all armies & I hope that I shall not be forced to witness the sack of Richmond."[27]

As he came ever closer to the climactic struggle, perhaps "one of the great historic battles of the world," as he described it for Ellen, his private letters were increasingly marked by expressions of fatalism. He had confidence in his men and was sure they had confidence in him, and his messianic vision remained bright — "When I see the hand of God guarding one so weak as myself," he confided to Burnside, "I can almost think myself a chosen instrument to carry out his schemes" — but there was also his sense that the contest was quite beyond his influence or control. "The will of God be done — what is given me to do I will try to do with all my might . . . ," he wrote his wife, and he prayed that he was worthy of this divine election. "How freely I shall breathe when my long task of months is over & Richmond is ours!" he told her in another letter. "I know the uncertainty of all human events — I know that God may even now deem best to crush all the high hopes of the nation & this army — I will do the best I can to insure success & will do my best to be contented with whatever result God sees fit to terminate our efforts."

Such a belief, held strongly enough, was the ultimate escape from responsibility. If, following this train of thought, it was predestined that victory in the struggle go to the Union, well and good; as God's instrument he would carry out God's will. If, however, the hand of God did not in fact predetermine winner and loser, if victory in battle might hang on whether General McClellan seized the moment and took control of events, it became a question of whether he was constitutionally able to do so. It was not the most promising state of mind for a general to take to the battlefield.[28]

"We are engaged in a species of warfare at which we can never win,'' Joe Johnston warned General Lee a few days before he evacuated Yorktown. By holding off the Federal besiegers for a month, the Confederacy had gained time it desperately needed to organize and equip its forces and to collect what new troops it could, but it was plain to Johnston that as the armies moved ever closer to Richmond, his opponent would ''depend for success upon artillery and engineering.'' He could compete in neither: ''We can have no success while McClellan is allowed ... to choose his mode of warfare.'' Now, in mid-May, as the Army of the Potomac began to shift its weight across the Chickahominy, Johnston confronted it with something over 62,500 men. Beyond anything else, McDowell at Fredericksburg must not be permitted to combine with McClellan before Richmond. Lee and Johnston had discussed with Stonewall Jackson ways to take advantage of the division of the Federal forces and to keep them divided, and on May 1 Lee gave Jackson discretion to act as he thought best in the Valley. As he phrased it when the campaign was under way, Jackson's objective was to move on General Banks and ''do it speedily, and if successful, drive him back towards the Potomac, and create the impression as far as practicable that you design threatening that line.''[29]

Back in February, when Jackson was operating on the upper Potomac, McClellan had warned one of his generals to be on the lookout for his one-time classmate, ''whom I know to be a man of vigor & nerve, as well as a good soldier.'' Jackson now demonstrated vigor and nerve and much else besides, moving with great speed and deception, striking first one Union detachment and then another, and finally driving Banks headlong down the Valley toward the Potomac. ''In consequence of Gen. Banks' critical position,'' the president telegraphed McClellan on May 24, he was suspending McDowell's movement to the Peninsula. The next day he telegraphed, ''I think the time is near when you must either attack Richmond or give up the job and come to the defence of Washington.''

McClellan was writing to his wife when he was handed this second dispatch, and it drove him to a fury of denunciation: ''Heaven save a country governed by such counsels!... I get more sick of them every day — for every day brings with it only additional proofs of their hypocrisy, knavery & folly....'' The one shred of silver lining was the fact that Washington was greatly alarmed by the fighting in the Valley: "A scare will do them good, & may bring them to their senses. . . ." He telegraphed the president that the time was "very near" when he would make his attack, and that Jackson's campaign was nothing but a diversion to prevent the Army of the Potomac from being reinforced. As he saw it, Washington was in no danger, and Jackson would retreat soon enough once he saw that his diversion had failed. It should be the government's "policy & duty" to send him every available soldier.[30]

He correctly judged Jackson's purpose, and presently Lincoln came to agree with him. What may have given the president pause, however, was the implication behind McClellan's argument. If McDowell went ahead to the Peninsula as scheduled, so (presumably) would Jackson, to reinforce Johnston, and it was hard to see how this would greatly alter McClellan's gloomy forecasts. Even admitting that McDowell brought more men with him than Jackson did, the best McClellan might say then was that he was outnumbered by perhaps five to three instead of the present two to one. Despite McClellan's later claims, it is highly unlikely that he would have moved any more swiftly against Richmond under such a circumstance.

Although McClellan regarded Jackson's operation as merely a distraction, something the enemy, with its great resources, could easily afford, the president saw it as an opportunity for a counterstroke. Shields's division was ordered back to the Shenandoah, to be followed by two more of McDowell's divisions. Frémont was told to march into the Valley from the mountains to the west. If everyone moved fast (ideally, as fast as Stonewall Jackson moved), Lincoln believed, the southern end of the Valley might be sealed in the manner of a cork in a bottle, trapping Jackson inside. It was a sound enough idea, but its execution would be plagued by bad luck and bad weather and especially by the decidedly modest military skills of the Union generals involved. Jackson slipped out of harm's way with barely hours to spare.

McClellan was meanwhile continuing his methodical preparations for the Battle of Richmond. He pushed two of his five corps, commanded by Samuel Heintzelman and Erasmus Keyes, across the Chickahominy at Bottom's Bridge to positions south of the river and half a dozen miles east of Richmond. With the change in McDowell's orders, he was now free to shift his line to the James if he so desired, but his approach continued to be along the axis of the York River Railroad. Aware of the risk he was running in having his army astride the river, he put crews to work on the construction of military bridges. "The net is quietly closing & some fish will soon be caught," he told Ellen.

On May 27 he sent Fitz John Porter to clear the enemy from his right flank at Hanover Court House, fifteen miles north of Richmond. In a small but brisk fight Porter drove the Rebels away, an accomplishment McClellan elevated into "truly a glorious victory" in reporting it to Washington. He had assured the president that once Porter disposed of this threat and returned to the main body, he would be free to strike. On the morning of May 30 he predicted, in a telegram to Stanton, "Another day will make the probable field of battle passable for artillery."

At that point, however, nature intervened with what a diarist in General Hooker's division described as "another of those rains in which the very sluice gates of heaven seem to be opened, and the water drops in masses for hours." Once more the roads turned to mud. On May 31 the Chickahominy rose alarmingly and came sweeping down between the two wings of the Federal army, flooding the bottomlands, smashing at the bridges and their approaches and washing away much of the engineers' work.

Through all this General McClellan was confined to bed with malarial fever — his "Mexican disease" — which had been troubling him for more than a week. It was close to 1:00 P.M. that Saturday when an explosion of musketry from across the river was plainly heard at headquarters. Joe Johnston had chosen this inauspicious moment to seize the initiative with an attack of his own.[31]

NINE

THE BATTLE FOR RICHMOND

AFTER THE LEFT WING of his army safely crossed the Chick-ahominy River, McClellan became increasingly confident of the course he was pursuing. He noted demands in the Richmond newspapers that Joe Johnston take the offensive against the Yankee invaders, but he doubted that Johnston would. "I think he is too able for that," he told Secretary Stanton on May 27. At the same time, he expressed satisfaction with his own preparations, with each day's efforts "making our result more sure...." What recourse this left his opponent he did not say, and apparently he did not give the matter a great deal of thought. Johnston's attack on May 31 took him by surprise, catching his left wing — the corps of Keyes and Heintzelman, 31,500 men in all — in an exposed and vulnerable position.

These Federals south of the river had pushed forward as far as the crossroads of Seven Pines and the Fair Oaks station on the York River Railroad, half a dozen miles beyond their river crossing. To be sure, they had a shorter link to Edwin Sumner's corps of the right wing by means of two bridges Sumner's men had thrown over the river, but these were nothing more than corduroyed roadways crossing the swampy bottomlands and spanning the meandering channels of the stream on log stringers. They were likely to break up and float away at the first rise in the river. It was McClellan's intention to continue clearing the south bank of the Chickahominy so that permanent trestle bridges could be built, but he postponed the operation until Fitz John Porter had driven the Rebels away from the area of Hanover Court House. There was some risk in this, he admitted, but he was considerably more concerned about his right wing than about his left across the river.

The Confederate high command had in fact decided it must strike at McClellan's right before it was braced by the First Corps from Fredericksburg, but when McDowell's troops were seen moving off in pursuit of Jackson in the Shenandoah Valley, Johnston switched to the more inviting target of the Federals south of the river. His attack was already scheduled when the great storm flooded the Chickahominy and threatened McClellan's communications, but whatever he gained on May 31 from the weather, he lost by poor execution of his tactical plan. Fair Oaks was a battle in which neither commanding general exercised much control of events on the field. Yankees and Rebels fought it out savagely with little reference to the high command, and when it was all over nothing very much had changed.[1]

By 1:00 P.M. on the thirty-first, General Keyes, whose corps held the advanced line, realized that the attack was a heavy one, and he sent back for help from General Heintzelman, in overall command of the left wing. For whatever reason, his messenger was delayed or misdirected, and as late as 2:30 Heintzelman was telegraphing headquarters that there was no word from Keyes and "therefore I presume there is nothing serious." Ten minutes later he finally forwarded a report from the front that Keyes was hard pressed, and at three o'clock he telegraphed that the enemy had broken through and he badly needed reinforcements from Sumner across the river.

McClellan was at his New Bridge headquarters upstream, "quite sick" (as he told Ellen) and resting as best he could. When the sound of the firing grew louder, he alerted Sumner to call his Second Corps to arms, but took no further action until there was news from the battlefield. Thus it was not until three o'clock or a few minutes before that he ordered Sumner to cross the river with his two divisions to support the left wing.

Sixty-five-year-old Edwin Sumner was an old regular of simple thought and great reverence for orders, and Fair Oaks was his finest hour. He had only to march to the sound of the guns that day, and he did so with singleminded determination. On McClellan's alert, he had called his men to arms and then took it upon himself to move them right up to the bridge approaches. When the order came to advance, he started across immediately, saving perhaps an hour of assembly time. It was a critical hour. The crossing was painfully slow, one of the two bridges was soon impassable, and all that kept the other one from floating away in the torrent was the weight of the marching men. It was only after 5 :00 P.M. that the first of Sumner's men began arriving on the field, and just one of his two divisions got into action before dark, but along with the reinforcements Heintzelman had sent forward from his corps it was enough to halt the enemy drive. McClellan, who left his sickbed for Sumner's headquarters north of the river at five o'clock and spent the night there, called in Heintzelman to report personally on the situation at the front. He also pressed his engineers hard. "It is absolutely necessary that several bridges be practicable for Artillery in the morning," he insisted. The entire army was to prepare for action on June 1.²

That Sunday morning the Confederates returned to the attack, but after a short and intense fight they were repulsed and withdrew to their original lines. Pale and weak from fever, McClellan rode onto the battlefield soon afterward and inspected the positions and inquired after the wounded. "During his progress he was greeted with great enthusiasm," a newspaper correspondent wrote. "It was a splendid ovation."

For a time that morning he debated an immediate counterstroke. Perhaps he remembered the Marshal Saxe maxim he had copied into his notebook a decade earlier, admonishing generals not to be simply content with possession of the battlefield. His engineers had managed to throw a bridge across the Chickahominy upstream, and there is evidence that he discussed with Fitz John Porter a plan to concentrate both wings of the army south of the river and pursue the Confederates toward Richmond. According to the recollection of the Comte de Paris, writing to McClellan after the war, nothing finally came of the idea because of Porter's "refusal to cross the Chickahominy as you suggested to him on the second day of Fair Oaks. . . ."

If Porter indeed opposed a counterattack, McClellan did not feel strongly enough about it to override him. His detractors would sharply criticize the decision, but as Francis W. Palfrey, one of Sumner's officers, wrote of Fair Oaks, the ease with which they claimed the Army of the Potomac might have marched into Richmond that day was largely an afterthought. "I know that the 1st of June was with us a most anxious day,'' Palfrey recalled. Communications across the unpredictable Chickahominy were far from secure and the enemy was present in vast (if imagined) force, and had George McClellan attempted to follow up the ''glorious victory'' he would have been acting with uncharacteristic boldness. Certainly his illness made him unfit to command and influenced his decision. After visiting the battlefield, he returned to headquarters that evening in a state of utter exhaustion. He was unable to venture out on horseback again for ten days.

In his report to Washington on June 2 he returned to his earlier theme: as soon as the weather improved and he was reinforced, he would go on the offensive. For the time being he could do nothing until his bridges were completed. His satisfaction with the outcome of the battle was tempered by what he had witnessed that Sunday. ''I am tired of the sickening sight of the battlefield, with its mangled corpses & poor suffering wounded!'' he wrote Ellen. ''Victory has no charms for me when purchased at such cost.'' In another letter he admitted, ''Every poor fellow that is killed or wounded almost haunts me!'' His consolation was that all his actions were designed to save as many lives as possible. He announced to his troops that the final, decisive battle was now at hand. ''The events of every day prove your superiority,'' he told them, and final victory would surely be theirs. ''Soldiers! I will be with you in this battle, and share its dangers with you,'' he promised.

The Federals suffered 5,000 casualties at Fair Oaks, and the Confederates just over 6,100 — a high price, considering how little was changed after those two days of fighting. McClellan was exceedingly (and unknowingly) fortunate that the enemy's forces were mishandled, and that General Sumner went beyond the letter of his orders and thereby got his men to the field in time to make the difference. Otherwise, in concentrating four fifths of his army for the offensive, Joe Johnston might well have overwhelmed two fifths of the Army of the Potomac. For Johnston the cost of Fair Oaks was more than a tactical defeat. Toward the end of the fighting on May 31 he was seriously wounded, first by a bullet and then by a shell fragment. McClellan's old friend G. W. Smith took over and directed the brief flurry of fighting on June 1, and that afternoon President Davis replaced Smith with Robert E. Lee, who was to lead the Army of Northern Virginia to the end of its days.[3]

McClellan's renewed call for reinforcements was met with considerable promptness by Washington. On June 6 George McCall's division of McDowell's corps was ordered to the Peninsula. At Fort Monroe General Wool was replaced by General Dix, and Dix's men put under McClellan's direct orders. (No doubt McClellan was glad to be rid of John Wool, who asked hard questions about the statements of Confederate strength; like his contemporary Winfield Scott, Wool was suspicious of the miraculous arithmetic practiced at Army of the Potomac headquarters.) McClellan ordered up nine regiments from Fort Monroe, and Secretary Stanton provided an additional seven from Washington and Baltimore, and together these added up to a second division of reinforcements. On June 13 General Burnside wrote McClellan that he had seen Lincoln and Stanton in Washington and they "expressed themselves anxious to grant you all you want. They both say that I can do anything you order me to do without reference to them...." However, McClellan could not make up his mind whether to have Burnside join him before Richmond or attack Confederate communications in North Carolina, and as it happened Burnside's command did neither and was of no help at all in the coming battles.[4]

Additional reinforcements were promised. General McDowell telegraphed on June 8 that all three divisions still under his command in northern Virginia would march for the Peninsula to join the Potomac army within ten days, but once again the good intentions were frustrated. Shields's troops who had chased after Stonewall Jackson in the Shenandoah were found to be, in Lincoln's homely phrasing, "terribly out of shape, out at elbows, and out at toes," and would be some time recovering. No doubt Shields and his worn-out men deserved a rest, but the division of James Ricketts was delayed for no better reason than disorganization among the various Valley commanders. McDowell's third division, under Rufus King, was at Fredericksburg by June 14 and might have gone on to McClellan but for the fact that by then the Federals had totally lost track of Jackson. He was thought to be somewhere between the Shenandoah Valley and Richmond and reportedly he was being reinforced, and until there was some

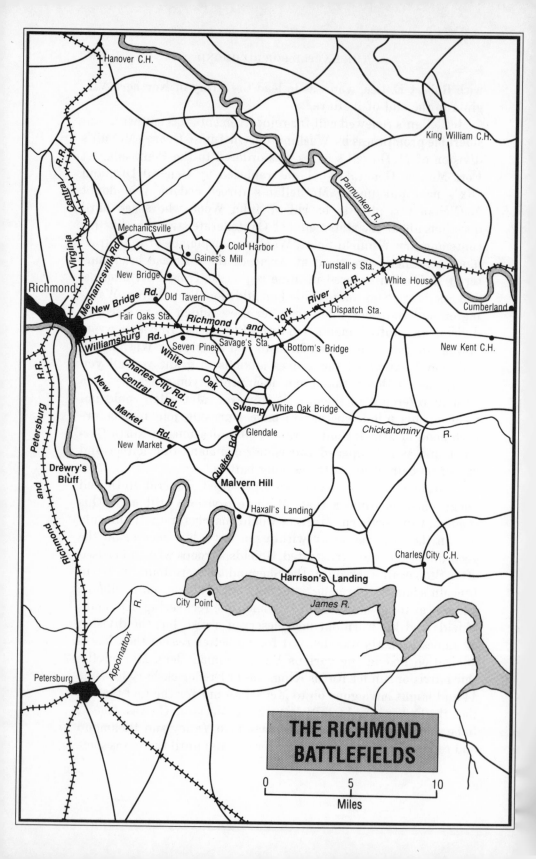

THE RICHMOND
BATTLEFIELDS

firm information on his whereabouts it seemed best to Washington not to leave any part of northern Virginia uncovered. General King stayed where he was.

In this manner the aftershocks of Jackson's Valley campaign continued for more than two weeks and kept the divisions of Ricketts and King — nearly 20,000 men — from the Peninsula battlefields. Yet there was another side to this coin. Despite all of Jackson's efforts at creating a diversion, two of McDowell's three original divisions — Franklin's and McCall's — had already joined McClellan. Moreover, during the course of the Peninsula campaign up until the last week in June, the threat that McDowell's corps might march south had kept Jackson's entire command out of the ranks of Richmond's defenders. As Mr. Lincoln often pointed out, every Confederate soldier otherwise occupied meant that many fewer Confederates facing the Army of the Potomac. Locked in his delusions, General McClellan could never see any advantage to himself in that fact.[5]

He was meanwhile seeking reinforcements from farther afield. In the western theater Beauregard's Confederate army had recently evacuated Corinth, Mississippi, under the threat of attack by General Halleck, and McClellan picked up rumors that Beauregard was in Richmond, or soon would be, with some sizable part of his army. He could not yet confirm this, he told Stanton, "but it is possible & ought to be their policy"; with Halleck no longer facing any organized resistance, he should be required to send the Army of the Potomac heavy reinforcements to counter this new threat. Henry Halleck was not one to give up a single soldier to such a scheme. He reported that Beauregard and all his troops were still very much in evidence in Mississippi, and the moment he sent any of his forces east he had no doubt that the Confederates "would immediately march back and attack us." McClellan began to realize he might have to confront Lee with the forces he had. "The rascals are very strong & outnumber me very considerably," he wrote Ellen on June 22, "... but I will yet succeed notwithstanding all they do & leave undone in Washington to prevent it."

In view of the pattern of conspiracy he detected in Washington, it is instructive to compare the size of the army he originally intended to command in the final contest for Richmond with the actual size of that army on the eve of the battle. On March 18 he had called on Secretary Stanton to furnish sufficient locomotives and cars for the York River Railroad, his lifeline for the final advance on Richmond, to carry supplies for 130,000 troops — the total number, that is, he would have to feed and supply while on campaign in the field. On June 20, when he was within half a dozen miles of his goal, and after the battle losses of Williamsburg and Hanover Court House and Fair Oaks and the considerable wastage from disease, the count of men present for duty in the Army of the Potomac on the Peninsula came to 127,327, and this figure did not include 7,000 of Burnside's troops who were also his to put to some purpose. To be sure, with better organization in the Valley command and with better intelligence sources Washington might have done more for General McClellan, but as it was it had done well enough.[6]

Through the month of June McClellan gradually shifted the bulk of his army south of the Chickahominy. "I shall be in perfect readiness to move forward to take Richmond the moment that McCall reaches here & the ground will admit the passage of artillery," he promised Stanton on June 7. A week later, after McCall's division arrived, he telegraphed that he would advance as soon as his bridges were completed and the ground had dried. On June 18, replying to the president's query as to when he might attack Richmond, he wrote, "After tomorrow we shall fight the rebel army as soon as Providence will permit. We shall await only a favorable condition of the earth and sky & the completion of some necessary preliminaries." Yet he was restrained by more than unfavorable conditions of earth and sky. Behind his promises was a caution that increasingly dominated his every action.

One important element of this caution was an obsessive preoccupation with the safety of the Army of the Potomac and of its commander. Allan Pinkerton returned from a trip to Washington bursting with gossip about Cabinet intrigues and the radicals' baneful influence on the president, and after hearing this tale McClellan wrote Ellen, "Honest A has again fallen into the hands of my enemies & is no longer a cordial friend of mine!..." He was as eager as anyone to finish the war, he continued, "yet when I see such insane folly behind me I feel that the final salvation of the country demands the utmost prudence on my part & that I must not run the slightest risk of disaster, for if anything happened to this army our cause would be lost. I feel too that I must not unnecessarily risk my life — for the fate of my army depends upon me & they all know it...." In another letter he remarked that if he were disabled, his senior general, Edwin Sumner, "would ruin things in about two days" should he succeed to the command. This defensiveness, combined with his sense of fatalism and his stubborn inflexibility of thought, formed a dangerous state of mind for a general certain to be tested to the limit before long.[7]

His view of the task he faced further ensured that he would act with caution. The failed flanking movement up the York River by Franklin was McClellan's last attempt at maneuver against the Confederate host. His tactics after Fair Oaks reflected what his West Point instructor Dennis Hart Mahan had termed an "active defense" — in effect, an advance toward battle from behind his own field fortifications. These works, he explained to the president, were his guard against "the consequences of unforeseen disaster." There could now be no doubt that he intended to lay siege to Richmond.

As Joe Johnston had predicted, the Federal campaign would be a matter of artillery and engineering, the only way McClellan could see to cope with the two-to-one odds he faced. He told Stanton that everything depended upon his artillery: "In this arm especially consists our great superiority over the enemy...." He called up pieces from his siege train that could be moved into the lines by teams — 30-pounder Parrott and four-and-a-half-inch Rodman rifles, 8-inch howitzers and mortars. The massive 13-inch seacoast mortars, the 100- and 200-pounder Parrotts, were meanwhile removed from the Yorktown batteries and loaded aboard barges, to be brought forward by river and rail when final siege operations began. His goal, he confided to Ellen, was to pin Lee in his Richmond lines. "If we gain that the game is up for Secesh — I will then have them in the hollow of my hand."[8]

At last the rains stopped and the skies cleared and the roads began to dry, and he prepared to advance one step at a time. "It now looks to me as if the operations would resolve themselves into a series of partial attacks, rather than a general battle," he wrote Ellen on June 23. The next day he notified Commander John Rodgers of the ironclad *Galena* that within a few more days he hoped to advance his lines far enough to send troops across to the James to take the Drewry's Bluff batteries from the rear, after which the river might be cleared "so that you can cooperate in the final attack." To support this operation, several vessels loaded with rations and forage were to move around from the White House base to the James.

McClellan later wrote that he undertook this movement of supplies in anticipation of changing his base to the James "if circumstances should render it advisable." It proved to be a fortuitous precaution, but at the time his primary interest was clearing the James of obstructions so that in due course the gunboats could add their firepower to the assault on Richmond. He remained firmly tied to the York River Railroad as the best means to move up his siege guns and deliver the 600 tons of supplies and forage his army required each day. Thus for both tactical and logistical reasons he kept a strong force of three divisions under the command of Fitz John Porter north of the Chickahominy to protect his railroad supply line. Even after Jeb Stuart's spectacular ride around the Federal army in mid-June demonstrated the vulnerability of the White House base, at least to cavalry raiders, McClellan was not inclined to give it up. Stuart's exploit, he later wrote a friend, "was a very minor consideration" in the decision to change his base of operations.[9]

Whatever his private concerns in these weeks, the face General McClellan displayed to the world was as confident as ever. Major Alexander S. Webb, a staff man with the artillery, thought his trials were enough to dishearten most generals, "but our little Mac is full of resource and only brightens as obstacles increase." The editor of the *New York Times*, Henry J. Raymond, remarked his capacity for detail. He seemed to be everywhere, Raymond wrote in a June 23 dispatch to his paper. "Every earthwork thrown up, every gun mounted, every position taken, every regiment moved, and almost every gun fired, are guided by his personal direction." McClellan often did his own reconnoitering, and one day the Prince de Joinville glimpsed him in a tall tree, perched with his officers on the high branches like a flock of crows, peering at the enemy through their glasses. Nothing in the campaign so far had diminished his popularity with the troops. A man in the 1st Minnesota watched him ride the lines on June 18 and wrote home, "I never before heard such cheering. It was one continuous cheer from one end of the line to the other. Regiment after Regiment threw their caps into the air and fairly went crazy ... the noise was awful.''

McClellan made no comparable effort to disguise his opinion of the administration in Washington. General Meade, who arrived on the Peninsula with McCall's division, recorded the scene on June 21 when he and Franklin and Baldy Smith called on the general commanding. McClellan "talked very freely of the way in which he had been treated,'' Meade wrote, ''and said positively that had not McDowell's corps been withdrawn, he would long before now have been in Richmond.'' At headquarters newspaper correspondents were told the same story of administration failures. Raymond of the *Times* called for 50,000 more men for the Peninsula. The *New York World*'s Edmund C. Stedman wrote that McClellan had been outnumbered from the first, and ''concentration and conscription alone have garrisoned Richmond in numbers far beyond the besiegers.'' Samuel Wilkeson of the *New York Tribune* ranked the Confederate army ''greatly superior to us in numbers'' and urged Washington ''to rectify the fearful mistake of weakening McClellan. ...'' On June 20 Fitz John Porter warned editor Manton Marble of the *World* that the army was in danger of a ''*defeat* or serious check'' on the Peninsula. ''The secy and Prest ignore all calls for aid. ... I wish you would put the question, — Does the President (controlled by an incompetent Secy) design to cause defeat here for the purpose of prolonging the war. ...''[10]

The general commanding meanwhile had been exploring larger issues. When General Lee designated Howell Cobb, a secretary of the treasury in the Buchanan administration and now a brigadier in the Army of Northern Virginia, to represent him in prisoner-exchange discussions, McClellan saw it as an opportunity for something more substantive. He assigned his aide Thomas M. Key, the former Cincinnati judge, to the talks, and gave him leeway to investigate informally with Cobb any possible basis for peace between the sections. Whether he discussed Key's approach with him beforehand is not clear; in any case, nothing Key said at the parlay, held on June 15, was contrary to McClellan's views.

In replying to Cobb's claim that the Confederacy had no choice but independence or subjugation, Key insisted that President Lincoln and the Northern people — and the army — had no thought of subjugating the South but were instead determined only to uphold the Constitution and to enforce the laws equally in all the states. "The slavery question has been settled," Key said. Its expansion was now halted by the law excluding it from federal territories, and it was abolished in the District of Columbia (by legislation drafted by Colonel Key himself); no longer need it be a divisive issue. Cobb was not convinced. He declared that the South could not return to the Union with security and without degradation: "We must become independent or conquered." In his report of their conversation, Key observed that the Confederacy would have to be defeated militarily before reunion was possible, and he added that he was certain the enemy was in Richmond in great force.

In forwarding Key's report to Washington, McClellan commented that among other points of interest it demonstrated what he had said from the beginning: "They will defend Richmond to the last extremity." Inspired by the interview and by the approaching climax to his campaign, he also offered to send the president his views "as to the present state of military affairs throughout the whole country." No doubt he was anticipating taking up his duties as general-in-chief again as soon as he completed the conquest of Richmond. He had to set the matter aside for later consideration, however, when Lincoln expressed concern about security in his sending such papers to Washington.[11]

At last, on June 24, McClellan was ready to order the first "decisive step" of the final advance on Richmond. The next day Heintzelman was to push his picket line forward a mile or so through a belt of thick woods in front of Seven Pines. This, in turn, would put him in position to support a longer step the following day, when Franklin's corps was scheduled to seize the Old Tavern crossroads, a choice spot for the Federal siege guns.

As preparations for the movement got under way on the twenty-fourth, a disturbing report from Allan Pinkerton reached headquarters. A deserter just in from Stonewall Jackson's command told his interrogators that Jackson's entire force had left the Shenandoah and was moving over the Virginia Central Railroad, intending to assail Fitz John Porter's corps north of the Chickahominy. McClellan asked Washington for the latest intelligence from the Valley. Secretary Stanton had to admit that there was no certain information on either Jackson's whereabouts or his strength.

McClellan went ahead with his offensive as planned, although perhaps with a sense of unease. He had written Ellen that the movements of the enemy were becoming mysterious, and he had a foreboding that something he could not yet begin to fathom was about to happen. Heintzelman's corps was moved forward on Wednesday, June 25, and was soon embroiled in a small but sharp fight christened the Battle of Oak Grove, an affair notable mainly for being the first of the Seven Days' battles.

That afternoon McClellan watched the clash from a redoubt in Heintzelman's lines and telegraphed Stanton that the troops were "behaving splendidly" and he was fully satisfied with the results. Some two hours later, however, a dispatch arrived that confirmed his worst fears and sent him galloping back to head-quarters.[12]

The dispatch was from Fitz John Porter, whose pickets had brought in a fugitive slave newly escaped from Richmond. The contraband reported that on the previous day the advance guard of Beauregard's western army had arrived in Richmond to the cheers of the citizenry, that Jackson was about to fall on the rear of the Yankee army, and that officers boasted of 200,000 troops available for the "big fight" soon to begin. Almost every day had brought such stories of reinforcements for Richmond (no reinforcements were actually from Beauregard's army, however; the cheers the day before were for a brigade from nearby Petersburg, called up by Lee to bolster his lines) and much evidence that Stonewall Jackson was on the move. Since Fair Oaks any number of deserters and contrabands and refugees carried tales of the Rebel host gathering in numbers ranging from 130,000 to 285,000 to defend their capital. McClellan accepted the latest contraband's story as part of an alarming pattern, and it shattered his fragile confidence.[13]

Early that evening he sent Secretary Stanton a despairing telegram, predicting disaster for his army and martyrdom for himself. He announced that he was contending against an army of 200,000, including the forces of both Beauregard and Jackson, but that he would try to hold his ground. "I regret my great inferiority in numbers but feel that I am in no way responsible

for it.... I will do all that a General can do with the splendid
Army I have the honor to command & if it is destroyed by overwhelming numbers can at least die with it & share its fate." In
that event "the responsibility cannot be thrown on my shoulders — it must rest where it belongs.... I feel that there is no
use in my asking for reinforcements."

Then he was in the saddle once more, crossing the Chickahominy to Porter's headquarters to plan the defense of his right flank.
The garrison and sentinel gunboats at the White House base were
alerted and the ordnance officer there ordered to send a supply
of ammunition around to the James in anticipation of a change
of base. McClellan was taking every possible precaution, he telegraphed Stanton. "If I had another good Division I could laugh
at Jackson.... Nothing but overwhelming forces can defeat us."

He returned to headquarters south of the river in the early
morning hours of Thursday, June 26, and then was off again at
first light to tour the positions facing Richmond, where he also
expected an attack. The corps commanders there were told to rest
their men and fight only from behind entrenchments. He snatched
but two or three hours sleep for himself. He was handed a report
from Pinkerton, who gave it as his official opinion that 180,000
Rebel soldiers faced the Army of the Potomac, a number "probably considerably short of the real strength of their army...."
At noon McClellan telegraphed Stanton that Porter's cavalry
pickets were being driven in, heralding Jackson's attack. "The
case is perhaps a difficult one but I shall resort to desperate
measures & will do my best to out manoeuvre & outwit & outfight
the enemy," he promised. Stanton should not be surprised if
communications were cut and even Yorktown lost. "Hope for the
best & I will not deceive the hopes you formerly placed in me."[14]

Like Joe Johnston before him, Robert E. Lee had concluded
that he could defend Richmond successfully only by taking the
offensive. He estimated that to resist a siege would require 100,000
men, and even that might merely prolong the agony. "McClellan
will make this a battle of posts," he wrote President Davis. "He
will take position from position, under cover of his heavy guns,
& we cannot get at him without storming his works...." His
solution was a turning movement against McClellan's right flank
north of the Chickahominy, which would at the same time threaten
the Federals' supply line to White House. In that event, they

must come out of their entrenchments to protect their communications or give up their siege and retreat down the Peninsula —
or, if Lee misread General McClellan's military character, they
might storm straight into Richmond while most of its defenders
were occupied with the turning movement. It was a plan as dangerous as it was bold, and it moved Jefferson Davis to write his
wife, "The stake is too high to permit the pulse to keep its even
beat...."

Yet Lee had taken careful measure of the general he faced. He
had seen the excessive caution that marked all of McClellan's
movements on the Peninsula. He noted his preoccupation with
siege warfare and his dependence on the York River Railroad to
carry his supplies and move his heavy guns. He knew from Northern newspapers passed through the lines the inflated estimates of
Confederate numbers that Potomac army headquarters had given
correspondents. In his offensive he would make his target McClellan
himself as much as McClellan's army.

Lee had set to work industriously to strengthen Richmond's
fortifications and to enlarge his army, although in no way did it
approach the numbers Federal intelligence suggested and General McClellan accepted. On the eve of the Seven Days the Army
of Northern Virginia counted some 85,000 troops, including Jackson's command, more men than it would ever again assemble for
any campaign. McClellan's force on the Chickahominy came to
104,300. Jeb Stuart's reconnaissance had given Lee a good idea
of the position and size of Porter's corps north of the river, and
he determined to throw two thirds of his troops against it. That
left fewer than 30,000 to defend Richmond (21,000 of them in
the fortifications facing the Federal lines) against McClellan's
74,300 south of the river. An important figure among those defenders was Prince John Magruder, who was preparing once
again to put his theatrical talents to the service of the Confederacy.[15]

Despite the pessimistic, self-fulfilling prophecy in his telegrams
to Washington, McClellan gave thought (for a time at least) to
putting up a fight for the initiative. He had earlier instructed
Porter that if attacked in force he was to hold his own long enough
for the general commanding "to make the decisive movement
which will determine the fate of Richmond." A "decisive movement" was certainly on his mind late on the afternoon of June

26, before the course of the attack on Porter was clear, when he telegraphed his wife, "I think the enemy are making a great mistake, if so they will be terribly punished. . . . You will hear that we are cut off, annihilated etc. Do not believe it. . . . I give you my word that I believe we will surely win & that the enemy is falling into a trap. I shall allow the enemy to cut off our communications in order to ensure success." Perhaps his thought was of Austerlitz, where in 1805 Napoleon had recognized his enemy's ill-considered turning movement and lured him to disastrous defeat. (That same thought crossed the minds of several nervous Confederate officers.) In the event, however, the Young Napoleon could not muster the resolution of the first Napoleon.

The telegram to Ellen was the only mention McClellan made of setting a trap for his opponent, and he never referred to it again, but it may be assumed that his idea "to ensure success" was to hold off the attackers along the line of the Chickahominy while, with the four corps of his left wing, he broke through and seized Richmond, supporting his army there from a new base on the James. Certain of his orders on the twenty-sixth seemed geared to such a plan. The corps commanders south of the river were alerted "to be ready to move in any direction called for." The quartermaster at White House was instructed to load all available freight cars and wagons with supplies and send them immediately to the front, and then be prepared to evacuate the base and establish new depots on the James. Porter was told to send his baggage and heavy guns back over the river and to "hold your position at least until after dark."

At the same time, there is evidence that McClellan considered that day the different and somewhat contradictory tactic of standing fast and fighting for a decisive victory north of the Chickahominy. In a letter to General Dix at Fort Monroe, written shortly after the Seven Days, he explained that, following "a marked success" north of the river, "I could have, by crossing the right wing, concentrated my forces, and on the succeeding day been in Richmond." For this tactic to work, however, Porter would have to be strongly reinforced. With that in mind, McClellan ordered Franklin, whose corps was posted just south of the Chickahominy, to hold Henry Slocum's division in readiness to cross the river and support Porter. Keyes, Heintzelman, and Sumner were asked how many of their men they needed to hold their ground for twenty-four hours and how many they could spare for the battle across the river. The cautious Keyes said he could spare none, Heintzelman offered a third of his troops, and stout old Sumner was willing to give up half his corps if called upon. These reinforcements would raise Porter's force to more than 50,000. The generals' replies reached McClellan that Thursday evening, but he postponed any decision on the matter until the next day.[16]

Meanwhile, in midafternoon, the Confederates had driven Porter's advance guard out of the village of Mechanicsville and at 5:00 P.M. opened an assault on his main line behind a tributary of the Chickahominy called Beaver Dam Creek. It was a strong natural position and Porter had his troops well posted, and the attackers made no headway at all. McClellan crossed the river to Porter's headquarters and witnessed part of the evening's fighting. When darkness ended the battle he was exultant. "We have completely gained the day . . . ," he reported to Randolph Marcy. "Tell our men on your side that they are put to their trumps & that with such men disaster is impossible." He telegraphed Stanton, "Victory of today complete & against great odds. I almost begin to think we are invincible."

In fact, Lee's battle plan for the twenty-sixth had gone badly awry, and if anything the defenders may have outnumbered the attackers. However seriously McClellan misjudged the weight of the assault — it was his first look at heavy fighting since the Mexican War — he did see that Porter was in danger of being outflanked if the battle was renewed the next day. During the night he ordered him back to a more defensible position near Gaines's Mill, overlooking the Chickahominy crossings. He did not leave Porter until 2:00 A.M. or later and then found more to do when he reached headquarters — including issuing an order to the staff to break camp in the morning and be ready to move — and if he took any rest at all, it was well after daylight. He was exaggerating somewhat when he telegraphed Ellen that he had not slept in two days, but there is no doubt that on Friday, June 27, a day he believed would be "decisive of the war," he had paced himself badly and had to make critical decisions in a state of near exhaustion.[17]

One of his first decisions was to put aside yesterday's thought of fighting his way into Richmond. In a 10:00 A.M. dispatch to

Stanton he announced the successful withdrawal of Porter's corps to its new position and assured the secretary that the whole army was now "so concentrated that it can take advantage of the first mistake made by the enemy." These were not the words of a general planning an offensive. All the information reaching his headquarters seemed to indicate that it was the Confederates who were bent on the offensive.

His corps commanders south of the Chickahominy reported the enemy threatening one point and then another. Two to four thousand Rebels were sighted marching through a clearing on Heintzelman's front, with an observation balloon rising nearby, perhaps heralding an attack on the Federal center. Franklin's pickets spotted six or eight regiments crossing their front. Dispatches from Sumner told of picket-line skirmishing and sharp exchanges of artillery fire. When word reached him at midday of an attack north of the river, McClellan telegraphed Washington, "We are contending at several points against superior numbers." He expected severe fighting on both banks of the river, and he might be forced "to concentrate between the Chickahominy & James. . . ." To that end he sent an engineer company to bridge White Oak Swamp at the crossing of the main road leading to the James. General McClellan may or may not already have decided on a retreat, but he was preparing for one.[18]

The menacing movements by the Confederates south of the Chickahominy were mostly the doings of Prince John Magruder. Lee had instructed Richmond's defenders to make feints and demonstrations while the rest of the army was in action north of the river, and if that was not enough they were to hold their lines at the point of the bayonet — another way of telling them they must fight to the last man. This grim choice moved General Magruder to new heights of dramatic art, and the revival of his Yorktown performance proved to be a considerable success. One attack was actually made by his troops late in the day, but it was a mistake, the result of a misunderstanding. All else was bluff, and effective enough that McClellan would report to Washington that his men had repulsed "several very strong attacks" south of the river. "They have outnumbered us every where," he told his wife the next day.

As skillfully as Magruder stage-managed his men, his success rested finally on the Federal high command's susceptibility to illusion. Fitz John Porter was convinced that in the Battle of Gaines's Mill he was attacked by 80,000 Rebels, and there is no reason to doubt that McClellan accepted his estimate. By such reckoning, that left at least 100,000 to defend Richmond. Consequently, McClellan considered it entirely logical that the Confederates were attacking him simultaneously on all fronts; it was precisely what he would do in Lee's position. Prince John's audience was willing to suspend belief even before he began his performance.[19]

Because of a peculiarity of atmospheric acoustics, the fighting at Gaines's Mill was heard only faintly at army headquarters, where it was first taken to be merely an artillery duel. McClellan remained at headquarters throughout the day, judging for himself none of the fighting on Porter's front and none of the bluffing on Magruder's. Slocum's division had started across the Chickahominy early in the morning to support Porter, but was recalled on McClellan's order; no reinforcements were to cross until called for. From that beginning General McClellan went on to play a passive role on June 27, as he had done to one degree or another in every battle his men had fought. He took no initiatives and attempted no decisive movements. Instead, he waited for events to shape his actions. As a consequence, Fitz John Porter lost a battle he might have won with more timely support.

Gaines's Mill was a bloody slugging match, the most intense fighting the two armies had yet experienced. Major Porter Alexander, who viewed the oddly silent field from the Confederates' observation balloon, wrote that he could see "the bursting of nearly every shell & the flash & smoke of every volley of musketry, making as grand & exciting a scene as the world ever shows." The struggle began at noon and lasted almost nine hours, and throughout its course it was believed at Porter's headquarters (according to Major Webb of the artillery staff) that they were fighting for time to enable the rest of the army to smash its way into Richmond.

At 2:00 P.M. Porter called for reinforcements, but it was not until 3:30 that Slocum's division finally arrived on the field. By then Porter was so hard pressed that he had to throw Slocum's brigades into action piecemeal to plug gaps opening in his lines. These troops, who increased his force to some 35,000, were the only help that reached him in time to do any good. At 5:30, on

McClellan's orders, Sumner started two brigades toward the river, but they could do no more than cover Porter's retreat. Through the critical hours of the fighting, 60,000 Federals sat idly facing Richmond, tested only by scattered artillery fire and Prince John Magruder's single small and misguided assault.[20]

Twice during the fighting McClellan experienced brief surges of hope. At Porter's request, he proposed that if Franklin saw an opportunity, he should send troops across the Chickahominy bridge nearest him to take Porter's attackers in the flank. Nothing came of that when Franklin replied that he had already destroyed the bridge to prevent the enemy from capturing it. Shortly after four o'clock Porter sent back a cheering dispatch that he had repulsed the Rebels repeatedly and "found everything most satisfactory." McClellan suggested a counterattack: "If the enemy are retiring and you are a chasseur, pitch in." Then the Confederates returned to the attack and Porter reported his situation growing critical. "You must beat them if I move the whole Army to do it & transfer all on this side," McClellan telegraphed him, but he apparently meant this promise simply to brace his subordinate. He had already ordered up the last reinforcements he would send. George McClellan never had a more devoted partisan than Fitz John Porter, but when Porter came to write of Gaines's Mill after the war, even he could muster but the faintest of praise for the conduct of his commander on that field.[21]

It was twilight before General Lee finally was able to mount an all-out coordinated attack — once again his offensive had not gone as he planned it — and under this pressure Porter's weakened line buckled and broke. In the confusion of defeat, 2,800 of his men and twenty-two of his guns were captured. McClellan revealed how little he grasped of the day's happenings when he telegraphed Heintzelman, at the center of the lines facing Richmond, "On the other side of the Chickahominy the day is lost. You must hold your position at all cost."

He warned Washington that he might have to pull back; if only he had 20,000 "fresh & good troops" he could be certain of "a splendid victory tomorrow." Briefly he debated gambling everything on winning that victory, but soon thought better of it. At 10:30 that night he made his decision official to change his base and put his army in retreat. "We have met a severe repulse to day having been attacked by vastly superior numbers," he telegraphed Flag Officer Goldsborough, "and I am obliged to fall back between the Chickahominy and the James River." He called for gunboats to cover the army when it reached the river.

The corps commanders were informed of the decision and assigned their roles in the retreat. Keyes, on the far left of the army, would lead the way, securing the crossings of White Oak Swamp, the major barrier between the Chickahominy and the James. Porter's battered command would follow. Heintzelman, Sumner, and Franklin were to hold their lines, forming a shield behind which the army's supply trains could make their way to safety, and then fall back as a rear guard. Orders went out to abandon the White House base and transfer everything remaining there to a new depot on the James, and at about midnight army headquarters was pulled back from the Chickahominy to Savage's Station on the railroad.[22]

When McClellan sat down shortly after midnight to report the day's events to Secretary Stanton, he had slept only ten or twelve hours in the last seventy-two. Beyond his exhaustion was the enormity of what had happened that day to all his hopes for taking Richmond, and it drove him to a state of emotional hysteria akin to what he had suffered the previous fall in Washington when he expected at any moment to be overwhelmed by the enemy host. His dispatch revealed him as a defeated, demoralized general, incapable of any thought beyond salvaging what he could from the wreck of his campaign.

His soldiers had done all that soldiers could do, he told Stanton, "but they were overwhelmed by vastly superior numbers even after I brought my last reserves into action." With 10,000 fresh men he could have won the battle across the river. With 20,000 or only 10,000 he could seize Richmond in a matter of hours, "but I have not a man in reserve & shall be glad to cover my retreat & save the material & personnel of the Army.... I have lost this battle because my force was too small. I again repeat that I am not responsible for this & I say it with the earnestness of a General who feels in his heart the loss of every brave man who has been needlessly sacrificed today." He might yet retrieve his fortunes, but only if very large reinforcements were sent to him. "I feel too earnestly tonight," he wrote; "— I have seen too many dead & wounded comrades to feel otherwise than that the Govt has not sustained this Army. If you do not do so now the game is lost.

If I save this Army now I tell you plainly that I owe no thanks to you or any other persons in Washington — you have done your best to sacrifice this Army.''

General McClellan had not ventured onto the battlefield that day nor (so far as the record shows) visited a field hospital, and his reference to dead and wounded comrades was as much inflated rhetoric as his claim that he had committed his last reserves to the fight. His insistence that nothing that had happened was his fault was predictable enough, but in accusing the administration of a treasonous conspiracy he was making public a charge that previously he had made only in private.

However overwrought he may have been, the accusation was made deliberately and with calculation. In anticipating that the worst might happen to him, he wanted the country to know the real authors of the disaster. ''It was pretty frank & quite true,'' he wrote Ellen of the dispatch; ''... I knew it when I wrote it, but as I thought it possible that it might be the last I ever wrote it seemed better to have it exactly true.'' (He went on to remark that the president was ''entirely too smart to give my correspondence to the public — it would have ruined him & Stanton forever.'')

To be doubly sure his message reached the world, he repeated the charge the next day in a letter to General Dix at Fort Monroe. ''May God forgive the men who have caused the loss this army has experienced,'' he wrote. ''It is now clear beyond a doubt that 20,000 more men would have given us a glorious victory. I for one can never forget nor forgive the selfish men who have caused the lives of so many gallant men to be sacrificed.'' They were not yet safe, and the entire army might be sacrificed, ''but I have at least the satisfaction of a clear conscience.'' He then made General Dix the executor of his last testament: ''If we get through this it will be better for you to keep this to yourself as confidential — if I lose my life make such use of it as you deem best.''

The dispatch to Stanton reached the War Department in midmorning on June 28 and created a considerable stir when it was deciphered. It was shown first to Edward S. Sanford, military supervisor of telegrams. Sanford adjudged McClellan's charge of treason against the administration false and refused to let it be seen by the secretary of war. He had the message recopied without the offending final sentence before it was delivered. Even expurgated it contained harsh enough accusations that Stanton carried it to the White House and said "with much feeling" that Lincoln must know that all his actions in regard to the Army of the Potomac had been authorized by the president. The complete dispatch was published only in 1864, in McClellan's official report. What Stanton and Lincoln may have said when they saw it then is not on record.

Lincoln's response on June 28, 1862, was mildly forbearing. "Save your Army at all events," he telegraphed. "Will send reinforcements as fast as we can. Of course they can not reach you to-day, to-morrow, or next day. . . . If you have had a drawn battle, or a repulse, it is the price we pay for the enemy not being in Washington"; neither the general nor the government was to blame. He appended a suggestion from General John Pope, just brought east from Halleck's command to head the new Army of Virginia, an assemblage of the various forces in Washington and northern Virginia. Pope hoped the Army of the Potomac would fall back on the York River rather than the James, to make cooperation between the two armies easier. McClellan did not reply before the Confederates cut his telegraph line, but there is no evidence that Pope's opinion caused him any second thoughts about his decision to retreat to the James. He remained out of touch with Washington for three days.[23]

When he came to review the Seven Days for Ellen, he wrote feelingly of the overwhelming sense of responsibility that pressed on him so relentlessly : "I *did* have a terrible time during that week — for I stood alone, without *anyone* to help me — I felt that on me rested everything. . . ." Through the worst of these times he had forced himself to display a mask of confidence and optimism despite "my heart full of care. . . ." In another letter he recalled, "I had no rest, no peace except when in front with my men. The duties of my position are such as often to make it necessary for me to remain in the rear — it is an awful thing."

He did it often enough, however. His duties in the rear, as he perceived them, were critically important to saving the army and were not to be entrusted to his staff or his quartermasters or his engineers. And despite his references to martyrdom and the promise in the Fair Oaks address to the troops to share the dangers of combat with them, he kept his distance from every battlefield during the retreat. On three straight days, while the Army of the Potomac fought to survive, he abdicated the position of commanding general and went to the rear, leaving it to others to direct all the fighting. General Heintzelman, asked about this by the Committee on the Conduct of the War, replied, ''Well, sir; he was the most extraordinary man I ever saw. I do not see how any man could leave so much to others; and be so confident that everything would go just right.'' Colonel Francis C. Barlow, a regimental commander in Sumner's corps who experienced much of the fighting on those three days, was more pointed when he wrote his mother, ''It is considered generally that McClellan has been completely outwitted. . . . I think the whole army feel that it was left to take care of itself and was saved only by its own brave fighting.''[24]

June 28 was a day of comparative quiet, with only limited fighting. It was like the calm in the eye of a great storm. McClellan remained at headquarters at Savage's Station, dealing with the complexities of starting the wagon trains and the artillery reserve through White Oak Swamp. Enormous columns of smoke signaled the burning of stores that could not be moved. Tons of artillery ammunition were loaded aboard a string of box cars, and the engineer opened the throttle wide and sent the train tumbling off a blazing railroad trestle into the Chickahominy in a spectacle of destruction. A field hospital containing 2,500 men too ill or too badly wounded to travel was left to the enemy. The corps of Sumner and Heintzelman and a division under Franklin were issued orders for the next day to abandon the fortifications and fall back along the railroad, holding their rear-guard position until dark to enable the last of the supply trains to escape across the swamp. In the small hours of the morning headquarters was moved across the swamp as well, to take up a new position beyond the main crossing point at White Oak Bridge.

General Lee's prediction that his opponent would retreat if he was defeated north of the Chickahominy proved accurate enough, but he misjudged the direction the retreat would take. Expecting McClellan either to fall back along his supply line to White House or withdraw down the Peninsula the way he had come, he had his army out of position for rapid pursuit when he discovered the Federals were moving south toward the James. McClellan thus gained a twenty-four-hour head start, and whatever else may be said of his decision to make the James his new line of operations, it most probably saved his army. Correspondent Samuel Wilkeson called it "a Napoleonic conception of the only salvation for his army from annihilation by fire, or loss by capture." In retrospect McClellan viewed it in the same light.[25]

The Federals needed every hour the enemy would grant them, for the movement of the trains was slow and labored. The artillery reserve had a hundred guns, a quarter of them heavy siege pieces that each weighed as much as two tons or more. The supply trains consisted of something over 3,000 wagons and ambulances, drawn by nearly 14,750 horses and mules. In the midst of it all was a lumbering herd of 2,500 beef cattle. Reconnaissance efforts were poor, and the whole movement was directed to a single road beyond White Oak Swamp. Only individual efforts, such as General Keyes's discovery of an overgrown and long-unused track leading to the river, prevented massive roadblocks from developing. Even so, reported the Potomac army's quartermaster, "The spectacle at times of entangled wagons with batteries and troops was frightful. . . ."[26]

While McClellan busied himself untangling traffic on the afternoon of the twenty-ninth, five miles away his rear guard fought a confused and misdirected battle around Savage's Station. He had designated no overall commander from among Sumner, Heintzelman, and Franklin, and although Sumner was the senior and assumed the command by default, the others acted independently. Heintzelman, judging there were enough troops on the scene to meet any attack, without notice marched his corps off to White Oak Swamp. In the midst of the fighting Sumner was startled to find his flank uncovered. Fortunately for the Federals, the Confederate command was in equal disarray, and the assault was beaten off.

Old Sumner, his blood up, refused to resume the retreat. "I never leave a victorious field," he told Franklin. "Why! if I had twenty thousand more men, I would crush this rebellion"; surely General McClellan did not realize the situation. In desperation, Franklin sent an aide to find McClellan and learn what he wanted done. McClellan sent back his inspector general, Colonel Delos Sacket, with marching orders for Sumner. If he did not obey, Sacket was to relieve him of command and put him under close arrest. A direct order was always enough for Edwin Sumner, and that night the rear guard pulled back across the swamp, destroying the crossings behind it.[27]

As June 30 dawned, McClellan could not fail to realize that it would be the critical day in his retreat to the James. A sizable part of the army's trains had still to pass down the Quaker Road to Haxall's Landing on the river, requiring the combat troops to remain in place to shield the long and vulnerable column. Soon after daylight he surveyed the likely battlefield and posted his forces. He marked the key to the position as the Glendale cross-roads, where two roads from Richmond intersected the Quaker Road. In late morning he conferred with Sumner, Heintzelman, and Franklin, laying out the day's plans. Confederate forces were reported to the north, threatening the rear guard at the White Oak Swamp crossings. Enemy troops were sighted in strength on the Richmond roads to the west, advancing toward the Glendale flank. At noon, with the sound of artillery exchanges and picket-line skirmishing in his ears, General McClellan mounted his horse and with most of his staff rode off to the James River, to be seen no more that day on the Glendale battlefield.

Whether he took this action because a battle was impending or in spite of it is impossible to say. He never offered an explanation. Perhaps in his frantic obsession with saving his army he needed to assure himself personally that there was indeed a safe haven on the James under the guns of the navy. Perhaps he believed his dispositions for battle were such that, as General Heintzelman observed of him, he was confident that everything would go just right. (One of his staff reflected this view when he later wrote that the generals left at Glendale faced only ''straightforward & plain work,'' requiring no major decisions.) Perhaps he had done all he could, leaving it to God's will to decide the outcome. Or perhaps, as he had confided to Ellen, for the sake of the army he, the indispensable man, genuinely feared to risk his life under fire. Whatever his reason, or combination of reasons, never in his military career was he so derelict of his duty. General Peter Michie, the distinguished soldier who wrote the first military biography of McClellan, could find no better word for his decision than ''astounding.''[28]

McClellan soon reached the James and inspected Malvern Hill, high ground that dominated the approaches to Haxall's Landing, where the trains were being parked as they arrived. Porter and Keyes already had their troops occupying the hill, and Chief Engineer John Barnard was at hand to lay out the defensive positions, as he had done at Gaines's Mill. The navy was at hand as well, in the person of Commander John Rodgers of the gunboat *Galena*. McClellan ordered Chief of Staff Marcy to bring the headquarters to Haxall's, explaining that Malvern Hill was only a temporary position and that the army must continue its retreat half a dozen miles downstream to Harrison's Landing; Rodgers could not guarantee the army's James River supply line as far upstream as Malvern. At 4:45 P.M., with McClellan and staff on board, the *Galena* steamed upriver to shell a column of Confederate troops approaching Malvern Hill. This was an important enough mission, but hardly one requiring the presence of the commanding general of the Army of the Potomac. Since mid-afternoon the roar of the guns and the rising clouds of battle smoke had announced that his army was fighting for its life at Glendale.[29]

General Lee had determined to make June 30 the decisive day. For the first time in the Seven Days he planned to commit virtually every man under his command to the battle in an all-out attempt to cut the Federal army in two and destroy it. Once again, however, nothing went as he planned it, and instead of 70,000 men going into action only 20,000 made the attack. It was a near thing even so, and the fighting was as bitter as any in the campaign, some of it hand to hand, with batteries overrun, McCall's division badly mauled, and a momentary breakthrough at the center of the Union line.

McClellan had again left no one in overall command, and his generals fought their troops ''entirely according to their own ideas,'' as Heintzelman phrased it, meeting assaults as they came or sending help where the fighting seemed heaviest. This haphazard command system worked well enough, because the battle was confined to the area near the Glendale crossroads; had Lee's original plan for a three-pronged offensive been carried out, the Federals would have been badly in need of central direction. And had the Army of the Potomac been defeated at Glendale, George McClellan would have been hard pressed to explain his absence from the field.

He knew little of the day's events and could not guess at the

failures of the enemy high command, and that evening, in his
first dispatch to Washington since reaching the James, he repeated the familiar litany of desperate fighting and assaults by
superior numbers. He was not certain he could save his trains
and artillery, but he would do his best to save his men. "If none
of us escape we shall at least have done honor to the country."
He had to have "very large" reinforcements and more gunboats.

While waiting that night at Porter's headquarters on Malvern
Hill for reports from Glendale, McClellan gave thought once
again, as he had after Gaines's Mill, to risking everything on the
day's battlefield. His trains had reached safety, and he was "as
willing to stake the last chance of battle in that position as any
other under the circumstances...." His generals decided the matter otherwise. Having no orders from McClellan, and assuming
that he had done his duty in holding position until nightfall,
Franklin set his troops marching for the river. Heintzelman and
Sumner had no choice but to follow. McClellan told Washington
he hoped to rest his weary men at Malvern Hill before moving
farther down the river. If the government intended reinforcing
him, "it should be done promptly, and in mass." With 50,000
fresh men he believed he might retrieve his fortunes; more would
be well, but that number "will, I think enable me to assume the
offensive."[30]

At first light on July 1 he inspected the position of the troops
and the placement of the guns on Malvern Hill and then returned
to his headquarters at Haxall's Landing. "The whole army is
here — worn out & war worn — after a week of daily battles,"
he wrote in a hasty note to Ellen that morning. "... The dear
fellows cheer me as of old as they march to certain death & I feel
prouder of them than ever. I am completely exhausted — no sleep
for days — my mind almost worn out — yet I *must* go through
it. I still trust that God will give me success & I cheerfully entrust
to his will...." He was benumbed by fatigue and depression.
"That Tuesday morning at Malvern was the gloomiest we have
had and never did I see a man more cut down than Genl. Mc-
Clellan was when I visited him ...," General Andrew A. Humphreys wrote his wife. "He was unable to do anything or say
anything."

At about the same hour he wrote Ellen, McClellan sent a dispatch to General Dix at Fort Monroe, calling on him for whatever

reinforcements might be available and reporting on the state of affairs. His men were exhausted and "in no condition to fight without 24 hours rest," he wrote; "— I pray that the enemy may not be in condition to disturb us today." However much he may have feared the outcome if there was an attack that day, he apparently was again satisfied to leave the matter to fate. At 9 :15 A.M. he boarded the *Galena*, and forty-five minutes later the gunboat steamed off down the river and out of sight. At 11 :30 she anchored off Harrison's Landing and McClellan went ashore in a tug to do (as he later wrote) "what I did not wish to trust to anyone else — i.e. examine the final position to which the Army was to fall back." He did not return to Haxall's Landing until midafternoon.

Nothing so publicly damaged George McClellan's military reputation as this expedition aboard the *Galena*. The canal boats at Harper's Ferry and the Quaker guns at Manassas were simply embarrassments, but this incident cast doubt not only on his competence but on his courage as well. One reporter called it "the meanest picture that this bloody rebellion has painted." Cartoons published during McClellan's 1864 presidential campaign took up the theme. One showed the general, drink in hand, taking his ease aboard ship while a battle raged in the background. Another, titled "The Gunboat Candidate, or the Battle of Malvern Hill," depicted him astride a saddle on the *Galena*'s spanker boom, peering at the distant fighting through a glass.

As it happened, McClellan was not aboard the *Galena* during the actual fighting at Malvern Hill, although he could not have anticipated the Confederates' delay in mounting their attack when he embarked for Harrison's Landing that morning. If the cartoonists were inaccurate in particulars, they had caught the larger implication of the episode (and of his lesser-known expedition aboard the *Galena* the day before). McClellan revealed his sensitivity on the subject in testimony to the Joint Committee on the Conduct of the War, when he professed not to remember whether he had boarded the gunboat that day.[31]

In late afternoon, when it became apparent that the Confederates were massing for a major attack, he returned to Malvern Hill and once again rode the lines and approved the placing of the defenders. Although he anticipated that the attack would be against his left, and massed most of his troops and guns there under the command of Fitz John Porter, he stationed himself on the right, some two miles away. ''My apprehensions were for the extreme right,'' he later said. Shortly after six o'clock Porter sent word that he had repelled the first strong attack. ''The enemy has renewed the contest vigorously — but I look for success again. The men cheer most heartily.'' Final success would be his, as the massed Federal guns took a terrible toll of Lee's men. An artillerist told him, one man wrote home, that ''it was horible to see the rebels advancing in a line of ten deep. They would let them get within half mile of them before our men fired a gun then they would let loose at them. He said that it made him heart sick to see how it cut roads through them some places ten feet wide. . . .''

A McClellan staff man recalled that from where he and the general were, on the right, they could hear the artillery fire but were too far away to hear the musketry. At dusk, once again having witnessed none of the day's fighting, McClellan returned to headquarters at Haxall's. Porter announced that after ''a hard fight for nearly four hours against immense odds, we have driven the enemy beyond the battle field. . . .'' If he was reinforced and his ammunition replenished, he added, ''we will hold our own and advance if you wish.'' Without waiting to hear from his victorious general, however, McClellan had already issued orders for the army to withdraw that night to Harrison's Landing.

At 11:00 P.M. he went aboard the *Galena* to spend the night, and the next morning the gunboat took him downriver to join his army. ''If not attacked during this day I will have the men ready to repulse the Enemy tomorrow,'' he telegraphed President Lincoln. ''. . . I have not yielded an inch of ground unnecessarily but have retired to prevent the superior force of the Enemy from cutting me off — and to take a different base of operations.'' It was the epitaph for his grand campaign to capture Richmond.[32]

TEN

IMPASSE
AT HARRISON'S LANDING

On July 2, in a driving, day-long rainstorm, the Army of the Potomac made good its retreat from Malvern Hill and took refuge at Harrison's Landing. "We camped in mud & slept in mud," the 2nd Michigan's Lieutenant Charles B. Haydon noted in his diary. "The enemy did not press." Even so, General McClellan did not yet feel safe from the Rebel army that had pursued him relentlessly for a week. He hurried Randolph Marcy off to Washington with a letter for Secretary Stanton. "The Army is thoroughly worn out & requires rest & very heavy reinforcements," he wrote. He would do his best to ready the men for the next battle, but the administration must finally realize the magnitude of the crisis. "To accomplish the great task of capturing Richmond & putting an end to this rebellion reinforcements should be sent to me rather much over than much less than 100,000 men."

He then turned to the more immediate task of restoring morale to his dispirited army. Like General Sumner at Savage's Station, the troops had been angered and discouraged by the recurring orders to retreat, especially when retreat meant abandoning wounded comrades to the enemy after every battle. By one estimate, of the nearly 16,000 Federal casualties 4,000 wounded had fallen into Confederate hands. Just two guns were taken, against fifty-two lost. Straggling was very heavy, and McClellan admitted in his letter to Stanton that just then he doubted whether there were 50,000 men with their regiments. "Either we have made an inglorious *skedaddle* or a brilliant retreat," a soldier wrote home from Harrison's Landing, and his bewilderment was common enough in the ranks.

On the morning of July 3 a burst of artillery fire foretold still another day of fighting, and McClellan seized the moment to make one of those dramatic gestures which always aroused his army. "I at once rode through the troops," he wrote Ellen, "clear in front of them — to let them see there was no danger — they began to cheer as usual, & called out that they were all right & would fall to the last man 'for little Mac'!" He looked over the ground and "saw at once where the trouble was," and soon had the whole army positioned to meet an attack. The trouble proved to be nothing more than harassing fire from Jeb Stuart's horse artillery, but to the Federals it was an assault repulsed and a boost to their spirits.

The next day, July 4, McClellan further raised morale by ordering the bands to play and the artillery to honor the nation's birthday. "All our banners were flung to the wind," Lieutenant Haydon wrote. "A national salute was fired. The music played most gloriously. Gen. McClellan came around to see us & we all cheered most heartily for country, cause & leader." Headquarters sent a dispatch to Washington announcing the festivities and the "first rate spirits" of the troops, and the War Department released it to the press so that the country would know that the Army of the Potomac was safe on the James and preparing to renew the contest.[1]

For a time it appeared the contest might resume sooner than later. A prisoner announced that the entire Confederate army was now at hand, and McClellan girded himself for the climactic struggle. "I go into this battle with the full conviction that our honor makes it necessary for me to share the fate of my army," he wrote Ellen in the predawn hours of July 6. If it was God's will that he die with his men, he would experience supreme happiness with her in a better world, but in any case she would have no cause to blush for him. The fight that day would "probably determine the fate of the country — I expect to be attacked by greatly superior numbers & hope to beat them." But the day passed quietly. General Lee had concluded that the Federals' position, and their gunboats, were too much for his strained army to overcome. "Enemy have not attacked," McClellan telegraphed the president on July 7; "— my position is very strong & daily becoming more so — if not attacked today I shall laugh at them.' "[2]

His final step in reinvigorating his army was to issue an address to the troops so that they might understand the Seven Days' battles and appreciate what they had accomplished. "Attacked by vastly superior forces, and without hope of reinforcements," he told them, "you have succeeded in changing your base of operations by a flank movement, always regarded as the most hazardous of military expedients... ; and under every disadvantage of numbers, and necessarily of position also, you have in every conflict beaten back your foes with enormous slaughter. Your conduct ranks you among the celebrated armies of history." It was not a claim of victory, certainly, but it was a proclamation of triumphant survival against adversity, precisely the mark that George McClellan would finally leave on this army. What was preserved, he wrote President Lincoln, was "above all honor," the ultimate palliative he had found for the shock of defeat.[3]

In a similar manner, he conjured up accomplishment from his own discreditable record during the Seven Days. He wrote his wife that the movement to the James was "one of the grandest operations in Military History." He told General Dix, "I have been able to extricate my army from difficulties sudden, unanticipated and almost overwhelming," and neither the country nor the military profession has "any cause for complaint of this army or its leader." When all the circumstances were fully known, he assured the president, "it will be acknowledged by all competent judges that the movement just completed by this Army is unparalleled in the annals of war."

In truth, although it was beyond his knowing, his army was safe at Harrison's Landing only because of repeated failures in the high command of the Army of Northern Virginia. Lee's staff system had proved faulty and none of his tactical plans was fully carried out on the Seven Days' battlefields, and several of his generals — including, most unaccountably, Stonewall Jackson — failed him at crucial moments. "Under ordinary circumstances the Federal Army should have been destroyed," Lee wrote, and it was a fair enough judgment.[4]

The Army of the Potomac's command system, by contrast, had worked effectively during the Seven Days, the measure of its success the fact that the army survived consecutive, critical days of fighting when it was abandoned by the general commanding. As early as the third of the Seven Days, at Gaines's Mill, McClellan surrendered the initiative and even the pretense of seeking victory. Whatever the merits of the strategy that had carried him to the gates of Richmond, he failed — and failed repeat-edly — the test of battle. Crisis on the battlefield left him incapa-ble of initiative and virtually deranged, desperately attempting to shift the responsibility and consequences of his failure. George McClellan was beaten in the battle for Richmond by an army that existed only in his mind's eye, its overwhelming numbers real enough to him so that he was able, in a final act of evasion, to make a plausible case to his own army and to the country and to himself that nothing of what had happened was actually his fault.

In reply to his call for massive reinforcements, Mr. Lincoln sought to reason with his general. "... I have not, outside your Army, seventyfive thousand men East of the mountains," he wrote McClellan on July 2. "Thus, the idea of sending you fifty thousand, or any other considerable force promptly, is simply absurd." He had called on the Northern governors for 300,000 new troops; McClellan must preserve his army "and I will strengthen it for the offensive again, as fast as I can." When Chief of Staff Marcy reached Washington, he was closely ques-tioned, particularly after he admitted that if McClellan was at-tacked again by overwhelming numbers and his communications cut, he might be forced to capitulate. That word was not to be used in connection with the army, Lincoln told him sharply. Marcy stammered that he spoke only of a hypothetical situation, which (he later wrote) "seemed to afford great relief to the President."

When he returned to Harrison's Landing on July 6, Marcy carried with him Lincoln's assurances that he would send what men he could, but McClellan was not to expect substantial re-inforcements for a month or six weeks. "Save the Army — first, where you are, if you *can* ; and secondly, by removal, if you must," he wrote. In a postscript he added that if McClellan felt able at any time to resume the offensive, "you are not restrained from doing so." Two days later the president himself arrived to see the condition of the army and to discuss what might be done with it.[5]

Lincoln reviewed the troops, corps by corps, and was encour-aged by what he saw. He later told his secretary, John Nicolay, that there were more men with their colors, and they were in better condition, than he had expected. McClellan confided to his wife that he had to order the men to cheer the president, ''& they did it very feebly,'' but others thought the welcome was a warm one. A New Yorker in Joe Hooker's division wrote his sister, ''Talk of McClellan's popularity among the soldiers. It will never measure 1/100th part of Honest Abe's. Such cheers as greeted him never tickled the ears of Napoleon in his palmiest days.'' After the review, McClellan joined Lincoln aboard the steamer *Ariel* and handed him what he described to Ellen as ''a strong frank letter.'' He added, ''If he acts upon it the country will be saved.''[6]

McClellan's famous Harrison's Landing letter originated in his offer to the president, before the Seven Days' battles, to detail his views on the state of military affairs throughout the country. The matter was postponed by mutual agreement. Now the war had reached a critical stage and (he told Ellen) he felt justified by conscience as well as duty to speak out plainly. The present letter, he admitted to Lincoln, went beyond the scope of his duties as an army commander, but events called for it: the time had come ''when the Government must determine upon a civil and military policy, covering the whole ground of our national trouble.''

Rebellion had become full-scale war, he wrote, and at stake was the survival of free institutions and self-government. To be won the war must be conducted ''upon the highest principles known to Christian Civilization.... Neither confiscation of property, political executions of persons, territorial organization of states or forcible abolition of slavery should be contemplated for a moment. In prosecuting the War, all private property and unarmed persons should be strictly protected....'' However, slaves seeking military protection should continue to be considered contraband of war, and military necessity might even require the manumission of all the slaves in a state, provided their masters were fully compensated. ''A system of policy thus constitutional and conservative, and pervaded by the influences of Christianity and freedom, would receive the support of almost all truly loyal men, would deeply impress the rebel masses and all foreign nations, and it might be humbly hoped that it would commend itself to the favor of the Almighty.'' Only if the president was pledged to such a policy would victory be possible. ''A declaration of radical views, especially upon slavery, will rapidly disintegrate our present Armies,'' he warned; raising new troops ''will be almost hopeless.''

His military advice was brief, general, and not new: ''The national forces should not be dispersed in expeditions, posts of occupation and numerous Armies; but should be mainly collected into masses and brought to bear upon the Armies of the Confederate States. . . .'' The president would require a general-in-chief who understood his views and had his confidence and was competent to direct the nation's forces. ''I do not ask that place for myself,'' he wrote. ''I am willing to serve you in such position as you may assign me. . . .'' The disclaimer aside, McClellan clearly envisioned being the executor of his own policy.[7]

Lincoln could not have been surprised by anything in the Harrison's Landing letter or by its mixing of political and military advice. General McClellan had treated the two as indivisible since the earliest months of the war. When he marched into western Virginia he had announced to the citizenry that neither his army nor the national government would interfere with the institution of slavery. (Soon after the president's visit, in a letter to the Virginia planter Hill Carter, McClellan renewed his pledge that he would not wage war ''upon the domestic institutions of the land.'') He had taken it upon himself to negotiate Kentucky's policy of neutrality. Just three weeks before he had used a flag-of-truce meeting to explore the possibilities of peace with Howell Cobb. To his mind, the political policy he advocated was as essential an element of military strategy as logistics or allocations of manpower. As he wrote a few weeks later, ''I . . . deprecate, and view with infinite dread, any policy which tends to render impossible the reconstruction of the Union and to make this contest simply a useless effusion of blood . . . and I regard the civil or political question as inseparable from the military. . . .''

What particularly alarmed him about the rising tide of radicalism he detected in the government, as reflected just then in the congressional debate over a new confiscation act, was his fear that it might demoralize his army. That tide must be stemmed, and he wanted his views on the subject circulated within the administration. That night he wrote Secretary Stanton that he had just spelled out for the president ''the policy which ought to govern this contest,'' and he urged Stanton to ask to see the letter when Lincoln returned to the capital. Under no other policy, he added, would the troops continue to fight. He was not very hopeful that his views would prevail, however. The president had read the letter in his presence, thanked him for it, and said nothing more about it. He wrote Ellen that he doubted whether Lincoln profited at all by his visit, ''for he really seems quite incapable of rising to the height of the merits of the question & the magnitude of the crisis.''[8]

This was the first time the two men had met in three months, yet they found little to say to each other. McClellan, as uncommunicative as ever when dealing with the president, apparently volunteered no hint of any concrete plan for renewing the campaign. In recounting the visit for Samuel Barlow, he wrote that Lincoln ''asked for no explanations, expressed no dissatisfaction — treated me with no confidence, & did not ask my opinion except in *three* questions. . . .'' The questions involved the state of the army, and (more ominously, in McClellan's view) if and how it could be removed safely from the Peninsula. He replied that it would be a delicate and very difficult maneuver. Questioning the army's five corps commanders on the same point, the president found only two of them, Keyes and Franklin, in favor of evacuation. Sumner, Heintzelman, and Fitz John Porter were positive in their opinion that the army was safe where it was and that to remove it would be ruinous to the Union cause. Whatever his impression of this counsel, Lincoln concluded that he needed a military man to oversee military operations. The day after he returned to Washington, he called Henry W. Halleck from the western theater to become general-in-chief of all the nation's armies. He neither consulted with McClellan on this action nor informed him of it.[9]

Debate in the newspapers over the Peninsula campaign had meanwhile become heated. As was now customary in any press commentary involving George McClellan, the tone was highly partisan. The Republican *Chicago Tribune*, for example, marveled at the ''amount of lying'' in the explanations for McClellan's retreat to the James. ''And the crowning deceit of the whole column of falsehoods is to call the affair a 'great strategic movement.' It was just as much a great strategic movement as the battle of Ball's Bluff, and not a whit more.'' A New Jersey paper described McClellan as ''the puffed-up little man who now

cowers on the banks of the James under the wing and protection
of our gunboats.'' Other papers, however, took the line that the
retreat was (as the *New York Times*'s Henry Raymond wrote)
''one of the boldest military conceptions ever formed.''

Papers supporting McClellan, such as the *New York Herald*,
located blame for the defeat in the War Department : ''The people
are furious against Secretary Stanton. They imperiously and
unanimously demand his removal.'' It was widely reported that
John Jacob Astor, who had recently resigned as one of Mc-
Clellan's volunteer aides, was telling everyone in New York who
would listen that Stanton had deliberately withheld reinforcements from the Peninsula to prevent McClellan from winning
and thus becoming the center of political opposition to the administration. The *New York World*, boasting of inside information
on the campaign — much of it from Fitz John Porter's venomous
letters to editor Manton Marble — made the same point, terming
Washington's treatment of McClellan and his army a ''suicidal
policy'' conceived by abolitionist radicals, the ''irresponsible''
Committee on the Conduct of the War, and ''an incompetent
civilian,'' Secretary Stanton.

Perhaps the most widely noticed newspaper story was that of
correspondent Samuel Wilkeson, which appeared in the *New York
Tribune* on July 3. Wilkeson termed the necessity for the change
of base a ''crime against the nation. . . . This crime is the refusal
to reenforce McClellan.'' In the peroration of a bitter assault on
the administration, he wrote, ''I say that the blackest crime that
Power can commit is to stalk upon the field of peril and say,
'Soldiers, I have no faith in your commander! Let your martyrdom proceed!' And so says this Army of the Potomac.'' As shocked
as he must have been, editor Greeley printed the entire dispatch,
although he wrote that it did not represent the *Tribune*'s views
and contained accusations believed to be mistaken and unjust.
Wilkeson's charges took on weight simply because they appeared
in the strongly anti-McClellan *Tribune*.[10]

In the wake of the Seven Days, for the first time since McClellan
took command (and reflecting the controversy in the press), there
was a noticeable undercurrent of disillusionment among the men
in the ranks. ''The army owes its safety to the 'splendid strategy
of McClellan' is the cry of the papers,'' one of Hooker's soldiers
wrote his sister. ''It may be so, perhaps he planned the movement,

I think he was *forced* to it. Anyhow, he gets too much credit for what other people do. McClellan kept at a respectable distance in action...." To be sure, the general retained the unquestioning loyalty of the largest share of his troops, such as the man in Sumner's corps who wrote home that McClellan had shown great skill in fighting off the Rebels in their overwhelming numbers. "We have abundant confidence in him, and believe that with an equal force to the rebels, he will take Richmond." A man in the 4th Michigan blamed the failure of the campaign on abolitionist plotting against the general. "The whole army knows these things and deep is the curse heaped on the heads of those who have nigh ruined us by designed neglect. We trust McClellan still...."

Yet even men whose faith in the general was unshaken admitted that others no longer felt that way. As a soldier in the 11th Massachusetts put it, "There is no use in denying the fact that the confidence of the Army is terribly shaken in Genl McClellan although I stick to my old opinion that the damned abolitionists ... have to bear the great share of the blame. That big fool Stanton I would also shoot with rare joy." An artillerist explained that "even now some have no faith in McClellan they say he was out Generaled but we know to the contrary...."

Officers reflected a similar division of opinion. Major Alexander Webb of the artillery staff wrote his father on July 10 that McClellan "stands higher this moment than he ever did before. In him all credit & damn the authorities who withheld reinforcements...." At the other extreme was Colonel Francis Barlow, who was in the midst of the hardest fighting during the retreat to the James. "You have no idea of the imbecility of management both in action & out of it," he wrote home. "McClellan issues flaming addresses though everyone in the Army knows he was outwitted...." In another letter he wrote, "I think officers & men are disgusted with & have lost confidence in McClellan & are disgusted with attempts of the papers to make him out a victorious hero.... The stories of his being everywhere among the men in the fights are all untrue." Perhaps a man in Hooker's division best expressed the common theme in many soldiers' letters when he wrote, "Who was to blame for all this? Some say 'the War Department', others 'the President', and not a few 'Our General'."[11]

The controversy erupted in Congress as well. Zach Chandler,

enraged by the news from the Peninsula, was convinced that the failure was entirely McClellan's doing. ''I shall open upon the traitorous cuss this week . . . ,'' he wrote his wife on July 6. ''I can hold my temper no longer & *will not try*. . . . McLelland is an *awful* humbug & deserves to be shot.'' True to his word, he took the Senate floor the next day to deliver the first of several vicious attacks on the general. When the Joint Committee on the Conduct of the War conveniently lifted the seal of secrecy from testimony it had taken, Chandler had fresh ammunition for his assault. He charged that McClellan repeatedly and deliberately threw away opportunities to take Richmond, and instead ''found another big swamp, and we sat down in the center of it, and went to digging.'' In the course of his philippic he missed no chance to defend Stanton's role in the campaign. Ben Wade added to the controversy by assuring the Senate that he had secret evidence showing that in 1860 General McClellan had been inducted into the Knights of the Golden Circle, a shadowy and notorious antiwar group that had its roots in the filibustering ventures of the 1850s.[12]

There was concern that the furious battle going on between the partisans of McClellan and Stanton would imperil the Northern war effort. David Tod, the new governor of Ohio, wired Stanton, ''For God's sake, stop the wrangling between the friends of McClellan and yourself in Congress. I ask this as the friend of both.'' In fact, Stanton had already proposed a truce, writing McClellan that ''wicked men'' had raised a cloud between them for base and selfish purposes. ''No man had ever a truer friend than I have been to you and shall continue to be,'' he insisted. McClellan replied that, although in the past the secretary of war had acted toward him ''in such manner as to be deeply offensive to my feelings,'' he was satisfied from his letter that they could now resume cordial relations.

The president took a hand in the matter as well. He told a rally at the Capitol in support of the war that the quarrel between general and secretary of war was not really as deep as those pretending to be their friends said it was, and he took the responsibility for everything relating to the administration's support of the army. ''I know Gen. McClellan wishes to be successful, and I know he does not wish it any more than the Secretary of War for him, and both of them together no more than I wish it.'' Other third parties sought a reconciliation. Edwards Pierrepont, a New York Democratic party leader and a friend of Stanton's, met with McClellan's friend Samuel Barlow in the hope of arranging an armistice. Stanton wanted the general to know (so Pierrepont reported) that on two occasions only his personal and vigorous intercession had kept Lincoln from removing him from command.

This was pure fabrication and typical of the hypocrisy behind Stanton's conciliatory efforts. George McClellan gave nothing away when it came to hypocrisy, however. Just five days after pledging to work in harmony with the secretary, he poured out his true opinion of Stanton in a letter to Ellen. "I think that he is the most unmitigated scoundrel I ever knew, heard or read of," he wrote; "I think that (& I do not wish to be irreverent) had he lived in the time of the Saviour, Judas Iscariot would have remained a respected member of the fraternity of the Apostles, & that the magnificent treachery & rascality of E. M. Stanton would have caused Judas to have raised his arms in holy horror & unaffected wonder — he would certainly have claimed & exercised the right to have been the Betrayer of his Lord & Master.... I *may* do the man injustice ... for I hate to think that humanity *can* sink so low...." Whatever may have been said for appearance's sake, there was not the slightest relaxation in the bitter enmity between the two men.[13]

In his meeting with the president McClellan was silent about plans for a new campaign probably because just then he had none. While promising both Lincoln and General Pope that "at whatever hazard" he would mount a threat to Richmond should the Confederates advance toward Washington, in fact he faced a considerable military dilemma in operating from Harrison's Landing.

Thus far he had sought to counter the overwhelming numbers he believed he faced on the Peninsula by one of two tactics: mounting siege operations that profited from his advantage in heavy artillery, or maneuvering so as to force the enemy to attack him in an entrenched position. For a campaign based on the James, however, his biggest guns were useless, for there was no practical way to transport them within range of the Richmond defenses. In the Yorktown siege a creek was used to bring up the guns by barge. On the Chickahominy the siege train was carried to the front on the York River Railroad. Now he had no railroad and no waterway, either, except the James itself, but to advance by that route meant he would have to do the attacking, and against strong defensive positions at Malvern Hill and Drewry's Bluff. Simply to use the James as a supply line for an advance required winning control of both banks. Harrison's Landing was no farther from Richmond than his old base at White House on the Pamunkey, but tactically it posed far greater difficulties.

He compounded his problem by clinging tirelessly to the role of underdog. He assured President Lincoln that according to Rebel prisoners the Army of the Potomac had indeed faced 200,000 men in the battle for Richmond. He made certain that his civilian supporters were also clear on this point. Any report that he had outnumbered the Confederates was "simply false," he wrote Barlow; "— they had more than two to one against me. I could *not* have gone into Richmond with my left." On July 15 he spelled out for Ellen the odds he was facing. Those who kept urging an offensive provoked him, he wrote. "I could not bring 70,000, at most 75,000, into battle — & it *is so easy to attack* from 150,000 to 170,000 brave men entrenched with that number!!"[14]

He did give thought to an alternative target. Twenty-two miles south of Richmond was the town of Petersburg, through which passed all but one of the rail lines that linked the Confederate capital with the states to the south. Before the *Merrimack* denied the James to him, McClellan had mentioned this approach to Richmond in his original campaign plans, and after reaching Harrison's Landing he wrote General Dix that there was a possibility his new line of advance might be along the south bank of the James. He sent Chief of Staff Marcy back to Washington with instructions to collect ferry boats and the army's pontoon bridge train at Fort Monroe, should he decide to put a force across the river.

That was as far as his thinking went, however. Rather than developing a plan for moving on Petersburg (or on Richmond) and submitting it to Washington, McClellan devoted the month of July to a drawn-out and bitter circular argument with the administration. He learned nothing from Washington as to policy and reinforcements, he complained. "Not a word from Gomorrah," he telegraphed Marcy; an advance "cannot occur without stupid insanity on my part until I have tools to work with. ..." At the same time, he gave Washington nothing on which to act.

He offered only generalities. All of Ambrose Burnside's troops then at Newport News ought to be attached to his army, he told the president, "to enable it to assume the offensive as soon as possible."[15]

His policy of refusing to take the president into his confidence met with far less patience in July than it had in January. Now his position was weakened by his record as a failed commander, and two weeks after the trip to Harrison's Landing the president decided that General McClellan was not indispensable. He and Stanton pressed General Burnside to take the command of the Army of the Potomac. Burnside refused, citing his incapacity and arguing that McClellan was the best qualified for the position. When Halleck arrived in Washington to take up his duties as general-in-chief, the president sent him to the Peninsula to assess the situation for himself, and confided to his friend Senator Browning (as Browning recorded it in his diary) "that he was satisfied McClellan would not fight and that he had told Halleck so, and that he could keep him in command or not as he pleased."[16]

As one scorching Virginia day after another passed without event, McClellan grew increasingly delusionary and embittered by his lot. He had received letters urging him to march on Washington and take over the government, he told Ellen, and sometimes it was tempting to imagine how much more politely he might be treated were he to take his "rather large military family" to the capital. In long, emotional letters to her he alternately justified his failure before Richmond and castigated his enemies for causing it.

With evangelical fervor he detected the hand of God in the outcome of the Seven Days' battles. "I think I begin to see his wise purpose in all this...," he wrote. "If I had succeeded in taking Richmond now the fanatics of the North might have been too powerful & reunion impossible." Perhaps, he admitted, with all the self-blindness about him he too had made mistakes, although they were committed unknowingly — but he did not carry the thought so far as to be specific about them. In truth, he found so much to blame on the government that he could not really fault his own actions. It was the administration's game to force him to resign, he wrote, and his to demand a leave of absence if it came to that: "When they begin to reap the whirlwind that they have sown I may still be in position to do something to save my country. With all their faults I *do* love my countrymen & if I can save them I will yet do so. . . .''

His delusions were if anything amplified by the adoring letters Ellen wrote in reply. She had left Washington in the spring for New York and then had gone to stay with her family in New Jersey and was now at a summer hotel on the Connecticut shore, and wherever she went she reported how widespread was his support among ''the better class of people.'' At each slight he described she expressed outrage and indignation. ''I almost wish you *would* march up to Washington & frighten those people a little,'' she wrote. ''I long to have the time come when you can have your revenge. . . .'' She echoed his complaints against the ''mean & contemptible'' actions of the administration. ''I am tired of you having to wait on the pleasure of fools & idiots. How *galling* it *must* be to you & how *bravely* you bear every thing. I dont believe there was *ever* such a man as you are George, and there is no flattery in *that*.'' No one could have served his country more honorably, she assured him, and he must promise that as soon as he had taken Richmond he would resign and return to her. ''You . . . deserve all the honors that the whole world can give you & will have your reward *some* day.''[17]

If Lincoln had made up his mind that General McClellan was expendable, McClellan in his turn had reached the limit of his tolerance for the president. ''I am confident that he would relieve me tomorrow if he dared do so,'' he wrote Ellen on July 27. ''His cowardice alone prevents it. I can never regard him with other feelings than those of thorough contempt — for his mind, heart & morality.'' When the War Department did not release his accusatory Gaines's Mill telegram to the press, he made sure his supporters in New York knew of his charge of treason against the administration. To William Aspinwall he explained that throughout the Peninsula campaign he had been the victim of an ''inveterate persecution,'' a calculated policy by Washington to weaken his command ''so as to render it inadequate to accomplish the end in view, & then to hold me responsible for the results. I am quite weary of this.'' He wrote Barlow that he had lost all respect for the ''heartless villains'' in the administration. ''I do not believe there is one honest man among them — & I know what I say — I fear none of them wish to save the Union — they prefer ruling a separate Northern Confederacy — God will yet foil their abominable designs & mete out to them the terrible punishment they deserve.'' They well knew, he wrote, that if he ever gained the victory, "my foot will be on their necks.'' Secretary Chase, for one, seemed to have suspected as much, and about this time he urged the president to dismiss General McClellan on the grounds of disloyalty — not disloyalty to the country but to the administration.[18]

The most important of McClellan's concerns, however, was the welfare of his army. "My fate is linked with that of the Army of the Potomac,'' he wrote his friend Joseph Alsop, who had urged him not to resign, "and so long as I can be useful with it I must remain with it.'' He was determined to restore it to full strength and fighting edge. One of his first acts, after he was secure at Harrison's Landing, was to seek changes in the officer corps, and when Chief of Staff Marcy went to Washington, he had with him a list of officers to be relieved or transferred to other duties.

Marcy advised proceeding slowly and generating as little dissatisfaction as possible, for McClellan's detractors were looking for any excuse to assail him, but eventually changes were made. The artillery was reorganized and put under Henry J. Hunt, who had directed the guns skillfully at Malvern Hill. Rufus Ingalls replaced the sluggish Stewart Van Vliet as quartermaster. Dissatisfied with John Barnard's engineering work, McClellan was able to have him transferred to the command of the Washington fortifications. At the top of his list for replacement was Erasmus Keyes, his former West Point artillery instructor, whose performance at Williamsburg and Fair Oaks he judged mediocre at best. He left Keyes as head of a corps, but managed it so that he did not again have a field command with the Army of the Potomac.

The campaign had also tested his staff. For what he described to Ellen as "the really serious work, especially under fire,'' he had come to rely primarily on officers from the regular army, particularly Albert Colburn, Nelson Sweitzer, Edward Hudson, Edward Wright, and a few "educated soldiers'' from foreign armies, such as Paul von Radowitz and Herbert Hammerstein. He also made use of "some youngsters I have caught,'' among them George Armstrong Custer and Charles Russell Lowell, nephew of the poet James Russell Lowell. But he had little good to say for the volunteers on his staff. "The most useless thing imaginable is one of these 'highly educated' civilians," he remarked; " — it takes them a long time to learn the fact that they know nothing & they are very apt to give offense by their assumption of manner etc. I have raked mine down so that they are now pretty regulated but I would not for the world have any new ones...." The lessons of the campaign did not convince him of the need for an operational staff.[19]

He did give priority to reforming the system for supplying reinforcements. Secretary Stanton had long since reopened the recruiting stations he so rashly closed in April, and the states were seeking to meet the president's new call for 300,000 men. McClellan strenuously argued that all depleted regiments be brought up to full strength before any new regiments were formed. A leavening of recruits in the veteran units, he wrote the Northern governors, would bring the army up to readiness far sooner than trying to fit raw new regiments (and their raw officers) into place. "I would prefer 50,000 recruits for my old regiments to 100,000 men organized into new regiments," he told them. To implement his plan he sent Brigadier Henry M. Naglee to Washington to press the administration and the Congress for an amendment to the regulations. The much-needed reform was not made, however. Congress adjourned without acting on the measure, and the governors could not be persuaded to put aside the patronage and political profit gained from organizing new regiments in favor of a less rewarding policy of recruiting replacements for the old regiments. As a consequence, when McClellan next took the field he would command an army in which one out of ten regiments was composed entirely of men who were experiencing war for the first time.[20]

A second evil he sought to remedy was absenteeism. Lincoln raised the problem with him in a dispatch of July 13, in which he calculated that 45,000 men carried on the rolls of the Army of the Potomac were "still alive, and not with it." He thought that half or two thirds of them might be fit for duty. "If I am right, and you had these men with you, you could go into Richmond in the next three days." In his reply McClellan scaled the figure down to 40,000, but he fully agreed with Lincoln's premise. "If I could receive back the absentees," he acknowledged, "could get my sick men up I would need but small reinforcements to enable me to take Richmond.''

Certain of these absentees, he pointed out, were in fact deserters, who had escaped aboard hospital ships after the Peninsula battles under the pretext of aiding the wounded. The majority, however, were absent with leave — wounded or sick men sent to recover in their home states, where, once they were out from under army control, there was little to impel them to return. He proposed that an officer from each regiment be sent to the place where it had been raised, armed with full authority to investigate ''all hospitals and places where soldiers may be detained,'' and order back to duty every healthy man found. He was convinced, he wrote, that there ''are two well men absent to one really sick man.'' Like the matter of replacements, however, his plan fell victim to the conflict between federal and state authority. The War Department duly issued orders on absenteeism but left the enforcement to local authorities, and predictably there was no rush of men to fill the Potomac army's ranks.[21]

On July 25 General-in-Chief Halleck arrived at Harrison's Landing to discuss the future of the Army of the Potomac. Pressed for his views, McClellan finally revealed his plan. If properly reinforced, he would cross the James and march on Petersburg. Few details are on record, but apparently it was his idea to rely on speed and surprise to gain him the town and its railroads — defended by perhaps 25,000 troops, he thought — before the mass of the enemy forces reacted, and then dig in astride their communications and force Lee either to attack him in this chosen defensive position or abandon his capital. By this reasoning (as Halleck reported it), it would not be necessary to assault Richmond at all.

Halleck argued that moving on Petersburg was both dangerous and impractical, and, he reported to Secretary Stanton, McClellan ''finally agreed'' with much of what he said. Writing after the war, and with General Grant's 1864–1865 campaign against Petersburg in mind, McClellan would give more weight to his plan. His defenders insisted that his wisdom antedated Grant's by two years. At the time, however, he quickly dropped the whole idea. What gave him pause was the news that General Buell would not be advancing any time soon against Chattanooga and the Confederacy's main east-west rail connection. Already outnumbered, as he supposed, by at least two to one, he would be vulnerable at Petersburg to having his communications cut or his flank turned (as Lee had turned it during the Seven Days) by an enemy heavily reinforced from the West. On July 26 he confirmed to his corps commanders that he had given up the Petersburg plan.

He then discussed with Halleck an advance on Richmond along the north bank of the James. McClellan said he might need to resort to siege tactics against the defenders, but he believed that with 30,000 reinforcements he had a "a good chance of success." Halleck said only 20,000 were available. Those would give him merely "a chance" for success, McClellan answered, but he was "willing to try it." In fact, 20,000 was the number he had told Ellen a week earlier that he needed in order to renew his campaign. In like manner, he enlarged on the difficulties facing him by telling Halleck that the enemy was 200,000 strong, a substantial increase over the 150,000 to 170,000 he told his wife he was confronting. At one point he even suggested that John Pope's Army of Virginia join him at Yorktown so that, thus strengthened, he might retrace his earlier march up the Peninsula.

As Halleck finally left it, he offered McClellan the choice of operating against Richmond from the James with 20,000 fresh men — giving him 110,00 in all — or withdrawing from the Peninsula. In the event of a withdrawal, his forces and those of Pope and Burnside, covering Washington at all times, would launch a land-based campaign from Fredericksburg against the Confederate army and capital. McClellan was assured that he would lead the combined armies.[22]

On first learning of Halleck's promotion McClellan had taken it as a slight, telling Ellen that the moment he was certain the Army of the Potomac could do without him, he would resign his commission and leave the war rather than take orders from "a man whom I know by experience to be my inferior...." The appointment was "a slap in the face," he assured Barlow, a deliberate act by the administration to humiliate him. Although he believed that Halleck would act toward him in good faith, he suspected that the general-in-chief (like the president) left Harrison's Landing no wiser than when he arrived.

In fact, the visit had confirmed Halleck's worst fears. He saw the strategic situation in the eastern theater violating certain of the most fundamental tenets of war, notably those of Baron Jomini that he had codified in his *Elements of Military Art and Strategy*. On the Peninsula McClellan was operating on exterior lines of communication rather than interior lines; worse, instead of being concentrated, the Federal forces were divided and beyond mutual supporting distance, with the enemy squarely between them. In Halleck's view, there was nothing to prevent Lee, with the 200,000 men attributed to him, from screening either Pope or McClellan and using his interior lines to fall on and destroy first one and then the other. (Lee, with substantially less than half the force McClellan officially credited him with, was of the same mind, and had already shifted Stonewall Jackson northward toward Pope.) Halleck wrote his wife soon after his visit that McClellan had many good qualities as a soldier, "but he does not understand strategy and should never plan a campaign."

Halleck had brought Burnside with him to Harrison's Landing to evaluate the condition of the Army of the Potomac and its officers. Burnside found the corps commanders divided on withdrawing the army — Sumner and Heintzelman opposing it, Keyes and Franklin in favor, and Porter expressing no opinion — but the majority of the divisional commanders he talked to supported evacuation. Many thought the climate would worsen in late summer and cripple the army through disease. He also detected an ugly undercurrent in the officer corps, with talk of marching on Washington to depose the civilians running the war. Hearing a group of generals discuss this one evening, Burnside snapped, "I don't know what you fellows call this talk, but I call it flat Treason, by God!" When told of the episode, Halleck dismissed it as loose camp talk, yet it was a disturbing echo of General McClellan's complaints. Too many of the officers of the Potomac army, taking their tone from the general commanding, were talking darkly of the need for a change in the government, and General Burnside's rebuke would not end the matter.[23]

The day Halleck returned to Washington he received a letter from McClellan that decided him finally on the course to take with the Army of the Potomac. McClellan wrote that he had learned the enemy in Richmond was being further reinforced, and so he must have more men before he could take the offensive.

The 20,000 already promised him were to be drawn from the commands of Burnside and David Hunter. Now he wanted not part of their troops but all of them, some 35,000. In addition, he repeated his contention that he should have troops from the western theater, to the number of 15,000 or 20,000. He was certain Halleck agreed with him "that the true defence of Washington consists in a rapid & heavy blow given by this Army upon Richmond." To deliver that blow, however, he was now raising his demand for reinforcements from 20,000 to 50,000 or 55,000. On July 30 Halleck told him to begin sending off all his sick immediately, and on August 3 he ordered the Army of the Potomac to abandon Harrison's Landing for the Rappahannock line.[24]

McClellan was stunned by this ignoble ending to his grand campaign. The dispatch "has caused me the greatest pain I ever experienced," he telegraphed Halleck, and he made an impassioned plea for the order to be rescinded. At Harrison's Landing he was but twenty-five miles from Richmond; a return to northern Virginia would put him three times as far from his target, in addition to depriving him of the advantages of water transportation and the support of the navy's gunboats. He predicted that retreat would demoralize his army and depress the war spirit in the North, and in Europe it would be a signal of Northern weakness and encourage the Powers to recognize the Confederacy. He repeated the argument he had first used with Secretary of War Cameron in the fall of 1861: go over to the defensive in every theater but his, suffer even "partial reverses" if necessary to strengthen the Army of the Potomac, and he would finally crush out the rebellion at its heart; "it is here on the banks of the James that the fate of the Union should be decided."

The order would stand, Halleck told him. He had already ordered Burnside to the Rappahannock, and he stressed again the danger to both McClellan's and Pope's armies so long as a powerful enemy was between them. "I find the forces divided, and I wish to unite them," he summed up, and pointed out that all of McClellan's counterproposals called for more reinforcements than it was possible to supply in any reasonable time. He must act quickly in carrying out the withdrawal. "Your reputation as well as mine may be involved in its rapid execution. I cannot regard Pope and Burnside as safe until you re-enforce them." None of this logic could affect McClellan's settled convictions.

Indulging his habit of self-fulfilling prophecy, he assured Ellen that withdrawing the army would be a fatal error. "Halleck has begun to show the cloven foot already," he wrote her on August 4; "— he will kill himself in less than two weeks...."[25]

He attempted one final initiative on the Peninsula. In the last days of July General Pope heard from deserters that the Confederate army was evacuating Richmond, and Halleck proposed to McClellan that he press the enemy on his front to learn the truth of the matter. To do so, McClellan replied, he first had to recapture Malvern Hill. He thought he could have an expedition ready for that purpose on August 1, but one thing and another went wrong, and it was not until the early hours of August 5 that two infantry divisions under Joe Hooker and a substantial cavalry force — some 17,000 men in all — completed the movement. Hooker chased away the Rebel outpost on Malvern Hill with little trouble, and McClellan went forward to see the situation for himself.

He had Chief of Staff Marcy telegraph Washington that he hated to give up the position. "Secesh is under cover, & tho' he is in strong force I can beat him if they will give me reinforcements," he told Marcy. (Marcy embroidered the case somewhat by telling Halleck, in McClellan's name, that if reinforced they could be in Richmond in five days.) After looking over the ground, McClellan returned to headquarters. On August 6, alarmed by the Federals' advance, Lee prepared to counterattack with some 24,000 men, nearly half the troops defending Richmond.

From the evidence of his private letters, it is clear enough that McClellan was seeking some engagement with the enemy before Richmond in order to forestall Halleck's evacuation order. Perhaps he could lure the foe into a trap, he wrote his wife, or he might make a desperate dash of his own ("If I succeed in my coup everything will be changed ... & my enemies will be at my feet"), and that thought was surely on his mind in deciding to reoccupy Malvern Hill. But Lee's aggressive reaction caused him second thoughts. The entire Rebel army must be rising to the challenge, and at the prospect of putting his own army at risk against this host his resolve abruptly vanished.

During the two days that Hooker occupied Malvern Hill, McClellan neither reinforced him nor readied any troops to act as reinforcement. On the night of August 6 he recognized that a battle was imminent, but notified Hooker that it would be impossible for him "to get the whole Army in position before some time tomorrow afternoon, which will be too late to support you. . . ." In any event, accepting battle at Malvern was too dangerous: it would "be necessary to abandon the whole of our works here & run the risk of getting back here should the enemy prove too strong for us." Since Washington would send him no reinforcements (how any could have reached him in time he did not explain), Hooker must give up the position immediately and return to Harrison's Landing.

On the morning of August 7 the Confederates were startled to find the Federals gone. General Lee gauged his opponent perfectly when he wrote Stonewall Jackson that day, "I have no idea that he will advance on Richmond now." In the fumbling direction and obsessive caution and anticlimactic result, the Malvern Hill episode was a clear reflection, in miniature, of George McClellan's entire Peninsula campaign. It demonstrated as well the emptiness of his argument, then and later, that the best defense of Washington was leaving him in command on the Peninsula to threaten Richmond.[26]

McClellan viewed any collaboration with General Pope as a cheerless prospect. From the first, he was certain that Pope (like Irvin McDowell) was a tool of the abolitionists and his rival for command of the Army of the Potomac, and his opinion hardened after Pope issued a maladroit address to his army on July 14. In it he urged his troops to discard such McClellanesque phrases as "bases of supplies" and "taking strong positions and holding them" and "lines of retreat"; his policy was attack, not defense. If anything more was needed to cement McClellan's antipathy, it was Pope's next act — a series of general orders to his army that appeared to inflict on Southern civilians living in the war zone a range of punishments from confiscation to execution without trial. McClellan reacted to these "infamous orders," and to the recently passed Second Confiscation Act, with a general order of his own, which he described for his wife as "directly the reverse instructions . . . forbid all pillaging & stealing & take the highest Christian ground for the conduct of the war. . . ." No army of his, he promised, was going to become "a set of wicked & demoralized robbers."

John Pope, for his part, had no illusions about the commander of the Army of the Potomac. Dining with Treasury Secretary Chase on July 21, he went on at some length about McClellan's incompetence and said he had urged the president to replace him. He also predicted that if in the coming campaign he should need help from General McClellan, he had no reason to expect he would get it. In his letters to his wife, McClellan made it plain that at the very least he would not go out of his way to render such aid. He took relish in reporting that with Stonewall Jackson pursuing the Army of Virginia the "Pope bubble" would soon collapse. Before long his relish turned to outright malice. "I have a strong idea that Pope will be thrashed during the coming week," he wrote on August 10; "— & very badly whipped he will be & ought to be — such a villain as he is ought to bring defeat upon any cause that employs him...."[27]

Finally, on August 14, the Army of the Potomac began its withdrawal from Harrison's Landing, bound for the tip of the Peninsula to board ship for northern Virginia. McClellan protested the movement to the last. On August 12, informed by his cavalry commander Alfred Pleasonton that Richmond now had only 36,000 defenders, he telegraphed Halleck that he could take and hold it — as long as reinforcements were sent to him. Later the same day, he insisted that if Washington was in danger "this Army can scarcely arrive in time to save it — it is in much better position to do so from here...." With equal persistence, Halleck urged him to hurry the evacuation. "I can't get General McClellan to do what I wish," he complained to his wife.

It was two weeks from Halleck's first order to send off the sick until the march from Harrison's Landing began, and to some, including Halleck, that argued unnecessary delay. He told Secretary Stanton that McClellan had not obeyed orders "with the promptness I expected and the national safety, in my opinion, required." McClellan heatedly insisted that in those two weeks not an hour was wasted; no power on earth could have started the army on its way any sooner. The two generals, however, were arguing entirely different cases.

As Halleck saw it, Pope's Army of Virginia and, with it, Washington were in grave and growing danger. Only the timely arrival of a steady stream of reinforcements from the Peninsula could retrieve the situation. As McClellan saw it, the immediate danger was to the Army of the Potomac. Withdrawal in the face of a powerful opponent was regarded as one of war's most difficult operations, requiring the most carefully coordinated movements to leave no opening for the enemy to exploit. For however long it took to evacuate the sick and remove the heavy baggage, the entire Army of the Potomac must remain in its Harrison's Landing lines. "Our material can only be saved by using the whole Army to cover it if we are pressed," he explained to Halleck.

That he was now once more at risk he had no doubt, and Pleasonton's modest count of the enemy was quietly put aside. The latest intelligence from Pinkerton was varied but alarming: Jackson had gone north with up to 100,000 men or more; as many as 130,000 remained at Richmond; Beauregard's entire western army was now in Virginia; and other such "general estimates," in greater or lesser numbers. During this welter of fanciful calculation it escaped notice that Lee, acting on the first evidence that the Army of the Potomac might withdraw, was rapidly shifting his field army northward to operate against Pope. (McClellan made it a point to be the last to leave the Harrison's Landing camp; the day before, Lee had left Richmond to take command on the Rappahannock.) General McClellan would depart the Peninsula under the eye of a single Confederate cavalry brigade, none the wiser about his foe than when he had arrived four and a half months earlier.[28]

Once the march began it proceeded swiftly, and by August 16 the great camp was empty except for dummy sentries stuffed with straw manning the fortifications at regular intervals. In his memoirs McClellan recalled that he sent his staff on ahead and remained alone in the works for a time, "my mind full of the fatal consequences of the order I was forced to carry into execution." He took some consolation in the arrival of Burnside from Washington, he wrote Ellen, carrying assurances that Halleck "is really my friend" and, more important, confirming that he would command all the forces in Virginia once they were combined. "I begin to think that I may still be master of the situation. . . ."

Had he started the army unit by unit for Fort Monroe a week or ten days earlier, instead of holding everyone to the last minute in anticipation of being attacked, the troops would probably all have sailed by about August 20. As it was, the entire army reached the embarkation points between August 18 and 22. Despite the best efforts, delays were inevitable, with troops arriving faster than the available transports could move them up the Potomac and return for the next load. The corps of Porter and Heintzelman began to embark promptly enough the day after they arrived, but Franklin's and Sumner's corps were delayed three days. McClellan took pride in having slipped from harm's way and conducted a successful retreat without demoralizing his men. "Strange as it may seem the rascals have not I think lost one particle of confidence in me & love me just as much as ever," he told Ellen. He was confident that no blame could attach to him if his troops did not arrive in time.[29]

He was at Fort Monroe on August 21 when he received an urgent summons from Washington. Pope and Burnside were hard pressed by the Confederates and needed support quickly. McClellan himself was to come to the scene at once. He viewed the crisis as retribution. "I believe I have triumphed!!" he wrote Ellen. "... Now they are in trouble they seem to want the 'Quaker,' the 'procrastinator,' the 'coward' & the 'traitor'! Bien...." He telegraphed ahead to have Porter tell his men and Heintzelman's that the general commanding would be with them in the next battle: "Whatever occurs hold out until I arrive."

Writing to Ellen the next morning, he speculated that whether he had the top command in the coming campaign, or any command at all, "will depend entirely upon the state of their nerves in Washn." The next afternoon, August 23, he and his staff boarded the steamer *City of Hudson*, bound for Aquia Landing, on the Potomac a dozen miles northeast of Fredericksburg. For George McClellan it marked the official end of the Peninsula campaign.[30]

ELEVEN

GENERAL WITHOUT AN ARMY

THE ARRIVAL of the *City of Hudson* at Aquia Landing at one o'clock in the morning on August 24 marked the beginning of a week that saw George McClellan's military fortunes fall to a point seemingly beyond recovery. The senior major general on active duty, commander of the North's largest army, he became a general without any army at all. "God grant that I may never pass through such a scene again," he wrote Ellen in the midst of his trials.

There was no small irony in his plight, for had he removed the Army of the Potomac from Harrison's Landing as rapidly as might be, he probably would have been (as he expected to be) the triumphant master of the situation. Arriving on the Rappahannock line several days earlier with the bulk of his forces, and with his seniority and a relatively stable military situation, he could have laid claim to command of the joint armies. As it was, he found a situation on August 24 that was anything but stable.

The Federal forces were widely scattered. Only the corps of Porter and Burnside were immediately at hand near Aquia. Heintzelman's corps had been shifted to Alexandria, and that day Franklin began to disembark his corps there as well. Sumner had not yet left the Peninsula. (Keyes's corps was posted at Yorktown and in due course one of its divisions would be called up, but McClellan kept Keyes himself well away from the Army of the Potomac.) The night before, Pope had pulled his command back from the Rappahannock — he "shamefully abandoned" Porter and Burnside, McClellan exclaimed to Ellen. "It was most infamous conduct & he deserves hanging for it" — and the enemy had a firm hold on the initiative. He could learn nothing about his own role. "They will suffer a terrible defeat if the present state of affairs continues," he wrote. "I *know* that with God's help I can save them...."[1]

Signals were mixed on the matter of command. Before leaving the Peninsula he had written Burnside that "confidential sources" led him to believe "that Halleck either will not or cannot carry out his intentions in regard to my position, as expressed to you." On the other hand, William Aspinwall canvassed influential opinion in Washington and told Ellen on August 24 that he was convinced the general would "be placed in full command of the large forces now concentrating on the Rappahannock." After talking to presidential secretary John Nicolay, Allan Pinkerton assured McClellan that at least he would not be placed under Pope. The one certainty in the situation, McClellan discovered, was that he could get no answers from Washington to his most pointed questions. He telegraphed Halleck the day he landed at Aquia to learn "whether you still intend to place me in the command indicated in your first letter to me, & orally through Genl Burnside.... Please define my position & duties." To that and similar inquires Halleck made no reply.

The general-in-chief hoped the whole thorny question would soon be resolved by the course of events, preferably by a victory on the battlefield. It is not even certain that he had told Lincoln and Stanton of his agreement with McClellan, but with a battle promised at any moment he could hardly now displace Pope. At any event, he was no doubt aware that both president and secretary of war would be well satisfied to see General Pope victorious on his own, with no need to share the laurels with General McClellan. For his part, McClellan concluded that his only possible ally among his superiors in Washington was Henry Halleck. Stanton was an inveterate enemy and beyond redemption, and in the nearly seven weeks since the Harrison's Landing letter the president had been aloof, communicating with him but four times. He wrote Ellen that he would serve Halleck loyally in the crisis "without regard to myself or my position" and "keep as clear as possible of the Presdt & Cabinet...."[2]

On August 26 Halleck telegraphed him that the enemy was thought to be moving into the Shenandoah Valley, and called him to Alexandria to straighten out certain "great irregularities.'' What in fact he wanted was a deputy to manage reinforcements and supplies at what would be the Federals' base of operations if the campaign did indeed shift northward. At nine o'clock that night, just as McClellan's steamer arrived, word reached Alexandria that Confederate raiders were striking at Manassas Junction, on the Orange and Alexandria Railroad just twenty-five miles away. Manassas was the Army of Virginia's main supply depot. This bad news was the last message received over the direct telegraphic link with General Pope. McClellan wrote Ellen the next morning that nothing could be learned from the front. ''Our affairs here now much tangled up & I opine that in a day or two your old husband will be called upon to unsnarl them,'' he told her. He would do what was asked of him and bide his time.[3]

When he first learned, early in August, that Stonewall Jackson was on the march toward the Rappahannock, he had little doubt (as he told Ellen) ''that Pope will catch his Tartar within a couple of days & be disposed of.'' Appraising matters in Alexandria, he was convinced that outcome could not be delayed much longer. Fitz John Porter helped him to this conclusion, writing scornfully of Pope in his dispatches from the field and pleading, ''Cant you get us all away. We pray for it.'' As was his habit in such cases, McClellan immediately set about preparing for the worst that might happen in the wake of Pope's certain defeat — a full-blooded Confederate assault on Washington — and in so doing he ensured that his prophecy would be fulfilled. The forecast he had made to Ellen on August 10 proved accurate in all respects but its timetable: ''I think the result of their machinations will be that Pope will be badly thrashed within two days & that they will be very glad to turn over the redemption of their affairs to me. I won't undertake it unless I have full & entire control. . . .''[4]

He began his first day at Alexandria, August 27, by promising to attend promptly to Halleck's order that Franklin's corps march ''as soon as possible'' for Manassas Junction. Then a dispatch reached him from Porter, sent roundabout through Burnside on the Rappahannock, warning that a battle was imminent, and he took alarm. He proposed making no advance from Alexandria until Sumner's corps was brought up to act in concert with Franklin's. The immediate priority, he told Halleck, must be to make

Washington ''perfectly safe.'' ''I am not responsible for the past
and cannot be for the future, unless I receive authority to dispose
of the available troops according to my judgment. Please inform
me at once what my position is.'' If Pope had to fight a battle,
Halleck replied, he must be reinforced; Franklin should join him
by forced marches. He had much to deal with, Halleck explained,
including a Confederate offensive in Kentucky and problems in
raising new troops. ''I have no time for details. You will therefore,
as ranking general in the field, direct as you deem best. . . .''[5]

That evening McClellan boarded a steamer for Washington
and was with the general-in-chief until three o'clock the next
morning discussing the growing crisis. They met on good enough
terms — McClellan wrote Ellen afterward, ''I find Halleck well
disposed, and has had much to contend against'' — but they came
away with very different ideas of what was decided. By Halleck's
account, he told McClellan to take charge of all the troops in the
Washington-Alexandria area, new men as well as old, and he made
it clear that Franklin must advance immediately. He telegraphed
Franklin to march promptly for Manassas if General McClellan
had not yet returned to his headquarters to issue the marching
orders himself.

Whatever he may have said to Halleck, McClellan had no intention of sending anyone under his command to General Pope
on August 28. ''Pope is in a bad way . . . ,'' he wrote Ellen that
morning, ''& I have not yet the force at hand to relieve him.''
Sumner's Second Corps was then landing at Alexandria, but
there was a shortage of cavalry and neither his artillery nor
Franklin's had arrived from the Peninsula — one more consequence of the shipping bottleneck McClellan had created by evacuating Harrison's Landing with the entire army at once. Reports
came in that it was Stonewall Jackson who had raided Manassas
Junction, and that alone was enough to give pause. McClellan
telegraphed Halleck in late afternoon, ''Neither Franklin's nor
Sumner's Corps are now in condition to move & fight a battle —
it would be a sacrifice to send them out now.'' He most clearly
expressed his view of the situation in a dispatch to one of the
garrison commanders. He would be able to decide what forces
were available to defend Washington, he wrote, only when ''I
know whether I must move my men to the front or not. . . .''[6]

Each telegram McClellan sent Washington on the twenty-eighth painted a darker and more ominous scene, as if he were describing an approaching thunderstorm. By midafternoon he was certain the Confederates were ''in large force between us & Pope.'' Pope must cut his way through and fall back to the capital; he would send Franklin and Sumner out to meet him halfway. ''The great object is to collect the whole Army in Washington ready to defend the works & act upon the flank of any force crossing the upper Potomac,'' he told Halleck.

Late in the day heavy and sustained gunfire was heard from the direction of the old Bull Run battlefield of 1861 — Jackson had decided it was time to bring Pope to battle and was attacking one of his columns — and Halleck insisted that there be no further delay in sending out Franklin's corps. Franklin would march the next morning, McClellan replied, but the general-in-chief should be aware of the full dimensions of the crisis. Reports ''numerous from various sources,'' he telegraphed at ten o'clock that night, indicated that General Lee himself was now at Manassas and that the Rebels ''with 120,000 men intend advancing on the forts near Arlington and Chain Bridge, with a view of attacking Washington & Baltimore.''[7]

There is nothing on record to show that this alarming intelligence — which, typically, more than doubled Lee's strength — rested on anything more substantial than overheated imagination. Some sightings sent to McClellan that day had enemy forces nearing Washington and the Potomac at the Chain Bridge, three miles upstream from the capital, but mentioned no numbers anywhere close to 120,000. The next day McClellan told Ellen of a ''terrible scare'' during the night: ''A rumor got out that Lee was advancing rapidly on the Chain Bridge with 150,000 men — & such a stampede!'' Apparently he had trimmed the rumor to a more reasoned estimate for the general-in-chief.

He employed his usual deductive process. Informants insisted they had seen Generals Lee and Jackson and A. P. Hill and Richard Ewell and Jeb Stuart at Manassas, which meant that the entire Army of Northern Virginia must be at hand. To George McClellan it was entirely logical to suppose that his opponent had assembled 120,000 troops for an offensive from among Richmond's 200,000 defenders. The same phantom army he had faced during the Seven Days now confronted him before Washington. He had the Chain Bridge prepared for demolition, should it come to that. "I have a terrible task on my hands now," he wrote Ellen, but he was determined "if possible to save the country & the Capital."[8]

Even before rumor magnified the danger, he had seen risk enough in sending Franklin's corps to the front without artillery. By the evening of August 28, however, Franklin's batteries and some of Sumner's were finally landed at Alexandria. Now nothing prevented him from ordering the two corps to set off together at first light the next morning to join the Army of Virginia by forced marches. The rest of Sumner's batteries were expected soon and could catch up. There was a shortage of wagons, but those used to carry supplies to the forts could be commandeered, at bayonet point if need be, on the unarguable ground that ammunition for combat troops going into action had priority over hardtack for garrison troops in the rear. In short, had General McClellan willed it, 25,000 reinforcements would have been at General Pope's call in time for the fighting on August 30, the second and decisive day of the Second Battle of Bull Run.[9]

During the Shenandoah Valley campaign in the spring one of Stonewall Jackson's men, picked up by the Yankees, was heard to complain "All old Jackson gave us, was a musket, a hundred rounds and a gum blanket, and he 'druv us so like hell'...." That was a concept of making war completely alien to George McClellan, as he demonstrated on August 29. On that day, acting on the alarm he had raised, he advanced Sumner's corps only as far as the city's outer fortifications. It was against his wishes and only because of Halleck's "pressing order" that he sent off Franklin at 6:00 A.M. General Jacob Cox recorded McClellan's parting words to Franklin: "Go and do all you possibly can. Let it not be said that any part of the Army of the Potomac failed in its duty to General Pope." His own sense of duty to General Pope led him to halt Franklin at the village of Annandale, hardly seven miles from his starting point. The Federals idled away the day listening to the steady rumble of guns from the direction of Bull Run. "We could distinctly hear the cannonading...," a man wrote home; "the firing was perfectly terrific...."[10]

In midafternoon President Lincoln, following events at the War Department telegraph office, wired McClellan for the latest news of the fighting. In his reply McClellan was blunt. Reports from the front were unreliable, but he was clear enough as to the choice that must be made: "1st To concentrate all our available forces to open communication with Pope — 2nd To leave Pope to get out of his scrape & at once use all our means to make the Capital perfectly safe. No middle course will now answer.... It will not do to delay longer." In fact that choice had been made two days earlier, when Halleck first ordered him to send out Franklin's corps; McClellan's telegram was simply his latest attempt to overturn the decision. He wrote Ellen a few minutes later, "Two of my Corps will either save that fool Pope or be sacrificed for the country.... I am heart sick with the folly & ignorance I see around me...."

He told her he had spoken very plainly in his telegram to the president, but he could not have guessed the effect he created by the phrase "leave Pope to get out of his scrape." It was a favorite figure of speech of his, one he used often and without particular malice, but Lincoln took it as expressing his true attitude toward his fellow general. He had never seen the president "so wrathful as last night against George," Adams S. Hill, head of the *New York Tribune*'s Washington bureau, would write his managing editor. In his diary John Hay recorded that Lincoln was "very outspoken" in regard to the dispatch: "He said it really seemed to him that McC. wanted Pope defeated."[11]

It is too much to say (as detractors later said) that George McClellan was deliberately conspiring to have the Army of Virginia beaten at Bull Run, if for no other reason than his strong feeling for the men of his own army fighting on that field. What can be said, however, is that his bruised sensibilities and his unreasoning contempt for Pope convinced him that general would be — and deserved to be — defeated. Nor can it be doubted that he would have acted far more vigorously at Alexandria had one of his favorites, such as Fitz John Porter, commanded the Army of Virginia. Instead, the captive of his delusions, he put his own interests and his messianic vision ahead of doing everything possible to push reinforcements to the battlefield.

To be sure, John Pope might have found another way to lose the Second Battle of Bull Run (or Robert E. Lee another way to win it), but however that may be, General McClellan saw in the outcome just retribution against his enemies. Others saw a more disagreeable lesson. Surveying the sorry results of the campaign, Attorney General Bates wrote of "a criminal tardiness, a

fatuous apathy, a captious, bickering rivalry, among our commanders who seem so taken up with their quick made dignity,
that they overlook the lives of their people & the necessities of
their country.'' Bates left no doubt that he had General McClellan
in mind when he wrote.

Correspondent Hill reported that day a growing hostility to
McClellan at the War Department. He learned from Peter H.
Watson, the assistant secretary, that if Pope suffered defeat,
''McClellan will justly be held responsible, since he received orders to move day before yesterday and had not budged an inch
at an early hour this morning.'' The general-in-chief's orders
were explicit. ''I want Franklin's corps to go far enough to find
out something about the enemy,'' he telegraphed McClellan. If
the Confederates were discovered in front of him in such force
''as to prevent his going farther'' than Annandale, he should
halt there; ''otherwise he will push on toward Fairfax.... Our
people must move more actively and find out where the enemy
is. I am tired of guesses.'' When that evening he learned that
Franklin had encountered no enemy but halted at Annandale
anyway, Halleck's anger matched the president's. ''This is all
contrary to my orders,'' he telegraphed McClellan; ''investigate
and report the facts of this disobedience.''

McClellan took quick offense. He had halted Franklin at Annandale, he replied, because it was not safe for him to go on —
in fact Franklin had found nothing before him that day but
civilian refugees fleeing the battle — and it was ''not agreeable
to me to be accused of disobeying orders when I have simply
exercised the discretion you committed to me.'' He expected a
row over this with the general-in-chief, he told Ellen: ''He sent
me a telegram I did not like & I told him so very plainly. He is
not a refined person at all....''[12]

On August 30 the sound of battle was heard once again from
Bull Run. Franklin had resumed his march in the morning, and
by afternoon Sumner's corps was also in motion. They ''should
be pushed forward with all possible dispatch,'' Halleck telegraphed. ''They must use their legs and make forced marches.
Time now is everything....'' McClellan replied that every man
at his command but his camp guard was on the way to the front.

''It is dreadful to listen to the cannonading & not be able to
take any part in it,'' he wrote Ellen, and in his restlessness he

rode out that afternoon to Upton's Hill, an advanced outpost manned by a brigade of Jacob Cox's Ohioans. He was casually dressed in a flannel hunting shirt and wore no sidearms or insignia of rank except inconspicuous shoulder straps. He seemed depressed, Cox thought, but as always he was courteous and he bore himself with quiet dignity despite the embarrassment of his position. He discussed the military situation freely. He obviously had a low opinion of Pope and McDowell, Cox recalled, but spoke of them without seeming rancor. He blamed the crisis on the withdrawal of his army from the Peninsula, and remarked that if the administration had lost confidence in him, it should have put Pope in his place and continued the campaign from the James. However personally bitter that might have been, he said, ''I would not have any cause for complaint.''

Back in Alexandria that evening he finished his daily letter to Ellen. He had sent off every man but a few aides and orderlies, he told her, and was literally a general without an army. It was the worst day of his life. ''I feel too blue & disgusted to write any more now, so I will smoke a cigar & try to get into a better humor.'' To Halleck he telegraphed that should the battle be renewed the next day, he wanted to go to the front with his men, where they would fight none the worse for his being there. ''If it is not deemed best to entrust me with the command even of my own Army I simply ask to be permitted to share their fate on the field of battle.'' Halleck replied that only the president could make that decision.[13]

Franklin's corps, marching some hours ahead of Sumner's, had finally reached the scene at dusk on the thirtieth, only in time to meet the outriders of defeat in the form of thousands of stragglers from the battlefield. Even the more steadfast and orderly of Pope's retreating units met a rude welcome when they encountered Franklin's men. ''. . . To them we were only a part of Pope's beaten army,'' a Massachusetts soldier recalled, ''and as they lined the road they greeted us with mocking laughter, taunts, and jeers on the advantages of the new route to Richmond ; while many of them, in plain English, expressed their joy at the downfall of the braggart rival of the great soldier of the Peninsula.''

By contrast, the fragmentary reports reaching Washington that Saturday evening seemed to herald a Union victory, made all the sweeter for being won on the same field where the Union had suffered defeat the year before. "Everything seemed to be going well and hilarious on Saturday & we went to bed expecting glad tidings at sunrise," John Hay wrote in his diary. But Sunday, August 31, dawned bleak and rainy and with tidings that were all bad. Major Hammerstein of McClellan's staff, whom he had sent to the front for authentic news, returned to report Pope "badly whipped." The news left McClellan unnerved with excitement and anxiety. "I feel like a fool here — sucking my thumbs & doing nothing...," he wrote Ellen. "I learn from Hammerstein that the men in front are all very anxious for me to be with them — it is *too* cruel!"

He found it equally cruel to discover the answer to his repeated questions about his status in that morning's *Washington Chronicle*. It was announced that General McClellan "commands that portion of the Army of the Potomac that has not been sent forward to General Pope's command." He learned that the order was the work of Secretary Stanton, and meant, he told Ellen, that "I am left in command of *nothing*." He would demand a leave of absence the moment the crisis was over, and intended to write William Aspinwall "a quiet moderate letter... explaining to him the exact state of the case, without comment, so that my friends in New York may know all...." At the moment everything was in a state of confusion. Ellen had written him of her concern for their Washington house and their silver, and he promised to try to slip into the capital and at least send the silver off. Without even a regiment to command, he would have time for that.[14]

General-in-chief Halleck was all but overwhelmed by the crisis. In these crowded days, he wrote his wife, he was "almost worn out" for want of sleep. "Few can conceive the terrible anxiety I have had." The grim news of the defeat at Bull Run was made all the worse by the latest dispatch from General Pope. It would have been "greatly better if Sumner and Franklin had been here three or four days ago," Pope commented, but he promised "as desperate a fight as I can force our men to stand up to." He then posed a chilling question: "I should like to know whether you feel secure about Washington should this army be destroyed."

McClellan's badgering telegrams on the thirty-first brought the general-in-chief no solace. Under Stanton's order, he said, he had no one to command and no right to do more than offer advice, but he understood that the armament in two of the main Washington forts was inadequate, and that 20,000 stragglers from Pope's army were wandering the roads between the battlefield and Alexandria. In his reply Halleck confessed that the situation was beyond his control, and he pleaded for help: "I beg of you to assist me in this crisis with your ability and experience. I am utterly tired out."

McClellan had just finished writing a "very severe" application for a leave of absence, he told Ellen, "when I received a dispatch from Halleck begging me to help him out of the scrape...." His response was sympathetic but unyielding: "I am ready to afford you every assistance in my power, but you will readily perceive how difficult an undefined position such as I now hold must be. At what hour in the morning can I see you alone, either at your house or the office?" In a second dispatch he summarized the latest bad news from the field and urged that Pope be ordered to bring the army back to the safety of the fortifications. He gave it as his frank opinion that "there appears to be a total absence of brains & I fear the total destruction of the Army.... The occasion is grave & demands grave measures. The question is the salvation of the country."[15]

When he reached Washington the next morning, September 1, he found the president as well as the general-in-chief waiting for him. In recounting the meeting in Halleck's office for Ellen, he wrote that he arrived "mad as a March hare, & had a pretty plain talk with him & Abe...." Halleck wanted him to take charge of the city's defenses, to which he consented only "reluctantly." It was a lesser assignment than he expected, and he told Ellen that if "when the whole army returns here (if it ever does) I am not placed in command of all I will either insist upon a long leave of absence or resign." He saw great danger in the situation. Porter had sent him a pessimistic message predicting that even if the army reached the Washington lines, it might be too badly crippled to defend them. He persuaded Halleck to send one of his staff officers to the front for a firsthand look at Pope's forces.

A dispatch soon reached the War Department from Pope that was the most disturbing of any he had sent. It was his duty, he wrote, to report the "unsoldierly and dangerous conduct of many brigade and some division commanders of the forces sent here from the Peninsula." Demoralization among these Army of the

Potomac officers was "calculated to break down the spirits of the men and produce disaster." He charged them with battlefield misconduct, stating the cause as personal resentment at the change in the high command, and he advised that the army be pulled back to the Washington fortifications and reorganized. "You may avoid great disaster by doing so."

At that McClellan was called back for a second meeting with Lincoln and Halleck. It was reported, the president told him, that the Army of the Potomac was not cooperating with and supporting General Pope, and he wanted him to telegraph Fitz John Porter or others of his friends and use his influence "in correcting this state of things." By McClellan's account, he cheerfully agreed simply to relieve the president's anxiety, and Lincoln, "much moved," expressed his profound thanks for the special favor. Considering the gravity of Pope's charge and the implied recognition McClellan gave it by agreeing to Lincoln's request, there must have been more steel in the president's manner than McClellan admitted. That day John Hay reported Lincoln "in a singularly defiant tone of mind."

"I ask of you for my sake that of the country & of the old Army of the Potomac," McClellan telegraphed Porter, "that you and all my friends will lend the fullest & most cordial cooperation to Genl Pope in all the operations now going on. . . . Say the same thing to my friends in the Army of the Potomac & that the last request I have to make of them is that for their country's sake they will extend to Genl Pope the same support they ever have to me." He closed with the announcement that he was now in charge of Washington's defenses. As he wrote, he could hear the rumble of the guns once again.[16]

Early on Tuesday morning, September 2, while he was breakfasting at his house on H Street, Lincoln and Halleck appeared at his door unannounced. The president said that Halleck's aide had returned from the front to report the situation there as bad as it might be. Then (as McClellan wrote Ellen) he "expressed the opinion that the troubles now impending could be overcome better by me than anyone else. Pope is ordered to fall back upon Washn & as he reenters everything is to come under my command again!" He considered it a thankless task, with many difficulties and immense responsibilities. "I only consent to take it for my country's sake & with the humble hope that God has called me to it — how I pray that he may support me! — Don't be worried — my conscience is clear & I trust in God."

He told General Cox later that day that the president's attitude toward him during their interview was "cordial," but in fact Lincoln put him in command of the joint armies only with great misgiving. When he announced the decision to the Cabinet a few hours later, Attorney General Bates observed that he was "in deep distress . . . wrung by the bitterest anguish. . . ." By Gideon Welles's account, Lincoln acknowledged that General McClellan suffered from the "slows" and was "good for nothing" in an offensive campaign. But in the present situation, with the need to defend Washington and reorganize the beaten troops and restore their morale, there was no one better. Beyond anything else, McClellan had the confidence of the army.

The Cabinet members were surprised and dismayed by the news, none more so than Secretary Stanton. He had intended their meeting that day to witness his final victory over McClellan. He had with him a petition, signed by a majority of his Cabinet colleagues, declaring to the president "our deliberate opinion that, at this time, it is not safe to entrust to Major General McClellan the command of any Army of the United States." Although Lincoln's action forestalled the petitioners, they registered their vociferous opposition to the decision — giving the top command to McClellan, Secretary Chase declared, was the same as giving Washington to the Rebels — but to no avail. The president said the decision was his and he would be responsible for it to the country.[17]

The three contemporaneous descriptions of the September 2 Cabinet meeting — those of Welles, Chase, and Bates — agree that it was Lincoln's intention at the time to limit General McClellan's responsibility to the defense of the capital. This seemed to be confirmed when at McClellan's request the order was put in writing. By direction of the president and by command of Secretary Stanton, it read, "Major General McClellan will have command of the fortifications of Washington, and of all the troops for the defense of the Capital." Apparently both Lincoln and Stanton had second thoughts about being held responsible for the decision, and presently the order was revised to remove mention of the president and to substitute Halleck's name for Stanton's. Halleck had written his wife, soon after reaching Washington,

The earliest known picture of George B. McClellan, a daguerreotype dating from about 1846, shows him as a West Point cadet. With him are his father, Dr. George McClellan, and his sister, Mary.

Captain McClellan (right), sent in 1855 to study Europe's armies, in Warsaw with his host and seated colleagues Alfred Mordecai and Richard Delafield.

Major General McClellan was photographed at the Mathew Brady studio soon
after reaching Washington to take command of the Army of the Potomac.

The Prince de Joinville, a member of France's royal family who served on McClellan's staff, did this water color at an outpost in the Washington lines in 1861. With McClellan are Fitz John Porter (right) and Randolph Marcy.

A ceremony to honor McClellan's appointment as general-in-chief of the army featured lighted transparencies and a torchlight parade reviewed by the general at headquarters. The drawing is by newspaper artist Alfred R. Waud.

Mary Ellen McClellan with the couple's first child, daughter Mary, or May as she was called. An 1861 carte de visite photograph.

McClellan and his staff, October 1862. From left: Hammerstein, Wright, Radowitz, Biddle, Colburn, Lowell, McClellan, Hudson, Abert, Arthur McClellan.

General and Mrs. McClellan posed for Mathew Brady in Washington in 1861 or early 1862, during the period when McClellan was general-in-chief.

Above, McClellan confronts Beauregard in a *Leslie's* newspaper cartoon, published in February 1862, titled "Masterly Inactivity, or Six Months on the Potomac." Below, wooden ordnance, the so-called Quaker guns, photographed in the abandoned Confederate defenses at Centreville a month later.

The "small politicians" of Congress cackling at General McClellan, by a *Harper's Weekly* cartoonist, January 1862.

This artist's composite based on photographs depicts McClellan at headquarters on the eve of the Peninsula campaign. His mother-in-law, Mary Marcy, and his wife are in the doorway, his daughter and a nursemaid in the upstairs window.

A Federal battery at Yorktown on the Peninsula, photographed by James F. Gibson. These thirteen-inch seacoast mortars, each weighing eight and a half tons, were emplaced only on the last day of the siege and saw no action.

David H. Strother, a Federal staff officer and an artist who used the name Porte Crayon, did the satirical drawing at right of President Lincoln with the siege-minded McClellan during the Peninsula campaign. The Currier and Ives cartoon below, based on the allegation that McClellan was aboard a gunboat during the Malvern Hill fighting, was widely distributed in the 1864 presidential campaign.

THE GUNBOAT CANDIDATE.
OR THE BATTLE OF MALVERN HILL.

McClellan took the brick farmhouse of Philip Pry, on a hill overlooking Antietam Creek, as his field headquarters during the Battle of Antietam.

Confederate dead along the Hagerstown turnpike, killed early in the fighting
at Antietam. This photograph, and the one above, are by Alexander Gardner.

The Philadelphia artist Christian Schussele intended the setting of his 1862
equestrian portrait of McClellan to represent the Antietam battlefield.

Alexander Gardner photographed Lincoln with McClellan in the general's headquarters tent at Antietam on October 4, 1862, the last time they would meet.

In November McClellan was removed from command. Waud's sketch of his farewell to the army shows him next to General Burnside, doffing his cap.

Sculptor John Quincy Adams Ward modeled this 1864 copper bas-relief on a drawing by F.O.C. Darley. McClellan presented moldings from it to friends.

THE BEGINNING.
ELECTION of M'CLELLAN!
PENDLETON, VALLANDIGHAM,
Vice-President.   Secretary of War.
ARMISTICE!
FALL OF WAGES!
NO MARKET FOR PRODUCE!
Pennsylvania a Border State!
INVASION! CIVIL WAR! ANARCHY!
DESPOTISM!!
THE END.

A Republican broadside issued during the 1864 presidential contest predicts a dismal progression of events after a McClellan victory.

Maj. Gen. George B. McClellan Whitewashing the Chicago Platform.

Candidate McClellan tries to hide the peace plank in the party platform with his acceptance letter as peace advocates Clement Vallandigham, Horatio Seymour, and Fernando Wood complain; running mate Pendleton looks on.

ELECT LINCOLN

AND THE

BLACK REPUBLICAN TICKET

You will bring on NEGRO EQUALITY, more
DEBT, HARDER TIMES, another

DRAFT!

Universal Anarchy, and Ultimate

RUIN!

ELECT McCLELLAN

AND THE WHOLE

Democratic Ticket

You will defeat NEGRO EQUALITY,
restore Prosperity, re-establish the

UNION!

In an Honorable, Permanent and Happy

PEACE

The Democrats engaged in the broadside war with their own predictions for
the future, such as this example contrasting the programs of the two parties.

THE TRUE ISSUE OR "THATS WHATS THE MATTER".

In this 1864 cartoon, Currier and Ives explain the true issue of the contest as
the preservation of the Union from the extremism of Lincoln and Jefferson
Davis, and put forth McClellan as the conservative candidate of compromise.

Thomas Nast titled his barbed comment on McClellan's 1877 bid for the New Jersey governorship "All Quiet on the Hudson," and recalled the gunboat candidate of 1864.

McClellan posed for this portrait while governor of New Jersey. His three-year term marked his last period of public service.

that the administration wanted him to do what it was afraid to do: dismiss General McClellan. Now, should any blame attach to restoring McClellan to command (or, more properly, restoring the army to McClellan), Halleck's was the only name on the order.

It was noticed that the general went to work with more energy than he had displayed for the past week. The scene was strikingly similar to that of thirteen months earlier when he arrived in Washington after the first debacle at Bull Run. Garrisons were alerted and every section of the city's fortifications inspected. Guides fanned out to bring in the army and its trains and to collect stragglers. The navy was put on notice to keep the Potomac open should the Rebels break the rail connections with the North. Stanton's order to send off to New York arms and ammunition from the city arsenal was countermanded. "I have been & am busily engaged in transmitting the necessary orders & obtaining the requisite information," McClellan assured the president. "If Pope retires promptly & in good order all will yet go well."[18]

In late afternoon he rode out, as he told his wife, "to pick up the Army of the Potomac." He thought he might have to fight if the enemy was in pursuit. Pope had reported a fierce engagement the evening before at Chantilly, on the army's flank, in which two of his best generals were killed — hard-fighting Phil Kearny and Isaac Stevens, McClellan's one-time nemesis from the Pacific railroad survey. "Unless something can be done to restore tone to this army," Pope warned Washington, "it will melt away before you know it."

When Jacob Cox encountered McClellan in the city's outer fortifications, he noted a considerable change since their last meeting. Now he was dressed in full uniform, wearing his general's yellow sash and dress sword, and he greeted Cox cheerfully, "Well, General, I am in command again!" Before long the first of the beaten troops appeared, with Pope and McDowell in the van. The enemy had not renewed the attack after all, and the retreat was orderly enough. McClellan rode out to meet them, announced the change of command and briefly discussed placing the troops, and with an exchange of salutes they went their separate ways. (In his memoirs McClellan would embroider this meeting, recounting that when he asked about the distant sound of artillery fire, Pope had replied indifferently that it must be the rear guard, and asked to go on to Washington. "I assented," McClellan wrote, "remarking at the same time that *I* was going to that artillery-firing." In preparing a review of *McClellan's Own Story*, Cox, a witness to the encounter, jotted in the margin of his copy, "Certainly *not* true.")

Brigadier John P. Hatch, whom Pope had recently demoted from the cavalry to an infantry command, heard the interchange and took the opportunity to settle accounts. Turning back to his brigade, he shouted, "Boys, McClellan is in command again! Three cheers!"

What followed was something unique and legendary in the history of the Army of the Potomac. Hatch's men erupted in a roar of cheers and shouts, "given with wild delight," Cox wrote. As the news spread down the long column and across the countryside that "Little Mac is back!" the scene was repeated again and again. "Such cheers I never heard before, and were never heard in Pope's army," Lieutenant Stephen Weld of Porter's staff wrote his father. "Way off in the distance as he passed the different corps we could hear them cheer him. Every one felt happy and jolly." A private wrote home, "We were so glad to see him that we cheered until we were hoarse...." To each unit he encountered McClellan said simply, "Boys, go back to your old camps." An army surgeon found the effect remarkable: "His presence seemed to act magically upon them: despondency is replaced by confidence...."[19]

"Everything now is changed," General Meade told his wife on September 3; "McClellan's star is again in the ascendant, and Pope's has faded away." It was now John Pope who was the general without an army. To anyone who would listen, he complained bitterly of the Army of the Potomac's failure to support him in the recent fighting. He demanded to know from Stanton if "I am to be deprived of my command because of the treachery of McClellan & his tools." The two armies would be consolidated, he was told, and presently Pope was sent to Minnesota to fight Indians, leaving behind him court-martial charges against Porter, Franklin, and Charles Griffin, one of Porter's brigade commanders. Pope's case was unfortunate, Lincoln told Gideon Welles, but there was no help for it; the army would not fight for him. "McClellan has the army with him," he said.

It was soon reported that the victorious Confederates were once again on the march, and once again the president faced the problem of command. On September 3 he wrote out, for Stanton's signature, an order to Halleck to prepare a force "for active operations," an invitation to the general-in-chief to take the field himself. Halleck cast a blind eye at the invitation and rewrote it for General McClellan. There was every possibility that the enemy would cross the Potomac "and make a raid into Maryland or Pennsylvania," he announced, and McClellan was to organize a field army to meet the threat. When McClellan questioned him, Halleck said it was not yet decided who would lead that army.[20]

There is a singular lack of agreement in the accounts of Halleck, Lincoln, and McClellan on the question of field command for the Maryland campaign. What is clear is that at about nine o'clock on the morning of September 5 the president and the general-in-chief once again called unannounced at McClellan's house on H Street and met alone with the general. Two hours later, in a state of high emotion, McClellan wrote Ellen, "Again I have been called upon to save the country — the case is desperate, but with God's help I will try unselfishly to do my best & if he wills it accomplish the salvation of the nation. . . . It is probable that our communications will be cut off in a day or two — but don't be worried."

This call to save the country could refer only to instructions to take the field against the enemy, and as in all such letters to his wife announcing milestones in his military career, he went on to ponder the deeper meaning of events and to renew his pledge of faith in the God who ordered all earthly happenings. He immediately began his preparations, and by afternoon headquarters was issuing marching orders to the various commands. "The General expects to take the field himself tomorrow," one order explained.

In Halleck's several accounts of this meeting, it was the president who made the decision regarding McClellan, and he knew nothing of it beforehand. In testimony to the Joint Committee on the Conduct of the War, he quoted Lincoln as saying, "General, you will take command of the forces in the field." For his part, the president told various listeners that in fact it was Halleck who gave McClellan his marching orders. "I could not have done it," he said to Secretary Welles on September 8, "for I can never feel confident that he will do anything." He explained that he did not countermand the order for fear of undercutting Halleck's authority. In view of Halleck's record of indecisiveness during these critical days, however, it is totally out of character that he would have made such a major decision by himself, and his version of events is surely the correct one. Lincoln's denials were most probably efforts to distance himself from the matter so as to avoid political repercussions.

McClellan's recollection of the meeting was equally selective. In his preliminary report on operations in Maryland, dated October 15, he wrote that the enemy's passage into Maryland "made an active campaign necessary. . . . Being honored with the charge of this campaign, I entered at once upon the additional duties. . . ." Yet when he testified to the Joint Committee in March 1863, he did not remember any such marching orders. "When the time came I went out," he said. As the years passed his recollection was increasingly warped by bitterness toward the Lincoln administration and its treatment of him. In a draft for his memoirs he labeled Halleck's testimony about his orders to repel the enemy invasion "simply false." In his final comment on the subject, just before his death, he said that he had marched into Maryland in September 1862 "with a halter around my neck"; had the Army of the Potomac been defeated, "I would, no doubt, have been tried for assuming authority without orders, and . . . would probably have been condemned to death."

He composed this tale of martyrdom risked after both Lincoln and Halleck were dead and in the knowledge that no written order on the subject was ever issued. In fact none was needed. He had not been relieved as head of the Army of the Potomac, and the order of September 2 only confirmed that the Army of Virginia was added to his forces. If that order did not expressly name him to command the army when it took the field, it did not deny him the command either. The president's real decision on September 5 was to affirm McClellan as commander of the Army of the Potomac; after that, telling him to take the field in pursuit of Lee's army was simply a formality.[21]

In any event, neither president nor general was satisfied that this interview was the last word on the subject. Shortly afterward, Lincoln called in Ambrose Burnside, who had arrived that day from Aquia Landing, and once again offered him the command of the Army of the Potomac. Once again Burnside refused it. The responsibility was too great and the consequences of defeat too momentous, he said; he aspired to nothing higher than a command under General McClellan. At last resigned to the situation, the president looked no further. "We must use what tools we have," he told John Hay.

For his part, McClellan debated going back to Lincoln and demanding, as his price of acceptance, the removal of Secretary of War Stanton and General-in-Chief Halleck. Burnside would tell editor Henry Raymond of the *New York Times* that he found McClellan "excessively stubborn" on the subject that day and had argued until three o'clock in the morning to convince him that if he imposed such conditions at a time of national peril, the country would turn against him. When the Danish minister saw McClellan a day or two later and advised him not to leave Washington with an opponent like Edwin Stanton at his back, McClellan replied that he had thought it all over and realized the risk, but to disorganize the government just then would be unpatriotic. Like the president, he would have to make do with the tools he had.[22]

By September 3 there was scarcely a Federal soldier in and around Washington who did not know that General McClellan was in command in place of the despised Pope, and that knowledge alone restored morale a hundredfold. Even the doubters recognized that things could only get better. "McClellan's reappointment gives great satisfaction to the soldiers. Whether right or wrong they believe in him," one of Burnside's officers wrote on September 4. "Our troops know of none other they can trust" was how Major Alexander Webb summed up opinion in the ranks. McClellan made a deliberate effort to reinforce this view by appearing in as many of the camps as he could. "I hear them calling out to me as I ride among them — 'George — don't leave us again!' 'They *shan't* take you away from us again' etc etc," he wrote Ellen. Looking back on his efforts a few days later, he told her, "I have been obliged to do the best I could with the broken & discouraged fragments of two armies defeated by no fault of mine...."

He acted with equal decisiveness to organize forces for the field and to guard Washington. Sumner's Second Corps and Franklin's Sixth, with no fighting in the recent campaign, were obvious choices for the field army, and both were substantially enlarged. Darius Couch's division, taken from Keyes's corps on the Pe-

ninsula, was attached to Franklin's command. Sumner was reinforced by a new division assembled from garrison troops, a
scattering of veterans of the Shenandoah Valley fighting, and
regiments of recruits fresh from home. Burnside's Ninth Corps
was also heavily reinforced for the new campaign by a division
from the North Carolina coastal expedition and the Kanawha
Division from western Virginia. From Fitz John Porter's Fifth
Corps McClellan took his favorite troops, George Sykes's division
of regulars. From the Army of Virginia he took the corps of
McDowell and Nathaniel Banks, renumbering them the First and
Twelfth corps, respectively. These raised the field army to five
corps and 85,000 men. Of the sixteen divisions, only six were from
the Peninsula army.

To support the Washington garrison he left three corps — Franz
Sigel's, the least effective in Pope's army; Heintzelman's Third
Corps from the Army of the Potomac, badly mauled in the Bull
Run fighting and in need of refitting; and, to provide solid brac-
ing, the balance of Porter's Fifth Corps. The capital's defenders,
including the garrison troops, came to 72,500. Pope's 16,000 casualties were made good from the dozens of regiments arriving in
response to the July call for new troops. Sixteen of them were
ordered to march with the field army and nineteen assigned to
the defenses.[23]

McClellan was determined to make major command changes a
part of his reorganization. First, and most important, he persuaded Stanton and Halleck to reinstate ''in the present crisis''
Porter, Franklin, and Charles Griffin, who had been relieved
pending a hearing on Pope's charges of misconduct at Second
Bull Run. (Writing of this to the president, McClellan described
his interview with Stanton as ''very pleasant.'' However, he could
not induce the secretary of war to give him General Charles P.
Stone, recently released from his imprisonment for alleged disloyalty, for a field command.)

He then revamped the command of the two corps inherited
from the Army of Virginia. The prejudice against Irvin Mc-
Dowell, both by his men and by McClellan, was so strong that
his removal, like Pope's, was inevitable. McClellan believed that
this corps, perhaps simply because it was McDowell's, was ''in
bad condition as to discipline & everything else,'' and he put Joe
Hooker in charge (as he told Ellen) to ''soon bring them out of

the kinks, & . . . make them fight if anyone can.'' Nathaniel Banks, a political general of only modest military ability, was disposed of by promotion to the command of the Washington defenses, where no doubt McClellan trusted that Porter and Heintzelman would take charge behind the scenes in case of an emergency. Banks was replaced by a veteran regular, Joseph K. F. Mansfield.

As early as September 3, when the Confederates were sighted crossing the upper Potomac, McClellan began to shift the weight of his army to the northern outskirts of Washington. It was soon reported that the enemy occupied Frederick, Maryland, twenty-three miles north of the Potomac, a position threatening Baltimore as well as Washington. To meet this threat and cover both cities, he devised a fan-shaped advance north and west into Maryland along three lines, and recast his command structure for the movement. He assigned the right wing to Burnside, with the Ninth Corps under Jesse Reno and the newly constituted First Corps under Hooker. Sumner commanded the center, with his own Second Corps and the other Army of Virginia corps, Mansfield's Twelfth. Franklin's Sixth Corps, with Couch's attached division, made up the left wing. Sykes's regulars were posted at headquarters as a general reserve.

All this reorganization and restoration of morale was accomplished, or well started, in the space of just five days, and George McClellan's skill as a military administrator never shone more brightly. As he had done the summer before, following the first defeat at Bull Run, he renewed the sense of order and purpose so essential to the functioning of an army. The transformation was remarkable. Lincoln told John Hay that if the general could not fight himself, ''he excels in making others ready to fight.'' General Alpheus Williams, who had endured the Valley defeats by Jackson and then Pope's debacle with bitter complaint, could write his family on September 12, ''There will be a great battle or a great skedaddle on the part of the Rebels. I have great confidence that we shall smash them terribly if they stand, more confidence than I have ever had in any movement of the war.'' As he prepared to leave Washington for the field, McClellan shared that spirit. ''I think we shall win for the men are now in good spirits — confident in their General & all united in sentiment . . . ,'' he wrote Ellen in a mood of optimism. ''I have now the entire confidence of the Govt & the love of the army — my enemies are crushed, silent & disarmed — if I defeat the rebels I shall be master of the situation. . . .''[24]

McClellan's enemies were hardly silenced, but to some extent they were disarmed in these early days of September. The *New York Tribune* had taken the lead in attacking him for delaying reinforcements to Pope in the recent battle, and the issue was violently debated in the press. If the *Tribune*'s charges were true, the *Springfield Republican* argued in a typical comment on the matter, ''Gen. McClellan ought to be dismissed and disgraced, if not punished as a traitor''; if the charges were false, the *Tribune* ought to be suppressed. When Lincoln subsequently restored McClellan to command, it was widely interpreted as a presidential vote of confidence. As a consequence, editor William C. Prime of the Democratic *Journal of Commerce* wrote a friend, ''Loyal and honest men . . . rejoice with exceeding joy'' while the radicals ''are indignant, outraged, and sullen or violent as they happen to be . . . , and they denounce *the President* with ferocity.''

As Prime saw it, the current military reverses were due entirely to administration bungling, and Northern conservative opinion was coming to the conclusion ''that the war be absolutely free from *political influences*, and that the government assume a *military aspect*. . . .'' The idea had widespread and powerful support. James Gordon Bennett's *New York Herald*, for example, called on General McClellan to become an American Cromwell and ''insist upon the modification and reconstruction of the Cabinet, in order to have it purged of the radical taint which may again infuse its poison over the whole.'' As master of the situation he had every right ''to demand indemnity for the past and security for the future. . . .'' August Belmont, national chairman of the Democratic party, also wanted men of proven military experience at the helm. Stanton should be replaced as secretary of war by General Halleck, he wrote the president, and General McClellan made commander of all Union forces east of the Alleghenies. With these changes ''new vigor & energy would be infused into our military operations & the exhausted ranks of our army would be speedily filled. . . .''[25]

On September 5 elements of the Army of the Potomac began moving into the field, and for hours on end Washington's avenues were filled with marching troops. Secretary Welles thought there was design in routing the columns past McClellan's house on H

Street, where the general was "cheered lustily," rather than past the White House to honor the president. On the seventh McClellan shifted his headquarters to Rockville, Maryland.

As his last official act in the capital that Sunday he rode to the White House, Secretary of State Seward's house, and the offices of Halleck and Stanton at the War Department and left calling cards bearing his name and the initials P.P.C. They stood for *pour prendre congé*, the French military phrase for formally taking leave to go on campaign. In later years he painted this act as a challenge to his enemies "to stop me if they dared." At the time, however, it seems to have been nothing more than a pallid, somewhat arrogant imitation of Napoleon, of a piece with taking the salutes of his army as it was marched past his house. He was feeling benign toward the administration that day. In a farewell telegram to Ellen, he said: "The feeling of the Govt towards me, I am sure, is kind & trusting. I hope with God's blessing, to justify the great confidence they now repose in me, & will bury the past in oblivion."

As he departed that evening he encountered Gideon Welles taking a walk along Pennsylvania Avenue. He halted his staff and escort to ride over and shake hands and say farewell. Welles asked where he was bound. He was taking command in the field, McClellan replied.

"Well, *onward*, General, is now the word — the country will expect you to go *forward*," Welles told him.

That was exactly his intention, McClellan said. "Success to you, then, General, with all my heart," Welles said as they parted, and McClellan rode off toward Maryland and a new campaign.[26]

TWELVE

OPPORTUNITY
OF A LIFETIME

ON THE EVENING of September 8, from his field headquarters at Rockville, fifteen miles northwest of Washington, General McClellan telegraphed General-in-Chief Halleck that the military situation in Maryland was shifting and uncertain. All the intelligence reaching him was "still entirely too indefinite to justify definite action." If the entire Army of Northern Virginia had indeed crossed the Potomac — which he cautioned was by no means certain — he could at least promise that it would not capture Washington or Baltimore without a fight. "As soon as I find out where to strike I will be after them without an hour's delay," he promised.

From the moment he entered on the Maryland campaign, he later recalled, it was his intention to fight offensively. "I hoped to attack, rather than to wait & receive battle in position," he wrote. "...I felt that the effect of being the attacking party would do very much towards restoring the old morale of my troops." In these first days he was optimistic about the outcome. "I expect to fight a great battle & to do my best at it," he told Ellen; "— I do not think secesh will catch me very badly — the men & officers have complete confidence in me...."

He made no immediate attempt to seize the initiative from his opponent, however. To Governor Andrew G. Curtin of Pennsylvania he explained that he would position his forces "to move against the Rebels whatever their plan may be." He remained at Rockville for four days, studying the situation, trying to form some calculation of the size, location, and intentions of the Rebel army.

These were days of reorganizing and waiting. He wrote Ellen

that "commanding such an army as this — picked up after a defeat, is no very easy thing — it does take a great deal of time & infinite labor." He wanted a breathing spell to get his men "rested & in good order for fighting." Headquarters was half a mile outside Rockville on a low hill in a field of clover, open to any breeze that stirred in the September heat. Lieutenant Colonel David H. Strother, newly transferred from Pope's staff to McClellan's, was impressed with the smooth-working and professional operation of the army's high command. "There is more appearance of military etiquette and soldierly bearing about it than I have yet seen," he noted in his diary. He had served under McClellan earlier in western Virginia, and found the general as cordial and personable as he remembered. "Our conversation was clear, unembarrassed, and agreeable," he wrote. He regarded this warm, genuine manner as one of the secrets of McClellan's popularity with officers and men.[1]

In these days a sense of crisis was growing across the North as rumor multiplied the Confederate menace. Governor Curtin called for 50,000 militia to repel the invaders, and there was great alarm among those who thought themselves in the enemy's path. "They may get to Philadelphia or New York or Boston, for fortune is apt to smile on audacity and resolution," the New York diarist George Templeton Strong wrote. Some believed the crisis went deeper than simply the fear of another Southern military success.

He had heard the "most alarming kind of talk," Strong wrote, from General McClellan's conservative Democratic supporters predicting that he and his lieutenants would strike a bargain with their opposite numbers in the Rebel army to enforce a compromise peace on the administration. Stories of a military conspiracy were also current in Washington. Henry Wilson, chairman of the Senate Committee on Military Affairs, told Gideon Welles that he had learned from a member of McClellan's staff that officers of the Army of the Potomac were plotting revolution "and the establishment of a provisional government." The controversy spilled over into the press. The *New York Herald* complained that "radical journals" were attempting to charge McClellan "with being in league with an unknown number of unknown conspirators for the purpose of usurping the authority of the government...."

The matter was given a certain plausibility by Thomas Key,

one of McClellan's most trusted staff officers. One evening during the advance into Maryland, Key confided to newspaperman Nathaniel Paige that the night before he had heard fellow staff officers seriously discussing a countermarch on Washington to intimidate the government into giving up its abolitionist policies, thus opening the way to a peaceful settlement of the conflict. Key said he spoke out against the plot — as Ambrose Burnside had spoken out in similar circumstances at Harrison's Landing in July — and thought he had silenced it. He did not believe McClellan knew about it. Yet he worried that it was more than just camp talk; the plotters apparently believed the general would give their plan a sympathetic hearing. Paige recalled that he was not surprised by the incident, for he believed McClellan had surrounded himself with like-minded officers disloyal to the administration and the way it was managing the war. Too many in the high command of this army, Colonel Key said, "were fighting for a boundary line and not for the Union."

It cannot be imagined that George McClellan would have lent himself to an attempted military coup. However little loyalty he felt for the Lincoln administration, there was never a doubt of his loyalty to the Union. To be sure, he was very ready to see major changes made in the War Department, and he unquestionably shared Secretary Welles's view of the matter. "Should McClellan in this Maryland campaign display vigor and beat the Rebels," Welles wrote in his diary on September 12, "he may overthrow Stanton as well as Lee."[2]

Discovering his opponent's designs promised to be complicated by the terrain in which the two armies were now operating. In a military sense, western Maryland's most prominent feature was a series of natural barriers running parallel to each other in a generally north-south direction. Parr's Ridge and the Monocacy River divided the area between McClellan's Rockville headquarters and Frederick, where the Rebels were said to be concentrated. Farther to the west there was opportunity for concealed maneuvering behind the successive barriers of Catoctin Mountain, South Mountain, and Elk Mountain. The entire region was crisscrossed by good roads, notably the National Road that led westward from Baltimore to Frederick, then northwestward through Hagerstown. Here the country opened out into the broad Cumberland Valley of Maryland and Pennsylvania, and it was here that General Lee intended to fight the Army of the Potomac. "I went into Maryland to give battle," he told an interviewer after the war, "and could I have kept Gen. McClellan in ignorance of my position and plans . . . I would have fought and crushed him." It was his judgment, he said, that his opponent was an able but timid commander.

From the first, Lee's movements posed a danger to the Federals in the lower Shenandoah Valley, especially the garrisons at Harper's Ferry under Colonel Dixon S. Miles and at Martinsburg under Brigadier Julius White, and before he left Washington McClellan urged Halleck to withdraw Miles and White and add their troops to the field army. Halleck refused. He was particularly adamant about Harper's Ferry, McClellan later wrote, and "insisted upon it that the garrison was perfectly safe where it was & that it should remain there." The general-in-chief regarded the Confederate advance into Maryland as nothing more than a feint to draw the Army of the Potomac away from Washington, Lee's real objective, and he was unwilling to see the abundant ordnance and supplies at Harper's Ferry abandoned without cause. Only on September 11 did he make Miles subject to McClellan's orders.

The intelligence reaching McClellan in these days came to him from new and different channels. Allan Pinkerton was still attached to army headquarters and sending agents "within the enemies' lines," but whatever intelligence they gained about the Confederate army in Maryland is not on record ; certainly it made little impression on McClellan. Instead, he consistently based his estimates of Lee's strength and intentions on reports from his cavalry and from an intelligence network set up by Governor Curtin.[3]

The main Federal cavalry force, reorganized as a unified command under Brigadier Alfred Pleasonton, had the primary responsibility for collecting information on the enemy and his movements. Pleasonton had attracted McClellan's notice for "most admirably" leading the rear guard during the army's withdrawal from Harrison's Landing, although at the time the danger of a Confederate attack was hardly as great as McClellan imagined. He was equally admiring of Pleasonton's efforts in clashes with

Jeb Stuart's cavalry in Maryland. Whatever record Pleasonton made in this fighting, however, was more than offset by his singular ineptitude in intelligence gathering.

He was unable to furnish any firsthand intelligence, for he never succeeded in breaking through Stuart's cavalry screen for a look at the Confederate army. He did collect and evaluate dozens of secondhand accounts, however. He interrogated captives taken in skirmishes and numerous deserters and stragglers, and any number of civilians eager to tell what they knew of the invaders. In his questioning Pleasonton might have exercised the wisdom of the Frederick civilian who, after trying to find out what he could from the Rebels occupying the town, noted in his diary, "Bragging is a favorite game with them, and they do it well." Instead, he fully credited virtually every prisoner's story and every tale from citizens professing loyalty to the Union. Like Pinkerton, Alfred Pleasonton combined great industry with small judgment.[4]

In his first effort at an overall evaluation, he notified headquarters that, according to the "most reliable information," the Confederates had crossed the Potomac 100,000 strong and intended to make a wide swing into Pennsylvania through Gettysburg and York so as to fall on Baltimore from the north. A Rebel officer was "drinking a little" when he revealed this to a Marylander of Unionist convictions, he said, and the facts were "firmly believed to be true." On the morning of September 9 McClellan forwarded the report to Washington, but added that he believed the source to be suspect.

As the day passed he put such doubts aside. A railroad telegrapher, citing civilian refugees, placed a Rebel army of 100,000 at Frederick. Pleasonton soon provided specifics : Stonewall Jackson with 80,000 and James Longstreet with 30,000 were encamped at Frederick. "These are the numbers that are given by the rebel officers & men to citizens as they have passed through & which appear to be consistent," he explained. Satisfied by this assurance, McClellan sent the report on to Washington without qualification. He was prepared for anything, he told Halleck, except overwhelming numbers. He wrote Ellen, "The enemy have 110,000 on this side of the river. I have not so many, so I must watch them closely & try to catch them in some mistake. . . . I think my present positions will check their advance into Penna & give me

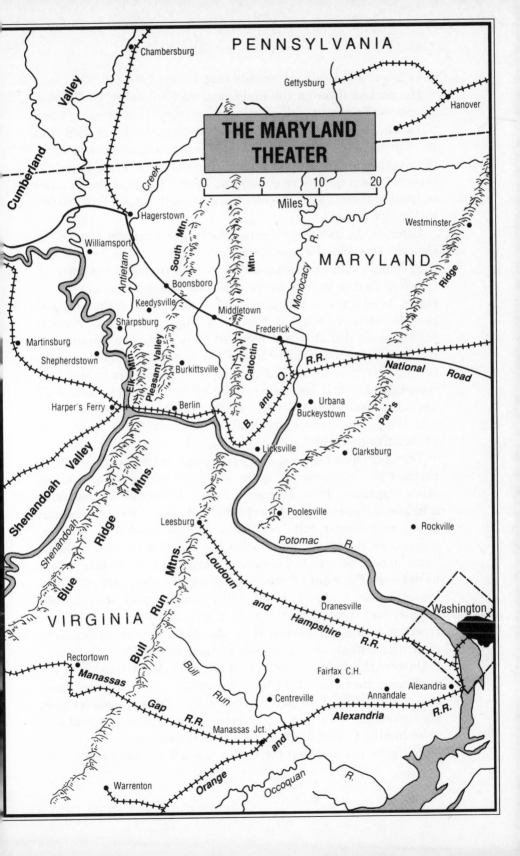

PENNSYLVANIA

Chambersburg

Gettysburg

Hanover

Valley

Cumberland

Creek

Hagerstown

Williamsport

THE MARYLAND THEATER

0   5   10   20

Miles

MARYLAND

Westminster

South Mtn.

Mtn.

Antietam

Monocacy R.

Boonsboro

Keedysville

Middletown

Ridge

Sharpsburg

Frederick

Martinsburg

Shepherdstown

Pleasant Valley

Catoctin

R.R.

Burkittsville

National   Road

Elk Mtn.

B. and O.

Paris

Harper's Ferry

Berlin

Urbana

Buckeystown

Shenandoah

Valley

Licksville

Clarksburg

Shenandoah R.

Ridge   Mtns.

Leesburg

Poolesville

Rockville

Blue

Potomac   R.

Loudoun   and

VIRGINIA

Bull Run Mtns.

Dranesville

Washington

Hampshire   R.R.

Rectortown

Manassas

Bull   Run

Fairfax C.H.

Alexandria

Centreville

Annandale

Gap   R.R.

Alexandria   R.R.

Manassas Jct.

and

Warrenton

Orange

Occoquan   R.

time to get some reinforcements that I need very much...."[5]

He worked through the night, and on September 10 outlined his plans. To the president, who telegraphed him often in these days with the query "How does it look now?" he replied that the Confederates were massed at Frederick and seemed to be threatening an advance eastward. To meet this threat he would seize the good defensive ground at Parr's Ridge, a dozen miles in front of them. Estimates of enemy strength ranged from 80,000 to 150,000, he said.

Later in the day he evaluated the larger strategic picture for General Halleck. His uncertainty was now gone, he wrote. "All the evidence that has accumulated from various sources since we left Washington goes to prove most conclusively that almost the entire Rebel army in Virginia, amounting to not less than 120,000 men, is in the vicinity of Frederick City." (He took this new count from a dispatch just received from Governor Curtin, who reported that a church elder from Frederick put the Rebel strength there at "not less than 120,000 men.") These were their best troops, led by their best generals, and they "intend to hazard all upon the issue of the coming battle. They are probably aware that their forces are numerically superior to ours by at least twenty-five per cent."

Therefore he must have every possible reinforcement — one or perhaps two of the army corps left at Washington, as well as Miles's garrison from Harper's Ferry. Otherwise the outcome could be "disastrous in the extreme." He did not see the capital in any real danger, but even if it should be taken while he campaigned in Maryland, that would not bear comparison with the "ruin and disasters" to follow if the Army of the Potomac should be defeated for want of reinforcements. He was confronting "a gigantic rebel army.... Every other consideration should yield to this; and if we defeat the army now arrayed before us, the rebellion is crushed.... But if we should be so unfortunate as to meet with defeat, our country is at their mercy."[6]

On this third day after taking the field McClellan drew the conclusion that shaped all his subsequent actions in Maryland: once again he faced the decisive battle with an army smaller than his opponent's. This prospect cannot have come as any real surprise to him. Called upon by God to save the country, he was no more likely to doubt that the enemy was a host than to doubt the call itself. The logic of the case was familiar : General Lee, having defended Richmond in June with 200,000 men and threatened Washington in August with 120,000, would hardly invade the North in September with an army of less than 120,000. That in fact General Lee commanded a third of that number — that he was daring to challenge the Army of the Potomac with so small a force — was a reality contrary to George McClellan's most strongly held conviction. Even had his intelligence network somehow discovered the truth about the Confederate army in Maryland, he would very likely have discounted it and gone on to act exactly as he did in the days that followed.

However that may be, the size of the Army of Northern Virginia remained Lee's secret. Following the lead of the general commanding, no one at Potomac army headquarters questioned this intelligence or expressed the least skepticism about its source, which almost without exception was the enemy — Rebels who spoke willingly and easily of great numbers to anyone who would listen, from gullible cavalrymen to trusting church elders. Stonewall Jackson confided to Marylanders at various times that he was marching on Chambersburg or Philadelphia or some other distant point. Jeb Stuart and his troopers planted false leads wherever they went. General Lee, well aware from reading Northern newspapers of the inflated numbers credited to him, was not averse to maintaining the fiction, and Pleasonton's remark about the consistency of the figures he collected suggests a deliberate Confederate campaign of misinformation.

The talkative Southerners must have marveled at Yankee credulity. At one point Pleasonton solemnly passed on to headquarters the tale of a certain Mr. Lotz, "said to be strong Union," who had it from the Rebels that while Lee lured McClellan on, Joe Johnston, recovered from his Fair Oaks wounds, was on the Potomac, about to spring on the rear of the Federals with an army of 150,000. The consequences of this, Pleasonton noted, "would if true be so tremendous that I must call the General's attention to it." Another civilian, vouched for as fully reliable by Governor Curtin, reported that he had just spent twenty-four hours in the enemy camps and was convinced that they had 190,000 men in Maryland and another 250,000 menacing Washington. Allan Pinkerton could not have brought any light to the subject ; he would assure President Lincoln that McClellan confronted

140,000 Confederates in Maryland. Nor was the general-in-chief immune to such speculations. He told the president and Secretaries Stanton and Chase that the Confederate army was 150,000 strong, of which probably 100,000 were in Maryland.[7]

General Pleasonton proved no better at divining enemy intentions than at estimating numbers, and his dispatch announcing that Jackson was on the National Road well to the east of Frederick and close to Parr's Ridge caused alarm at headquarters. (Jackson was just then twenty miles from that point and moving in the opposite direction.) On September 11 McClellan prepared to meet an attack and urgently telegraphed Washington for reinforcements. Lincoln replied that Porter's command would join him as soon as possible: "I am for sending you all that can be spared, & I hope others can follow Porter very soon." The president gave thought to going north himself to meet with his general in the field, but was finally talked out of it. It was too dangerous, he was told; there was a chance he might be intercepted by the wide-ranging Confederate cavalry.[8]

By the eleventh, too, there was evidence that the Rebel army was on the move. To this point McClellan had handled his forces with methodical care, making no attempt to close with the enemy, taking Parr's Ridge as his line of defense. Commands were moved in short steps, always within mutual supporting distance in case Lee made a thrust eastward toward Baltimore or southeastward toward Washington. Now, suddenly, Confederate troops were sighted at virtually every other point on the compass, south, west, and north.

One column, reversing the course of the invasion, was said by Pleasonton to be crossing the Potomac back into Virginia. Governor Curtin telegraphed that refugees from Frederick had seen a large force of Rebels on the National Road to the west. "General Jackson commanded in person," he added. Another refugee told the cavalry that Jackson had marched out of Frederick toward Harper's Ferry. Other reports said he was bound for Harrisburg and Philadelphia. The governor reported enemy cavalry in Hagerstown, just half a dozen miles from the Pennsylvania line. "It is believed that Jackson will move down the Cumberland Valley with at least part of his column and may attack White at Martinsburg with the balance." About the only certainty in all this was that the Rebels were leaving Frederick, and McClellan telegraphed Washington that he would try to occupy the town the next day. He promised to "follow up the rebels as rapidly as possible."[9]

On September 12 he hazarded an opinion on his opponent's movements. He telegraphed Halleck that he was "perfectly confident" the Confederates had marched out of Frederick on two roads: the National Road running northwest toward Hagerstown and the road leading southwest toward Harper's Ferry. In this he was only half right — they had not taken the Harper's Ferry road from Frederick — but in any case he quite misjudged Lee's purposes. "From all I can gather secesh is skedadelling & I don't think I can catch him unless he is really moving into Penna ...," he wrote Ellen that afternoon. "I begin to think that he is making off to get out of the scrape by recrossing the river at Williamsport — in which case my only chance of bagging him will be to cross lower down & cut into his communications near Winchester. He evidently don't want to fight me — for some reason or other. ..."

He gave the same opinion to President Lincoln, in reply to a telegram urging him not to let the enemy return to Virginia "without being hurt." His advance had occupied Frederick that evening, he said, and he assured the president that the cavalry would set out in pursuit the next morning. "My apprehension is that they may make for Williamsport & get across the river before I can catch them." The apprehension was understandable; he would be starting his pursuit seventy-two hours behind the quarry.[10]

Perplexity about the Rebels' movements was widespread in the high command. "Where they have gone, or what their plans are, is as yet involved in obscurity, and I think our generals are a little puzzled," General Meade wrote his wife. It was the "received opinion" at headquarters, Colonel Strother noted in his diary, that the enemy's designs in Maryland had been frustrated and that he was retreating into the Shenandoah Valley through Hagerstown and the nearby Potomac crossing at Williamsport. To compensate for their reversal of fortune, Strother wrote, it was thought the Rebels might seek the "additional éclat" of capturing the Harper's Ferry and Martinsburg garrisons. That General Lee was not searching for a way out of a scrape but instead was moving deliberately against these garrisons so as to secure his supply line before continuing his northern campaign apparently did not occur to McClellan.

He expressed concern for Harper's Ferry, to be sure, and told the president that he thought he could save the garrison if it put up a fight, yet he did nothing beyond ordering Pleasonton's cavalry to try to open communications with Colonel Miles. He made no serious effort either to relieve the garrison or to put pressure on the enemy. His advance on September 12 averaged six miles. "The troops have marched today as far as was possible and proper for them to move," he told Washington. He ordered an equally modest advance for September 13. General Lee, in his confidence that he could complete the Harper's Ferry operation and reunite his army without interference, once again displayed an intuitive ability to read his opponent's mind. It was an ability that General McClellan conspicuously lacked.[11]

On the morning of September 13 McClellan and the headquarters staff rode into Frederick to a tumultuous greeting. After five days of Confederate occupation, Frederick's Unionists welcomed the Federals as liberators, and the occasion had something of the look of a Roman triumph about it. Men, women, and children crowded into the street to cheer the general and shake his hand; mothers held up their babies to be kissed. Young women, General John Gibbon wrote, "kissed his clothes, threw their arms around his horse's neck and committed all sorts of extravagances." *Harper's Weekly* would devote its front page to a drawing of the scene, showing citizens in windows and on balconies waving flags and handkerchiefs and tossing flowers as McClellan, astride Dan Webster, raised his cap in acknowledgment. He wrote Ellen that he was "nearly overwhelmed & pulled to pieces. I enclose with this a little flag that some enthusiastic lady thrust into or upon Dan's bridle. As to flowers!! — they came in crowds!" He had seldom ever been so affected, he told her.[12]

September 13 was also the day the Federals' dismal intelligence-gathering record took a startling upward turn with the discovery of the famous Lost Order. The Twelfth Corps reached Frederick that morning, and in the bivouac of the 27th Indiana Corporal Barton W. Mitchell came on an envelope lying in the meadow grass that contained three cigars wrapped in a sheet of paper covered on both sides with official-looking writing. Bearing the heading "Hd Qrs Army of Northern Va Special Orders No 191" and marked confidential, it was signed "By Command of Gen. R. E. Lee." The document was filled with the names of other

Confederate generals equally well known to Corporal Mitchell. He took it to his company commander, who soon sent it on its way up the chain of command to Twelfth Corps headquarters.

General Alpheus Williams, in temporary command until General Mansfield arrived from Washington, examined the paper and then forwarded it to McClellan without delay. "I enclose a Special Order of Gen. Lee commanding Rebel forces which was found on the field where my corps is encamped," he wrote in a covering note. "It is a document of interest & is also thought genuine." Terming it "a document of interest" was a considerable understatement. McClellan was meeting with a delegation of local citizens when he was handed the paper and Williams's note, and after a quick reading he threw up his hands and exclaimed (according to one of his visitors), "Now I know what to do!"[13]

Special Orders No. 191, dated September 9, was Lee's operational plan for the capture of Harper's Ferry. It was detailed and explicit. Jackson's command was directed to leave Frederick on the National Road, take the Old Sharpsburg Road across South Mountain to a Potomac crossing near Shepherdstown, capture the Martinsburg garrison, and come in on Harper's Ferry from the west. John G. Walker's division would cross the river back into Virginia near the ford the army had used earlier and seize Loudoun Heights, the high ground south of Harper's Ferry. To complete the ring, Lafayette McLaws, with his division and R. H. Anderson's, would make a left turning off the National Road at Middletown, cross South Mountain into Pleasant Valley, and take Maryland Heights, overlooking Harper's Ferry on the north.

The operation would begin on September 10, and by the twelfth all the commands were to be in position for the attack. Longstreet's command, with D. H. Hill's division as rear guard, would follow the National Road across South Mountain and wait two miles beyond at Boonsboro until Harper's Ferry was taken. The army would reunite at Boonsboro or at Hagerstown, according to circumstances. All this was spelled out for General McClellan in the copy addressed to D. H. Hill and lost in a manner never explained. It so happened that Hill received a duplicate of the order from Jackson, and no one in the Confederate chain of command suspected that a copy was missing.[14]

McClellan's exuberance at the find was evident in the telegram he sent the president at noon that day: "I have the whole Rebel force in front of me but am confident that no time shall be lost.... I think Lee has made a gross mistake and that he will be severely punished for it. The Army is in motion as rapidly as possible. I hope for a great success if the plans of the Rebels remain unchanged.... I have all the plans of the Rebels and will catch them in their own trap if my men are equal to the emergency." He was uncharacteristically effusive, offering his respects to Mrs. Lincoln and remarking on the enthusiastic greeting he had received from the ladies of Frederick. "Will send you trophies," he promised.

He gave no thought to the possibility that the paper was a ruse. "I was satisfied in regard to the genuineness of the order & made no further inquiries," he told D. H. Hill after the war. Nor did he underestimate its importance. From Order 191 he knew that beyond South Mountain Lee's army was divided into four widely separated parts, and that at least two of those parts were vulnerable to being cut off and beaten in detail. At Boonsboro, distant fifteen miles from the right wing and center of the Army of the Potomac at Frederick, were the commands of Hill and Longstreet. The three divisions of Franklin's right wing were at that moment about the same distance from McLaws's two divisions besieging Harper's Ferry, with the prospect of defeating this second segment of Lee's army and rescuing Colonel Miles's garrison in the bargain. Here was the promise of almost certain victory, potentially as decisive as any McClellan had ever imagined in his various strategy papers. The Lost Order represented the opportunity of a lifetime.

He understood that as well. That evening, discussing current operations with his old West Point friend John Gibbon, McClellan turned down a fold of the Lost Order so that Gibbon could see the signature of Lee's adjutant, and said, "Here is a paper with which if I cannot whip Bobbie Lee, I will be willing to go home." It revealed the movement of every segment of the Rebel army, he went on. "Tomorrow we will pitch into his centre and if you people will only do two good, hard days' marching I will put Lee in a position he will find hard to get out of." He remarked, "Castiglione will be nothing to it," a reference to Napoleon's 1796 victory over an Austrian general who had incautiously divided his forces.

In drawing the parallel to Castiglione, perhaps McClellan did

not recall that it was Napoleon's rapid and well-timed marches
that had made the victory possible. Not even his remarkable good
fortune inspired him to change his deliberate habits. In his noon
telegram he assured the president that the army was ''in motion
as rapidly as possible,'' but like so many such pledges of prompt
action, this one was not quite what it seemed. Only Jacob Cox's
Kanawha Division was being put in motion, routinely ordered
forward earlier that morning to support Pleasonton's cavalry.
Nearly all the army's other fifteen divisions had finished their
short prescribed marches for the day or had not moved at all.
The only movement McClellan ordered on September 13 in response to the Lost Order was the advance of two other Ninth
Corps divisions to join Cox that evening.[15]

Had he resolved to waste not a moment of his opportunity,
seven hours of daylight were available on the thirteenth for
Franklin's left wing to press forward ten miles to the base of
South Mountain, to be in position to move against McLaws at
dawn. At the same time, on his own front at Frederick, a ten-
mile march would put Hooker's First Corps alongside the Ninth
Corps facing South Mountain, ready for an advance by the entire
right wing toward Boonsboro in the morning. This would require
an extra effort by the troops — a total march for the day of
seventeen miles for Franklin's men, and ten, sixteen, and twenty-
one miles, respectively, for Hooker's three divisions — but
McClellan told Gibbon that under the exceptional circumstances
of the moment he was going to demand hard marching. Yet the
afternoon hours of September 13 passed without a decision, and
finally he ordered these movements to begin only the next day.

Issuing those orders at noon that day instead of in the evening
would have required George McClellan to step out of character,
which he had demonstrated repeatedly he was incapable of doing.
In spite of his initial excitement on seeing the Lost Order and
his bold predictions to General Gibbon, the find had a paradoxical
effect on him. Thus far in the campaign he had been content to
march to his opponent's pace and not be accountable for events.
Abruptly, for the first time since before the Seven Days, he was
invited to take the military initiative. He reacted as he had before
Richmond in June: realizing it was now his decisions that would
shape events and decide the fate of the nation, and borne down
by the added responsibility, he became more sensitive to risk than

ever. The battle's outcome might be predestined — he told Ellen
the next day that he was as confident as one could be "who trusts
in a higher power & does not know what its decision will be" —
but in approaching battle he must weigh each possibility and
every consequence with extra care before acting.

However great a find the Lost Order might be, for example,
parts of it troubled him. It confirmed some intelligence reports
but contradicted others. The force Pleasonton had said was re-
tracing its steps to cross the Potomac into Virginia was no doubt
Walker's division bound for Loudoun Heights. It must be McLaws
who had left Frederick for Harper's Ferry and Maryland Heights.
Governor Curtin had been right in naming General White at
Martinsburg as Jackson's quarry. And a report just received of
heavy firing from the direction of Harper's Ferry seemed to
confirm that the siege had begun.

Yet nothing in the Lost Order accounted for the persistent
reports of large Rebel forces in Hagerstown and Williamsport;
neither was on the routes of march Lee specified. McClellan told
the president he hoped for a great success "if the plans of the
Rebels remain unchanged." Upon reflection it appeared they had
changed, and as always the unexpected gave him pause. (Lee's
plans were indeed altered, and to McClellan's further advantage.
Jackson had made a wider swing to the west, crossing the Potomac
at Williamsport, and Lee had moved to Hagerstown with Longstreet, leaving only D. H. Hill's division at Boonsboro. Moreover,
the whole operation was a day behind schedule.) He would hold
up his movements until he had more information.

At three o'clock that afternoon he sent a copy of Order 191 to
Pleasonton and asked him whether the routes of march had actually been followed. Although he lacked any real knowledge of
the matter, Pleasonton replied that evening, "As near as I can
judge the order of march of the enemy that you sent me has been
followed as closely as circumstances would permit." This was the
wrong answer, but it was reassuring to McClellan, and he went
ahead with his orders for the next day's movements.[16]

The dispatch he sent Halleck at 11:00 P.M. revealed his second
thoughts about the Lost Order. He explained that an order of
General Lee's addressed to D. H. Hill "which has accidentally
come into my hands this evening . . . discloses some of the plans
of the enemy. . . ." At noon he had telegraphed the president that

he then possessed "all the plans of the Rebels." Now it was "some of the plans," and they had reached him only "this evening," an apparently deliberate effort to make it seem that everything possible was done on September 13 to take advantage of his good fortune. The next morning the army would advance and by forced marches attempt to relieve Harper's Ferry, although "we may be too late." He assured the general-in-chief that he was facing the entire Confederate army, 120,000 men or more, commanded by General Lee in person, "& they outnumber me when united." Unless Lee had changed his plans, he concluded, "I expect a severe general engagement tomorrow."

Earlier that evening he had sent a long dispatch to Franklin, who was camped with his two divisions near Buckeystown, on the Monocacy River half a dozen miles south of Frederick. After summarizing the Confederates' Harper's Ferry operation, he outlined his own plans for September 14. The main body, with Burnside's right wing leading, would advance on the National Road to cross South Mountain at Turner's Gap and move on Boonsboro, where he expected to encounter Longstreet and D. H. Hill. Franklin was instructed to march "at daybreak in the morning" to the village of Burkittsville, at the foot of South Mountain, and make his way through Crampton's Gap into Pleasant Valley. Couch's division, then some five miles farther south at Licksville, would be ordered to join him. Franklin was cautioned that if he encountered opposition at Crampton's Gap, he was not to assault the position until half an hour after hearing the sound of firing at Turner's Gap, "where the main column will attack."

Franklin's first duty was to "cut off, destroy or capture McLaws' command & relieve Col Miles." He was then to return northward through Pleasant Valley, either to support the main army if it was still fighting or to cut off the escape route of the Rebels north of the Potomac while at the same time preventing Jackson from crossing the river to come to their aid. "My general idea is to cut the enemy in two & beat him in detail," McClellan explained. ". . . I think the force you have is, with good management, sufficient for the end in view."

Initiative was not William Franklin's strong point — even McClellan admitted his friend was "perhaps a little slow to move & somewhat cautious" — but the most resourceful of generals would have been taken aback by this array of tasks. Franklin faced half a day's march just to reach Burkittsville, and even if he found Crampton's Gap unguarded, he could hardly hope to defeat McLaws and lift the siege of Harper's Ferry, and then march a dozen miles or so to aid the main army. He may have wondered why General McClellan, with four army corps to pit against the commands of Longstreet and D. H. Hill, should need his help at all.

This division of labor resulted from McClellan's view of enemy numbers. When Burnside remarked to him that perhaps he was giving Franklin too much to do, he replied that there was no help for it; he could spare the Sixth Corps no reinforcements. In crediting Lee with an army of 120,000, he did not spell out how he apportioned that total among the generals named in the Lost Order. However, from his references to Jackson, Longstreet, and D. H. Hill leading "commands" or "corps," he apparently concluded that theirs were the largest units in the Confederate army, some 30,000 men each, while the other five generals he listed in his telegram to Halleck — McLaws, Anderson, Walker, A. P. Hill, and John B. Hood — led normal divisions averaging about 6,000 men each.

By this method of counting he made the seemingly logical deduction that Lee had put half his army into the Harper's Ferry operation, including 12,000 men in the divisions of McLaws and Anderson; thus he assured Franklin that his three divisions (19,500 men) were "sufficient for the end in view." On the other hand, it would require every man then under his direct command at Frederick to contend with the second half of the Rebel army, the corps of Longstreet and D. H. Hill, at Boonsboro. Evidence of his line of reasoning is found in the diary of his brother Arthur, his aide-de-camp, who wrote on the day after the fighting at South Mountain that Generals Longstreet and D. H. Hill were taking a stand at Sharpsburg in "two strong lines of battle 50,000 strong."[17]

Sunday, September 14, was the first of five consecutive days on which General McClellan was in close contact with all or some part of Lee's forces. Not once in that time would he discover, by observation or intuition or with the aid of the Lost Order, his opponent's critical situation or the true strength and condition of his army. In the Seven Days' battles he had surrendered to defeat almost as soon as the fighting began. In Maryland, once more facing odds existing only in his mind's eye, he would not dare to pursue decisive victory for fear of being defeated again.

His directions for Franklin's left wing were clear enough, but he was less clear about his intentions for the rest of the army on September 14. He wrote his wife in the morning that he anticipated "a serious engagement today & perhaps a general battle — if we have one at all during this operation it ought to be today or tomorrow." His dispatch to Franklin recognized that there might be a fight for the South Mountain passes. Yet on the evidence of his actions and his orders for the day, he cannot have taken the possibility very seriously. The Lost Order made no mention of any defense of South Mountain, and he judged cavalry and a single brigade of infantry to be sufficient to take and hold Turner's Gap in the morning.

The day's order of march was further indication that on September 14 he intended to position only the center and right wing of his army for battle, probably at Boonsboro and not before the following day. In spite of his now-familiar promise to Washington — "The whole Army is moving as rapidly as possible," he telegraphed at 9:00 A.M. — his lead columns were not going to reach much beyond the summit of South Mountain that day even under the best of circumstances.

The Ninth Corps would lead the march from its advanced posting at Middletown, but next in line was to be the other half of the right wing, Hooker's First Corps. McClellan's failure to order Burnside's wing united on the thirteenth left the First Corps still camped on the Monocacy east of Frederick, and with the farthest to march of any unit in the army it would be afternoon before it could reach even Middletown. As a further consequence of this order of march, only the Ninth Corps would be available for action for the best part of the day should any serious opposition be encountered at Turner's Gap.[18]

That morning General Gibbon announced to his brigade that General McClellan had told him that "if we would do two good honest days marching he would have the rebels in such a tight place they could never get out." The promise earned Gibbon three cheers. For his part, McClellan left the direction of the march to his subordinates and remained at headquarters in Frederick for most of the morning. At nine o'clock he received disturbing news from a cavalry captain who had managed to slip out of Harper's

Ferry during the night. He reported that Colonel Miles had given up Maryland Heights and pulled all his forces back into the town. General White was there with the Martinsburg garrison as well, and the Rebels had them surrounded. If not relieved by the fifteenth, Miles had said, he would be forced to surrender. The captain testified that General McClellan was greatly surprised to learn that Maryland Heights had been abandoned.

McClellan reported these developments to Franklin, urging him to occupy Crampton's Gap and to ''bear in mind the necessity of relieving Colonel Miles if possible.'' He sent a message to Miles, assuring him that he would do his best to relieve him but that he must hold out ''to the last extremity.'' Three of Pinkerton's men were recruited to attempt to reach Harper's Ferry with copies of the dispatch. If they failed (as in fact they did), McClellan could only hope that his orders to Pleasonton's horse artillery to fire rounds periodically as a signal that Federal forces were nearby would encourage Miles to keep fighting.[19]

Meanwhile, musketry and artillery could be heard in growing volume from the direction of Turner's Gap. The advance had encountered more opposition than McClellan anticipated. At about 11:00 A.M. general and staff rode to Middletown, where McClellan joined Burnside at his headquarters. He learned that Cox's Kanawha Division, attempting to outflank Turner's Gap by way of Fox's Gap, a mile to the south, was meeting sharp resistance. Cox had called for reinforcements, but they were slow in arriving. McClellan had not shared the finding of the Lost Order with his senior generals and his orders for the day carried no particular sense of urgency, and Burnside and Jesse Reno, the Ninth Corps commander, had not hurried the rest of the corps forward.

It was not until two o'clock in the afternoon, five hours after the fighting began, that the first of these reinforcements reached Cox's front. It was midafternoon before Hooker's entire First Corps was on the scene. Hooker deployed his forces for a turning movement against the other flank of the Turner's Gap position. In the interval, columns of Confederate troops were seen arriving on the mountaintop. While the Federals slowly marshaled their forces, Longstreet had marched the thirteen miles from Hagerstown to reinforce D. H. Hill's hard-pressed division.

With his entire right wing finally committed to the battle, McClellan advanced headquarters two miles to a knoll alongside the National Road and near the foot of South Mountain, where there was a clear view of the widening conflict. Trusted generals were at hand to direct the fighting, Reno on the left and Hooker on the right, and there was little that now required his direction. He surveyed the battlefield, recalled the war correspondent George W. Smalley, with a singular air of detachment, "as a chess-player surveys the board."

There was a theatrical quality to the moment, and with his surpassing talent for the dramatic gesture, McClellan rose to the occasion. Artillery batteries nearby were dueling with the enemy guns at Turner's Gap. The mountain ahead was wreathed in eddies of battle smoke in which the gun flashes shone like brief, hot sparks. The opposing battle lines on the heights were marked by heavier layers of smoke, and columns of Federal troops were visible winding their way up the mountainside, each column, one of Reno's men wrote, looking like "a monstrous, crawling, blue-black snake. . . ." McClellan posed against this spectacular back-drop, sitting motionless astride his war horse Dan Webster with his arm extended, pointing Hooker's passing troops toward the battle. The men cheered him until they were hoarse, one of them recalled, and some broke ranks to swarm around the martial figure and indulge in "the most extravagant demonstrations." All that was lacking was a painter to celebrate the Young Napoleon in his moment of triumph, in the manner of Antoine Gros's cele-bration of the first Napoleon at Eylau.[20]

Late in the afternoon battle smoke was seen to rise over Cramp-ton's Gap to the south, indicating that the Sixth Corps had also met opposition trying to break through South Mountain. Pres-ently a dispatch arrived from Franklin confirming the fact. "The force of the enemy is too great for us to take the pass to night I am afraid," he wrote; he would resume his attack in the morning. (As it happened, his officers did not share his pessimism, and after this dispatch was written they attacked and routed the Confederates defending the pass.) Whatever the outcome, there could be no relief for Harper's Ferry that day. Darkness found the main body advanced as far as the summit of the range, with Fox's Gap secure and a hold on the heights on both sides of Turner's Gap. The Federals had won the fight, but the Confed-erates had won twenty-four hours of time.

General Cox recalled that the general commanding expressed

no disappointment at the outcome of events on September 14, "but on the other hand congratulated me in very warm terms." McClellan never gave notice even to the possibility that his forces and Franklin's might have been across South Mountain well before midday on the fourteenth. He testified to the Joint Committee on the Conduct of the War that as soon as he learned the contents of Order 191, "I at once gave orders for a vigorous pursuit...." That assertion guided his subsequent accounts of the battle. "It has been a glorious victory," he telegraphed Halleck that night; "I cannot yet tell whether the enemy will retreat during the night or appear in increased force in the morning." He was preparing for any eventuality. The only damper on his satisfaction was the report that his friend and West Point classmate Jesse Reno had been killed in the fighting.[21]

In the light of day on September 15 he magnified the South Mountain victory beyond all plausibility. On the basis of a series of imaginative reports from Joe Hooker, whose source was "some citizens from Boonsboro," he announced to Washington that the Rebel army was in flight for the Potomac "in a perfect panic, & that Genl Lee last night stated publicly that he must admit they had been shockingly whipped." At midmorning he telegraphed, "Information this moment rec'd completely confirms the rout & demoralization of the rebel Army.... It is stated that Lee gives his loss as fifteen thousand." The War Department released the dispatches to the press, and by afternoon they were being posted on newspaper bulletin boards across the North. "The long catalogue of disaster is closed," the *Journal of Commerce* editorialized the next day. "... The army, led by McClellan, redeems its name and restores hope to the hearts of the people.... McClellan's history for the past few weeks has been more like a romance than a truth."

In his diary Gideon Welles tartly remarked of these dispatches that they neglected to explain to whom General Lee made these confessions that they might be brought to General McClellan so promptly. "A tale like this from Pope would have been classed as one of his lies," he wrote. "... I shall rejoice if McC. has actually overtaken the Rebels which is not altogether clear." From his inflated claim of victory — Lee was not in fact shockingly whipped and fleeing in rout and he had not lost anything close to 15,000 men, nor was he given to making such confessions — McClellan seized the thought that the campaign was all but over. "How glad I am for my country that it is delivered from immediate peril," he wrote Ellen that morning. "... If I can believe one tenth of what is reported, God has seldom given an army a greater victory than this...."[22]

He gave Washington the usual assurances that he was hurrying everything forward to press the enemy to the utmost, with the army marching "as rapidly as the men can move," but once again the reality was considerably different. Under the circumstances it might be supposed that he would have been at the front early that morning, personally directing a strong, effective pursuit to try to finish the work begun the day before. Instead, he remained well to the rear for nearly the entire day, savoring his success and sending victory telegrams to his wife and his brother John and Winfield Scott.

Not until more than three hours after first light on September 15 were any orders for an advance sent out from headquarters, and subsequent orders were conflicting and hedged about with cautions. Without direction the pursuit floundered. Units became intermixed and blocked one another's way; supply trains lumbered into the middle of columns of fighting men. The first Federal infantry reached Boonsboro only at ten that morning, two hours after Lee's rear guard had left. McClellan would blame General Burnside for holding up the march on the Fox's Gap road, yet it was not until midday that the problem was even discovered. General and staff then took time to look over the battlefield at Fox's Gap where the Ninth Corps had fought, and to see the spot where Jesse Reno had received his mortal wound. The party rode along the summit to Turner's Gap to examine the ground over which Hooker's First Corps put in its attack. Finally McClellan proceeded down the western face of the mountain and established headquarters at Boonsboro.[23]

These actions spoke louder than his brave words. The Confederates were retreating along the turnpike running from Boonsboro through Sharpsburg to Shepherdstown on the Potomac, apparently intending to recross the river into Virginia, and he was content to see them go. That afternoon the president telegraphed him, "Your dispatches of to-day received. God bless you, and all with you. Destroy the rebel army, if possible." General McClellan, however, was well satisfied with the prospect of simply driving the invading host from Northern soil without further fighting. He would welcome the time to make his army truly ready for battle.

In any event, by late morning on September 15 all his cautionary instincts had been aroused by a dispatch from Franklin in Pleasant Valley, written shortly before 9:00 A.M. The sound of artillery firing had ceased at Harper's Ferry, Franklin wrote, and he took it as the signal that Colonel Miles had surrendered. Fearing that the enemy on his front was now free to attack him, he called for large reinforcements. Presently he sent a second dispatch, announcing that he was outnumbered two to one: "It will, of course, not answer to pursue the enemy under these circumstances."

General Franklin was being hoodwinked that morning, just as he had been hoodwinked in the Crampton's Gap fighting the day before, by a greatly inferior force. In later years McClellan was privately critical of his old friend for his lack of energy and his failure to attack early on September 15 and relieve Harper's Ferry. At the time, however, he found Franklin's excuses plausible and an echo of his own views. If Franklin was in danger in Pleasant Valley, the left flank of the main army was also in danger, and he diverted five divisions from his pursuit to guard his flank and to support the Sixth Corps should it become necessary.[24]

Other cautionary dispatches soon arrived. From a vantage point on South Mountain the army's signal officer warned that the Confederates were no longer retreating but were instead taking up a line of battle "on the other side of Antietam creek and this side of Sharpsburg." At 1:00 P.M. Captain Custer of the headquarters staff, riding with the advance, confirmed the sighting. Rebel infantry occupied the forward slope of a low ridge, he reported: "They are in full view. Their line is a perfect one about a mile and a half long. . . . We can employ all the troops you can send us." Edwin Sumner, the ranking general in the pursuit, reached the front about 3:00 P.M. and reported the Confederates to be in large force. "As we don't know the number of their lines it is impossible to estimate their *entire* force," he wrote. "Shall I make the necessary dispositions to attack? And shall I attack without further orders?" McClellan had forbidden any assault until he was on the scene, and now he decided to go to the front to investigate the situation personally.

It was three miles from Boonsboro to the village of Keedysville, where Sumner was waiting, and for the cavalcade of general, staff, and headquarters escort it was a scene of uninterrupted triumph. "The whole ride was through masses of troops and our movement was escorted by one continuous cheering," Colonel Strother noted in his diary. Of the many such occasions in his wartime service General McClellan remembered this one particularly, and he wrote pridefully in his memoirs that he was received by the troops "with the wildest enthusiasm." It was late in the afternoon when he arrived and saw for the first time the field that would witness the climax of his military career.[25]

The general and his officers and staff made a large party as they inspected the enemy's position from a ridgeline overlooking Antietam Creek, and a Confederate battery promptly took them under fire. The group dispersed, and McClellan continued his reconnaissance accompanied only by Fitz John Porter, who had arrived the day before in advance of his troops. "The examination of the enemy's position and the discussion of it continued till near the close of the day," General Cox wrote. The Confederate gunners meanwhile continued to act aggressively, firing on any Federal troops who showed themselves.

In a draft for his memoirs, referring to his differences with those who constantly urged immediate action on him, McClellan wrote, "It has always been my opinion that the true course in conducting military operations, is to make no movement until the preparations are as complete as circumstances permit, & never to fight a battle without some definite object worth the probable loss." This was the credo he applied to the situation facing him on September 15. Only two hours or so of daylight remained, and any attack would be an improvised affair, lacking careful preparation. No doubt the enemy had concealed reserves and was too strong for him to gain a definite object in that time. His own count of Lee's forces is not on record, but he certainly talked that afternoon to Joe Hooker, who was heard by one of his men to say that they were confronting at least 40,000 Rebels. The figure of 50,000 noted in Arthur McClellan's diary that day suggests an estimate widely accepted at headquarters. With General

McClellan's constantly reiterated accounts of huge enemy numbers fixed in their collective mind, the Federal high command apparently never suspected that Lee was running a defiant bluff against them with hardly 15,000 men of all arms.[26]

McClellan wrote nothing of his plans and little of his intentions during these critical days and hours on the Antietam. In his solitary reconnaissance with Porter that afternoon the two men certainly discussed an attack, but neither left any record of the conversation. He called no conference of his generals or staff that evening to describe his plans for the next day, issued no general orders, advanced no troops to positions from which they might open an attack. A dispatch he sent to Franklin at 9:00 P.M. explained that it had not been possible to bring enough troops to the front that day for an assault, but he would reconnoiter the enemy at daylight ''and if he is found to be in position, he will be attacked.'' There was an unstated qualification in this, however: only when he knew the enemy was still there would he begin preparations for an offensive. As had increasingly become his custom, General McClellan would do nothing until he felt certain of his enemy's intentions. Rather than act he would only react, and in this peculiar attitude of command he surrendered much of the initiative to his opponent.

The single contemporary account of his thoughts on the pivotal night of September 15 is a dispatch that Captain William J. Palmer sent the next day to Governor Curtin. Palmer, the governor's chief scout and probably the only trained Federal observer to have actually seen much of Lee's army, reached McClellan's headquarters at Keedysville late that night and reported what he had learned of the enemy. ''The general believes,'' Palmer told Curtin, ''that Harper's Ferry surrendered yesterday morning'' — that is, on September 15 — ''and that Jackson reenforced Lee at Sharpsburg last night.... Rebels appear encouraged at arrival of their re-inforcements.'' He added that when he left, at noon on the sixteenth, he expected a battle to begin that afternoon.

If Captain Palmer's account is substantially correct — and his strong record in intelligence gathering makes him a credible witness — it meant that in McClellan's mind the usefulness of the Lost Order, however much he believed he had already benefited from it, was now at an end. He need be under no pressure to act aggressively or to hurry his attack against the divided enemy forces; with the arrival of Jackson's command at Sharpsburg on the fifteenth the Confederate army was reunited, or nearly so — the troops facing Franklin in Pleasant Valley were not yet accounted for — and he was once again outnumbered.

Messages had arrived during the afternoon confirming the surrender of Harper's Ferry, and Governor Curtin telegraphed him a warning to "look out for Jackson's column from Harper's Ferry . . . ," but otherwise McClellan received not a scrap of factual evidence on September 15 (for there was none) that Jackson's command had actually reached Sharpsburg: no reports from the cavalry, no information from deserters or prisoners, no sightings by civilians. He simply made one of his deductive leaps, first imagining the worst that might happen, then believing that it had happened. His exercise in unreason ensured that the worst did in fact happen. When at last he fought the Battle of Antietam, he would face the entire Army of Northern Virginia.[27]

THIRTEEN

THE BATTLE OF ANTIETAM

In THE MORNING LIGHT on September 16 a heavy ground fog masked the Confederate positions across Antietam Creek. At seven o'clock General McClellan reported to Washington that he was uncertain whether the enemy was still there or in what force. "Will attack as soon as situation of the enemy is developed," he said. Forty-five minutes later, in a dispatch to Franklin in Pleasant Valley, he observed that while the fog made it difficult to determine, he believed Lee had abandoned his lines and withdrawn across the Potomac. He added, however, "If the enemy is in force here, I shall attack him this morning."

These promises were by now a matter of habit, a reflexive delaying action against possible criticism or even comment. He remained willing enough to see the Confederates depart and was in no manner prepared to attack them that morning or at any other time on September 16. Presently the fog burned off, but his perplexity remained. The lines of infantry clearly visible the previous afternoon were gone, although Rebel gunners continued their shelling. This, McClellan later wrote, "was interpreted by many to be the demonstrations of a rear guard to cover a retreat across the Potomac." He began what he described as a "careful examination," and was soon convinced that Lee was still there, with all his numbers, "concealed behind the opposite heights, collecting his energies for a desperate effort." As the *New York Tribune*'s George Smalley phrased it, "It was all a rebel stronghold beyond."

McClellan was correct, in an unintended sense, that General Lee was collecting his energies on September 16. Not until midday did the first of Jackson's troops begin to arrive at Sharpsburg from Harper's Ferry, and they trailed slowly into the lines throughout the afternoon. By day's end three of the six divisions that had besieged Colonel Miles were at hand. Two more would arrive at dawn on the seventeenth. Marching orders went out to the sixth division, A. P. Hill's, which had been left at Harper's Ferry to parole the 11,500 Federal prisoners and to send off the huge stock of captured armaments. General McClellan was not aware of any of these movements. Three and a half days had passed since he was handed the Lost Order, and his remarkable opportunity to duplicate Napoleon's feat at Castiglione and conquer a divided foe was now entirely gone.[1]

After a further reconnaissance, he determined that if the Rebel army was still confronting him the next day, he would accept the challenge and attack it. It was not a decision he reached easily; the evidence suggests that he would have preferred to find the enemy gone on September 17 and not have need to fight at all until he had further reorganized and trained and enlarged his army. He was already well enough pleased with his accomplishments. "Have reached thus far & have no doubt delivered Penna & Maryland," he telegraphed Ellen early on the sixteenth. "All well & in excellent spirits." He would give battle at Antietam against his best judgment, and the fact that he did not suffer the great defeat he predicted might be his fate that day gave him more satisfaction and pride than any other of his Civil War accomplishments.

It was noon on September 16 before he settled on a plan of action. Joe Hooker was ordered to advance his First Corps across the Antietam during the afternoon to take a position from which to assault the Confederates' left flank. The Ninth Corps, under Jacob Cox since Jesse Reno's death at Fox's Gap, was posted downstream to move against the enemy's right. As McClellan explained it to Colonel Strother that afternoon, these flanking movements, if properly supported by the rest of the army, should cut off all the escape routes to the Potomac. He used the image, Strother wrote, of pinching the enemy in a vice.

The only officer besides Strother to leave a description of McClellan's thinking on September 16 was Joe Hooker. His recollection was not unlike Strother's: when he left with his corps to cross the Antietam, as he testified to the Joint Committee on the Conduct of the War, "I had been assured that, simultaneously with my attack, there should be an attack upon the rebel army in the centre and on the left the next morning.''[2]

McClellan wrote no instructions outlining his plan of battle, nor did he call his generals together to explain it, nor are his later descriptions of it consistent one with another. Yet from what he said to Strother and Hooker on the day he formulated his "design," as he called it, apparently he intended to attack both of Lee's flanks in strength and, if he hoped to press the enemy in a vice, more or less simultaneously. If this was in fact his design, one of the key figures in the scheme, Ambrose Burnside, did not understand it.

Burnside's role at Antietam — and Burnside himself — would in time be the subjects of much heated controversy. The friendship between "Burn" and "Mac," dating back to West Point and their years together with the Illinois Central, had remained cordial until as recently as the fighting at South Mountain and the delayed pursuit afterward. McClellan's poor opinion of Burnside's efforts on those occasions owed much to Fitz John Porter, who was acting as his confidant and unofficial second-in-command. Porter was a bearer of grudges, and in charging the failed pursuit to Burnside he was no doubt influenced by personal enmity. During the Second Bull Run campaign Burnside had forwarded Porter's messages disparaging John Pope to the president and the War Department, an action Porter saw as one cause of his pending court-martial. McClellan felt strongly enough about Burnside's failings to make a major command change on the eve of battle. In posting his forces along the Antietam on September 15, he cut Burnside's command responsibility in half by disbanding his wing and sending the First and Ninth corps to opposite ends of the line.

Burnside did not hide his resentment at the rebuke. By Jacob Cox's account, he took the cause of it as Joe Hooker's conniving for independent command, but he could hardly ignore the fact that it was his old friend Mac who gave the order. Cox offered to step down as head of the Ninth Corps and return to his Kanawha Division, but Burnside said this would only signal acceptance of the humiliating demotion. He would instead make his headquarters with the Ninth Corps and retain what was now a supernumerary position, simply transmitting orders from army headquarters to corps commander Cox. Both men in effect commanded the Ninth Corps, and neither understood just where his duties and responsibilities began or ended.[3]

McClellan spent most of September 16 performing administrative tasks and reconnoitering as much of the Confederate positions west of the Antietam as could be seen. From his headquarters in the large brick house of a prosperous farmer named Philip Pry, on high ground near the center of his lines east of the creek, he rode far downstream to make sure that the Ninth Corps was positioned both to meet the threat of a flanking attack from Pleasant Valley and to move against the Rebels' flank across the stream. In what must have been a strained meeting with Burnside, he ordered the corps to be advanced to a point overlooking the Rohrbach Bridge, which carried the Sharpsburg-Rohrersville road across the Antietam. As he recorded it later, he told Burnside "he would probably be required to attack the enemy's right on the following morning."

Normally McClellan delegated the details of tactical decisions to his generals, but in this instance he fueled Burnside's resentment by bringing along his staff engineers to inspect the ground and mark out just where all the Ninth Corps troops were to be placed. General Cox shared the resentment. Had he considered himself in full command of the corps, he said, he would have taken it as his duty to reconnoiter the ground personally and to post the troops accordingly. When there was a delay in moving the men into the new positions, McClellan sent Burnside a sharply worded rebuke — the general commanding, it read, "cannot lightly regard such marked departure from the tenor of his instructions" — that did nothing to embolden Burnside when the fighting began.

In the midst of all this, General Burnside lost sight of exactly what the Ninth Corps was supposed to do in the next day's battle, if in fact McClellan had made it plain to him in their conference. The Rohrbach Bridge — to become famous on September 17 as the Burnside Bridge — was a stone span only twelve feet wide, and the terrain on the Southerners' side of the creek was ideally suited to defense, and it was obvious that any attack on such an exceedingly narrow front would be (as McClellan himself described it) a "difficult task." Burnside assumed that what was wanted of him was simply a diversion, to keep the Rebels from sending troops from their right to reinforce their left, where

McClellan's main blow would fall. The diversion included marching part of the corps downstream to cross at a ford below the
bridge and take its defenders in the flank.

McClellan inspected this part of the field more closely than
any other on September 16, and he went to more trouble here
than elsewhere to see that the troops were readied for action, yet
he made remarkably little impression for all his efforts. Whether
he did not make his intentions clear, or whether Burnside did
not understand them, is uncertain, but in the event so many things
went wrong on the Ninth Corps's front on September 17 that
there would be blame enough for everyone. McClellan's failures
to make his plan understood and to establish a workable command
system for the Ninth Corps — and to act decisively once the fighting began — made his record as discreditable as Burnside's.[4]

In positioning the Ninth Corps, McClellan continued to be
concerned about an attack on his left flank and rear by the enemy
column facing the Sixth Corps in Pleasant Valley. At about midday on the sixteenth, as he worked out his plan of battle, he
received word from Franklin that the Confederate forces had
left his front for Harper's Ferry. Even that did not fully relieve
his mind. Only in the evening did he send orders to Franklin to
join the main army, and he was only to start his march the next
morning. (At the same time, General Lee was ordering the divisions of McLaws and Anderson, Franklin's erstwhile opponents, to start for Sharpsburg at midnight. They arrived at dawn;
Franklin arrived when the battle was half over.)

Furthermore, the Sixth Corps would set out for the battlefield
with just two of its three divisions. In the morning Couch's division marched off in the opposite direction, for Harper's Ferry.
McClellan never explained this assignment, but apparently it
reflected his comment to Franklin on September 15 that the only
reason to hold Harper's Ferry was "to secure a tête du pont"
should Lee retreat into the Shenandoah Valley and a bridgehead
be needed from which to pursue him. In consequence of this
indecision about what role Franklin's left wing should play —
to guard the army's flank, or to hold Harper's Ferry, or to reinforce the main body — Franklin arrived too late to take any
effective part in the Federal offensive on September 17, and
Couch never reached the battlefield at all.[5]

McClellan acted with more decision that day in dealing with

what he had come to regard as the problem of Edwin Sumner. He later wrote privately that in many respects old Sumner was a model soldier, ''but unfortunately nature had limited his capacity to a very narrow extent.'' After experiencing the effects of Sumner's want of judgment at Williamsburg and Savage's Station on the Peninsula, McClellan was determined to keep him on a checkrein. Given a specific objective and kept under direct control, he was often enough the model soldier; in an independent command he was totally unpredictable. McClellan believed he had the solution to the problem when on the evening of September 16 Hooker pointed out that he was isolated on the enemy's flank and needed support. Deliberately disbanding Sumner's command (as he had disbanded Burnside's), McClellan sent Mansfield's Twelfth Corps across the Antietam that night and made Mansfield subject to Hooker's direction rather than Sumner's. Sumner was ordered to hold the Second Corps behind the Antietam and be prepared to advance an hour before daylight. By Hooker's account, McClellan assured him that when Sumner reached the scene of the fighting, he would come under Hooker's orders as the general commanding on the field of battle.[6]

In reviewing Antietam for his wife, McClellan would complain that his opponent ''possessed an immense advantage in knowing every part of the ground, while I knew only what I could see from a distance. . . .'' From Burnside's headquarters on September 16 he was able to get a fairly good idea of the position of the enemy facing the Ninth Corps, but elsewhere on the field it was uncommonly difficult to learn what an attacking force might encounter. Antietam Creek flows into the Potomac some three miles south of Sharpsburg, and Lee had taken as his general line of defense the ridgeline bisecting the angle of land between the two streams. Where the angle narrows, south of Sharpsburg, the ground was seen to be broken and marked by ravines and steeply sloped hills, but north of the town it appeared more open and better suited to maneuvering troops. McClellan decided as early as his first look at the field, on the fifteenth, that in his tactic of a double envelopment he would make the main effort here, against the enemy's left flank.

It was, however, nearly two miles from his headquarters to the crest of the ridgeline where he supposed that flank to be, and it was impossible to form any impression of how strongly it was

held. "All along this ridge the rebels had batteries placed...,"
one of Porter's staff wrote home. "Their infantry, according to
their custom, was hidden in the woods." Although McClellan
crossed the Antietam and rode with Hooker's advance for a time
that afternoon, he returned to his headquarters no wiser than
when he left. Gaining information on the Rebel positions on September 17 would be a trial-and-error experience, both for him
and for his field commanders.[7]

When facing what he supposed were superior forces in the
battle for Richmond, McClellan had opened his offensive from
behind entrenchments, and he might have repeated the tactic on
September 17 but for the fact that Antietam Creek ran along the
full length of his front. A winding stream averaging some twenty
to twenty-five yards wide, it formed an effective barrier to military movements. Three stone bridges crossed the stream in the
vicinity of Sharpsburg: the Rohrbach Bridge on Burnside's front;
the Middle Bridge on the Boonsboro turnpike, at about the center
of the Federal line; and, several miles upstream, the Upper Bridge,
where Hooker crossed with the First Corps. Since an attacking
force's artillery and ammunition trains could cross the creek only
at these bridges or at a few nearby fords, and since the Federals
controlled all the crossing points except those in front of Burnside, he felt secure enough to dispense with fortifications. Nevertheless, on September 17 he would be exceedingly cautious in
advancing units beyond the Antietam for fear that an enemy
counterstroke would find a gap in his defenses.[8]

His most current estimate gave his opponent 120,000 men that
day, less whatever he reckoned the Rebels' casualties at South
Mountain to have been. The diaries and letters of staff officers
suggest that the same general opinion prevailed at headquarters.
Colonel Strother entered a figure of 100,000 "in round numbers"
in his diary on September 17. Alexander Webb, Fifth Corps chief
of staff, put the Confederate numbers at between 100,000 and
130,000, and another Fifth Corps aide, Stephen Weld, wrote home,
"The enemy greatly outnumbers us ..."; both men certainly took
their counts from Fitz John Porter, McClellan's chief adviser.
The course of events on September 17 would only serve to reinforce McClellan's convictions. Ten days later he reported to
Washington, "In the last battles the enemy was undoubtedly
greatly superior to us in numbers...," and it was only by the

hardest fighting that the Army of the Potomac had survived.

He had available to him (including the entire Sixth Corps, had he called it up promptly) just over 95,000 men present for duty, of whom perhaps 75,000 could actually be put on the firing line. That General Lee would stand and fight with hardly 38,000 men (when his army was finally reunited) was to McClellan unimaginable, and on September 17 he repeated precisely his pattern of command in the Seven Days. Antietam was the only battle that George McClellan ever planned and directed — indeed, it was the only Civil War battle he ever witnessed from start to finish — and he fought it less to gain a victory than to forestall a defeat.[9]

As it finally took shape, his design had Hooker making the main assault on Lee's left with the First Corps, with the Twelfth Corps available to him should he call for it. There was a sharp clash at dusk on the sixteenth as Hooker took position opposite the enemy's flank, and he notified headquarters that he would resume the fighting at dawn, so that McClellan "might direct the other attacks to be made at the same time." His corps and Mansfield's, made up entirely of former Army of Virginia troops, would be reinforced if need be by the Peninsula veterans of Sumner's Second Corps, the largest in the army. McClellan intended the three corps, totaling just over 31,000 fighting men, to be under Hooker's overall direction on the field.

He would keep under his own control the actual commitment of Sumner's troops to the battle, and also the timing of Burnside's movement against the Confederate right. Fitz John Porter's Fifth Corps was positioned in the center as a "reserve in the first line," as McClellan termed it, strongly suggesting that Porter's role was as much defensive as offensive. When Franklin's two Sixth Corps divisions arrived from Pleasant Valley, they would be placed behind the army's center, available to reinforce success anywhere on the field. Pleasonton's cavalry division was also massed behind the center "should it be required to make pursuit of the enemy," as his orders read. As an offensive plan it was well suited to the circumstances and the terrain; indeed, McClellan had unknowingly devised perhaps the most effective tactics possible against an opponent he outnumbered two to one.[10]

At first light on September 17 artillery firing was heard on Hooker's front, and soon the infantrymen who had battled there

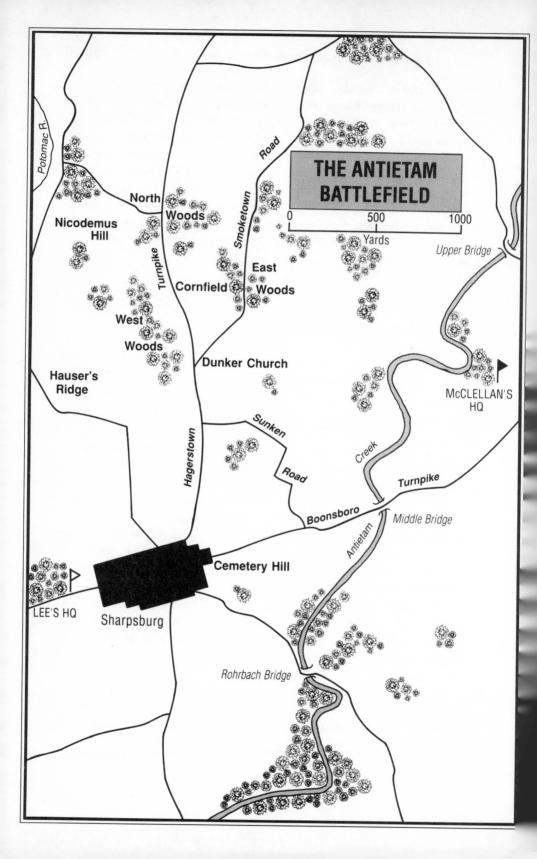

the evening before resumed their fight. Then, at 6:00 A.M., Hooker opened a full-fledged assault with the First Corps, driving southward on the line of the Hagerstown turnpike that ran along the ridgeline into Sharpsburg. The roar of the guns became continuous, and battle smoke blanketed the fields and woodlots north of the town. Edwin Sumner, who had his men up and breakfasted and in marching order before daylight in expectation of going to the front, was at the Pry house by six o'clock to see about the delay and to get his orders personally. According to his son and aide, Captain Samuel S. Sumner, he was impatient and uneasy about how long it was going to take him to join the Second Corps with the Twelfth to support Hooker's offensive. He saw no point, he testified, in starting a battle with an attack made "in driblets." The headquarters staff did not let him see the general.

The story would be told that in fact General McClellan was asleep in these first hours of the Battle of Antietam, and that his staff refused to disturb him in the belief that the noise of battle was nothing but a rear-guard defense by the Rebels retreating across the Potomac. One staff officer assured Captain Sumner that Robert E. Lee was too good a soldier to fight a battle with a river at his back. The story is plausible enough. McClellan had stayed up most of the night trying to make sure everything was in order, and as he had done in a similar situation before the fight at Gaines's Mill on the Peninsula, he may well have sought an hour or two of sleep at dawn. He would fall ill the next day when (as he told Ellen) "the want of rest & anxiety" seriously debilitated him. At any event, he remained true to his habit of only reacting to his opponent's actions; asleep or awake, he did not appear and issued no orders much before 7:00 A.M. General Sumner was left to pace Mr. Pry's yard or sit on his front steps for more than an hour while Hooker's attack was fought to a standstill by Stonewall Jackson.[11]

At first the news from the front was encouraging, and McClellan was heard to remark "All goes well. Hooker is driving them." According to his design, this ought to have been the signal for him to order Burnside to open a simultaneous attack, but General McClellan was not yet ready to make so decisive a commitment to the offense. He sent an aide to Burnside simply to alert him to have the Ninth Corps ready for action. In the yard in front of the Pry house the staff crowded around telescopes strapped to stakes driven into the ground to try to gain some sense of the distant fighting.

Soon the course of the battle was seen to change. Rebel infantry stormed out of a woodlot west of the Hagerstown turnpike — labeled the West Woods on the military maps — in a powerful counterattack against Hooker's advance. At 7:20 McClellan finally ordered Sumner to the front. His men had to cross the creek and march nearly two miles to reach the scene, however, and for most of the next two hours Hooker's only reinforcement was Mansfield's Twelfth Corps.

Each movement that McClellan ordered at Antietam, beginning with Sumner's, had an element of defense attached to it. Of the Second Corps' three divisions, only two marched immediately for the fighting. The third, under Israel B. Richardson, was kept on the Antietam Creek line until its place was taken by George W. Morell's Fifth Corps division, then camped a mile to the rear at Keedysville. For reasons never explained, Morell required more than ninety minutes to march that one mile, and it was nine o'clock before Richardson was released.

Since Pleasonton's cavalry could have protected the batteries east of the creek where Richardson was posted (as it would later protect the guns at the center of the line), the only apparent reason to hold back Richardson's division was McClellan's fear of a counterstroke against his right flank. This concern, however, makes his handling of the cavalry that day all the more inexplicable. It was the "practice of the centuries" (as a Federal trooper put it) to guard an army's flanks with cavalry to give timely warning of an enemy's approach. In his own cavalry manual, adopted by the army in 1861, McClellan wrote that a principal duty of the mounted forces was "to secure the detachment to which they belong, as well as the rest of the army, against sudden attacks." Yet from the first hours of September 17 to the last, both flanks of the Army of the Potomac were left entirely unguarded.

It was not until just before noon that McClellan called up Pleasonton's troopers from Keedysville, and then it was only to protect batteries at the Middle Bridge. In a postscript to this order he asked Pleasonton, "Can you do any good by a cavalry charge?" To propose a Napoleonic-style cavalry charge against the center of an opposing army that he supposed to be substantially larger than his own and that he knew to be equipped with rifled muskets and rifled artillery was to invite nothing less than a mass slaughter. Pleasonton pointedly replied that in fact he needed infantry to protect his cavalry even where it was. One of Pleasonton's officers later observed that at Antietam the Federal cavalry arm ''had not yet fallen into the hands of those who knew the proper use to make of it.''[12]

In search of a better view of the fighting, the commanding general and his staff presently left the Pry house and rode to Porter's headquarters on a commanding knoll south of the Boonsboro turnpike, from where McClellan had first glimpsed the Antietam battlefield two days earlier. A small redan had been built of fence rails for protection against artillery fire, and McClellan took this as his field headquarters. Porter stood by his side, observing the action through a telescope resting on the top rail and passing on his observations, Colonel Strother wrote, ''by nods, signs, or in words so low-toned and brief that the nearest bystanders had but little benefit from them. When not engaged with Porter, McClellan stood in a soldierly attitude intently watching the battle and smoking with the utmost apparent calmness; conversing with surrounding officers and giving his orders in the most quiet under-tones. . . . Every thing was as quiet and punctilious as a drawing-room ceremony.''

The most rapid means of communicating with Hooker's front was by flag signal, using a station set up near the Hagerstown turnpike beyond the Confederate flank. To supplement the information collected by the signalmen, McClellan sent aides to the scene to report directly on the situation. By contrast, on the Ninth Corps front the site of the Rohrbach Bridge was hidden from the headquarters observers by trees and the contours of the ground, and a signal station was not established there until the afternoon. Consequently, all communication with Burnside during the most critical hours of the fighting had to be delivered by aides.[13]

The roar of battle reached a new intensity. The men of these two armies had never experienced anything like this, not at Gaines's Mill or Glendale or Malvern Hill, nor at Bull Run less than three weeks earlier. There was the most savage kind of fighting in the West Woods and the East Woods and a thirty-acre cornfield between them that would gain a terrible fame that day as *the* Cornfield. Alpheus Williams, who took command of the Twelfth Corps when General Mansfield was mortally wounded soon after reaching the field, wrote home a few days later that the sound of the musketry was almost beyond belief: "If all the stone and brick houses of Broadway should tumble at once the roar and rattle could hardly be greater, and amidst this, hundreds of pieces of artillery, right and left, were thundering as a sort of bass to the infernal music." The rumble of the guns could be distinctly heard in Hagerstown, a dozen miles away.

The Twelfth Corps took the place of the First and was seen to press the Rebel infantry and artillery back across the Hagerstown turnpike and into the West Woods. Federal troops followed them into the woods near a small white building assumed to be a schoolhouse but which in fact was a church of the German Baptist Brethren, known locally as Dunkers. Clearly the tide of battle was reversing once more, but still McClellan made no move to open the assault on the enemy's other flank. From their headquarters on high ground east of the Antietam, Burnside and Cox saw columns of Confederate troops leaving their positions opposite and marching northward toward the fighting around the Dunker church. Whatever else the Ninth Corps might accomplish that day, it would not succeed in any diversionary role.

Sumner's lead division, 5,400 men under John Sedgwick, meanwhile advanced up the sloping ground toward the ridgeline and the early morning's battleground. A staff officer recalled that from McClellan's headquarters "it was a thrilling sight. With flags flying and the long unfaltering lines rising and falling as they crossed the rolling fields, it looked as though nothing could stop them...." As Sedgwick reached the East Woods at 9:00 A.M. there was a sudden lull in the firing, as if an audience were quieting in expectation of a new act in the drama.

A rush of messages reached headquarters from the field. "The signal officer on the right reports Gen. Mansfield wounded and that the work goes bravely on," read one. A signal soon arrived with fuller information from Major Hammerstein, of McClellan's staff: "General Hooker is wounded in the foot. General Sumner is coming up. The enemy is driven on our left and retiring.... General Mansfield killed." Alpheus Williams, reporting from the "field of battle," confirmed that the two Federal corps commanders had been hit. "Please give us all the aid you can. It is reported that the enemy occupy the woods in our advance in strong force.'' At 9 :10 a message went out from headquarters for Sumner, warning him that the general commanding ''desires you to be very careful how you advance, as he fears our right is suffering.'' It was sent too late. Impatient with any further delay, Sumner had pushed ahead with Sedgwick's division, crossing the Hagerstown turnpike north of the Dunker church and disappearing from view into the West Woods.

Word also reached headquarters that the leading division of Franklin's Sixth Corps was nearing Keedysville on its march from Pleasant Valley. It was this news, rather than the shifting fortunes on Hooker's front, that finally decided McClellan to commit Burnside to the battle. Just as Richardson was not released until Morell took his place on the Antietam Creek line, Burnside was held back until Franklin arrived to replenish the tactical reserve. Burnside's orders went out at 9 :10 A.M. : ''General Franklin's command is within one mile and a half of here. General McClellan desires you to open your attack. As soon as you shall have uncovered the upper Stone Bridge'' — the Middle Bridge, on the Boonsboro turnpike — ''you will be supported, and, if necessary, on your own line of attack. So far all is going well.''[14]

Some thirty minutes later, Baldy Smith, commanding the lead division of the Sixth Corps, rode up to headquarters to get instructions for posting his men. General McClellan was optimistic, Smith recalled, saying that Sumner was doing ''very well'' on the right and that he expected to hear Burnside's guns opening at any minute on the left. He told Smith to keep his troops near the Boonsboro turnpike, at the center of the line, so that he might put them into action where they would ''be of the most service.'' The battle appeared to be going just as he had planned.

Shortly afterward, at about 10 :00 A.M., McClellan's optimism evaporated rapidly as the fighting on the northern flank took still another dramatic turn. The Confederate soldier who had fired a bullet through Joe Hooker's foot not only put one of the most aggressive generals in the Potomac army out of action, but also put General Sumner in field command in his place. This was the last place McClellan wanted him to be. The belated warning from headquarters was evidence of his concern that Sumner would act rashly, and the concern was well founded. With characteristic obtuseness, Sumner ignored what George Meade of the First Corps and Alpheus Williams of the Twelfth tried to tell him of the situation at the front, and instead rushed forward incautiously at the head of Sedgwick's division. Stonewall Jackson routed him with a surprise flank attack made up largely of fresh troops whom Lee had shifted to this part of the field. "Re-enforcements are badly wanted," Sumner signaled. "Our troops are giving way." One of McClellan's aides with him described the situation more succinctly: "Things look blue."

To this point, however cautiously he was committing his forces, McClellan had held the initiative in the fighting. With the rout of Sedgwick's division, however, he surrendered control of events and never regained it. Indeed, he made no attempt to regain it. Sedgwick's disaster in the West Woods confirmed his worst fear: using his thousands concealed in reserve about Sharpsburg, General Lee was responding to any Federal advance with a heavy counterattack. The northern half of the battlefield that invited an offensive against the Confederate left was just as inviting for a Confederate counteroffensive against the Federal right. Orders went immediately to Baldy Smith to march his division to the right to support Sumner. On reporting to Sumner, Smith wrote, "I was told to close my division in mass facing a certain way from which point he expected an attack." As it arrrived Henry Slocum's Sixth Corps division was also ordered to the right.[15]

At the same time, without McClellan's bidding it, the entire focus of the Union offensive shifted from Lee's left to his center. This assault was made without direction or purpose. William H. French's division, the second of Sumner's Second Corps divisions ordered to Hooker's aid, had fallen behind during the advance, and when French reached the East Woods, Sedgwick's division was nowhere to be seen — once it had crossed the Hagerstown turnpike, it was out of French's line of sight behind the ridge — and he found himself without instructions from either Sumner or McClellan. The initiative he exercised was ill chosen. Without reconnoitering and without identifying even those Federal troops who were within view, he slanted off to the left and went into action beyond what turned out to be two Twelfth Corps brigades holding the ground in front of the Dunker church. French never explained why he believed he was supporting Sedgwick by putting in an attack almost three quarters of a mile due south of his original line of march.

The center of Lee's line, commanded by D. H. Hill, was a salient formed by a farm lane that ran eastward from the Hagerstown turnpike and then turned to follow a southerly course, intersecting the Boonsboro turnpike midway between Sharpsburg and Antietam Creek. Weather and travel had worn down the lane over the years until its surface was several feet lower than the adjoining fields. Hill's men strengthened this natural trench with a breastwork of fence rails, and a ridge that ran along its front made it even more formidable: an attacking force had to close to within fifty to eighty yards before it could even see its target. Hill's position would be called the Sunken Road or, more appropriately, Bloody Lane.

French rushed into action as incautiously as had Sumner and was repulsed with losses only somewhat less severe. Casualties in Sedgwick's division came to 40 percent; in French's, 30 percent. A Confederate officer wrote that his regiment's first volley "brought down the enemy as grain falls before a reaper," and subsequent charges simply multiplied the casualties. The battle for the Sunken Road was clearly visible from McClellan's headquarters, and a newspaper reporter there described the panorama: "On the great field were riderless horses and scattering men, clouds of dirt from solid shot and exploding shells, long dark lines of infantry swaying to and fro, with columns of smoke rising from their muskets, red flashes and white puffs from the batteries — with the sun shining brightly on all this scene of tumult...."

French's attack had spent its force when Richardson finally appeared on the field. Like French, he was without instructions from headquarters. About the time the Bloody Lane fighting began, two brigades under George Sears Greene of the Twelfth Corps stormed into the West Woods and regained the important ground around the Dunker church. Greene's sortie apparently made little impression, however, and McClellan did not attempt to reinforce him. Richardson's 4,000 veteran troops, instead of exploiting Greene's foothold, joined the battle for Bloody Lane. (Two hours later Greene was driven out, and the Federals had seen the last of the West Woods.) Like every Potomac army command that morning — Hooker's First Corps and Mansfield's Twelfth, the divisions of Sedgwick and French — Israel Richardson's division would go into battle on its own, neither supporting nor supported by any other forces. His opening assault shattered against the impenetrable Rebel defenses.[16]

Suddenly, without apparent reason, the Confederate battle line in the Sunken Road, the strongest defensive position on the battlefield, collapsed completely. Rebel soldiers by the hundreds were seen clambering out of the road and running for the rear. It was a mixup in orders that caused the line to be abandoned, the only significant command failure in Lee's army that day. Ironically, what had been a senseless frontal attack promising only failure and fearful casualties was now on the verge of becoming a spectacular success. Richardson drove his men forward in pursuit.

Colonel Strother was standing with McClellan during this newest turn of events, and he sensed a surge of excitement in his manner. '' It is the most beautiful field I ever saw and the grandest battle!'' Strother heard him exclaim. ''If we whip them today it will wipe out Bull Run forever.'' Yet beyond this display of satisfaction he did nothing. By his reckoning there was nothing he could do : he had no troops available to exploit the opportunity. He had committed Franklin's Sixth Corps to defending the right flank. Porter's Fifth Corps was guarding the Antietam Creek line and the army's trains. General Richardson would have to make what he could of his sudden success.

Richardson made a valiant effort. When he was stymied by batteries the enemy rushed into the breached line, he broke off the attack temporarily to reorganize and resupply ammunition for a further effort, and called for rifled artillery to break this gun line. Word came back that no rifled pieces could be spared from the batteries massed immediately to the north on Sumner's front, where Lee's counterstroke was expected. Leading from up front, Richardson understood what McClellan far to the rear did not — that Lee's center was held now by little more than artillery and that one more hard push could cut the Rebel army in half. Then Richardson was mortally wounded by an artillery burst, and the opportunity vanished. His replacement, Winfield S. Hancock, had orders directly from McClellan to stand on the defensive and hold his position at any cost.

With Richardson's wounding at 1:00 P.M. a lull settled over the battlefield north of Sharpsburg. The four Federal corps there — First, Second, Sixth, and Twelfth — were now everywhere on the defensive. Only on Burnside's front was McClellan still offensive-minded, but with a purpose different from when he issued the attack order shortly after nine o'clock. It was critical that the Ninth Corps open a new front south of Sharpsburg to distract his opponent from assaulting Sumner to the north. From mid-morning onward gunfire had been heard from the direction of the Rohrbach Bridge, but with no visible result. A series of staff officers was hurried off to find the cause of the delay. "What is Burnside about?" McClellan asked impatiently. "Why do we not hear from him?" Alexander Webb of Porter's staff heard him say to one of the aides, "Tell him if it costs him 10,000 men he must go on now."[17]

The Ninth Corps operations were dogged by misfortune and poor direction. As obtuse in his way as Sumner, Burnside had planned for nothing more than creating a diversion. The first attack on the bridge, at 10:00 A.M., miscarried when the assaulting column lost its way in the woods. A second attack was shot to pieces at virtually pointblank range by the well-posted defenders. Meanwhile, the flanking column that was intended to clear the way for the bridge assault encountered problems of its own. No one had inspected the ford chosen the day before by McClellan's engineers, and when it proved unusable and another crossing point had to be searched out farther downstream, so much time was lost that any chance for a rapid success on this flank was gone.

It was only at 1:00 P.M. that the Rohrbach Bridge was successfully stormed. Colonel Thomas Key of McClellan's staff brought word from Burnside that he believed he could hold the newly won position. McClellan sent Key back with positive orders to advance on Sharpsburg at whatever cost. Key also carried with him an order relieving Burnside of his command if he did not act promptly.[18]

Shortly after 1:30 McClellan reported on the course of the day's events to General-in-Chief Halleck. "We are in the midst of the most terrible battle of the war, perhaps of history," he wrote; " — thus far it looks well but I have great odds against me. . . . Our loss has been terrific, but we have gained much ground." He explained that he had thrown his main attack against the enemy's left, that Burnside was attacking the right, and his "small reserve" of Porter's corps was ready to attack the center when the flanking movements were developed. "It will be either a great defeat or a most glorious victory. I think & hope that God will give us the latter.'' He had second thoughts about admitting the possibility of defeat, and before he sent the telegram he crossed out the final two sentences and substituted his hope ''that God will give us a glorious victory.''

A few minutes later he telegraphed his wife, ''We are in the midst of the most terrible battle of the age. So far God has given us success but with many variations during the day.... I trust that God will smile upon our cause.'' General McClellan was clearly preoccupied by the prospect of defeat; equally clearly, once again he found escape from his responsibility in the belief that the outcome was predetermined by God rather than shaped by man.[19]

The chief cause for his concern was no doubt the reports he was receiving from General Sumner. Old Sumner had been in the midst of the bloodiest fighting in the attack on Sedgwick and had witnessed the worst scenes of rout, and the experience had demoralized him. To one of McClellan's staff sent to learn the situation he pointed to the suffering and straggling in his corps and those of Hooker and Mansfield, and said, ''Sir, I have rallied these troops in the woods and behind the fences and got them in line — Sir, tell the General I will *try* and hold my position — tell him, Sir, I *will* hold it, I *will* hold it, Sir!'' He warned that he must have reinforcements at once if there was to be any hope of saving the day on the right.

When Wiliam Franklin reached the scene, he and his divisional commanders viewed matters very differently. They determined to mount an attack by the Sixth Corps in the area of the West Woods, their target the high ground of Nicodemus Hill, to the left and rear of the Confederates' position. When Sumner heard of the plan he was vehemently opposed and took the responsibility for canceling it. Franklin's men were now the only reliable troops on this part of the field, he said, and if they were defeated there would be no one left to meet a Rebel counterattack.

Franklin felt strongly enough about the case to send Major Hammerstein to headquarters to appeal Sumner's decision. Hammerstein's account created a surge of optimism in McClellan, much like the one he had experienced at Gaines's Mill when Porter reported that the battle seemed to be turning his way. At about two o'clock, with a few of his staff, he set out for Sumner's headquarters. He told artillerist Henry J. Hunt that he intended to take command and direct an attack himself. On the way he encountered his West Point classmate George H. Gordon, who had commanded in some of the Twelfth Corps' hottest fighting that morning. He told Gordon to collect his troops and be ready to fight. "If we cannot whip the enemy now, we may as well die upon the field. If we succeed we end the war."

This sense of decision deserted him when he reached the front. He knew only too well Edwin Sumner's lack of military judgment, and earlier he had ordered Burnside relieved if he did not act aggressively, yet after listening to Franklin and Baldy Smith and others who favored the attack, and to Sumner's stubborn opposition to it, he gave way to Sumner. In Fitz John Porter's account — certainly based on what he was told by McClellan — Sumner said that the three corps that had fought on the right were scattered and demoralized, and that he would not risk another attack; he would advance only if General McClellan "was willing to risk a total defeat if he failed. . . ."

General McClellan accepted that as his choice and would not overrule Sumner or relieve him or take the command himself. In his memoirs he wrote that at about this time he rode in among some of Sedgwick's dispirited men and rallied them, and thus he might have rallied all his admiring troops on that field, as he had done at Harrison's Landing when the final crisis seemed at hand, and at South Mountain, when he dramatically pointed his army into battle. But he could not bring himself to it; the risk seemed too great. By Franklin's testimony he said that "things had gone so well on all the other parts of the field that he was afraid to risk the day by an attack there on the right at that time." With his decision he suppressed his last remaining impulse to seek a decisive victory at Antietam. Baldy Smith would term it the "nail in McC's coffin as a general. . . ."[20]

McClellan was back at his headquarters vantage point in time to watch the great battle reach its climax. Burnside's forces had been finally reorganized and massed for the advance on Sharpsburg, and at 3:00 P.M. they had moved forward, seemingly as inexorable as a blue tide. "His advancing rush was in full view and magnificently done," Colonel Strother wrote in his diary. The Rebels were steadily forced back on the town and the road leading to the Potomac crossing. Then, dramatically, the battle took its final turn. A. P. Hill's division reached the field from Harper's Ferry and without warning slashed into the unguarded left flank of Burnside's advance. Now it was the Federals who were forced back, toward the Antietam and Burnside's Bridge.

The *New York Tribune*'s George Smalley was a witness to the scene at headquarters. "McClellan's glass for the last half-hour has seldom been turned away from the left," he wrote. "He sees clearly enough that Burnside is pressed — needs no messenger to tell him that. His face grows darker with anxious thought." Before them was the Fifth Corps, the "reserve in the front line," as McClellan called it. The general, Smalley wrote, "turns a half-questioning look on Fitz-John Porter, who stands by his side, gravely scanning the field. . . . But Porter slowly shakes his head, and one may believe that the same thought is passing through the minds of both generals. 'They are the only reserves of the army; they cannot be spared.' "

Smalley read the generals' minds accurately. Porter's forward troops, posted across the Antietam beyond the Middle Bridge, had earlier advanced to support Burnside, only to be recalled and cautioned about the risk. At 4:30, about the time Smalley was describing, a dispatch went to General Pleasonton, whose cavalry and batteries were also across the bridge. "Gen. McClellan particularly desires that your operation should be *cautiously* conducted," it read. "Gen. Porter has sent off as much of his infantry as he can spare. . . . The infantry he has is the *only* infantry the General in Chief has now to rely on in reserve. . . ."

With Porter and a few staff officers, McClellan presently rode toward the left to confer with Burnside. On the way they were intercepted by a Ninth Corps courier carrying Burnside's plea for reinforcements. By Smalley's account, McClellan glanced at the western sky and the setting sun and said to the courier, "Tell Gen. Burnside this is the battle of the war. He must hold his ground till dark at any cost. I will send him Miller's battery. I can do nothing more. I have no infantry." The courier started to ride away, but McClellan called him back. "Tell him if he *cannot* hold his ground, then the bridge, to the last man! — always the bridge! If the bridge is lost, all is lost!"

This Napoleonesque pronouncement proved to be McClellan's final battlefield decision of the day. Burnside continued his fight unaided, but in the end the Confederates lacked the strength to drive the Ninth Corps into the Antietam, and the Federals held on to their bridgehead. At dusk there was another brief surge of hope at headquarters when a signalman on high ground to the rear thought the Rebels at Sharpsburg appeared "disordered" and in retreat. If the report could be confirmed, Burnside was told, McClellan would commit Porter's corps to the pursuit.

Nothing came of this, however, and the fighting died down and finally darkness ended the bloodiest single day of the Civil War. "The general," Colonel Strother wrote, "then led us back to the headquarters camp, established in the rear of Keedysville, where, forgetting the events of the day for a time, we supped heartily and slept profoundly."[21]

FOURTEEN

THE LAST COMMAND

GENERAL MCCLELLAN was not one of those who slept profoundly during the night following the great battle. Colonel Strother was awakened in the early hours of September 18 by the sounds of couriers' horses outside the general's tent, and he heard McClellan say to someone, "They are to hold the ground they occupy, but are not to attack without further orders." Like others on the staff, Strother had assumed that if the enemy did not retreat across the Potomac in the night, the battle would resume in the morning. What he heard led him to fear that any fruits of victory might be lost, and he was so disturbed that he slept no more that night.

McClellan telegraphed Washington at 8:00 A.M. that they held most of the gains made in the previous day's fighting except what had been abandoned on Burnside's front, and that their losses were very heavy, especially in general officers. "The battle will probably be renewed today," he predicted. At the same hour, he telegraphed Ellen that the battle had been a desperate one, and would probably be resumed that day. He then took a few minutes to write her a letter revealing his innermost thoughts about the struggle he had witnessed.

The fighting on both sides had been superb, he told her, and he believed the general result was in his favor: "that is to say we gained a great deal of ground & held it." Whether it proved to be a decided victory would depend on what happened during the day. "I hope that God has given us a great success. It is all in his hands, where I am content to leave it." The battlefield spectacle "was the grandest I could conceive of — nothing could be more sublime. Those in whose judgment I rely tell me that I

fought the battle splendidly & that it was a masterpiece of art.''
It had required someone of Fitz John Porter's ingratiation to
deliver that compliment, and someone of George McClellan's self-
delusion to accept it.[1]

Taken at his word, at that hour on September 18 he had yet
to make a final decision about resuming the contest. He could
expect Darius Couch's Sixth Corps division from Pleasant Valley
as well as Andrew Humphreys's Fifth Corps division called up
from Frederick. (It was also reported that several thousand
Pennsylvania militia would join him, but he placed little reliance
on these Sunday soldiers. In the event, many of them refused to
leave their state to fight in ''foreign'' Maryland.) The 12,000
men of these two divisions, when added to the four divisions under
Franklin and Porter that saw almost no action on September 17,
would give him better than 32,000 fresh troops to put into action.
To at least support such an offensive there were approximately
30,000 available from the four corps that had done the fighting
the day before. McClellan had committed only some 50,000 men,
two thirds of his available force, to battle on the seventeenth; he
had substantially more than that number with which to give battle
on the eighteenth.

Presently he rode to the front to confer with his principal
officers. Franklin again urged his plan to seize Nicodemus Hill
with the Sixth Corps. Whatever may have been McClellan's resolve on this point, it did not survive his conference with Edwin
Sumner. Sumner remained adamantly opposed to resuming the
offensive, and once more McClellan deferred to his judgment.
By now, too, he was suffering the intense pain of a neuralgia
attack brought on by ''the want of rest & anxiety'' and was even
less inclined than ever to take active command himself. His only
directions were for repelling an enemy assault. Batteries were
added to the line of artillery on the right that commanded the
ground over which any Rebel flanking column would have to
march. Cavalry was this time posted in Pleasant Valley and along
the Antietam downstream to guard against another surprise attack against Burnside. When he granted a truce to bury the dead
and exchange the wounded, it was plain to all that General
McClellan would initiate no fighting that day. He was content,
as he told Ellen, to leave the matter in God's hands. The men in
the ranks wondered what it all meant. According to ''rumor no.

5," a First Corps soldier noted in his diary, "Little McC has given the Rebs 7 hours to make up their minds whether they will surrender."[2]

A legion of critics would descend on McClellan for deciding to stand on the defensive on September 18. Walt Whitman was more tolerant than most of them when he looked back on that day and wrote, "The fault seems to have been in neglecting to follow out an opportunity . . . ; in McClellan's 'no, no — the army must be rested.' " At the time, however, those like Franklin and Baldy Smith who urged an offensive were a minority in the Potomac army's officer corps. In describing the battle a few days later for his father, Major Webb of Porter's staff wrote, "Now that all is over you will hear that we ought to have advanced the next day. Well I say that myself but no one thought so at the time. . . . I know of no advocates for a continuance of the battle on the 18th." Colonel Charles S. Wainwright, arriving that day to take command of the First Corps artillery, found a similar attitude. In his diary he noted that virtually every officer he talked to expected Lee to make an attack on the eighteenth.

It is not in fact surprising that so many in the Potomac army, beginning with the general commanding, failed to grasp how near they had come to crushing the Army of Northern Virginia on September 17, and how great a bluff General Lee was running by holding his lines on September 18. To those who had experienced the worst of the fighting, or had witnessed it, it seemed that the enemy met each attack in the sequence of Federal attacks with strong forces and stronger counterattacks. Few guessed how skillfully Lee had maneuvered his army or how often it was stretched nearly to the breaking point. The flank attacks by Jackson on Sedgwick and by A. P. Hill on Burnside were made with substantially inferior forces, and succeeded only because of position and surprise. By holding back so many troops from the action, McClellan had (albeit unwittingly) cut his advantage in manpower from two to one to perhaps five to four, and Lee was never so hard pressed that he could not muster the strength to fight off the disjointed Federal assaults. At the end of the day — and on the next day — the myth of a huge Rebel army remained intact.

That myth became McClellan's defense against his critics. In his preliminary report on Antietam, prepared a month later, he explained that on September 18 his duty "to the army and the country forbade the risks involved in a hasty movement, which might result in the loss of what had been gained the previous day." He dramatized those risks in the report on his tenure as commander of the Army of the Potomac, written in 1863: "At this critical juncture I should have had a narrow view of the condition of the country had I been willing to hazard another battle with less than an absolute assurance of success." He pointed to an estimate, compiled after the battle by a member of General Banks's staff in Washington, that gave Lee's strength at Antietam as more than 97,000, comfortably close to his own estimate at the time. This figure, based on a fairly accurate order of battle for the Confederate army but a remarkably inaccurate count of its numbers, gained credibility by being produced independently of the Army of the Potomac's intelligence service. "One battle lost," McClellan concluded, "and almost all would have been lost. Lee's army might then have marched as it pleased on Washington, Baltimore, Philadelphia, or New York,"[3]

He intended, he wrote, to renew the battle on September 19, but his one order on the subject suggests something considerably less than a full-blooded assault. Franklin had proposed that an entire division attack Nicodemus Hill beyond the Confederate left; Franklin's orders for September 19 were to advance two companies of skirmishers. In any case, Lee did not grant his opponent a second chance, and during the night he withdrew across the Potomac into the Shenandoah Valley. By morning's first light Federal observers reported the quarry gone. The high command seemed pleased, Colonel Strother wrote, "but I feel as if we had not done enough to wipe out Harper's Ferry, and had lost an opportunity which may never again be presented to us. The empty name of victory is not sufficient. . . ." General McClellan had no such reservations. "Our victory was complete," he telegraphed Halleck at midmorning. "The enemy is driven back into Virginia. Maryland & Penna. are now safe."

Still pained by the neuralgia attack, he went forward in an ambulance through Sharpsburg and toward the river to reconnoiter. There was no rush to pursue. Infantry was ordered to close up to the Potomac ford but not to cross without further orders. Pleasonton was to make no pursuit with the cavalry unless he saw "a splendid opportunity to inflict great damage upon the enemy without loss to yourself." Presently Porter was sent across the river to attempt a pursuit, but it was poorly coordinated and on September 20 he was counterattacked by A. P. Hill and driven back to Maryland. Except for reoccupying Harper's Ferry, McClellan was content to hold his army north of the Potomac. Finally free of the anxiety that had pressed on him since the South Mountain battles, he rapidly regained his health.[4]

He experienced an overwhelming sense of relief at having escaped defeat and an upsurge of self-esteem at having preserved the army and thus the country. He had the satisfaction, he wrote Ellen, "of knowing that God has in his mercy a second time made me the instrument for saving the nation. . . ." He felt "some little pride in having with a beaten and demoralized army defeated Lee so utterly, & saved the North so completely." The campaign, he believed, would secure his military reputation. Perhaps one day, he wrote, "history will I trust do me justice in deciding that it was not my fault that the campaign of the Peninsula was not successful. . . . I have shown that I can fight battles & *win* them !"

His claim was the traditional one that to the army that holds the battlefield goes the victory. In that long day's struggle, however, the Confederate line had been pressed back but never broken, and the casualties Lee inflicted were one fifth greater than those he suffered, 12,400 against 10,300. The campaign as a whole cost the Federals 27,000 men, including the Harper's Ferry captives, compared with the Confederates' 14,000. (In his official report McClellan more than doubled the enemy's loss, to 30,000.) That Maryland and Pennsylvania were now safe from invasion was a more just claim, although this was due less to any achievement of General McClellan's than to the Lost Order, which brought Lee to battle sooner and with considerably fewer troops than he had anticipated.

Paradoxically, both commanding generals would take pride from the same accomplishment — that at Sharpsburg on September 17 each had saved his army. George McClellan did not understand — in his self-delusion he was incapable of understanding — that however the actual results of Antietam might be measured, he had squandered the unique opportunity of winning a battle of annihilation. Since the first months of the war he had predicted for himself the command in one great decisive battle that would go far toward ending the rebellion; when he actually came face to face with that reality, he was unable to recognize it.

Antietam was also McClellan's ultimate test as a battlefield tactician, and the only explanation for his failing on so many counts is that once again, in common with his failings in the Seven Days' battles, he lost his inner composure and with it the courage to command under the press of combat. Colonel Strother remarked on his calm demeanor on September 17; what he witnessed was actually a near paralysis of will. The phantom army McClellan attributed to his opponent perhaps accounted for his overall obsessive caution, but many of his battlefield decisions were, for a trained soldier, simply irrational.

He faced what he took to be a superior foe, yet he failed to order all his forces to the battlefield in good time, and then held fully a third of them out of the fighting. He developed a workable plan, then abandoned it at the first sight of enemy resistance. No attack was coordinated with any other attack; no success was reinforced and no reverse salvaged. He failed to impose his will on the fumbling Burnside and the demoralized Sumner, and shied from taking command himself. He failed to collect timely intelligence and to take the elementary precaution of guarding his flanks. He lacked the instinct to anticipate and exploit — or to understand — the events of the day, even when they took place under his own eye, and he lacked the will to finish the fight the next day. "He made absolutely no use of the magnificent enthusiasm which the army then felt for him," wrote Francis W. Palfrey, a veteran of Antietam and its first historian. Ezra A. Carman, another Antietam veteran and the author of the most detailed tactical study of the battle, delivered the hard but measured judgment that on September 17, 1862, "more errors were committed by the Union commander than in any other battle of the war. . . ."[5]

For General McClellan, the fruits of Antietam proved to be bitter. He had hoped that victory on the battlefield would lead to victory over his archenemies, Secretary of War Stanton and General-in-Chief Halleck. "The only safety for the country & for me is to get rid of both of them — no success is possible with them," he told Ellen on September 20. The people must rally to his cause and remove these obstacles from his path: "If my countrymen will not open their eyes & assert themselves they must pardon me if I decline longer to pursue the thankless avocation of serving them...." Unless these conditions were met, he told her, he would resign his commission.

He had already taken a first step to effect these changes. "An opportunity has presented itself through the Governors of some of the states to enable me to take my stand," he wrote; " — I have insisted that Stanton shall be removed & that Halleck shall give way to me as Comdr in Chief." The Northern governors were meeting on September 24 at Altoona, Pennsylvania, but which of them he importuned to speak for him is not known. Most probably it was David Tod of Ohio, a Democrat and an acquaintance from his days with the Ohio and Mississippi Railroad. Possibly he also expected Governor Curtin of Pennsylvania to be his spokesman. In any event, he quite misjudged the temper of the Altoona meeting. Rather than a call for the removal of Stanton and Halleck, there was a concerted effort at the conference to have General McClellan removed. A resolution to that effect was deflected only by the efforts of Tod, Curtin, and Governor Augustus W. Bradford of Maryland. After this disappointment, McClellan concluded that only through some great success of his own could he drive Stanton from office. "If I can crush him I will — relentlessly & without remorse....," he assured Ellen.[6]

Even before learning of the failure of his Altoona initiative, he was stunned by news of two presidential proclamations that ran counter to the most fundamental tenets of his political philosophy. On September 22 Lincoln disclosed the preliminary Emancipation Proclamation, and two days later he suspended the habeas corpus privilege and specified military trial for anyone charged with discouraging enlistments and militia drafts or with any "disloyal practice" giving aid and comfort to the enemy.

To George McClellan these acts were hallmarks of social revolution and a surrender to radical subverters of the Constitution. He would never fight for the "accursed doctrine" of abolitionism, he told Ellen: "It is too infamous." On September 26 he wrote William H. Aspinwall that he was "very anxious to know how you and men like you regard the recent Proclamations of the Presdt inaugurating servile war, emancipating the slaves, & at one stroke of the pen changing our free institutions into a despotism — for such I regard as the natural effect of the last Proclamation suspending the Habeas Corpus throughout the land."

He would have been even more appalled had he realized how large a role he had unwittingly played in the issuing of the two proclamations. The suspension of habeas corpus was a consequence of the pressing need to raise new troops in the wake of his Peninsula defeat. Emancipation had been decided upon by the president two months earlier, but he was persuaded to delay until it could be announced from a position of strength rather than of weakness. Lincoln viewed Antietam as a flawed victory, but enough of a victory for him to act. He told the Cabinet that in the midst of the campaign he vowed to issue the proclamation if God granted the army a victory. "God had decided this question in favor of the slaves," he said. In the Battle of Antietam General McClellan had been willing enough to be God's instrument for saving the nation; he hardly considered also being God's instrument for abolishing slavery to be part of the bargain.[7]

Members of his military family echoed his views. Once again taking his case to the chief opposition newspaper, Fitz John Porter wrote editor Manton Marble of the *New York World* that the emancipation decree demoralized the Army of the Potomac. "The proclamation was ridiculed in the Army — caused disgust, discontent, and expressions of disloyalty to the views of the administration and amount, I have heard, to insubordination . . . ," he wrote. Abolitionists prolonged the war by arousing bitter feeling in the South, he said; soldiers did their best to end the conflict honorably, only to see their efforts "upset by the absurd proclamations of a political coward. . . ." Porter was not alone. A *New York Herald* correspondent wrote to James Gordon Bennett that if the sampling of officers he talked to was at all typical, emancipation "will go far towards producing an expression on the part of the Army that will startle the Country and give us a Military Dictator."

There is little evidence, however, that the men in the ranks were as demoralized as Porter and other like-minded generals supposed. They might write home to praise or damn emancipation and to express every shade of opinion in between, yet calls for a military dictatorship were largely confined to the overheated imagination of those in the officer corps. McClellan, too, misread the soldiers' attitudes. He had never seen anything like their enthusiasm for him, he told Ellen: "It surpasses anything you ever imagined, & I don't believe that Napoleon even ever possessed the love & confidence of his men more fully than I do of mine. . . ." That they would follow his lead elsewhere than on the field of battle was another matter.[8]

His first impulse was to register strong opposition to emancipation, and he drafted a protest to Lincoln, repeating the warning in his Harrison's Landing letter that the army would disintegrate under such a radical policy. Before he sent it off he sought the comments of his old friend Baldy Smith. Smith warned him that neither the army nor the country would sustain him if he aligned himself against the government on this issue, and persuaded him to destroy the letter.

At about this time, in late September, McClellan called in Ambrose Burnside, Jacob Cox, and John Cochrane, three generals he understood had the confidence of the administration, and over dinner asked their advice about what course he should follow regarding emancipation. Politicians and certain generals of rank were urging him to take a public stand against it, he said. He was not opposed to emancipation in principle — he admitted to another visitor that as an institution slavery was dead — but he believed it must be carried out gradually, over the full course of time, and not be allowed to disrupt the war effort. By Cox's account, he was convinced that his troops were so devoted to him that they would "as one man enforce any decision he should make. . . ." His guests told him emphatically that going on record in opposition to the Emancipation Proclamation would be "a fatal error"; not a corporal's guard would stand by him if he violated the subordination of the military to the civil authority. McClellan promised to give their views the closest attention.[9]

Advice reached him from other quarters as well. Montgomery Blair, his sole ally in the Cabinet, wrote him on September 27 to urge him to clarify his views on slavery. This would be especially wise, he said, in light of a recent incident involving Major John J. Key, a staff man in the War Department and a brother of Colonel Thomas M. Key of McClellan's staff. The president had learned of Major Key's statement, Blair wrote, "that the reason why the Rebel army had not been destroyed at Sharpsburg was that the plan was to exhaust our resources so that a compromise might be made which would preserve Slavery & the Union at the same time." Lincoln was cashiering the major to make an example of him, Blair continued, and McClellan must not be tarred by his supporters' talk of a compromise peace. He felt sure the general had gone to war to preserve the Union but now realized that reunion would inevitably result in slavery's extinction. "I think it would have a salutary effect if you could ... declare yourself on the point in question," Blair wrote, particularly "if you had the ambitions to the Presidency ... for I can assure you that no appreciable portion of the nation will favor the long continuation of Slavery after this war is over or will tolerate any guarantees for its perpetuity as the price of peace."

His father, Francis P. Blair, seconded his views. The senior Blair, whose political influence went back to the administration of Andrew Jackson, wrote McClellan on September 30 that the proclamation was a war measure designed to destroy one of the foundations of the Confederacy; slaves formed "the sinews of war, whether in the trenches, the cotton field or the corn field." For the sake of Northern unity "you should manifest in every way, a fixed purpose to give full affect to the proclamation." To do so would "baffle those who follow you with 'fire in the rear' while you advance on that of the enemy."[10]

Presently William Aspinwall visited McClellan in his camp near Sharpsburg to add his influential voice to the debate. "Mr. Aspinwall is decidedly of the opinion that it is my duty to submit to the Presdt's proclamation & quietly continue doing my duty as a soldier," McClellan wrote Ellen. "I presume he is right...." In the face of this unanimous counsel, he finally abandoned the idea of opposing the proclamation publicly and instead issued a general order to the army explaining that it was every soldier's duty to obey the acts of the government. "Discussions by officers & soldiers concerning public measures ... when carried at all beyond temperate and respectful expressions of opinion," he wrote, substituted "the spirit of political faction" for the higher duty of respect and support for the civil authority. The only legitimate remedy for political error was at the ballot box. The elder Blair thought McClellan's order "in much better taste and in a more decisive authoritative style than I could have devised," and even the *New York Tribune* approved. Whatever the general's private thoughts on the matter, it editorialized, his response was given "temperately, deferentially, and with profound respect for the constituted authorities of the Nation."[11]

It was no doubt equally discouraging to McClellan to find that the North did not entirely share his view of Antietam. Newspaper opinion divided as usual along partisan lines. The *Journal of Commerce* described the battle as a triumph gained over superior numbers — the Rebels, it explained, "have never had less than four times the strength radicals give them credit for" — and Manton Marble's *New York World* ascribed victory to the gallantry of the troops "and the splendid management of Gen. McClellan." However, due in large measure to the *Tribune*'s George Smalley, whose Antietam account was more widely reprinted in newspapers at home and abroad than any other battle report of the war, it was the more common opinion that an opportunity for a truly decisive victory had been lost. When Smalley left the field to get his story of the fighting on the seventeenth to the *Tribune*, he wrote, "If not wholly a victory to-night, I believe it is the prelude to a victory to-morrow." After McClellan refused to renew the fighting on the eighteenth and the Confederates withdrew unopposed, the *New York Times* reported widespread disappointment "that they should have eluded our grasp. All the talk about bagging the rebels was mere bragging." As a result, an officer wrote, "the effect of the great battle at Antietam was to produce a feeling at home in which there was quite as much disgust as gratification."

Once more all was quiet on the Potomac. Days and then weeks of good campaigning weather passed, and still the army rested in its camps. "The country groans but nothing is done," Gideon Welles wrote in his diary. "Certainly the confidence of the people must give way under this fatuous inaction." There were "sinister rumors of peace intrigues," Welles wrote, and many believed McClellan guilty of "acting on the army programme avowed by Key." General Meade told his wife that everyone returning to camp from Washington reported the commanding general's position to be most precarious, "and that if he does not advance soon and do something brilliant, he will be superseded."[12]

General McClellan was reliving his experience at Harrison's Landing in July, brooding over his misfortunes and bitterly resentful of the incompetence of his superiors. He also revealed a reluctance to test himself again on the battlefield, a reluctance that went beyond his abhorrence of the new course the war seemed to be taking. He believed Antietam had removed any stain on his military reputation, and he told Ellen he was willing to retire from active command on that note. "I feel now that this last short campaign is a sufficient legacy for our child, so far as honor is concerned. . . ." He was certain "the poison still rankles in the veins of my enemies at Washn" and they would attempt to "throw me overboard again. I don't care if they do. . . . I have seen enough of public life." He made a similar point to Randolph Marcy, remarking that if the "good men" of the country did not come to his support and "press a proper policy over the Govt." he would retire to private life. Before retiring, however, he would try once more to regain the post of general-in-chief.

Following the dinner conference on the emancipation decree, he sent General Cochrane to Washington to press his claim. Cochrane confided to a *New York Herald* correspondent that he would tell the president that McClellan must be vested with "more authority and power than he now has" or he would resign; he was unwilling to serve longer under a general-in-chief who did not support him. When he did discuss this with Lincoln, Cochrane recalled, the president acknowledged that such a plan had occurred to him, and he supposed another place could be found for Halleck so as to make room for McClellan. More specifically, it was the president's design, the political insider T. J. Barnett assured Samuel Barlow, to transfer Halleck to a western command "& promote Mc out of the Army of the Potomac & place Hooker there. . . . I presume Mc will be promoted as the pressure is intense. . . ."

Another part of Cochrane's mission was to try to repair the breach between McClellan and Treasury Secretary Chase, his one-time advocate, and thus gain Chase's support for the change in the high command. As Chase recorded it in his diary, Cochrane told him that McClellan "would like to retire from active command if he could do so without disgrace . . . which could be accomplished . . . by restoring him to the chief command. . . ."[13]

However strong the pressures on him might be, Mr. Lincoln continued to make his own decisions regarding General Mc-Clellan, as he had from the beginning. He was willing enough to accept McClellan's claim of victory on the Antietam battlefield, but he was considerably less tolerant of an aftermath that left the enemy's army (by the general's own account) just as dangerous as ever. To claim a great victory simply because Maryland and Pennsylvania were safe, Lincoln later remarked to John Hay, was a hollow boast. "The hearts of 10 million people sunk within them when McClellan raised that shout. . . ."

McClellan's dispatches had soon enough resumed their old tone: he must be heavily reinforced, the army must be reorganized, the enemy was growing stronger and more threatening each day. "A defeat at this juncture would be ruinous to our cause," he telegraphed on September 23. In talking to Lincoln that day, T. J. Barnett found him noticeably cool toward his general, and he wrote Barlow that he was sure the president would not hesitate to remove McClellan if he could find a competent replacement and thought he could manage the reaction in the army and the country. When McClellan gave increasing evidence of remaining on the defensive north of the Potomac for the foreseeable future — "This Army is not now in condition to undertake another campaign nor to bring on another battle . . . ," he wrote ten days after Antietam — Lincoln determined to visit the Army of the Potomac and press its reluctant commander into action.[14]

The president arrived at the army's camps on October 1 and remained for four days, reviewing troops and visiting hospitals and touring the battlefields of South Mountain and Sharpsburg. Those were his ostensible purposes, McClellan confided to Ellen, but he thought that the "real purpose of his visit is to push me into a premature advance into Virginia." Except that Lincoln did not judge an advance to be premature, McClellan was right in his surmise. The two spoke privately and at length on the subject. The president "was very affable & I really think he does feel very kindly towards me personally," McClellan wrote Ellen; " . . . told me he was convinced I was the best general in the country etc etc." However kindly the tone, however, Lincoln apparently spoke of his purpose with candor. In a later letter, reminding the general of their conversations, he wrote, "You remember my speaking to you of what I called your over-cautiousness." When he related the visit to his old friend David Davis, Lincoln said he had told McClellan (as Davis recorded it) "that he wd be a ruined man if he did not move forward, move rapidly and effectively."

Just how McClellan responded to this urging is not known — there is no record of the conversations — but privately he left no doubt of his determination to resist. He told Ellen on October 2 that his men were still "completely tired out" and that the troops formerly in Pope's army remained demoralized and ought not to be made to fight again for some time yet. "The real truth is that my army is not fit to advance.... These people don't know what an army requires & therefore act stupidly...." Lincoln seems to have sensed this stubborn intransigence. The same day that McClellan wrote these thoughts to his wife, the president, standing on a hilltop with his friend Ozias M. Hatch and observing the vast encampment of the army, abruptly asked Hatch whether he knew what they were looking at. It was the Army of the Potomac, of course, Hatch replied. "So it is called, but that is a mistake," Lincoln said ; "it is only McClellan's bodyguard."[15]

If retained in field command and left to his own devices, McClellan intended that all other concerns give way to the restoring of his army. In addition to stocking new supplies and equipment, he planned to fill up all the battle-thinned veteran regiments, train and drill the new units, and add reinforcing divisions from Washington and elsewhere. By his reckoning, time was his ally. While he rested and refitted the Army of the Potomac and brought it up to parity with the enemy — intelligence estimates once again gave Lee 150,000 men — the North would be able to muster its resources and answer the call for new troops for the next campaign. Any premature movement, he told Colonel Strother, would risk a defeat that "at this crisis would be fatal to the Government and the cause."

When in due course the Potomac rose enough to limit the crossing places and make guarding them practicable, he might open a brief fall campaign, advancing on Winchester and either fighting Lee there or pushing him farther up the Shenandoah Valley. The lack of a railroad made it impossible to supply such an advance much beyond twenty-five miles. His next step would be to secure the entire upper Potomac area by constructing permanent rail and wagon bridges over the Potomac and the Shenandoah at Harper's Ferry and fortifying that place, repairing existing railroads, and enlarging the supply network by building two new railroads, one connecting Hagerstown with the Baltimore and Ohio line, the other linking Winchester and Strasburg in the Valley. Finally, presumably in the spring of 1863, he would return to his grand campaign against Richmond by the Peninsula route. It was the view at headquarters, a correspondent wrote his editor, that General McClellan "clings to the Peninsula. As far as I can judge from Key and his other echoes, he is in favor of going into winter quarters. If he is kept at the head of the army, it *will* go into winter quarters. . . .''[16]

In his memoirs McClellan claimed that Lincoln told him ''not to stir an inch until fully ready,'' but that is a recollection difficult to credit. Just two days after they parted, the president sent him orders through Halleck to ''cross the Potomac and give battle to the enemy or drive him south. Your army must move now while the roads are good.'' If he chose to make his advance east of the Blue Ridge — between Lee's army and the capital — he was assured of 30,000 reinforcements. If he advanced into the Shenandoah, only 12,000 to 15,000 men could be spared him from the capital's defenders. The president, Halleck added, ''advises the interior line, between Washington and the enemy, but does not order it. . . .''

The dispatch opened a thirty-day war of words between McClellan and Washington. Unwilling either to obey the order and make the best of the situation or to resign in protest against it, McClellan generated one excuse after another to delay the movement. Nothing so clearly reveals his design than the fact that while Lincoln and Halleck pressed him almost daily to march, he was playing host to his wife and his year-old daughter and his mother-in-law in a farmhouse near his camp in Pleasant Valley, where they remained in domestic tranquillity for nearly two weeks. ''My wife is with me here,'' he wrote Barlow on October 17, ''. . . & we are having a very quiet & pleasant time. . . .'' A frustrated General Halleck would tell a friend that there was an immobility about the Army of the Potomac that exceeded belief: ''It requires the lever of Archimedes to move this inert mass. I have tried my best, but without success.''[17]

McClellan explained that he could not move because of supply shortages, especially of shoes and clothing for the men and horses for the cavalry. The shortages were real enough. General Meade, for example, complained that hundreds of men in his division were without shoes, and Alpheus Williams wrote home, ''We want shoes and blankets and overcoats — indeed, almost everything.'' McClellan laid the blame for the problem on the quartermaster department in Washington, but in fact it had other sources as well.

The Army of the Potomac's chief quartermaster, Rufus Ingalls, admitted that the problem originated with the failure of brigade commanders and their quartermasters to make timely supply requisitions. With his characteristic energy, Herman Haupt, the director of military railroads, quickly discovered transportation bottlenecks. Through poor management in Washington and in the field, supply trains were being dispatched to the wrong depots and by roundabout routes, and after they finally arrived they stood on sidings, or blocked main lines, for days before they were unloaded. The shortage of cavalry horses was also largely a creation of red tape. For want of clear requisitions, many were sent to the Potomac army's cavalry stationed around Washington instead of to the units in the field. "Had you so ordered," Quartermaster Meigs telegraphed McClellan on the subject, "not less than 10,000 so distributed to troops under your command would have been sent to Harper's Ferry or Frederick."

In short, there was blame enough to go around, but a less obvious factor in the supply crisis was the commander of the Army of the Potomac, probably the best military administrator in the United States Army. It was not until three weeks after Antietam that McClellan even informed Washington of supply difficulties that were by then of long standing. He had applied no strong pressure for timely and rapid resupply for the reason that he had no immediate plans for a campaign that depended upon it; the army was unprepared for an advance simply because General McClellan had not ordered it to be prepared. His discovery of a crisis coincided exactly with the arrival of the president's order to cross the Potomac and take the offensive in Virginia.[18]

In the midst of this debate, he suffered the grievous embarrassment of seeing Jeb Stuart and 1,800 troopers once again ride completely around his army, collecting 1,200 horses from Pennsylvania farmers in the bargain. Stuart's audacity was rewarded by good fortune, and hardly a shot was fired at the Confederates by their badly directed pursuers. The raid climaxed a dismal record for the Army of the Potomac's cavalry under McClellan. Tactical independence was as lacking as ever, with cavalry detachments again scattered broadcast among the infantry. At Antietam, however they were misused, Pleasonton had counted 4,300 troopers under his command; in pursuing Stuart he could muster but 800. Colonel Wainwright wrote in his diary that the whole affair was "a burning disgrace. . . . I fear our cavalry is an awful botch."

Stuart's exploit frayed President Lincoln's temper in a manner reminiscent of the canal-lock fiasco at Harper's Ferry the previous winter. By the latest official returns, there were over 108,000 men present for duty on the upper Potomac, yet once again the enemy had made this host look exceedingly foolish. When McClellan blamed the affair on the overworked condition of his cavalry and the failure of the government to furnish remounts, Halleck replied, "The President has read your telegram, and directs me to suggest that, if the enemy had more occupation south of the river, his cavalry would not be so likely to make raids north of it." On another occasion, after receiving further complaint about the exhaustion of the cavalry force, Lincoln sent McClellan the barbed query "Will you pardon me for asking what the horses of your army have done since the battle of Antietam that fatigue anything?"

The president's telegram left him mad as a March hare, McClellan told Ellen: "It was one of those dirty little flings that I can't get used to when they are not merited." He sent Washington a lengthy catalogue of the cavalry's accomplishments and elaborate explanations for its shortcomings, but he did not address, or acknowledge, Lincoln's fundamental point: as long as the Army of the Potomac remained inactive, the war effort would be stalled on dead center and the Confederacy would profit thereby. Time was not the North's ally but its enemy.[19]

In response to the October 6 directive to advance, McClellan said that he would take the Shenandoah Valley route, although he warned that it promised no lasting strategic result; afterward he would have to "adopt a new & decisive line of operations which shall strike at the heart of the rebellion." No movement could be made, however, until the supply problem was resolved. When a week passed and it was clear that he was no closer to starting, the president determined to try one more time — perhaps for the last time — to reach some understanding with his general. The letter he wrote him on October 13 was the longest and most closely reasoned of all his letters to McClellan, and it probed most deeply into the general's failings as he perceived them.

His purpose, above everything else, was to convince McClellan that he must overcome his greatest failing — his reluctance to fight. His objective was the Rebel army, not some geographic area or strategic gain, and he must fight that army as soon as possible and to the best advantage he could. To wait to build railroads "ignores the question of *time,* which can not, and must not be ignored," he wrote. At the moment, he thought the situation very much in McClellan's favor. From his position on the Potomac he was closer to Richmond than General Lee was at Winchester, well to the west in the Shenandoah Valley; he was on the chord of the circle and Lee on the arc. A swift march southward that threatened the enemy's communications should force a battle: "I would press closely to him, fight him if a favorable opportunity should present, and, at least, try to beat him to Richmond on the inside track. I say 'try'; if we never try, we shall never succeed." If instead Lee turned northward again, as McClellan seemed to dread, "he gives up his communications to you absolutely, and you have nothing to do but to follow, and ruin him. . . ." Was he not being overcautious when he assumed that his army could not do what the enemy was constantly doing? "Should you not claim to be at least his equal in prowess, and act upon the claim?" The advance he proposed, Lincoln concluded, "is all easy if our troops march as well as the enemy; and it is unmanly to say they can not do it."

Before dispatching his letter, Lincoln showed it to Vice President Hannibal Hamlin and expressed his doubts that it would do much good and that he would be compelled to dismiss General McClellan. He made the same point to another visitor. He had grown weary of the general's endless excuses, he said, and were it not for the midterm elections taking place just then he would dismiss him. He had concluded that for the moment keeping him in command was the more politic thing to do. Nevertheless, it was clear that the president was giving McClellan his final chance to make good as commander of the Army of the Potomac.[20]

The letter's last-chance character did not escape McClellan's notice. The same day he received it, he was told by one of his staff just back from Washington that according to General John A. McClernand, one of those in the president's party when he visited the army, Lincoln was thinking of removing him from the Army of the Potomac and sending him west to take the supreme command there. Subsequently McClellan showed the president's letter to General Darius Couch and remarked, "Lincoln is down on me." Couch said he found no ill feeling in the letter, but McClellan disagreed. "Yes, Couch, I expect to be relieved from the Army of the Potomac, and to have a command in the West...." He wrote Lincoln on October 17 that he would give his views "the fullest & most unprejudiced consideration," and that he would open his advance the moment there were shoes for his men and horses for his cavalry.

Lincoln had described his letter as "in no sense an order," but from its general tone it was obvious that he would tolerate nothing like McClellan's plan for a brief expedition into the Shenandoah before going into winter quarters in expectation of a return to the Peninsula in the spring. McClellan mulled it over for another five days, and finally, on October 22, telegraphed Halleck that he had decided "to move upon the line indicated by the Presdt...." He sent his family north and on October 26 began crossing the Potomac with the bulk of the army, over 100,000 strong.[21]

The crossing required nine days, and during that time his disputes with Washington continued unabated. True to his habit of imagining the worst that might happen, he once again raised the specter of the Confederates reinforcing Lee with their western army, now under Braxton Bragg. With some asperity Halleck told him he need not worry: he was 20 miles from Lee's army and Bragg was 400 miles distant. To argue his case for railroad building and defensive measures on the upper Potomac, McClellan sent his aide Albert Colburn to see Halleck, but Colburn reported that he had little success with the general-in-chief: "The only answer I could get was that they had nothing to do with the present campaign.... There was no use of trying to explain matters to him because he would not listen to anything." On October 30 McClellan telegraphed the president a listing of the government's many failings in preparing the Army of the Potomac for the campaign, and explained, "I write this only to place the responsibility where it belongs...."

This barrage of charge and countercharge widened the breach between McClellan and his superiors until nothing could bridge it but a prompt and convincing victory by the Army of the Potomac. "The sword hangs over Mc — the pressure is awful and before long you will see a move," the Washington tipster Barnett warned Samuel Barlow. "If you could know the mean & dirty character of the dispatches I receive you would boil over with anger," McClellan burst out to Ellen; "... whenever there is a chance of a wretched innuendo — there it comes. But the good of the country requires me to submit to all this from men whom I know to be greatly my inferiors socially, intellectually & morally! There never was a truer epithet applied to a certain individual than that of the 'Gorilla.' "[22]

He told Ellen that he did not anticipate a battle any time soon. "I don't think Lee will fight me nearer than Richmond," he wrote on October 25; "— I expect no fight in this vicinity. . . ." So that he could exchange his Harper's Ferry supply base for one at Washington, he set as his objective Culpeper Court House, on the Orange and Alexandria Railroad some thirty miles northwest of Fredericksburg. Beyond that his intentions were less clear. If he had not brought Lee to battle by then, any continued advance very far south of the Rapidan River would dangerously lengthen his supply line. In that event, once across the Rapidan he probably intended to shift the army eastward to Fredericksburg and a shorter supply line running to Aquia Landing on the Potomac. From there, in due course, presumably he would advance overland toward Richmond, as the president and Halleck had long urged on him. Allan Pinkerton's intelligence gathering remained true to form, and in his final report to McClellan, on October 31, he estimated enemy strength at 130,000. On that day General Lee had some 70,000 men present for duty.[23]

Although McClellan told Washington nothing of his plans, it was quickly apparent that he was paying no heed to the president's injunction that he march swiftly along the chord of the circle to get between General Lee and his capital. Instead he advanced cautiously, taking eleven days to cover the first thirty-five miles. Anticipating using the same tactics against McClellan that he had employed against John Pope, Lee divided his army, holding Stonewall Jackson in the Shenandoah to operate on the enemy's communications and directing Longstreet's corps to Culpeper. Marching nearly twice as far as the Federals in half the time, Longstreet reached Culpeper comfortably ahead of the Army of the Potomac. "All goes well except secesh who are travelling too fast to meet my views," McClellan told his wife.

The report that the Confederates were across McClellan's line of advance reached Washington on November 4, the same day that New Yorkers voted in the last of the midterm elections. Possibly the two events bore equally on his decision, but however that may be, the president acted promptly. He had lost all patience with McClellan's constant delays "on little pretexts of wanting this and that," he later told John Hay. "I began to fear he was playing false — that he did not want to hurt the enemy. I saw how he could intercept the enemy on the way to Richmond. I determined to make that the test. If he let them get away I would remove him." On November 5 he directed Halleck to relieve General McClellan of command of the Army of the Potomac and replace him with Ambrose Burnside.[24]

Lincoln was straightforward and consistent in stating the military failings for which he dismissed General McClellan, and had frequently considered dismissing him earlier: he was the general with the "slows," the general who would not fight. The day after he made his decision he told Francis P. Blair that he had "tried long enough to bore with an auger too dull to take hold." In telling John Hay that he feared McClellan was playing false and did not want to hurt the enemy, however, the president was accusing him of the same offense for which he had cashiered Major Key. That charge was false. There is no credible evidence that George McClellan was anything less than completely patriotic and loyal to the Union cause, yet there is no small irony in the fact that his obsessive caution on campaign and his repeated loss of will in battle produced exactly the effect of a conspiracy to gain a compromise peace.

Another central flaw in his military character that led to his removal was his failure to grow as a commander. The general he was on his first campaigns was as good a general as he ever became. When he could not summon the courage to order Franklin's corps to attack at Antietam, he was echoing his failure to attack at Rich Mountain in western Virginia fourteen months earlier. His inability to exploit the opportunity presented him by the Lost Order in Maryland was a repetition of his inability to seize the moment at Yorktown on the Peninsula. The movement into Virginia toward Culpeper in October was as lumbering and beset by overcaution as the labored advance toward the Chickahominy the previous May. His chorus of complaints about unpreparedness and his dire warnings about enemy superiority were as loud in his last days of command of the Army of the Potomac as they were in his first days.

The president's other, unstated reason for relieving McClellan was political. The general had become the most prominent opponent of the administration and its policies. It was not a role forced on him by unscrupulous supporters (as some would believe) but one he had chosen deliberately and pursued for a year and more. He had consistently informed such Democratic leaders as William Aspinwall and Samuel Barlow of his charges against the government, particularly his accusation that Secretary Stanton had led a traitorous conspiracy to destroy him and his army on the Peninsula. He made his case to anti-administration newspapers like the *New York Herald* and especially to the *New York World*, now a Democratic party organ in which Barlow held a major interest. He did nothing to restrain his supporters in their attacks and indeed sometimes encouraged them. Chief of Staff Marcy wrote Barlow after Antietam that the general had not the slightest confidence in Stanton, ''and so far as he is concerned you are at perfect liberty to open your batteries upon him as soon as you please.''

Nor was it a secret in Washington that in the higher councils of the Army of the Potomac the active opposition to the administration took its tone from the general commanding. The talk in the Potomac army of disloyalty and military takeover ''has long been known to me,'' Stanton wrote Horace Greeley of the *Tribune*, ''& has been stimulated and fostered for twelve months against all my warnings and efforts.'' General McClellan might proclaim to his soldiers that the military was subordinate to the civil authorities, but clearly he did not feel that the principle applied to him, and he made every effort to have his superiors removed. No government, especially one in the midst of a civil war, could tolerate such actions by the commander of its largest army — nor restore him to the post of general-in-chief — and in the debate over McClellan's dismissal the point was frequently made that it was long overdue. Secretary Chase had said it months before: General McClellan might not be disloyal to the country, but beyond any doubt he was disloyal to the Lincoln administration.[25]

Another much-argued point in the debate was that General

McClellan was on the threshold of a great military success when he was relieved. Had he remained in command and forced a divided enemy to battle, he wrote in his *Report*, "I cannot doubt that the result would have been a brilliant victory for our army." Fitz John Porter asked editor Marble of the *New York World*, "What can be the notion, what the justification, of relieving a successful general in the midst of a campaign, on the eve of, perhaps, an important, and general battle... ?" Yet in truth McClellan could hardly have seriously expected to divide and conquer an enemy superior in numbers (by his count) and falling back along its communications while his own supply line was lengthening. Having James Longstreet free to maneuver on his front and Stonewall Jackson on his flank was not the enviable position he later made it out to be. Robert E. Lee's comment when he learned of McClellan's removal — "I fear they may continue to make these changes till they find some one whom I don't understand" — suggests that he had not found his situation greatly alarming.[26]

Secretary Stanton's suspicions of treachery at Potomac army headquarters led him to engineer the change of command with some care. To give maximum authority to the proceeding he had a War Department general officer, Brigadier Catharinus P. Buckingham, deliver the orders, and directed him to use every possible argument to persuade Burnside to accept the command. If he refused it, however, Buckingham was not to relieve McClellan but was to return to Washington. Stanton wanted no interval in the changeover that would allow General McClellan time to reflect on giving up his army. On November 7, in a snowstorm, Buckingham reached the army and delivered Burnside's orders, and after some argument persuaded him to accept. The two then went to McClellan's headquarters at the village of Rectortown.

It was 11:00 P.M. when they reached his tent. The staff had gone to bed and he was alone, writing his nightly letter to his wife. Having been alerted by a telegram from Washington that General Buckingham was arriving by special train with dispatches, he suspected the purpose of the visit. As he read his orders, he told Ellen, "I am sure that not a muscle quivered nor was the slightest expression of feeling visible on my face.... They shall not have that triumph." He turned to his successor and said, "Well, Burnside, I turn the command over to you."

He discussed details briefly and agreed to remain a few days
to help Burnside with the changeover, and then his visitors left
and he returned to his letter. "Poor Burn feels dreadfully, almost
crazy," he told Ellen; "— I am sorry for him, & he never showed
himself a better man or truer friend than now." (The next day
he wrote Mrs. Burnside that her husband "is as sorry to assume
command as I am to give it up. Much more so.") As to the larger
question of his relief, he wrote, "They have made a great mistake — alas for my poor country — I know in my innermost heart
she never had a truer servant." He had always tried to do his
duty and although he knew he must have made many mistakes,
"I do not see any great blunders — but no one can judge of
himself." He took his final consolation, as he always did, in finding blame elsewhere: "We have tried to do what was right — if
we have failed it was not our fault...."27

Headquarters was moved to Warrenton the next day, and
McClellan told Ellen that he felt very bad when he rode among
the troops "& saw how bright & cheerful they looked & how glad
they were to see me. Poor fellows, they did not know the change
that had occurred...." Soon the news spread through the ranks,
first by rumor and then officially. Marsena Patrick, the army's
provost marshal, wrote that night in his diary, "The Army is in
mourning & this is a blue day for us all."

On Sunday, November 9, General McClellan began the painful
process of bidding farewell to his army. That evening he received
the officers of his staff and escort in a highly emotional scene.
The side curtains of his tent were raised and the area was lit by
a large log fire nearby, and as each man entered he greeted him
and ushered him inside. To expressions of dismay at his removal
he replied, "It was very unexpected to me, I assure you," and
to those who made protest he said simply, "We have only to obey
orders." Champagne was served, and he raised his glass to the
assembled company and offered a toast: "To the Army of the
Potomac, and bless the day when I shall return to it."

The next morning the forces around Warrenton — First, Second, and Fifth corps — were assembled for review, and his farewell address was read to them. "In parting from you I cannot
express the love and gratitude I bear to you," he wrote. "As an
army you have grown up under my care.... The battles you have
fought under my command will proudly live in our Nation's

history. The glory you have achieved, our mutual perils and fa-
tigues, the graves of our comrades fallen in battle and by disease,
the broken forms of those whom wounds and sickness have disabled — the strongest assocations which can exist among men —
unite us still by an indissoluble tie. Farewell!''[28]

Presently McClellan, with Burnside at his side, rode past the
solid ranks in review. ''The line of soldiers was perhaps 3 miles
long,'' a Massachusetts man wrote home. ''We could hear the
cheers approach nearer and nearer till little Mac came in sight
and I can tell you we gave him 3 rousing cheers. He had not the
usual smile on. . . .'' At one point General Patrick thought the
cheers ragged, and he swung his hat ''with a call for a Once More
& All Together. It was magical in its effect & the result was
splendid.'' The *New York Times*'s William Swinton considered
the whole business contrived for ''scenic effect,'' with officers
leading each division to cheer on cue. In fact there had always
been this contrivance in McClellan's grand reviews, yet the cheers
were given no less sincerely. Even without orchestrated cheering,
the drama of the moment was real. When McClellan reviewed
the First Corps, Colonel Wainwright wrote in his diary, ''Not a
word was spoken, no noisy demonstration of regret at losing him,
but there was hardly a dry eye in the ranks.'' Some wept like
children, he noted; ''others could be seen gazing after him in
mute grief, one may almost say despair. . . .''

McClellan was deeply moved by this final display of affection
from his men. ''I did not know before how much they loved me
nor how dear they were to me,'' he wrote to Ellen. '' . . . The
scenes of today repay me for all that I have endured.'' Following
the review, he made his farewells to his field officers. All expressed
regret at the command change, Colonel Wainwright wrote, ''and
a few even going so far as to beg him to resist the order, and
saying that the army would support him. These last he reproved
gently but strongly.'' Whatever anyone may have thought of
George McClellan as a general, Wainwright concluded, on this
day he demonstrated that he was ''great in soul if not in mind.''[29]

As far as they can be finally counted, reactions in the army to
McClellan's removal most often divided along the same partisan
lines that divided the press. The *New York World* printed a letter
sent to Barlow by General Thomas F. Meagher that described
the government's action as notorious and criminal, ''which the

Army of the Union will never forgive." By contrast, the *Times* claimed that its correspondents found no such sentiments among the troops, and that in fact most were pleased by the change, while the *Tribune* welcomed the end at last of the "stubborn, criminal, fatal paralysis" of the Army of the Potomac.[30]

Soldiers' comments ranged almost as widely. A great many blamed McClellan's downfall on the "hellish influences" of Republican radicals, and a diarist in the 14th Indiana described the entire army as "melancholy" at losing the only general in whom it had any confidence. Yet another man in the 14th Indiana wrote home that McClellan had been in command eighteen months and accomplished nothing, "& I think he should have given some evidence of military genius in that time." Evidence that the command change caused any real demoralization is slight and is limited to the officer corps. In spite of McClellan's efforts to calm unrest, there was much campfire talk of mass resignations. The announcement that any officer seeking to resign "in the face of the enemy" would be dishonorably cashiered soon quelled the impulse. In the end, the Army of the Potomac proved to be no weapon for a coup d'état, and George McClellan no general to lead one.

The next morning, November 11, McClellan and members of his staff boarded a special train at Warrenton Junction that was bound for Washington. There was a brief display of protest by the honor guard at his leaving, but he came out on the train's rear platform and told them that if they would follow General Burnside as loyally as they had followed him all would be well. "The tears ran down his cheeks as he spoke & it was quite a while before he could speak," one of the soldiers wrote. Then the train left, and the Army of the Potomac — his army, he always called it — saw George McClellan no more.[31]

FIFTEEN

THE POLITICAL ARENA

O<small>NCE IT HAD RELIEVED</small> its senior general and best-known critic, the Lincoln government faced the problem of what to do with him. There was no available administrative post befitting McClellan's rank, and he had no home where he might be stationed, having given up the house in Washington where he had lived the previous winter, and in any event the capital was the last place the government wanted him to be. Secretary Stanton decided to order him to Trenton, New Jersey, apparently for no better reason than its proximity to Orange, where Ellen was staying in the Marcys' home.

In a scene that would be repeated wherever he went in the next few months, McClellan was welcomed in Trenton as a hero home from the wars. There was a crowded reception on November 13, with a serenade by the Trenton Cornet Band and much patriotic oratory. He responded with a brief speech, urging his listeners to be sure the war was prosecuted "for the preservation of the Union and the Constitution, for your nationality and rights as citizens." According to the *New York Express*, "No such demonstration, political or otherwise, was ever before witnessed in Trenton."

McClellan remained in relative obscurity at Trenton barely a week before taking up residence in the Fifth Avenue Hotel in New York. The city was the largest Democratic stronghold in the North, and his greeting there was tumultuous. On the day of his arrival the street in front of the hotel was solidly packed with people hoping for a glimpse of him, the *Herald* reported, and soon a band appeared and local militiamen with a small fieldpiece, and "amid the music . . . and the occasional thunder of artillery arose the voices of the people in loud shouts and huzzas for their favorite General." His appearance on the hotel's balcony "was the signal for an outburst of enthusiasm simply impossible to describe." After three weeks there McClellan blandly applied to the War Department for permission to change his posting to New York to prepare his final report as commander of the Army of the Potomac. Permission was slow in coming, but faced with the prospect of making the general a martyr in the camp of the enemy if he refused, Secretary Stanton finally yielded.[1]

New York newspapers began to carry regular features headed "McClellan's Movements," listing his attendance at the theater and the opera and at dinner parties and grand balls. It was noticed that he was courted by Democrats of every station. New York's newly elected governor, Horatio Seymour, arranged to confer with him, as did August Belmont, national chairman of the party, John Van Buren, state chairman, and Dean Richmond, a leading party strategist. He became close to the editors of the two leading Democratic papers, Manton Marble of the *World* and William C. Prime of the *Journal of Commerce*. He was seen regularly with such major corporate and financial figures — and party supporters — as Samuel Barlow, William Aspinwall, John Jacob Astor, and William B. Duncan. Presently they demonstrated their admiration for him by the gift of a handsome, fully furnished, four-story brick house on West 31st Street, in one of Manhattan's most desirable residential areas.

These men not only easily qualified as the "best people" whose company McClellan had always favored, but their Democratic politics (like his) had a decidedly conservative cast. This latter fact alarmed others among his friends. Edward H. Eldredge, Dr. John McClellan's father-in-law, wrote the doctor on November 28 that he had recently called on General McClellan and observed the scene around him, and he warned of danger "if he is not careful of his surroundings." When McClellan attended the opera one evening, Eldredge wrote, the orchestra struck up national airs and the audience cheered when he entered, and "he was brought forward to bow an acknowledgment by John Van Buren. He was in Duncan's box, with Belmont & Sam Barlow. . . ." New Yorkers, he went on, "know full well the political attitudes of all these gentlemen — they are known to be ultra democrats . . . , as near secessionists as they dare to be. Regret was everywhere expressed that he had fallen into such hands." He urged Dr. McClellan to put his brother on guard against such company, lest he be caught in "the snares of seeming friends who may prove his worst enemies."

Eldredge was not alone in raising this warning. T. J. Barnett, who professed himself devoted to McClellan's cause, cautioned Barlow about the widespread belief that "men of doubtful loyalty have had hold of Mac since he was relieved," which to many seemed proof that his heart had never been in the war. A man in the Army of the Potomac wrote home that from what he read in the papers General McClellan was associating with Copperheads, the peace-at-any-price Democrats likened to poisonous reptiles. "He must be some like Benedict Arnold; for I do not believe he was a traitor while in command, but he thinks he has been injured & now seems to be trying to injure his country in every possible way...." However much this misjudged the motives of both McClellan and those he associated with, it was a widely accepted view. Former Ohio governor William Dennison told McClellan directly that his "dangerous surroundings" were jeopardizing any hope he might have for a further command.[2]

McClellan's friendship with both Barlow and Aspinwall was of long standing, and Astor had been a volunteer on his staff on the Peninsula, and it was natural that he would renew these acquaintances when he moved to New York. At the same time, he was hardly the "poor, confiding McClellan," naïvely susceptible to designing politicians, that some thought him to be. He was now no more innocent of the implications of associating with leaders of the conservative wing of the Democratic party than he had been in corresponding with them for a year past. Their cause was his cause; like them he was convinced that the war could never be won nor the nation successfully reunited under Lincoln and the Republicans. As he later phrased it to Barlow, he could not find it in himself to support "a party & a policy which I conscientiously believe will bring ruin upon us all."

The strength of his appeal to conservatives was expressed by the lawyer George Ticknor Curtis in a letter to editor Prime of the *Journal of Commerce.* "Let it be understood," Curtis wrote, "that Genl. McClellan's character and powers stand between the Constitution and the radicalism and the disorganizing doctrines of the dominant party, and something may yet be saved from the wreck to which all things now seem to be tending.'' To be sure, McClellan was in fundamental disagreement with the party's Copperhead faction in his insistence that the war must be vigorously prosecuted until reunion was assured, yet reunion was his sole condition for peace. Slavery should not and must not be at issue in this war, and he had no actual quarrel with the Copperhead slogan, ''The Constitution as it is, the Union as it was.''

There is nothing to indicate that during the winter of 1862–1863 McClellan's ambition was strongly focused on the presidency, yet there is nothing either to indicate any effort on his part to discourage those who wanted him as a candidate. At any time he might have made it clear that he would not be the Democrats' nominee in 1864. Instead, he regarded the whole question as a matter of duty. In his first recorded reference to the subject, when writing to his mother in December 1863, McClellan professed to be indifferent to the White House, but in any event he judged any call to that position (like his call to command the Army of the Potomac) to be predestined: ''I shall do nothing to get it & trust that Providence will decide the matter as is best for the country.''[3]

Three weeks after McClellan's relief from command Albert Colburn wrote him from Washington that he had learned ''from a reliable source that there is no chance of your being assigned to duty.'' The administration dared not name him to any lesser post than head of the Army of the Potomac or general-in-chief, Colburn said, and had no plans to give him either one. It was equally apparent that Secretary Stanton's suspicions had not been put to rest by the peaceful command change at Rectortown. McClellan reported that his mail was being opened, and he began to send correspondence by messenger when he could. In his interview with Edward Eldredge, he said he was under constant surveillance by government agents, who noted down every place he went and everyone he saw. (That same day, the *New York Herald* added a nice twist to the matter by charging this spying to Allan Pinkerton. An enraged Pinkerton wanted McClellan's help in putting down this ''gross slander.'') At about this time McClellan or someone on his staff developed a telegraphic cipher that included code words for such ominous phrases as ''Secrete all important papers'' and ''I have been arrested.''

McClellan detected an undercurrent of suspicion directed at

him when he was called to Washington to testify in military court regarding the charges lodged against Irvin McDowell and Fitz John Porter for their conduct in the Second Bull Run battle. "Fitz & I are the 'great tabooed,' " he wrote Ellen; "— you would laugh to see how *some* officials fight shy in public, & then come to me privately to protest their devotion!" The verdicts in the two cases — his enemy McDowell cleared of all charges, his friend Porter found guilty and cashiered — were further proof to McClellan that the government, most particularly Secretary Stanton, was still conspiring against him. He was assured by Porter and others that (as Porter put it) under pressure by Republican radicals "the court began to smell your return to power and were influenced by it in their decision."[4]

The matter of his return to power had been given sudden currency by the disastrous collapse of Ambrose Burnside's Fredericksburg campaign. In the aftermath of the failed battle on December 13, 1862, a disgusted soldier in the 17th Michigan wrote, "The Fates seem against this Army of the Potomac. We have tried strategy under McClellan, dash under Pope, bulldog fighting under Burnside & failed with all. Who shall we find combining all?" The call for McClellan's reinstatement was strongest in the army's officer corps. "We *must* have McClellan back with unlimited and unfettered powers," Brigadier G. K. Warren of the Fifth Corps wrote. "His name is a tower of strength to everyone here...."

The six weeks following Fredericksburg were a time of crisis in the Army of the Potomac, remembered ever after as the Valley Forge of its existence. This was chargeable in part to General Burnside's many failings, particularly his neglect of his men. Army administration fell into a shambles. Every day soldiers by the scores died senselessly in the wretched hospitals and filthy camps. The food was so bad that they even died from scurvy. It was estimated that desertions averaged 200 a day. There was another factor in the collapse of morale, however, that was a consequence of General McClellan's unique legacy to the Potomac army.

McClellan had linked morale so directly to the personal popularity of the general commanding that this characteristic had come to be weighed equally with military ability. Burnside was appointed to the army command (and twice before invited to take it) not so much for his supposed military talents as for the fact that he was a favorite with the troops; the government hoped they would follow him as faithfully as they had followed McClellan. When there proved to be no way to explain away the glaring Fredericksburg defeat, as McClellan had explained away his defeats, Burnside fell abruptly from grace and carried morale down with him. At a review of the veteran Second Corps after the battle, a call for a cheer for the general commanding was met by a stony silence. When it became necessary to replace Burnside, Joe Hooker's popularity with the men would be a decisive factor in selecting him over John Reynolds or George Meade.[5]

Even more noticeable in the wake of Fredericksburg was McClellan's mark on the army's officer corps. His detractors called it McClellanism and described its symptoms as bad blood and general paralysis. So systematically was Burnside undercut by generals friendly to McClellan that the army soon became unmanageable. William Franklin and Baldy Smith collaborated on a criticism of the Fredericksburg campaign and urged a return to McClellan's Peninsula strategy, and they sent their letter over Burnside's head directly to the president. Generals John Cochrane and John Newton made complaint directly to the White House, painting for Lincoln a bleak picture of demoralization stemming from a total loss of confidence in Burnside. Other generals said much the same thing to anyone who would listen. (Hooker was one of these, although unlike the others his intention was to see Joe Hooker in command rather than McClellan.) There was, old Sumner complained, "a great deal too much croaking; there is not sufficient confidence."

The situation finally reached the point that Burnside drew up a list of eight generals to be dismissed from the service or transferred from the Potomac army if he was to remain in command. Forced to a choice between evils, Lincoln accepted Burnside's resignation. In doing so, however, he did not discount the threat of McClellanism. Colonel Wainwright wrote in his diary that "the disaffection produced by Franklin's and others' talk was very evident. The whole army seems to know what they have said. . . ." The worst offenders on Burnside's list were transferred, beginning with Generals Franklin and Smith. And however the justice of the court-martial verdict against Fitz John Porter may be judged, it was hardly coincidence that Lincoln approved Porter's cashiering in the midst of this officers' revolt. No one in the

Potomac army was closer to McClellan than Porter, and there is reason to believe that the president intended his action in this case, like his action in Major Key's case, to be taken as an object lesson. The Army of the Potomac's officer corps was put on notice that loyalty to the commander-in-chief was a higher duty than loyalty to that army's first commander.[6]

Late in January 1863 the McClellans visited Boston at the invitation of a group of prominent men whose common coin was political conservatism, although unlike the general's New York supporters they were mostly Republican conservatives. The nine-day visit was a triumph, and McClellan pronounced himself overwhelmed by the welcome. "Dinners, balls, and serenades succeeded each other in rapid succession," one of his hosts wrote. An estimated 10,000 people appeared at a public reception at the Tremont House, and a citizens' committee honored him with a presentation sword. He made no public addresses, although the *Boston Post* quoted his remark that he was pleased to note an upsurge in conservatism in New England, a trend he regarded as "the hope and strength of the nation."

The Boston publisher William D. Ticknor wrote a friend that he did not expect the visit would restore McClellan to command of an army or make him president. It was instead "simply a graceful tribute to his services, . . . not forgetting at the same time, that it damages the men who have treated him so ill," and no doubt that sort of revenge was on McClellan's mind when he accepted the invitation. The *Worcester Spy* thought the "work of lionizing the chieftain" was a deliberate effort by Boston's political Brahmins "to concentrate all the hostile political elements in the loyal states about a hero. . . ." After all, the *Springfield Republican* commented, Boston never invited strangers to visit unless it wanted something of them, and strangers never visited Boston unless they sought something. At the very least, General McClellan sought the approbation of like-minded political conservatives.[7]

His political future was of interest to a great many people, none more so than the Blair clan. Late in 1862 Francis P. Blair and his sons Montgomery and Frank began to evolve a complicated strategy to steer the general's political popularity away from the New York Democrats and into what they regarded as a more constructive channel. The elder Blair had counseled against relieving McClellan, and in a letter written to Lincoln on December 18 he argued that it was better to have him within the administration than outside it. Blair saw the Fredericksburg debacle as an opportunity to restore McClellan to the Army of the Potomac. ''We must look to the Army as a great political as well as war machine,'' he wrote. ''The soldiers are to give us success in the field & at the polls. McClellan is dear to them. He will bring them to the support of the country & you.''

By the president's reckoning, putting General McClellan again in a field command simply to dampen his political prospects was a bad bargain, but there is evidence that at about this time he did give thought to returning him to the post of general-in-chief. When he held that position he had actively directed the armies, and Lincoln was sorely disappointed that General Halleck played the role very differently. Repeatedly Halleck refused to provide direction and recommendations, most recently during the Burnside controversy, and the president was not averse in principle to replacing him. On February 24, 1863, reportedly with Lincoln's concurrence, Montgomery Blair discussed the matter with McClellan in New York. There is no record of their conversation beyond the fact that it took place. Some months afterward McClellan told a friend of the meeting, and Blair described it to Gideon Welles. By Welles's account, Blair claimed he had negotiated an agreement with McClellan, but when he returned to Washington he ''found his plans frustrated, and the President unwilling to give them consideration.'' Blair blamed Secretary of State Seward for thwarting the scheme, but however that may be, it did not put an end to the efforts of the Blairs to bring General McClellan back into command.[8]

Shortly after the interview with Blair, McClellan was called to testify before the Joint Committee on the Conduct of the War. He expected an ordeal. ''I have many — very many — bitter enemies here — they are making their last grand attack,'' he wrote Ellen when he reached Washington. ''. . . I am in a *battle* & must fight it out.'' He considered the committee, he later wrote, ''the most accomplished set of villains and blaguards that were ever collected together.'' Yet however hostile most of the committee members may have been, their two-day examination of him turned out to be comparatively mild. He was well prepared and handled himself with his usual assurance, and they seemed reluctant to

challenge him. Nearly all the questioning was done by Representative Daniel Gooch of Massachusetts, who was content simply
to elicit information. Such fierce opponents as Senators Zach
Chandler and Ben Wade sat by and said nothing.

"I have been tramping up & down the Committee room for I
don't know how long," McClellan told Ellen after the first day's
testimony; "— my brain on a constant stretch, watching like a
hawk for the training of every question, for fear that I should
be tripped in some way or other." He was never tripped as he
narrated the history of his command of the Army of the Potomac.
He said he had always faced stronger enemy forces and had
always advanced the moment it was possible to do so. He fended
off the few probing questions with confident replies: "In my best
judgment...," or "No, I think it was better as it was...," or
simply "I think not...." On occasion he had no recollection of
some point (such as whether he was aboard a gunboat on the day
of Malvern Hill). In all respects he gave the committee the record
he would stand on, then and thereafter.

It was clear enough that the committee had reopened its hearings on the Army of the Potomac primarily to discredit General
McClellan's military record once and for all. Hurriedly it prepared its report for publication. Let the people see this display
of incompetence, Senator Chandler predicted, and "McClelland
is deader than the prophets. He will *never* be heard from again."
The report appeared early in April, followed later in the month
by the testimony on which it was based as well as a substantial
number of the dispatches sent during McClellan's operations. At
the same time, as a counter to this, the McClellan camp released
to the press his preliminary reports on the Peninsula and Maryland campaigns, and on April 28 the *New York Herald* devoted
most of its front page to his committee testimony. As a consequence of all this publishing activity, McClellan partisans and
detractors found all the evidence they needed to confirm their
respective views, and he remained in the public eye.[9]

Lacking any other official duties, he devoted most of his time
in these early months of 1863 to the report on his fifteen months
as commander of the Army of the Potomac. It was a work designed to refute his critics and to justify his military conduct to
his countrymen and to history, and when it was published the
New York Times sarcastically termed it "nothing less than the

Military Memoirs of George B. McClellan, printed at the expense of the Government.'' In fact the barb was close to the mark. The *Report* would form a sizable part of the narrative of *McClellan's Own Story,* his posthumously published memoirs. In a letter to Edward Everett, the noted orator, whom he had met on his Boston tour, he described the writing as tedious and difficult: ''It is much easier to conduct campaigns & fight battles than to write their history — at least I find it so.''

An outline prepared for the staff members who drafted various sections of the *Report* suggests how large a role rationalization played in its writing. The ''reasons for delays'' and the ''controverted points of this period'' were to be part of the narrative of the first eight months of McClellan's command. About the Peninsula, the outline read, ''Note insufficiency of troops & ... reasons for so much delay before active operations,'' and there was to be a ''full & copious'' discussion ''as to the propriety of abandoning Harrison's Landing.'' In the Second Bull Run campaign it would be demonstrated that General McClellan ''assisted Genl Pope all he could''; in the Maryland campaign, ''Show why did not fight on the 18th of September'' and ''why did not cross the Potomac at once in obedience to President's order.'' ''Enemy's positions & numbers'' were to be shown by including all the dispatches containing important intelligence estimates. The lesson was pointed concerning ''interference from civilians'' and ''meddling'' by members of Congress. James Russell Lowell detected an important truth about the *Report* when he wrote in 1864 that General McClellan ''makes affidavit in one volume octavo that he is a great military genius, after all.''[10]

The amount of pressure on the administration to restore McClellan to command varied in inverse proportion to the fortunes of the Army of the Potomac, and following Joe Hooker's defeat at Chancellorsville in early May of 1863 McClellan stock (as T. J. Barnett remarked to Samuel Barlow) ''was pulsating in the market.'' A Federal soldier wrote home that he hoped the president ''will be 'honest old Abe' enough to just put George B. McClellan back in command ..., that is if old Lee dont bag them all before he can get around to it. ...'' As Lee's army began marching northward toward Pennsylvania, Edward Everett was one of those urging Lincoln to put McClellan in Hooker's place immediately, insisting that such an act would be worth 50,000 men to the Union cause. "Right or wrong," Everett wrote, "the mass of the People confide in him," for he possessed the confidence not only of the Democrats but of the conservative wing of Lincoln's party as well. Governor Joel Parker of New Jersey wanted him at least put in charge of the militia mobilizing to meet the invasion, a suggestion echoed by the Pennsylvania editor Alexander K. McClure. The *Herald* was the most prominent of the newspapers demanding the dismissal of Stanton and Halleck and the reinstatement of McClellan.

What was most needed in the crisis was a general willing to fight, and Mr. Lincoln had already made up his mind about General McClellan on that count. He told Governor Parker that there were "difficulties and involvements" in reinstating McClellan, but he was more blunt to his friend McClure. "Do we gain anything by opening one leak to stop another?" he asked. "Do we gain anything by quieting one clamor, merely to open another, and probably a larger one?" When the time came, it was General Meade who replaced Hooker, and McClellan's only role in the Gettysburg campaign was to help Governor Seymour prepare New York's militia to march to the defense of Pennsylvania.[11]

In drafting his memoirs, McClellan gave it as fact that "most of the army thought at Gettysburg that they were fighting under my command. . . . I have been told by many officers that 'McClellan's ghost' won the battle, because the men would not have fought as they did had they not supposed that I was in command." This particular conceit, which also appeared in the newspapers at the time, was based on a letter of July 1863 from one of Fitz John Porter's former staff officers, which Porter sent to McClellan and also copied and distributed to Democratic editors with the notation "Make what use of it you choose." There is no doubt that some men in the Army of the Potomac believed the rumor that their favorite general had returned, but to attribute victory to that cause was of a piece with the counter-rumor, sweeping Boston, that on the eve of Gettysburg McClellan conspired with Democratic leaders to march on Washington and depose the Lincoln government.[12]

While he waited to be recalled to military duty, McClellan was repeatedly importuned to declare his political views. In late May, at the request of Montgomery Blair, he had granted an interview to Charles C. Fulton, editor of the *Baltimore American*. To correct what he termed the "general misapprehension prevailing as to your views on . . . the vigorous prosecution of the war," Fulton sought McClellan's permission to publish the interview. He had understood the general to say that "all talk of 'terms of peace' and 'conciliation' and 'compromise,' with men arrayed in armed hostility to the Government, was simply ridiculous," and that anything standing in the way of reunion, including holding "property in men," must be thrust aside and the administration supported. He also understood McClellan to deny any connection with such notorious Copperheads as James Brooks, editor of the *New York Express,* and Congressmen Clement L. Vallandigham of Ohio and the brothers Fernando and Benjamin Wood of New York, whom detractors had tried to tie him to. This was altogether too much of a stand for McClellan. He told Fulton that he had recorded his views "in some cases rather stronger & wider than I intended, & in others less so," and he refused him permission to publish.

He was no more responsive to Samuel S. Cox, the Democratic leader in the House of Representatives, who wanted him to commit himself to the opposition by running for governor of Ohio on the Democratic ticket that fall. Let his name be mentioned, Cox wrote, and the nomination — and election — were foregone conclusions. McClellan rejected the proposal, and the nomination went to Vallandigham.

A third supplicant was the Republican political manager Thurlow Weed, who wanted him to preside over a mass meeting in New York on June 15 to rally support to the government in this time of military crisis. McClellan's avowal of the principle that peace could only follow the re-establishment of the authority of the government, Weed wrote him, "would refresh the country." In declining the invitation McClellan assured Weed, in a letter meant for publication, of his conviction that the war must be prosecuted "at whatever cost of time treasure & blood," and that he would support any policy leading to ultimate reunion while preserving "the rights of all Union loving citizens" (including, that is, the right to hold "property in men") wherever they might be.

On his return from organizing the militia in Albany, McClellan and Ellen and daughter May moved out of their new 31st Street home to live in a rented house on Orange Mountain in New Jersey.

In part this was an escape from the summer heat of the city, but it was also an escape from the growing pressures he was exposed to as a public figure. He made no comment on the draft riots that convulsed New York for four days in mid-July, and, contrary to reports, he gave Governor Seymour no advice on dealing with the street mobs (one newspaper had him recommending grape and canister instead of argument), but privately he condemned the administration's emancipation policy as the root cause of the rioting. "The Govt must come back to the true & original issues before it can hope to have the support of the great mass of the people," he wrote Samuel Cox on July 14, "— & without their cordial support I see but little hope for ultimate success."[13]

On August 4, 1863, McClellan saw his final report off to the War Department in the care of his brother Arthur. "In view of all the circumstances of the case," he wrote Adjutant General Lorenzo Thomas, "I respectfully request permission to publish the Report." Apparently he expected the accompanying 263 reports of his subordinates to be published as well, and he included five of Pinkerton's intelligence summaries to document his case for enemy superiority. The main report alone came to 756 manuscript pages, making it unique among the wartime writings of Civil War generals, and the War Department was understandably reluctant to have to publish a vindication of its best-known critic. "Messrs Stanton & Halleck are puzzled what to do with Gen. Mac's long Report and documents," T. J. Barnett wrote. "They threaten not to print it, unless by an appropriation for the purpose." Finally the House of Representatives passed a resolution calling for the report (but not the subordinates' reports) to be submitted to Congress and published by the Government Printing Office, and it appeared as a book of 242 pages in February 1864.[14]

One cause of Secretary Stanton's complaint about publishing McClellan's report was that six weeks after it was submitted, the general publicly committed himself to the political arena — and on the side of the opposition party. The occasion he chose for entering politics was the Pennsylvania gubernatorial election, held on October 13, 1863.

To oppose Governor Curtin, the Democrats nominated George W. Woodward, chief justice of the Pennsylvania supreme court. Woodward was strongly conservative in outlook, and in 1860 had been one of those willing to see the South leave the Union unchallenged. He labeled as unconstitutional the Legal Tender Acts, on which much of the war's financing rested, and the Draft Act, on which its manpower needs now depended. Republicans painted Judge Woodward as at the very least a peace Democrat and at worst a Copperhead. The party's press also insisted that General McClellan, who as head of the Army of the Potomac had worked closely with Governor Curtin, was committed to Curtin's re-election.

On Election Day the *Philadelphia Press* published a letter from McClellan denying that he had pledged his support to Governor Curtin. On the contrary, he wrote, he had recently met Judge Woodward and found that "our views agree, and I regard his election as Governor of Pennsylvania called for by the interests of the nation." He understood Woodward to favor fighting the war according to "the principles of humanity and civilization, working no injury to private rights and property," and to believe that the "sole great objects of this war are the restoration of the unity of the nation, the preservation of the Constitution, and the supremacy of the laws of the country." He fully concurred on these points: "I would, were it in my power, give to Judge Woodward my voice and vote."

McClellan's supporters would regard the Woodward letter as unfortunate — especially after Woodward lost the election — and attribute its writing to the general's political naïveté and his understandable annoyance at having his views distorted for partisan purposes. Naïveté played no part in the matter, however. George McClellan knew precisely what he was doing when he wrote the Woodward letter, and knew what he must include in it if he was to have any chance of becoming president of the United States.

The Pennsylvania Democratic leaders had made it clear that a wholehearted endorsement by General McClellan was vital to Woodward's chances, and that if the general expected the party to nominate him for the presidency in 1864, he would have to pay his party dues here and now in Pennsylvania. Two weeks before the election he had made a supposedly nonpolitical appearance in Philadelphia, but without apparent effect on the campaign. He then discussed the matter with Barlow and Manton Marble of the *World,* and Marble wrote out for him a careful, point-by-point analysis of the situation. "Without a plump authoritative word from you we shall certainly be beaten," he explained, and in that event "your silence will certainly be deemed by the leading Democratic politicians as the cause of the defeat. The effect of this in the future is obvious enough." McClellan's endorsement of Woodward was expected to be particularly effective among soldier voters, of which Marble estimated there were as many as 12,000 in Pennsylvania. Such an endorsement appearing at the last minute, he added, would be "too late to be attacked or denied. . . ." Reluctantly, McClellan accepted these arguments.

Marble told him afterward that the decision to write the Woodward letter had been a choice between two evils, but a necessary choice: party leaders were satisfied, and now "the people's eyes are turned all one way in their search for the candidate who will win in 1864." He was greasing the axis of the *World*, he said, to keep it rolling toward that goal. Samuel Cox wrote from Ohio that "our whole people — from the lake to the river — are full of McClellan. Our papers are coming out for him." On the other hand, Edward Eldredge detected widespread disappointment in New England that McClellan had given his support to a man "who is generally believed to be at heart an out and out Copperhead." T. J. Barnett also thought it a serious misjudgment. "Why should *he* step from a dignified & secure position into the depths of partizan mud?" he asked Barlow. "He has hazarded everything by this 'change of base' & I think & fear, lost all. The Oracle is unveiled, & a partizan is presented — that's all he has done!"[15]

Recognizing that the Woodward letter and his commitment to the Democratic opposition probably ended any chance for a command under the Lincoln administration, McClellan determined to resign his commission and return to private life. Doing so, however, would end his main source of income, his $6,000 salary as a major general. The problem appeared to be resolved when John Jacob Astor notified him on November 19 that he was being considered for the presidency of the New Jersey Railroad at an annual salary of $5,000. This prospect was enough for McClellan to draft a letter of resignation to the president. Intending it to be made public, he was at pains to recite the history of his military services, his final service being "to free the Capital a second time from danger and the loyal states from invasion." Now that it was obvious "that my services are no longer desired by your Excellency," and since "a fitting opportunity has offered," he could resign in good conscience. "I cannot, nor ought I to restrain myself from bidding through you a last farewell to the heroic men who so long fought under my command," he wrote, and he thanked Lincoln for "the confidence and kind feeling you once entertained for me...."

This self-indulgent defense of his record never reached the eyes of the electorate, however. Nothing came of the offer of the railroad presidency after all, and he decided to remain in the army. He took as his model Winfield Scott, who ran for the presidency on the Whig ticket in 1852 without resigning his commission. As it happened, his financial picture brightened considerably during 1864, thanks to another gift from his wealthy friends. He was given a one-sixth share in the proceeds of the liquidation of Ohio and Mississippi Railroad stock, a process handled by William Aspinwall, and in one year this brought him just under $20,000.

He added further to his income by writing articles of military analysis anonymously for a new weekly journal of opinion called *The Round Table*, which during the winter of 1863–1864 published five of his pieces. Three dealt with unexceptional topics — military ordnance, battlefield communications, a comparison of American and European military practices — but the other two offered a critical view of the forthcoming spring campaigns. He argued anew for operations in the West to be merely supportive of the eastern army; any advance on Atlanta, he wrote, "is open to the objection that it renders impossible all concert of action with the troops on the Eastern line." He expressed concern for the Army of the Potomac "for the reason that its line of operations is not well selected." The only proper line was the James River, "but this is not in accordance with the theories of the Washington strategists, and we have only to anticipate another fruitless attempt to reach Richmond overland 'on wooden legs.'" As for the government's overall policy toward the South, McClellan echoed his Harrison's Landing letter by urging it "be in accordance with the enlightened maxims of the New Testament, not with the bloody and barbarous code of the nations of old time, who fought solely to destroy and enslave."[16]

McClellan seldom ventured away from Orange Mountain as political activity intensified in the election year of 1864. Publication of his *Report* early in the year served as an unofficial opening of his presidential campaign. "I hear from all quarters that the Report is doing much good, & opening many eyes," he wrote. Newspapers printed many of the dispatches and long excerpts from the narrative, and there was column after column of commentary and editorializing. The *New York Times* assigned reporter William Swinton to do a series based on the *Report*, eventually running to eleven articles, that "exposed" McClellan's military ineptitude. The *New York World* countered with a highly laudatory series by Hiram Ketchum, who consulted with McClellan on the articles. McClellan's Harrison's Landing letter received perhaps the widest attention. The *World* called it a remarkable document, forecasting "with a statesman's vision the sound political as well as the sound military policy upon which the war should have been conducted...." The *Times* called it an "intolerable insult to the soldier to say that he will break from his ranks, if Slavery is not spared."

Soon after the congressional printing appeared, the New York publisher Sheldon & Company issued a more widely available edition of the *Report,* containing an opening section McClellan wrote for it on the western Virginia campaign. The royalties furthered his financial independence. To meet the demand for a more personal history, a Boston attorney, G. S. Hillard, embarked on an authorized campaign biography, for which McClellan allowed himself to be interviewed. Hillard announced to his readers that the treatment the general had received "has made it ... necessary sometimes to take the attitude of controversy, and to assail others in order to do him justice." Certainly no other American general ever had his military history so widely read or closely analyzed so soon after it ended.[17]

His military record was at issue simply because more than anything else it made him, in Democratic eyes, a viable candidate against President Lincoln. If he had failed on the Peninsula to capture Richmond and end the war, it was because the administration (as his *Report* persuasively argued) failed to reinforce him and, in the case of McDowell's corps, actually withheld forces essential to his strategy. And as McClellan had made clear in his anguished dispatch from Gaines's Mill — printed in full for the first time in the *Report* — these actions were taken with the deliberate, treasonous intent to destroy him and further radical

Republican designs. On the other hand, for his opponents to damage his military reputation, as Senators Wade and Chandler had sought to do in the hearings of the Joint Committee on the Conduct of the War, was to damage him as a candidate. Horace Greeley wanted voters to understand that, as bad as Generals Pope and Burnside and Hooker might be, they were no worse than General McClellan. "He is essentially not a soldier, but a politician, and his fighting and writing have alike been intended to train him for the Presidential race," Greeley wrote.

In these months McClellan's backers acted in perfect confidence that he would accept the Democratic nomination at the party's national convention in Chicago that summer. "I think no underhanded work can prevent his getting Ohio," Cox wrote Barlow in February in reference to the state Democratic organization. "He is getting Indiana, Pa. & N.Y." While disclaiming ambition for the presidency, as always McClellan would follow Providence's command. He had earlier told his mother that he was indifferent to the White House, and on March 13 he wrote her, "I know that all things will prove in the end to have been arranged for the best and am quite willing to accept what I cannot avoid."[18]

One of the things he could not avoid, as the party's apparent candidate, was responding to charges concocted by his political enemies. Cox told him, for example, that the Republicans were circulating a particularly harmful story that he was behind the arrest of the Maryland legislature in September 1861. McClellan replied that he had only been carrying out orders, and in any event those legislators intended to take Maryland out of the Union, a very different case from the controversial arbitrary arrests now taking place in the loyal states, and he added, "I have no apology to make." He wrote Reverdy Johnson, Democratic senator from Maryland, to say that there was nothing to the story that he had been aboard a gunboat during the fighting at Malvern Hill. The canard that he had offered his sword to the Confederacy, which he blamed on the radical press, surfaced once again, this time in the western armies. He had not before dignified such charges with denials; now he felt compelled to.

The most sensational charge of all was that he had met with General Lee on the Antietam battlefield and agreed that the Confederate army would withdraw across the Potomac without interference, clearing the way for a compromise peace settlement preserving slavery. The *Tribune* and *Times* made capital of the story for several days until it was revealed that the Joint Committee on the Conduct of the War had investigated and found the bearer of the tale, a Maryland schoolteacher named Francis Waldron, to be an alcoholic who suffered from what the *World* termed "maniacal hallucinations." The *Journal of Commerce* charged Republican editors with having so great an enmity toward the general "that common rules of editorial caution and decency are forgotten." In the case of the *Tribune*'s coverage, at least, there was considerable justice in the charge. "I shall fight like a savage in this campaign," editor Greeley assured John Nicolay. "I hate McClellan."[19]

In contrast to the political gains they made in 1862, the Democrats had fared poorly in the 1863 by-elections. Woodward in Pennsylvania, Vallandigham in Ohio, and Thomas H. Seymour in Connecticut, perhaps the three most visible figures in the peace wing of the party, were defeated in gubernatorial elections. Nevertheless, party chairman August Belmont and his fellow strategists believed there were important issues in their favor in 1864. The suspension of the privilege of habeas corpus and the widespread arbitrary arrests seemed to threaten fundamental American liberties. The government's treatment of the press, notably its brief suppression in the spring of 1864 of the *Chicago Times*, the *New York World*, and the *Journal of Commerce*, the three leading Democratic organs, were labeled acts of despotism. In the wake of the victories at Gettysburg and Vicksburg and Chattanooga, the war was not then an issue for the Democrats, but it might become one if the 1864 military campaigns went badly. Above all, there were the issues that divided the two parties most deeply: emancipation, the Negro, subjugation of the South, and the eventual reconstruction of the Union.

With the memory of the party's breakup in 1860 still fresh, unity was on every Democratic leader's mind. Samuel Cox called General McClellan's candidacy a "necessity" for unifying the party faithful. His stand on the war might be too strong for the peace men, but he was sound on other issues and was the best-known figure in a party that had lacked a national leader since the death of Stephen A. Douglas in 1861. By putting reunion first and peace second he appealed to all conservatives, Republican as well as Democratic. Vallandigham's followers "are the fiercest party disciplinarians, & they dare not bolt," Cox explained to Barlow. "Our efforts should be directed to pouring balm into the hearts of the soi disant Peace Democrats. Let them understand they are of some account, in the making up of our organization in 1864." Keeping these peace men satisfied and pulling in harness with the rest of the party promised to be the Democrats' greatest challenge in 1864.[20]

In one of his few public appearances in that election year, McClellan traveled to West Point to deliver an address on June 15 dedicating the site of a monument to honor the Civil War dead of the regular army. By his choice this address, along with his Harrison's Landing letter to Lincoln, would make up his personal platform for the presidency. To be sure, he delivered an oration rather than a speech, and as befitted the occasion it was nonpolitical, yet he was at pains to clarify his position on the war and its origins. The conflict, he said, had originated among extremists from both sections, men "with whom sectional and personal prejudices and interests outweighed all considerations for the general good." It was being fought, however, for a cause "just and righteous, so long as its purpose is to crush rebellion and save our nation from the infinite evils of dismemberment" and to enforce the government's "just power and laws. . . ." The Civil War should be, in short, a war for Union and Constitution and no other object. Barlow told him that the address "is right, every word of it and strikes the true chord in each sentence," and arranged to have it printed for circulation as a campaign document. Delegates to the Chicago convention would be presented with copies of the West Point address and the Harrison's Landing letter, labeled "McClellan's Platform."[21]

As his political prominence increased, Secretary Stanton's animosity grew apace. Stanton operated by his rule that any army officer (such as General McClellan) who played the sport of politics "must risk being gored." Once in that game, he could no longer "claim the procedural protections and immunities of the military profession." Stanton's resort was often to petty harassment. Former members of McClellan's staff found difficulty obtaining commissions in other commands. A movement in the Army of the Potomac to raise money for a presentation sword to honor the army's first commander was halted on Stanton's order. Following the West Point address, Stanton dismissed or transferred the three members of the committee (including the Academy's superintendent) who had invited McClellan to speak.

In other instances the threat seemed greater than simple harassment, or so McClellan and his supporters believed. In March, T. J. Barnett had written Samuel Barlow from Washington to warn him that Stanton's detectives considered Barlow and other Democratic leaders "fit subjects for summary acts." Barnett urged him to be cautious, and added, "A noble chivalric fellow *near* you — beg him to be prudent." McClellan had no doubt that in this election year he was under constant War Department surveillance.[22]

In the meantime, the Blair family had resumed its attempt to reshape the political scene. The Blairs' path to an objective typically went by twists and turns and hidden ways, and this effort was no exception. Pointing to his unbroken record of support for the general, Montgomery Blair opened a correspondence with Samuel Barlow designed to gain a number of goals — to see Mr. Lincoln re-elected and General McClellan restored to army command, while in the process frustrating the objectives of the radical Republicans. McClellan was making a great mistake and mortgaging his future, Blair wrote Barlow on May 1, by giving the impression that, in a nation torn by civil war, "as a General he was ready to hand himself to a party to supplant the chief magistrate. . . ." He wanted him instead to renounce political ambition — he was young enough to wait a term or two for the presidency — and make common cause in a conservative mandate for Lincoln's re-election. "I believe if he would unbosom himself unreservedly & in confidence directly with the President that he would give him a military place in which he could be most useful. . . ."

Barlow sent the letter to McClellan for his thoughts on how to answer it, and McClellan made a reply that flatly rejected Blair's contentions. He insisted that he had never played politics while in command and was not doing so now. He had raised his voice only once, in the Woodward letter, and then merely to exercise "the right of a citizen to repel attack & express an opinion." To do as Blair suggested would be to endorse the policies of the administration, and that he could not do. "I will not sacrifice my friends my country & my reputation for a command. I can make

no communication to Mr Lincoln on the subject.'' Barlow wrote
Blair that he did not see how he could ask the general to compromise his principles by making his peace with the president.[23]

At the time there was a certain theoretical quality to Blair's
efforts to have McClellan recalled. No obvious military command
was available to him in the spring campaigns just then opening
in Virginia and Georgia under General-in-Chief Grant, recently
called from the western theater to direct the war effort. By July,
however, the situation was different. Neither Richmond nor Atlanta had been taken and the two offensives seemed stalemated,
and long casualty lists filled the newspapers nearly every day.
McClellan mourned many army friends, notably John Sedgwick,
killed by a sharpshooter in the Wilderness. ''I have been utterly
upset by poor Sedgwick's death — a sad blow to the Army & the
country,'' he wrote his sister when he heard the news. Then, with
the Army of the Potomac settled into siege warfare at Petersburg,
General Lee sent Jubal Early on a raid through the Shenandoah
Valley to threaten Washington. On July 11, amid great alarm,
Early's forces came within sight of the Capitol dome before withdrawing. There was a chorus of demands for McClellan's recall.

Francis P. Blair now took it upon himself to confer with
McClellan and renew his son's proposition, and they met in Blair's
room at the Astor House in New York on July 21. Blair explained
that, although he was not acting on instructions from the president, he was confident that if McClellan declared he would not
accept the Democratic presidential nomination, he would be appointed to a command befitting his rank. Possibly he mentioned
a specific position; it was no secret that a commander was needed
to unify and organize the scattered forces defending Washington
and the Shenandoah. By McClellan's count, it would be the third
time he was called on to save the capital. Blair presented it as a
matter of duty to his country, to ensure national unity in prosecuting the war. The general seemed to consider the idea but was
noncommittal, Blair wrote. When he returned to Washington, he
told the president of his effort and said that he might soon be
hearing from General McClellan. Lincoln ''neither expressed approval nor disapprobation of what I had done . . . ,'' Blair noted.

McClellan drafted an answer to this proposition that was the
clearest statement yet of his political views and his attitude toward the presidency. Repeating his response to Montgomery Blair's

earlier proposal, he said he would not compromise his principles by asking Lincoln for a command. He insisted that he was not an aspirant for the Democratic presidential nomination. "It is my firm conviction that no man should seek that high office, and that no true man should refuse it, if it is spontaneously conferred upon him...." His differences with the president were fundamental, he wrote. "I think that the original object of the war, as declared by the Govt., viz: the preservation of the Union, its Constitution & its laws, has been lost sight of,... & that other issues have been brought into the foreground which either should be entirely secondary, or are wrong or impossible of attainment." This was an obvious reference to emancipation, which, he declared, "unnecessarily embitters the inimical feeling between the two sections, & much increases the difficulty of attaining the true objects for which we ought to fight." Change this policy, he said, and peace was attainable: "Our antagonists should be made to know that we are ever ready to extend the olive branch, & make an honorable peace on the basis of the Union of all the states."[24]

It is virtually certain that McClellan had second thoughts about this letter and decided not to send it. Had he done so, Blair would have shown it to the president, who would then hardly have done what he soon did, which was to discuss with Grant the question of recalling McClellan to the army. The president and the general-in-chief met at Fort Monroe on July 31 to confer about command problems in the eastern theater, and in his list of matters to discuss Lincoln included McClellan's name. The two men no doubt considered him for the overall command on the upper Potomac, and possibly for command of a kind of reserve army that he would recruit, or even for his old position as head of the Army of the Potomac. When the elder Blair learned of the meeting, he understood Lincoln and Grant had agreed that if the Democrats did not make the general their candidate, or if he took himself out of the running, "Gen. McClellan would be invited to return to the army." Simon Cameron confirmed the story, naming the president himself as his authority.

Nothing finally came of the matter. Grant seemed willing enough to restore McClellan to the service — he said later that when he came east to assume his new command he had hoped to employ McClellan in some capacity — and the president was at least willing to discuss it. But McClellan refused to make the overture urged on him by the Blairs, either out of principle or in the belief that the whole affair had too much of the odor of a bargain about it, and there could be no waiting until the end of August for the Democratic convention to announce its candidate. On August 6 Grant put General Philip Sheridan in charge in the Shenandoah Valley, and retained General Meade as head of the Potomac army. McClellan later told one of his correspondents that it was "the wish of my heart ... to command the Army of the Potomac in one more great campaign," but whatever the chances for that may have been, he was not willing to trade a presidential nomination for the possibility.[25]

He was becoming a more formidable political presence every moment, and no doubt the prospect of removing him from the election picture had been on the president's mind in his meeting with Grant. "The great election of next November looks more and more obscure, dubious, and muddled every day," George Templeton Strong noted in his diary on August 16. The war was now very much an issue favoring the Democrats. By August Federal casualties in the 1864 campaigns were nearing 90,000, with no apparent prospect for an end to the killing, and the government had been forced to call for an additional 500,000 men. War-weariness pervaded the North, and the calls for peace — including peace at whatever price, as advocated by the Copperheads — grew louder.

The mood among the president's advisers was pessimistic. "The tide is setting strongly against us," Henry J. Raymond, editor of the *New York Times* and Republican national chairman, wrote Lincoln on August 22. If the election were held the next day, he reported, such key states as New York, Pennsylvania, Indiana, and Illinois would go to the Democrats. Thurlow Weed regarded Lincoln's re-election as "an impossibility.... The People are wild for Peace." Like Raymond, he blamed the party's problems on the want of military success and the widespread belief that "the President will only listen to terms of Peace on condition Slavery be abandoned." Observing a gathering of party strategists at the White House, John Nicolay wrote, "Everything is darkness and doubt and discouragement."

The president judged the case the same way, and determined on a course of action. In a memorandum dated August 23 he wrote, "This morning, as for some days past, it seems exceedingly probable that this Administration will not be re-elected. Then it will be my duty to so co-operate with the President elect, as to save the Union between the election and the inauguration; as he will have secured his election on such ground that he can not possibly save it afterwards." He sealed it and had his Cabinet members endorse it, sight unseen, by signing their names on the outside.

He told them later the specifics of his plan if General McClellan, who he assumed would be his Democratic opponent, were elected president in November. He would go to him and say that in the four months remaining in his term "let us together . . . try to save the country. You raise as many troops as you possibly can for this final trial, and I will devote all my energies to assisting and finishing the war." Secretary Seward said he could imagine the scene: "And the General would answer you 'Yes, Yes;' and the next day when you saw him again and pressed these views upon him, he would say, 'Yes, Yes;' & so on forever, and would have done nothing at all.'"[26]

Lincoln had detected the paradox in the situation. The better the Democrats' prospects for winning the election, the deeper became the fissure in their party. "They must nominate a Peace Democrat on a war platform, or a War Democrat on a peace platform," he predicted to a newspaperman a few days before the Chicago convention. Democratic strategist Samuel Cox saw the same thing and was worried. "I am satisfied that there is an *immense — immense* change going on among the people against the adminis.," he wrote McClellan, "& that the peace men (the ne plus ultras) will use it to the disservice of the Democracy & the country — if we do not answer & control it." He wanted McClellan and his managers to counter this threat by granting concessions in the party platform and pledging to take "all the steps known to civilization, for the attainment of peace & Union, at every opportunity of tender from the South, or decided success of our arms." Barlow saw in the situation the danger of over-confidence among the peace men, leading them to think "they can win with any one, & thus defeat the clearly developed feeling in your favor.'"[27]

McClellan was decidedly unhappy with any thought of compromise. There had already been one such concession, to his regret. The Chicago convention was originally scheduled to open on July 4, but the peace advocates had succeeded in having it postponed to August 29, with the argument that the party could be better unified in the interim while at the same time the worsening military situation eroded Lincoln's support. McClellan opposed the change, seeing the real motive behind it (accurately enough) as an attempt to manipulate the growing mood of Northern war-weariness into a demand for a peace platform and a peace candidate, and he named Governor Horatio Seymour of New York as the chief instigator.

He insisted he would not be the tool of these peace men. One of them even told him, he complained, that if he called for an immediate armistice he could double his chances for the nomination. "If these fools will ruin the country I won't help them," McClellan told editor Prime of the *Journal of Commerce*. He had been willing enough — or at least dutiful enough — to be the candidate of a conservative-dominated "Union before peace" Democratic party; he would not be the candidate of a peace party willing to treat with the South on conditions that did not include reunion. "I feel now perfectly free from any obligation to allow myself to be used as a candidate," he wrote Manton Marble. "It is very doubtful whether anything could now induce me to consent to have my name used."[28]

Marble and other supporters hastened to assure him that he would not become the captive of the peace wing. All signs pointed to victory, Marble told him on August 10; he had only to do nothing and say nothing for nineteen more days, and the nomination would be his. "This is your only fortnight of peace & quietness for four years," he predicted. Barlow's assessment was the same. McClellan would control the soldier vote and the army and thus make it certain that the Republicans could not stay in power by the rule of the bayonet. Assuming that the Democrats in Chicago "do not absolutely throw away success," Barlow told Marble, "I have no doubt of our ability to elect McClellan and to restore the Union." McClellan was mollified and agreed that unless "distasteful" conditions were attached to the nomination, he would accept it.

As the delegates gathered in Chicago in the last days of August, McClellan remained on Orange Mountain, keeping in touch with events through Barlow in New York. On the eve of the convention Barlow wrote him that everything looked well. None of the

McClellan managers had "private powers" to make political deals behind the scenes, he said, and as matters stood he would be the nominee with "a wise platform and a good V.P. . . ." McClellan replied in high spirits. "Things are just as I would have them — if we win we win everything and are free as air," he wrote. "If we lose we lose like gentlemen. I would not for the world have given any powers to make bargains. . . . If I am nominated . . . I shall want to talk to you about many things."[29]

SIXTEEN

CAMPAIGN
FOR THE PRESIDENCY

SAMUEL L. M. BARLOW served, without title, as George McClellan's political manager in 1864 and took the part of chief strategist during his presidential campaign, yet he refused to attend the Democratic nominating convention. After Manton Marble arrived there and tested the delegates' mood, he telegraphed McClellan, "Barlow must come out to Chicago ... with full decision as to platform & with authority general & full." McClellan did not intervene, however, for Barlow explained that his presence in Chicago would in fact be "positively harmful." He argued that the McClellan managers at the convention were so jealous of one another's influence with the general that he, the closest confidant of all, would be rendered ineffectual by their envy.

His reasoning was dubious at best and proved to be a serious mistake. The McClellan forces at Chicago contained many officers but no commanding general, and the consequence was a political disaster for the party second only to its fatal split at the Charleston convention in 1860. On August 29, the day the convention opened, August Belmont remarked ruefully, "It will not be as easy as we expected — the people are all right but the leaders have learned *nothing* since Charleston."

Except for Samuel Cox of Ohio, all the most prominent managers of McClellan's candidacy at the convention were New Yorkers from the party's conservative wing — national chairman Belmont, state chairman Dean Richmond, Samuel J. Tilden, Sanford E. Church, and editor Marble of the *New York World*. During the preconvention politicking, they had made two discoveries that raised Belmont's sudden doubts about the inevitability of the McClellan bandwagon.

For one thing, although the peace wing of the party was a minority centered most strongly in Ohio, Indiana, and Illinois, under the leadership of Clement Vallandigham it was a far larger and more effective minority than they had bargained for. "Ohio is the *worst* of all," one of the delegates told McClellan; "her peace men are *rampant* & for peace men most bloodthirsty." The second discovery was that Governor Horatio Seymour of New York was not at all unwilling to be drafted as the compromise candidate of the two contending factions. "Seymour is being used against McClellan," Marble cautioned, and Belmont added that the governor "blows hot & cold . . . professes not to be a candidate *& will be none if I can help it.*"[1]

In contradiction of Barlow's assurance to McClellan that no pledges or bargaining would be necessary to gain the nomination, Marble telegraphed on August 27, "If we lose it will be because private powers have been begrudged but in the ultimate pinch Richmond and Tilden will be urged by me to assume all that is necessary." Preoccupied with overcoming Seymour's threat to the nomination, McClellan's managers left the task of securing a platform that complemented their candidate largely to Tilden, the New York representative on the Committee on Resolutions, as the platform committee was called.

Samuel Tilden, however, was by nature vacillating and a compromiser and no match for the determined Vallandigham, the Ohio representative on the committee. Vallandigham's attempt to gain the committee chairmanship was deflected, but in a major concession to the peace faction he was named to the seven-man subcommittee charged with the actual writing of the platform. "I fear there may be trouble as to the platform," Barlow warned McClellan when he learned the news, but he added hopefully, "Our friends understand what is necessary so fully that they will not allow any mistakes that can be prevented."

The friends were not equal to the test, however. Gaining a four-to-three majority on the subcommittee, Vallandigham forced through his famous "war-failure" resolution as the platform's second plank. After four years of failure to restore the Union "by the experiment of war . . . ," he wrote, "justice, humanity, liberty and the public welfare demand that immediate efforts be made for a cessation of hostilities, with a view to an ultimate convention of the States, or other peaceable means, to the end that at the earliest practicable moment peace may be restored on the basis of the Federal Union of the States.'' Behind the polished phrasing was the Copperheads' call for peace at any price — an armistice without conditions and a negotiated settlement, with nothing to guarantee that the Confederacy would in fact exchange reunion for peace.

The McClellan men on the subcommittee attempted to insert a substitute plank making reunion the precondition for peace talks, but they could muster only three votes against Vallandigham's four. Belmont would write apologetically to McClellan that they had done their best to gain a less objectionable platform, ''but we had to fight against the western peace men, who are very ultra & as it is, the present wording is quite a concession to us...." The concession can hardly have been anything more than substituting the euphemism ''cessation of hostilities'' for the word ''armistice.''[2]

Tilden might have led a fight against Vallandigham's peace plank in the full Committee on Resolutions, where the vote on the chairmanship had demonstrated that the peace men lacked a majority, or even on the floor of the convention itself, but he chose conciliation over confrontation, and no other McClellan manager overruled him. ''We might have altered the platform ... by an appeal from the Committee on Resolutions to the Convention,'' a delegate explained to Barlow, ''but it would have involved a fight & probably rupture.''

There can be little doubt that Vallandigham used the threat of a bolt by the peace men as a weapon to save his second plank. He made his position unmistakably clear in a letter of advice to McClellan a few days later: ''If any thing implying war is presented, two hundred thousand men in the West will withhold their support, & many go further still.'' When the platform was quickly approved by a voice vote of the delegates, a newspaperman wrote that Samuel Cox ''clasped his hands in his lap and dropped his head, a picture of despair,'' and he observed that August Belmont ''also looked profoundly sad.'' The Washington correspondent for the *World* later wrote his managing editor, ''The Chi. platform gave me a *chill* in the convention when it was read that I still feel.''

Having approved a peace platform, on August 31 the Chicago convention with hardly less dissent nominated a war candidate.

Seymour's hopes had faded, and on the first ballot McClellan polled 174 votes, comfortably above the 151 needed for nomination. Soon states began switching their votes to gain a place on the bandwagon, and finally Vallandigham himself moved that the nomination be made unanimous, and it was done. "Instantly the pent-up feelings of the crowd broke forth in the most rapturous manner," a reporter wrote; "cheers, yells, music, and screams indescribable rent the air, and outside . . . a park of cannon volleyed a salute in honor of the nominee."

In a final act of political self-destruction, the convention then provided its war candidate for president with a peace candidate for a running mate. The New York delegation, making a further ill-considered attempt to unify the party, led the movement to George H. Pendleton as the vice-presidential nominee. Pendleton was a peace Democrat from Ohio whose opposition to the war was almost as vehement and well known as Clement Vallandigham's. When Pendleton was first spoken of for the post, Thomas Key wrote McClellan, it was the prediction of the general's supporters "that he would be a very heavy load for you to pack. . . ."

McClellan and Ellen were at their house on Orange Mountain, waiting with a few friends, when news of the nomination arrived. "I congratulate you and the country equally," Barlow wrote. "I have no doubt of our success, nor of your ability to restore one Govt. over all the States." That evening a procession of supporters made its way by torchlight up the mountain from the village of Orange and crowded around the McClellans' front porch. A band brought over from Newark "struck up a serenade of spirited music," a newspaper reported, and there were speeches and barrages of cheering. The general acknowledged the cheers with what the paper described as "a few informal remarks." They must not expect a speech from him, McClellan said. The day's events were entirely too new, "and he could scarcely realize the position in which he had been placed."[3]

His position was in fact a dilemma. "I need not tell you how bitterly I am disappointed by the want of wisdom manifested at Chicago," George Ticknor Curtis wrote him. "Their second resolution looks as if it had been concocted to destroy their candidate." Thomas Key assured him that he owed nothing to those who had nominated him: "The convention was disunion; the nomination for vice-president was disunion — those who con-

trolled platform and this nomination are for disunion. . . ." Even
his closest friends would not vote for him if he accepted Vallandigham's handiwork, William Aspinwall cautioned. "The Chicago platform is simply an effort to unite the opposing elements
of the Democratic party, & is unworthy of the crisis in which our
country is placed." The common thread in letters from party
leaders such as Belmont and Barlow was an almost pathetic hope
that in his acceptance letter General McClellan could somehow
repair all the political damage done at Chicago and paper over
the party's divisions and make everything right again. Barlow
wrote him on September 2, "In your hands & without any conflict,
without any question as to your right, you have it in your favor
to render complete success. . . ."[4]

While there is no evidence that McClellan seriously considered
refusing the nomination, he left no doubt that in his letter of
acceptance he would reject the Vallandigham peace plank. He
told Ellen he was taking a stand "& am not afraid to go down
to posterity on it." "I could not have run on the platform . . . without violating all my antecedents — which I would
not do for a thousand Presidencies," he explained to Samuel Cox.
He added that as a matter of practical politics, if he accepted
the peace plank he could never win Pennsylvania and New York,
two states he had to have to gain election. On September 6 he
wrote William Aspinwall that his letter "will be acceptable to
all true patriots, & will only drive off the real adherents to Jeff
Davis this side of the line."

He labored through six drafts in composing his acceptance,
but from first to last he consistently rejected an unconditional
armistice and made reunion a precondition for any peace settlement with the Confederacy. Anything less, he declared, and "I
could not look in the face of my gallant comrades of the Army
and Navy, who have survived so many bloody battles, and tell
them that their labors, and the sacrifice of so many of our slain
and wounded brethren had been in vain. . . ."

To be sure, changes were made from draft to draft, particularly
after he consulted with Barlow and other advisers. "We have
fought enough to satisfy the military honor of the two sections,
and to satiate the vengeance of the most vindictive" was a sentiment in the first draft that was soon dropped. His blunt declaration that if peace negotiations failed "we must continue the

resort to the dread arbitrament of war" was watered down to
"The responsibility for ulterior consequences will fall upon those
who remain in arms against the Union"; indeed on Barlow's
urging the word "war" was deleted entirely from the letter.
Much verbiage was eliminated and favorable mention of the other
platform planks added. Barlow sharpened the message with such
phrasing as "The Union is the one condition of peace. We ask no
more." Significantly, the subject of slavery, like the word itself,
was absent from every draft of McClellan's acceptance letter, as
it was from the Chicago platform. In this respect the letter was
addressed as much to the people of the South as to the voters of
the North.

Beyond anything else, in accepting the nomination McClellan
expressed his stand on ending the fighting and gaining peace.
President Lincoln had stated the two conditions for a peace settlement as reunion and the abolition of slavery. Presidential candidate McClellan wrote that as soon as the Confederate States of
America, or any of them individually, stated a readiness for peace
simply on the basis of reunion, "we should exhaust all the resources of statesmanship . . . to secure such peace, reestablish the
Union, and guarantee for the future the Constitutional rights of
every State." Had the war been conducted solely for that object
from the first, as he had urged when in command, "the work of
reconciliation would have been easy, and we might have reaped
the benefits of our many victories on land and sea." On September
8 he presented his acceptance letter to the convention's nomination committee and made it public. "The effect thus far has
been electric," he wrote Ellen the next day; "— the peace men
are the only ones who squirm — but all the good men are delighted
with it."[5]

The promise of gaining peace and reunion with honor would
be a mainstay of his presidential campaign. With General
McClellan's election, peace would become inevitable, Manton
Marble's *New York World* editorialized, "for the simple reason
that, after his inauguration, the character of the war will have
so changed that the southern people will no longer have a sufficient motive to stand out. They will then see that submission to
the Union does not involve the overthrow of their institutions,
the destruction of their property, industrial disorganization, social chaos, negro equality, and the nameless horrors of a servile

war.... On the election of General McClellan ... a peace party will spring up, as if by magic, in every part of the South.''

In 1861 George McClellan had committed himself to exactly this view of the Confederacy, and as was his custom he clung to the judgment tenaciously, ignoring all evidence to the contrary. Once defeated in a major test of arms, he insisted, the South would willingly trade secession for reunion. That a great many Southerners were in deadly earnest in fighting for their independence rather than for reunion with constitutional guarantees, that they had no more interest in ''the Union as it was'' than the most outspoken abolitionist, was something he could not admit. The message he intended his letter of acceptance to deliver fell on deaf ears in the South far more than he imagined. His West Point friend Cadmus Wilcox, for example, now a Confederate general, opposed McClellan's election because of its threat to the Rebels' resolve to fight on for independence. Any cessation of hostilities that promised less than victory, warned the Confederate ordnance chief Josiah Gorgas, and ''Our armies would dissolve like frost before the rising sun.'' Jefferson Davis even expressed a willingness to trade the emancipation of the South's slaves for recognition by the European powers and the independence that might follow.[6]

On September 1, the day following McClellan's nomination, Atlanta fell to General Sherman. In combination with Admiral Farragut's earlier victory at Mobile Bay and General Sheridan's subsequent victories over Early's Rebel army in the Shenandoah Valley in September and October, the capture of Atlanta effectually removed the ''failure of the war'' issue from the Democratic campaign. This was not by itself necessarily fatal to the party's chances in November. Make the best of it, William Aspinwall urged Barlow; make sure that McClellan supporters ''burnt as much powder as the Republicans in celebrating the victories announced from time to time.'' Other issues separated the two parties, and they were clear-cut and fundamental, presenting the electorate with a genuine choice between political philosophies. Even without the war issue, there was at least a fair possibility that had the Chicago convention given him a platform on which he could stand comfortably, George McClellan might have been elected seventeenth president of the United States.

His acceptance letter was welcomed by those campaigning for

him, and at least tolerated by most of the peace faction except for the most "ultra" extremists. "If the election shall go as we hope," Robert Winthrop wrote him, "you will have won the victory by your own pen, as surely as you won Antietam by your sword." Yet there was no disguising the distance between the candidate and both his platform and his running mate. He had not so much rejected Vallandigham's peace plank as rewritten it, and then added, with bland assurance, "Believing that the views here expressed are those of the Convention...., I accept the nomination." Opponents were quick to exploit the contradiction. The general would like the voters to take him on his acceptance letter alone, a Republican pamphlet writer observed. "But, alas! we can no more take the letter without the platform as an exposition of the party, than we can take Hebrews without John and James ... as an exposition of the New Testament."[7]

The Democratic party would suffer the aftereffects of the 1864 Chicago convention for a generation, and General McClellan was the first victim. Republican orators and campaign literature bound him tightly to the Chicago platform and the party's peace wing, labeling him at the very least the creature of the Copperheads and at worst a Copperhead himself. They painted the Democrats of 1864 as the party of disloyalty and treason, and tarred McClellan with the brush. One Republican pamphleteer, comparing him with peace-at-any-price Copperheads, wrote, "It is true that their treason is more open and noisy than his, but his is nevertheless as real and earnest as theirs." George Templeton Strong recorded in his diary that the most dangerous public enemy was not the Confederate army "but the party of malcontents at home — traitors represented by 'little Mac'clellan and Pendleton, H. Seymour, Vallandigham, Cox & Co.'"

It was a heaven-sent opportunity for political cartoonists. *Harper's Weekly* portrayed candidate McClellan as a circus rider attempting a "Marvelous Equestrian Performance on Two Animals," the steed of war and Pendleton's donkey of peace. Another cartoonist showed the general with a brush and a bucket of whitewash labeled "Letter of Acceptance," covering over disloyal slogans scrawled on the Chicago platform while Vallandigham and Seymour and Fernando Wood protested. Currier and Ives depicted Vallandigham and Wood, along with Jefferson Davis and Satan, holding up a rickety platform on which a

Janus-like McClellan simultaneously proclaims, "I accept the nomination and of course stand on the platform," and, "If you don't like the platform, I refer you to my letter of acceptance." (With bipartisan evenhandedness, Currier and Ives also issued a print of a patriotic McClellan collaring Presidents Lincoln and Davis as they sought to tear a map of the country in half.)

Cartoonists pursuing this theme of McClellan versus his party's platform often included in their drawings figures of Federal soldiers scorning their once-beloved commander. "I would vote for you General, if you were not tied to a Peace Copperhead," one says, and his companion adds, "Good bye 'little Mac' — if thats your company, Uncle Abe gets my vote." It was perceptive commentary. No theme in soldiers' letters of the period is more common than disillusionment with General McClellan.[8]

A Vermonter in the Army of the Potomac wrote his home-town paper that he and his fellow soldiers had talked over the whole question, and the most popular opinion was that of a veteran who said he had always stood up for McClellan, "was a McClellan man clear to the bone, but he couldn't vote for him on the Chicago platform. Rather than have peace by surrendering to the rebels, he would let his bones manure the soil of Virginia." A colonel in the Potomac army wrote his wife that he had not found a single officer or enlisted man who would vote Democratic. "Why, we don't touch the Chicago platform! The former friends of George B. McClellan have abandoned him because he has got in *such bad company*." When it came time to cast their votes, the survivors of the Iron Brigade's 2nd Wisconsin, which had fought so desperately for the general at Antietam, gave him one vote to Lincoln's seventy, and the single ballot was cast so that "he would know that we have not entirely forgotten him." McClellan had never been particularly popular in the western armies, and he was less so now. It was widely believed, one of Sherman's men wrote, that he would compromise with the Rebels "by letting them have their slaves. Then we can fight them again in ten years. But let Old Abe settle it, and it is always settled."[9]

McClellan assumed a dignified stance above the hurly-burly of politics, remaining in virtual seclusion during the campaign. Ellen was frequently absent on visits to friends and relatives, and he handled campaign business with only the aid of a secretary. He stood on his record and issued no statements of purpose after writing his acceptance letter. He made only two public appearances, at a party rally in Newark in September and, shortly before Election Day, at a massive torchlight parade in New York, where he reviewed his political army from the balcony of the Fifth Avenue Hotel. He refused repeated urgings to show himself to the party faithful in the pivotal state of Pennsylvania. Although appreciating the importance of carrying the state, he wrote a supporter, "I have made up my mind on reflection that it would be better for me not to participate in person in the canvass." Except for a week spent with Ellen at the country home of Joseph Alsop in Connecticut and an occasional trip to New York on campaign matters, he seldom left Orange Mountain.

While General McClellan was not the political innocent he was often portrayed as being, he displayed little interest in the actual workings of politics and was as intolerant as ever of politicians as a group. Before the convention he wrote to William Prime from Orange, "Don't send any politicians out here — I'll snub them if they come — confound them!" During the campaign, although he recognized the necessity of greeting the politically influential, he did so no more often than he had to. In response to one delegation's request for a meeting, he pleaded with Prime, "Can't you invent *some* way of getting me out of the scrape?" He dutifully corresponded with party leaders and campaign organizers, and if it was a task he clearly did not relish, he preferred writing them to having to meet them. After one particularly busy correspondence session, he informed Barlow that he had written to everyone on his list and was now satisfied that "it don't make much difference if I don't see them provided I don't avoid them."[10]

One of his few partisan forays was a visit in October to the estate of James Gordon Bennett to secure the *New York Herald* to his cause, but it was a failure. Bennett shied away from his previous support and finally backed Lincoln's re-relection. "Little Mac's visit to Fort Washington was like most of his advance movements — altogether unsuccessful," one of Bennett's associates wrote the president. McClellan also made an effort to encourage the McClellan Legion, a grouping of veterans' clubs organized to get out the votes of discharged soldiers and of men home on furlough or sick leave. The Legion bluntly rejected the Chicago platform in favor of McClellan's acceptance letter. He wrote as well to many of his army friends in the hope that they would display their loyalty to him by distributing Democratic campaign literature to the men in the ranks. Beyond these efforts, he left the campaign work and the campaign strategy to his managers.[11]

Their strategy was to hammer at what they called the tyranny of the Lincoln administration, with its subversion of the Constitution and individual liberties and its revolutionary altering of the social order. Democrats might not now be able to label the war a failure, but they could campaign against the "abolitionist fanaticism" and the economic chaos unleashed by the war. Elect Lincoln and his black Republican ticket, a Democratic poster proclaimed, and "You will bring on NEGRO EQUALITY, more DEBT, HARDER TIMES, another DRAFT!" The consequences would be "Universal Anarchy, and Ultimate RUIN!"

Perhaps the party's most effective spokesman was Robert Winthrop of Massachusetts, whose addresses in Union Square in New York and in New London, Connecticut, were widely reported and reprinted as pamphlets. Let there be no cavil about platforms, Winthrop told his New York listeners. General McClellan had made his own platform, "broad enough and comprehensive enough for every patriot in the land to stand upon." His letter of acceptance was "worth an army with banners to the cause of the Union." In New London he declared that Lincoln's forcible emancipation would produce nothing "but mischief and misery for the black race, as well as the white. . . . We are not for wading through seas of blood in order to reorganize the whole social structure of the South." McClellan wrote Winthrop to thank him for his "noble oration. . . . I know of no political speech of the present or the past that will bear comparison with yours. . . ."[12]

For a time the McClellan strategists counted on John Charles Frémont's third-party candidacy to take important votes from Lincoln, especially in such states as New York and Pennsylvania, where traditional Democratic strength promised a close outcome. Frémont's role in the 1864 contest was decidedly peculiar. Trading on the fact that in 1856 he had been the first presidential candidate of the new Republican party, he originally hoped to displace Lincoln on the Republican ticket in 1864. When nothing came of that, he accepted the nomination of a new third party, the Radical Democracy, on a platform designed to appeal to the extreme radicals among Republicans. Even before that, however,

Frémont seems to have sought an alliance of sorts with General McClellan. In March 1864 his spokesman approached Edward H. Wright with the proposition that if Frémont and McClellan became the two presidential candidates, the winner would name the loser general-in-chief, to bring the conflict to a prompt end. McClellan labeled the interview ''a strange one.''

Frémont continued to court the Democrats. His former military aide Justus McKinstry was believed to have arrived at the Chicago convention bearing Frémont's commitment to an armistice, hoping it would gain him the party's nomination. A few weeks later Randolph Marcy was approached in St. Louis by a Frémont man who offered to swing the votes of the Radical Democracy to McClellan. Marcy suggested making some arrangement with Frémont. ''I think a good office would command his influence,'' he wrote. A week later, on September 20, McKinstry himself sought out Marcy, saying he was authorized by Frémont ''to make any arrangement which the Democrats determined to be best in regard to running or withdrawing from the Presidential contest.''

Exactly what McClellan thought of all this is not on record, but it is difficult to imagine him considering a bargain of any kind with John Charles Frémont. He thought little of him as a general and less of him for his abolitionist beliefs, and as general-in-chief he had once authorized his arrest in an investigation of fraud in the western command. At any event, nothing came of the attempted alliance, and on September 22 Frémont withdrew from the race. Whatever support the Radical Democracy had gained gravitated naturally to Lincoln, and Democratic hopes for a split in the enemy ranks evaporated.[13]

McClellan was convinced that during the campaign Secretary Stanton's detectives were as interested in him as ever. He had information he considered reliable, he wrote Barlow on September 21, that ''My steps are dogged & every person reported who comes to see me.'' He continued to use codes when writing or telegraphing anything confidential, and to employ messengers instead of the mails whenever he could. On one occasion a telegrapher friendly to his cause secretly forwarded a telegram intended for him that had been suppressed by the authorities.

Stanton's perfidy reached its peak, as far as McClellan was concerned, some two weeks before the election. A message reached him from Allan Pinkerton warning of a threatened action by the government, the details of which he would impart to a trusted go-between. McClellan sent Edward Wright. After elaborate cloak-and-dagger precautions, Pinkerton met Wright at a hideaway in Baltimore. He told him that the administration had information about a conspiracy by "the friends of McClellan," including August Belmont, George Ticknor Curtis, Thomas M. Key, and Wright himself, to assassinate the president. They were being watched, Pinkerton said, "and on the slightest movement on their part all would be arrested and hung."

There is no knowing the source of Pinkerton's fantastic tale. On receiving his first message, McClellan had told Barlow that those in the party "who have papers which could in any way commit them should be at once advised to destroy them or to conceal them," but when he heard Wright's report he dismissed the whole matter as the nonsense it was. By Wright's account, he said "he would not insult any of his friends by repeating such a charge to them." He had no doubt that whatever ploy was intended by all this, Stanton was behind it.[14]

Local and congressional elections in Ohio, Indiana, and Pennsylvania on October 11 were expected to be forecasts of November. The Democrats in Ohio faced an uphill battle. They started with a 100,000-vote handicap, Vallandigham's margin of defeat in his 1863 race for governor, and in any case the party there was badly split between moderates and peace men. They conceded defeat a week before the election, and took consolation from the fact that in losing by 54,000 votes they improved on their 1863 record. Nor were expectations high in Indiana, and the outcome — Republican governor Oliver P. Morton was re-elected by 20,000 votes — came as no real surprise. An Indiana campaigner wrote McClellan that the election had been a farce, and he hoped for a better result in November. Fraud was indeed common, especially in the army voting. The 60th Massachusetts, a regiment stationed near Indianapolis to guard Confederate prisoners, was marched to the polls to help elect Governor Morton. A Massachusetts man wrote home, "Most of our regiment went down to the city and voted. Some of the boys voted twenty-five times each. . . ." Despite the instances of fraud, however, Morton's plurality was large enough that most Democratic strategists wrote off Indiana for November.

Pennsylvania also went to the Republicans, by 13,000 votes,

but both sides agreed that the result might be different on November 8. The winning margin was furnished by soldier ballots, with the home vote virtually even. Republican editor Alexander McClure warned of a struggle in Pennsylvania. "Don't feel too sure of the State," he wrote. "It is in our hands, but we have to earn our victory dearly." A Democratic politician reminded McClellan that these were only local elections, and predicted a different outcome in the presidential canvass. "The thousands who will vote for you in Nov. could not be induced to go to the polls," and he foresaw "a decided if not overwhelming majority."[15]

McClellan's managers remained optimistic during the closing weeks of the campaign. On October 20 William Prime sent him an analysis of the electoral vote based on the latest estimates from his correspondents across the North. He counted New York and Pennsylvania, with half the votes needed for an electoral victory, as certain for the Democrats. With the border and far western states, Illinois and one other populous midwestern state, and at least one New England state, he forecast victory. He was certain, he wrote, "that a strong current is now setting in our favor. . . . We cant tell what will happen within a fortnight or three weeks, but the *set* of the tide is now with us." Only a week earlier, President Lincoln had drawn up a strikingly similar tally of the electoral vote. He too gave New York and Pennsylvania and the border states, along with Illinois and Missouri, to McClellan. Although he calculated that he would be re-elected, 120 electoral votes to 114, he clearly anticipated a very close contest.[16]

McClellan later wrote that he was prepared for defeat, but in fact he was confident of victory at least as late as a few days before the election. He told August Belmont that all his reports from the army were encouraging, and on October 27 he wrote Barlow that Governor Seymour had assured him "that all is favorable in New York, & I hear that the Penna people feel very jubilant." In another letter to Barlow that day he wrote, "All the news I hear is *very* favorable. There is every reason to be most hopeful." During the first week in November visitors heard him say that he was certain of carrying New York, Pennsylvania, Connecticut, and Illinois, states that were pivotal to his election. He expected to be unpopular among certain Democrats during his first year in the White House, he confided to an army friend, for he would expend every effort to press the war and enforce the draft, and he would listen to no remonstrance until the rebellion was crushed. On November 8, before the outcome of the election was known, he wrote the adjutant general to resign his commission.[17]

In the light of his unwavering insistence on seeing the war through, it is impossible to imagine his election producing a military outcome different from the actual one. George McClellan assuming the role of commander-in-chief on March 4, 1865, would hardly have given new life to a visibly crumbling Confederacy. As he expressed it to Barlow a year later, ''Of course I can't tell what the secesh expected to be the result of my election — but if they expected to gain their independence from me they would have been woefully mistaken. . . .'' It is equally certain, however, that his policy toward the defeated South and the Negro would have been immeasurably different from the course pursued by his Republican opponents. On those topics his views also proved to be unwavering. Carrying out such a policy would have depended on the election of a sufficient number of Democrats to Congress to support him. After the fact, he shuddered at what might have been. ''I can now fully realize,'' he wrote William Prime in December 1865, ''what my position would have been if I had been elected, with such a Congress!''

As it happened, his defeat on November 8 was decisive enough to leave little room for might-have-beens. Of just over four million votes cast, President Lincoln received 55 percent and General McClellan 45 percent, a margin of victory of 403,000. In the electoral college McClellan won but three states — New Jersey, Delaware, and Kentucky — giving him 21 electoral votes against Lincoln's 212. The most surprising of the election statistics, and for McClellan surely the most shocking, was the soldier vote. It was always supposed that if he ran he would capture the soldier vote, and, in theory, had he received an overwhelming share of the votes of the men in the field and on leave and of the ex-soldiers at home, it is possible that he would have won the election. In fact, however, in every instance where the soldier vote was recorded, it was overwhelmingly in favor of his opponent.

A total of 154,000 ballots were cast in the field, and over three quarters of them (78 percent) went to Lincoln. The men in Sherman's army from states where statistics are complete voted against

McClellan by an extraordinary 86 to 14 percent. Even in the Army of the Potomac the percentage of voters for Lincoln was vastly greater than in the home vote as a whole. Of just over 23,000 voting, seven out of ten favored the president over the army's first commander. Among the Potomac army's Pennsylvania forces, which had the largest number voting in the field, just six of fifty-one regiments recorded a majority for McClellan. The New York soldier votes were cast at home by proxy and not separately recorded, but there is no reason to believe the voting ratio there was any different. Nor is there reason to believe that the voting fraud charged by both parties appreciably changed the outcome. This lopsided vote was not essential to the president's re-election — only in New York is it likely that the Democrats could have gained the state had the soldier-vote and home-vote percentages been the same — but it signaled an unmistakable repudiation of the Chicago platform and of General McClellan himself.[18]

Addressing his supporters afterward, McClellan took comfort from his conclusion that he bore no responsibility for the outcome of the election campaign. "As I look back upon it," he wrote Manton Marble, "it seems to me a subject replete with dignity — a struggle of honor patriotism & truth against deceit selfishness & fanaticism, and I think that we have well played our parts. The mistakes made were not of our making — & before the curtain falls ... I trust that we will see that these apparent mistakes were a part of the grand plan of the Almighty, who designed that the cup should be drained even to the bitter dregs, that the people might be made worthy of being saved." He told Samuel Barlow that personally he was just as happy not to have the burdens of the presidency. "For my country's sake I deplore the result — but the people have decided with their eyes wide open and I feel that a great weight is removed from my mind." He was done now with public service and satisfied to "leave to others the grateful task of serving an intelligent, enlightened and appreciative people!"[19]

SEVENTEEN

THE OLD SOLDIER

DECEMBER 3, 1864, marked the start of George McClellan's thirty-ninth year, an event that must have occasioned sober reflection. In the less than three and a half years since he was summoned to Washington from western Virginia, he had commanded all the nation's armies, led the largest of those armies through great campaigns and battles, and run for the presidency, receiving the votes of close to two million of his countrymen. No doubt he wondered what possible turning the life of an old soldier could now take that would not be anticlimactic.

The president had accepted his resignation from the army without comment, and he was bruised enough by his defeat at the polls to assure his mother "I can imagine no combination of circumstances that will draw me into public life again." Nor was his temper improved by a recent foray into the business world. Earlier in the year he had done some engineering consulting work for the industrialist Abram Hewitt, and after the election Hewitt negotiated on his behalf for the presidency of New Jersey's Morris and Essex Railroad. Concerned that McClellan's political notoriety would endanger the line's dealings with the government, however, the board of directors (as Hewitt phrased it) "did not think it expedient to make you President...."

McClellan considered it a denial of his right to make a living "merely because a great & honest party chose to make me their leader," and he told Samuel Barlow that he saw no reason to remain longer in a country where that could happen. "I suppose I must make up my mind now to shake the dust off my shoes & go elsewhere — so be it." He was sorely tempted, he said, to offer his sword to Czar Alexander or to Maximilian, the puppet emperor the French had installed in Mexico. In the event, he decided on self-imposed exile in Europe.[1]

Thanks to his benefactors, his exile, if not luxurious, was comfortable enough. The New York house they had given him produced rental income of $5,000 a year, and his $20,000 return on the donated Ohio and Mississippi Railroad stock was invested for him by Barlow in a highly profitable mining venture. At the time it was possible to live moderately well in Europe for considerably less than in the United States, and except for one brief business venture he did not find it necessary to seek employment during his more than three and a half years abroad.[2]

He sailed with his family for Europe on January 25, 1865, and wherever they went in the following months in England and on the Continent, they found that his military reputation (as enhanced by his *Report*) had preceded him. ''The feeling for the General in England is enthusiastic,'' Ellen wrote her father; ''— they look upon him as *the* American General. . . .'' He was much gratified by this reception, McClellan wrote Barlow from Rome : ''I hear no slanders — all treat me as a gentleman, & seem disposed to exaggerate very much the importance of my part in the war. . . . Here we are the equals of the best — at home there is always the wretched feeling of partisan to be encountered. I should be glad to be able to remain abroad until the expiration of Uncle Abraham's term of service — if gold keeps down, & quicksilver up, I may be able to do it.'' By contrast, were he home ''there would probably be nothing for me to do but to go into exile in Nevada or Utah for some years. . . .''

He closely followed the war news from home. He had expressed his doubts about Sherman's bold advance through the South — ''I think Sherman will come to grief,'' he predicted when he first learned of the March to the Sea — but he was soon caught up in the excitement of the final campaigns and of Richmond's fall and Lee's surrender at Appomattox. The news of the president's assassination filled him with ''unmingled horror & regret,'' he wrote. ''How strange it is that the military death of the rebellion should have been followed with such tragic quickness by the atrocious murder of Mr Lincoln! Now I cannot but forget all that had been unpleasant between us, & remember only the brighter parts of our intercourse.'' In his only public statement on the war's ending, he told a group of Americans in Switzerland who were celebrating the Fourth of July that he prayed the occasion would signal a new era in reunited America. "I trust . . . that, since we have completely vindicated our national strength and military honor by the entire defeat & ruin of our late enemies, our people will pursue a magnanimous and merciful course towards a fallen foe — one that will tend to soften the bitter feelings inevitably caused by a long & earnest war. . . ." The advent of peace, however, caused no change in his plans to continue living abroad.[3]

The McClellans spent much of that spring of 1865 in Rome, living in the splendid Palazzo Barberini with the American sculptor William Wetmore Story and his wife, the sister of Dr. John McClellan's wife, Maria. They marveled at the city's historical wonders and artistic treasures. "This is certainly the most interesting place in the world . . . ," McClellan wrote his army friend William Franklin. "I feel fully compensated for all the miseries of the last few years by the privilege of seeing Rome." For the summer they took lodgings in a small hotel on Switzerland's Lake Geneva, where they lived quietly. He rowed on the lake and walked in the mountains and began work on his memoirs. He wrote William Prime that he was concentrating on "the secret history of my connection with Lincoln, Stanton, Chase, etc; it may be valuable for history one of these days." Ellen was pregnant with their second child, a fact that with Victorian delicacy he kept private. No doubt William Aspinwall and Samuel Barlow were puzzled by his cryptic rejections of attractive job offers they obtained for him.

In October they took what he termed winter quarters in Dresden, where Mrs. Marcy and her daughter Fanny joined them for Ellen's confinement. On November 23, 1865, she gave birth to a son, christened George Brinton McClellan like his father but always called Max. "The boy is a dear little fellow — strong and bright — he looks about him as wisely as a young owl and bids fair to be a good specimen," McClellan wrote his mother.

During 1866 and 1867 the McClellans continued their travels about Europe, summering in Switzerland and wintering in the south of France. For much of this time Ellen's health was poor, and although the nature of her ailment is not recorded, the homeopathic physicians they consulted usually prescribed the baths of Europe's leading spas. The waters of Switzerland's Saint-

Moritz seemed to offer her the most relief. In December 1866 McClellan wrote Barlow that he had finally found a physician "who has, I am satisfied, at last found out the true cause of my wife's troubles, & under whose care she is doing splendidly." By the autumn of 1867 he felt confident enough of Ellen's health to embark on his first important employment since he was displaced as commander of the Army of the Potomac.[4]

In September of that year, in Paris, he signed a contract with the American marine engineer Edwin A. Stevens to seek out a European buyer for the so-called Stevens Battery. This vessel had been under construction, in one form or another, for almost thirteen years and had gained considerable notoriety. Conceived by the brothers Robert L. and Edwin A. Stevens in 1842, she was originally intended as an ironclad floating battery for harbor defense, and a halting start was made on her in Hoboken, New Jersey, in 1854. During the Civil War the design was revamped into a powerful oceangoing ironclad 420 feet long, driven by eight steam engines delivering 8,600 horsepower. In spite of an infusion of $500,000 from the government, however, the Stevens Battery remained unfinished at war's end. Stevens turned his attention to finding a buyer abroad.

McClellan's contract called for payment of his expenses and a commission ranging from a minimum of $50,000 to a maximum of $150,000, depending on the sale price he negotiated. He traveled to Berlin and Dresden and Vienna, where his name and reputation opened the doors of government officials. The reputation of the Stevens Battery was apparently also well known, and the navies of Prussia, Russia, and Austria were unwilling to risk its purchase.

For McClellan the high point of the journey was his interview with Helmuth von Moltke, the celebrated chief of staff of the Prussian army. Moltke confided details of the recent Austro-Prussian War and flattered him with the observation that his Peninsula campaign of 1862 would surely have ended the Civil War had he not been "shamefully deserted" by the Lincoln government. (Since Moltke's opinion was no doubt derived from a reading of McClellan's *Report,* he could hardly have reached any other conclusion.) Several months later, in Paris, McClellan had an interview with eighty-nine-year-old Baron Jomini, whom he admired as "the greatest of military writers," and listened, fascinated, as the old soldier reminisced about his service with Napoleon. He drew on the interview for an article on Jomini he wrote the next year for *The Galaxy*.[5]

Although he was titular head of the Democratic party, McClellan took care to make no public comment on the American political scene while he was in Europe, although privately he continually scourged the radicalism "running rough-shod over the land." He expressed little interest in reports that President Andrew Johnson was considering him for the post of secretary of war and, later, minister to Great Britain. He was certain, he said, that his enemies in the Senate would never consent to either nomination.

As he began his fourth year abroad, however, he confided to William Prime, "I am becoming very homesick and tired of this rambling life and Europe." Yet to demonstrate his divorce from politics he determined not to return until after the Democrats had chosen their presidential candidate for 1868, and probably he would not have returned until after the campaign itself except that he had decided to continue his connection with the Stevens Battery, this time in the United States.

Initially there was interest among Democrats in running him for the presidency again in 1868, but his support dwindled after the Republicans nominated General Grant. Now, a newspaper remarked, the party would only ensure a Republican victory "by running the man who didn't take Richmond against the man who did." Nevertheless, McClellan was still politically popular in the eastern cities, and he was enthusiastically welcomed by the party faithful when his ship reached New York, on September 29. Three days later he reviewed the war veterans of the McClellan Legion from the balcony of the Fifth Avenue Hotel, as he had done four years earlier. The audience, according to the *World*, "swelled in rising accumulating tides into Madison Square from dusk till nearly midnight."

McClellan's diary in these first days home contains such comments as "A good deal bothered by politicians," and "Bored entirely by politicians." On October 8, after a personal plea by the party's nominee, Horatio Seymour, he reviewed a massive Democratic rally in Philadelphia. "The greatest ovation I have ever experienced," he noted with pleasure. With that appearance, and a public statement, he bowed out of the campaign. He had the highest personal regard for General Grant, his statement read, but the party that had nominated him was the party of strife and discord, "and can never restore peace or constitutional supremacy. . . ." On Election Day he wrote Samuel Cox, "I had the satisfaction of putting the largest possible Democratic ticket into the box this morning — I sincerely wish the *one* could have been multiplied by many thousands." Grant's margin of victory over Seymour was 100,000 less than Lincoln's margin over McClellan in 1864.[6]

Meanwhile McClellan had gone to work on the Stevens Battery. Edwin Stevens had died, but in his will he designated $1 million for the completion of the battery, on condition that McClellan be chief engineer of the project. When completed, the battery was to be given to the state of New Jersey — for what purpose was never made entirely clear. McClellan accepted the post and its $12,000 annual salary, rented a house in Hoboken, and for the next eighteen months labored on what was increasingly coming to resemble a nautical white elephant. Eventually the Stevens money ran out and McClellan resigned, leaving the vessel with its iron hull and machinery largely finished but still a year short of completion. A dozen years later she was scrapped and (as a newspaper reported) "made into Queen Ann fireplaces and other ornaments."[7]

Among the positions offered McClellan in these years was the presidency of the new University of California, but he wanted to remain in the New York area, and in July 1870 he accepted the post of chief engineer for New York City's Department of Docks. He remained for almost three years in what must have been something less than a full-time job, for at the same time he was also trustee and then (in 1872) president of the Atlantic and Great Western Railroad, where he earned $15,000 a year. In 1870 his income had exceeded $20,000 for the first time, and thereafter it climbed steadily to the point where he could be regarded as moderately wealthy. In 1870, too, he completed the construction of a large, rambling house on Orange Mountain that he named Maywood, after his daughter. For the first time in their marriage he and Ellen truly had a home of their own.[8]

In 1871, when the massive corruption of the Tweed Ring began to be exposed, McClellan was invited by New York's mayor to accept the post of city comptroller, the office from which one of the principals in the ring, Richard (Slippery Dick) Connolly, had been operating. Seeing it at first as his duty to help reform the city's finances, McClellan drafted a letter of acceptance. However, his long-time adviser William Aspinwall urged him to reject the offer, which was being made, he wrote, only "for the purpose of whitewashing parties who are as deep in the mud as Connolly is in the mire. . . ." McClellan recognized the wisdom of the advice and declined the position. The next year, when the Democrats endorsed Horace Greeley for the presidency against Grant, McClellan backed away from politics entirely. Since he could never forgive editor Greeley and his *Tribune* for its abuse of him during the war, he could never support candidate Greeley, he wrote, "& preserve my self-respect."⁹

In the spring of 1873 McClellan resigned his post with the Department of Docks to organize his own firm, Geo. B. McClellan & Co., Consulting Engineers & Accountants. The company prospectus described his specialty as "representing the interests of European investors in American Railroad Securities." When such investments became "impaired or endangered" — and many did, in this age of brass-knuckle American capitalism, when railroad stocks were counters in various schemes — McClellan & Co. pledged to restore the investments to health or to liquidate them on the best terms possible.

That October the McClellans once again sailed for Europe, where they remained for nearly two years. In London, Paris, Berlin, Frankfurt, and other cities McClellan introduced his new firm to banking houses and securities holders. The rest of the time was spent visiting leading spas and traveling for pleasure in France and Italy and Sicily and, for five months, in Egypt. Egyptology was a particular interest of McClellan's, and he reveled in voyaging up the Nile and seeing Luxor and Thebes and Abu Simbel. In Cairo he met General Charles P. Stone, the wartime victim of Secretary of War Stanton and the Joint Committee on the Conduct of the War, now chief of staff to the khedive of Egypt. Stone "was kind & agreeable as can be," McClellan recorded in his diary. "He looks very well & is happy."¹⁰

During intervals in these travels he prepared a three-part article on the fundamentals of army organization, taking the European powers as his examples, which *Harper's Monthly* published in 1874. After his return to America, late the next year, he continued to devote time to writing. *Scribner's* published three essays he derived from his travels in Switzerland, Sicily, and on the Nile, and *The North American Review* ran his military analyses of the 1877 war between Russia and Turkey, and the British conflict with the khedive of Egypt in 1882. In 1877 he returned to the theme of military organization for *Harper's Monthly,* this time focusing on the American regular army. Stressing an idea he had first proposed after the Mexican War, he called for reform of the peacetime army so that it would be organized and officered in such a way as to be readily expandable in wartime by adding volunteers while still maintaining high standards of discipline and training. Whatever the topic, his writing style in these articles was well informed and informative, free of the self-pleading that marked his accounts of his own campaigns.

He wrote Samuel Barlow early in 1876 that he was also resuming work on his memoirs, "not with any intention of publishing them at present, but only availing myself of the opportunity to place my side of the story on record." In notes written in 1866 during his European exile, he had explained his rationale for undertaking this effort: "Few, if any, know fully the motives by which my action was influenced and the circumstances by which I was often necessarily controlled; as yet, no competent person has come forward to lay before the world a full account of my career." For the sake of his family and the benefit of history, he wrote, "I desire to leave behind me, when removed from this earth, a true and plain account ... of my connection with that civil war which will never be forgotten in the history of America." To refresh his recollections he wrote to subordinates and staff members for their versions of disputed points during his time of command, and made notes of meetings with wartime comrades and opponents during which they refought old campaigns. After one of these congenial gatherings his daughter wrote in her diary, "He enjoyed it very much as he did not come home until twelve o'clock which for him is immoral dissipation."[11]

When the Democrats nominated Samuel J. Tilden to run against Republican Rutherford B. Hayes in 1876, McClellan re-entered the political scene with enthusiasm. He became an active campaigner for the first time, embarking on a month-long tour that included speeches in Reading and Philadelphia in Pennsylvania;

Boston; Indianapolis; Orange, New Jersey; Dayton, Ohio; and Elmira, New York. His Elmira address, delivered on the eve of Election Day, typified his message to the voters.

The issue in 1876 was the legacy of the Civil War, he told his audience. Defeated Southerners had accepted every condition imposed upon them by the victors — emancipation and citizenship and suffrage for blacks, and abandonment of the theory of secession — and now their "rights, privileges, and duties under the Constitution and the laws" must be fully restored. Radical Republican reconstruction must cease. Southern whites had demonstrated that they would live up to their new obligations, he said, and "it is only by trusting them, treating them kindly, and doing our best to restore kind feeling between all parts of the country, that we can accomplish the real, hearty restoration of the Union which was the true purpose of the war. ..." Except for his acknowledgment that slavery was dead and that, legally at least, blacks were citizens and could vote, his sentiments had not changed the smallest fraction since 1861. Sectional harmony was paramount; states' rights must prevail in all social — and racial — questions.

The disputed results of the election — Tilden victorious by some 250,000 in the popular vote, but the electoral-vote count in doubt — roused McClellan to action against what he saw as the Republican threat to remain in power by fraud and force. While the electoral-vote tangle was being unraveled, he wrote his mother that the only fair result would be to declare Tilden elected: "Any opposition to that must be forcible & revolutionary, & must be met by force." The Democrats would remain within the bounds of law whatever the result, he said. Any overt act, if there was one, would come from the other side, "& we shall know how to meet it when the time arrives."

To prepare for such a crisis, he set out to organize the successors to the McClellan Legion of 1864, political clubs of ex-soldiers or militia units that were loyal to the Democrats. After Tilden was officially declared president, he said, they would appear in Washington to ensure that there would be no interference with the inauguration. "The 18th regiment (Dusquesne Grays) Col Guthrie, one of the finest in the country, known as a Democratic regiment, will be in Washington the 4th of March to witness the inauguration of Tilden," one of his correspondents promised. The project was quietly abandoned when the Electoral Commission found in favor of Hayes, 185 electoral votes to 184.[12]

McClellan continued his new association with politics. In September 1877 New Jersey's fractious Democratic party met in convention to select a candidate for governor. A bitter fight was predicted, but in a surprise move one of the factions nominated General George B. McClellan. The name swept over the delegates "like a hurricane . . . , fell on them like a thunderbolt," the *New York Herald* reported. ". . . The applause was so deafening that it was useless to name any other candidate for several minutes. . . . The effect was electrical." He surged into the lead on the first ballot, and the vote was made unanimous.

Not anticipating the nomination, McClellan told a reporter, he had gone to Boston to attend the dedication of a Civil War memorial on the fifteenth anniversary of Antietam, where he was warmly received and (his son recalled) "was happier than he had been for many a long day." He told the press he had known that his name might be presented to the convention but did not suppose there was one chance in fifty he would be nominated. He promptly accepted.

It was George McClellan's lifelong habit to insist that he had never sought any of the positions he accepted, either as soldier or civilian, and that therefore he always accepted selflessly, beholden only to his patriotism and his sense of duty. He saw this as the case with his nomination to the New Jersey governorship, and at the age of fifty he finally envisioned a future for himself in a return to public service. He recalled his role in 1864 as that of scapegoat, but in this contest he was virtually certain of winning. Possibly another factor influenced him to accept. A few months earlier the New York legislature, in a straight party vote, had rejected him as superintendent of public works, a post involving the management of the state's extensive canal system (and one that, for once, he had actively sought), and this unanimous vote of confidence from another political body surely gave him particular satisfaction.[13]

Wherever he appeared during the campaign his audiences were large and enthusiastic. Asked at one rally what he did to make himself so popular, he replied, "I don't remember ever to have done more than my duty. . . . When I hear the shouts of a crowd like this outside my carriage window, and realize that I am the occasion of it all, I feel as though I were traveling in an unknown world. It's like a dream...." Thomas Nast took notice of the campaign with a cartoon picturing General McClellan aboard a Hudson River ferryboat that bore the sign "Little Mac's Head-Quarters ... N.B. This is *not* a gunboat," scanning the New Jersey shore and calling for reinforcements of Democratic voters. On Election Day his margin of victory was a comfortable 12,700 votes.

Governor McClellan's three-year term was marked by careful, conservative executive management and minimal political rancor. In a photographic portrait of the period he looks the part, well-tailored and holding a top hat, with graying hair and imperial beard. Within a year he had reduced expenditures by $400,000 and cut the state debt by $600,000, or 23 percent, and by the end of his term he had abolished direct state taxes on the citizenry. He reformed the militia organization and encouraged trade schools and local industry. A newspaper remarked approvingly of his 1879 annual message that it was "as devoid of party allusion and party spirit as one of Paul's epistles."

Being New Jersey's governor in that day was not an especially time-consuming occupation. His West Point friend Cadmus Wilcox, the former Confederate general, visited him at Maywood during the summer of 1878 and noted that Governor McClellan was able to handle the state's business by traveling to Trenton one day a week, on Tuesday, and returning in the evening. He found time to pursue his varied business interests and to complete his memoirs. Two months before the end of his term he moved into a house on New York's Gramercy Park for the winter, and on December 11, 1880, a thousand guests attended nineteen-year-old May's coming-out party. McClellan wrote his mother early in the new year that he was well pleased to be done with the governorship, "as it was becoming a nuisance to be obliged to go to Trenton in all matters."[14]

That spring of 1881, feeling "the need of a few weeks at St. Moritz," McClellan once again took his family to Europe. For May McClellan the Atlantic voyage was enlivened by the attentions of thirty-two-year-old Brooks Adams, grandson and great-grandson of presidents, who was taking a European tour to mark his transition from practicing law to writing history. He was "perfectly charming," May wrote in her diary. Their paths would cross again in Munich and Paris. The McClellans traveled from Germany into Austria, then spent the summer at Saint-Moritz. In the fall they toured France, where on September 17, visiting the Comte de Paris at the Orléans family château, they drank a champagne toast to the Battle of Antietam. McClellan gathered impressions for an article on the House of Orléans that he would write for *The Century* magazine. When they reached London they found that Brooks Adams had just departed. "I feel suicidal," May noted in her diary. (Their romance would flare up again that winter in America, then finally subside. "I shall never see him again," she wrote sadly.)

On his return from Europe in the fall of 1881 McClellan received shocking news. The warehouse in New York where during his stay abroad he had stored his collection of fine china and ceramics and the only copy of his completed memoirs had been totally destroyed by fire. A friend urged him to emulate Thomas Carlyle, who when his manuscript on the French Revolution was burned immediately set out to reconstruct it. "I have not the heart to begin it," McClellan replied.

Before very long he changed his mind, however, and did begin anew, although in an unsystematic and less ambitious way than with his earlier effort. On the evidence of the drafts and notes that survive, his original memoirs had covered his early life and military career in fair detail, including West Point, the Mexican War, and his assignments in the 1850s, although they focused most heavily on the Civil War. It is not known whether he wrote of his political career as well. His new effort was more limited and entirely military, framed by the contents of his wartime *Report*. For the next several years he worked sporadically on the manuscript.

His life in these years followed a consistent pattern. Most winters were spent in New York and the rest of the year at Maywood on Orange Mountain. Each August, to escape the summer heat, the family visited the White Mountains in New Hampshire or Mount Desert Island in Maine. They entertained often, and the McClellans' receptions became a fixture of New York's winter social season. McClellan & Co. continued to prosper, and he sat on the boards or was a trustee of a number of companies. His holdings in stocks and bonds were substantial. McClellan was restless, however, for in all this there was little that challenged him. In her diary on May 7, 1882, May wrote, "Papa & I went to Doctor Crosby's church today. I am worried about him — he is so depressed — if he only had something to do that would occupy his mind."[15]

In 1884 presidential politics once again attracted McClellan's interest when it appeared that the Democrats had a good chance to capture the White House for the first time since before the Civil War. He campaigned vigorously for Grover Cleveland and regarded the Democrats' victory in November as signaling a new era for the nation. "This family is in a state of wild excitement over it," May wrote. "Papa is blissful. ..." As an elder statesman of the party and as a loyal campaigner for the president-elect, McClellan expected to be rewarded by an invitation to join the Cabinet as secretary of war. There was no denying his qualifications for the office and no denying that he wanted it. To hold the Cabinet seat from which he had been so long abused by Edwin Stanton would be sweet vindication. "I have always held to my old position of neither asking nor expecting any office or reward from my country, or from the party ... ," he wrote highmindedly, but this can only have meant that he did not ask Cleveland directly for the appointment. By his son's account, he had received "positive assurance" that the post would be his.

He did not reckon with New Jersey's senator John R. McPherson, however. A member of the state's Democratic faction that had considered itself hoodwinked by McClellan's nomination for governor in 1877, McPherson pressed a candidate of his own from New Jersey for the Cabinet and strongly opposed McClellan. President-elect Cleveland finally resolved the dilemma by deciding not to invite anyone from New Jersey into his Cabinet. Ironically, it was precisely the sort of politically motivated decision that McClellan always scorned.[16]

The May 1885 issue of *The Century* carried an article by McClellan on the Peninsula campaign, a part of the "Battles and Leaders of the Civil War" series the magazine had initiated the year before. It was the first time he had published anything on his campaigns since his wartime *Report*, and not surprisingly he enlarged on the theme that the failure on the Peninsula was entirely the fault of the administration, particularly Secretary of War Stanton. He recounted his versions of important private meetings with Stanton and with President Lincoln, which, both men being dead, could not be controverted. He ended the article with the observation that to him, at least, it had been clear in 1862 (as it later became clear to all in 1865) that the fate of the Union would be decided on the banks of the James. He agreed to the request of the *Century* editors that he write a second article for the series, on the Maryland campaign.

That same month he relived the war more directly by returning for the first time since 1862 to the Antietam battlefield, for him the scene of his greatest triumph. He walked the field with Kyd Douglas, who had served on Stonewall Jackson's staff during the battle, and according to a newspaper reporter the two "indulged in good-humored criticisms of each other...." On Decoration Day, at the Antietam military cemetery, McClellan addressed an audience made up largely of ex-soldiers from both armies. He spoke of the Army of the Potomac, "so very dear to me ..., ever worthy of its fame, whether in adversity or success — and never more so than on this field...." He described the "ability and virtues of Robert Lee, and the achievements of the magnificent Army of Northern Virginia...." The fame and exploits of these two great armies, he said, "have already become a part of the common heritage of glory of all the people of America." The reporter wrote that "Gen. McClellan's oration was a scholarly production, and was delivered with an ease and grace of manner and speech that were cordially recognized. He was awarded several rousing cheers at the close."

Three months later he relived still another memorable experience from his past when he and Randolph Marcy traveled through the Red River country of Texas that they had first explored in 1852. The purpose this time was to inspect a mining venture that McClellan had organized. He enjoyed the outdoor life as much as he had thirty-three years earlier. He and Marcy continued westward by rail, to Denver and Salt Lake City and San Francisco, and in his journal he noted the pleasure it gave him when at every stopover old soldiers called to pay their respects. By September 17 he was back at Maywood to mark, as he did every year, the anniversary of the Battle of Antietam.[17]

Early in October he suffered a severe attack of angina pectoris. Under his doctor's care and with rest he seemed to make a complete recovery. On the evening of October 28, however, while working on his Antietam article for *The Century*, he complained of returning chest pains. Rapidly his condition worsened. At three o'clock the next morning, October 29, 1885, he was heard to murmur "I feel easy now. Thank you ...," and then he died.

McClellan's unexpected death — he was only fifty-eight — was featured on the front page of newspapers across the country. It was noted that of all the men who had commanded the Army of the Potomac in battle, now only John Pope remained alive. Messages of condolence arrived by the hundreds in Orange, from President Cleveland and other national leaders, from generals who had fought with him and against him, from men who had served in the ranks of the Potomac army. The country had lost "one of her purest and most patriotic sons," August Belmont said. His death, Fitz John Porter wrote, "is crushing to me." P. G. T. Beauregard described the great esteem he felt for General McClellan "as a man and soldier," and Joe Johnston mourned "a dear friend whom I have so long loved and admired."

Lengthy obituaries recounted and evaluated the events of McClellan's crowded life. In the opinion of the *New York Evening Post*, "Probably no soldier who did so little fighting has ever had his qualities as a commander so minutely, and we may add, so fiercely discussed." There was universal recognition of his role in organizing the Army of the Potomac. The *New York Times* thought his failures were due less to circumstances than to temperament. "His error was in expecting and requiring a degree of perfection in preparation and of absolute safeguard against the possibility of failure, such as the highest generalship would not, under the circumstances, have exacted." The *New York World* was unrepentantly partisan to the end : "No General who fought in the war from its outbreak to its close was ever actuated by nobler sentiments and purer and more patriotic motives. Yet no soldier was ever more unjustly dealt with or more harshly, cruelly and unfairly criticised."

A brief and simple funeral service was held on November 2 at the Madison Square Presbyterian Church in New York, which McClellan had attended during his stays in the city. The day was dark and rainy and as mournful as the occasion. The honorary pallbearers included old friends from the business and political world, such as Samuel Barlow, William Prime, and Abram Hewitt, and old comrades from the army years, such as Fitz John

Porter, William Franklin, Winfield Scott Hancock, Edward Wright, and Joe Johnston. Burial was in the McClellan and Marcy family plot in Riverview cemetery in Trenton, overlooking the Delaware. The *World*'s obituary had concluded with an epitaph for General McClellan, one that he would surely have approved: "History will do him justice."[18]

EPILOGUE:
A MEMOIR FOR HISTORY

NOW THAT General McClellan has passed away,'' a newspaper editor wrote, "even those who were most disposed to criticise or condemn him will regret that he did not leave behind him, for permanent reference, his own account of the campaigns...." Publishers sought writings of any sort that the general might have left. An editor of *The North American Review,* his appetite whetted by the unfinished sketch of the Maryland campaign that appeared posthumously in *The Century,* promised William C. Prime, McClellan's literary executor, that he would publish any of the general's observations on the Civil War "without regard to the men or parties whom such publication will offend." Prime put them off. He was himself preparing McClellan's military recollections for publication. Honoring his friend's wish to have his side of the story on record, he titled these posthumous memoirs *McClellan's Own Story.*[1]

When the book was published, in 1887, it gave the impression that General McClellan, speaking from the grave, had deliberately sought to stir up anew every controversy that had ever swirled around his head in the war years. A few reviews were complimentary. *The North American Review* thought it conclusively proved "that the history of the Civil War could not be accurately written until McClellan's story had been told." Far more reviewers were sharply critical. *McClellan's Own Story,* far from persuading history to do him justice at last, irreparably damaged his military reputation. "It were better for his memory had he left his story all untold," one commentator remarked.

John C. Ropes and Jacob D. Cox, two of the most knowledgeable historians of the war then writing, demolished McClellan's contentions point by point. They could not understand how, two decades after the war, the general could remain so deluded. "Never was there a controversial work in which the other side was more calmly ignored," Ropes wrote in the *Atlantic Monthly*. "... His egotism is simply colossal, — there is no other word for it." In his review for *The Nation*, Cox was astonished that McClellan had apparently paid no attention to the documentation on the war being published, especially in the early volumes of the *Official Records of the Union and Confederate Armies*, even as he was writing. "The facts, as he believed them then, and as we know them now, differ in such essential particulars that arguments which were plausible then are now worthless," Cox wrote. "It is worse than blindness to repeat the old accusations and the old justifications, without acknowledging or showing any sign of recognition of the truth that his assumed facts are essentially wrong."[2]

Not Ropes nor Cox nor anyone else realized the extent to which William Prime was responsible for this impression. To be sure, when he set out to tell his side of the story, General McClellan had avenged himself on everyone he believed had wronged him. Secretary of War Stanton was his primary target, but others such as Irvin McDowell and Ambrose Burnside were also portrayed as the real architects of events for which McClellan had been blamed. He was explicit in his charge that the Lincoln adminsitration had deliberately and traitorously conspired to see him defeated. Yet he had not been entirely unaware of the new evidence that, for example, gave the true size of the Confederate forces he had faced. In the manuscript he wrote in the early 1880s he did not use several of the papers and dispatches from his wartime *Report* that contained hugely inflated estimates of enemy numbers. He further narrowed the difference in size between the two armies by arguing that the Army of the Potomac was never as large in effective fighting strength as had been said.

However, he had not come close to finishing his memoirs before his death. His manuscript narrative ends in May 1862, with the Army of the Potomac arriving on the Chickahominy River on the Peninsula, with all the great battles of that campaign still to be fought, and with no account at all of the Second Bull Run and Maryland campaigns. When Prime wrote in his introduction to *McClellan's Own Story*, "Of course his work was unfinished when he left it,'' he seriously understated the case. A good half of McClellan's own story remained to be told.

It was Prime who assembled the second half of the story out of bits and pieces. He relied most heavily on McClellan's wartime *Report,* and reprinted long sections of it unchanged. He inserted portions of the two articles published in *The Century* in 1885 and 1886. He used notes and rough drafts that McClellan had written as early as 1865 and 1866 when in exile in Europe. In the earlier manuscript portion he restored dispatches McClellan had not included, and added others, previously unpublished, that he found among the general's papers. One of these, for example, was the letter to Simon Cameron in September 1861 announcing the alarming news that the Confederate army facing him at Washington was 130,000 strong, including a column of 100,000 preparing to attack. It was hardly surprising that this miscellany of unconnected and often raw material, written at different times over the course of twenty years and patched together so thoughtlessly, caused a puzzled John Ropes to wonder why ''McClellan has chosen to let the original and erroneous statements stand.''

To compound his crimes as a literary executor, Prime added excerpts from more than 250 of McClellan's letters to his wife. It is beyond question that McClellan never intended these excerpts to be published. Prime found them in a notebook McClellan compiled after the war when he was working on the original memoirs later destroyed by fire. Obviously his purpose was simply to refresh his memory of events when he came to write his narrative; in his surviving manuscript he had quoted but a single brief passage from these letters to Ellen. Deciding that these excerpts failed to disclose enough of the personal side of his friend's character, Prime had May McClellan go through the original letters and copy more revealing passages for him.

By the time he finished his labors, two thirds of the contents of *McClellan's Own Story* were selected on Prime's decision alone. He further put his stamp on the work by censoring and altering material freely in both letters and manuscript. This is most noticeable in McClellan's characterizations of people, particularly in the numerous aspersions he had cast on the now-martyred Lincoln. Prime had considered it his duty, he wrote in his introduction, ''to withhold such portions as I think he would not have published now.'' What guided his efforts, he said, was his desire to present to others the same view of his friend "which those nearest to him always had. . . .''[3]

There is no indication that Ellen McClellan had any role in the preparation of her husband's memoirs. She left the country before their publication. In June 1886, following Max's graduation from college, she took Max and May with her to Europe for an extended period. In fact it was in Europe that Ellen spent most of the rest of her life. She died in 1915, at the age of seventy-nine, while visiting her daughter in Nice. May, too, lived abroad much of her life. In 1893 she married Paul Desprez, a French diplomat, and she died, childless, in 1945 at the Villa Antietam, her home in Nice. Max — George B. McClellan, Jr. — achieved a political career of some distinction, serving as congressman from New York from 1895 to 1903 and as mayor of New York City from 1903 to 1909. In 1889 he had married Georgianna Heckscher, but like May he had no children. He died in 1940.

It was Max McClellan who was responsible for preserving his father's papers and presenting them to the Library of Congress, and he wrote several works of history, but nothing about the Civil War or his father's role in it. Thus *McClellan's Own Story*, for better or worse, remained George McClellan's record as his contemporaries saw it. William Prime concluded his introduction with the "guiding trust" that his friend "will approve what I have done when I again meet him.'' Historians have been grateful enough to Prime, certainly, but if his wish was ever granted it required truly saintly forgiveness on McClellan's part.[4]

SOURCES AND
ACKNOWLEDGMENTS
NOTES
BIBLIOGRAPHY
INDEX

SOURCES AND
ACKNOWLEDGMENTS

The principal collection of primary material on George B. McClellan is the McClellan Papers in the Manuscript Division of the Library of Congress. The collection contains some 33,000 items, including private and official correspondence and telegrams, dispatch books, diaries, notebooks, manuscripts, newspaper clippings, and business and financial records. It details McClellan's life from his appointment to West Point in 1842 to his death in 1885, focusing most heavily on the Civil War years. The collection also includes material relating to other McClellan family members, papers of the Marcy family, and correspondence of William C. Prime, McClellan's literary executor.

The McClellan Papers are a unique source of information on the military history of the war, particularly in the years 1861 and 1862. Although George B. McClellan, Jr., loaned some of his father's dispatch books to the compilers of the *Official Records of the Union and Confederate Armies* in 1896 for use in their supplemental volumes, the Papers contain thousands of pieces of military correspondence never made available for publication. In a like manner, the Papers are a unique resource for the political history of the period.

McClellan's wartime letters to his wife, which constitute an invaluable guide to his thinking, survive in the Papers in the form of extensive excerpts he himself copied, probably in the mid-1870s, when he was working on his memoirs, and in additional copies made by his daughter, May, after his death. Although the original letters have not been found, I am satisfied that these copies contain their substantive content, complete and uncensored, with only personal matter deleted. Other useful elements of the Papers are the manuscripts, drafts, and notes for his memoirs, presenting his unvarnished thoughts on events before the deletions and censorship applied to *McClellan's Own Story* by literary executor Prime.

I canvassed manuscript collections across the country for material by and about McClellan, and my indebtedness to their curatorial staffs is great. Among the many who gave generously of their time and effort, I want to thank particularly James H. Hutson and his staff at the Library of Congress; Howard Wehmann, Michael P. Musick, and Robert B. Matchette at the National Archives; Harriet McLoone at the Huntington Library, San Marino, California; Mark A. Greene at the Bentley Historical Library, University of Michigan; Steven Eric Nielsen at the Minnesota Historical Society, St. Paul; Margaret A. Fusco at the University of Chicago Library; Jean F. Preston and John Delaney at the Princeton University Library; Lee Meininger at the Historical Society of Pennsylvania, Philadelphia; Margaret R. Goostray at the Boston University Library; W. E. Bigglestone at the Oberlin College Archives; Karl Kabelac at the Rush Rhees Library, University of Rochester; Richard J. Somers at the U.S. Army Military History Institute, Carlisle Barracks, Pennsylvania; Carolyn Autry at the Indiana Historical Society Library, and Marybelle Burch at the Indiana State Library, both in Indianapolis; and John Y. Simon at the Ulysses S. Grant Association, Southern Illinois University.

No facet of General McClellan's military character was more important than his picture of the enemy, and I am grateful to Edwin C. Fishel of Arlington, Virginia, for sharing with me his knowledge of intelligence gathering and allowing me to read portions of his unpublished manuscript on Civil War intelligence. Frederick W. Chesson of Waterbury, Connecticut, also provided valuable guidance in this area. Mark Grimsley of Columbus, Ohio, generously made available portions of his translation of the Comte de Paris diary. Betty Peebles of Alexandria, Virginia, Brinton D. McClellan of Darien, Connecticut, and Robert J. Smith of Pomfret Center, Connecticut, furnished information on the McClellan family, and Dr. John Moses of Scarsdale, New York, advised me on McClellan's medical record.

Valuable assistance in research and information about McClellan material were furnished me by Linda McCurdy of Chapel Hill, North Carolina; Jeffrey A. Sears of New York City; Russell B. Bailey of Covington, Tennessee; Michael O. Berry of San Jose, California; Paul Kallina of Arlington, Virginia; Edward Maturniak of Allendale, New Jersey; David Black of New York City; and John Hennessey of Selkirk, New York.

Brian C. Pohanka of Time-Life Books, Alexandria, Virginia, and Peter Harrington of the Anne S. K. Brown Military Collection, Brown University, were generous with their help on illustrations. My special thanks are once again due Stanley Crane of the Pequot Library, Southport, Connecticut. Geoffrey C. Ward, my editor, provided a valuable commentary on the manuscript.

NOTES

Works cited by author and short title will be found in full in the Bibliography. Consecutive citations from the same source are separated by dashes. The following abbreviations and manuscript citations are used in the Notes:

GBM George Brinton McClellan

HL Huntington Library

LC Library of Congress

NA National Archives. Citations are by Record Group, followed by microfilm series and reel number. Thus, ''RG 107 (M-473:102), NA'' refers to Record Group 107, microfilm series M-473, reel 102, National Archives. These National Archives collections are listed under ''Manuscript Collections'' in the Bibliography.

NOR U.S. Naval War Records Office, *Official Records of the Union and Confederate Navies in the War of the Rebellion.* Reference is to Series 1 unless otherwise stated.

OR U.S. War Department, *The War of the Rebellion: A Compilation of the Official Records of the Union and Confederate Armies.* Reference is to Series 1 unless otherwise stated.

Papers George B. McClellan Papers, Manuscript Division, Library of Congress. Citations are by volume, followed by microfilm reel number. Thus, ''Papers (B-11:48)'' refers to volume B-11, microfilm reel 48, McClellan Papers. ''Papers (C-7:63/D-10:72)'' refers to the special case of a letter preserved in the form of a copy partly by McClellan in volume C-7 and partly by his daughter in volume D-10.

Virtually all the quotations from McClellan's letters and dispatches used in the text are taken from manuscript sources. Those from the Civil War years, arranged chronologically and printed in full, will be found in Stephen W. Sears, ed., *The Civil War Papers of George B. McClellan: Selected Correspondence, 1860–1865* (New York: Ticknor & Fields, forthcoming in 1989).

Chapter 1. The Making of a Soldier

1. GBM to Frederica M. English, June 28, 1842, Papers (A-1:1); GBM's cadet information card, U.S. Military Academy Archives.
2. GBM, "Notes on Childhood," c. 1882 — reminiscence of G. W. Smith, undated — GBM to John H. B. McClellan, Feb. 27, 1848 — GBM to Elizabeth B. McClellan, July 20, 1884, Papers (D-23:79, A-108:42, B-1:43, A-101:40). For GBM's ancestry, see: family genealogies, Papers (D-4:67, D-5:68); *Appleton's Cyclopaedia of American Biography* (1888); Clarence W. Bowen, *The History of Woodstock, Connecticut* (Norwood, Mass.: Plimpton Press, 1926–43), I, pp. 142–44, VII, pp. 311–24; McClellan biographical record, J. M. Winterbotham Collection, State Historical Society of Wisconsin; Richard Buel, Jr., *Dear Liberty: Connecticut's Mobilization for the Revolutionary War* (Middletown, Conn.: Wesleyan University Press, 1980), pp. 78, 126, 131.
3. *McClellan's Own Story*, draft — GBM, "Notes on Childhood," c. 1882, Papers (D-9:71, D-23:79); Dr. George McClellan to John C. Spencer, Mar. 5 — Spencer to GBM, Apr. 19, 1842, RG 94 (M-688:135), NA.
4. Frederica M. English to May McClellan, Feb. 17, 1886 — GBM to Elizabeth B. McClellan, July 20, 1884 — GBM to his wife, July 22, 1862 — GBM, "Notes on Childhood," c. 1882, Papers (A-105:41, A-101:40, C-7:63/D-10:72, D-23:79).
5. GBM to Elizabeth B. McClellan, Aug. 5 — GBM to Frederica M. English, Sept. 10, 1842, Papers (A-1:1).
6. James L. Morrison, Jr., *"The Best School in the World": West Point, the Pre–Civil War Years, 1833–1866,* pp. 4, 73, 103, 160; Lenoir Chambers, *Stonewall Jackson,* I, pp. 60, 62; Engineer Department to West Point superintendent, Apr. 23, 26, May 26, June 26, 1842, RG 94 (M-91:10), NA; GBM to John H. B. McClellan, Jan. 21, 1842, Papers (A-1:1); Peter S. Michie, *General McClellan,* pp. 11–12.
7. Thomas H. Neill to Edward D. Neill, Nov. 2, 1843, Neill Papers, Minnesota Historical Society; GBM to John H. B. McClellan, Jan. 21, 1843, Papers (B-1:43).
8. James L. Morrison, Jr., ed., "Getting Through West Point: The Cadet Memoirs of John C. Tidball, Class of 1848," *Civil War History,* 26:4 (Dec. 1980), p. 321; GBM to Elizabeth B. McClellan, Feb. 1, [1845], Papers (A-1:1); Thomas H. Neill to Edward D. Neill, Jan. 7, 1844, Neill Papers, Minnesota Historical Society. For West Point's curriculum in the 1840s, see: Morrison, *"The Best School in the World,"* pp. 160–63.
9. E. D. Keyes, *Fifty Years' Observation of Men and Events,* p. 197; Dabney H. Maury, *Recollections of a Virginian in the Mexican, Indian, and Civil Wars,* p. 59; Michie, *General McClellan,* p. 12; GBM to Frederica M. English, Jan. 18, 1843, Papers (A-1:1).
10. GBM to Elizabeth B. McClellan, Feb. 1, [1845] — GBM to Frederica M. English, Jan. 6, 1845, Papers (A-1:1).
11. GBM to Elizabeth B. McClellan, Mar. 18, 1846, Papers (A-1:1).

12. Edward Hagerman, "From Jomini to Dennis Hart Mahan: The Evolution of Trench Warfare and the American Civil War," *Civil War History*, 13:3 (Sept. 1967), pp. 201–203; James L. Morrison, Jr., "The United States Military Academy, 1833–1866: Years of Progress and Turmoil," Ph.D. diss., Columbia University, 1970, pp. 159–66, 173; Dennis Hart Mahan to GBM, Aug. 3, 1861, Papers (B-8:47).

13. Morrison, "Getting Through West Point," p. 323; GBM to Elizabeth B. McClellan, Mar. 18, 1846, Papers (A-1:1).

14. Morrison, *"The Best School in the World,"* p. 20; GBM to Elizabeth B. McClellan, Mar. 18 — GBM to Frederica M. English, May 13, 1846, Papers (A-1:1).

15. GBM, Dialectic Society address, June 1842, Papers (A-1:1); James L. Morrison, Jr., "The Struggle Between Sectionalism and Nationalism at Ante-Bellum West Point, 1830–1861," *Civil War History*, 19:2 (June 1973), pp. 141–43; Morrison, *"The Best School in the World,"* p. 75.

16. GBM to Frederica M. English, Aug. 16, 1846, Papers (A-1:1); *Registrar of Graduates and Former Cadets of the United States Military Academy* (West Point Alumni Foundation, 1960 ed.), pp. 194–99.

17. Joseph G. Totten to GBM, July 9 — GBM to Frederica M. English, Aug. 16 — Totten to A. J. Swift, May 19, 1846, Papers (A-1:1); GBM to John H. B. McClellan, c. Aug. 25, 1846, Papers (B-1:43).

18. GBM to Elizabeth B. McClellan, Aug. 23 — GBM to Thomas C. English, Aug. 28, Sept. 22, 1846, Papers (A-1:1).

19. GBM to Frederica M. English, Oct. 16, 1846 — GBM, Mexican War diary, Oct. 16, 1846, Papers (A-1:1, D-3:67); GBM to Charles S. Stewart, Dec. 1, 1846, Houghton Library, Harvard University. GBM worked up his Mexican War journal periodically but retained the format of a daily diary. A copy he made, probably in Mexico City in the winter of 1847–48, is the version preserved in his Papers. A heavily edited transcription by William Starr Myers was published in 1917 under the title *The Mexican War Diary of General George B. McClellan.*

20. Cadmus M. Wilcox, *History of the Mexican War* (Washington, D.C.: Church News Publishing Co., 1892), pp. 113–14; GBM to Elizabeth B. McClellan, Nov. 14, 1846 — GBM, Mexican War diary, Jan. 2, 1847, Papers (A-1:1, D-3:67).

21. GBM to Elizabeth B. McClellan, Feb. 4 — GBM to Dr. George McClellan, Jan. 25, Feb. 14, 1847, Papers (A-1:1, B-41:61, B-1:43).

22. GBM, Mexican War diary, Mar. 13, 22, 25, 29, 1847, Papers (D-3:67); Ethan Allen Hitchcock, Mar. 16, 1847, Hitchcock, *Fifty Years in Camp and Field: Diary of Major-General Ethan Allen Hitchcock, U.S.A.,* p. 241; Maury, *Recollections of a Virginian,* p. 34.

23. Robert E. Lee to his wife, Apr. 25, 1847, quoted in Douglas Southall Freeman, *R. E. Lee: A Biography,* I, p. 239; GBM, Mexican War diary, c. Apr. 20, 1847 — GBM to unnamed senator, Oct. 31, 1847, Papers (D-3:67, B-1:43).

24. G. S. Hillard, *Life and Campaigns of George B. McClellan, Major-General U.S. Army,* pp. 19–20; GBM to Frederica M. English, Aug. 16, 1846, Papers (A-1:1).

25. GBM to Robert C. Winthrop, Mar. 25, 1863, Winthrop Papers, Massachusetts Historical Society; William White to GBM, May 11, 1847 — reminiscence of G. W. Smith, undated — GBM to John H. B. McClellan, Oct. 24, 1847, Feb.

27, 1848, Papers (B-1:43, A-108:42, B-1:43, B-41:61).

26. Justin H. Smith, *The War with Mexico*, II, p. 89; Hillard, *Life of McClellan*, pp. 24–25; Chambers, *Stonewall Jackson*, I, pp. 104–5; D. H. Hill diary, Aug. 23, 1847, Southern Historical Collection, University of North Carolina; Hitchcock, Aug. 20, 1847, *Diary*, pp. 277, 278; Joseph G. Totten to GBM, Aug. 30, 1848, Papers (A-1:1); P. F. Smith in *Mexican Reports*, House Exec. Doc. No. 1, 30th Cong., 1st Sess., 1849, p. 332.

27. Hitchcock, Sept. 11, 13, 1847, *Diary*, pp. 301, 303; Freeman, *Lee*, I, pp. 277–78; Michie, *General McClellan*, p. 21.

28. GBM to John H. B. McClellan, Oct. 24, 1847 — Roger Jones to GBM, Sept. 25, 1848 — GBM to Elizabeth B. McClellan, Jan. 19, 1849, Papers (B-1:43, A-1:1, B-1:43).

29. Stephen E. Ambrose, *Duty, Honor, Country: A History of West Point* (Baltimore: Johns Hopkins Press, 1966), p. 140; GBM to Abraham Lincoln, Apr. 20, 1862, Lincoln Papers, LC; GBM to unnamed senator, Oct. 31, 1847 — GBM, Mexican War memorandum, Jan. 4, 1848, Papers (B-1:43, A-1:1).

30. GBM to John H. B. McClellan, Feb. 22, 1848 — GBM to Winfield Scott, May 7, 1861 — Joseph E. Johnston to GBM, Mar. 21, 1856, Papers (B-1:43, C-3:62, B-3:44).

31. GBM to Elizabeth B. McClellan, Oct. 24, 1847, Mar. 22, 1848, Papers (B-1:43); GBM, 1852 journal — James Stuart to GBM, July 29, 1848 — Robert E. Lee to GBM, June 6, 1848, Papers (D-3:67, B-1:43, A-1:1).

Chapter 2. On Peacetime Service

1. GBM, West Point diary, Sept. 22, 1849, Papers (D-3:67); GBM to Totten, Nov. 1 — Totten to GBM, Oct. 31, Nov. 3, 1848, Papers (A-1:1).

2. GBM outlined his duties at West Point in a letter to Charles T. Baker, Nov. 29, 1849, Papers (A-2:1). That he instructed only the men of the engineer company is evident from his grading notebooks: Papers (D-13:75).

3. GBM to Totten, June 23 — Totten to GBM, June 26, 1848, Papers (A-1:1); Charles T. Baker to GBM, Nov. 26, 28 — GBM to Baker, Nov. 29 — GBM to Totten, Dec. 16, 1849, Papers (A-2:1); GBM to Totten, Aug. 5, 1850 — GBM to Seth Williams, Nov. 5, 1850 — GBM to Maria E. McClellan, c. Apr. 1851, Papers (A-2:1, A-3:2, B-41:61).

4. GBM to Totten, Feb. 14 — GBM to Scott, Mar. 8, 1850, Papers (A-2:1); GBM to J. M. Jones, Jan.–, Mar. 12, 1851, Papers (A-3:2); GBM to Totten, Sept. 16 — Totten and Charles M. Conrad endorsements, Oct. 4, 1850, Papers (A-2:1, A-3:2); GBM to William H. Chase, c. Dec. 27, 1850 — GBM to John H. B. McClellan, c. Mar. 1851, Papers (A-3:2, B-41:61).

5. GBM to John H. B. McClellan, c. Mar. 1851 — GBM to Maria E. McClellan, Jan. –, 1849, Papers (B-41:61, A-1:1); Maury, *Recollections of a Virginian*, pp. 50, 53; Maury to GBM, Mar. 28, 1856, Papers (B-5:45).

6. GBM to Maria E. McClellan, c. Apr. 1851, Papers (B-41:61); Maury, *Recollections of a Virginian*, p. 62; G. W. Smith to GBM, June 26, 1852, Papers (A-3:2). Neither of GBM's papers has been located. Their subject matter is given in Maury, *Recollections of a Virginian*, p. 50, and Michie, *General McClellan*, p. 24. The Marshal Saxe notes, marked "West Point, May 1851," are in the Papers (D-3:67).

7. GBM to Elizabeth B. McClellan, Mar. 3, 1850 — GBM to Maria E. McClellan, c. Apr. 1851, Papers (A-2:1, B-41:61); Dr. George McClellan to William A. Graham, Feb.

14, 1842, North Carolina State Archives; GBM to Frederica M. English, Sept. 25, 1848, July 21, 1851, Papers (A-1:1, A-3:2).

8. Joseph G. Totten to GBM, June 12 — GBM to Elizabeth B. McClellan, July 18, 1851, Papers (A-3:2, B-4:45). GMB's notation of Stuart's death is written on a blank page of his Mexican War diary: Papers (B-3:67).

9. GBM to John G. B. McClellan, Feb. 3 — Totten to GBM, Mar. 5, 1852, Papers (B-1:43, A-3:2).

10. William H. Goetzmann, *Army Exploration in the American West, 1803–1863,* pp. 213–18; GBM, Red River diary, [Apr. 12, 1852] — GBM to Maria E. McClellan, Sept. 12 — GBM to John H. B. McClellan, Apr. 21, 1852, Papers (D-3:67, B-2:44, A-3:2).

11. GBM to John H. B. McClellan, Apr. 21, 1852, Papers (B-2:44); GBM to Elizabeth B. McClellan, Mar. 12, 1853, May 7, 1852, Papers (B-2:44, A-3:2). The Marcys' elder daughter is listed incorrectly in some sources as Ellen Mary Marcy. Her correct name is given in full in (for example) an affidavit application: Mary Ellen Marcy McClellan to Edward D. Neill, Jan. 24, 1893, Neill Papers, Minnesota Historical Society.

12. GBM to John H. B. McClellan, May 14 — GBM to Elizabeth B. McClellan, May 7, 1852, Papers (A-3:2); GBM, Red River diary, June 11, 16, July 1, 28, 1852, Papers (D-3:67); GBM to John H. B. McClellan, Sept. 3, 1852, Papers (A-4:2); GBM to Maria E. McClellan, Sept. 12, 1852 — GBM to Arthur McClellan, Apr. 14, 1853, Papers (B-2:44). Marcy's report was published as Senate Exec. Doc. No. 54, 32nd Cong., 2nd Sess., 1854. The expedition is detailed in W. Eugene Hollon, *Beyond the Cross Timbers: The Travels of Randolph B. Marcy, 1812–1887,* pp. 126–58.

13. GBM to Elizabeth B. McClellan, Sept. 26 — GBM to Maria E. McClellan, Sept. 12, 1852, Papers (A-4:2, B-2:44).

14. Totten to GBM, Sept. 28, Nov. 30 — GBM to John H. B. McClellan, Oct. 25, 1852, Papers (A-4:2); Texas rivers and harbors payroll account, 1852–53 — GBM to Elizabeth B. McClellan, Dec. 24, 1852 — GBM to Frederica M. English, Jan. 1, 1853, Papers (D-11:73, B-2:44, A-4:2).

15. GBM to Totten, Jan. 13, 1853, Papers (C-1:61); GBM to Maria E. McClellan, Mar. 9 — GBM to Elizabeth B. McClellan, Jan. 15, Mar. 12, 1853, Papers (B-2:44). An inventory of GBM's personal library, c. Oct. 1, 1864, includes all of Jomini's works, in their French editions: Papers (D-18:76).

16. GBM, Texas diary, Apr. 7, 1853, Papers (D-14:75); Isaac I. Stevens teleg. to P. G. T. Beauregard, Mar. 29 — Beauregard to GBM, Mar. 30 — Totten teleg. to GBM, Apr. 5, 1853, Papers (A-4:2); GBM to Arthur McClellan, Apr. 14, 1853, Papers (B-2:44).

17. Goetzmann, *Army Exploration,* pp. 262–77; GBM, Texas diary, Apr. 25, 1853, Papers (D-14:75).

18. Stevens to GBM, May 9, 1853, Papers (D-11:73); GBM, Pacific railroad diary, May 20, June 5, 22, 27, 1853, Papers (D-3:67).

19. Henry C. Hodges to William C. Church, Jan. 7, 1897, Church Papers, LC, cited in Lloyd Lewis, *Captain Sam Grant* (Boston: Little, Brown, 1950), pp. 319–20; GBM to Elizabeth B. McClellan, July 12 — GBM, Pacific railroad diary, July 18, 1853, Papers (B-2:44, D-3:67).

20. GBM to John H. B. McClellan, Sept. 18, 1853, Papers (B-2:44); GBM, Pacific railroad diary, Aug. 24, 26, Oct. 18, 28, Nov. 9, 1853, Papers (D-3:67); GBM to Jefferson Davis, Sept. 18 — GBM to

Frederick W. Lander, Nov. 8, 1853, Papers (C-1:61, A-5:2). The route of the party is traced in Philip Henry Overmeyer, "George B. McClellan and the Pacific Northwest," *Pacific Northwest Quarterly*, 32:1 (Jan. 1941).

21. GBM to Stevens, Jan. 31, Feb. 8, 1854, Papers (C-1:61); Abiel W. Tinkham to Stevens, Feb. 1, 1854, U.S. War Dept., *Pacific Railroad Reports*, 1855, I, p. 631; Overmeyer, "McClellan and the Pacific Northwest," pp. 56–57. GBM's report is in his Papers (C-1:61) and in *Pacific Railroad Reports*, I, pp. 188–202.

22. Goetzmann, *Army Exploration*, pp. 295–304; GBM to Stevens, June 3 — Stevens to GBM, Sept. 27 — GBM to Stevens, Oct. 31, 1854, Papers (C-1:61, A-6:3, C-1:61).

23. Elizabeth B. McClellan to GBM, Apr. 15, [1854] — GBM to Mary M. Marcy, May 14, [1854] — Randolph B. Marcy to his wife, June 18, [1854] — GBM to his wife, [Feb. 28, 1863] — GBM to Mary M. Marcy, Aug. 27, 1854, Papers (B-2:44, B-3:44, B-1:43, A-12:48, A-3:44). GBM's promotion to first lieutenant dated from July 1, 1853.

24. GBM to Mary M. Marcy, June 21, [1854] — Davis to GBM, June 19, 1854, Papers (B-3:44, B-2:44); GBM, Caribbean diary, July 18, 25, Aug. 1, 1854, Papers (D-3:67); GBM to Davis, Aug. 27, Sept. 30, 1854, Papers (C-1:61); Michie, *General McClellan*, p. 35.

25. GBM to Mary M. Marcy, Sept. 10, [1854], [Oct. 4, 1854], Nov. 1, [1854], Dec. 5, 1854, Jan. 4, [1855], Mar. 22, [1855], Papers (B-3:44).

26. GBM to Mary M. Marcy, Apr. 6, [1855] — GBM's 1855 passport — GBM to John H. B. McClellan, Sept 9, 1855, Papers (B-3:44, D-27:81, A-6:3).

27. GBM to Mary M. Marcy, May 21 — GBM to Elizabeth B. McClellan, May 12, 1855, Papers (B-3:44, A-

6:3). GBM's European itinerary is traced in his six military commission diaries, May 6, 1855–Apr. 30, 1856: Papers (D-16:76).

28. GBM to John H. B. McClellan, Oct. 12, 1855 — GBM, military commission diary 3, Oct. 16, 20, 1855 — GBM to his wife, Apr. 23, 1862, Papers (A-7:3, D-16:76, C-7:63); GBM to John H. B. McClellan, Dec. 29, 1855, Feb. 2, 1856, Papers (A-7:3); GBM to Mary M. Marcy, Jan. 14, 1856, Papers (B-3:44).

29. Military commission library inventory, Papers (A-108:43); GBM to Mary M. Marcy, June 24 — GBM to Mary Ellen Marcy, July–, 1856, Papers (B-3:44); Stephen Z. Starr, *The Union Cavalry in the Civil War*, I, p. 50; Richard Delafield to Davis, Oct. 6, 1856, Papers (A-8:4). GBM's cavalry manual was published as *Regulations and Instructions for the Field Service of the United States Cavalry in Time of War* in 1861.

30. GBM, *The Report of Captain George B. McClellan, One of the Officers Sent to the Seat of War in Europe, in 1855 and 1856*, pp. 16, 10; *Atlantic Monthly*, 8 (Dec. 1861), p. 771; Hagerman, "Jomini to Mahan," p. 210; GBM, military commission diary 6, Mar. 6, 1856, Papers (D-16:76).

31. GBM to Samuel Cooper, Nov. 26, 1856 — GBM to Marcy, Feb. 15, 1857, Papers (A-8:4, A-11:5).

Chapter 3. Life in a Civilian World

1. J. K. Duncan to GBM, Jan. 12, 1857 — Johnston to GBM, Apr. 13, Oct. 25, 1856, Papers (B-3:45, B-3:44, A-8:4).

2. A. H. Bowman to GBM, Sept. 19, Nov. 5 — Smith to GBM, Nov. 5, 1856, Papers (A-8:4); William H. Osborn to Executive Committee, Illinois Central Railroad, Nov. 26, 1856, Newberry Library; GBM to Samuel L. M. Barlow, Nov. 6, 1856, Jan. 3, 1858, Papers (A-8:4); Bar-

low to GBM, Jan. 8, 1858, Papers (B-5:45).

3. Paul W. Gates, *The Illinois Central Railroad and Its Colonization Work,* pp. 43, 78–79; GBM to Marcy, Feb. 15, 1857, Papers (A-11:5); William H. Osborn to GBM, Nov. 24, 1856, Newberry Library; Carlton J. Corliss, *Main Line of Mid-America: The Story of the Illinois Central,* pp. 90–91; Marcy to Mary Ellen Marcy, Feb. 4, 1857, Papers (B-3:45); GBM to Mary Ellen Marcy, Feb. 15, May 16, 1857, Papers (B-4:45).

4. Fitz John Porter to GBM, July 14, 1857 — Mansfield Lovell to GBM, Feb. 25, 1858, Papers (B-4:45, B-5:45); Duncan to GBM, July 23, Aug. 19, Nov. 9, 11, 1857, Papers (B-4:45); G. W. Smith to GBM, Oct. 26 — Johnston to GBM, Dec. 6, 1857, Papers (B-5:45). Comparatively few of GBM's letters relating to filibustering are on record, and his connection with the movement is in part extrapolated from letters of his correspondents that paraphrase or quote his views.

5. Gates, *Illinois Central,* p. 79; GBM to John Newall, Aug. 28 — GBM to Osborn, Aug. 29, Sept. 1 — GBM to Jonathon Sturges, Sept. 11, 1857, Papers (C-2:61).

6. Corliss, *Main Line of Mid-America,* pp. 94–97; Gates, *Illinois Central,* pp. 79–80; GBM to Jonathon Sturges, Oct. 11 — GBM to J. N. Perkins, Sept. 27 — GBM to Osborn, Oct. 28, 1857, Papers (C-2:61).

7. A. H. Bowman to GBM, Nov. 29 — GBM to Mary M. Marcy, Nov. 21 — GBM to Mary Ellen Marcy, Dec. 8, 1857, Papers (B-5:45); Allan Nevins, *The Emergence of Lincoln: Douglas, Buchanan, and Party Chaos, 1857–1859,* pp. 319–22; GBM to Barlow, Jan. 3, Feb. 12, 1858 — GBM to Mary M. Marcy, Dec. 5, 1854, Papers (A-8:4, A-11:5, B-3:44); Smith to

GBM, Dec. 29, 30, 1857, Papers (B-5:45).

8. Lovell to GBM, Feb. 25 — GBM to Mary Ellen Marcy, Feb. 28, 1858, Papers (B-5:45); Johnston to GBM, Apr. 7 — Chicago Light Guard commission, Mar. 7, 1859, Papers (A-11:5). In 1859 GBM apparently also explored a position with the Sardinian army in the War for Italian Unification: Joseph E. Johnston to GBM, May 12, 1859, Papers (A-11:5).

9. GBM library inventory, c. Oct. 1, 1864 — GBM to Mary Ellen Marcy, Jan. 25, 1860, Papers (D-18:76, A-11:5). Although there is no inventory of GBM's library before 1864, when it numbered over 500 volumes, there are references to its contents in earlier letters suggesting that it was of substantial size in the late 1850s.

10. Corliss, *Main Line of Mid-America,* pp. 100–101; GBM to William H. Osborn, Jan. 31, 1858, Newberry Library; GBM to Osborn, June 3, 1858, Papers (A-11:5).

11. Corliss, *Main Line of Mid-America,* pp. 59, 97; Ambrose E. Burnside to GBM, May 4, 1858 — GBM to Mary Ellen Marcy, c. Jan. 1860, Papers (A-11:5).

12. *McClellan's Own Story,* p. 36, and manuscript and draft, Papers (D-9:71); May McClellan diary, Nov. 7, 1883, Papers (D-6:68). GBM placed this incident in Bloomington, but no debate was held there; which of the seven debates he was describing is unknown.

13. *McClellan's Own Story,* notes, Papers (D-9:71); John M. Douglas to GBM, Jan. 26, 1861, Papers (B-6:46).

14. GBM to Mary Ellen Marcy, Feb. 28, Mar. 17, 1858, Papers (B-5:45). The letters from her various suitors are in the Papers (B-5:45, B-6:46).

15. GBM to Mary M. Marcy, July 22 — Marcy to Mary Ellen Marcy, May

22, 28, 1856, Papers (B-3:44); A. P. Hill to Marcy, May 29, 1857, Papers (B-4:45); James I. Robertson, Jr., *General A. P. Hill: The Story of a Confederate Warrior* (New York: Random House, 1987), pp. 8–9, 24–25; GBM to Mary Ellen Marcy, July –, 1856 — Mary M. Marcy to Mary Ellen Marcy, c. Sept. 1856, Papers (B-3:44, B-3:45).

16. GBM to Mary Ellen Marcy, Sept. 25, 1858, Papers (B-6:46). Other quotations are from GBM's letters to his wife-to-be, preserved in the form of excerpts copied by their daughter, May, after GBM's death; most of the excerpts do not bear dates, but the originals were written during the winter of 1859–60: Papers (A-11:5).

17. *New York Herald,* May 23, 1860; GBM diary (1860), May 22 — GBM to Elizabeth B. McClellan, June 6, 1860, Papers (D-4:67, B-6:40).

18. Barlow to GBM, June 21 — GBM to Mary Ellen Marcy, c. Jan. 8, 1860, Papers (B-6:46, A-11:5); William H. Aspinwall to Barlow, July 2, 17, 1860, Barlow Papers, HL; John H. B. McClellan to GBM, July 22, 1860, Papers (B-6:46); GBM to Charles S. Stewart, Aug. 3, 1860, Houghton Library, Harvard University. GBM confirmed to J. Lyttleton Adams on Sept. 23, 1864, that the cause of his leaving the Illinois Central was (in Adams's words) "a personal matter between yourself and some of the officers. . . .": Papers (B-21:52).

19. GBM to Thomas C. English, Feb. 7, 1861 — GBM to adjutant of Guthrie Grays, undated, Papers (A-11:5, B-40:60); Joseph W. Alsop to GBM, Sept. 26, 1860 — GBM to Alsop, May 6, 1861 — Alsop to GBM, Jan. 15, 1862, Papers (A-11:5, B-6:46, B-10:47); Barlow to GBM, May 13, 1861 —

Aspinwall to GBM, Mar. 21, 1864, Papers (B-6:46, B-15:49).

20. GBM to Barlow, Dec. 27, [1860], Barlow Papers, HL; GBM to Thomas C. English, Feb. 7, 1861, Papers (A-11:5); *McClellan's Own Story,* p. 29.

21. Welles, Sept. 3, 1862, Gideon Welles, *Diary of Gideon Welles,* ed. Howard K. Beale, I, p. 107; *McClellan's Own Story,* p. 38, and draft, Papers (D-9:71); GBM to Porter, Apr. 18, 1861, Nicholson Collection, HL; Cadmus M. Wilcox to GBM, Mar. 24, 1861, Papers (B-6:46); Wilcox to David L. Swain, Feb. 20, 1864, Swain Papers, North Carolina Division of Archives and History; *Confederate Veteran,* 16 (Apr. 1908), p. 178; Lovell to GBM, Apr. 15, 1861, Papers (B-6:46).

22. Duncan to GBM, Jan. 12, 1857, Papers (B-3:45). GBM's commission as a major general of volunteers dated from Apr. 23, 1861; that of a major general in the regular army, from May 14, 1861.

Chapter 4. The Call to War

1. Porter to GBM — William F. Smith to GBM, Apr. 15, 1861, Papers (A-11:5).

2. None of these messages of proffered command has been found. For Gen. Patterson's and Gov. Morgan's offers, see: *McClellan's Own Story,* draft, Papers (D-9:71); GBM to Robert Patterson, Apr. 18, 1861, Miscellaneous Collections, HL. For Gov. Curtin's offer, see: GBM to Porter, Apr. 18, 1861, Nicholson Collection, HL; GBM to his wife, Apr. 18, 1861, George B. McClellan, Jr., Papers, LC; GBM teleg. to Andrew G. Curtin, Apr. 24, 1861, McClellan Papers, Illinois State Historical Library. For the Ohio command, see: *McClellan's Own Story,* draft — GBM to William Dennison, Apr. 18, 1861, Papers (D-9:71, A-11:5); William H. Aspinwall to Winfield Scott,

Apr. 21, 1861, *OR*, Ser. 3, I, pp. 97–98; GBM to Joseph W. Alsop, Apr. 24, 1861, Alsop Family Papers, Yale University Library; John G. Nicolay and John Hay, *Abraham Lincoln: A History*, IV, pp. 281–83.

3. GBM to Scott, Apr. 23, 1861, Papers (A-11:5); Jacob D. Cox in *Battles and Leaders of the Civil War*, eds. Robert U. Johnson and Clarence C. Buel, I, p. 89; Cox interview in *Cincinnati Commercial Gazette*, Nov. –, 1885, clipping, Cox Papers, Oberlin College Archives; John C. Ropes to John C. Gray, Feb. 7, 1863, Gray and Ropes, *War Letters, 1862–1865*, p. 78.

4. Simon Cameron to Dennison, Apr. 15 — Dennison to Cameron, Apr. 22 — Union Defense Committee to Cameron, May 3, 1861, *OR*, Ser. 3, I, pp. 68–69, 101, 148–49; GBM to Lorenzo Thomas, Apr. 27, 1861, RG 94 (M-619:37), NA.

5. Cox in *Battles and Leaders*, I, pp. 94–95; GBM to E. D. Townsend, May 4, 1861, *OR*, LI, Part 1, pp. 370–71.

6. GBM to E. D. Townsend, May 11, 1861 — Alsop to GBM, May –, 1861 — N. P. Willis in *The Home Journal*, c. Oct. 1861, clipping, Papers (C-3:62, A-12:5, D-29:81); *New York Tribune*, June 19, 1861.

7. *McClellan's Own Story*, pp. 45–53.

8. Allan Pinkerton to GBM, May 4 — GBM to Scott, May 7, 1861, Papers (A-11:5, C-3:62); GBM to Lorenzo Thomas, May 21, 1861, RG 94 (M-619:37), NA; Salmon P. Chase to GBM, July 7, 1861, Jacob S. Schuckers, *The Life and Public Services of Salmon Portland Chase*, pp. 427–28.

9. GBM to Scott, Apr. 23, 1861, Papers (A-11:5); GBM to Scott, Apr. 28, 1861, Andre De Coppet Collection, Princeton University Library; GBM to Scott, May 9, 1861, McClellan Papers, New-York Historical Society; E. D. Townsend to

GBM, Apr. 30, May 15, 1861, *OR*, LI, Part 1, pp. 342–43, 379–80; Dept. of the Ohio, G.O. 7, 8, May 14 — G.O. 9, May 15, 1861, *OR*, LI, Part 1, pp. 377, 379; GBM to Lincoln, June 1, 1861, RG 107 (M-492:10), NA.

10. John Russell Young, *Around the World with General Grant* (New York: American News Co., 1879), I, pp. 214–15; *McClellan's Own Story*, p. 47. In a contemporary letter Grant implied that his calls at GBM's headquarters were on June 11 and 12. GBM only left Cincinnati on an inspection tour the evening of June 12: Grant to his wife, June 10, 1861, Ulysses S. Grant, *The Papers of Ulysses S. Grant*, ed. John Y. Simon (Carbondale: Southern Illinois University Press, 1967–), II, pp. 40–41 and n.

11. GBM, *Report on the Organization and Campaigns of the Army of the Potomac, To which Is Added an Account of the Campaign in Western Virginia* (New York, 1864), p. 8; GBM to Dennison, May 13, 1861, Papers (C-3:62).

12. GBM teleg. to Simon Cameron, May 20, 1861, Papers (C-3:62); Scott to GBM, May 21, 1861, *OR*, LI, Part 1, pp. 386–87; William Dennison, Richard Yates, and O. P. Morton to Scott, May 24, 1861, *OR*, LII, Part 1, pp. 146–47; GBM teleg. to Dennison, May 25, 1861, Papers (A-12:5).

13. GBM to Scott (with Scott's annotations), Apr. 27, 1861, RG 94 (M-619:41), NA; Scott to GBM, May 3, 21, 1861, *OR*, LI, Part 1, pp. 369–70, 386–87; GBM to Scott, May 7, 1861, Papers (C-3:62). GBM mentioned railroad logistical support for the Nashville movement in a draft of his April 27 plan: Papers (A-11:5).

14. Lincoln to Orville H. Browning, Sept. 22, 1861, Abraham Lincoln, *The Collected Works of Abraham*

Lincoln, ed. Roy P. Basler, IV, p. 532; Beriah Magoffin proclamation, May 20, 1861, in Frank Moore, ed., *The Rebellion Record: A Diary of American Events,* I, Documents, pp. 264–65; GBM to E. D. Townsend, May 10, 1861, *OR,* LI, Part 1, p. 375.

15. Allan Pinkerton, *The Spy of the Rebellion,* pp. 182–202; GBM to E. D. Townsend, May 4, 1861, *OR,* LI, Part 1, p. 371; William M. Dickson to Lincoln — GBM to Lincoln, June 10, 1861, Lincoln Papers, LC. Letters from GBM's Kentucky informants are in the Papers (A-12:5, A-13:6).

16. GBM to John Rodgers, May 19, 1861, Rare Book Collection, HL; GBM to E. D. Townsend, May 17, 1861, Papers (C-3:62).

17. Scott teleg. to Dennison, May 20, 1861, Papers (B-7:46); Scott teleg. to GBM, May 24, 1861, *OR,* II, p. 648. In an undated letter received May 30, John S. Carlisle wrote GBM that Gen. Scott confirmed to him that "you had full authority — that you will be sustained in taking the responsibility of doing all that is necessary" to protect Unionists in western Virginia: Papers (B-7:46).

18. GBM teleg. to Scott, [May 24], 1861, RG 107 (M-504:9), NA; GBM to E. D. Townsend, May 27, 1861, *OR,* II, pp. 44–45; GBM to Scott, June 4, 1861, Papers (C-3:62); *McClellan's Own Story,* draft, Papers (D-9:71); GBM proclamations (two), May 26, 1861, Papers (A-12:5); GBM to Lincoln, May 30, 1861, Lincoln Papers, LC; Russell, July 7, 1861, William Howard Russell, *My Diary North and South,* p. 194.

19. GBM teleg. to E. D. Townsend, June 3 — GBM to Scott, June 10, 1861, *OR,* II, pp. 64–65, 65–66; "Active Service; or, Campaigning in Western Virginia," *Continental Monthly,* I (Mar. 1862), p. 334;

William S. Rosecrans to GBM, June 5, 1861, Papers (A-13:6); *Appleton's American Annual Cyclopaedia,* 1861, p. 743.

20. GBM to Lincoln, May 30, 1861, Lincoln Papers, LC; GBM to Scott, June 5, 1861, Papers (C-3:62).

21. GBM to Scott, June 11, 1861, *OR,* II, p. 674; GBM teleg. to Scott, June 26, 1861, Lincoln Papers, LC; Thomas M. Key to GBM, June 7 — Samuel Gill to GBM, June 26, 1861, Papers (A-13:6, A-15:7); Simon B. Buckner to Magoffin, June 10, 1861, in Moore, *Rebellion Record,* II, Documents, p. 163; *Cincinnati Commercial,* June 23, 1861; GBM to Nathaniel Lyon, July 6 — William Nelson, Allan Pinkerton telegs. to GBM, June 26, 1861, Papers (A-18:8, A-23:11, A-15:7). Pinkerton's name appears throughout in citations rather than E. J. Allen, the nom de guerre he often used. GBM and Buckner met a second time, on June 13, at Cairo, Illinois, but added little if anything to their Cincinnati discussion: GBM to Scott, June 26, 1861, *OR,* LII, Part 1, pp. 182–83.

22. Anson Stager teleg. to Marcy, June 23 — GBM to his wife, June 21 — Mary Ellen McClellan to Elizabeth B. McClellan, June 28, 1861, Papers (A-23:11, C-7:63/D-10:72, B-41:61).

23. GBM to his wife, June 23 — GBM to Chase, June 26 — GBM to Army of the West, June 25, 1861, Papers (C-7:63, A-15:7, B-7:46); Cox in *Battles and Leaders,* I, p. 135; Sophia Peabody Hawthorne to Annie Adams Field, c. Mar. 18, 1862, Boston Public Library.

24. GBM to People of Western Virginia, June 23 — GBM to Dennison, July 6 — GBM to Jacob Beyers, July 14 — court-martial report, Co. C, 19th Ohio, July 3 — GBM to his wife, July 7, 1861, Papers (B-7:46, A-18:8, A-19:9, A-17:8, C-7:63/D-10:72).

25. GBM to E. D. Townsend, July 5, 6, 1861, Papers (A-17:8, A-18:8), Robert S. Garnett report, *OR*, II, p. 237.

26. GBM to his wife, July 3, 1861 — *McClellan's Own Story*, draft, Papers (C-7:63/D-10:72, D-9:71); Rosecrans to GBM, June 29, 1861, *OR*, II, p. 213; GBM to his wife, July 2, 1861, Papers (C-7:63); Thomas A. Morris to GBM, July 2 — GBM to Morris, July 3, 1861, Papers (B-7:46). GBM was unforgiving of Morris, who saw no further wartime service. "I more than once told the Presdt that he was unfit to be retained in command," he recalled: GBM to Henry B. Carrington, Nov. 30, 1862, Carrington Family Papers, Yale University Library.

27. GBM to E. D. Townsend, July 5, 1861, Papers (A-17:8); GBM to Townsend, July 14, 1861, *OR*, II, p. 205. Confederate strength is estimated in Jed Hotchkiss, *Confederate Military History*, III: *Virginia* (Atlanta: Confederate Publishing Co., 1899), p. 47. For the Federal table of organization, see: Dept. of the Ohio, G.O. 21, July 6, 1861, Papers (A-18:8). Returns of the period in the Papers suggest that Jacob Cox's figure of about 700 men per Union regiment is a reasonable estimate: Cox in *Battles and Leaders*, I, p. 130.

28. GBM to his wife, July 5, 1861, Papers (C-7:63); GBM teleg. to E. D. Townsend, July 10, 1861, Morris Library, Southern Illinois University at Carbondale; GBM teleg. to Townsend, July 6, 1861, Papers (C-9:63).

29. GBM described the Rich Mountain action in his report of July 14, 1861, *OR*, II, pp. 205–208; and in his 1864 *Report* (New York ed.), pp. 28–31. Rosecrans's account is in his report, *OR*, II, pp. 214–18; in a letter to Salmon P. Chase, Mar. 14, 1862, Chase Papers, LC; and

in his testimony in *Report of the Joint Committee on the Conduct of the War*, III (1865), pp. 1–7.

30. John Beatty, *The Citizen-Soldier; or, Memoirs of a Volunteer* (Cincinnati: Wilstach, Baldwin, 1879), p. 27; GBM to E. D. Townsend, July 14, 1861, *OR*, II, p. 206; GBM, *Report* (New York ed.), p. 30; *McClellan's Own Story*, draft, Papers (D-9:71); Rosecrans testimony, *Report of the Joint Committee*, III (1865), p. 6; GBM to Ezra A. Carman, Feb. 25, 1880, Civil War Collection, HL.

31. GBM telegs. to E. D. Townsend, July 14, 19, 1861, Papers (A-19:8, A-21:10); Milo S. Hascall teleg. to GBM, July 20, 1861, Papers (A-21:10); Cox to his wife, July 25, 1861, Cox Papers, Oberlin College Archives; GBM to his wife, July 21, 1861, Papers (C-7:63).

32. GBM to Army of the West, July 16 — GBM to his wife, July 21, 1861, Papers (B-8:47, C-7:63); GBM to E. D. Townsend — Seth Williams to William S. Rosecrans, July 12, 1861, Papers (A-19:9).

33. Anson Stager teleg. to GBM, July 15, 1861, Papers (A-20:9); Scott teleg. to GBM, July 13, 1861, *OR*, II, p. 204; Moore, *Rebellion Record*, II, Diary, p. 31; Zachariah Chandler to his wife, July 16, 1861, Chandler Papers, LC; *New York Tribune*, July 16, 1861; *Louisville Journal*, July 20, 1861; *New York Times*, July 20, 1861; *New York Herald*, July 15, 1861.

34. GBM to his wife, July 19 — GBM to Scott, July 18 — Marcy teleg. to GBM, July 20 — GBM teleg. to Marcy, c. July 21, 1861, Papers (C-7:63, A-21:10, C-7:63, A-23:11); Scott teleg. to GBM, July 18 — Lorenzo Thomas teleg. to GBM, July 22, 1861, *OR*, II, pp. 743, 753. Nothing on record indicates that it was Lincoln who called GBM to Washington, and Gen. Scott's later remark to Cameron — "if I did not

call for him, I heartily approved of the suggestion" — indicates that it was the secretary of war who took the initiative: Scott to Cameron, Oct. 4, 1861, *OR*, LI, Part 1, p. 491.

Chapter 5. Building an Army

1. *McClellan's Own Story*, draft, Papers (D-9:71); GBM to his wife, July 27, 30, Aug. 4, 1861, Papers (C-7:63/D-10:72); Camille Ferri Pisani, *Prince Napoleon in America, 1861: Letters from his Aide-de-Camp*, trans. Georges J. Joyaux (Bloomington: Indiana University Press, 1959), pp. 110–13.
2. GBM to Edwin M. Stanton, [Feb. 3], 1862, Lincoln Papers, LC; Henry J. Hunt to George Stoneman, July 29, 1861, *OR*, II, pp. 768–69; Nicolay and Hay, *Lincoln*, IV, pp. 352–54.
3. Div. of the Potomac, G.O. 2, July 30, 1861, *OR*, II, p. 769; GBM to his wife, Aug. 2, 1861, Papers (C-7:63/D-10:72); *New York Tribune*, Aug. 1, 1861; Charles B. Haydon diary, Aug. 9, 11, 24, 28, 1861 — Jonas D. Richardson to his family, Oct. 5, 1861, Michigan Historical Collections, Bentley Historical Library, University of Michigan; James W. Riggs to Montgomery Blair, Aug. 5, 1861, Salmon P. Chase Papers, LC.
4. Comte de Paris, *History of the Civil War in America*, I, p. 270; GBM to 79th N.Y. regiment, Aug. 14, 1861, in *McClellan's Own Story*, pp. 99-100; GBM to his wife, Aug. [14], 1861, Papers (C-7:63).
5. GBM to his wife, Aug. 2, 1861, Papers (C-7:63/D-10:72); GBM to Lincoln, Aug. 2, 1861, Lincoln Papers, LC.
6. For GBM's headquarters and military routine, see: GBM to his wife, Aug. 13, [14], 23, 31, [Sept.] 6, 1861, Papers (C-7:63/D-10:72); her teleg. to GBM, Sept. 4, 1861, RG 107 (M-504:9), NA; Comte de

Paris diary, Sept. 26, 1861, Fondation Saint-Louis; Salmon P. Chase, Jan. 6, 1862, Chase, *Inside Lincoln's Cabinet: The Civil War Diaries of Salmon P. Chase*, ed. David Donald, p. 57. GBM's balloon ascensions are noted in Moore, *Rebellion Record*, III, Diary, p. 38, and *OR*, Ser. 3, III, p. 260.
7. Army of the Potomac, G.O. 1, Aug. 20, 1861, *OR*, V, p. 575; *Washington Evening Star*, Aug. 5, 1861; *Philadelphia Inquirer*, Aug. 28, 1861; William Howard Russell, "Recollections of the Civil War," *North American Review*, 166 (June 1898), p. 745; Russell, Aug. 2, 1861, *My Diary*, p. 240.
8. GBM telegs. to div. commanders, Aug. 4, 1861, Papers (A-23:11); GBM teleg. to Irvin McDowell, Aug. 6, 1861, *OR*, V, p. 553; GBM to Scott (endorsed: copy delivered to Lincoln by Thomas M. Key), Aug. 8 — GBM to his wife, Aug. 8, 1861, Papers (A-24:11, C-7:63); *OR*, V, pp. 884-87; Edward B. McMurdy to Henry W. Halleck, Sept. 26, 1862, RG 94 (M-619:121), NA.
9. Scott to Cameron, Aug. 9, 1861, *OR*, XI, Part 3, pp. 3–4; GBM to his wife, Aug. 8, 1861, Papers (C-7:63); *OR*, II, pp. 718–23; *OR*, V, p. 932; Scott to Cameron, Oct. 4, 1861, *OR*, LI, Part I, pp. 491–92.
10. GBM to his wife, Aug. [10], 16, 19, 20, 25, 1861, Papers (C-7:63/D-10:72); GBM to Cameron, Sept. 8, 11, 1861, RG 94 (M-619:41), RG 107 (M-221:197), NA; GBM to Cameron, Sept. 13, 1861, Cameron Papers, LC. The arrest of the Maryland legislators was carried out primarily by Allan Pinkerton, and GBM wrote his wife that it "has no doubt taken them by surprise & defeated their calculations. ...": c. Sept. 18, 1861, Papers (C-7:63).
11. *McClellan's Own Story*, p. 39, and manuscript, Papers (D-9:71);

GBM to Barlow, Nov. 8, 1861, Barlow Papers, HL; GBM to Edwin M. Stanton, [Feb. 3], 1862, Lincoln Papers, LC; GBM to his wife, Aug. [10, Oct. 30, 31], 1861, Papers (C-7:63/D-10:72); Orville H. Browning, July 25, 1862, Browning, *The Diary of Orville Hickman Browning*, eds. Theodore C. Pease and James G. Randall, I, p. 563.

12. Edwin C. Fishel, "The Mythology of Civil War Intelligence," *Civil War History*, 10:4 (Dec. 1964), pp. 349–50; Prince de Joinville, *The Army of the Potomac*, p. 38; Pinkerton to GBM, Aug. 31, Oct. 28, Nov. 26, 1861, Papers (A-24:11, A-29:13, A-31:13); *OR*, V, pp. 932, 974; Pinkerton to Edwin M. Stanton, Mar. 18, 1862, *OR*, Ser. 2, II, pp. 1303–1305. Some two dozen of Pinkerton's reports for the fall months of 1861 are in the Papers (A-23:11–A-34:14).

13. Pinkerton to GBM, Oct. 4, Nov. 15, 1861, Apr. 1862, Papers (A-27:12, A-31:13, A-43:17). It is not known if the arithmetical errors in Pinkerton's reports were noticed.

14. *Harper's Weekly*, Aug. 24, 1861; GBM to Cameron, Sept. 13, 1861, Cameron Papers, LC; Pinkerton to GBM, Nov. 15, 1861, Papers (A-31:13); *OR*, Ser. 4, I, p. 822; William B. Franklin testimony, *Report of the Joint Committee*, I (1863), p. 127; Charles A. Dana to Cameron, Dec. 29, 1861, Cameron Papers, LC.

15. GBM to Lincoln, Aug. 20, 1861, Lincoln Papers, LC; James H. Wilson, *Under the Old Flag*, I, p. 123. Returns — July 27, 1861: *OR*, V, p. 11; Sept. 13, 1861: GBM to Cameron, Cameron Papers, LC; Oct. 15, Dec. 1, 1861, Jan. 1, 1862: *OR*, V, p. 12.

16. George B. Sanford, *Fighting Rebels and Redskins: Experiences in Army Life of Colonel George B. Sanford, 1861–1892* (Norman: University of Oklahoma Press,

1969), pp. 191–92; John Gibbon, *Personal Recollections of the Civil War*, pp. 78–79; GBM to his wife, Sept. [11], 1861, Papers (D-10:72); Meade to his wife, Nov. 21, 1861, George G. Meade, *The Life and Letters of George Gordon Meade*, I, p. 229; Charles E. Davis, *Three Years in the Army: The Story of the Thirteenth Massachusetts Volunteers* (Boston: Estes & Lauriat, 1894), pp. 156–57; Henry W. Bellows to his wife, Sept. 12, 1861, Bellows Papers, Massachusetts Historical Society; Edward D. Neill to his wife, Sept. 13, 1861, Neill Papers, Minnesota Historical Society; A. M. Stewart, *Camp, March and Battle-Field; or, Three Years and a Half with the Army of the Potomac*, p. 88.

17. Russell F. Weigley, *History of the United States Army*, pp. 241–42; Edward Hagerman, "The Professionalization of George B. McClellan and Early Civil War Field Command: An Institutional Perspective," *Civil War History*, 21:2 (June 1975), p. 118; Emory Upton, *The Military Policy of the United States*, p. 255; GBM, *Report on the Organization and Campaigns of the Army of the Potomac* (Washington, 1864), pp. 10–11; GBM, Instructions to General Officers, c. Aug. 4, 1861, Papers (A-16:7).

18. *Congressional Globe*, 37th Cong., 1st Sess., 1861, p. 113; Jen-Wha Lee, "The Organization and Administration of the Army of the Potomac Under General George B. McClellan," Ph.D. diss., University of Maryland, 1960, pp. 35–39; GBM to Cameron, Sept. 8 — GBM endorsement, Aug. 24, on John A. Andrew to GBM, Aug. 22, 1861, RG 94 (M-619:41, M-619:38), NA. Statistics cited by Emory Upton on the availability of regular officers do not reflect the realities of the situation in 1861: Upton, *Military Policy*, pp. 236–37.

19. *McClellan's Own Story*, pp. 115, 117–19; Starr, *Union Cavalry*, I, pp. 234–43; GBM, Instructions to General Officers, c. Aug. 4, 1861, Papers (A-16:7); Hampton S. Thomas, *Some Personal Reminiscences of Service in the Cavalry of the Army of the Potomac* (Philadelphia: L. R. Hammersley, 1889), p. 2.

20. GBM report (unissued), c. Nov. 15, 1861, Papers (A-32:14); *Congressional Globe*, 37th Cong., 2nd Sess., 1862, Part 1, p. 206; *OR*, Ser. 3, I, pp. 382–83; Army of the Potomac HQ journal, Sept. 20, 1861, Papers (A-23:11); *New York Tribune*, Sept. 27, Nov. 1, 16, 1861, cited in Fred A. Shannon, *The Organization and Administration of the Union Army, 1861–1865*, I, pp. 186–87.

21. *McClellan's Own Story*, p. 143; R. J. Amundson, "Sanford and Garibaldi," *Civil War History*, 14:1 (Mar. 1968), pp. 40–45; Comte de Paris diary, Sept. 26, 1861, Fondation Saint-Louis; Margaret Leech, *Reveille in Washington, 1860–1865*, p. 113.

22. John G. Barnard to GBM, Nov. 2, 1861, Papers (A-30:13); Barnard to Joseph G. Totten, Dec. 10, 1861, *OR*, V, p. 683; GBM to his wife, [Sept. 29], 1861, Papers (C-7:63/D-10:72).

23. *McClellan's Own Story*, pp. 33, 35, 149, and manuscript and draft, Papers (D-9:71); GBM to Marcy, Aug. 20, 1865 — GBM to his wife, c. Nov. 14, 1861 — GBM to William C. Prime, Dec. 24, 1865, Papers (A-92:36, C-7:63, B-25:54); E. D. Townsend to Jacob D. Cox, Jan. 25, 1887, Cox Papers, Oberlin College Archives; Aspinwall to GBM, Aug. 27, 1861, Papers (B-8:47); Welles, Sept. 8, 1862, *Diary*, I, p. 117

24. *New York Tribune*, Oct. 7, 1861; GBM to his wife, Oct. 6, 1861, Papers (C-7:63); Chandler to his wife,

Oct. 12 — Benjamin F. Wade to Chandler, Oct. 8, 1861, Chandler Papers, LC.

25. Louis M. Goldsborough to Gideon Welles, Oct. 17, 1861, *NOR*, VI, pp. 333–34; Pinkerton to GBM, c. Dec. 16, 1861, Papers (A-34:11); Thomas O. Selfridge to Gustavus V. Fox, Nov. 11, 1861, Fox, *Confidential Correspondence of Gustavus Vasa Fox*, eds. Robert M. Thompson and Richard Wainwright, I, pp. 397–400; Barnard to GBM, Dec. 6 — David D. Porter to GBM, Nov. 22, 24, 1861, Papers (A-32:14, B-9:47, A-31:13); GBM to Edwin M. Stanton, [Feb. 3], 1862, Lincoln Papers, LC.

26. GBM to Cameron, Sept. 30, 1861, Cameron Papers, LC; Fox, GBM testimony, *Report of the Joint Committee*, I (1863), pp. 240–41, 421–22; L. G. Young to his uncle, Nov. –, 1861, Robert N. Gourdin Papers, William R. Perkins Library, Duke University; Edward Bates, Sept. 30, 1861, Bates, *The Diary of Edward Bates: 1859–1866*, ed. Howard K. Beale, p. 194.

27. GBM to his wife, Oct. 19, 1861, Papers (C-7:63); A. V. Colburn teleg. to Charles P. Stone, Oct. 20, 1861, *OR*, V, p. 290; George A. Bruce, *The Twentieth Regiment of Massachusetts Volunteer Infantry, 1861–1865* (Boston: Houghton Mifflin, 1906), p. 55; *OR*, V, p. 308; GBM to div. commanders, Oct. 24, 1861, RG 107 (M-504:66), NA; GBM to his wife, Oct. 25, 1861, Papers (C-7:63); GBM, Stone testimony, *Report of the Joint Committee*, II (1863), pp. 506, 488–89; Alpheus S. Williams to his family, Nov. 5, 1861, Williams, *From the Cannon's Mouth: The Civil War Letters of General Alpheus S. Williams*, ed. Milo M. Quaife, p. 27.

28. Welles, Feb. 25, 1863, *Diary*, I, pp. 241–42; GBM to his wife, Sept. 27, 1861, Papers (D-10:72); Scott to

Cameron, Oct. 4, 1861, *OR*, LI, Part 1, p. 492; Thurlow Weed to William H. Seward, Oct. 27, 1861, Lincoln Papers, LC; Comte de Paris diary, Nov. 2, 1861, Fondation Saint-Louis; Bates, Oct. 18, 1861, *Diary*, pp. 196-97; GBM to his wife, Oct. 19, 1861, Papers (C-7:63).

29. Chandler to his wife, Oct. 27, 1861, Chandler Papers, LC; Hay, Oct. 26, 1861, John Hay, *Lincoln and the Civil War in the Diaries and Letters of John Hay*, ed. Tyler Dennett, p. 31; GBM to his wife, Oct. 26, [31], 1861, Papers (C-7:63/ D-10:72); GBM to Cameron, [Oct. 31, 1861], Papers (A-29:13); Comte de Paris diary, Nov. 2, 1861, Fondation Saint-Louis.

Chapter 6. General of All the Armies

1. Lincoln to GBM, Nov. 1, 1861, Papers (A-30:13); Army HQ, G.O. 19, Nov. 1, 1861, Simon Gratz Autograph Collection, Historical Society of Pennsylvania; GBM to his wife, Nov. 7, 1861, Papers (C-7:63); Hay, Nov. –, 1861, *Diaries and Letters*, pp. 32-33.

2. Unidentified clipping, Papers (D-29:81); Stewart, *Camp, March and Battle-Field*, p. 55; GBM to his wife, [Nov. 2], 1861, Papers (C-7:63); *New York Tribune*, Nov. 4, 1861; *New York Times*, Nov. 6, 1861.

3. Weigley, *History of the U.S. Army*, pp. 192-93; GBM to his wife, Nov. 2, 1861 — GBM to Ulysses S. Grant, Dec. 26, 1866 — Cameron to GBM, Sept. 7, 1861, Papers (C-7:63, A-92:36, A-26:12).

4. Mahan to GBM, Aug. 3, 1861, Papers (B-8:47); Russell F. Weigley, *Quartermaster General of the Union Army: A Biography of M. C. Meigs*, pp. 217-18; GBM to Totten, Mar. 28, 1862, Pierpont Morgan Library; GBM teleg. to John C. Frémont, Nov. 1, 1861, McClellan Papers, New-York Historical Society.

5. GBM to Barlow, Nov. 8 — Barlow to GBM, Nov. 11, 1861, Barlow Papers, HL; Barlow to Edwards Pierrepont, Jan. 28, 1862, Edwin M. Stanton Papers, LC.

6. Zachariah Chandler to his wife, Oct. 27, 1861, Chandler Papers, LC; GBM to Cameron, [Oct. 31, 1861], Papers (A-29:13); GBM to Halleck, Nov. 11 — GBM to Don Carlos Buell, Nov. 12, 1861, Papers (D-7:69); *McClellan's Own Story*, manuscript, Papers (D-9:71); Malcolm Ives to James Gordon Bennett, Jan.15, 1862, Bennett Papers, LC; GBM to Edwin M. Stanton, Feb. 20, 1862, *OR*, Ser. 3, I, pp. 896-97.

7. Pinkerton to GBM, Oct. 28, 1861 — GBM memorandum, [Mar. 2, 1862], Papers (A-29:13, A-88:35); Lincoln to GBM, c. Dec. 1 — GBM to Lincoln, Dec. 10, 1861, Lincoln Papers, LC.

8. Aspinwall to GBM, Aug. 27, 1861 — Barnard to GBM, Dec. 6, 1861 — Stewart Van Vliet to Seth Williams, Jan. 3, 1862, Papers (B-8:47, A-32:14, B-9:47); Goldsborough testimony, *Report of the Joint Committee*, I (1863), p. 631; topographical study, c. Jan. 1862, Papers (A-34:14); Chase memorandum, Sept. 2 — Chase to John Young, Oct. 27, 1862, Schuckers, *Chase*, pp. 445, 458; Chase, July 27, 1862, *Diaries*, p. 102.

9. GBM to his wife, c. Oct. 11, [Oct. 31], 1861, Papers (C-7:63/D-10:72); Fanny Seward diary, Mar. 30, 1862, William Henry Seward Papers, Rush Rhees Library, University of Rochester; George Bancroft to his wife, Dec. 16, 1861, M. A. DeWolfe Howe, *The Life and Letters of George Bancroft* (New York: Scribner's, 1908), II, p. 47.

10. *McClellan's Own Story*, p. 152; GBM to his wife, c. Oct. 11, [Oct. 31], Nov. 17, 1861, Papers (C-7:63/ D-10:72); Samuel P. Heintzelman

diary, Nov. 11, 1861, LC; Hay, Nov. 13, 1861, *Diaries and Letters*, pp. 34–35; Russell, Oct. 9, 1861, *My Diary*, p. 205; Virginia Fox diary, Nov. 14, 1861, Blair Family Papers, LC. It has been suggested, regarding his snub of Lincoln, that GBM was the worse for drink after the wedding he attended, yet nothing on record indicates he ever drank to excess; in any event, a simple message to the president that he was "indisposed" would have covered such a situation. It is claimed, too, that John Hay's account is suspect in view of the bias against GBM he later admitted to when writing his Lincoln biography. Hay's diary, however, reveals no evidence of such bias at this time. For these assertions, see: J. G. Randall, *Lincoln the President* (New York: Dodd, Mead, 1956), II, pp. 68, 72.

11. GBM to his wife, Oct. 16, Nov. 17, 1861, Papers (D-10:72, C-7:63); GBM to Lincoln, Feb. 22, 1862, Lincoln Papers, LC; *McClellan's Own Story*, draft, Papers (D-9:71); Hay, Oct. 10, 1861, *Diaries and Letters*, p. 27; GBM to his wife, Oct. [29, 1862] — Alexander K. McClure to Mary Ellen McClellan, Jan. 13, 1892, Papers (C-7:63, B-39:60).

12. Harrison Thompson to GBM, Dec. 9, 1861, Papers (B-9:47); Jonas D. Richardson to his family, Nov. 10, 1861, Michigan Historical Collections, Bentley Historical Library, University of Michigan; Moore, *Rebellion Record*, III, Diary, p. 85; *Harper's Weekly*, Dec. 7, 1861; GBM to his wife, [Nov. 20, 1861], Papers (C-7:63).

13. GBM to Barlow, Nov. 8, 1861, Barlow Papers, HL; GBM to Elizabeth B. McClellan, Nov. 9, 1861 — GBM teleg. to Marcy, Dec. 4, 1861, Papers (B-9:47, A-23:14); Meade to his wife, Feb. 6, 1862, *Life and Letters*, I, p. 244; E. O. C. Ord to his wife, Feb. 7, 1862, Ord Papers, Stanford University Libraries; GBM to Mary M. Marcy, [Jan. 23, 1862] — Mary Ellen McClellan to Elizabeth B. McClellan, c. Dec. 23, 1861, Papers (B-40:60, B-41:61).

14. Joseph Casey to David Davis, Dec. 11, 1861, Davis Papers, Illinois State Historical Library; *New York Tribune*, Dec. 18, 1861; *Journal of Commerce*, Jan. 14, 1862; *New York Herald*, Dec. 11, 1861; Barlow to Stanton, Dec. 11, 1861, Barlow Papers, HL.

15. *Report of the Joint Committee*, I (1863), p. 70; John A. Logan to John A. McClernand, Dec. 27, 1861, McClernand Papers, Illinois State Historical Library; William W. Harding teleg. to Thomas A. Scott, Jan. 2, 1862, RG 107 (M-473:98), NA; *New York Tribune*, Dec. 27, 1861; *New York Express*, Dec. 30, 1861; Meade to his wife, Jan. 5, 1862, *Life and Letters*, I, p. 242; GBM to Don Carlos Buell, Jan. 6, 1862, *OR*, VII, p. 531.

16. Heintzelman diary, Dec. 16, 1861, LC. For the generals' testimony, see: *Report of the Joint Committee*, I (1863), pp. 113–235 *passim*; Wade's remarks are on pp. 130, 140, 155.

17. Hans L. Trefousse, *The Radical Republicans: Lincoln's Vanguard for Racial Justice*, p. 184; Lincoln telegs. to Buell and Halleck, Dec. 31, 1861, *Works*, V, p. 84; Buell and Halleck telegs. to Lincoln, Jan. 1, 1862, *OR*, VII, p. 526; Chase, Jan. 6, 1862, *Diaries*, pp. 56, 57–58; Lincoln to GBM, Jan. 9, 1862, *Works*, V, p. 94.

18. Lincoln to Buell and Halleck, Jan. 13, 1862, *Works*, V, pp. 98–99; GBM to Lincoln, Dec. 10, 1861, Lincoln Papers, LC.

19. Buell teleg. to Lincoln, Jan. 5 — Lincoln to Cameron, Jan. 10, 1862, *OR*, VII, pp. 530–31, 533; Mont-

gomery C. Meigs, "General M. C. Meigs on the Conduct of the Civil War," *American Historical Review*, 26:2 (Jan. 1921), p. 292.

20. "Memorandum of General McDowell," in Henry J. Raymond, *The Life and Public Services of Abraham Lincoln* (New York: Derby and Miller, 1865), pp. 272–77; Franklin testimony, *Report of the Joint Committee*, I (1863), p. 122; Chase, Jan. 11, 1862, *Diaries*, pp. 59–60; *McClellan's Own Story*, pp. 155–56, and draft, Papers (D-9:71); GBM teleg. to Mrs. Nathan B. Rossel, Jan. 7, 1862, RG 107 (M-504:66), NA; GBM to Buell, Jan. 13, 1862, *OR*, VII, p. 547; Meigs, "General Meigs on the Conduct of the Civil War," pp. 292–93; Montgomery C. Meigs diary, Jan 10, 13, 1862, Meigs Papers, LC.

21. John G. Barnard, *The Peninsula Campaign and Its Antecedents*, p. 21; Jacob D. Cox, *Military Reminiscences of the Civil War*, I, p. 367; Henry W. Raymond, ed., "Excerpts from the Journal of Henry J. Raymond," *Scribner's Monthly*, 19:3 (Jan. 1880), p. 423; Franklin in A. K. McClure, ed., *The Annals of the War*, p. 79; GBM to Lincoln, [Jan. 14, 1862], Lincoln Papers, LC; GBM to his wife, Aug. 22, 1862, Papers (C-7:63).

22. *McClellan's Own Story*, pp. 153, 161; GBM in *Battles and Leaders*, II, p. 163; GBM to Barlow, Jan. 18, 1862, Barlow Papers, HL.

23. Ives to Bennett, Jan. 15, 27 — Ives to Frederic Hudson, Jan. 16, 1862, Bennett Papers, LC; GBM to Marcy, [Jan. 29, 1862], Papers (A-106:42); GBM to Barlow, Nov. 8, 1861, Barlow Papers, HL; Detroit Post and Tribune, *Zachariah Chandler: An Outline of His Life and Public Services* (Detroit: Post and Tribune Co., 1880), pp. 225–26. In many respects the eccentric Ives is an unreliable witness. In this instance, however, what he sent Bennett was undeniably military secrets, and from the Jan. 29 letter to Marcy it is clear that GBM leaked those secrets to Bennett through him.

24. Richard B. Irwin in *Battles and Leaders*, II, pp. 132–33; *Report of the Joint Committee*, I (1863), pp. 78–79, II (1863), pp. 295–97, 18, 489, 510; Stanton to GBM, Jan. 28, 1862, *OR*, V, p. 341; Stone teleg. to James A. Hardie, Jan. 7, 1862, Papers (A-35:15); Hardie teleg. to Stone, Jan. 8, 1862, *OR*, LI, Part 1, p. 517; GBM to Stone, Dec. 5, 1862, Papers (A-88:35); Bates, Feb. 3, 1862, *Diary*, p. 229.

25. Pinkerton to GBM, Feb. 6 — GBM to Andrew Porter, Feb. 8 — George Gibbs to GBM, c. Jan. 20, 1862, Papers (A-39:16, A-40:16, A-34:14).

Chapter 7. The Grand Campaign

1. GBM to Buell, Jan. 13, 1862, *OR*, VII, p. 547; Stanton to Dana, Jan. 24, 1862, Charles A. Dana, *Recollections of the Civil War: With the Leaders at Washington and in the Field in the Sixties* (New York: D. Appleton, 1898), p. 5; GBM to Marcy, [Jan. 29, 1862], Papers (A-106:42); GBM, *Report*, p. 42; Lincoln Occoquan memorandum, undated, *Works*, V, p. 119; *McClellan's Own Story*, manuscript, Papers (D-9:71). Here and hereafter, references to GBM's *Report* are to the 1864 Washington edition.

2. GBM to Stanton, [Jan. 26, 1862] — Scott to Stanton, Feb. 2, 1862, Stanton Papers, LC; GBM, "The Peninsula Campaign" manuscript (*Battles and Leaders*, II), Papers (A-109:43); Barlow to GBM, Feb. 6, 1862, Barlow Papers, HL; GBM teleg. to Scott, Feb. 20, 1862, RG 107 (M-473:12), NA; Buell teleg. to GBM, Feb. 10, 1862,

OR, LII, Part I, p. 208; Stanton to Scott, Feb. 21, 1862, Stanton Papers; Heintzelman diary, Feb. 21, 1862, LC; Welles, *Diary*, III, p. 674.

3. President's General War Order No. 1, Jan. 27 — President's Special Order No. 1, Jan. 31, 1862, Lincoln, *Works*, V, pp. 111–12, 115; GBM to Stanton, [Feb. 3], 1862, Lincoln Papers, LC; Lyman Trumbull to Yates, Feb. 6, 1862, Chicago Historical Society; GBM to Halleck, Jan. 29, 1862, *OR*, VII, p. 931; John Tucker to Stanton, Apr. 5, 1862, *OR*, V, p. 46.

4. GBM telegs. to Buell, Halleck, Jan. 29, 1862, RG 107 (M-473:10), NA; Scott to Stanton, Feb. 14, 1862, Stanton Papers, LC; GBM teleg. to Halleck, Feb. 15, 1862 — GBM to Stanton, [Feb. 16, 1862], RG 107 (M-473:11, M-473:96), NA; GBM to Halleck, Mar. 3, 1862, James S. Schoff Collection, William L. Clements Library, University of Michigan.

5. *New York Times*, Feb. 16, 1862; *Journal of Commerce*, Feb. 18, 1862; Robert Henry Newell, *The Orpheus C. Kerr Papers: First Series* (New York: Blakeman and Mason, 1862), p. 205; Chase memorandum, Sept. 2, 1862, Schuckers, *Chase*, p. 446; Richard Smith to Joseph H. Barrett, Feb. 9, 1862, University of Chicago Library; *New York Tribune*, Feb. 22, 1862; *Journal of Commerce*, Feb. 27, 1862; Barlow to GBM, June 17, 1862, Papers (A-65:26); *New York Express*, Feb. 28, 1862; Gibbs to GBM, Mar. 13 — GBM to Edmund C. Stedman, Mar. 17, 1862, Papers (B-10:48).

6. *Report of the Joint Committee*, I (1863), p. 85; Marsena R. Patrick, Feb. 27, Mar. 6, 1862, Patrick, *Inside Lincoln's Army: The Diary of Marsena Rudolph Patrick*, ed. David S. Sparks, pp. 45, 48; Bar-

nard to GBM, Dec. 6, 1861, Barnard, *Peninsula Campaign*, pp. 54–55; GBM, *Report*, pp. 50, 53.

7. Gilbert Thompson diary, Feb. 27, 1862, Thompson Papers, LC; GBM telegs. to Stanton, Feb. 26, 27, 1862, RG 107 (M-473:12, M-473:98), NA; GBM to War Dept., c. Mar. 1, 1862, Papers (A-43:17); John G. Nicolay notes, Feb. 27, 1862, Helen Nicolay, *Lincoln's Secretary: A Biography of John G. Nicolay*, pp. 42–44; Charles Sumner to John A. Andrew, Mar. 2, 1862, Andrew Papers, Massachusetts Historical Society; Horace White to Joseph Medill, Mar. 3, 1862, Charles H. Ray Papers, HL.

8. GBM memorandums, [Mar. 1, 2, 1862] — John G. Barnard to GBM, Mar. 4, 1862, Papers (A-88:35, A-43:17); Heintzelman diary, Mar. 4, 1862, LC; GBM to Halleck, Mar. 3, 1862, James S. Schoff Collection, William L. Clements Library, University of Michigan; Meade to his wife, Mar. 18, 1862, *Life and Letters*, I, p. 253; Mary Ellen McClellan to Elizabeth B. McClellan, c. Mar. 12, 1862, Papers (B-24:53).

9. *McClellan's Own Story*, pp. 195–96, and drafts, Papers (D-9:71, D-10:72); Stanton notes, Mar. 8, 1862, Stanton Papers, LC; Henry M. Naglee to William D. Kelley, Sept. 27, 1864, in *New York World*, Oct. 1, 1864; Barnard to E. D. Townsend, Oct. 3, 1864, Lincoln Papers, LC; Barnard, *Peninsula Campaign*, p. 52; Heintzelman diary, Mar. 8, 1862, LC; McDowell testimony, *Report of the Joint Committee*, I (1863), p. 260; Hay, *Diaries and Letters*, p. 36; McDowell speech, San Francisco, Oct. 21, 1864, in *New York Herald*, Dec. 4, 1864.

10. President's General War Orders Nos. 2 and 3, Mar. 8, 1862, Lincoln, *Works*, V, pp. 149–50, 151; GBM

to Halleck, Mar. 3, 1862, James S. Schoff Collection, William L. Clements Library, University of Michigan; Heintzelman diary, Mar. 8, 1862, LC; Lincoln to GBM, May 9, 1862, *Works*, V, pp. 208–209; GBM to John A. Dix, Jan. 14, 1862, Dix Papers, Rare Book and Manuscript Library, Columbia University. GBM sketched out a six-corps organization, probably in Jan. 1862, under Gens. Sumner, McDowell, Heintzelman, Fitz John Porter, Franklin, and Andrew Porter, but apparently did not pursue the matter: Papers (A-50:20).

11. GBM to Buell, Dec. 5, 1861, Buell Papers, Woodson Research Center, Rice University Library; GBM to Stanton, Feb. 5, 1862, Cincinnati Historical Society; GBM to John W. Garrett, Mar. 7, 1862, *OR*, LI, Part 1, p. 548; topographical study, c. Jan. 1862, Papers (A-34:14); Barnard testimony, *Report of the Joint Committee*, I (1863), p. 393. The Duc de Chartres and the Comte de Paris summarized the Pinkerton reports but made no interpretations.

12. Nicolay notes, Mar. 9, 1862, Helen Nicolay, *Lincoln's Secretary*, pp. 136–38; GBM teleg. to Dix, Mar. 9, 1862, RG 107 (M-473:50), NA; GBM to Stanton, Mar. 9, 1862, McClellan Papers, New-York Historical Society; Nathaniel P. Banks teleg. to Marcy, Mar. 8 — Joseph Hooker teleg. to Seth Williams, Mar. 9 — Leavitt Hunt teleg. to Heintzelman, Mar. 9, 1862, Papers (A-44:18); GBM teleg. to Lincoln and Stanton, Mar. 9, 1862, Papers (A-50:20).

13. Army of the Potomac return, Mar. 2, 1862, Papers (A-43:17); Rufus R. Dawes diary, Mar. 12, 1862, Dawes, *Service with the Sixth Wisconsin Volunteers*, p. 36; *New York Tribune*, Mar. 15, 1862;

Joinville, *Army of the Potomac*, p. 24.

14. Comte de Paris diary, Feb. 21, 1862, Fondation Saint-Louis; Pinkerton to GBM, Mar. 8, 1862, *OR*, V, p. 736; *OR*, V, pp. 53, 1086; GBM to Barlow, Mar. 16, 1862, Barlow Papers, HL; GBM teleg. to Stanton, Mar. 11, 1862, RG 107 (M-504:66), NA; Pinkerton to GBM, Jan. 27, 1862, Papers (A-38:16); *St. Louis Republican*, Mar. 25, 1862; George Templeton Strong, Mar. 16, 1862, Strong, *The Diary of George Templeton Strong: The Civil War, 1860–1865*, eds. Allan Nevins and Milton H. Thomas, p. 213; *New York Tribune*, Mar. 15, 1862; GBM to Stanton, Mar. 14, [Feb. 3], 1862, Lincoln Papers, LC.

15. President's Special War Order No. 3, Mar. 11, 1862, Lincoln, *Works*, V, p. 155; A. K. McClure, *Abraham Lincoln and Men of War-Times*, pp. 204–205; GBM to his wife, July 20 — Dennison teleg. to GBM, Mar 14 — Marcy teleg. to GBM, Mar. 11 — GBM to Edmund C. Stedman, Mar. 17, 1862, Papers (C-7:63, A-46:18, B-10:47, B-10:48); GBM teleg. to Marcy, Mar. 11, 1862, RG 107 (M-504:66), NA; GBM to his wife, Mar. 11 — Marcy teleg. to GBM, Mar. 12, 1862, Papers (C-7:63, A-45:18); GBM in *Battles and Leaders*, II, p. 168; GBM to Lincoln, Mar. 12, 1862, Lincoln Papers, LC.

16. *McClellan's Own Story*, p. 225; Anson Stager to Jeptha H. Wade, Mar. 20, 1862, Western Reserve Historical Society; GBM to Barlow, Mar. 16, 1862, Barlow Papers, HL.

17. GBM teleg. to Stanton, Mar. 13, 1862, Papers (A-46:18); Stanton teleg. to GBM, Mar. 13, 1862, *OR*, V, p. 56; GBM to Army of the Potomac, Mar. 14, 1862, Papers (A-46:18); William W. Folwell diary, Mar. 14, 1862, Folwell Papers,

Minnesota Historical Society;
GBM to Barlow, Mar. 16, 1862,
Barlow Papers, HL.

Chapter 8. On the Peninsula

1. Tucker to Stanton, Apr. 5, 1862,
   OR, V, p. 46; Joinville, *Army of
   the Potomac*, p. 34; Barnard, *Peninsula Campaign*, p. 74. The Apr.
   13 return indicates that Tucker's
   figure for troops was somewhat too
   high: *OR*, XI, Part 3, p. 97.
2. Nathaniel Hawthorne to his
   daughter, Mar. 16, 1862, Julian
   Hawthorne, *Hawthorne and His
   Wife* (Boston: Houghton Mifflin,
   1889), II, p. 310; Samuel Ward
   to Barlow, Mar. 16, 18, 22, 1862,
   Barlow Papers, HL; Hitchcock,
   Mar. 15, 1862, *Diary*, p. 439;
   Browning, Apr. 2, 1862, *Diary*, I,
   pp. 537–39; Benjamin Stark to
   Barlow, Mar. 20, 1862, Barlow
   Papers.
3. President's General War Order No.
   3, Mar. 8, 1862, Lincoln, *Works*, V,
   p. 151; council of war report, Mar.
   13 — Seth Williams to Banks, Mar.
   16, 1862, *OR*, XI, Part 3, p. 58, V,
   p. 56; Marcy teleg. to GBM, Mar.
   25 — GBM to Banks, Apr. 1, 1862,
   Papers (A-48:19, A-50:20).
4. Lincoln to GBM, Mar. 31, 1862,
   Works, V, pp. 175–76; GBM to
   Lincoln, Mar. 31 — GBM to Lorenzo Thomas, Apr. 1, 1862, Lincoln Papers, LC; James S.
   Wadsworth to Stanton, Apr. 2,
   1862, *OR*, XI, Part 3, pp. 60–61;
   Sumner to John A. Andrew, May
   28, 1862, Andrew Papers, Massachusetts Historical Society.
5. *McClellan's Own Story*, p. 241;
   GBM to Banks — GBM to his wife,
   Apr. 1, 1862, Papers (A-50:20, C-
   7:63).
6. Hitchcock and Lorenzo Thomas to
   Stanton, Apr. 2, 1862, *OR*, XI, Part
   3, pp. 61–62; War Board minutes,
   Mar. 27, 1862, Stanton Papers, LC;
   Lincoln to GBM, Apr. 9, 1862,
   Works, V, p. 184; Stanton to

Heman Dyer, May 18, 1862, *OR*,
XIX, Part 2, p. 726; G. W. Smith,
Confederate War Papers (New
York: Atlantic Publishing, 1884),
p. 41; Joseph E. Johnston to Rob-
ert E. Lee, Apr. 30, 1862, *OR*, XI,
Part 3, p. 477.

7. GBM teleg. to his wife, Apr. 2, 1862,
   RG 107 (M-504:66), NA; John E.
   Wool teleg. to Stanton, Apr. 4, 1862,
   OR, XI, Part 3, p. 66; GBM to his
   wife, Apr. 3, 1862, Papers (C-7:63).
8. GBM teleg. to Gustavus V. Fox,
   Mar. 12, 1862, Lincoln Papers, LC;
   John E. Wool teleg. to Stanton —
   Gideon Welles to Stanton, Mar. 13,
   1862, *NOR*, VII, pp. 102, 103; GBM
   to Stanton, Mar. 19, 1862, Papers
   (D-7:69); Fox, Goldsborough testimony, *Report of the Joint Committee*, I (1863), pp. 630, 631–32;
   McClellan's Own Story, manuscript — John G. Barnard to GBM,
   Mar. 20, 28 — Marcy to GBM, Mar.
   22, 1862, Papers (D-9:71, A-47:19,
   A-49:19, A-48:19); GBM to Totten, Mar. 28, 1862, Pierpont Morgan Library; GBM teleg. to
   Stanton, Apr. 3, 1862, Papers (C-
   10:63); GBM to Goldsborough,
   Apr. 3, 1862, RG 45 (M-625:85),
   NA.
9. Porter report, *OR*, XI, Part 1, p.
   286; GBM to Winfield Scott, Apr.
   11, 1862, Papers (A-51:20); Pinkerton to GBM, Mar. 29 — Seth
   Williams to Stewart Van Vliet,
   Apr. 5, 1862, *OR*, XI, Part 1, pp.
   266–68, Part 3, pp. 71–72; GBM
   to Goldsborough, Apr. 5, 1862, RG
   45 (M-625:85), NA. The order
   calling for the siege train bears no
   time of sending, but has the date-
   line Big Bethel, and by 1:00 P.M.
   on Apr. 5 headquarters had been
   shifted forward from Big Bethel
   to a point near Yorktown: Yorktown siege journal, *OR*, XI, Part
   1, p. 321; Arthur McClellan diary,
   Apr. 5, 1862, Papers (D-2:66).
10. John B. Magruder report, *OR*, XI,
    Part 1, p. 405; Edmund D. Pat-

terson, Apr. 5, 1862, Patterson, *Yankee Rebel: The Civil War Journal of Edmund DeWitt Patterson*, ed. John G. Barrett (Chapel Hill: University of North Carolina Press, 1966), p. 17; Heintzelman diary, Apr. 5, 1862, LC; Barnard, *Peninsula Campaign*, p. 74.

11. Lorenzo Thomas to GBM, Apr. 4, 1862, *OR*, XI, Part 3, p. 66; GBM teleg. to Lincoln, Apr. 5, 1862, Lincoln Papers, LC; GBM to his wife, Apr. 6, 1862, Papers (C-7:63/D-10:72).

12. GBM, *Report*, p. 77; GBM to Barlow, July 15, 30, 1862, Barlow Papers, HL; Marcy to McDowell, Apr. 1 — GBM to McDowell, Apr. 4, 1862, *OR*, LI, Part 1, p. 565, XI, Part 3, p. 68; GBM to Stanton, c. Apr. 27, 1862, Papers (A-88:35); Barton S. Alexander report, *OR*, XI, Part 1, p. 134; GBM teleg. to Stanton, Apr. 11 — GBM to his wife, Apr. 18 — GBM to Winfield Scott, Apr. 11, 1862, Papers (A-51:20, C-7:63/D-10:72, A-51:20).

13. GBM to his wife, Apr. 11 — Franklin to GBM, Apr. 7, 1862, Papers (C-7:63/D-10:72, A-50:20); *McClellan's Own Story*, pp. 150–51, and notes and manuscript, Papers (D-9:71).

14. George H. Bangs intelligence report, [Apr. 7, 1862] — GBM teleg. to Stanton, Apr. 7, 1862, Papers (A-107:42, A-50:20); James Russell Lowell, "General McClellan's Report," *The North American Review*, 203 (Apr. 1864), p. 558.

15. Lincoln to GBM, Apr. 6 (teleg.), 9, 1862, *Works*, V, pp. 182, 184–85; Blair to GBM, Apr. 9 — GBM to his wife, Apr. 8, 1862, Papers (A-50:20, C-7:63); Pinkerton to GBM, May 3, 1862, *OR*, XI, Part 1, p. 268. On the size of the Army of the Potomac, see: return of Mar. 31, 1862, *OR*, XI, Part 3, p. 53; Stanton memorandum, Mar. 30, 1862, Stanton Papers, LC; GBM teleg. to Lincoln, Apr. 7, 1862 (annotations on retained copy), Papers (A-50:20). Miscalculations in the assignment of cavalry units account for some of the difference, but the largest part of it resulted from the counting methods.

16. Magruder to George W. Randolph, Apr. 11, 1862, *OR*, XI, Part 3, p. 436; Benjamin C. Stevens to his parents, Apr. 19, 1862, Stevens Papers, William R. Perkins Library, Duke University; GBM to his wife, Apr. 19, 1862, Papers (C-7:63).

17. Johnston to Lee, Apr. 22, 1862, *OR*, XI, Part 3, p. 456; GBM to Lincoln, Apr. 20, 1862, Lincoln Papers, LC.

18. Hay to Nicolay, Apr. 9, 1862, Hay, *Diaries and Letters*, pp. 40–41; Sidney Deming telegs. to Associated Press: Apr. 9, 1862, Lincoln Papers, LC, Apr. 10, 1862, RG 107 (M-473:99), NA; Ward to Barlow, May 3, 1862, Barlow Papers, HL; Porter to Manton Marble, Apr. 26, 1862, Marble Papers, LC; Jonas D. Richardson to his family, May 4, 1862, Michigan Historical Collections, Bentley Historical Library, University of Michigan.

19. GBM to his wife, May 3, 1862, Papers (C-7:63); William F. Barry report, *OR*, XI, Part 1, p. 348.

20. Comte de Paris diary, May 12, 1862, Fondation Saint-Louis; GBM telegs. to Stanton, May 4, 1862 (two), Papers (A-55:22); GBM to his wife, [May 8, 1862], Papers (C-7:63); GBM to Burnside, May 21, 1862, *OR*, IX, p. 392; GBM teleg. to Winfield Scott — GBM teleg. to his wife, May 4, 1862, Papers (A-55:20, C-13:64).

21. *OR*, XI, Part 3, p. 484; GBM teleg. to Stanton, May 5 — GBM to his wife, May 6, 1862, Papers (A-56:22, C-7:63); GBM telegs. to Stanton, May 5, 8, 1862, Stanton Papers, LC; GBM to his wife, [May 8, 1862] — Franklin to GBM, May 7, 1862, Papers (C-7:63, A-56:22).

22. GBM teleg. to Stanton, May 10, 1862, Papers (A-57:22); Goldsborough testimony, *Report of the Joint Committee*, I (1863), p. 633; W. Smith to Goldsborough, May 20, 1862, *NOR*, VII, p. 404; GBM teleg. to Lincoln, May 21, 1862, Papers (A-58:23); Goldsborough to his wife, June 13, 1862, Goldsborough Papers, William R. Perkins Library, Duke University.

23. GBM to Burnside, May 21, 1862, *OR*, IX, p. 392; Chase to Horace Greeley, May 21, 1862, Chase Papers, LC; GBM teleg. to Stanton, May 7, 1862, *OR*, XI, Part 3, pp. 148–49; Adams S. Hill to Sydney H. Gay, July 8, 1862, Gay Papers, Rare Book and Manuscript Library, Columbia University.

24. Barlow to GBM, May 10, 1862, Barlow Papers, HL; GBM to his wife, May 10, 15, 22, 1862, Papers (C-7:63/D-10:72); Moore, *Rebellion Record*, V, Diary, p. 6; Lincoln teleg. to GBM, May 21, 1862, *Works*, V, p. 227; GBM teleg. to Lincoln, May 22, 1862, RG 107 (M-504:66), NA; GBM teleg. to Stanton, May 8, 1862, Stanton Papers, LC; Heintzelman diary, Apr. 29, 1862, LC; Lincoln to GBM, May 9, 1862, *Works*, V, pp. 208–209; *OR*, XI, Part 3, p. 181; *McClellan's Own Story*, manuscript, Papers (D-9:71).

25. Pinkerton to Andrew Porter, May 6, 7, 1862, Papers (A-56:22); GBM teleg. to Stanton, May 10, 1862, Stanton Papers, LC; GBM teleg. to Lincoln, May 14, 1862, Papers (A-57:22); *McClellan's Own Story*, p. 76; *OR*, XI, Part 3, p. 184; Hay, *Diaries and Letters*, p. 53.

26. Stanton teleg. to GBM, May 18, 1862, *OR*, XI, Part 1, p. 27; McDowell testimony, *Report of the Joint Committee*, I (1863), pp. 267–68; Lincoln telegs. to GBM, May 21, 24, 1862, *Works*, V, pp. 226, 231–32; Banks teleg. to Stanton, Apr. 30 — McDowell teleg. to

Stanton, May 19, 1862, *OR*, XII, Part 3, pp. 118–19, 202.

27. GBM to his wife, May 18 — GBM teleg. to Lincoln, May 21, 1862, Papers (C-7:63, A-58:23); Lincoln teleg. to GBM, May 21, 1862, *Works*, V, p. 226; GBM, *Report*, pp. 96–97; GBM in *Battles and Leaders*, II, pp. 173–74; GBM to his wife, May 22, 1862, Papers (C-7:63/D-10:72).

28. GBM to his wife, May 22, 1862, Papers (C-7:63/D-10:72); GBM to Burnside, May 21, 1862, *OR*, IX, p. 392; GBM to his wife, May 10, 1862, Papers (C-7:63).

29. Johnston to Lee, Apr. 30, 1862, *OR*, XI, Part 3, p. 477; *Battles and Leaders*, II, p. 219; Lee to Thomas J. Jackson, May 1, 6, 1862, Robert E. Lee, *The Wartime Papers of R. E. Lee*, ed. Clifford Dowdey, pp. 162–63, 175.

30. GBM teleg. to Frederick W. Lander, Feb. 2, 1862, RG 107 (M-473:11), NA; Lincoln telegs. to GBM, May 24, 25, 1862, *Works*, V, pp. 232, 236; GBM to his wife, May 25 — GBM teleg. to Lincoln, May 25 — GBM teleg. to Stanton, May 28, 1862, Papers (C-7:63, A-58:23, A-59:23).

31. GBM teleg. to his wife — GBM teleg. to Lincoln, May 26, 1862, Papers (C-13:64, A-58:23); GBM telegs. to Stanton, May 28, 30, 1862, Papers (A-59:23); Charles S. Wainwright, May 31, 1862, Wainwright, *A Diary of Battle: The Personal Journals of Colonel Charles S. Wainwright, 1861–1865*, ed. Allan Nevins, p. 75; GBM to his wife, May 26, June 2, 1862, Papers (C-7:63).

Chapter 9. The Battle for Richmond

1. GBM to his wife, May 22 — GBM teleg. to Stanton, May 27, 1862, Papers (C-7:63/D-10:72, A-58:23); *OR*, XI, Part 3, p. 204; GBM teleg. to Stanton, May 28, 1862, *OR*, XI, Part 1, p. 36; Joseph E. Johnston,

Narrative of Military Operations (New York: D. Appleton, 1874), pp. 131–33.

2. Keyes, GBM, Sumner, Heintzelman testimony, *Report of the Joint Committee*, I (1863), pp. 608, 432, 362, 352; Heintzelman telegs. to Marcy, May 31, 1862 (three), Papers (A-59:23); GBM to his wife, June 2, 1862, Papers (C-7:63); Marcy teleg. to Sumner, May 31, 1862, *OR*, XI, Part 3, p. 203; Chauncey McKeever teleg. to A. V. Colburn — Arthur McClellan diary, May 31, 1862, Papers (A-59:23, D-2:66); Heintzelman diary, June 1, 1862, LC; GBM teleg. to Marcy, May 31, 1862, McClellan papers, New-York Historical Society.

3. Moore, *Rebellion Record*, V, Documents, p. 93; John G. Barnard to Marcy, June 2, 1862, *OR*, LI, Part 1, pp. 650–51; Comte de Paris to GBM, Mar. 13, 1875, Papers (A-95:38); Military Historical Society of Massachusetts, *The Peninsular Campaign of General McClellan in 1862*, p. 145; GBM to his wife, June 2, 11, 23, 1862, Papers (C-7:63); GBM teleg. to Stanton — GBM to Army of the Potomac, June 2, 1862, Papers (C-13:64, D-12:74); *OR*, XI, Part 1, pp. 762, 942, 991.

4. Stanton teleg. to McDowell, June 6 — Adj. Gen. Office, G.O. 57, June 1 — Wool teleg. to Stanton, May 24 — Dix teleg. to Stanton, June 9 — Stanton teleg. to GBM, June 7, 1862, *OR*, XI, Part 3, pp. 216, 207, 189–90, 221, 219; Burnside teleg. to GBM, June 13 — GBM teleg. to Burnside, June 20, 1862, Papers (A-63:25, A-66:26).

5. McDowell teleg. to GBM, June 8, 1862, *OR*, XI, Part 3, pp. 220–21; Lincoln to GBM, June 15, 20 (teleg.), 18 (teleg.), 1862, *Works*, V, pp. 272, 277–78, 276; *OR*, XII, Part 3, p. 448.

6. GBM teleg. to Stanton, June 10,

1862, Papers (A-62:24); Halleck telegs. to Stanton, June 12, 16, 1862, *OR*, XVI, Part 2, pp. 14, 26; GBM to his wife, June 22, 1862, Papers (C-7:63/D-10:72); GBM teleg. to Stanton, Mar. 18, 1862, RG 107 (M-473:98), NA; *OR*, XI, Part 3, p. 238. The June 20 return included some 10,000 men stationed at Fort Monroe. This was a number far in excess of need, and had GBM reduced the garrison to a reasonable size and utilized Burnside's troops, his field army before Richmond would have reached the intended 130,000 figure.

7. GBM teleg. to Stanton, June 7, 1862, RG 107 (M-473:102), NA; GBM teleg. to Stanton, June 14 — GBM teleg. to Lincoln, June 18 — GBM to his wife, June 22, 11, 1862, Papers (A-63:25, C-10:63, C-7:63/D-10:72, C-7:63).

8. Hagerman, "Jomini to Mahan," pp. 214–15; GBM teleg. to Lincoln, June 20 — GBM teleg. to Stanton, June 15, 1862, Papers (C-13:64, A-64:25); Robert O. Tyler report, *OR*, XI, Part 1, pp. 273–74; James H. Van Alen teleg. to Seth Williams, June 10 — GBM to his wife, June 15, 1862, Papers (A-62:24, C-7:63/D-10:72).

9. GBM to his wife, June 23 — GBM teleg. to Rodgers, June 24, 1862, Papers (C-7:63, C-13:64); Henry F. Clarke, Stewart Van Vliet reports, *OR*, XI, Part 1, pp. 169, 159; GBM, *Report*, p. 123; GBM to Samuel S. Cox, c. 1884, Papers (A-107:42). About this time, GBM reportedly met with Gen. Porter and they agreed that a change of base to the James would be undertaken only as a last resort: Alexander S. Webb, *The Peninsula: McClellan's Campaign of 1862*, p. 128.

10. Alexander S. Webb to his father, June 9, 1862, Webb Papers, Yale University Library; *New York Times*, June 26, 1862; Joinville, *Army of the Potomac*, p. 84; John

McEwen to his cousin, June 22, 1862, Benton Family Papers, Minnesota Historical Society; Meade to his wife, June 22, 1862, *Life and Letters,* I, pp. 277–78; *New York World,* June 20, 1862; *New York Times,* June 24, 1862; *New York Tribune,* June 10, 1862; Porter to Marble, June 20, 1862, Marble Papers, LC.

11. Key to Stanton, June 16, 1862, *OR,* XI, Part 1, pp. 1052–56; Chase to Key, Apr. 18, 1862, Schuckers, *Chase,* pp. 434–35; GBM teleg. to Stanton, June 15 — GBM teleg. to Lincoln, June 20, 1862, Papers (A-64:25, C-13:64); Lincoln teleg. to GBM, June 21, 1862, *Works,* V, p. 279.

12. GBM telegs. to Heintzelman, Stanton, June 24, 1862, Papers (C-13:64, A-67:27); Stanton teleg. to GBM, June 25, 1862, *OR,* XI, Part 1, p. 49; GBM to his wife, June 23, 1862, Papers (C-7:63); GBM teleg. to Stanton, June 25, 1862, McClellan Papers, New-York Historical Society.

13. Fitz John Porter teleg. to Marcy, June 25, 1862, Papers (A-68:27); Robert Ransom, Jr., report — J. K. F. Mansfield teleg. to GBM, June 15, 1862, *OR,* XI, Part 2, p. 791, Part 3, p. 231; Pinkerton to Andrew Porter, June 15, 23, 1862, Papers (A-64:25, A-67:27); Fitz John Porter to Manton Marble, July 22, 1862, Marble Papers, LC; Pinkerton to GBM, June 26, 1862, *OR,* XI, Part 1, p. 269.

14. GBM telegs. to Stanton (two), Stewart Van Vliet, Heintzelman, June 25, 1862, Papers (A-68:27); Pinkerton to GBM, June 26, 1862, *OR,* XI, Part 1, p. 269; GBM teleg. to Stanton, June 26, 1862, Papers (C-13:64).

15. Lee to Davis, June 5, 1862, *Wartime Papers,* p. 184; Lee report, *OR,* XI, Part 2, p. 490; Davis to his wife, June 21, 1862, Dunbar Rowland, ed., *Jefferson Davis,*

Constitutionalist: His Letters, Papers and Speeches (Jackson: Mississippi Department of Archives and History, 1923), V, p. 283; Freeman, *Lee,* II, p. 116; *OR,* XI, Part 3, p. 238. The count of GBM's field army is the number present for duty, equipped. Lee's estimated strength appears to be counted the same way.

16. Marcy teleg. to Porter, June 23, 1862, *OR,* XI, Part 3, p. 247; GBM teleg. to his wife, June 26, 1862, Papers (C-10:63); D. H. Hill in *Battles and Leaders,* II, p. 326; John B. Magruder report, *OR,* XI, Part 2, p. 662; Marcy telegs. to corps commanders — Stewart Van Vliet teleg. to Rufus Ingalls — GBM teleg. to Porter, June 26, 1862, Papers (A-69:27, A-69:28, A-69:27); GBM to Dix, July 4, 1862, Dix Papers, Rare Book and Manuscript Library, Columbia University; A.V. Colburn teleg. to Franklin — Marcy teleg. to Colburn, June 26, 1862, Papers (A-69:27).

17. GBM teleg. to Marcy, [June 26] — GBM teleg. to Stanton, June 26, 1862, Papers (A-69:27); GBM to his wife, July 2, June 27 (teleg.), 1862, Papers (C-7:63, C-10:63); William F. Biddle to John C. Ropes, Mar. 27, 1895, Ropes Collection, Boston University Library; GBM teleg. to Porter, June 27, 1862, *OR,* XI, Part 3, p. 265.

18. GBM telegs. to Stanton (three) — Heintzelman teleg. to Marcy, June 27, 1862, Papers (A-70:28); Marcy teleg. to Sumner — Sumner telegs. to Marcy (two), June 27, 1862, *OR,* XI, Part 1, p. 58; Seth Williams teleg. to Heintzelman, June 27, 1862, Papers (A-70:28).

19. Lee to Benjamin Huger, June 26, 1862, *Wartime Papers,* pp. 201–202; Magruder report, *OR,* XI, Part 2, pp. 661–62; GBM teleg. to Stanton — GBM teleg. to his wife, June 28, 1862, Papers (A-71:28, C-

10:63); Porter to Manton Marble, July 22, 1862, Marble Papers, LC.

20. Andrew A. Humphreys to his wife, July 17, 1862, Humphreys Papers, Historical Society of Pennsylvania; Marcy teleg. to Franklin, June 27, 1862, Papers (A-70:28); E. Porter Alexander to his father, July 24, 1862, Alexander Papers, Southern Historical Collection, University of North Carolina; Webb, *The Peninsula*, p. 187; GBM, *Report*, p. 127; George Montieth to Marcy — Sumner teleg. to Marcy, June 27, 1862, Papers (A-70:28).

21. Porter teleg. to Marcy, June [27], 1862, Papers (A-71:28); GBM teleg. to Franklin — Franklin teleg. to GBM, June 27, 1862, Papers (A-70:28); Porter telegs. to GBM, [June 27], 1862 (two), Papers (A-69:27); GBM telegs. to Porter, June 27, [June 27], 1862, Papers (A-70:28, A-69:27); Porter in *Battles and Leaders*, II, pp. 336–37. Stephen M. Weld of Porter's staff later wrote: "General Porter always took the ground . . . that if he could have been supported then with one or two more divisions, he would have won a victory." Weld, *War Diary and Letters of Stephen Minot Weld, 1861–1865*, p. 79.

22. GBM telegs. to Heintzelman, Stanton, June 27, 1862, Papers (A-70:28); Heintzelman diary, June 27, 1862, LC; GBM teleg. to Goldsborough, June 27, 1862, Papers (A-71:28); GBM, *Report*, p. 131; GBM in *Battles and Leaders*, II, p. 182.

23. GBM teleg. to Stanton, June 28 — GBM to his wife, July 20, 1862, Papers (A-71:28, C-7:63); GBM to Dix, June 29, 1862, Dix Papers, Rare Book and Manuscript Library, Columbia University; David H. Bates, *Lincoln in the Telegraph Office* (New York: Century, 1907), pp. 109–10; Browning, July 14,

1862, *Diary*, I, p. 559; GBM, *Report*, pp. 131–32; Lincoln teleg. to GBM, June 28, 1862, *Works*, V, pp. 289–90. The source for the full text of GBM's June 28 telegram to Stanton, as printed in his 1864 *Report* and repeated in the *Official Records*, was his retained copy.

24. GBM to his wife, July 17, 10, 4, 1862, Papers (C-7:63); Heintzelman testimony, *Report of the Joint Committee*, I (1863), p. 359; Francis C. Barlow to his mother, July 4, 1862, Barlow Papers, Massachusetts Historical Society.

25. GBM, *Report*, pp. 131, 132; Lee report, *OR*, XI, Part 2, pp. 493–94; *New York Tribune*, July 3, 1862.

26. Robert O. Tyler report, *OR*, XI, Part 1, p. 274; *OR*, XI, Part 3, p. 238; Montgomery Meigs report, *OR*, Ser. 3, II, p. 798; Henry F. Clarke, Erasmus Keyes reports, *OR*, XI, Part 1, p. 170, Part 2, p. 193; GBM, *Report*, p. 135; Rufus Ingalls to Meigs, July 18, 1862, *OR*, XI, Part 3, p. 327.

27. Heintzelman, Sumner reports, *OR*, XI, Part 2, pp. 99, 50–51; Franklin in *Battles and Leaders*, II, p. 375; Arthur McClellan diary — A.V. Colburn to Delos B. Sacket, June 29, 1862, Papers (D-2:66, A-71:28); Heintzelman diary, June 30, 1862, LC.

28. A.V. Colburn to GBM, Apr. 16, 1863, Papers (A-90:35); Franklin in *Battles and Leaders*, II, p. 377; Sumner, Heintzelman testimony, *Report of the Joint Committee*, I (1863), pp. 364, 359; William F. Biddle to John C. Ropes, Mar. 27, 1895, Ropes Collection, Boston University Library; Michie, *General McClellan*, p. 354.

29. Barnard report, *OR*, XI, Part 1, p. 120; GBM to Marcy, June 30, 1862, Papers (A-71:28); log of the *Galena* (copy), June 30, 1862, Lincoln Papers, LC.

30. Freeman, *Lee*, II, p. 192; Hein-

tzelman testimony, *Report of the Joint Committee*, I (1863), p. 358; GBM teleg. to Stanton, June 30, 1862, Lincoln Papers, LC; A.V. Colburn to GBM, Apr. 16, 1863, Papers (A-90:35); GBM teleg. to Lorenzo Thomas, July 1, 1862, RG 107 (M-473:50), NA; Franklin in *Battles and Leaders,* II, pp. 379–80.

31. Arthur McClellan diary — GBM to his wife, July 1, 1862, Papers (D-2:66, C-7:63); Humphreys to his wife, July 11, 1862, Humphreys Papers, Historical Society of Pennsylvania; GBM to Dix, July 1, 1862, Dix Papers, Rare Book and Manuscript Library, Columbia University; log of the *Galena* (copy), July 1, 1862, Ropes Collection, Boston University Library; GBM to Reverdy Johnson, Mar. 9, 1864, Johnson Papers, LC; *Cincinnati Commercial,* 1864 clipping, quoted in J. Cutler Andrews, *The North Reports the Civil War,* p. 215; cartoons: Anne S. K. Brown Military Collection, Brown University Library; GBM testimony, *Report of the Joint Committee,* I (1863), pp. 436–37. The *Galena*'s log does not record GBM's return from Harrison's Landing, but other witnesses place him on board.

32. Arthur McClellan diary, July 1, 1862, Papers (D-2:66); GBM testimony, *Report of the Joint Committee,* I (1863), p. 437; Porter to GBM, July 1, 1862 (two), Papers (A-72:29); George W. Faucett to his father, July 18, 1862, Indiana Historical Society; William F. Biddle to John C. Ropes, Mar. 27, 1895, Ropes Collection, Boston University Library; Andrew A. Humphreys to GBM, Feb. 28, 1864, Papers (B-14:49); Porter in *Battles and Leaders,* II, pp. 422–23; log of the *Galena* (copy), July 1, 2, 1862, Ropes Collection; GBM teleg. to Lincoln, July 2, 1862, Lincoln Papers, LC.

Chapter 10. Impasse at Harrison's Landing

1. Haydon diary, July 2, 4, 1862, Michigan Historical Collections, Bentley Historical Library, University of Michigan; GBM to Stanton, July 3, 1862, Houghton Library, Harvard University; Thomas L. Livermore, *Numbers and Losses in the Civil War in America, 1861–65* (2nd ed., Boston: Houghton Mifflin, 1902), p. 86; E. P. Alexander, *Military Memoirs of a Confederate* (New York: Scribner's, 1907), p. 171; G. F. Newhall to his father, July 4, 1862, Boston Public Library; GBM to his wife, July 4, 1862, Papers (C-7:63); A. V. Colburn teleg. to Thomas T. Eckert, July 4, 1862, RG 107 (M-473:107), NA; Eckert teleg. to Colburn, July 6, 1862, Papers (A-72:29).

2. Seth Williams to Franklin, July 5, 1862, *OR,* XI, Part 3, p. 301; GBM to his wife, July 6, 1862, Papers (C-7:63/D-10:72); Lee to Jefferson Davis, July 4, 1862, *Wartime Papers,* p. 208; GBM teleg. to Lincoln, July 7, 1862, RG 107 (M-473:50), NA.

3. GBM to Army of the Potomac — GBM teleg. to Lincoln, July 4, 1862, Papers (A-11:48, A-72:29).

4. GBM to his wife, July [7], 1862, Papers (C-7:63); GBM to Dix, July 4, 1862, Dix Papers, Rare Book and Manuscript Library, Columbia University; GBM teleg. to Lincoln, July 4, 1862, Papers (A-72:29); Lee report, *Wartime Papers,* p. 221.

5. Lincoln to GBM, July 2 (teleg.), 4, 1862, *Works,* V, pp. 301, 305–306; Browning, July 14, 1862, *Diary,* I, p. 559; Marcy memorandum, undated, Papers (A-107:42).

6. Nicolay to Therena Bates, July 13, 1862, Nicolay Papers, LC; GBM to his wife, July 17, 8, 1862, Papers (C-7:63, C-7:63/D-10:72);

Felix Brannigan to his sister, July 16, 1862, Brannigan Papers, LC.

7. GBM teleg. to Lincoln, June 20 — GBM to his wife, July 17, 1862, Papers (C-13:64, C-7:63); GBM to Lincoln, July 7, 1862, Lincoln Papers, LC.

8. GBM to Hill Carter, July 11 — GBM to Halleck, Aug. 1 — GBM to Stanton, July 8, 1862, Papers (B-11:48, A-73:29, A-72:29); *McClellan's Own Story*, p. 487; GBM to his wife, July 9, 1862, Papers (C-7:63/D-10:72).

9. GBM to Barlow, [July] 23, 1862, Barlow Papers, HL; Lincoln memorandum, July 8–9, 1862, *Works*, V, pp. 309–12; Heintzelman diary, July 9, 1862, LC.

10. *Chicago Tribune*, July 14, 1862; *Paterson (N.J.) Daily Guardian*, July 4, 1862; *New York Times*, July 7, 1862; *New York Herald*, July 6, 1862, Strong, July 11, 1862, *Diary*, p. 239; *New York World*, Aug. 7, 1862; *New York Tribune*, July 3, 1862.

11. Felix Brannigan to his sister, July 16, 1862, Brannigan Papers, LC; George W. Lambert to his brother and sister, July 28, 1862, Indiana Historical Society; Edward H. Taylor to his mother, July 14, 1862, Michigan Historical Collections, Bentley Historical Library, University of Michigan; "George" to his brother, July 29, 1862, University of Virginia Library; "Johnnie" to his father, July 17, 1862, William R. Perkins Library, Duke University; Webb to his father, July 10, 1862, Webb Papers, Yale University Library; Barlow to his brother, July 8, 12, 1862, Francis Channing Barlow Papers, Massachusetts Historical Society.

12. Chandler to his wife, July 6, 1862, Chandler Papers, LC; *Report of the Joint Committee*, I (1863), p. 102; *Congressional Globe*, 37th Cong., 2nd Sess., 1862, Chandler:

pp. 3149–50, 3219–21, 3386–92, Wade: p. 1736.

13. David Tod teleg. to Stanton, July 11, 1862, *OR*, Ser. 3, II, p. 219; Stanton to GBM, July 5 — GBM to Stanton, July 8, 1862, Papers (A-72:29); Lincoln address, Aug. 8, 1862, *Works*, V, pp. 358–59; Barlow to GBM, Aug. 9 — GBM to his wife, July 13, 1862, Papers (A-74:29, C-7:63/D-10:72).

14. GBM teleg. to Lincoln, July 4, 1862, Lincoln Papers, LC; GBM to John Pope, July 7 — GBM teleg. to Lincoln, July 11, 1862, Papers (C-6:63, A-72:29); GBM to Barlow, [July] 23, 1862, Barlow Papers, HL; GBM to his wife, July 15, 1862, Papers (C-7:63/D-10:72). GBM approximated his combat strength by reducing the number of enlisted men present for duty by one-sixth: *OR*, XI, Part I, p. 312. He arrived at Lee's strength by subtracting estimated casualties for the Seven Days from the 180,000–200,000 he believed he had faced in those battles.

15. GBM to Stanton, [Feb. 3], 1862, Lincoln Papers, LC; GBM to Burnside, Apr. 2, 1862, *OR*, IX, p. 374; GBM to Dix, July 4, 1862, Dix Papers, Rare Book and Manuscript Library, Columbia University; Colburn teleg. to Marcy, July 8, 1862, Stanton Papers, LC; GBM teleg. to Marcy, July 19 — GBM teleg. to Lincoln, July 17, 1862, Papers (A-73:29).

16. Burnside testimony, *Report of the Joint Committee*, I (1863), p. 650; Browning, July 25, 1862, *Diary*, I, p. 563. It is probable that Burnside was offered the command of the Potomac army when he was in Washington on July 22–23: Burnside teleg. to GBM, July 21, 1862, Papers (A-73:29); *Washington Star*, July 23, 1862; GBM to Barlow, July 30, 1862, Barlow Papers, HL.

17. GBM to his wife, July 11, 29, 10,

17, 18, 1862, Papers (C-7:63), Aug. 8, 1862, Papers (C-7:63/D-10:72); she to GBM, Aug. 3, July 31, Aug. 6, July 22, 1862, Papers (B-11:48).

18. GBM to his wife, July 27 — GBM to Aspinwall, July 19, 1862, Papers (C-7:63/D-10:72, A-73:29); GBM to Barlow, July 15, 30, 1862, Barlow Papers, HL; Chase, July 22, 1862, *Diaries,* p. 98.

19. Alsop to GBM, July 24 — GBM to Alsop, July 26, 1862, Papers (A-73:29); A. V. Colburn teleg. to Marcy, July 8, 1862, Stanton Papers, LC; Marcy to GBM, July 13 — GBM to his wife, July 31, 1862, Stanton Papers (B-11:48, C-7:63).

20. GBM teleg. to Lorenzo Thomas, July 10, 1862, Papers (C-3:63); GBM to Nathaniel S. Berry, July 15, 1862, Houghton Library, Harvard University; Naglee to Seth Williams, Aug. 3, 1862, Papers (A-73:29).

21. Lincoln teleg. to GBM, July 13, 1862, *Works,* V. p. 322; GBM teleg. to Lincoln, July 14, 1862, Papers (C-12:64); GBM teleg. to Lorenzo Thomas, July 27, 1862, McClellan Papers, New-York Historical Society; Adj. Gen.'s Office, G.O. 92, July 31, 1862, *OR,* Ser. 3, II, pp. 286–87.

22. Halleck to Stanton, July 27, 1862, *OR,* XI, Part 3, pp. 337–38; GBM teleg. to Lincoln, July 18, 1862, Papers (C-15:64); GBM in *Battles and Leaders,* II, p. 548; Heintzelman diary, July 26, 1862, LC; Halleck to GBM, Aug. 6, 7, 1862, *OR,* XII, Part 2, pp. 9–11, XI, Part 3, pp. 359–60; GBM to his wife, July 17, 15, 1862, Papers (C-7:63, C-7:63/D-10:72).

23. GBM to his wife, July 20, 1862, Papers (C-7:63); GBM to Barlow, July 23, 30, 1862, Barlow Papers, HL; GBM to Joseph W. Alsop, July 26, 1862, Papers (A-73:29); Halleck to GBM, Aug. 6, 1862, *OR,* XII, Part 2, p. 10; Halleck to his wife, July 28, 1862, James Grant

Wilson, "General Halleck — A Memoir," *Journal of the Military Service Institution of the United States,* 36 (May–June 1905), p. 557; Burnside testimony, *Report of the Joint Committee,* I (1863), p. 638, Burnside testimony, Porter court-martial, *OR,* XII, Part 2 Suppl., p. 1005; Meigs, "General Meigs on the Conduct of the Civil War," p. 294.

24. GBM to Halleck, July 26, 1862, RG 94 (159:Halleck Papers), NA; *OR,* IX, p. 414, XIV, p. 367, LI, Part 1, p. 726; Halleck telegs. to GBM, July 30, Aug. 3, 1862, *OR,* XI, Part 1, pp. 76–77, 80–81.

25. GBM teleg. to Halleck, Aug. 4, 1862, Papers (A-74:29); Halleck to GBM, Aug. 6, 7, 1862, *OR,* XII, Part 2, pp. 9–11, XI, Part 3, p. 360; Halleck teleg. to Burnside, Aug. 1, 1862, *OR,* XII, Part 3, p. 524; GBM to his wife, Aug. 4, 1862, Papers (C-7:63).

26. Halleck telegs. to GBM, July 30, 31, 1862, *OR,* XI, Part 1, pp. 76–77; GBM to Halleck, Aug. 1 — Hooker to Marcy, Aug. 3, 1862, *OR,* XI, Part 2, pp. 935–36, 951–52; GBM to his wife, Aug. 4 — GBM to Marcy, Aug. 5, 1862, Papers (C-7:63); *OR,* XI, Part 3, pp. 312, 645; GBM [Marcy] teleg. to Halleck, Aug. 5, 1862, *OR,* XI, Part 1, pp. 77–78; Lee to Jefferson Davis — Lee to Jackson, Aug. 7, 1862, *Wartime Papers,* pp. 246–47, 247–48; GBM to his wife, Aug. 8, 10 — GBM to Hooker, Aug. 6, 1862, Papers (C-7:63/D-10:72, C-7:63, A-74:29); Halleck teleg. to GBM, Aug. 6, 1862, *OR,* XI, Part 1, p. 78.

27. Pope to Army of Virginia, July 14 — Army of Virginia, G.O. 5–7, 11, July 18–23, 1862, *OR,* XII, Part 3, pp. 473–74, Part 2, pp. 50–52; Army of the Potomac, G.O. 54, Aug. 9, 1862, *OR,* XI, Part 3, pp. 362–64; GBM to his wife, Aug. 8, 1862, Papers (C-7:63/D-10:72); Chase,

July 21, 1862, *Diaries*, p. 97 ; Pope
to Halleck, Sept. 30, 1862, *OR*, XII,
Part 3, p. 818 ; GBM to his wife,
July 22, Aug. 10, 1862, Papers (C-
7 :63/D-10 :72, C-7 :63).

28. Alfred Pleasonton to Marcy, Aug.
11, 1862, *OR*, XI, Part 3, p. 369 ;
GBM telegs. to Halleck, Aug. 12,
1862 (two), Papers (C-10 :63, A-
74 :29) ; Halleck to his wife, Aug.
13, 1862, *Collector*, 21, p. 52 ; Halleck to Stanton, Aug. 30, 1862, *OR*,
XII, Part 3, p. 739 ; Pinkerton to
Andrew Porter, Aug. 10, 1862, Papers (A-74 :29) ; Pinkerton to GBM,
Aug. 14, 1862 (summary), *OR*, XI,
Part 1, pp. 269-72 ; Freeman, *Lee*,
II, pp. 272-74. Previous to Aug.
14, a brigade of infantry, a regiment of cavalry, and five batteries
of artillery were sent by water to
Burnside : *OR*, XI, Part 1, pp. 84,
86.

29. Howell Cobb to unknown, Aug. 18,
1862, Chicago Historical Society ;
McClellan's Own Story, p. 328 ;
GBM to his wife, Aug. 17, 18, 1862,
Papers (C-7 :63, C-7 :63/D-10 :72) ;
GBM to Burnside, Aug. 20, 1862,
OR, XII, Part 3, p. 605. Franklin
reached Yorktown on Aug. 19,
found no transports, and embarked from Fort Monroe on Aug.
23 ; Sumner arrived at Newport
News on Aug. 22, began to embark
on Aug. 24, and was delayed a day
by bad weather : *OR*, XI, Part 1,
p. 93, XII, Part 3, pp. 599, 612-
13, 645, 660.

30. Halleck teleg. to GBM, Aug. 21,
1862, *OR*, XI, Part 1, p. 92 ; GBM
to his wife, Aug. 21, 22, 23, 1862,
Papers (C-7 :63) ; GBM teleg. to
Porter, Aug. 21, 1862, Papers (C-
15 :64).

*Chapter 11. General Without an
Army*

1. Arthur McClellan diary, Aug. 24,
1862, Papers (A-74 :29) ; GBM to
his wife, Aug. 29, 24, 1862, Papers
(C-7 :63). GBM became senior

serving general in the regular
army when John Charles Frémont,
whose commission dated from the
same day as his, resigned his
command rather than serve under
Pope.

2. GBM to Burnside, Aug. 20, 1862,
OR, XII, Part 3, p. 605 ; Aspinwall
to Mary Ellen McClellan, Aug.
24 — Marcy teleg. to GBM, Aug.
26, 1862, Papers (B-11 :48, A-
74 :30) ; Pinkerton to GBM, Aug.
23, 1862, cited in Nevins, *The War
for the Union: War Becomes Revolution, 1862-1863*, p. 173n ; GBM
teleg. to Halleck, Aug. 24, 1862,
McClellan Papers, New-York Historical Society ; GBM to his wife,
Aug. 27, 28, 1862, Papers (C-7 :63).

3. Halleck teleg. to GBM — Herman
Haupt teleg. to Halleck, Aug. 26,
1862, *OR*, XI, Part 1, p. 94, XII,
Part 3, p. 680 ; Arthur McClellan
diary, Aug. 26 — GBM to his wife,
Aug. 27, 1862, Papers (A-74 :29, C-
7 :63).

4. GBM to his wife, Aug. 10, 1862,
Papers (C-7 :63) ; Porter to Burn-
side (copy to GBM), Aug. 27, 1862,
OR, XII, Part 3, pp. 699-700 ;
Porter teleg. to GBM, Aug. 27, 1862,
Papers (A-75 :30).

5. Halleck telegs. to GBM, Aug. 27,
1862 (three), *OR*, XI, Part 1, pp.
94, 95, XII, Part 3, p. 691 ; GBM
telegs. to Halleck, Aug. 27, 1862
(four) : RG 107 (M-504 :65), NA
(two), Papers (C-15 :64, A-75 :30) ;
Burnside teleg. to Halleck (copy
to GBM), Aug. 27, 1862, *OR*, XII,
Part 3, p. 701.

6. GBM to his wife, Aug. 28, 1862,
Papers (C-7 :63) ; Halleck testimony, *Report of the Joint Committee*, I (1863), p. 453 ; Halleck
to Stanton, Aug. 30 — Halleck
teleg. to Franklin, Aug. 28, 1862,
OR, XII, Part 3, pp. 739-41, 707 ;
GBM telegs. to Halleck, Aug. 28,
1862 (four) : *OR*, XII, Part 3, pp.
706, 707, RG 107 (M-473 :50, M-
504 :65), NA ; GBM teleg. to Amiel

W. Whipple, Aug. 28, 1862, RG 107 (M-504:65), NA.

7. GBM telegs. to Halleck, Aug. 28, 1862 (two): RG 107 (M-473:50), NA, Papers (A-75:30); Franklin to GBM, Aug. 28, 1862, Papers (A-75:30); Halleck teleg. to GBM, Aug. 28, 1862, *OR*, XII, Part 3, p. 710.

8. Amiel W. Whipple teleg. to GBM, Aug. 27, 1862, Papers (A-75:30); Whipple teleg. to John G. Barnard, Aug. 28, 1862, *OR*, XII. Part 3, p. 707; GBM to his wife, Aug. 29, 1862 (two), Papers (C-7:63); GBM teleg. to Halleck, Aug. 28, 1862, *OR*, XII, Part 3, p. 709; GBM teleg. to Barnard, Aug. 29, 1862, RG 107 (M-504:65), NA.

9. GBM teleg. to Halleck, Aug. 28, 1862, *OR*, XII, Part 3, p. 709; GBM to Halleck, Aug. 30, 1862, RG 94 (159:Halleck Papers), NA. At least three of Sumner's batteries must have reached Alexandria on Aug. 28, for they were shipped along with Franklin's guns from the Peninsula: C. G. Sawtelle teleg. to Montgomery C. Meigs, Aug. 26, 1862, *OR*, XII, Part 3, pp. 681–82. Yet in GBM's telegram to Halleck at 10:00 P.M. he said that none of Sumner's artillery was "here," that is, at Alexandria. Possibly Sumner's batteries were earmarked for Washington's defense, for at 2:00 A.M. on Aug. 29 GBM ordered one of them to the Chain Bridge: GBM teleg. to John G. Barnard, Aug. 29, 1862, RG 107 (M-504:65), NA.

10. Dawes. *Service with the Sixth Wisconsin*, p. 47; GBM telegs. to Halleck, Aug. 29, 1862 (two), RG 107 (M-504:65), NA; Cox interview in *Cincinnati Commercial Gazette*, Nov. –, 1885, clipping, Cox Papers, Oberlin College Archives; William H. Brearley to his sister, Sept. 1, 1862, Burton Historical Collection, Detroit Public Library.

11. Lincoln teleg. to GBM, Aug. 29, 1862, *Works*, V, p. 399; GBM teleg. to Lincoln — GBM to his wife, Aug. 29, 1862, Papers (C-15:64, C-7:63); Hill to Sydney H. Gay, Aug. 31, 1862, Gay Papers, Rare Book and Manuscript Library, Columbia University; Hay, Sept. 1, 1862, *Diaries and Letters*, p. 45.

12. GBM to his wife, Sept. [9], Aug. 29, 1862, Papers (C-7:63/D-10:72, C-7:63); Bates to Francis Lieber, Sept. 2, 1862, Lieber Collection, HL; Hill to Sydney H. Gay, [Aug. 29, 1862], Gay Papers, Rare Book and Manuscript Library, Columbia University; Halleck telegs. to GBM, Aug. 29, 1862 (two), *OR*, XII, Part 3, pp. 722, 723; GBM teleg. to Halleck, Aug. 29, 1862, Papers (C-15:64); Franklin to GBM, Aug. 29, 1862, *OR*, XII, Part 3, pp. 723–24.

13. Halleck telegs. to GBM, Aug. 30, 1862 (two), *OR*, XII, Part 3, p. 747, XI, Part 1, p. 102; GBM telegs. to Halleck, Aug. 30, 1862 (two), RG 107 (M-504:65), NA; GBM to his wife, Aug. 30, 1862, Papers (C-7:63/D-10:72); Cox, *Military Reminiscences*, I, pp. 241–43; Cox interview in *Cincinnati Commercial Gazette*, Nov. –, 1885, clipping, Cox Papers, Oberlin College Archives.

14. Military Historical Society of Massachusetts, *The Virginia Campaign of 1862 Under General Pope*, p. 144; Hay, Sept. 1, 1862, *Diaries and Letters*, p. 46; GBM to his wife, Aug. 31 — she to GBM, Aug. 30, 1862, Papers (C-7:63, B-11:48); Adj. Gen.'s Office, S.O. 89, Aug. 30, 1862, *OR*, XI, Part I, p. 103; E. D. Townsend teleg. to Seth Williams, Aug. 31, 1862, Papers (A-75:30).

15. Halleck to his wife, Sept. 2, 5, 1862, Wilson, "General Halleck," p. 558; Pope teleg. to Halleck, Aug. 31, 1862, *OR*, XII, Part 2, p. 80; GBM telegs. to Halleck, Aug. 31, 1862

(four) : *OR*, XI, Part 1, p. 102, RG 107 (M-504 :65), NA (two), Papers (C-15 :64) ; Halleck teleg. to GBM, Aug. 31, 1862, *OR*, XI, Part 1, pp. 102–103 ; GBM to his wife, Sept. 2, 1862, Papers (C-7 :63).

16. GBM to his wife, Sept. 1, 2, 1862, Papers (C-7 :63) ; Porter to GBM, Aug. [31], 1862, *OR*, XII, Part 3, pp. 768–69 ; GBM, *Report*, pp. 182–83 ; Pope teleg. to Halleck, Sept. 1, 1862, *OR*, XII, Part 2, pp. 82–83 ; Hay, Sept. 1, 1862, *Diaries and Letters*, p. 46 ; GBM teleg. to Porter, Sept. 1, 1862, Papers (A-76 :30).

17. GBM, *Report*, pp. 183–84 ; GBM to his wife, Sept. 2, 1862, Papers (C-7 :63) ; Cox, *Military Reminiscences*, I, p. 243 ; Bates memorandum, Sept. 2, 1862, Lincoln Papers, LC ; Welles, Sept. 2, 1862, *Diary*, I, pp. 104–106 ; Chase, Aug. 29–Sept. 2, 1862, *Diaries*, pp. 116–20 ; Cabinet petition, undated, Stanton Papers, LC.

18. Halleck testimony, *Report of the Joint Committee*, I (1863), p. 453 ; Adj. Gen.'s Office, G.O. 122, Sept. 2, 1863 (three versions) : *McClellan's Own Story*, p. 546, RG 94 (M-619 :121), NA, *OR*, XII, Part 3, p. 807 ; Halleck to his wife, Aug. 9, 1862, Wilson, "General Halleck," p. 557 ; Hay, Sept. 5, 1862, *Diaries and Letters*, p. 47 ; GBM to Lincoln, Sept. 2, 1862 (two), Lincoln Papers, LC ; GBM to Halleck, Sept. 2, 1862, *OR*, XII, Part 3, p. 802.

19. GBM to his wife, Sept. 3, 1862, Papers (C-7 :63) ; Pope teleg. to Halleck, Sept. 2, 1862, *OR*, XII, Part 3, pp. 796–97 ; Cox, *Military Reminiscences*, I, pp. 243–45 ; *McClellan's Own Story*, p. 537, and Cox copy, Oberlin College Library ; George Kimball in *Battles and Leaders*, II, p. 550 ; Weld to his father, Sept. 4, 1862, *War Diary and Letters*, p. 136 ; A Davenport to his father, Sept. 3, 1862, Lydia Mintern Post, *Soldiers' Letters*

from Camp, Battle-field and Prison (New York : Bunce & Huntington, 1865), p. 155 ; Warren L. Goss, *Recollections of a Private: A Story of the Army of the Potomac* (New York : T. Y. Crowell, 1890), p. 91 ; Thomas T. Ellis, *Leaves from the Diary of an Army Surgeon* (New York : J. Bradburn, 1863), p. 214.

20. Meade to his wife, Sept. 3, 1862, *Life and Letters*, I, p. 307 ; Pope to Stanton, Sept. 5, 1862, Stanton Papers, LC ; Welles, Sept. 7, 8, 1862, *Diary*, I, pp. 113, 116 ; Stanton to Halleck — Halleck to GBM, Sept. 3, 1862, *OR*, XIX, Part 2, p. 169 ; GBM testimony, *Report of the Joint Committee*, I (1863), pp. 438–39.

21. GBM to his wife, Sept. 5, 1862, Papers (C-7 :63) ; Marcy telegs. to div. commanders, Sept. 5, 1862, *OR*, LI, Part 1, p. 788 ; Marcy teleg. to Nathaniel Banks, Sept. 5, 1862, Papers (A-77 :31) ; Halleck, GBM testimony, *Report of the Joint Committee*, I (1863), pp. 451, 453, 438–39 ; Halleck to Pope, Oct. 10, 1862, *OR*, XII, Part 3, pp. 819–20 ; Welles, Sept. 8, 10, 12, *Diary*, I, pp. 116, 122, 124 ; Pope to V. B. Horton, Mar. 25, 1863, Pope Papers, New-York Historical Society ; GBM report (Oct. 15, 1862), *OR*, XIX, Part 1, p. 25 ; *McClellan's Own Story*, p. 551, and draft, Papers (D-9 :71) ; GBM in *Battles and Leaders*, II, p. 552 ; Henry Kyd Douglas, *I Rode with Stonewall*, p. 177.

22. Burnside testimony, *Report of the Joint Committee*, I (1863), p. 650 ; Browning, Nov. 29, 1862, *Diary*, I, pp. 589–90 ; Hay, Sept. 5, 1862, *Diaries and Letters*, p. 47 ; Henry W. Raymond, "Journal of Henry J. Raymond," p. 423 ; A. E. Edwards to GBM, Apr. 12, 1883, Papers (A-101 :40). Tracing the movements of Lincoln, Halleck, and Burnside on Sept. 5 makes it clear that Lincoln's interview with GBM

preceded his offer of the command to Burnside: Hay's diary for Sept. 5; Burnside teleg. to GBM, Sept. 4, 1862, *OR*, XIX, Part 2, p. 175; Pope to V.B. Horton, Mar. 25, 1863, Pope Papers, New-York Historical Society. When Raymond's journal containing the Burnside interview was published in 1880, Randolph Marcy sought to discredit it by claiming Burnside was not then in Washington, and GBM endorsed his argument: "There is not a word of truth" in Burnside's account. However, Burnside was in the capital on Sept. 5-6, and there is no evidence that he fabricated the story. It is lent plausibility by GBM's remark to the Danish minister and by GBM's effort after Antietam to have Stanton and Halleck removed.

23. William T. Lusk to his father, Sept. 4, 1862, Lusk, *War Letters of William Thompson Lusk* (New York: privately printed, 1911), p. 181; Webb to his father, Sept. 4, 1862, Webb Papers, Yale University Library; GBM to his wife, Sept. 5, [9], 1862, Papers (C-7:63, C-7:63/D-10:72); Richard D. Irwin to Seth Williams, Sept. 11, 1862, *OR*, XIX, Part 2, p. 265; "Assignment of Regiments," c. Sept. 7, 1862, Papers (B-41:61).

24. GBM to Lincoln, Sept. 6, 1862, Papers (A-77:31); GBM to Halleck, Sept. 6, 1862, RG 94 (159:Halleck Papers), NA; GBM to Stanton, Sept. 7, 1862, *OR*, V, p. 342; GBM to his wife, Sept. 7, 12, 1862, Papers (C-7:63, C-7:63/D-10:72); GBM, *Report*, pp. 184–86; Hay, Sept. 5, 1862, *Diaries and Letters*, p. 47; Williams to his family, Sept. 12, 1862, *From the Cannon's Mouth*, pp. 120–21.

25. *New York Tribune*, Sept. 1, 1862; *Springfield* (Mass.) *Republican*, Sept. 3, 1862; Prime to J. C. G. Kennedy, Sept. 6, 1862, Papers (B-

11:48); *New York Herald*, Sept. 11, 1862; August Belmont to Lincoln, Sept. 4, 1862, Lincoln Papers, LC.

26. GBM, *Report*, p. 185; Welles, Sept. 6, 7, 1862, *Diary*, I, pp. 111, 114–15; *McClellan's Own Story*, p. 551, and draft, Papers (D-9:71); GBM teleg. to his wife, Sept. 7, 1862, Papers (C-7:63).

Chapter 12. Opportunity of a Lifetime

1. GBM teleg. to Halleck, Sept. 8, 1862 — *McClellan's Own Story*, draft — GBM to his wife, Sept. [9], 1862, Papers C-15:64, D-9:71, C-7:63/D-10:72); GBM teleg. to Curtin, Sept. 8, 1862, RG 107 (M-504:66), NA; GBM to his wife, Sept. 9, 1862 (two), Papers (C-7:63); D. H. Strother, Sept. 9, 11, 1862, Strother, *A Virginia Yankee in the Civil War: The Diaries of David Hunter Strother*, ed. Cecil B. Eby, pp. 103, 104.

2. Curtin teleg. to Halleck, Sept. 10, 1861, *OR*, XIX, Part 2, p. 248; Strong, Sept. 13, 1862, *Diary*, pp. 255–56; Welles, Sept. 10, 12, 1862, *Diary*, I, pp. 118, 129; *New York Herald*, Sept. 15, 1862; Nathaniel Paige interview, *New York Tribune*, Mar. 14, 1880.

3. Stephen W. Sears, *Landscape Turned Red: The Battle of Antietam*, pp. 82–83; E. C. Gordon to William Allan, Nov. 18, 1886, in Douglas Southall Freeman, *Lee's Lieutenants: A Study in Command*, II, pp. 716–17; *McClellan's Own Story*, draft, Papers (D-9:71); Halleck telegs. to GBM, Sept. 7, 11, 1862 — Halleck report, *OR*, XIX, Part 2, p. 201, Part 1, pp. 758, 4; Secret Service accounts, Sept.–Oct. 1862, RG 110 (entry 95), NA.

4. GBM to his wife, Aug. 18, 1862, Papers (C-7:63/D-10:72); Lewis H. Steiner, Sept. 6, 1862, *Report*

of Lewis H. Steiner, M.D.... Containing a Diary Kept During the Rebel Occupation of Frederick, Md. (New York: Anson D. F. Randolph, 1862).

5. Alfred Pleasonton telegs. to Marcy, Sept. 8, 9 (two), 1862, Papers (A-78:31); GBM telegs. to Halleck, Sept. 9, 1862 (three): RG 107 (M-473:50), NA, Papers (C-18:65, C-15:64); Thomas A. Scott teleg. to GBM, Sept. 9, 1862, OR, XIX, Part 2, p. 230; GBM to his wife, Sept. 9, 1862, Papers (C-7:63).

6. GBM teleg. to his wife, Sept. 10, 1862, RG 107 (M-504:66), NA; Lincoln teleg. to GBM, Sept. 10, 1862, OR, XIX, Part 2, p. 232; GBM teleg. to Lincoln, Sept. 10, 1862, Papers (C-16:65); GBM to Halleck, Sept. [10], 1862, Stanton Papers, LC; Curtin teleg. to GBM, Sept. 10, 1862, OR, XIX, Part 2, p. 248.

7. Curtin teleg. to John E. Wool, Sept. 7, 1862, OR, XIX, Part 2, p. 203; Douglas, I Rode with Stonewall, p. 151; Lee interview, Feb. 15, 1868, in Freeman, Lee's Lieutenants, II, p. 718; Pleasonton teleg. to Marcy, Sept. 13, 1862, Papers (A-79:31); Curtin teleg. to Lincoln, Sept. 12, 1862, OR, XIX, Part 2, p. 277; Pinkerton to GBM, Sept. 22, 1862, cited in Nevins, The War for the Union: War Becomes Revolution, 1862–1863, p. 326; Chase, Sept. 11, 1862, Diaries, pp. 133–34.

8. Pleasonton teleg. to Marcy, Sept. 10 — GBM teleg. to Halleck, Sept. 11, 1862, Papers (A-78:31, C-18:65); Lincoln teleg. to GBM, Sept. 11, 1862, Works, V, p. 415; Nathaniel Banks to Lincoln, Sept. 12, 1862, Lincoln Papers, LC.

9. Pleasonton teleg. to Marcy, Sept. 10, 1862, Papers (A-78:31); Curtin teleg. to Halleck, Sept. 10 — Curtin teleg. to Lincoln, Sept. 11, 1862, OR, XIX, Part 2, pp. 247, 268; W. P. Sanders to Pleason-

ton — Curtin teleg. to GBM, Sept. 11, 1862, Papers (A-79:31); GBM teleg. to Halleck, Sept. 11, 1862, Papers (C-16:65).

10. GBM teleg. to Halleck, Sept. 12, 1862, RG 107 (M-473:50), NA; GBM to his wife, Sept. 12, 1862, Papers (C-7:63/D-10:72); Lincoln teleg. to GBM, Sept. 12, 1862, Works, V, p. 418; GBM teleg. to Lincoln, Sept. 12, 1862, Papers (C-15:64).

11. Meade to his wife, Sept. 13, 1862, Life and Letters, I, p. 310; Strother, Sept. 11, 12, 1862, Diaries, p. 105; GBM teleg. to Lincoln, Sept. 12, 1862, Papers (C-15:64); GBM teleg. to Halleck, Sept. 12, 1862, RG 107 (M-473:50), NA.

12. Strother, Sept. 13, 1862, Diaries, p. 105; Gibbon to his wife, Sept. 16, 1862, Personal Recollections, p. 74; Harper's Weekly, Oct. 4, 1862; GBM to his wife, Sept. 14, 1862, Papers (C-7:63).

13. Richard C. Datzman, "Who Found Lee's Lost Order?" 1973, Antietam National Battlefield; Army of Northern Virginia, S.O. 191, Sept. 9 (D. H. Hill copy) — Williams to GBM, Sept. 13, 1862, Papers (A-78:31, A-79:31); Lee interview, Feb. 15, 1868, in Freeman, Lee's Lieutenants, II, p. 718.

14. Army of Northern Virginia, S.O. 191, Sept. 9, 1862, OR, XIX, Part 2, pp. 603–604; D. H. Hill in Battles and Leaders, II, p. 570. In fact, the loss should have been noted at Lee's headquarters. The delivery envelope is with the Lost Order in the McClellan Papers, suggesting that a headquarters courier was at fault in the incident. Normally a courier was required to bring back the envelope, signed by the recipient, as proof of delivery. "If the envelope was with it, the paper was never delivered," D. H. Hill wrote GBM on Apr. 17, 1869: Papers (A-93:37).

15. GBM teleg. to Lincoln, Sept. 13, 1862, RG 107 (M-473:50), NA; GBM to Hill, Feb. 1, 1869, D. H. Hill Papers, Virginia State Library; Gibbon, *Personal Recollections*, p. 73; GBM, *Report*, p. 195. The fourth Ninth Corps division was also ordered forward, but took the wrong road and returned to Frederick.

16. Marcy to Franklin, Darius N. Couch, Sept. 12, 1862, *OR*, LI, Part 1, p. 822; First Corps, S.O. 10, Sept. 13, 1862, *OR*, LI, Part 1, p. 828; GBM to his wife, Sept. 14, 1862, Papers (C-7:63); Pleasonton to Marcy, Sept. 13, 1862 (two), Papers (A-79:31); Sears, *Landscape Turned Red*, p. 116; Marcy to Pleasonton, Sept. 13, 1862, *OR*, LI, Part 1, p. 829.

17. GBM teleg. to Halleck — GBM to Franklin — Marcy to Couch, Sept. 13, 1862, Papers (A-79:31, C-16:65, C-18:65); *McClellan's Own Story*, draft, Papers (D-9:71); William F. Biddle to John C. Ropes, Mar. 27, 1895, Ropes Collection Boston University Library; GBM telegs. to Halleck, Sept. 13, 15, 1862, Papers (A-79:31, C-16:65); Arthur McClellan diary, Sept. 15, 1862, Papers (A-79:31). The 30,000 men GBM cited in his *Report* (p. 199) as the enemy's strength at Turner's Gap was taken from a set of figures only compiled later, on Oct. 6, 1862: *OR*, XIX, Part 2, p. 453.

18. GBM to his wife, Sept. 14, 1862, Papers (C-7:63); Jacob D. Cox in *Battles and Leaders*, II, p. 585; Pleasonton to Marcy — GBM teleg. to Halleck, Sept. 14, 1862, Papers (A-79:31, C-16:65); GBM, *Report*, p. 195.

19. Frank M. Bull diary, Sept. 14, 1862, Minnesota Historical Society; Charles H. Russell testimony, Harper's Ferry court of inquiry, *OR*, XIX, Part 1, pp. 720-22; GBM to Franklin, Dixon S. Miles, Sept. 14, 1862, Papers (C-18:65); Marcy to Pleasonton, Sept. 13, 1862, *OR*, LI, Part 1, p. 829.

20. Strother, Sept. 14, 1862, *Diaries*, p. 106; Cox in *Battles and Leaders*, II, p. 587-88; George W. Smalley, *Anglo-American Memories* (New York: G. P. Putnam's Sons, 1911), pp. 140, 143; David L. Thompson, George Kimball in *Battles and Leaders*, II, pp. 558, 551.

21. Franklin to GBM, Sept. 14, 1862, Papers (A-81:32); Cox to Ezra A. Carman, Jan. 27, 1897, Civil War Collection, HL; GBM testimony, *Report of the Joint Committee*, I (1863), p. 440; GBM teleg. to Halleck, Sept. 14, 1862, RG 107 (M-473:50), NA.

22. Hooker to Seth Williams (two) — George A. Custer to A.V. Colburn, Sept. 15, 1862, Papers (A-79:31); GBM telegs. to Halleck, Sept. 15, 1862 (two), Papers (C-16:65); *Journal of Commerce*, Sept. 16, 1862; Welles, Sept. 15, 1862, *Diary*, I, p. 130; GBM to his wife, Sept. 15, 1862, Papers (C-7:63).

23. GBM telegs. to Halleck, Sept. 15, 1862 (two), Papers (C-16:65); GBM telegs. to his wife, John H. B. McClellan, Winfield Scott, Sept. 15, 1862, RG 107 (M-504:66 [two], M-473:50), NA; Ezra A. Carman, "The Maryland Campaign of September 1862," ch. 9, p. 48, LC; C. B. Comstock to GBM, [Sept. 15, 1862], Papers (A-81:32); George D. Ruggles to Burnside, Sept. 15, 1862, *OR*, LI, Part 1, p. 837; Strother, Sept. 15, 1862, *Diaries*, p. 108; *McClellan's Own Story*, p. 586.

24. Lincoln teleg. to GBM, Sept. 15, 1862, *Works*, V, p. 462; Franklin to GBM, Sept. 15, 1862 (two), *OR*, XIX, Part 1, p. 47; William Allan, *The Army of Northern Virginia in 1862*, p. 364; *McClellan's Own Story*, draft — Comte de Paris to GBM, May 31, 1875, Papers (D-9:71, A-95:38).

25. Albert J. Myer to GBM — Custer to A. V. Colburn — Sumner to Marcy, Sept. 15, 1862, Papers (A-81 :32, A-80 :32, A-79 :31) ; *New York Tribune*, Sept. 19, 1862 ; Strother, Sept. 15, 1862, *Diaries*, p. 108 ; *McClellan's Own Story*, p. 586.

26. Cox in *Battles and Leaders*, II, pp. 630–31 ; *McClellan's Own Story*, draft, Papers (D-9 :71) ; Dawes, *Service with the Sixth Wisconsin*, p. 86 ; Arthur McClellan diary, Sept. 15, 1862, Papers (A-79 :31). Cox's assertion that GBM reached the front about 3 :00 P.M. on Sept. 15 is surely in error. GBM drafted a dispatch to Franklin from Boonsboro (although it was not sent) as late as 4 :00 P.M. : Papers (C-16 :65).

27. [James A. Hardie] to Franklin, Sept. 15 — Curtin teleg. to Lincoln, Sept. 16, 1862. *OR*, XIX, Part 2, pp. 297, 311 ; McClure, *Lincoln and Men of War-Times*, pp. 366–67 ; Thomas T. Eckert teleg. to GBM, Sept. 15, 1862, Papers (A-79 :31) ; Franklin to GBM — Curtin teleg. to GBM, Sept. 15, 1862, *OR*, XIX, Part 2, pp. 296, 306.

Chapter 13. The Battle of Antietam

1. GBM teleg. to Halleck — GBM to Franklin, Sept. 16, 1862, Papers (C-16 :65, C-18 :65) ; GBM, *Report*, draft, Papers (D-8 :70) ; *New York Tribune*, Sept. 19, 1862 ; Allan, *Army of Northern Virginia*, pp. 368–69.

2. GBM teleg. to his wife, Sept. 16, 1862, RG 107 (M-504 :66), NA ; D. H. Strother, "Personal Recollections of the War by a Virginian, Antietam," *Harper's New Monthly Magazine*, 36 (Feb. 1868), p. 281 ; Hooker testimony, *Report of the Joint Committee*, I (1863), p. 581.

3. GBM report (Oct. 15, 1862), *OR*, XIX, Part 1, p. 30 ; GBM, *Report*, pp. 201–202 ; *McClellan's Own Story*, p. 590 ; Marcy to Porter,

Sept. 15, 1862, *OR*, XIX, Part 2, p. 296 ; Cox, *Military Reminiscences*, I, pp. 380–81 ; Cox in *Battles and Leaders*, II, p. 631.

4. Henry J. Hunt to GBM, Jan. 12, 1876, Papers (A-95 :38) ; GBM, *Report*, p. 208 ; Carman, "Maryland Campaign," ch. 21, p. 11 ; Lewis Richmond to Seth Williams, Sept. 17, 1862 — [James A. Hardie] to Burnside, Sept. 16, 1862 — GBM report (Oct. 15, 1862), *OR*, XIX, Part 2, pp. 314, 308, Part 1, p. 31 ; Cox in *Battles and Leaders*, II, pp. 633–34.

5. Franklin to GBM, Sept. 16, 1862, Papers (A-80 :32) ; George D. Ruggles to Franklin, Sept. 16, 1862, *OR*, LI, Part 1, pp. 839–40 ; Lafayette McLaws report, *OR*, XIX, Part 1, p. 857 ; GBM to Franklin, Sept. 15, 1862, Papers (C-18 :65).

6. *McClellan's Own Story*, draft, Papers (D-9 :71) ; Hooker report, *OR*, XIX, Part 1, p. 217 ; George D. Ruggles to Sumner, Sept. 16, 1862, *OR*, LI, Part 1, p. 839 ; Hooker testimony, *Report of the Joint Committee*, I (1863), p. 582.

7. GBM to his wife, Oct. 1, 1862, Papers (C-7 :63) ; Sears, *Landscape Turned Red*, pp. 168–69 ; *McClellan's Own Story*, p. 587 ; Weld to his sister, Sept. 23, 1862, *War Diary and Letters*, p. 140.

8. Carman, "Maryland Campaign," ch. 21, pp. 27–28 ; Henry J. Hunt to GBM, Jan. 27, 1876, Papers (A-95 :38).

9. GBM teleg. to Halleck, Sept. 13, 1862, Papers (A-79 :31) ; Strother, Sept. 17, 1862, *Diaries*, p. 112 ; Webb to "Mr. Remsen," Sept. 28, 1862, Webb Papers, Yale University Library ; Weld to his father, Sept. 18, 1862, *War Diary and Letters*, p. 138 ; GBM teleg. to Halleck, Sept. 27, 1862 — "Memorandum Showing the Strength of the Army of the Potomac at the Battle of Antietam," Papers (C-18 :65, A-80 :32) ; Car-

man, "Maryland Campaign," ch. 23 *passim.*

10. GBM, *Report,* pp. 201-202, 206-207; Hooker testimony, *Report of the Joint Committee,* I (1863), p. 581; Comte de Paris to GBM, May 31, 1875, Papers (A-95:38); George D. Ruggles to Pleasonton, Sept. 16, 1862, *OR,* LI, Part 1, p. 840.

11. S. S. Sumner to George B. Davis, Apr. 4, 1897, John C. Ropes Collection, Boston University Library; Edwin V. Sumner testimony, *Report of the Joint Committee,* I (1863), p. 368; Rufus R. Dawes to Jacob D. Cox, Apr. 30, 1887, Cox Papers, Oberlin College Archives; Carman, "Maryland Campaign," ch. 17, p. 2 (S. S. Sumner interview); GBM to his wife, Sept. 20, 1862, Papers (C-7:63).

12. William Child, *A History of the Fifth Regiment New Hampshire Volunteers in the American Civil War, 1861-1865* (Bristol, N.H.: R. W. Musgrove, 1893), p. 120; Burnside report, *OR,* XIX, Part 1, p. 419; Charles Coffin in *Battles and Leaders,* II, p. 683; Sumner report, *OR,* XIX, Part 1, p. 275; Carman, "Maryland Campaign," ch. 18, p. 25, ch. 20, p. 9; GBM, *Regulations and Instructions for the Cavalry,* p. 45; GBM to Pleasonton, Sept. 17, 1862, private collection; Pleasonton to Marcy, Sept. 17, 1862, Papers (A-80:32); John C. Tidball, "The Artillery Service in the War of the Rebellion, 1861-65," *Journal of the Military Service Institution of the United States,* 12 (1891), p. 955.

13. Strother, "Personal Recollections," pp. 281-82; Benson J. Lossing, *Pictorial History of the Civil War in the United States of America* (Philadelphia: G. W. Childs, 1866-68), II, p. 476; B. F. Fisher report, *OR,* XIX, Part 1, pp. 128-29.

14. Williams to his daughters, Sept. 22, 1862, *From the Cannon's Mouth,* p. 127; Wilson, *Under the Old Flag,* I, p. 109; B.F. Fisher to Marcy — Herbert Hammerstein to A.V. Colburn — Williams to Marcy, Sept. 17, 1862, Papers (A-80:32); George D. Ruggles to Sumner — Ruggles to Burnside, Sept. 17, 1862, *OR,* LI, Part 1, pp. 842, 844.

15. William F. Smith to George B. Davis, May 9, 1897, Walter Wilgus Collection; S. S. Sumner to Davis, Apr. 4, 1897, John C. Ropes Collection, Boston University Library; Williams to Lewis Allen, Sept. 24, 1862, *From the Cannon's Mouth,* p. 135; Edwin V. Sumner to GBM, Sept. 17, 1862, *OR,* XIX, Part 1, p. 134; W. S. Abert to Marcy, Sept. 17, 1862, Papers (A-80:32); Cox in *Battles and Leaders,* II, p. 657; GBM, *Report,* p. 206.

16. William H. French report, *OR,* XIX, Part 1, p. 324; Sears, *Landscape Turned Red,* pp. 236-37; Carman, "Maryland Campaign," ch. 19, p. 53; *OR,* XIX, Part 1, pp. 192-93; Walter Clark, ed., *Histories of the Several Regiments and Battalions from North Carolina in the Great War, 1861-'65* (Raleigh: State of North Carolina, 1901), II, p. 500; Albert D. Richardson, *The Secret Service, the Field, the Dungeon, and the Escape* (Hartford, Conn.: American Publishing, 1865), p. 284; Carman to John C. Ropes, May 23, 1899, Ropes Collection, Boston University Library.

17. Strother, Sept. 17, 1862, *Diaries,* p. 110; Henry J. Hunt, Winfield S. Hancock, William M. Graham reports, *OR,* XIX, Part 1, pp. 206, 407, 343-44; Strother, "Personal Recollections," p. 283; Webb to "Mr. Remsen," Sept. 28, 1862, Webb Papers, Yale University Library.

18. Carman, "Maryland Campaign," ch. 21, pp. 25-26; Strother, "Personal Recollections," p. 284; Wil-

liam F. Biddle, "Recollections of McClellan," *United Service Magazine*, 9 (May 1894), p. 467.

19. GBM teleg. to Halleck, Sept. 17, 1862, Papers (A-80:32); GBM teleg. to his wife, Sept. 17, 1862, RG 107 (M-504:66), NA.

20. Nelson H. Davis to GBM, Jan. 31, 1876, Papers (A-95:38); Franklin testimony, *Report of the Joint Committee*, I (1863), pp. 626–27; Franklin in *Battles and Leaders*, II, p. 597; Hunt to GBM, Jan. 12, 1876, Papers (A-95:38); *New York Tribune*, Sept. 29, 1862; William F. Smith to George B. Davis, May 9, 1897, Walter Wilgus Collection; Porter to Manton Marble, Sept. 30, 1862, Marble Papers, LC; *McClellan's Own Story*, p. 606; Smith to John C. Ropes, Feb. 11, 1897, Ropes Collection, Boston University Library.

21. Strother, Sept. 17, 1862, *Diaries*, p. 111; *New York Tribune*, Sept. 19, 1862; W. H. Powell in *The Century*, 33 (Mar. 1897); Joseph Kirkland to Pleasonton, Sept. 17, 1862, private collection; N. H. Gloskoski to William S. Stryker, Sept. 17, 1862, Papers (A-81:32); Marcy to Burnside, Sept. 17, 1862, *OR*, LI, Part 1, p. 844; Strother, "Personal Recollections," p. 284.

Chapter 14. The Last Command

1. Strother, "Personal Recollections," p. 285; GBM teleg. to Halleck — GBM teleg. to his wife — GBM to his wife, Sept. 18, 1862, Papers (C-18:65, A-80:32, C-7:63).

2. Humphreys to GBM, Apr. 13, 1863, *OR*, LI, Part 1, pp. 1005–1006; Humphreys to Porter, Sept. 17 — John F. Reynolds teleg. to Marcy, Sept. 18, 1862, Papers (A-80:32); Reynolds teleg. to Halleck, Sept. 19, 1862, *OR*, XIX, Part 2, p. 332; Sears, *Landscape Turned Red*, pp. 300–303; Franklin to GBM — Sumner to Marcy, Sept. 18, 1862, Papers (A-80:32); Porter to Man-

ton Marble, Sept. 30, 1862, Marble Papers, LC; Marcy to Burnside, Pleasonton, Sept. 18, 1862, *OR*, LI, Part 1, pp. 848–49; Frank M. Bull diary, Sept. 18, 1862, Minnesota Historical Society.

3. Walter Lowenfels, ed., *Walt Whitman's Civil War* (New York: Knopf, 1960), p. 250; Webb to his father, Sept. 24, 1862, Webb Papers, Yale University Library; Wainwright, Sept. 19, 1862, *A Diary of Battle*, p. 104; GBM report (Oct. 15, 1862), *OR*, XIX, Part 1, p. 32; GBM, *Report*, p. 211; John S. Clark, "Return of Forces Under Command of Major General Robert E. Lee C.S.A. Previous to Battle of Antietam," Oct. 20, 1862, Papers (A-82:33).

4. GBM report (Oct. 15, 1862), *OR*, XIX, Part 1, p. 32; Marcy to Franklin, Sept. 18, 19, 1862, *OR*, LI, Part 1, pp. 848, 851; Strother, "Personal Recollections," p. 287; GBM teleg. to Halleck, Sept. 19, 1862, Papers (A-80:32); Marcy to Pleasonton, Sept. 19, 1862, *OR*, LI, Part 1, p. 853; Francis W. Palfrey, *The Antietam and Fredericksburg*, p. 128.

5. GBM to his wife, Sept. 20, 22, 1862, Papers (C-7:63); Sears, *Landscape Turned Red*, pp. 296, 309; GBM report (Oct. 15, 1862), *OR*, XIX, Part 1, p. 32; Strother, "Personal Recollections," p. 282; Palfrey, *Antietam*, p. 119; Carman, "Maryland Campaign," ch. 21, p. 98.

6. GBM to his wife, Sept. 20 (two), Oct. 31, 1862, Papers (C-7:63); *New York Herald*, Sept. 26, 1862.

7. Preliminary Emancipation Proclamation, Sept. 22 — habeas corpus proclamation, Sept. 24, 1862, Lincoln, *Works*, V, pp. 433–36, 436–37; GBM to his wife, Sept. 25, 1862, Papers (C-7:63); GBM to Aspinwall, Sept. 26, 1862, Civil War Collection, HL; Welles, Sept. 22, 1862, *Diary*, I, p. 143.

8. Porter to Marble, Sept. 30, 1862, Marble Papers, LC; L. A. Whitely to Bennett, Sept. 24, 1862, Bennett Papers, LC; Sears, *Landscape Turned Red*, pp. 320–21; GBM to his wife, Sept. 20, 1862, Papers (C-7:63).

9. John Gregory Smith to Lincoln, Dec. 30, 1864, Special Collections, University of Vermont Library; Cox, *Military Reminiscences*, I, pp. 359–61; O. M. Hatch to Joseph Medill, Oct. 14, 1862, Charles H. Ray Papers, HL. The Baldy Smith interview is related here in the corrected form furnished by Gen. Smith's cousin, Gov. John Gregory Smith of Vermont, in 1864. Originally, Gov. Smith, acting on garbled information, told Lincoln — and Lincoln told John Hay (Hay, Sept. 25, 1864, *Diaries and Letters,* pp. 217–18) — that on the Peninsula and again after Antietam GBM succumbed to the blandishments of the New York politician Fernando Wood and agreed to be the Democratic nominee for president in 1864, only to be dissuaded by Baldy Smith. After clarifying the matter with his cousin, Gov. Smith sent a corrected version of the story to Lincoln.

10. Montgomery Blair to GBM, Sept. 27 — Francis P. Blair to GBM, Sept. 30, 1862, Papers (A-81:32).

11. GBM to his wife, Oct. 5, 1862, Papers (C-7:63); Army of the Potomac, G.O. 163, Oct. 7, 1862, Lincoln Papers, LC; Francis P. Blair to John A. Andrew, Oct. 9, 1862, Andrew Papers, Massachusetts Historical Society; *New York Tribune,* Oct. 9, 1862.

12. *Journal of Commerce,* Sept. 22, 1862; *New York World,* Sept. 20, 1862; *New York Tribune,* Sept. 19, 1862; *New York Times,* Sept. 23, 1862; John C. Gray to his mother, Oct. 23, 1862, Gray and Ropes, *War Letters,* p. 9; Welles, Oct. 18, 1862, *Diary,* I, pp. 176–77; Meade to his wife, Oct. 20, 1862, *Life and Letters,* I, p. 320.

13. GBM to his wife, Sept. 20, 22, 1862, Papers (C-7:63); Marcy to Barlow, Sept. 21, 1862, Barlow Papers, HL; L. A. Whitely to James Gordon Bennett, Oct. 5, 1862, Bennett Papers, William R. Perkins Library, Duke University; John Cochrane, *The War for the Union: Memoir of Gen. John Cochrane* (New York: 1875), pp. 30–32; Cochrane to Lincoln, Oct. 26, 1862, Lincoln Papers, LC; T. J. Barnett to Barlow, Oct. 27, 1862, Barlow Papers; Chase, Oct. 7, 1862, *Diaries,* p. 168.

14. Hay, July 14, 1863, *Diaries and Letters,* p. 67; GBM telegs. to Halleck, Sept. 23, 27, 1862, Papers (C-18:65); Barnett to Barlow, Sept. 23, 1862, Barlow Papers, HL.

15. GBM to his wife, Oct. 2, 5, 1862, Papers (C-7:63); *McClellan's Own Story,* pp. 627–28; Lincoln to GBM, Sept. 13, 1862, *Works,* V, p. 460; David Davis to Leonard Swett, Nov. 26, 1862, Davis Papers, Illinois State Historical Library; Nicolay and Hay, *Lincoln,* VI, p. 175.

16. GBM telegs. to Halleck, Sept. 24, 27, 1862, Papers (C-18:65); Darius N. Couch to Marcy, Oct. 7, 1862, Papers (A-82:33); Heintzelman diary, Oct. 9, 1862, LC; Strother, "Personal Recollections," p. 291; GBM to his wife, Sept. 25, Oct. 7, 1862, Papers (C-7:63); Benjamin A. Latrobe to GBM, Oct. 17, 1862, Papers (A-83:33); GBM, *Report,* p. 236; A. D. Richardson to Sydney H. Gay, Oct. 31, 1862, Gay Papers, Rare Book and Manuscript Library, Columbia University.

17. *McClellan's Own Story,* p. 628; Halleck teleg. to GBM, Oct. 6, 1862, *OR,* XIX, Part 1, p. 72; *Philadelphia Press,* Oct. 15, 1862; GBM to Barlow, Oct. 17, 1862, Barlow Papers, HL; Halleck to Hamilton R. Gamble, Oct. 30, 1862, *OR,* Ser. 3, II, pp. 703–704.

18. GBM telegs. to Halleck, Oct. 7, 12, 1862, Papers (A-83:33, C-16:65); Meade to his wife, Oct. 20, 1862, *Life and Letters*, I, p. 320; Williams to his daughter, Oct. 26, 1862, *From the Cannon's Mouth*, p. 140; GBM teleg. to Halleck, Oct. 18, 1862, RG 94 (159:Halleck Papers), NA; Ingalls teleg. to Marcy, Oct. 17, 1862, Papers (A-83:33); Haupt to Stanton, Oct. 20, 23, 1862, RG 107 (M-492:31), NA; Meigs teleg. to GBM, Oct. 22, 1862, *OR*, XIX, Part 2, pp. 464–65.

19. Starr, *Union Cavalry*, I, pp. 318–19, 320–21; Wainwright, Oct. 14, 1862, *Diary of Battle*, p. 115; *OR*, XIX, Part 2, p. 410; Halleck teleg. to GBM, Oct. 14, 1862, *OR*, XIX, Part 2, p. 421; Lincoln teleg. to GBM, Oct. 25, 1862, *Works*, V, p. 474; GBM to his wife, Oct. 26, 1862, Papers (C-7:63); GBM teleg. to Lincoln, Oct. 26, 1862, *OR*, XIX, Part 2, pp. 490–91.

20. GBM teleg. to Halleck, Oct. 7, 1862, Papers (A-83:33); Lincoln to GBM, Oct. 13, 1862, *Works*, V, pp. 460–61; Charles E. Hamlin, *The Life and Times of Hannibal Hamlin* (Cambridge, Mass.: Riverside Press, 1899), p. 442; Adams S. Hill to Sydney H. Gay, Oct. 13, 1862, Gay Papers, Rare Book and Manuscript Library, Columbia University.

21. Wilson, *Under the Old Flag*, I, pp. 122–23; Couch in *Battles and Leaders*, III, pp. 105–106; GBM to Lincoln, Oct. 17, 1862, Lincoln Papers, LC; GBM teleg. to Halleck, Oct. 22, 1862, Papers (C-15:64); *OR*, XIX, Part 2, p. 569.

22. GBM teleg. to Halleck, Oct. 25, 1862, Papers (C-19:66); Halleck teleg. to GBM, Oct. 26, 1862, *OR*, XIX, Part 1, pp. 84–85; Colburn teleg. to GBM, Oct. 25 — GBM teleg. to Lincoln, Oct. 30, 1862, Papers (A-86:34, C-15:64); Barnett to Barlow, Oct. 24, 1862, Barlow Papers, HL; GBM to his wife, [c.

Oct. 29, 1862], Papers (C-7:63).

23. GBM to his wife, Oct. 25, 1862, Papers (C-7:63); GBM, *Report*, pp. 235–36; Wainwright, Nov. 17, 1862, *Diary of Battle*, p. 127; GBM telegs. to Herman Haupt, Oct. 26, 27, 1862, Papers (C-19:66); Pinkerton to GBM, Oct. 31, 1862, Papers (A-87:34); *OR*, XIX, Part 2, pp. 674, 713.

24. Lee to George W. Randolph, Nov. 10, 1862, *Wartime Papers*, p. 332; GBM teleg. to his wife, Nov. 4, 1862, RG 107 (M-504:66), NA; Hay, Sept. 25, 1864, *Letters and Diaries*, pp. 218–19; Lincoln to Halleck, Nov. 5, 1862, *Works*, V, p. 485.

25. Francis P. Blair to Montgomery Blair, Nov. 7, 1862, William Ernest Smith, *The Francis Preston Blair Family in Politics*, II, p. 144; GBM to Aspinwall, July 19, 1862, Papers (A-73:29); GBM to Barlow, July 15, 30 — Marcy to Barlow, Sept. 21, 1862, Barlow Papers, HL; George T. McJimsey, *Genteel Partisan: Manton Marble, 1834–1917*, pp. 39–40; Stanton to Greeley, Oct. 4, 1862, Lincoln Papers, Lincoln Memorial University; Chase, July 22, 1862, *Diaries*, p. 98.

26. GBM, *Report*, p. 238; Porter to Marble, Nov. 9, 1862, Marble Papers, LC; James Longstreet in *Battles and Leaders*, III, p. 70.

27. C. P. Buckingham account in *Chicago Tribune*, Sept. 4, 1875, quoted in Comte de Paris, *Civil War in America*, II, pp. 555–57n; Herman Haupt teleg. to GBM, Nov. 7, 1862, Papers (A-87:34); *McClellan's Own Story*, pp. 651–52; GBM to his wife, Nov. 7, 1862, Papers (C-7:63); GBM to Mary B. Burnside, Nov. 8, 1862, Charles B. Phillips Library, Aurora University.

28. GBM to his wife, Nov. 9, 1862, Papers (C-7:63); Patrick, Nov. 8, 1862, *Diary*, p. 173; *New York World*, Nov. 12, 1862; *New York*

Times, Nov. 12, 1862; GBM to Army of the Potomac, Nov. 7, 1862, Papers (B-12:48). To this broadside version of his address, issued to the army, GBM added a concluding sentence — "We shall also ever be comrades in supporting the Constitution of our country & the nationality of our people" — which appeared in official printings: Alexander S. Webb Papers, Yale University Library.

29. James Ford to his brother, Dec. 2, 1862, Henry Ford Papers, William R. Perkins Library, Duke University; Patrick, Nov. 11, 1862, *Diary,* p. 174; *New York Times,* Nov. 12, 1862; Wainwright, Nov. 10, 1862, *Diary of Battle,* p. 125; GBM to his wife, Nov. 10, 1862, Papers (C-7:63).

30. Thomas F. Meagher to Barlow, Nov. 10, 1862, Barlow Papers, HL; *New York World,* Nov. 12, 1862; *New York Times,* Nov. 12, 1862; *New York Tribune,* Nov. 10, 1862.

31. George W. Salter to James M. Wilson, Nov. 9, 1862, John Hay Library, Brown University; George W. Faucett diary, Nov. 10 — Gus Van Dyke to his brother, Nov. 11, 1862, Indiana Historical Society; Charles W. Hughes to his sister, Nov. 13, 1862, Minnesota Historical Society; George Ticknor Curtis, *McClellan's Last Service to the Republic,* pp. 81–83; Electus W. Jones to his parents, Nov. 16, 1862, William R. Perkins Library, Duke University.

Chapter 15. The Political Arena

1. *New York Express,* Nov. 14, 1862; *New York Herald,* Nov. 21, 1862; GBM to Lorenzo Thomas, Dec. 9, 1862, Papers (A-88:35).

2. Barlow to Horatio Seymour, Dec. 2, 1862, Seymour Papers, New-York Historical Society; GBM to Belmont, Dec. 7, 1862, Belmont Family Collection, Rare Book and Manuscript Library, Columbia

University; Aspinwall to Barlow, Dec. 12, 1862 — GBM to Barlow, Jan. 20, 1863, Barlow Papers, HL; Edward H. Eldredge to John H. B. McClellan, Nov. 28, 1862, Papers (B-12:48); Barnett to Barlow, May 15, 1863, Barlow Papers; Darius Starr to his brother, June 18, 1863, Starr Papers, William H. Perkins Library, Duke University; Dennison to GBM Aug. 4, 1863, Papers (B-12:48).

3. Strong, July 6, 1863, *Diary,* p. 330; GBM to Barlow, c. May 3, 1864 — George T. Curtis to Prime, Feb. 6, 1863 — GBM to Elizabeth B. McClellan, Dec. 6, 1863, Papers (B-23:53, A-89:35, B-13:49).

4. Colburn to GBM, Nov. 27 — GBM to Leslie Combs, Dec. 11, 1862, Papers (A-88:35, A-72:29); *New York Herald,* Nov. 28, 1862; Pinkerton to GBM, Nov. 28, 1862 — telegraphic cipher, 1863 — GBM to his wife, Dec. 12, 1862 — Porter to GBM, Jan. 13, 1863, Papers (B-12:48, A-107:42, D-10:72, A-89:35).

5. W. H. Withington to his sister, Dec. 23, 1862, Michigan Historical Collections, Bentley Historical Library, University of Michigan; G. K. Warren to his brother, Dec. 18, 1862, Warren Papers, New York State Library; Walter H. Hebert, *Fighting Joe Hooker,* p. 179; Francis A. Walker, *History of the Second Corps in the Army of the Potomac* (New York: Scribner's, 1887), p. 198; Charles F. Benjamin in *Battles and Leaders,* III, pp. 239–40.

6. Strong, Feb. 11, 1863, *Diary,* p. 297; Franklin and Smith to Lincoln, Dec. 20, 1862, *OR,* XXI, pp. 868–70; Nicolay and Hay, *Lincoln,* VI, pp. 213–14; Sumner testimony, *Report of the Joint Committee,* I (1863), p. 660; Army of the Potomac, G.O. 9, Jan. 23, 1863, *OR,* XXI, pp. 998–99; Wainwright, Jan. 21, 1863, *Diary of Battle,* p. 158;

approval of Porter sentence, Jan. 21, 1863, Lincoln, *Works*, VI, p. 67.

7. J. Jefferson Coolidge, *Autobiography* (Boston: Houghton Mifflin, 1923), p. 39; Edith Ellen Ware, *Political Opinion in Massachusetts During Civil War and Reconstruction* (New York: Columbia University, 1916), pp. 120–22; *Boston Post*, Feb. 3, 1863; William D. Ticknor to George T. Curtis, in Curtis to William C. Prime, Feb. 6, 1863, Papers (A-89:35); *Worcester* (Mass.) *Spy*, Feb. 7, 1863; *Springfield* (Mass.) *Republican*, Feb. 9, 1863.

8. Francis P. Blair to Lincoln, Dec. 18, 1862, Lincoln Papers, LC; Browning, Jan. 26, 1863, *Diary*, I, p. 619; Herman Haupt, *Reminiscences of General Herman Haupt* (Milwaukee: Wright & Joys, 1901), p. 177; GBM to Mrs. Francis P. Blair, Feb. 25, 1863, Blair Family Papers, LC; George T. Curtis to GBM, Oct. 4, 1864, Papers (B-21:52); Welles, June 26, 1863, *Diary*, I, p. 345.

9. GBM to his wife, Feb. 26, 28, 1863, Papers (B-12:48); GBM to Franklin, Mar. 10, 1865, Franklin Papers, LC; GBM testimony, *Report of the Joint Committee*, I (1863), pp. 419–41; Chandler to his wife, Mar. 31, 1863, Chandler Papers, LC; *New York Herald*, Apr. 28, 1863.

10. *New York Times*, Jan. 6, 1864; GBM to Edward Everett, Feb. 20, 1863, Everett Papers, Massachusetts Historical Society; "Scheme of Report," Papers (A-87:34); GBM, *Report*, p. 239; Lowell, "General McClellan's Report," p. 552.

11. Barnett to Barlow, June 22, 1863, Barlow Papers, HL; B. C. Stevens to his parents, June 29, 1863, Stevens Papers, William R. Perkins Library, Duke University; Everett to Lincoln, June 16, 1863, Everett Papers, Massachusetts

Historical Society; Joel Parker teleg. to Lincoln, June 29 — McClure teleg. to Lincoln, June 30, 1863, *OR*, XXVII, Part 3, pp. 409, 436; *New York Herald*, June 18, 1863; Lincoln telegs. to Parker, McClure, June 30, 1863, *Works*, VI, pp. 311–12; GBM to Barlow, June 15, 1863, Barlow Papers.

12. *McClellan's Own Story*, draft — Porter to GBM, July 22, 1863, Papers (D-9:71, A-90:35); Porter to Barlow, July 22, 1863, Barlow Papers, HL; Edward Everett to GBM, July 25, 1863, Papers (A-90:35).

13. Charles C. Fulton to GBM, May 27 — GBM to Fulton, May 28 — Samuel S. Cox to GBM, May 31 — GBM to Cox, June 8 — Weed to GBM, June 12, 1863, Papers (A-90:35); GBM to Weed, June 13, 1863, Weed Papers, Rush Rhees Library, University of Rochester; *New York Express*, July 31, 1863; GBM to Cox, July 14, 1863, Thomas F. Madigan Collection, Rare Books and Manuscripts Division, New York Public Library.

14. GBM to Thomas, Aug. 4, 1863 — "List of documents to accompany Maj. Gen. McClellan's Report," Papers (A-90:35); *Journal of Commerce*, Dec. 23, 1863; Barnett to Barlow, Sept. 5 — Samuel S. Cox to Barlow, Dec. 16, 1863, Barlow Papers, HL.

15. William B. Hesseltine, *Lincoln and the War Governors*, p. 328; GBM to Charles J. Biddle, Oct. 12, in *Philadelphia Press*, Oct. 13, 1863; D. Solomon to Marble, Nov. 12, 1863, Papers (B-91:36); *New York Times*, Sept. 30, 1863; Marble to GBM, [Oct. 11, 1863], McClellan Papers, New Jersey Historical Society; Marble to GBM, Nov. 14 — Eldredge to GBM, Dec. 4, 1863, Papers (A-91:36, A-13:49); Cox to Barlow, Oct. 21 — Barnett to Barlow, c. Oct. 15, 1863, Barlow Papers, HL.

16. John Jacob Astor to GBM, Nov.

19, 1863 — GBM, draft of resignation, Nov. 1863, Papers (A-91:36); Aspinwall to GBM, Mar. 21, July 6, Dec. 8, 1864, Papers (B-15:49, B-16:50, B-23:53); [GBM], "The Coming Campaign in the West," *The Round Table*, 1 (Mar. 19, 1864), pp. 209–210; [GBM], "The Coming Campaign Foreshadowed," *The Round Table*, 1 (Mar. 12, 1864), p. 194. GBM's authorship of these articles is identified through manuscript drafts in the Papers (B-39:60).

17. GBM to Edward H. Wright, Mar. 2, 1864, Miscellaneous Collections, HL; Hiram Ketchum to GBM, Mar. 9, 1864, Papers (B-14:49); *New York World*, Jan. 7, 1864; *New York Times*, Jan. 6, 1864; GBM to Barlow, Mar. 9, 1864, Barlow Papers, HL; G. S. Hillard to George T. Curtis, Dec. 18, 1863, McClellan Papers, New Jersey Historical Society; Hillard, *Life of McClellan*, p. 5. Both the Swinton and Ketchum series were issued as campaign pamphlets in 1864.

18. Horace Greeley, "Gen. McClellan — The Presidency," *Independent*, Mar. 5, 1864; Cox to Barlow, Feb. 12, 1864, Barlow Papers, HL; GBM to Elizabeth B. McClellan, Mar. 13, 1864, Papers (B-14:49).

19. Cox to GBM, Feb. 11, 1864, Papers (B-14:49); GBM to Cox, Feb. 12, 1864, Charlton L. Lewis Papers, Yale University Library; GBM to Reverdy Johnson, Mar. 9, 1864, Johnson Papers, LC; *McClellan's Own Story*, p. 38; A. J. Daugherty to GBM, Feb. 21, 1864, McClellan Papers, New Jersey Historical Society; *New York Tribune*, Mar. 7, 9, 14, 1864; *New York Commercial Advertiser*, Mar. 12, 1864; *New York World*, Mar. 15, 1864; *Journal of Commerce*, Mar. 19, 1864; Nicolay to Lincoln, Aug. 30, 1864, Lincoln Papers, LC.

20. Irving Katz, *August Belmont: A*

Political Biography, p. 121; Joel H. Silbey, *A Respectable Minority: The Democratic Party in the Civil War Era, 1860–1868*, pp. 78, 121; Cox to Barlow, Oct. 21, Dec. 16, 1863, Barlow Papers, HL.

21. Hillard, *Life of McClellan*, pp. 376, 388–89; Barlow to GBM, June 16 — Hiram Ketchum to GBM, Aug. 24, 1864, Papers (B-15:50, B-17:50).

22. Stanton to Lincoln, Jan. 1863, quoted in Benjamin P. Thomas and Harold M. Hyman, *Stanton: The Life and Times of Lincoln's Secretary of War*, p. 262; Arthur McClellan to GBM, Sept. 24, 1863 — GBM to Elizabeth B. McClellan, July 3, 1864, Papers (A-90:35, B-41:61); Barnett to Barlow, Mar. 20, 1864, Barlow Papers, HL.

23. Montgomery Blair to Barlow, May 1 — Barlow to Blair, May 3, 1864, Barlow Papers, HL; GBM to Barlow, c. May 3, 1864, Papers (B-23:53).

24. GBM to Mary McClellan, May 12, 1864, Papers (B-15:49); Francis P. Blair to editor, Oct. 5, in *National Intelligencer*, Oct. 8, 1864; Montgomery Blair to Fitz John Porter, Dec. 1, 1874, Porter Papers, Massachusetts Historical Society; GBM to Francis P. Blair, c. July 22, 1864, Papers (B-16:50).

25. Bruce Catton, *Grant Takes Command* (Boston: Little, Brown, 1968), pp. 157, 336–38; Lincoln endorsement, Grant teleg. to Lincoln, July 30 — Edwin D. Morgan to Lincoln, July 27, 1864, Lincoln Papers, LC; James C. Welling to GBM, Oct. 8 — Franklin to GBM, Aug. 22, 1864, Papers (B-21:52, B-17:50); Barlow to Manton Marble, Aug. 26, 1864, Marble Papers, LC; GBM to Charles A Whittier, Sept. 27, 1864, William Alvord Papers, Bancroft Library, University of California at Berkeley.

26. Strong, Aug. 16, 1864, *Diary*, p. 473; Henry J. Raymond to Lin-

coln — Weed to William H. Seward, Aug. 22, 1864, Lincoln Papers, LC; Nicolay to John Hay, Aug. 25, 1864, Helen Nicolay, *Lincoln's Secretary*, p. 212; Lincoln memorandum, Aug. 23, 1864, *Works*, VII, p. 514; Hay, Nov. 11, 1864, *Diaries and Letters*, p. 238.

27. Noah Brooks, "Two War-Time Conventions," *The Century*, 49 (Mar. 1895), p. 732; Cox to GBM, Aug. 4, 1864, Papers (B-16:50); Barlow to GBM, [Aug. 1864], Barlow Papers, HL.

28. Samuel S. Cox to GBM, June 9, 1864, Papers (B-15:50); Fernando Wood to Barlow, June 15 — GBM to Barlow, June 17, 1864, Barlow Papers, HL; GBM to Cox, June 20, 1864, Thomas F. Madigan Collection, Rare Books and Manuscripts Division, New York Public Library; George W. Morgan to GBM, Aug. 4 — GBM to Prime, Aug. 10, 1864, Papers (B-16:50, B-17:50); GBM to Marble, June 25, 1864, Marble Papers, LC.

29. Marble to GBM, [Aug. 10, 1864], Papers (B-40:60); Barlow to Marble, Aug. 21, 1864, Marble Papers, LC; James Lawrence, to GBM, Aug. 31 — Barlow to GBM, Aug. 28, 1864, Papers (B-17:51, B-22:52); GBM to Barlow, [Aug. 28, 1864], Barlow Papers, HL.

Chapter 16. Campaign for the Presidency

1. Marble teleg. to GBM, c. Aug. 26 — Barlow to GBM, Aug. 28, 1864, Papers (B-40:60, B-22:52); Belmont teleg. to Barlow, Aug. 29, 1864, Barlow Papers, HL; H. S. Lansing to GBM, Aug. 28, 1864, Papers (B-17:50); Marble teleg. to Barlow, Aug. 17, 1864, Barlow Papers.

2. Barlow to GBM, Aug. 28, 29, 1864, Papers (B-22:52, B-17:50); Marble teleg. to Barlow, Aug. 27, 1864, Barlow Papers, HL; Clement L. Vallandigham to editor, *New York News*, Oct. 22, 1864, in Edward McPherson, *The Political History of the United States of America, During the Great Rebellion*, p. 423; McPherson, *Political History*, p. 419; Amasa J. Parker to GBM, Sept. 5 — Belmont to GBM, Sept. 3, 1864, Papers (B-18:51).

3. William Cassidy to Barlow, Sept. 5, 1864, Barlow Papers, HL; Vallandigham to GBM, Sept. 4, 1864, Papers (A-91:36); Brooks, "Two War-Time Conventions," pp. 733, 734; McPherson, *Political History*, p. 420; George W. Adams to David G. Croly, Oct. 16, 1864, Marble Papers, LC; Noah Brooks to John G. Nicolay, Sept. 2, 1864, Lincoln Papers. LC; Key to GBM, Sept. 4 — Barlow to GBM, Aug. 31, 1864, Papers (B-18:51, B-17:51); *Newark Advertiser*, Sept. 1, 1864.

4. Curtis to GBM, Sept. 1 — Key to GBM, Sept. 4 — Aspinwall to GBM, Sept. 4, 1864, Papers (A-91:36, B-18:51, A-91:36); Belmont to GBM, Sept. 3 — Barlow to Washington McLean, Sept. 2 — Barlow to GBM, Sept. 2, 1864, Papers (B-18:51).

5. GBM to his wife, [Sept. 6, 1864], Papers (B-35:54); GBM to Cox, Sept. 15, 1864, Thomas F. Madigan Collection, Rare Books and Manuscripts Division, New York Public Library; GBM to Aspinwall, [Sept. 6, 1864], James S. Schoff Collection, William L. Clements Library, University of Michigan; Barlow to GBM, Sept. 3, 1864, Papers (B-18:51); "To Whom It May Concern," July 18, 1864, Lincoln, *Works*, VII, p. 451; Vallandigham speech, Sept. 24, 1864, in McPherson, *Political History*, p. 421; GBM to his wife, [Sept. 9, 1864], Papers (B-12:48). Drafts One, Two, Three, and Five of GBM's acceptance letter are in the Papers (B-21:52 [two], A-96:38, B-23:53); drafts Four and

Six are in the Barlow Papers, HL. In "McClellan's Changing Views on the Peace Plank of 1864," *American Historical Review*, 38:3 (Apr. 1933), pp. 598–605, Charles R. Wilson incorrectly states that GBM wavered on the "reunion before peace" issue in drafting his acceptance letter.

6. *New York World*, Sept. 1, 1864; Wilcox to his wife, Nov. –, 1864, Andrew Jackson Donelson Papers, LC; Josiah Gorgas to George W. Rains, Sept. 3, 1864, Rains Papers, Southern Historical Collection, University of North Carolina Library; Larry E. Nelson, *Bullets, Ballots, and Rhetoric: Confederate Policy for the United States Presidential Contest of 1864* (University: University of Alabama Press, 1980), pp. 168–69.

7. Aspinwall to Barlow, Sept. 26, 1864, Barlow Papers, HL; Robert C. Winthrop to GBM, Sept. 19, 1864, Papers (A-80:32); Charles A. Bristed, *The Cowards' Convention* (New York, 1864), in Frank Freidel, ed., *Union Pamphlets of the Civil War*, II, p. 1147.

8. Gerrit Smith, *Gerrit Smith on McClellan's Nomination and Acceptance* (New York, 1864), p. 12; Strong, Oct. 7, 1864, *Diary*, p. 497; *Harper's Weekly*, Oct. 8, 1864; cartoons: Anne S. K. Brown Military Collection, Brown University Library; Prints and Photographs Division, LC; New-York Historical Society.

9. Wilbur Fisk to *Green Mountain Freeman*, Oct. 12, 1864, Ruth and Emil Rosenblatt, eds., *Anti-Rebel: The Civil War Letters of Wilbur Fisk* (Croton-on-Hudson, N.Y.: Emil Rosenblatt, 1983), pp. 264–65; Robet McAllister to his wife, Oct. 8, 1864, James I. Robertson, Jr., ed., *The Civil War Letters of General Robert McAllister* (New Brunswick, N.J.: Rutgers University Press, 1965), p. 518; Eugene

Cole to his father, Nov. 22, 1864, RG 15 (Civil War Pension Records), NA; John Brobst to "Mary," Sept. 27, 1864, Margaret B. Roth, ed., *Well Mary: Civil War Letters of a Wisconsin Volunteer* (Madison: University of Wisconsin Press, 1969), p. 92.

10. *New York Tribune*, Sept. 23, 1864; *New York World*, Nov. 6, 1864; GBM to Charles Mason, Oct. 3, 1864, Mason Papers, Iowa State Historical Department; GBM to Prime, Aug. 10, Sept. 28, 1864, Papers (B-17:50, B-41:61); GBM to Barlow, [Oct. 4, 1864], Barlow Papers, HL.

11. William O. Bartlett to Lincoln, Nov. 5, 1864, Lincoln Papers, LC; Albert C. Ramsey to GBM, Oct. 18 — J. Henry Liebenau to GBM, Oct. 8, 1864, Papers (B-22:52, B-21:52); GBM to Liebenau, Oct. 13, in *New York World*, Oct. 16, 1864.

12. Poster: Louis A. Warren Lincoln Library and Museum; Robert C. Winthrop, *Speech by Hon. Robert C. Winthrop, at the Great New York Ratification Meeting, September 17, 1864* (Boston, 1864), pp. 12–13; Winthrop, *Great Speech of Hon. Robert C. Winthrop, at New London, Conn., Oct. 18* (New York, 1864), in Freidel, *Union Pamphlets*, II, pp. 1098, 1101; GBM to Winthrop, Oct. 22, 1864, Winthrop Papers, Massachusetts Historical Society.

13. Wright to GBM, Mar. 15, 1864, Papers (B-14:49); GBM to Wright, Mar. 19, 1864, Miscellaneous Collections, HL; Barlow to Marble, Aug. 24, 1864, Marble Papers, LC; Marcy to GBM, Sept. 13, 20, 1864, Papers (B-19:51, B-20:52); GBM teleg. to Samuel R. Curtis, Nov. 7, 1861, RG 107 (M-504:9), NA.

14. GBM to Barlow, Sept. 21, 1864, Barlow Papers, HL; GBM to Marcy, Sept. 18, 1864 — Edward W. Kulgan to GBM, Sept. 23, 1864 — Wright to Curtis, Dec. 28,

1886, Papers (B-41 :60, B-20 :52, B-39 :60) ; GBM to Barlow, [Oct. 27, 1864], Barlow Papers.

15. William Frank Zornow, *Lincoln and the Party Divided,* pp. 191-95; John Love to GBM, Oct. 13, 1864, Papers (B-21 :52) ; Oscar O. Winther, "The Soldier Vote in the Election of 1864," *New York History,* 25 :4 (Oct. 1944), p. 453; McClure to Leonard Swett, Oct. 14, 1864, Lincoln Papers, LC ; John C. Mather to GBM, Oct. 13, 1864, Papers (B-21 :52).

16. Prime to GBM, Oct. 20, 1864, Papers (B-22 :52) ; "Estimated Electoral Vote," Oct. 13, 1864, Lincoln, *Works,* VIII, p. 46.

17. GBM to Barlow, Nov. 10, 1864, Barlow Papers, HL ; GBM to Belmont, Oct. 13, 1864, Belmont Family Collection, Rare Book and Manuscript Library, Columbia University; GBM to Barlow, Oct. 27, 1864 (two), Barlow Papers; Monroe Porter to Horace N. Congar, Nov. 11, 1864, Congar Papers, New Jersey Historical Society, quoted in Daniel W. Crofts, "Re-Electing Lincoln : The Struggle in Newark," *Civil War History,* 30 :1 (Mar. 1984), p. 77 ; Wainwright, Oct. 26, 1864, *Diary of Battle,* p. 477 ; GBM to Lorenzo Thomas, Nov. 8, 1864, RG 94 (M-619 :278), NA ; GBM to Barlow, Nov. 12, 1865, Barlow Papers; GBM to Prime, Dec. 24, 1865, Papers (B-25 :54).

18. McPherson, *Political History,* p. 623; Winther, "The Soldier Vote," p. 457; Joseph T. Glatthaar, *The March to the Sea and Beyond: Sherman's Troops in the Savannah and Carolinas Campaigns* (New York : New York University Press, 1985), pp. 47, 200–202 ; *OR,* XLII, Part 3, pp. 560–78 *passim.* Lincoln's electoral count was actually 213, but one elector died and his vote was not counted.

19. GBM to Marble, Nov. 28, 1864, Marble Papers, LC ; GBM to Barlow, Nov. 10, 1864, Barlow Papers, HL.

Chapter 17. The Old Soldier

1. GBM to Elizabeth B. McClellan, Nov. 11 — Abram Hewitt to GBM, May 19, Nov. 26, 1864, Papers (B-22 :52, B-17 :50, B-22 :52) ; GBM to Barlow, Nov. 28, 1864, Barlow Papers, HL.

2. GBM to Frederic Goodridge, Aug. 17, 1864, Papers (B-91 :36) ; GBM to Barlow. Jan. 24, 1865, Barlow Papers, HL.

3. Mary Ellen McClellan to Marcy, Feb. 9, 1865, Papers (A-92 :36) ; GBM to Barlow, Apr. 15, 1865, Nov. 28, 1864, Mar. 18, 1865, Barlow Papers, HL; GBM to August Belmont, Mar. 19, 1865, Belmont Family Collection, Rare Book and Manuscript Library, Columbia University ; GBM to William Adams, May 4, 1865, George B. McClellan, Jr., Papers, LC ; GBM to Charles E. Whitehead, July 4, 1865, Chicago Historical Society.

4. GBM to Franklin, Mar. 10, 1865, Franklin Papers, LC; GBM to William Adams, July 14, 1865, George B. McClellan, Jr., Papers, LC; GBM to Prime, Sept. 17 — GBM to Elizabeth B. McClellan, Dec. 3, 1865, Papers (B-25 :54) ; GBM to Barlow, Dec. 24, 1865, Dec. 4, 1866, Barlow Papers, HL.

5. E. A. Stevens to GBM, Sept, 30, 1867 — GBM to king of Prussia, Dec. 1867 — Stevens to GBM, Jan. 31, 1868 — Rear Adm. Jackmann to GBM, Jan. 15, 1868 — Russian minister of marine to GBM, Jan. 20, 1868, Papers (B-26 :55) ; GBM European diary (1867–68), Jan. 1868, May 13, 1868, Papers (D-4 :67).

6. GBM to Prime, Mar. 24, 1867, Mar. 2, 1868, Papers (B-41 :61, B-26 :55) ; GBM to Barlow, Nov. –, 1867, Mar. 13, 1868, Barlow Papers, HL ; Katz, *August Belmont,* p. 167 ; *New York World,* Oct. 3, 1868 ; GBM diary

(1868–69), Sept. 30, Oct. 1, 8, 1868, Papers (D-4:67); Seymour to GBM — GBM to Douglas Taylor, Oct. 2, 1868, Papers (B-27:55); GBM to Cox, Nov. 3, 1868, Thomas F. Madigan Collection, Rare Books and Manuscripts Division, New York Public Library.

7. Michie, *General McClellan*, p. 453; GBM to Prime, May 8, 1870, Papers (B-37:55); *New York Commercial Advertiser*, Oct. 29, 1885.

8. Andrew J. Moulder to GBM, Nov. 12, 1868 — James McHenry to GBM, May 4, 1872 — 1870 income memorandum, May 1871, Papers (A-93:37, A-94:37, A-93:37).

9. A. Oakey Hall to GBM, Sept. 16, 17, 1871 — GBM to Hall, undated draft — Aspinwall to GBM, Sept. 18, 1871, Papers (A-94:37); GBM to Hall, Sept. 18, 1871 — GBM to Thomas F. Randolph, July 6, 1872, Papers (A-93:37, A-94:37).

10. McClellan & Co. prospectus, Oct. 1, 1874 — GBM diary (1874–75), Papers (A-94:37), D-5:68).

11. GBM to Barlow, Jan. 29, 1876, Barlow Papers, HL; *McClellan's Own Story*, draft — May McClellan diary (1881–82), Mar. 12, 1882, Papers (D-9:71, D-6:68). GBM's articles are cited in the Bibliography.

12. GBM, *Speeches of Gen. George B. McClellan During the Presidential Campaign of 1876*, pp. 60–61; GBM to Elizabeth B. McClellan, Nov. –, 1876, Papers (A-95:38); John M. Tobin to GBM, Dec. 15, 19, 1876, Jan. 5, 1877 — W. W. H. Davis to GBM, Jan. 11, 15, 1877, Papers (A-96:38).

13. William Starr Myers, *General George Brinton McClellan: A Study in Personality*, pp. 494–97; *New York Herald*, Sept. 20, 1877; *New York Sun*, Sept. 21, 1877; George B. McClellan, Jr., *The Gentleman and the Tiger: The Autobiography of George B. McClellan, Jr.*, p. 49; GBM to Barlow, Mar. 13, 1868, Barlow Papers, HL; Lucius Robinson to GBM, Mar. 17, 23, 1877, Papers (A-96:38, A-97:38).

14. Myers, *General McClellan*, pp. 498–502; *Harper's Weekly*, Oct. 27, 1877; *Newark Weekly Journal*, Jan. 14, 1879; *Orange* (N.J.) *Journal*, Jan. 14, 1879; Wilcox to H. B. McClellan, July 24, 1878, H. B. McClellan Papers, Virginia Historical Society; May McClellan diary (1880–81), Dec. 11, 1880 — GBM to Elizabeth B. McClellan, Feb. 1881, Papers (D-5:68, B-33:57).

15. GBM to Elizabeth B. McClellan, Apr. 27, 1881 — May McClellan diaries (1880–81, 1881–82), Papers (B-33:57, D-5:68, D-6:68); *New York Evening Post*, Oct. 29, 1885; GBM financial ledger, 1870–80, Papers (D-22:78).

16. May McClellan diary (1882–84), Nov. 15, 1884 — GBM to John R. McPherson, Dec. 27, 1884, Papers (D-6:68, A-103:41); George B. McClellan, Jr., *Gentleman and the Tiger*, p. 55; *New York Herald*, Feb. 22, 1885; *New York Tribune*, Dec. 3, 1884; Myers, *General McClellan*, p. 507.

17. Douglas, *I Rode with Stonewall*, p. 177; *Baltimore Sun*, May 31, 1885; *Hagerstown* (Md.) *Mail*, June 5, 1885; GBM diary (1885), Papers (D-19:77); Hollon, *Beyond the Cross Timbers*, pp. 252–53; *New York World*, Oct. 30, 1885.

18. *Philadephia Times*, Oct. 30, Nov. 3, 1885; telegrams received Oct.–Nov. 1885, Papers (D-24:80); *New York Evening Post*, Oct. 30, 1885; *New York Times*, Oct. 30, 1885; *New York World*, Oct. 30, 1885.

Epilogue: A Memoir for History

1. *New York Commercial Advertiser*, undated clipping — William Appleton to Barlow, undated — H. O. Houghton to Prime, Nov. 7, 1885 — James

Redpath to Prime, Mar. 15, 1886, Papers (D-25:80, A-109:42, A-105:41, B-39:60).

2. *The North American Review,* 363 (Feb. 1887), p. 214; Donn Piatt, *Memories of the Men Who Saved the Union* (New York: Belford, Clarke, 1887), p. 280; John C. Ropes, ''General McClellan,'' *Atlantic Monthly,* 59 (Apr. 1887), p. 546; Jacob D. Cox, ''McClellan's Own Story — I,'' *The Nation,* 44 (Jan. 20, 1887), p. 57.

3. *McClellan's Own Story,* introduction, pp. 22–24; Ropes, ''General McClellan,'' p. 547. Manuscripts, drafts, notes, and other material relating to *McClellan's Own Story* are in the Papers (D-9:71, D-10:72). GBM's excerpts from his letters to his wife, and May McClellan's excerpts from those letters, are also in the Papers (C-7:63, D-10:72).

4. George B. McClellan, Jr., *Gentleman and the Tiger,* pp. 48n, 78n; *McClellan's Own Story,* introduction, p. 24.

BIBLIOGRAPHY

Manuscript Collections

Alsop Family Papers, Yale University Library
John A. Andrew Papers, Massachusetts Historical Society
Samuel L. M. Barlow Papers, Huntington Library
Belmont Family Papers, Rare Book and Manuscript Library, Columbia
    University
James Gordon Bennett Papers, Manuscript Division, Library of Con-
    gress
Blair Family Papers, Manuscript Division, Library of Congress
Simon Cameron Papers, Manuscript Division, Library of Congress
Ezra A. Carman Papers: "The Maryland Campaign of September 1862,"
    Manuscript Division, Library of Congress
Centennial History of the Civil War, Bruce Catton: Research Notes,
    Doubleday & Co., Manuscript Division, Library of Congress
Zachariah Chandler Papers, Manuscript Division, Library of Con-
    gress
Salmon P. Chase Papers, Manuscript Division, Library of Con-
    gress
Civil War Collection, Huntington Library
Civil War Records, National Archives
        RG 45   Naval Records Collection, Office of Naval Records and
                  Library: Area File, 1775–1910 (M-625)
        RG 94   Records of the Adjutant General's Office:
                  Letters Received, Main Series, 1861–70 (M-619)
                  Generals' Papers and Books (159:Halleck Papers)
                  U.S. Military Academy Cadet Application Papers,
                    1805–66 (M-688)
                  Records Relating to the U.S. Military Academy, 1812–
                    67 (M-91)

RG 107   Records of the Office of the Secretary of War:
         Letters Received, Main Series, 1801–70 (M-221)
         Letters Received, Irregular Series, 1861–66 (M-492)
         Telegrams Collected (Bound), 1861–82 (M-473)
         Telegrams Collected (Unbound), 1860–70 (M-504)
RG 108   Records of the Headquarters of the Army:
         Letters Sent, Main Series, 1828–1903 (M-857)
RG 393   Records of the United States Army Commands:
         Army of the Potomac, 1861–65

Jacob D. Cox Papers, Oberlin College Archives

Samuel S. Cox Letters, Thomas F. Madigan Collection, Rare Books and
    Manuscripts Division, New York Public Library

John A. Dix Papers, Rare Book and Manuscript Library, Columbia
    University

Edward Everett Papers, Massachusetts Historical Society

Gustavus V. Fox Papers, New-York Historical Society

William B. Franklin Papers, Manuscript Division, Library of Congress

Sydney H. Gay Papers, Rare Book and Manuscript Library, Columbia
    University

Samuel P. Heintzelman Diary, Manuscript Division, Library of Congress

Reverdy Johnson Papers, Manuscript Division, Library of Congress

Abraham Lincoln Papers, Manuscript Division, Library of Congress

George B. McClellan Papers
    Houghton Library, Harvard University
    Illinois State Historical Library
    Manuscript Division, Library of Congress
    New Jersey Historical Society
    New-York Historical Society

George B. McClellan, Jr., Papers, Manuscript Division, Library of
    Congress

Manton M. Marble Papers, Manuscript Division, Library of Congress

Comte de Paris Diary, Fondation Saint-Louis, Amboise, France

Fitz John Porter Papers, Manuscript Division, Library of Congress

Charles H. Ray Papers, Huntington Library

John C. Ropes Collection, Papers of the Military Historical Society of
    Massachusetts, Boston University Library

James S. Schoff Collection, William L. Clements Library, University
    of Michigan

William Henry Seward Papers, Rush Rhees Library, University of
    Rochester

Edwin M. Stanton Papers, Manuscript Division, Library of Congress

Alexander S. Webb Papers, Yale University Library

Robert C. Winthrop Papers, Massachusetts Historical Society

Writings by George B. McClellan

The Mexican War Diary of George B. McClellan. Ed. William Starr
Myers. Princeton: Princeton University Press, 1917.

*Bayonet Exercise, or School of the Infantry Soldier, in the Use of the
Musket in Hand to Hand Conflicts.* Translated from the French of
Gomard. Washington, D.C.: U.S. War Department, 1852. Reissued
as *Manual of Bayonet Exercise: Prepared for the Use of the Army
of the United States.* Philadelphia: Lippincott, 1862.

"Railroad Practicability of the Cascades . . ." *Pacific Railroad Reports*
[*Reports of Explorations and Surveys to Ascertain the Most Practicable and Economical Route for a Railroad from the Mississippi
River to the Pacific Ocean*]. Washington, D.C.: U.S. War Department, 1855, Vol. I, pp. 188–202.

*The Report of Captain George B. McClellan, One of the Officers Sent
to the Seat of War in Europe, in 1855 and 1856.* Washington, D.C.:
Senate Exec. Doc. No. 1, 35th Cong., Special Sess., 1857. Reissued
as *The Armies of Europe.* Philadelphia: Lippincott, 1861.

*European Cavalry, Including Details of the Organization of the Cavalry
Service Among the Principal Nations of Europe.* Philadelphia:
Lippincott, 1861.

*Regulations and Instructions for the Field Service of the United States
Cavalry in Time of War.* Philadelphia: Lippincott, 1861. Reissued
as *Regulations for the Field Service of Cavalry in Time of War.*
Philadelphia: Lippincott, 1862.

"American and European Warfare." *The Round Table*, Part I: 1 (December 19, 1863), pp. 6–7; Part II: 1 (December 26, 1863), p. 21;
Part III: 1 (January 2, 1864), pp. 36–37.

"Balloons, Telegraphs, and Signals in War." *The Round Table*, 1 (January 30, 1864), p. 101.

*Report on the Organization of the Army of the Potomac, and of Its
Campaigns in Virginia and Maryland.* Washington, D.C.: Government Printing Office, 1864.

*Report on the Organization of the Army of the Potomac, to which Is
Added an Account of the Campaign in Western Virginia.* New
York: Sheldon, 1864.

"About Rifled Ordnance." *The Round Table*, 1 (February 27, 1864),
pp. 167–68.

"The Coming Campaign Foreshadowed." *The Round Table*, 1 (March
12, 1864), pp. 193–94.

"The Coming Campaign in the West." *The Round Table*, 1 (March 19,
1864), pp. 209–210.

"Jomini." *The Galaxy*, 7 (July 1869), pp. 874–88.

"Army Organization." *Harper's New Monthly Magazine*, Part I: 48 (April 1874), pp. 670–80; Part II: 49 (June 1874), pp. 101–111; Part III: 49 (August 1874), pp. 401–411.

"A Winter on the Nile." *Scribner's Monthly*, Part I: 13 (January 1877), pp. 368–83; Part II: 13 (February 1877), pp. 452–59.

"The War in the East." *The North American Review*, Part 1: 125 (July–August 1877), pp. 35–59; Part II: 125 (September–October 1877), pp. 246–70; Part III: 125 (November–December 1877), pp. 439–61.

"The Regular Army of the United States." *Harper's New Monthly Magazine*, 55 (October 1877), pp. 774–82.

"Capture of Kars and Fall of Plevná." *The North American Review*, 126 (January–February 1878), pp. 132–55.

"The Engadine." *Scribner's Monthly*, 16 (September 1878), pp. 639–51.

"From Palermo to Syracuse." *Scribner's Monthly*, 20 (July 1880), pp. 400–416.

"The War in Egypt." *The Century*, 24 (September 1882), pp. 784–88.

"The Princes of the House of Orléans." *The Century*, 27 (February 1884), pp. 614–23.

"The Peninsular Campaign." *The Century*, 30 (May 1885), reprinted in *Battles and Leaders of the Civil War*. Eds. Robert U. Johnson and Clarence C. Buel. New York: Century, 1887–88, II, pp. 160–87.

"From the Peninsula to Antietam." *The Century*, 32 (March 1886), reprinted in *Battles and Leaders of the Civil War*, II, pp. 545–55.

McClellan's Own Story. Ed. William C. Prime. New York: Charles L. Webster, 1887.

Books and Articles

Adams, Michael C. C. *Our Masters the Rebels: A Speculation on Union Military Failure in the East, 1861–1865*. Cambridge, Mass.: Harvard University Press, 1978.

Allan, William. *The Army of Northern Virginia in 1862*. Boston: Houghton Mifflin, 1892.

Ambrose, Stephen E. *Halleck: Lincoln's Chief of Staff*. Baton Rouge: Louisiana State University Press, 1962.

Andrews, J. Cutler. *The North Reports the Civil War*. Pittsburgh: University of Pittsburgh Press, 1955.

Barnard, John G. *The Peninsular Campaign and Its Antecedents*. New York: Van Nostrand, 1864.

Bates, Edward. *The Diary of Edward Bates, 1859–1866*. Ed. Howard K. Beale. Washington, D.C.: Government Printing Office, 1933.

Battles and Leaders of the Civil War. Eds. Robert U. Johnson and Clarence C. Buel. 4 vols. New York: Century, 1887–88.

Biddle, William F. "Recollections of McClellan." *United Service Magazine*, 11 (May 1894), pp. 460–69.

Brooks, Noah. "Two War-Time Conventions." *The Century*, 49 (March 1895), pp. 723–36.

Browning, Orville H. *The Diary of Orville Hickman Browning*. Eds. Theodore C. Pease and James G. Randall. 2 vols. Springfield: Illinois State Historical Library, 1925, 1933.

Campbell, James Havelock. *McClellan: A Vindication of the Military Career of General George B. McClellan, A Lawyer's Brief*. New York: Neale, 1916.

Catton, Bruce. *The Centennial History of the Civil War*. 3 vols. New York: Doubleday, 1961–65.

Chambers, Lenoir. *Stonewall Jackson*. 2 vols. New York: Morrow, 1959.

Chase, Salmon P. *Inside Lincoln's Cabinet: The Civil War Diaries of Salmon P. Chase*. Ed. David Donald. New York: Longmans, Green, 1954.

Cooling, Benjamin Franklin. *Symbol, Sword, and Shield: Defending Washington During the Civil War*. Hamden, Conn.: Archon Books, 1975.

Corliss, Carlton J. *Main Line of Mid-America: The Story of the Illinois Central*. New York: Creative Age Press, 1950.

Cox, Jacob D. "McClellan's Own Story." *The Nation*, Part I: 44 (January 20, 1887), pp. 57–59; Part II: 44 (January 27, 1887), pp. 79–81.

Cox, Jacob D. *Military Reminiscences of the Civil War*. 2 vols. New York: Scribner's, 1900.

Curtis, George Ticknor. *McClellan's Last Service to the Republic*. New York: Appleton, 1886.

Dawes, Rufus R. *Service with the Sixth Wisconsin Volunteers*. Marietta, Ohio: Alderman & Sons, 1890.

Dell, Christopher. *Lincoln and the War Democrats*. Rutherford, N.J.: Fairleigh Dickinson University Press, 1975.

Douglas, Henry Kyd. *I Rode with Stonewall*. Chapel Hill: University of North Carolina Press, 1940.

Eckenrode, H. J., and Bryan Conrad. *George B. McClellan: The Man Who Saved the Union*. Chapel Hill: University of North Carolina Press, 1941.

Elliott, Charles W. *Winfield Scott, the Soldier and the Man*. New York: Macmillan, 1937.

Fishel, Edwin C. "The Mythology of Civil War Intelligence." *Civil War History*, 10:4 (December 1964), pp. 344–67.

Fox, Gustavus V. *Confidential Correspondence of Gustavus Vasa Fox, Assistant Secretary of the Navy, 1861–1865*. Eds. Robert M. Thompson and Richard Wainwright. 2 vols. New York : Naval History Society, 1920.

Freeman, Douglas Southall. *Lee's Lieutenants: A Study in Command*. 3 vols. New York : Scribner's, 1942–44.

Freeman, Douglas Southall. *R. E. Lee, A Biography*. 4 vols. New York : Scribner's, 1934–35.

Freidel, Frank, ed. *Union Pamphlets of the Civil War, 1861–1865*. 2 vols. Cambridge, Mass. : Harvard University Press, 1967.

Fry, James B. "McClellan and His 'Mission.' " *The Century*, 48 (October 1894), pp. 931–46.

Gates, Paul W. *The Illinois Central Railroad and Its Colonization Work*. Cambridge, Mass. : Harvard University Press, 1934.

Gibbon, John. *Personal Recollections of the Civil War*. New York : Putnam's, 1928.

Goetzmann, William H. *Army Exploration in the American West, 1803–1863*. New Haven : Yale University Press, 1959.

Gray, John C., and John C. Ropes. *War Letters: 1862–1865*. Boston : Houghton Mifflin, 1927.

Hagerman, Edward. "From Jomini to Dennis Hart Mahan : The Evolution of Trench Warfare and the American Civil War." *Civil War History*, 13 :3 (September 1967), pp. 197–220.

Hagerman, Edward. "The Professionalization of George B. McClellan and Early Civil War Field Command : An Institutional Perspective." *Civil War History*, 21 :2 (June 1975), pp. 113–35.

Harsh, Joseph L. "On the McClellan-Go-Round." *Civil War History*, 19 :2 (June 1973), pp. 101–118.

Hassler, Warren W., Jr. *General George B. McClellan: Shield of the Union*. Baton Rouge : Louisiana State University Press, 1957.

Hay, John. *Lincoln and the Civil War in the Diaries and Letters of John Hay*. Ed. Tyler Dennett. New York : Dodd, Mead, 1939.

Hebert, Walter H. *Fighting Joe Hooker*. Indianapolis : Bobbs-Merrill, 1944.

Hendrick, Burton J. *Lincoln's War Cabinet*. Boston : Little, Brown, 1946.

Hesseltine, William B. *Lincoln and the War Governors*. New York : Knopf, 1948.

Hillard, G. S. *Life and Campaigns of George B. McClellan, Major-General U.S. Army*. Philadelphia : Lippincott, 1864.

Hitchcock, Ethan Allen. *Fifty Years in Camp and Field: Diary of Major-General Ethan Allen Hitchcock, U.S.A.* Ed. W. A. Croffut. New York : Putnam's, 1909.

Hollon, W. Eugene. *Beyond the Cross Timbers: The Travels of Randolph B. Marcy, 1812–1887.* Norman: University of Oklahoma Press, 1955.

Horan, James D. *The Pinkertons: The Detective Dynasty That Made History.* New York: Crown, 1967.

Hurlbert, William H. *General McClellan and the Conduct of the War.* New York: Sheldon, 1864.

Joinville, Prince de. *The Army of the Potomac: Its Organization, Its Commander, and Its Campaign.* New York: Anson D. F. Randolph, 1862.

Katz, Irving. *August Belmont: A Political Biography.* New York: Columbia University Press, 1968.

Keyes, E. D. *Fifty Years' Observation of Men and Events, Civil and Military.* New York: Scribner's, 1885.

Klement, Frank L. *The Copperheads in the Middle West.* Chicago: University of Chicago Press, 1960.

Klement, Frank L. *The Limits of Dissent: Clement L. Vallandigham and the Civil War.* Lexington: University Press of Kentucky, 1970.

Lee, Jen-Wha. "The Organization and Administration of the Army of the Potomac Under General George B. McClellan." Ph.D. dissertation, University of Maryland, 1960.

Lee, Robert E. *The Wartime Papers of R. E. Lee.* Ed. Clifford Dowdey. New York: Bramahall House, 1961.

Leech, Margaret. *Reveille in Washington, 1860–1865.* New York: Harper, 1941.

Lincoln, Abraham. *The Collected Works of Abraham Lincoln.* Ed. Roy P. Basler. 9 vols. New Brunswick, N.J.: Rutgers University Press, 1953–1955.

Lowell, James Russell. "General McClellan's Report." *The North American Review,* 203 (April 1864), pp. 550–66.

Macartney, Clarence E. *Little Mac: The Life of General George B. McClellan.* Philadelphia: Dorrance, 1940.

McClellan, George B. *Speeches of Gen. George B. McClellan During the Presidential Campaign of 1876.* Philadelphia: Lippincott, 1877.

McClellan, George B. *[West Point] Oration by General McClellan.* New York: C. W. Westcott, 1864.

McClellan, George B., Jr. *The Gentleman and the Tiger: The Autobiography of George B. McClellan, Jr.* Ed. Harold C. Syrett. Philadelphia: Lippincott, 1956.

McClure, A. K., ed. *The Annals of the War, Written by Leading Participants, North and South.* Philadelphia: Times Publishing, 1879.

McClure, A. K. *Lincoln and Men of War-Times.* Philadelphia: Times Publishing, 1892.

McJimsey, George T. *Genteel Partisan: Manton Marble, 1834–1917*. Ames: Iowa State University Press, 1971.

McPherson, Edward. *The Political History of the United States of America, During the Great Rebellion*. 2nd ed. Washington, D.C.: Philp & Solomons, 1865.

McWhiney, Grady, and Perry D. Jamieson. *Attack and Die: Civil War Military Tactics and the Southern Heritage*. University: University of Alabama Press, 1982.

Maury, Dabney H. *Recollections of a Virginian in the Mexican, Indian, and Civil Wars*. New York: Scribner's, 1894.

Meade, George G. *The Life and Letters of George Gordon Meade*. 2 vols. New York: Scribner's 1913.

Meigs, Montgomery C. "General M. C. Meigs on the Conduct of the Civil War." *American Historical Review*, 26:2 (January 1921), pp. 285–303.

Michie, Peter S. *General McClellan*. New York: Appleton, 1901.

Military and Historical Society of Massachusetts. *The Peninsular Campaign of General McClellan in 1862*. I, Boston, 1881.

Military and Historical Society of Massachusetts. *The Virginia Campaign of 1862 Under General Pope*. II, Boston, 1895.

Mitchell, Stewart. *Horatio Seymour of New York*. Cambridge, Mass.: Harvard University Press, 1938.

Moore, Frank, ed. *The Rebellion Record: A Diary of American Events*. 11 vols. and supplement. New York: Putnam's, 1861–63; Van Nostrand, 1864–68.

Morrison, James L., Jr. *"The Best School in the World": West Point, the Pre–Civil War Years, 1833–1866*. Kent, Ohio: Kent State University Press, 1986.

Morrison, James L., Jr. "The United States Military Academy, 1833–1866: Years of Progress and Turmoil." Ph.D. dissertation, Columbia University, 1970.

Myers, William Starr. *General George Brinton McClellan: A Study in Personality*. New York: Appleton-Century, 1934.

Nevins, Allan. *The Emergence of Lincoln*. 2 vols. New York: Scribner's, 1950.

Nevins, Allan. *The War for the Union*. 4 vols. New York: Scribner's, 1959–71.

Nicolay, Helen. *Lincoln's Secretary: A Biography of John G. Nicolay*. New York: Longmans, Green, 1949.

Nicolay, John G., and John Hay. *Abraham Lincoln: A History*. 10 vols. New York: Century, 1886–90.

Overmeyer, Philip Henry. "George B. McClellan and the Pacific Northwest." *Pacific Northwest Quarterly*, 32:1 (January 1941), pp. 3–60.

Palfrey, Francis A. *The Antietam and Fredericksburg.* New York: Scribner's, 1882.

Paris, Comte de. *History of the Civil War in America.* 4 vols. Philadelphia: Porter & Coates, 1875–88.

Patrick, Marsena R. *Inside Lincoln's Army: The Diary of Marsena Rudolph Patrick, Provost Marshal General, Army of the Potomac.* Ed. David S. Sparks. New York: Yoseloff, 1964.

Pinkerton, Allan. *The Spy of the Rebellion; Being a True History of the Spy System of the United States Army During the Late Rebellion.* New York: G. W. Dillingham, 1883.

Rawley, James A. *The Politics of Union: Northern Politics During the Civil War.* Hinsdale, Ill.: Dryden Press, 1974.

Raymond, Henry W., ed. "Excerpts from the Journal of Henry J. Raymond." *Scribner's Monthly,* 19:3 (January 1880), pp. 419–24.

Report of the Joint Committee on the Conduct of the War. 3 vols. Washington, D.C.: Government Printing Office, 1863; 5 vols., 1865.

Ropes, John C. *The Army Under Pope.* New York: Scribner's, 1882.

Ropes, John C. "General McClellan." *Atlantic Monthly,* 59 (April 1887), pp. 546–59.

Ropes, John C. *The Story of the Civil War.* 2 vols. New York: Putnam's, 1895–98.

Russell, William Howard. *My Diary North and South.* 1863; reprinted, New York: Harper, 1954.

Schuckers, Jacob S. *The Life and Public Services of Salmon Portland Chase.* New York: Appleton, 1874.

Sears, Stephen W. *Landscape Turned Red: The Battle of Antietam.* New York: Ticknor & Fields, 1983.

Shannon, Fred A. *The Organization and Administration of the Union Army, 1861–1865.* 2 vols. Cleveland: Arthur H. Clark, 1928.

Silbey, Joel H. *A Respectable Minority: The Democratic Party in the Civil War Era, 1860–1868.* New York: Norton, 1977.

Smith, George Winston, and Charles Judah, eds. *Chronicles of the Gringoes: The U.S. Army in the Mexican War, 1846–1848; Accounts of Eyewitnesses and Combatants.* Albuquerque: University of New Mexico Press, 1968.

Smith, Justin H. *The War with Mexico.* 2 vols. New York: Macmillan, 1919.

Smith, William Ernest. *The Francis Preston Blair Family in Politics.* 2 vols. New York: Macmillan, 1933.

Starr, Stephen Z. *The Union Cavalry in the Civil War.* 3 vols. Baton Rouge: Louisiana State University Press, 1979–85.

Stewart, A. M. *Camp, March and Battle-Field; or, Three Years and a Half with the Army of the Potomac.* Philadelphia: J. B. Rodgers, 1865.

Strong, George Templeton. *The Diary of George Templeton Strong: The Civil War, 1860–1865*. Eds. Allan Nevins and Milton H. Thomas. New York: Macmillan, 1952.

Strother, D. H. "Personal Recollections of the War by a Virginian, Antietam." *Harper's New Monthly Magazine,* 36 (February 1868), pp. 275–91.

Strother, D. H. *A Virginia Yankee in the Civil War: The Diaries of David Hunter Strother*. Ed. Cecil D. Eby, Jr. Chapel Hill: University of North Carolina Press, 1961.

Swinton, William. *Campaigns of the Army of the Potomac*. New York: Charles B. Richardson, 1866.

Thomas, Benjamin P., and Harold M. Hyman. *Stanton: The Life and Times of Lincoln's Secretary of War*. New York: Knopf, 1962.

Trefousse, Hans L. *The Radical Republicans: Lincoln's Vanguard for Racial Justice*. New York: Knopf, 1969.

Upton, Emory. *The Military Policy of the United Sates*. Washington, D.C.: Government Printing Office, 1917.

U.S. Naval War Records Office. *Official Records of the Union and Confederate Navies in the War of the Rebellion*. 30 vols. Washington, D.C.: Government Printing Office, 1894–1922.

U.S. War Department. *The War of the Rebellion: A Compilation of the Official Records of the Union and Confederate Armies*. 128 parts in 70 vols. and atlas. Washington, D.C.: Government Printing Office, 1880–1901.

Wainwright, Charles S. *A Diary of Battle: The Personal Journals of Colonel Charles S. Wainwright, 1861–1865*. Ed. Allan Nevins. New York: Harcourt, Brace & World, 1962.

Webb, Alexander S. *The Peninsula: McClellan's Campaign of 1862*. New York: Scribner's, 1881.

Weigley, Russell F. *History of the United States Army*. New York: Macmillan, 1967.

Weigley, Russell F. *Quartermaster General of the Union Army: A Biography of M. C. Meigs*. New York: Columbia University Press, 1959.

Weld, Stephen M. *War Diary and Letters of Stephen Minot Weld, 1861–1865*. 2nd ed. Boston: Massachusetts Historical Society, 1979.

Welles, Gideon. *Diary of Gideon Welles*. Ed. Howard K. Beale. 3 vols. New York: Norton, 1960.

Williams, Alpheus S. *From the Cannon's Mouth: The Civil War Letters of General Alpheus S. Williams*. Ed. Milo M. Quaife. Detroit: Wayne State University Press, 1959.

Williams, Kenneth P. *Lincoln Finds a General: A Military Study of the Civil War*. 5 vols. New York: Macmillan, 1949–59.

Williams, T. Harry. *Lincoln and His Generals*. New York: Knopf, 1952.

Williams, T. Harry. *Lincoln and the Radicals*. Madison: University of Wisconsin Press, 1941.

Williams, T. Harry. *McClellan, Sherman, and Grant*. New Brunswick, N.J.: Rutgers University Press, 1962.

Wilson, Charles R. "McClellan's Changing Views on the Peace Plank of 1864." *American Historical Review*, 38:3 (April 1933), pp. 498–505.

Wilson, James Grant. "General Halleck — A Memoir." *Journal of the Military Service Institution of the United States*, 36 (1905), pp. 537–59.

Wilson, James H. *Under the Old Flag*. 2 vols. New York: Appleton, 1912.

Winther, Oscar O. "The Soldier Vote in the Election of 1864." *New York History*, 25:4 (October 1944), pp. 440–58.

Zornow, William Frank. *Lincoln and the Party Divided*. Norman: University of Oklahoma Press, 1954.

INDEX